From the Gracchi to Nero

'Still the best introduction to **Roman history**'
Miriam Griffin, University of Oxford, UK

'For a concise, factual narrative of the **Roman** world's traumatic transformation from **Republic** to **Empire**, [it] remains unsurpassed. **As a foundation for university and college courses, it is invaluable.**'
Richard Talbert, University of North Carolina, Chapel Hill, USA

'Without a rival as a guide to the intricacies of **Republican** politics.'
Greg Woolf, University of St. Andrews, UK

'A classic textbook: clear, authoritative and balanced in its judgements . . . it has established itself as the fundamental modern work of reference for teachers, sixth-formers and university students . . . it is still the best and most reliable modern account of the period.'
Tim Cornell, University of Manchester, UK

'This book is a modern classic. It provides a clear narrative of the two centuries from 133 B.C. to 68 A.D., but it is especially valuable for Scullard's extensive footnotes which provide undergraduates with both the ancient sources and the most important scholarly contributions.'
Ronald Mellor, University of California at Los Angeles, USA

Routledge Classics contains the very best of Routledge publishing over the past century or so, books that have, by popular consent, become established as classics in their field. Drawing on a fantastic heritage of innovative writing published by Routledge and its associated imprints, this series makes available in attractive, affordable form some of the most important works of modern times.

For a complete list of titles visit
www.routledge.com/classics

H. H. Scullard

From the Gracchi to Nero

A history of Rome from 133 B.C. to A.D. 68

With a new foreword by Dominic Rathbone

 London and New York

First published 1959 by Methuen & Co.

First published in Routledge Classics 2011
by Routledge
2 Park Square, Milton Park, Abingdon, Oxon OX14 4RN

Simultaneously published in the USA and Canada
by Routledge
711 Third Avenue, New York, NY 10017

Routledge is an imprint of the Taylor & Francis Group, an informa business

© 1959, 1963, 1970, 1976, 1982 H. H. Scullard

Foreword © 2011 Dominic Rathbone

Typeset in Joanna by RefineCatch Limited, Bungay, Suffolk

British Library Cataloguing in Publication Data
A catalogue record for this book is available from the British Library

Library of Congress Cataloging in Publication Data
A catalog record for this book has been requested

ISBN10: 0–415–58488–4 (pbk)
ISBN10: 0–203–84478–5 (ebk)

ISBN13: 978–0–415–58488–3 (pbk)
ISBN13: 978–0–203–84478–6 (ebk)

Printed and bound in Great Britain by
CPI Group (UK) Ltd, Croydon, CR0 4YY

Contents

CHRONOLOGICAL TABLE   x
PREFACE   xxi
PREFACE TO SECOND EDITION   xxii
PREFACE TO THIRD, FOURTH AND FIFTH EDITIONS   xxii
FOREWORD   xxiv

I   Rome at the Cross-Roads   1
    1.   Introductory   1
    2.   The Growth of Rome's Empire   2
    3.   The Senatorial Government   4
    4.   The People and the Knights   7
    5.   Greek Cultural Influences on Roman Life   8
    6.   The Effects of Wealth and Slavery   11
    7.   Rome's Allies   13
    8.   Economic Changes and the Land Problem   16

II The Gracchi   19
    1.   Attempts at Reform   19
    2.   Tiberius Gracchus   20
    3.   The Land-bill of Tiberius Gracchus   22
    4.   The Importance of Gracchus' Attempt   24
    5.   The Land Commission, Scipio Aemilianus
         and the Allies   25
    6.   The Legislation of Gaius Gracchus   27
    7.   The Opposition to Gaius Gracchus   30

	8.	The Importance of the Gracchi	32
	9.	Foreign Affairs: Asia and Gaul	33
III		The Rise and Fall of Marius	36
	1.	The Senatorial Settlement	36
	2.	The Metelli and Marius	37
	3.	The Outbreak of War against Jugurtha	39
	4.	The Defeat of Jugurtha	41
	5.	The Northern Menace and its Political Repercussions	44
	6.	L. Appuleius Saturninus	46
	7.	Marius' Victory over the Germans	47
	8.	Marius' Sixth Consulship (100 B.C.)	49
IV		The Rise and Fall of Sulla	52
	1.	The Nineties	52
	2.	The Younger Drusus	53
	3.	The Outbreak of the Italian or Social War	54
	4.	The Italian or Social War	56
	5.	Sulpicius' Tribunate and Sulla's Capture of Rome	58
	6.	Cinna	60
	7.	Mithridates, King of Pontus	61
	8.	The First Mithridatic War	63
	9.	Civil War	65
	10.	Sullanum Regnum	67
	11.	Sulla's Reforms	68
	12.	Sulla's Retirement	71
V		The Rise of Pompey	73
	1.	The Counter-revolution of Lepidus	73
	2.	Q. Sertorius	74
	3.	The Senate's Administration	77
	4.	Spartacus	79
	5.	The Consulship of Pompey and Crassus (70 B.C.)	80
	6.	Pompey's Commands	82
	7.	The Pirates	83
	8.	The Third Mithridatic War: Lucullus	84
	9.	Pompey's Victory	86
	10.	Pompey's Settlement of the East	88
VI		Pompey and Caesar	90
	1.	Crassus and Caesar	90
	2.	Catiline's Conspiracy	93

	3.	The Return of Pompey	95
	4.	The First Triumvirate	96
	5.	Caesar's First Consulship (59 B.C.)	97
	6.	Clodius	99
	7.	The Renewal and Breakdown of the Triumvirate	101
	8.	Crassus and Parthia	105

VII	The Domination of Caesar		107
	1.	Conditions in Gaul	107
	2.	The Reduction of Gaul (58–56 B.C.)	109
	3.	Germany and Britain (55–54 B.C.)	111
	4.	Revolt and Reconquest	112
	5.	Civil War in Italy, Africa and Spain (49 B.C.)	114
	6.	War in Greece, Egypt and Asia (48–47 B.C.)	116
	7.	The End of the Civil War	119
	8.	Reform and Reconstruction	121
	9.	Policy and Administration	124
	10.	Caesar's Autocracy	125

VIII	The Second Triumvirate		131
	1.	The Rise of Antony	131
	2.	The Rise of Octavian	132
	3.	The Second Triumvirate and Philippi	134
	4.	Octavian's Consolidation of the West	137
	5.	Antony in the East	140
	6.	The Final Break and War: Actium	143

IX	Economic and Social Life in Italy and the Provinces in the Late Republic		146
	1.	Agriculture, Industry and Trade	146
	2.	The Aristocracy	149
	3.	The Knights	151
	4.	Other Classes	151
	5.	The City	153
	6.	The Provinces	154

X	Art, Literature and Thought in the Late Republic		159
	1.	Graeco–Roman Culture	159
	2.	Art and Architecture	161
	3.	The Poets	163
	4.	Historical Writing	166
	5.	Oratory	169
	6.	Education and Learning	170
	7.	Law	171

| | | 8. | Philosophy and Religion | 173 |

XI The Augustan Principate — 176
1. Octavian's Problem — 176
2. The First Settlement (27 B.C.) — 178
3. The Second Settlement (23 B.C.) — 180
4. Consolidation of the Principate — 181
5. The Last Twenty-five Years of Augustus' Principate — 183
6. Princeps and Senate — 185
7. The Executive: Magistrates and Officials — 189
8. Rome and Italy — 192
9. Social Reforms — 195
10. Religious Reforms — 197
11. Virgil, Horace and Livy — 199
12. Other Writers of the Augustan Age — 203

XII Frontiers and Provinces — 205
1. Imperial Problems — 205
2. The Army — 205
3. The Eastern Frontier — 208
4. Africa, Spain and Gaul — 212
5. The Northern Frontier — 214
6. Provincial Administration — 219
7. Augustus — 223

XIII Tiberius and Gaius — 226
1. The Accession of Tiberius — 226
2. Germanicus — 228
3. The Civil Government of Tiberius — 230
4. Sejanus — 232
5. Provincial Affairs under Tiberius — 234
6. Tiberius' Last Years — 236
7. Gaius (Caligula) — 239
8. The Provincial Policy of Gaius — 240

XIV Claudius and Nero — 243
1. The Accession of Claudius — 243
2. Claudius and the Senate — 245
3. Claudius' Centralized Administration — 246
4. The Provincial Policy of Claudius — 249
5. The Conquest of Britain — 252
6. Court History under Claudius — 255
7. Nero's First Years — 256

	8.	The Administration of Seneca and Burrus	258
	9.	Nero the Artist	259
	10.	The Gathering Storm	260
	11.	The Provinces and Foreign Affairs	263
	12.	The Storm Breaks	268
XV		Economic and Social Life in the Early Empire	272
	1.	Agriculture	272
	2.	Industry and Trade	273
	3.	Trade Beyond the Empire	277
	4.	General Economic Conditions	279
	5.	The Senatorial Class	283
	6.	Social Life	285
XVI		Art, Literature and Religion in the Julio-Claudian Period	292
	1.	Architecture and Art	292
	2.	Post-Augustan Literature	295
	3.	The Writers	297
	4.	Philosophy and Religion	302
	5.	Judaism and Christianity	306

ABBREVIATIONS	311
NOTES	313
SELECT BIBLIOGRAPHY	396
INDEX	399

MAPS AND TABLE

The Roman Empire *circa* A.D. 68	xxx–xxxi
The Roman Empire *circa* 133 B.C.	224
The Roman Empire at the Death of Augustus	224
Genealogical Tree of the Chief Members of the Julio-Claudian Dynasty	270
Italy	290

CHRONOLOGICAL TABLE

133   Tiberius Gracchus, tribune, proposes a land law. Opposed by tribune Octavius who is deposed; land law passed and land-commission established. Pergamum bequeathed to Rome by Attalus III. Gracchus murdered. Scipio Aemilianus storms Numantia and settles Spain. Slave war continues in Sicily

132   Court established to punish Gracchus' supporters. Land-commission working. Slave-war ended and Sicily reorganized. Revolt of Aristonicus in Asia Minor

131   *Lex tabellaria* of tribune Papirius Carbo establishes secret ballot for legislation

130   Aristonicus defeated by Perperna

129   Death of Scipio Aemilianus. Organization of province of Asia

126   Law of tribune Pennus *de peregrinis*. Sardinia restless

125   M. Fulvius Flaccus, consul, proposes enfranchisement of the Latins. Revolt of Fregellae

124   Defeated Fregellans settled at Fabrateria. War against Arverni and Allobroges in Gaul

123   First tribunate of Gaius Gracchus who proposes many laws. *Lex Rubria* (or 122) establishes Junonia on the site of Carthage; later repealed. *Castellum* at Aquae Sextiae near Massilia

122   Second tribunate of Gaius Gracchus and further legislation. Opposition of M. Livius Drusus. Gracchus fails to win re-election for 121. Balearic Islands subdued and colonies founded at Palma and Pollentia

121   Senate passes the 'last decree'. Civil disorder in which Gaius Gracchus is killed; his followers executed by Opimius. Defeat of Arverni and Allobroges; Via Domitia constructed in southern Gaul

120   Trial and acquittal of Opimius
119   Marius, as tribune, carries legislation to improve voting methods. Gracchan land-commission abolished. *Lex agraria*
118   Colony at Narbo Martius in southern Gaul. Adherbal, Hiempsal and Jugurtha become joint rulers of Numidia
117   Death of Hiempsal
116   Jugurtha consolidates his position. Senatorial commission sent to settle Numidian affairs
115   Aemilius Scaurus, consul, regulates apportionment of freedmen in tribes
114   Marius in Spain. Scordisci defeat C. Cato in Macedonia
113   Cn. Carbo defeated at Noreia by Cimbri
112   Jugurtha sacks Cirta. Rome declares war on Jugurtha
111   *Lex agraria (lex Thoria?)*. Temporary agreement with Jugurtha
110   Mamilian enquiry. Renewal of war in Africa; surrender of Aulus Albinus
109   Metellus gains some success against Jugurtha
107   Marius, elected consul, enlists volunteers and *proletarii*; succeeds Metellus and captures Capsa. Tigurini defeat Cassius in Gaul
106   Birth of Cicero and Pompey. Caepio's *lex iudiciaria*. Marius advances into western Numidia. Bocchus of Mauretania surrenders Jugurtha to Sulla
105   Cimbri and Teutones destroy armies of Caepio and Mallius at Arausio
104   Judiciary law of Servilius Glaucia. Marius, consul II, reorganizes Roman army. *Lex Domitia* concerning election to the priestly colleges. Second Sicilian Slave War
103   Saturninus tribune: corn law, *lex de maiestate*, land-allotments for Marius' veterans. Marius, consul III, trains army in Gaul
102   Marius, consul IV, defeats Teutones near Aquae Sextiae. M. Antonius sent to Cilicia to deal with pirates
101   Marius, consul V, and Catulus defeat Cimbri near Vercellae
100   Marius consul VI. Legislation of Saturninus. Marius breaks with Saturninus and Glaucia; rioting in Rome; *senatus consultum ultimum*; Marius restores order. Death of Saturninus and Glaucia. Birth of Julius Caesar. Second Sicilian Slave War ended. Colony settled at Eporedia in Gallia Cisalpina
99   Reaction in favour of Senate
98   *Lex Caecilia Didia*. Marius leaves Rome for Asia. Revolt in Lusitania
97   Sulla praetor (rather than in 93?) and ordered to install Ariobarzanes as king of Cappodocia in 96
96   Ptolemy Apion dies; bequeaths Cyrene to Rome
95   *Lex Licinia Mucia*: expulsion order. Rome orders Mithridates out of Paphlagonia and Cappadocia. Tigranes becomes king of Armenia

94   Death of Nicomedes III (Euegetes) of Bithynia

92   Condemnation of Rutilius Rufus *de repetundis*. Suppression of Latin *rhetors* by censors

91   Tribunate of M. Livius Drusus, whose plans for the allies fail; his assassination. Outbreak of Social War; massacre of Romans at Asculum

90   Roman reverses in Social War. *Lex Iulia*

89   Victories of Strabo and Sulla. *Lex Plautia Papiria. Lex Pompeia*

88   Sulpicius Rufus tribune. Proposal to transfer the Mithridatic command from Sulla to Marius. Sulla marches on Rome with his army, captures the city, repeals Sulpicius' legislation and passes some laws to strengthen the Senate. Marius escapes. Social War limited to Samnites who gradually yield. Mithridates overruns Asia Minor; massacres many Romans and Italians; joined by Athens

87   Cinna and Marius occupy Rome; massacre of Sulla's supporters. Sulla lands in Greece and besieges Athens. Carbo consul 87–84

86   Marius, consul VII, dies. Flaccus and Fimbria sent to Asia. Sulla takes Athens and defeats Mithridates' armies at Chaeronea and Orchomenus

85   Sulla negotiates Treaty of Dardanus with Mithridates. Settlement of Asia

84   New citizens distributed through all the tribes. Cinna killed by mutineers. Carbo remains sole consul

83   Sulla lands in Italy and is supported by Pompey. Murena begins a Second Mithridatic War

82   Civil War in Italy; Sulla victorious at the battle of the Colline Gate. Proscriptions. Sertorius leaves for Spain. Pompey defeats Sulla's opponents in Sicily. Sulla orders Murena to stop fighting against Mithridates

81   Sulla dictator; constitutional settlement and reform of criminal law. Pompey defeats Marians in Africa. Sertorius driven out of Spain

80   Sulla consul. Sertorius returns to Spain. Ptolemy Auletes installed as king of Egypt

79   Sulla, no longer consul, resigns dictatorship in 79 (if not already in 80). Sertorius defeats Metellus Pius in Spain

78   Death of Sulla. Aemilius Lepidus challenges Sulla's constitution. P. Servilius campaigns against the pirates for three years in Lycia, Pamphylia and Isauria

77   Lepidus defeated by Catulus and Pompey; dies in Sardinia. Pompey appointed against Sertorius

76   Attempts to restore powers to tribunes. Sertorius successful against Metellus and Pompey

75   *Lex Aurelia* allows tribunes to hold other offices later. Cicero quaestor in Sicily.

75–74 Death of Nicomedes who bequeaths Bithynia to Rome

74   Cyrene made a Rome province. Reinforcements sent to Spain. M. Antonius given command against the pirates. Mithridates invades Bithynia; Lucullus sent against him

73   Tribune Licinius Macer agitates for reform. Lex Terentia Cassia deals with distribution of corn. Rising of Spartacus at Capua. Lucullus relieves Cyzicus and defeats Mithridates on the Rhyndacus

72   Spartacus continues successfully. Sertorius assassinated by Perperna; Pompey defeats Perperna and settles Spain. L. Lucullus campaigns against Mithridates in Pontus. M. Lucullus defeats Thracian tribes. M. Antonius defeated by pirates of Crete

71   Spartacus defeated by Crassus. Pompey returns from Spain. Lucullus defeats Mithridates who flees to Tigranes

70   First consulship of Pompey and Crassus. Restoration of tribunician powers. Iudicia publica reorganized. Trial of Verres, governor of Sicily. Birth of Virgil

69   Lucullus invades Armenia and captures the capital, Tigranocerta

68   Mithridates returns to Pontus. Unrest in Lucullus' army but he captures Nisibis

67   Lex Gabinia invests Pompey with extraordinary command against the pirates whom he clears from the whole Mediterranean

66   Lex Manilia gives Pompey command against Mithridates, who is finally defeated. First Catilinarian 'conspiracy'. Cicero, praetor, delivers speech de imperio Pompei

65   Crassus censor; his intrigues for influence in Spain and Egypt fail. Pompey campaigns in the Caucasus. Birth of Horace

64   Pompey in Syria; end of Seleucid monarchy

63   Cicero consul. Lex agraria of Rullus. Caesar elected Pontifex Maximus. Birth of Octavian (Augustus). Conspiracy of Catiline; execution of conspirators. Pompey in Damascus and Jerusalem; end of Hasmonean power. Mithridates dies in Crimea

62   Defeat and death of Catiline at Pistoia. Clodius profanes Bona Dea festival. Pompey settles the East (including making Syria a province), returns to Italy and dismisses his army (Dec.)

61   The Senate opposes Pompey's acta; his triumph. Trial of Clodius. Caesar governor of Further Spain. Revolt of the Allobroges. Aedui appeal to Rome

60   Caesar returns from Spain; his agreement with Pompey and Crassus, the 'first triumvirate'

59   Caesar consul; carries legislation. Pompey marries Julia, Caesar's daughter. Caesar receives Cisalpine Gaul and Illyricum under lex

Vatinia; Senate adds Transalpine Gaul. Senate recognizes Ptolemy Auletes as king of Egypt

58 Tribunate of Clodius: corn-law. Cicero exiled; Cato sent to Cyprus which is annexed. Caesar defeats Helvetii and Ariovistus. Ptolemy driven out of Alexandria

57 Rioting in Rome between Clodius and Milo. Return of Cicero (Sept.). Pompey concerned with food-supply. Caesar defeats Belgae and Nervii

56 Disagreement among the triumvirs. Cicero attacks Caesar's land-law. Conference at Luca (April). Cato returns from Cyprus. Caesar campaigns against Veneti and Morini

55 Second consulship of Pompey and Crassus. The three triumvirs receive fresh commands. Caesar massacres Usipetes and Tencteri; bridges the Rhine; invades Britain

54 Pompey remains near Rome and governs Spain through legates. Death of Julia (Sept.). Rioting in Rome. Caesar's second British expedition; revolt in north-east Gaul. Crassus, in Syria, prepares for Parthian campaign. Gabinius, governor of Syria, restores Ptolemy to his throne

53 Continued rioting in Rome; no consuls elected until July. Crassus defeated and killed by Parthians at Carrhae. Unrest in Gaul partly pacified by Caesar

52 Milo kills Clodius (Jan.). Pompey sole consul until August. Law of the Ten Tribunes. Revolt of central Gaul under Vercingetorix. Caesar repelled from Gergovia. Besieges Alesia; Vercingetorix surrenders

51 Optimate attacks on Caesar, who gains support of Curio. Revolt of Bellovaci; siege of Uxellodunum. Parthian invasion of Syria; Cicero sent as governor to Cilicia. Death of Ptolemy Auletes. Ptolemy XIII marries Cleopatra; joint rulers

50 Curio vetoes discussion of a successor to Caesar. Pompey ill during summer. Curio proposes that both Caesar and Pompey disarm: vetoed. Pompey asked by consul Marcellus to save the State (Nov.). Tribunes leave Rome. Caesar organizes Gaul and crosses the Rubicon into Italy

49 Civil War. Pompey crosses to Greece. Caesar, dictator I for eleven days, carries emergency legislation and goes to Spain where he defeats Pompeian forces at Ilerda. Surrender of Massilia. Curio defeated and killed in Africa

48 Caesar consul II. Disturbances in Italy; Milo killed. Caesar crosses to Greece: campaign of Dyrrachium; defeats Pompey at Pharsalus. Pompey murdered in Egypt. Caesar arrives in Egypt; Alexandrine War; Cleopatra queen. Pharnaces of Bosporus defeats Domitius Calvinus in Pontus

47   Caesar dictator II (*in absentia*); Antony, his Master of Horse, tries to maintain order in Italy. Caesar defeats Pharnaces at Zela, settles the East and returns to Italy; quells a mutiny in Campania. He passes legislation on debt and sails against the Pompeian forces in Africa

46   Caesar defeats Pompeians at Thapsus; organizes Africa Nova. Suicide of Cato. Caesar, dictator II and consul III, returns to Rome and holds triumph. Legislation. Reform of calendar. Caesar leaves for Spain (Nov.)

45   Caesar, dictator III and consul IV, defeats Pompeians at Munda (March). Returns to Rome and receives exceptional honours

44   Caesar dictator IV (for life) and consul V. Refuses crown at Lupercalia. Conspiracy and murder of Caesar (15 March). Octavian returns from Greece. Antony receives command in Cisalpine and Transalpine Gaul. Cicero's first *Philippic* against Antony

43   Antony's siege of Mutina raised. Deaths of consuls Hirtius and Pansa. D. Brutus killed in Gaul. Octavian declared consul (Aug.). Triumvirate of Octavian, Antony and Lepidus (Nov.). Proscriptions: death of Cicero. M. Brutus in Macedonia, Cassius in Syria

42   Julius Caesar deified as Divus. Sextus Pompeius controls Sicily. Brutus and Cassius, defeated at Philippi, commit suicide (Oct.). Birth of emperor Tiberius

41   Perusine War in Italy. Antony in Asia Minor; meets Cleopatra and visits Alexandria

40   L. Antonius surrenders Perusia to Octavian. Agreement at Brundisium partitions the Roman world (Oct.). Antony marries Octavia. Parthians invade Syria. Herod recognized as king of Judaea by Senate. Virgil's *Fourth Eclogue*

39   Agreement at Misenum between Antony, Octavian and Sextus Pompeius. Ventidius defeats Parthians at Mt. Amanus

38   Octavian marries Livia (Jan.). Naval successes of Sextus Pompeius. Victory of Ventidius at Gindarus; Antony captures Samosata

37   Pact of Tarentum; triumvirate probably renewed. Herod and Sosius capture Jerusalem. Antony marries Cleopatra at Antioch. Amyntas made king of Galatia, and Polemo of Pontus; Archelaus succeeds in Cappadocia

36   Tribunician sacrosanctity granted to Octavian. Offensive against Sextus Pompeius who is defeated off Naulochus in Sicily. Lepidus ceases to be a triumvir. Antony fails to capture Phraaspa and retires through Armenia

35   Octavian campaigns in Illyria. Death of Sextus Pompeius

34   Octavian in Illyria. Antony invades Armenia; celebrates a triumph at Alexandria. The 'Donations of Alexandria'

33 Octavian consul II. Antony in Armenia; winters (33–32) with Cleopatra at Ephesus

32 Octavian justifies his acts to the Senate. Antony divorces Octavia. Octavian publishes Antony's will in Rome. Antony and Cleopatra winter (32–31) in Greece

31 Octavian consul III (and each year until 23); defeats Antony at Actium (Sept.) and winters in Asia

30 Tribunician power offered to Octavian but probably declined. Suicide of Antony. Octavian enters Alexandria. Suicide of Cleopatra

30–28 M. Crassus campaigns in Balkans. Cornelius Gallus in Egypt

29 Octavian's triple triumph. Dedication of temple of Divus Iulius

28 Octavian and Agrippa hold census: *lectio Senatus*. Temple of Apollo on Palatine dedicated. Mausoleum of Augustus begun. Messalla campaigns in Spain

27 Constitutional settlement. Octavian receives name of Augustus and *imperium* for ten years (Jan.). Triumph of Crassus. Augustus in Gaul and Spain until 25. The first Pantheon built by Agrippa

26 Disgrace and suicide of Cornelius Gallus. Arabian expedition of Aelius Gallus launched

25 Marriage of Julia and Marcellus. Varro defeats the Salassi. Tarraconensis organized as a province. Annexation of Galatia on death of Amyntas. Gallus in Arabia Felix. Success of C. Petronius in Ethiopian War (25–23)

23 Augustus ill. Conspiracy of Caepio and Murena. Constitutional resettlement. Augustus resigns consulship and receives *proconsulare imperium maius* and full tribunician powers. Death of Marcellus. Agrippa sent to East. Publication of first three books of Horace's *Odes*

22 Augustus refuses dictatorship, and consulship for life, but accepts the *cura annonae*. Augustus in Greece and Asia for three years

21 Agrippa marries Julia

20 Parthia returns Roman standards. Tiberius enters Armenia and crowns Tigranes

19 Augustus returns to Rome. Arch of Augustus in Rome. Agrippa pacifies Spain. Cornelius Balbus campaigns against the Garamantes. Deaths of Virgil and Tibullus

18 Augustus' *imperium* renewed for five years. Agrippa co-regent with *imperium maius* and *tribunicia potestas. Leges Iuliae. Lectio Senatus*

17 Augustus adopts Gaius and Lucius, his grandsons. Ludi Saeculares celebrated; Horace's *Carmen Saeculare*

16–13 Augustus in Gaul

16 Agrippa in East. Noricum incorporated

15	Tiberius and Drusus defeat Raeti and Vindelici and reach Danube
14	Agrippa assigns Bosporan kingdom to Polemo
13	Return of Augustus; renewal of his imperium for five years. Tiberius consul. Return of Agrippa. Death of Lepidus. Dedication of theatre of Marcellus. Vinicius campaigns in Pannonia
12	Augustus becomes Pontifex Maximus. Death of Agrippa. Tiberius in Pannonia. Drusus dedicates altar near Lugdunum and campaigns in Germany until 9
11	Tiberius divorces Agrippina and marries Agrippa's widow, Julia
9	Death of Drusus near the Elbe. Dedication of Ara Pacis in Rome
8	Augustus' imperium extended for ten years. Census. Deaths of Horace and Maecenas. Tiberius in Germany
7	Rome divided into fourteen regiones
6	Tiberius given tribunicia potestas for five years. He retires to Rhodes. Paphlagonia added to Galatia
5	Augustus' twelfth consulship. C. Caesar introduced to public life
4	Death of Herod the Great
2	Augustus consul for thirteenth time; becomes Pater Patriae. Exile of Julia. Dedication of temple of Mars Ultor

A.D.

1	C. Caesar in Syria
2	Tiberius returns to Rome from Rhodes. Death of L. Caesar. C. Caesar settles Armenia
3	Augustus' imperium renewed for ten years
4	Death of C. Caesar in Lycia. Augustus adopts Tiberius who receives tribunicia potestas for ten years. Tiberius adopts Germanicus and goes to the German front. Lex Aelia Sentia
5	Tiberius advances to the Elbe
6	Aerarium militare and office of Praefectus Vigilum created. Revolt in Pannonia and Illyricum. Maroboduus recognized as king of the Marcomanni. Judaea made a province; assessment made by Sulpicius Quirinius, legate of Syria
8	Claudius becomes an augur. Ovid banished. Pannonians surrender
9	Lex Papia Poppaea. Revolt in Dalmatia crushed. Defeat of Varus by Arminius in Germany with loss of three legions
12	Triumph of Tiberius
13	Augustus' imperium renewed for ten years. Tiberius receives tribunicia potestas for ten years and proconsular imperium co-ordinate with that of Augustus
14	Lustrum held. Death of Augustus (19 Aug.). Accession of Tiberius. Sejanus made a Praetorian Prefect. Legions in Pannonia and Germany

	revolt. Drusus sent to crush mutiny in Pannonia. Germanicus crosses the Rhine against the Marsi
15	Germanicus attacks the Chatti. Achaea and Macedonia transferred from the Senate to the *princeps* and attached to Moesia
16	Libo Drusus accused; suicide. Germanicus again invades Germany; he is recalled
17	Triumph of Germanicus. Cn. Piso legate of Syria. Earthquake in Asia Minor. Cappadocia and Commagene organized as imperial provinces. Revolt of Tacfarinas in Africa. Death of Livy
18	Tiberius, consul III, with Germanicus. Germanicus in East. Armenia granted to Artaxias. Germanicus goes to Egypt
19	Jews expelled from Rome. Arminius killed. Piso leaves Syria. Death of Germanicus at Antioch
20	Trial and suicide of Piso
21	Tiberius, consul IV, with his son Drusus. Tiberius retires for a time to Campania. Revolt of Florus and Sacrovir in Gaul. Trouble in Thrace
21–22	Castra Praetoria built in Rome
22	Drusus granted tribunician power
23	Death of Drusus
24	Defeat and death of Tacfarinas in Africa
25	Cremutius Cordus accused; suicide
26	Trouble checked in Thrace. Pontius Pilate appointed prefect of Judaea
27	Tiberius withdraws to Capreae
28	Revolt of the Frisii
29	Death of Livia. Banishment of Agrippina the elder
30	Publication of the *History* of Velleius Paterculus
31	Tiberius, consul V, with Sejanus. Gaius receives *toga virilis*. Sejanus put to death. Macro appointed Praetorian Prefect
33	Death of Agrippina on island of Pandateria. Gaius quaestor. Financial difficulties in Rome. Possible date of the Crucifixion of Jesus Christ
34	Tetrachy of Philip incorporated into Syria
36	Pontius Pilate sent to Rome by L. Vitellius, governor of Syria
37	Death of Tiberius (16 March). Accession of Gaius (Caligula); he is consul with Claudius. Commagene reestablished as a client kingdom
38	Death and deification of Drusilla. Jewish disturbances in Alexandria. Polemo II receives Pontus and Cotys Armenia Minor
39	Gaius goes to the Rhine. Julia and Agrippina exiled
40	Gaius' expedition to the Channel; returns to Rome. Ptolemy of Mauretania murdered in Rome; revolt in Mauretania. Jewish embassy from Alexandria to Rome. Agrippa I receives kingdom of Antipas. Judaea restless
41	Gaius murdered (24 Jan.). Claudius made emperor. The Chauci

defeated. Claudius settles Alexandrian trouble. Agrippa I receives Judaea and Samaria. Exile of Seneca to Corsica

42   Revolt of Scribonianus in Dalmatia; his suicide. Mauretania organized as two provinces

43   Expedition to Britain. Lycia made an imperial province

44   Claudius' triumph over Britain. Achaea and Macedonia transferred to Senate. Death of Agrippa I; Judaea reverts to provincial status

46   Thrace made a province

47   Triumph of Aulus Plautius for conquest of Britain. Claudius and L. Vitellius censors. *Ludi Saeculares*. Corbulo campaigns against the Frisii. Ostorius Scapula in Britain

48   Messalina killed. Claudius marries Agrippina

49   Seneca recalled from Corsica and made praetor and Nero's tutor

50   Claudius adopts Nero as guardian for Britannicus. Agrippa II rules in Chalcis

51   Burrus made Praetorian Prefect. Vespasian consul. Caratacus defeated in Wales. Vologeses king of Parthia (or in 52). Gallio proconsul in Achaea (51–52)

53   Nero marries Octavia. Parthians occupy Armenia and Tiridates recovers the throne

54   Death of Claudius. Accession of Nero. Claudius deified

55   Britannicus poisoned. Pallas dismissed. Corbulo goes to the East

56   *Praefecti aerarii* replace *quaestores aerarii*

57   Nero orders senators and knights to take part in Games

58   Nero refuses perpetual consulship. Corbulo captures Artaxata

59   Nero murders Agrippina; establishes Greek Games. Corbulo takes Tigranocerta

60   Neronia established. Corbulo settles Armenia; governor of Syria. Festus succeeds Felix as governor of Judaea

61   Revolt of Boudicca and Iceni in Britain

62   Death of Burrus. Tigellinus made Praetorian Prefect. Seneca disgraced. Nero divorces Octavia and marries Poppaea. Octavia murdered. Paetus surrenders to the Parthians at Rhandeia

64   Great fire at Rome. Persecution of the Christians. Domus Aurea begun. Mission to Ethiopia. Cottian Alps made a province (64–65); Pontus incorporated into Galatia

65   Conspiracy of Piso. Suicides of Seneca and Lucan. Death of Poppaea. Musonius Rufus exiled

66   Nero crowns Tiridates king of Armenia in Rome and goes to Greece. Thrasea Paetus condemned. Conspiracy of Vinicius at Beneventum. Nero marries Statilia Messalina. Temple of Janus closed. Suicide of Petronius. Rebellion in Palestine

67   Nero at Corinthian canal. Corbulo ordered to commit suicide.
     Vespasian in command in Judaea; Josephus surrenders to him
68   Nero returns to Italy. Death of Nero (6 June). Galba, accepted by
     Senate and Praetorians, enters Rome (autumn). Verginius Rufus
     opposes Vindex's rebellion in Gaul. Defeat and death of Vindex.
     Vespasian attacks Jerusalem
69   After death of Galba and brief reigns of Otho and Vitellius, Vespasian
     becomes emperor and reaches Rome in the summer of 70

PREFACE

Reflection on the existing number of histories of Rome might well raise doubt about the desirability of adding to them. But since research does not stand still and its more assured results often take long to reach the handbook, there may be a place for a brief account of this period which lays no claim to originality of interpretation but which attempts to benefit from the work of recent years and to put the reader on the track of some of this for further study. I am conscious of the risks involved in trying to include much in small compass, but present-day production-costs suggest that an author owes a debt of reasonable brevity to both publisher and reader. If some of my younger readers should feel that this book might profitably have been still shorter, I can only assure them that I have tried to be ever mindful of a phrase of Cicero: 'ut brevissime potui'. The purpose of the Notes that I have included is manifold. I hope that they may help to temper the dogmatism inevitable in a book of this kind, to give some indication of the sources and of some of the problems that they raise, to afford the slightly more advanced student a few hints about where to seek further information, and by no means least to give some clues to the immense obligations that I owe to modern writers. As this debt is very wide, I cannot define it in detail here, but I would mention in particular both the individual contributors to volumes IX and X of *Cambridge Ancient History*, and the work of my friend, the late Professor M. Cary whose generous help and wise advice in the field of ancient history I have enjoyed for over thirty years. I am greatly indebted also to another friend and colleague, Professor A. Momigliano, for his kindness in reading through the typescript of this book and for his helpful suggestions: it is hardly necessary to add the time-honoured note that this kindness does not involve any suggestion of his concurrence with any of the views expressed in it or responsibility for any of its shortcomings.

H. H. S.

January 1958

Preface to Second Edition

In this new edition I am glad of the opportunity to correct some misprints and errors of the first, and I am most grateful to friends, reviewers and some unknown correspondents who have been kind enough to draw my attention to some of these. In order not to disturb the pagination of the text, changes in this part of the book have been kept down to a bare minimum. It is for this practical reason that I have not availed myself of the suggestion made by some reviewers that schoolchildren would have found it useful if a number of technicalities had received fuller explanation and if Latin phrases had been translated; it may be hoped that where this need exists it may lead them to make enquiries of their sixth-form teachers or else to turn to the fuller histories or encyclopaedias (as *The Oxford Classical Dictionary*). In the Notes, I have tried to take fuller advantage of work done in the last four years. If the additions are greater for the period 133–70 B.C., this is a tribute to the work of Dr E. Badian, whose *Foreign Clientelae* and numerous articles have made such a deep impact on the study of these years.

H. H. S.

September 1962

Preface to Third, Fourth and Fifth Editions

I am glad, at the request of the publishers, to have this opportunity of trying to keep this book reasonably up-to-date. For practical reasons, as in earlier revisions, I have made relatively few changes in the text but considerable additions in the Notes.

In this latest edition I have also added a Chronological Table and a Select Bibliography.

H. H. S.

February 1970
April 1975
July 1981

FOREWORD

From the Gracchi to Nero has become the most popular book on Roman history in the anglophone world since Gibbon's *The Decline and Fall of the Roman Empire*. In the fifty and more years since its first publication in 1959, the year that Scullard was promoted to Professor of Ancient History at King's College London, it has been through four revised editions (1963, 1970, 1976 and 1982) and numerous reprints, and has sold tens of thousands of copies. Although it has not been revised since Scullard's death in 1983 and several competitor volumes have since appeared, it still leads the field as the book on their shelf to which teachers, students and the general reader turn for a clear and sensible introduction to any episode in the story of the central two hundred years of Roman history from 133 B.C. to A.D. 68. How do we explain its success, and what has been its impact?

The success is easy to explain: *From the Gracchi to Nero* fills a large need and does it very well. In 1959 and still today school and university syllabuses focus on the pivotal periods of the fall of the Republic and establishment of the Principate. Although Hannibal and Hadrian lie outside the book's chronological range, it efficiently covers the most generally familiar events of Roman history and the best known figures including Tiberius and Gaius Gracchus, Marius and Sulla, Pompey and Caesar, Cicero and Cato, Mark Antony and Augustus, and the emperors Tiberius, Gaius, Claudius and Nero. Here in one compact volume of 500 pages, notes and indices included, we have it all.

While the chronological centrality is important, the deeper reason for this book's vibrant longevity lies in its qualities as a general introduction or textbook. Like Scullard himself, it bears a quiet air of authority. As is attested by the bibliographies for 'Ancient history to A.D. 500' which he compiled for the *Annual Bulletin of Historical Literature* from 1949 to 1968, Scullard was a dedicated reader of modern scholarship on ancient history. His knowledge of Roman history, both the ancient evidence and modern debates, was broad and deep. In each new edition the footnotes were meticulously updated, and the text amended where he judged it necessary, which was not frequent. Despite his learning, however, Scullard had the knack of not assuming too much of his readers, and *From the Gracchi to Nero* is mostly open to those with no prior knowledge of Rome (although it is curious that Scullard left some citations in Latin through to the 1982 edition). Its clarity and authority also owe much to his avoidance of polemic and disavowal of originality of inter-pretation: the book, like the man, is unfailingly modest and polite. The writ-ing too is concise and clear, excepting the occasional overpacked sentence, in itself a monumental achievement which is now all the more outstanding amid the often linguistically untidy products of word processors. And so the reader is quietly, even unconsciously, persuaded of the dispassionate reliability of Scullard's narrative and judgments.

The question of impact, that is the view of Rome which the book has propagated, is more complex. Because *From the Gracchi to Nero* was presented by Scullard in its Preface as a 'handbook' and has been used as such, it has received no critical notice from other historians after the few and brief reviews of the first edition, even though Scullard himself noted in the Preface that writing a handbook inevitably involved 'dogmatism'. In fact *From the Gracchi to Nero*, which he sub-titled *A History of Rome from* 133 B.C. *to* A.D. 68, completed a whole history of the rise and fall of the Republic and its meta-morphosis into the Principate. It had been preceded by his *A History of the Roman World 753–146* B.C., first published in 1935, on the basis of which he was that year appointed Reader in Ancient History at King's College London. This earlier history, a volume of similar size and structure, was almost as popular, with re-editions in 1951, 1961 and 1980. The unity of conception of the two works was recognized in their joint translation into Italian as a two-volume *Storia del mondo romano* (1983), for which Scullard himself cut out the now unnecessary background sections in the first chapter of the second work. A third element in the equation is Scullard's *Roman Politics 220–150* B.C. (1951, second edition 1973), which had developed out of his doctoral dissertation on Scipio Africanus. This was his principal overtly theoretical contribution to the interpretation of Roman history and its ideas underpin the approach to Roman political history adopted in the two handbooks between which it was first published.

Scullard's project to record the history of the Roman Republic 'from the foundation of the city' (*ab urbe condita*) would have made obvious sense to a Roman, although most would not have seen its concision as a virtue. So too would his focus on political and military history – to which his chapters on social, economic and cultural developments, while important, are subordinate

– and his conviction that the central issue of Republican history was political morality. Noting Rome's dominance of the Mediterranean world by 146 B.C. and the killing of Tiberius Gracchus in 133, Scullard begins *From the Gracchi to Nero* with the rhetorical question, 'She was gaining the whole world: must she at the same time lose her own soul?'. The question is adapted from a quotation from Warde Fowler on changes in Roman religion, which Scullard had cited on the penultimate narrative page of the earlier history, 'Rome gained the world and lost her soul'.

Scullard's overview of Roman history is grounded in early twentieth-century liberalism. Rome's destiny was to unite Italy and bring peace and prosperity to its empire. The senate's refusal to address the grievances of Rome's Italian allies was 'criminally short-sighted', and although Scullard asserts that the allies' revolt in 91 B.C. was for independence, he saw no need a page later to explain their rapid acceptance of Roman citizenship; this was a necessary step for Romans and Italians to form a nation. Rome's overseas conquests, whose motivation is more fully discussed in his earlier book, are presented as necessary to maintain and extend peace, prosperity and, where it was lacking, civilization. Roman aggression and brutality, although usually noted, are underplayed. Some statements use revealingly modern names: the need for intervention in the Balkans, and Caesar preventing the Germans from flooding across the Rhine so that Gaul could be civilized and eventually become France. Rome's Mediterranean and European empire is often referred to as 'the world', for which Rome had taken on 'responsibility'. The undeniable maladministration under the late Republic was rectified by Augustus who instituted fair taxation based on censuses (no mention of the novel and hated poll-tax) and made governors 'salaried professionals' who were promoted for 'efficiency' (only the salary might pass scrutiny). The emperors Tiberius and Claudius and Nero's advisers, Seneca and Burrus, are all praised for promoting the well-being of the provinces.

Scullard's view of Roman politics was conservative. The Republic fared best when controlled by the Senate, the repository of experience and 'political wisdom'. Although also part of the elite, to Scullard the Equites formed a 'Third Estate' which represented business interests and sought greater political power in the late Republic to further their sectional interests. The people are damned throughout as an 'unrepresentative' urban mob, 'irresponsible' and 'unworthy to govern'. The Republic therefore fell in 60 B.C. when the so-called First Triumvirate 'backed by armed force, by the urban populace and by many of the Equites, imposed their will on the State and destroyed the power of the Senate'. The crisis of the late Republic was one of moral leadership: 'could (Rome) produce sufficient men of insight and goodwill who would persuade both the governing class and people to face squarely the pressing problems of the day?'

In the middle Republic men like Scipio Africanus and the elder Cato had competed to provide such leadership, building up factions of supporters; thus a few families had 'shaped the destiny of Rome and the world'. Factions around leaders continued into the late Republic, and indeed into the Principate, although in From the Gracchi to Nero Scullard did not have space to analyse them as he had in his Roman Politics (and anyway others had done the job for Caesar and Augustus). But upper-class politics became polarised between Optimates and Populares, whom Scullard introduces as individuals choosing different ways, oligarchic and populist, to achieve personal aims, but later tends to treat as obstinate ideological groupings with the Optimates defending traditional senatorial dominance at any cost. Scullard's Republic fell because of personal ambitions which exploited rather than sought to solve the problems Rome faced. A number of leading Romans are praised for trying to address the problems, such as Tiberius and Gaius Gracchus and Julius Caesar, or to encourage a unity of purpose among the upper classes, such as Cicero. Augustus' achievement on both fronts is grudgingly recognized ('not a man of genius'), but also the cost which was replacement of the Republic by a thinly disguised autocracy. Thereafter emperors are judged, as they are in the Roman elite tradition, by their willingness to respect and work with the Senate, although the underlying and inevitable trend was towards absolutism. The key virtue now becomes 'stable government and sound administration', more to the benefit of the empire than Rome: 'although it was too late to save the Republic, Augustus at least saved the provinces'. The broad view tacitly echoes that of the third-century Greek senator Cassius Dio whose history of Rome includes our only, albeit incomplete, ancient narrative of the period from 133 B.C. to A.D. 68.

For the political and military narrative a new Scullard would insert the evidence from new inscriptions such as those illustrating the turbulent annexation of the province of Asia around 130 B.C. or the record of the senate's decision in A.D. 19 to acquit Calpurnius Piso of poisoning Germanicus but condemn him for treason. There is a considerable literature since 1982 to digest on topics including the nature of later Republican politics and the monumentalization of the Augustan regime. More difficult to integrate would be the enormous volume of work on socio-economic aspects, much drawing on the boom in archaeology of private life. When first published From the Gracchi to Nero was almost ahead of its time in devoting chapters, two each for the Republic and Principate, to economic and social life and art, literature and thought. Scullard was aware of the growing archaeological evidence, and his discussion of the agrarian law of Tiberius Gracchus, although we would not now use the term latifundia, is still a useful survey of the problems. However, these chapters buttress Scullard's narrative: culture is part of the nation-building process, and socio-economic development the product of good government. The broad sweep of socio-economic history, including the political 'problems' which the late Republic's inadequate leadership failed to solve, were not part of Scullard's conception of the purpose of his books. For issues such as the economic and demographic impact of Roman militarism and imperialism, the cultural and political background to the Social War and its effects, changes in social structures and attitudes, the expansion of Rome into a megalopolis, religious developments including the introduction of ruler worship, whether and how 'Romanization' of the provinces occurred, and so on, the reader must turn elsewhere. But for a succinct and sensible narrative account – with due awareness of its presuppositions – of the fall of the Republic and emergence of the Principate, still one of the great stories of world history, *From the Gracchi to Nero* remains without peer.

Dominic Rathbone
Professor of Ancient History
King's College London

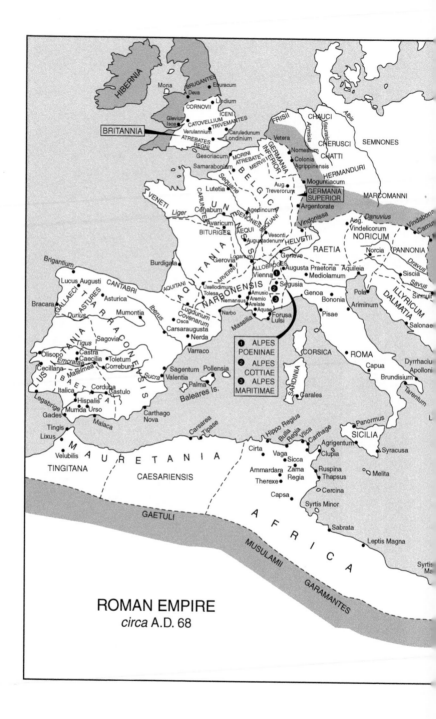

HIBERNIA

Mona
Deva
BRIGANTES • Eburacum
CORNOVII
Lindium
CATOVELLIUM ICENI
Glevium TRIVEMANTES
Isca
Verulannium
Caruledunum
ATREBATES Londinium
REGNI

BRITANNIA

FRISII CHAUCI
Vetera
CHERUSCI SEMNONES
Nomessum
Colonia CHATTI
Agrippinensis
HERMANDURI
Aug. Moguntiacum
Treverorum GERMANIA
SUPERIOR MARCOMANNI
Argentorate

VENETI
Liger
Cenabum
Lutetia
Agedincum
Avaricum
BITURIGES AEQUI
Augustadunum
HELVETII
Vindonissa

Gesoriacum
MORINI
Samarabonum ATREBATE
MERVII BELGIC
GERMANIA
INFERIOR

Brigantium
Lucus Augusti CANTABRI
Asturica
Bracara GALLAECI ASTURES
Durius Mumontia
Ibenus
CARSARAUGUSTA
TARRACONENSIS
Sagovia
Tigus
Olisopo Castra
Cecillana Caecilia Toletum
Emeratae Mafelmea Correburd
Italica Sucra
Hispalis
BAETICA
Legabrige Munda Urso
Gades
Tingis Malaca
Lixus

AQUITANI
Uxellodunum
Tolesa
NARBONENSIS
Lugdunum
Covenarum
Osca
Nerda
Varraco
Sagentum
Valentia Pollensia
Palma
Baleares Is.
Carthago
Nova

Burdigala
Gerovia
ARVERNI
Logarum
VIENNA
ALLOBROGES
Augusta Praetoria
Aquileia
Mediolamum

NORICUM
Aug.
Vindelicorum
Norcia
PANNONIA
RAETIA

Genoa
Bonona
Pisae
Ariminum

Vindabone
Carnu
Danuvius
Dravus
Savus
Siscia
Simmu
DALMATIA
Salonae

Aremio
Arelate
Aquae
Forusa
Luisi
Massilia
Narbo
Segusia
Pola

❶ ALPES
POENINAE
❷ ALPES
COTTIAE
❸ ALPES
MARITIMAE

CORSICA
ROMA
Capua
Brundisium
Tarentum
SARDINIA
Carales

Dyrrhaciu
Apolloni

Carsarea
Tipase
Cirta
Vaga
Ammardara
Therexe
Capsa

Hippo Regius
Bulla
Regia Vilica
Carthage
Sicca
Zama Clupia
Regia Ruspina
Thapsus
Cercina
Syrtis Minor
Sabrata

Agrigentum
SICILIA
Panormus
Syracusa
Melita
Leptis Magna

TINGITANA

MAURETANIA

CAESARIENSIS

GAETULI

AFRICA

MUSULAMII

GARAMANTES

Syrtis
Ma

ROMAN EMPIRE
circa A.D. 68

Miles
0 100 200 300 400 500

SARMATAE

SCYTHAE

ALANI

Tanais

Olbia

Panticapaeum

Chersonesus

COLCHIS

Phasis

IBERI

ALBANI

Gidunum

Viminacium

Terni

Pontus Euxinus

Sinope

Amisus

Thamiscyra

Trapezus

ARMENIA

Artaxata

MOESIA

Serdica

THRACE

Byzantium

Chalcedon

NIA ET PONTUS

Eupatoria

A

Nicopolis

Lake
Van

CEDONIA

Philippopolis

Nicomedia

Amasia

Cabeira

ARMENIA

Rhandeie

Tigranoceria

Thessalonica

Philippi

BITHY

Ancyra

Zela

CAPPADOCIA

Metitene

Phraspa

Cyzicus

G

A

L

A

T

Nisibis

Rhyndacus

Pegamum

Samasata

Tigris

iersalus

Lesbos

Smyrna

Sardes

Antiochia

Icanium

CILICIA

Zeugma

Carrhae

Actium

Chaer

Delphi

Euboea

Samos

Ephesus

Tennessus

Lystra

Jersus

Seleuceia

Euphrates

Ctesiphen

pla

Petras

Corinth

Miletus

HOMANDES

Coracesium

Antiochia

ACHAE

Sparta

LYCIA

Xanthus

Elmesa

Palmyra

Babylon

Rhodus

Salamis

Heliopolis

CRETA

CYPRUS

Berytus

Sidas

Damascus

Tyrus

Caesarea

Sammaria

Jammia

Bostra

Cyrene

Hirrosolymae

Gaza

Masada

Alexandria

Petusium

Petra

CYRENAICA

Memphis

Oxyrhynchus

MARMARIDAE

A E G Y P T U S

Myoshermos

Sinus
Arabicus

Coptos

Thebes

I

ROME AT THE CROSS-ROADS

1. INTRODUCTORY

Carthage and Corinth, two great cities of the ancient world, crashed to their ruin amid smoke and flame in 146 B.C., destroyed and sacked by Roman troops. Thirteen years later a Roman tribune, Tiberius Gracchus, was clubbed to death in a fracas led by an ex-consul. These tragic episodes showed clearly that Rome's power throughout the Mediterranean world was dominant and unchallengeable, but that her internal stability was weakened and threatened. She was gaining the whole world: must she at the same time lose her own soul? Could a city-state govern an empire? Could Rome adapt her institutions to meet the challenge of her increasing responsibilities? Above all, could she produce sufficient men of insight and goodwill who would persuade both the governing class and people to face squarely the pressing problems of the day and to seek solutions for the common good even when this might involve some sacrifice of individual gain by leaders and common man alike? If statesmen failed to grapple with urgent political, economic and social problems, and if sections of the community selfishly set their own interests before the well-being of the whole which now embraced Rome, Italy and an overseas Empire, then stresses and tensions might overstrain the stability of the body politic and the days of the Roman Republic would be numbered.[1]

First, therefore, we must see very briefly how Rome reached this perilous position and glance at the various sections of Rome and her Empire in an attempt to envisage their needs and responsibilities in light of the changes that they were undergoing. Then we come to the two chief themes of this book: first the century in which the Republic failed to meet the challenge and in consequence crashed to its ruin amid civil war and military dictatorship, and then the following century when the war-weary world was given peace and a stable government though at the cost of seeing the Republic restored only in name by a First Citizen whose authority did not differ widely from that of a constitutional monarch and whose successors became increasingly autocratic.

2. THE GROWTH OF ROME'S EMPIRE

Since many of the problems which faced Rome in 133 B.C. arose from her acquisition of an empire overseas, we must first see briefly how she had come to possess it. In the course of the preceding four hundred years Rome had developed from a small city-state on the banks of the Tiber into the dominant power throughout the Mediterranean. After the expulsion of the Etruscan king, Tarquinius Superbus, at the end of the Regal Period (510 B.C.), the Romans had established a Republic which gradually came to control all Italy. This process was not achieved by military conquest alone, and in fact Roman religious law (the *ius fetiale*) did not countenance wars of aggression designed to gain new territory. But in alliance with neighbouring Latin cities Rome did not hesitate to hit back when the hill tribes of central Italy began to press down against the more fertile plain of Latium. Very slowly, partly by accident and partly by design, Roman interests extended throughout central Italy and ultimately throughout the peninsula, so that by 264 B.C. she had become the dominant political and military power. But more than that, she had united all Italy within the framework of a Confederacy. Unlike many peoples of the ancient world, the Romans were most generous in sharing their own citizenship with others: thus they had incorporated a considerable part of Italy in their own State by granting all or some of the privileges of Roman citizenship to many of the cities and tribes with which they had come into contact. With the rest of Italy they had contracted alliances of varying conditions, the most favoured allies being the Latin cities. Thus the early period of fighting was ended, Italy was to a large extent united through the central power of Rome, while law and order were maintained the more easily because of the roads which Rome had constructed, and the colonies (both Roman and Latin) which had been established at strategic points.[2]

One of the chief consequences of the consolidation of Roman power in Italy was that she now stepped into the front rank of the Great Powers. The Greeks and the Hellenistic monarchs, who had carved kingdoms for themselves out of the empire of Alexander the Great, had hitherto regarded the inhabitants of central Italy as barbarians in so far as they had thought of them at all, but they received a sudden shock when news came that Pyrrhus king of Epirus, who had invaded Italy at the request of Tarentum, had been driven out of Italy by Roman arms in 275 B.C. Indeed two years later Ptolemy II king of Egypt hastened to enter into a formal 'friendship' with the Roman Republic. Thereafter for the next half century Rome and the Greek world paid little attention to one another and were content to live and let live. This was also the policy which Rome had hitherto adopted towards the dominant power in the western Mediterranean, Carthage. The main interest of Carthage was commerce, while the Romans were primarily an agricultural people who had no reason to wish to stop the Carthaginians gaining a complete trading monopoly in the western Mediterranean and closing this area to all foreign shipping. But the attention of Carthage was arrested when Rome came to control southern Italy, because at its toe lies Sicily, where both Carthage and Rome's Greek allies in southern Italy had interests. This led to the First Punic War (264–241 B.C.) when after a long and bitter struggle the Romans drove the Carthaginians out of Sicily. This they achieved only because they ventured on the sea, built up a strong fleet and smashed the naval power of Carthage. For Rome the consequences were far-reaching: she had not only become a naval power, but she had acquired control of Sicily. She decided not to include the island in her Italian confederacy but to govern a considerable part of it directly as the overseas *provincia* of a magistrate whom she sent out annually as governor. She treated in the same way Sardinia and Corsica, which she also took from Carthage.

Carthage, however, built up her influence in Spain, from which Hannibal later launched an attack on Italy (218 B.C.). For fifteen years Rome grappled with him in a life-and-death struggle in Italy until he was forced by Scipio's landing in N. Africa to return to defend his country, but in vain. Carthage was beaten for a second time, and though Rome sought no territory in Africa she found that, having ejected the Carthaginians from Spain, she had the peninsula left on her hands. This she organized into two new provinces in the south and east, but for the next sixty years she had to spend much time and energy in crushing the wilder independent tribes of the interior: the process was not essentially completed until the Celtiberian capital of Numantia was destroyed in 133 B.C., nor was the yet wilder north-west corner finally pacified until the time of Augustus.

Thus by 200 B.C. Rome had become the unchallenged mistress of the western Mediterranean. She next faced the Hellenistic East, where she intervened in response to appeals from Greek cities who were the victims of aggression by Antiochus of Syria and Philip of Macedon, the latter having in fact sided with Hannibal against Rome during the Second Punic War. After defeating Philip (Second Macedonian War, 200–196), Rome at first proclaimed a policy of 'freedom for the Greeks' and withdrew her armies from Greece, but she was soon drawn back in order to eject Antiochus who had entered Greece. After defeating him and pushing him back into his own kingdom, Rome again allowed the Greeks to manage their own internal affairs, even after Philip's son Perseus had involved them in another war in Greece (171–167). But Rome gradually and inevitably was becoming the dominant influence throughout the Hellenistic world and when the Greeks failed to live at peace with one another and a pretender attempted to seize the Macedonian throne, her patience at length gave way. She established peace by armed intervention, and then decided after more than fifty years of restraint that peace could only be maintained in the Balkans if she herself governed the area directly; she therefore created a new province, Macedonia, and sacked Corinth as an example to the rest of Greece (146).

In this same year Rome also destroyed Carthage after a three-years' siege. For half a century after the Hannibalic War Rome and Carthage had lived at peace. Roman interests in N. Africa had been watched by Masinissa, king of Numidia, which lay to the west of Carthaginian territory. He had consolidated and civilized his kingdom, but at length by his eastwards aggressions he had provoked Carthage to war. Rome intervened and decided this time to destroy her old rival completely. Carthaginian intransigence and courage merely postponed her fate for three years. Finally the city was razed to the ground and her territory was turned into a new Roman province named Africa (roughly equivalent to modern Tunisia).

Between 241 and 200 Rome had thus gained four provinces and then after a lull of over fifty years she had acquired two more: and all of them, except Macedonia, had come to her as a result of her prolonged struggles with Carthage. Now throughout the length and breadth of the Mediterranean world there was no state that could hope successfully to challenge the dominant power of Rome, who owed not a little to the central position of Italy in the Mediterranean: East and West had been beaten, and the future lay with Rome. She had in fact introduced a political unity into world history such as Alexander the Great and others had dreamed about. This was Rome's great achievement. An acute contemporary Greek statesman, Polybius, realizing this challenging fact, wrote a Universal History covering the years 220–145 B.C. because he could not believe that anyone could be so dull as not to want to know how 'the Romans in less than fifty-three years succeeded in subjugating nearly the whole inhabited world to their sole government – an achievement unexampled in history'.[3]

3. THE SENATORIAL GOVERNMENT

This spectacular spread of Roman influence naturally created many new problems with which the government must grapple if it was to remain in control of events. But before these problems are considered, a question arises: who was the government? The answer may in theory have been Senatus Populusque Romanus (and each of these two partners must be examined separately), but in practice the Senate was the effective governing body throughout the second century, until in 133 B.C. Tiberius Gracchus challenged it in the name of the People.

The Senate had acquired this leading position not by constitutional enactment but simply through its own initiative: custom, not law, enabled it to govern. It comprised some three hundred men, drawn mainly from the landed aristocracy; they remained senators for life and held the chief magistracies. It thus contained the men who possessed the greatest administrative experience and political wisdom. Its steady direction of policy during the dark days of the Hannibalic War had given it great prestige, while the growing complication of foreign policy, when the Romans had to master countless details about the domestic affairs of numbers of Greek cities and states, made the Roman People willing to acquiesce in the Senate taking a lead in foreign affairs and also in financial matters. This the People may have been the more ready to do since it was they who elected the magistrates from whom the Senate was normally recruited.

Naturally not all senators had equal influence and the business of the Senate was in fact very largely in the hands of the *nobiles*. These were an inner circle of senators, drawn from a very limited number of families; only a man who could boast a consul among his ancestors could claim to be a noble, and the consulship was the closely guarded prerogative of comparatively few families. During the hundred years preceding the tribunate of Tiberius Gracchus, practically half the consulships went to only ten *gentes*, while 159 of the 200 were gained by twenty-six *gentes*. Few men outside this charmed circle managed to force their way in: when such a one did win a consulship, he was known as a *novus homo* and ennobled his family for ever. A slightly greater number of 'outsiders' might gain a lower magistracy and access to the Senate, but they would not be able to exercise much influence there, because the business of the House was arranged in such a way as to give greater control to senior members who had held the higher (curule) magistracies. Thus the effective management of the State rested in the hands of some twenty or less families: they supplied the men who commanded the armies, governed the provinces, and by guiding senatorial policy shaped the destiny of Rome and the world.

Real power does not always reside where it officially appears to belong. If the Senate exercised its control through customary rather than official recognition, the way in which the nobles maintained their influence was even less 'constitutional'. One of the most vital, but less advertised, aspects of Roman life was patronage: most of the nobles had a considerable number of 'clients' whose interests, personal, economic, social, legal or political, they protected and advanced. Political relationships were fundamentally of a personal character, and it was largely on this basis that the nobles built up their own political careers. Through patronage they were generally able to control the elections; this in turn gave them control of the Senate, where the influence of the higher magistrates was out of all proportion to their numbers. They also controlled the State religion through the priesthoods which were held by themselves and not by a special class of professional clergy: since most official acts had to be accompanied by some religious observances (e.g. the taking of auspices), the nobles gained much political control through their member-ship of the priestly colleges of Augurs and Pontiffs.[4]

Not all the nobles would think alike on every matter, and each family would naturally wish to advance its own members. Thus the nobility tended to split up into groups, based on families or *gentes*. These often formed polit-ical alliances (*amicitiae*), sometimes strengthened by inter-marriage, while some of the more powerful *gentes* would tend to act as patrons of less influen-tial families. These groups did not develop into political parties in any mod-ern sense of the term, but the first half of the second century had witnessed some fierce electoral tussles between rival coteries.[5] Such struggles may have become slightly less tense by 133, when another division within the nobility soon becomes observable: that into Optimates and Populares.[6] These words have often been misunderstood and difficulties have arisen from thinking of the Optimates as a Senatorial Party, and of the Populares as a Popular, Democratic or Reform Party. But in fact both groups, designated by these political catchwords, were members of the same class: one group, the Optimates, gained control of the Senate and by blocking the wishes of the others forced the latter to seek tribunician support for their measures in the Tribal Assembly: these were called the Populares, the demagogues, by their opponents. The real difference lay, not in class nor even in the pro-grammes that they proclaimed, but in the methods that they followed. Many of the Populares sought a personal predominance, while in contrast the Optimates tried to uphold the oligarchy that they controlled. But if the Populares as a group frequently shared a common background and used similar tactics, they often varied in motive. Many wooed the Populus as a means rather than as an end, their objective being to break the dominant oligarchy, and by using various slogans they urged the People to assert its freedom against the *potentia, dominatio, superbia* or *libido* of the Few. Others, as the Gracchi, were genuine reformers who sought popular support because they had at heart the well-being of the people rather than their own personal position. But whether selfish adventurers or altruistic reformers, the Populares in their struggles against the Optimate faction dominated the political scene in Rome for many decades to come.

4. THE PEOPLE AND THE KNIGHTS

Senatus Populusque Romanus. What then of the *populus Romanus*? In 287 B.C. the *lex Hortensia* had asserted the sovereign authority of the People and had enacted that their resolutions (*plebiscita*) should have the force of law, binding on the whole community. But this development towards full democracy was checked, partly through the skill with which the Senate gained the lead, and partly because the People were quite content to leave more and more responsibility to the Senate. They seldom questioned the Senate's control of the chief military commands, of finance or of foreign policy; and they allowed the Senate to appoint judicial commissions to deal with matters that concerned the safety of the State and to supply the jury when the first permanent court (*quaestio perpetua*) was established in 149 B.C. Further, the People's representatives, the tribunes, were always in the city; they could keep an eye on proceedings in the Senate and they carried much legislation through the Tribal Assembly. But most of the measures had already been shaped in the Senate, and the tribunes were in fact becoming an instrument of the senatorial oligarchy, although a single tribune, by exercising his right of veto, could bring the whole machinery of government to a standstill.[7] The trouble was that the People meeting in their Assemblies were becoming less representative of the needs of the Roman People as a whole. They largely reflected the wish of the urban plebs, which was very different in 133 B.C. from what it had been a hundred years earlier. But on important occasions many small landowners within reach of the city could still come in to vote, and thus a sturdy independent country opinion might continue to make itself felt. At times therefore the Senate might have to listen to public opinion, but on the whole the Sovereign People was content with the Senate's leadership.

The Roman constitution was the remarkable product of a long period of trial and error on the part of a practical and conservative people, and it had achieved that 'balance' which many Greek political theorists so much admired. The historian Polybius concluded that it contained a nicely mingled and balanced blend of three fundamental principles: the consuls represented regal power, the Senate aristocratic, and the People democratic.[8] This theoretical balance was not destroyed, perhaps not even seriously threatened, by the increasing influence of the Senate, thanks to the Roman aptitude for practical compromise. But another element emerged which might disturb the equilibrium, because though remaining outside the government it yet gained increasing social and economic influence. Between the Senate and the People there grew up a Third Estate, that of the so-called Knights (Equites). They owed their rise partly to the fact that senators, who formed a landed aristocracy, were forbidden by law (the *lex Claudia* of 218 B.C.) to take any part in commerce: a sharp distinction was drawn between land and trade, between the governing and the commercial classes. The Equites had originally formed Rome's cavalry and were enrolled in eighteen groups called *centuriae*, but in the third century the censors had drawn up a supplementary list of those whose property warranted cavalry service at their own expense; probably in the second century this *census* was fixed by law. It was these men that were commonly called the Equestrian Order.

Rome's conquest of the Mediterranean opened up a wide field for commercial activities for rich Equites and smaller *negotiatores*, who went in for money-lending, banking and trading. They helped to supply the armies with equipment and stores, and to convert war-booty into more transportable cash. The *publicani* also received contracts from the censors for the performance of public works and for the collection of certain taxes, and they were allowed to take over the operation of mines in Spain and Macedonia. This came about because the Senate had failed to build up a Civil Service. As Rome acquired her empire, she had tried to adapt her existing institutions to enable her to administer it instead of devising completely new machinery. She turned naturally to the business men who were available and allowed them to undertake many tasks for the performance of which she would otherwise have had to create a body of professional financial agents. The Equites thus received many opportunities for advancing themselves, and this growing body of rich and intelligent men would naturally demand some political influence though at the same time avoiding political responsibility. In consequence some friction and jealousy developed between them and the Senate, and this increased when, as will be seen, Gaius Gracchus greatly added to the power of the Equites. But although a sharp political division existed between these two groups, socially they were not necessarily far apart, since many came from the same class: some men of this social group turned to public life and politics, others preferred business or even the quieter life of a country squire. Further, some senators began to indulge secretly in business deals and by Cicero's day, though the political rivalry between senators and Equites might remain sharp, the ban imposed on senators by the *lex Claudia* was widely disregarded.[9]

5. GREEK CULTURAL INFLUENCES ON ROMAN LIFE

The moral and intellectual background of Roman society in 133 B.C. was very different in many respects from that of a century earlier. Without some realization of these changes it is scarcely possible to understand the events of subsequent years, but it is clearly not feasible here to trace this revolution, for it was little less, in any detail. One major factor was the impact of the Greek world on Roman thought and customs.[10] This manifested itself in all the chief cultural aspects of life. Private tutors in the houses of the nobility and teachers in schools taught the study of Greek language and literature, so that with an increasing number of Romans learning Greek, by 133 probably most educated Romans were bilingual. Stimulated by Greek examples, Naevius and Ennius created an epic poetry, which however was infused with a deep religious belief in Rome's destiny; writers of comedy, such as Plautus and Terence, produced Greek plays in Roman form for Roman audiences; dramatists, as Ennius, adapted Greek tragedies for the Roman stage; the satirist Lucilius developed a new branch of poetry in which Rome was to excel; and Roman senators wrote histories of Rome in Greek, partly to justify Roman policy to the Greek world. Greek architecture and art also exercised powerful influences: in the second century many public buildings and private houses began to reflect Greek models, while Greek statues and paintings were increasingly admired, imported and copied.

Even more profound were the changes in religion and thought. From early times Rome had enjoyed some knowledge of Greek religion, through contacts with the Etruscans in northern and Greeks in southern Italy, but hitherto the State religion, though formal, had largely sufficed; by traditional observances the *pax deorum* had been preserved and thereby also the ancestral customs of Rome, the *mos maiorum*. This native attitude was now threatened by an influx of religious ideas from the cosmopolitan culture of the eastern Mediterranean. The cult of the Phrygian nature-goddess Cybele (Magna Mater) had been officially brought to Rome in 205, and the mystical worship of the Greek wine-god, Dionysus (Bacchus), became very popular in Italy, but its celebration was often accompanied by crime and immorality so that the Senate in 186 checked the spread of this cult which it regarded as a threat to public order, a *coniuratio*.[11] Rome's reaction to such novelties was typical: without persecuting any religion as such, the government tried to regulate them and to tone down their more exuberant and less healthy aspects. Excess of excitement (*superstitio*) must be curbed: where accepted, foreign cults must be brought into line with Roman tradition and common sense. But the tide from the East kept seeping in: in 139 a praetor expelled by edict from Rome and Italy all astrologers because 'by their false interpretation of the stars and by their lies they were confusing shallow minds for their own financial profit'. Some Jews, who worshipped Juppiter Sabazios, were also sent packing.

The first reaction of the Romans to the impact of Greek philosophy had been equally sharp. This was perhaps to be expected, since they were a practical people who distrusted speculative inquiry unless directed to purely utilitarian ends. Law, engineering and architecture demanded careful and logical thought, but metaphysical speculation was alien to their traditional ways of thinking. It might even endanger their *mos maiorum*. Thus they were repelled by the scepticism of the New Academics and the emphasis that

Epicurus gave to pleasure, albeit pleasure of the intellect; consequently they expelled some Greek philosophers from Rome in 173 and again in 161.

But philosophy includes ethics within its ambit, and ethics have a practical bearing on life. Hence the Romans gave a less frigid welcome to Stoicism which taught a new doctrine of the relation of man to God and offered a new way of life.[12] Its appeal lay largely in the possibility of applying its teaching to everyday life. One of the leading Stoic teachers of the day, Panaetius of Rhodes, who came to Rome, won the personal friendship of Scipio Aemilianus. The interest of Scipio's friends was aroused and under Panaetius' guidance the teaching of the Porch was adapted to the Roman way of life. Whereas earlier Stoics had held the view that, since virtue is based on knowledge, only the absolutely wise man can be virtuous, Panaetius rather gave encouragement to those who were struggling to make progress in wisdom and virtue: the Wise Man was no longer to be merely an abstract ideal but was to be realized in practical life. Panaetius adapted ethics to the needs of Roman statesmen, and provided a philosophic sanction for many of the traditional characteristics of Roman behaviour, such as *virtus*, *pietas* and *gravitas*. He was also interested in political theory. Unlike the older Stoics who did not expect the wise man to be politically-minded, Panaetius brought him down to earth and into relation with the needs of society; the Stoic sage may share in human feelings of love, loyalty and companionship, and may even have a desire to lead, an 'appetitio quaedam principatus', so that moral superiority might be harnessed to practical politics. Panaetius' attitude to religion was to reject many of the popular manifestations (e.g. the gods of Greco-Roman mythology) but to regard it as a valuable method of popular control in the hands of a statesman. But Stoics also believed in divine imma-nence, God being reason immanent in the universe; divine reason in man provided a religious impulse for morality and thus offered a new basis for religion in Rome. This seed fell on fertile ground: if the Stoic was self-sufficient and hard, an appeal to follow unflinchingly the call of Reason and Will met with a ready response in the Roman temperament, while the cosmopolitan outlook of Stoicism broadened the narrower parochial perspective of the Roman.

Such ethical, religious and philosophical ideas were among the matters discussed by a group of 'intellectuals' that gathered around Scipio Aemilianus: besides Panaetius there were the historian Polybius, Scipio's friend Laelius the 'Wise', the dramatists Terence and Pacuvius and the satirist Lucilius. Through the discussions of such men an attempt was made to blend the best elements of Greek and Roman life.[13] And of all this we can learn something from Cicero, who looked back to this period as an ideal era of aristocratic govern-ment and chose it as the dramatic setting of some of his philosophic and political treatises.

6. THE EFFECTS OF WEALTH AND SLAVERY

The countries of the eastern Mediterranean provided Rome with material goods in addition to ideas, and in this traffic the western provinces also took their part. Though Rome had not acquired any of her provinces for commercial purposes, nevertheless their products began to enrich both state and individuals: war-booty, war-indemnities and the profits of administration, tax-collecting and trade all poured in. With these material aids the lives of many Roman nobles became more luxurious, and sumptuary laws were passed to check extravagance, though to little purpose. For the first few decades of the second century the deterioration was probably slight but the annalist Calpurnius Piso, who was consul in 133, dates the overthrow of Roman modesty to the year 154 ('a quo tempore pudicitiam subversam') and another contemporary witness, Polybius, attests the general extravagance and dissoluteness of the young Roman nobles when Scipio Aemilianus was growing up. This decline was probably confined mainly to Rome itself and affected the nobility in the first instance, but there lay the danger: if the governing class became rotten, there would be little hope for the Republic. One way in which wealth was seriously misused was in the increasing bribery of the urban population at elections. Not unconnected with this was the growing elaboration of public festivals, games and gladiatorial shows with which the people demanded to be entertained. Other social changes included the greater emancipation of women, greater freedom of divorce, the increase of celibacy, a decline in family life and above all the increase of slavery.

Before the third century slavery[14] had existed at Rome, but on a small scale, and since emancipation was frequent a considerable body of freedmen had come into existence. With the Punic and overseas wars, however, and the consequent influx of large numbers of war captives, slavery began to bulk much larger in Roman life. It took two forms: while the more barbarian captives would be sent by their Roman masters to work on their lands, the more cultivated Greek slaves were kept in their town houses and employed as secretaries, teachers and doctors. Though subject to the arbitrary whims and possible cruelty of their masters, these domestic slaves were often well treated and they had a good chance of saving up sufficient pocket-money (*peculium*) to buy their freedom before they were too old to enjoy it. Some alleviated their lot by pandering to the luxurious tastes of their masters, others more usefully helped to acquaint them with Greek culture, while yet others were employed in the manual trades and were often, after emancipation, set up by their former masters in small businesses of their own. The fate of the rougher slaves who were put to work on their masters' estates, often under the control of slave-bailiffs, was much more pitiful; they were often treated as mere beasts with revolting callousness; the lot of those who worked in the State mines in Spain or Macedon was still more wretched.

Such conditions led to insecurity even in Italy: runaway slaves naturally turned to brigandage and conspiracies became frequent. Most serious was a rising of the slaves in Sicily against their Greek and Roman masters in 135; from small beginnings soon no less than 70,000 slaves were organized into a disciplined fighting force by their leaders, a Syrian named Eunus and the Sicilian Cleon. This revolt was accompanied by sporadic outbreaks elsewhere, in Italy at Minturnae and Sinuessa, in Attica and Delos (this island being a main centre of the slave-trade) and in Asia Minor under Aristonicus (see p. 33): although there is little evidence to suggest that this development was due to concerted action or an 'international' organization, it at least shows the widespread nature of the evil of slavery. Though King Antiochus, as Eunus called himself, began to consolidate his power in central Sicily at Enna and gained control of Agrigentum, Tauromenium and Catana, the Romans' first reply was half-hearted: the forces that they sent were at first defeated, including those led by a consul of 134. L. Calpurnius Piso, consul of 133, however, improved discipline among the Roman troops and reached Enna;[15] his successor, P. Rupilius in 132, who had more soldiers at his disposal after Rome's final victory in Spain at Numantia, brought the war to an end, reorganized the province of Sicily and, with ten senatorial commissioners, drafted a charter for its administration (*lex Rupilia*). The insurrection was thus crushed, but it vividly indicated the need for reform.

The fighting in Sicily demonstrated another widening chink in Rome's armour: her standards of military conduct were declining. Though the prospect of spoils may have rendered campaigning in the East not unattractive, harsher conditions of service in Spain made both officers and men unwilling to serve there. Cases of mutiny or insubordination are reported as far back as the 190s; generals, in pursuit of booty or triumphs, sometimes conducted campaigns in defiance of the wishes of the Senate; the management of the wars in Spain was marked by increasing treachery and bad faith; difficulties in raising the levies reached such a pitch that some tribunes in 151 arrested one of the consuls and others again in 138 threatened similar action. To meet this changing mood, conditions of service were ameliorated: Roman citizens on military service were first granted immunity from scourging and then allowed the right of appeal, like civilians; their period of service was reduced to six years; their rations were improved. But despite concessions, discipline deteriorated. When Scipio Aemilianus arrived in Spain in 134 he took over a demoralized army: he had to rid the camp of traders and women and put his men through some toughening drill before he could turn to fighting, and even then he could not think of trying to storm Numantia by assault but had to reduce it by blockade. Things had come to such a pass that campaigns tended to open with defeats before victories could be won.

The standard of provincial administration was threatened by the selfishness of individual governors and by the growing pressure of Roman business interests in their provinces. As a body the Senate no doubt wished to maintain high standards, if not for moral reasons, at least for practical ones: they would not want to see either individual governors gaining undue personal independence and power or members of the equestrian order becoming richer and so potentially more threatening to the Senate's own predomin- ance. Thus in 149 a tribune, L. Calpurnius Piso (the future consul of 133), proposed a measure to set up in Rome a permanent court to try cases of extortion (*quaestio de rebus repetundis*); this court was to consist of senators and its judgements were subject neither to appeal to the People nor to the tribune's veto. Its establishment gave senators greater control over provincial gov- ernors, but at the same time its existence would not tend to improve relations with the Equites, since if some of them hoped to work hand-in-glove with corruptible governors, such governors would clearly be more chary of con- doning their exactions in the future. On the other hand if a governor, himself a senator, had sufficient friends in the jury court, he could hope that his peers might be ready on occasion to judge his misdemeanours more lightly. On the whole, however, the establishment of the court must be reckoned as an honest recognition of a growing evil and a deliberate attempt to check it. Further, though abuses existed, and later reached an unparalleled pitch of shame in Verres' governorship in Sicily (see p. 81 f.), the standard of provincial administration in the main was still high: Polybius paid a glowing tribute to the uprightness of Roman magistrates, and even Verres' prosecutor admitted that hitherto Roman rule in Sicily had been popular.[16]

7. ROME'S ALLIES

A more pressing source of discontent and danger nearer home was the fester- ing sore of Rome's relations with her allies in Italy. This became so inflamed that it poisoned the whole political system, and Rome's failure to tackle the problem finally threatened to split Italy into two in the Social War of 90 B.C. In view of its importance, it is necessary to see how the Italian Confederacy stood in 133 B.C. after several centuries of development. Regarded in detail, a political map of Italy at this time resembles a complex mosaic pattern, but all its inhabitants fall into one of two categories, Roman citizens or allies, sharply differentiated groups which might interlock territorially but not politically.

The Roman citizens comprised several sections. These were: (*a*) ordinary citizens in Rome itself; (*b*) cities on which Rome had conferred full Roman citizenship (e.g. Tusculum, perhaps in 381); the inhabitants continued to live in their own cities which enjoyed administrative autonomy; these oppida civium Romanorum later became known as pro municipiis or municipia, which originally meant something different; (c) municipia civium Romanorum; in origin these were strictly cives sine suffragio, who had received some of the rights and duties of Roman citizenship without all its privileges (this device of 'half-citizenship' proved a very valuable training in civic responsibility for some of the more backward peoples of Italy); they were gradually raised to the status of full citizenship so that by 133 the class of half-citizens had virtually disappeared, and the two sorts of municipia differed only in their origin and history. For their local administration these municipia had a council, a popular assembly and magistrates whose titles varied greatly according to their origins (aediles, praetors or octoviri); (d) some 27 colonies of Roman citizens, which were established from the mid-fourth century to 177 B.C. normally on the coast. The colonists, who usually numbered only 300, retained their Roman citizenship, including their right to vote, though they could exercise this only in Rome itself. In early times they were excused from normal military service in return for garrison duty, their purpose being to protect the coast from sudden raids. From 183 B.C. some larger citizen colonies were founded inland in N. Italy. These approximated more closely to the Latin colonies (on which see below), but the Roman colonies, unlike the Latin, were not true respublicae, though very gradually they acquired a municipal character; (e) members of small rural centres, fora and conciliabula civium Romanorum.

Rome's allies consisted of two groups: the more privileged socii nominis Latini and the rest of the civitates foederatae. The Latins comprised (a) some original Latin towns as Tibur and Praeneste, whose status was established when the Latin League was dissolved in 338 B.C.; (b) some early Latin colonies (e.g. Signia, Norba, Ardea) which were joint foundations of Rome and the Latin League before 340; (c) the much larger number of Latin colonies founded by Rome after the dissolution of the Latin League. Most of the colonists were Romans who gave up their citizenship in return for land in the colony. The colonies were normally larger than the Roman colonies (e.g. 3000–6000 men) and over forty of them had been founded before 180 B.C.; then the process ceased, partly because by then Roman citizens were unwilling to lose their citizenship by entering a new community. It was no doubt because they were composed so largely of ex-Roman citizens that they enjoyed so many privileges. These included (i) rights of connubium and commercium with Romans and presumably also, at this time, with each other; (ii) ius migrandi: by going to live at Rome and registering himself in the Roman census, a Latin could obtain Roman citizenship, provided he had left a son behind him at home. This process was unpopular with the Latin cities, who did not wish to become depopulated, and the right gradually disappeared. It was replaced sometime in the second century by the *ius adipiscendi civitatem Romanam per magistratum*, i.e. by holding local office in a Latin colony; thus a small body of Roman citizens would now form a nucleus of the governing class of the colony, while the principle was changed, since Roman citizenship could now be obtained without domicile at Rome; (iii) *ius suffragii ferendi*: any Latins who happened to be in Rome could vote in a tribe which was chosen by lot in the Comitia Tributa. As independent states the Latins were not subject to tax or tribute, but as Rome's allies they had to supply a quota of troops to fight alongside the Roman legions. Each colony had its own constitution with council and popular assembly, its own laws and magistrates (often called praetors or *duoviri*, though other titles are found), its own jurisdiction, census and coinage.

The rest of the allies were bound to Rome by treaties (*foedera*) which might be either *aequa* or *iniqua*; the latter may on occasion have bade the allies 'imperium maiestatemque populi Romani comiter conservanto'. The conditions would vary in accordance with the circumstances in which the state had first come into permanent relationship with Rome. The chief obligation of the allies, who like the more privileged Latins paid no tribute, was to supply troops when required.[16a] They retained the rights of sovereign states when these did not clash with the supremacy of Rome. A large proportion of the cities of Etruria and of Italy south of Naples were in this legal position.

During the first half of the second century Rome's relations with her allies deteriorated.[17] The Senate did not maliciously begin to intervene in their internal affairs, but unless Rome adopted a totally new policy, her growing centralized power would inevitably tilt the balance against them: Roman control (as exemplified in the suppression of the Bacchic conspiracy) would gradually overshadow the local authorities until at length they became part of the machinery worked by the central government. Further, the degree of tact shown by the Senate or individual Roman magistrates varied on occasion: the way in which L. Postumius, consul in 173, abused his *imperium* by making outrageous demands on Praeneste when he was visiting the town, became a notorious scandal. Again in 177 the allies did not get their fair share of war-booty, which hitherto had been divided equitably between Romans and Latins, while some harsh aspects of Roman military law had been modified by some *Leges Porciae* in respect of Roman citizens only and not the Latins. Further, economic conditions began to make life more difficult for many of the allies. Thus numbers of them began to desire Roman citizenship either for its positive benefits or for the protection against oppression that it would confer, while others later began to consider the possibility of breaking away from Rome altogether.

8. ECONOMIC CHANGES AND THE LAND PROBLEM[18]

Many Italians and Romans alike were suffering from changing economic conditions. The changes arose partly from the upheaval caused by the Hannibalic War, but chiefly from the influx of wealth from the provinces: this upset the older economy which was based on the peasant farmers who also formed the main bulk of the Roman army. Hannibal's invasion of Italy had caused widespread devastation so that in some parts of Italy farms and land were neglected and abandoned, but hard work would have restored this deterioration if it had not been accompanied by other difficulties. One complication that faced the small independent farmer who was still trying to make both ends meet was that more corn was being imported into Italy from the provinces, especially Sicily and Sardinia. This competition from abroad is often alleged to have ruined Italian farmers, but until 167 and perhaps until 146 most of this foreign corn was used by the Roman armies fighting overseas and did not reach the home market.[19] By the time of the Gracchi, however, the pinch may have been felt by many farmers in the relatively limited area around Rome which had hitherto supplied the capital with corn and around some of the coastal towns (transport by sea was cheap, by land extremely dear); Italy as a whole was less affected. Further, conscription fell heavily upon the peasant when overseas wars demanded long periods of service: the rich could ensure that their farms were looked after during their absence, but the poorer man might often return to a ruined homestead.

Two other factors depressed the small farmer's prospects still further: wealth and slaves. War and provincial administration filled the pockets of senators and Equites, who often returned to Italy and looked around for safe investments. Land attracted most of their capital and it so happened that as a result of the Hannibalic War the State had much *ager publicus* of which to dispose: when unable to attract the peasant-farmer back to it, the State was ready to lease it out in large assignments to anyone who had the capital and vision to undertake the venture. Thus a slow revolution took place: land now became an object of speculation to be exploited as a regular source of profit. The owner might no longer live on his estate or take any personal interest in it, but would entrust its management to a steward (*vilicus*) while he himself joined the ranks of the aristocracy in Rome or some other city. At the same time the foreign wars had flooded the Italian slave-markets, so that servile labour, being abundant, began to oust free labour on the bigger estates. In many parts of Italy, especially in Etruria and the South, peasant husbandry, devoted to arable farming and cereal cultivation, gave place to a capitalist system of large estates (*latifundia*) worked by slaves and given over to pasturage and stock-rearing or to the cultivation of the vine and olive. Mixed farming could be quite profitable in Campania and Latium, and Cato in his handbook *De Agri Cultura* wrote for men, senatorial nobles or others, who would invest in a mixed estate of 100–300 *iugera* (66–200 acres), worked by slaves and with grazing on public land. These mixed farms could supply the towns with oil, wine, fruit, vegetables, meat and wool; together with the larger ranches, they might in fact represent the best use to which the land could be put in some parts of Italy. But few of the small farmers would have the capital or skill to switch over from corn-growing to other forms of production.[20] The result was therefore disastrous: free men began to abandon their land to the larger proprietors. Forced off the land, some were absorbed by commercial enterprise abroad, since the number of Italians trading in the eastern Mediterranean greatly increased; some may have moved northwards to the Po valley, but most drifted to Rome and the other cities. Since no new industries were developed to absorb their labour and since the number of slaves was increasing in the cities as well as in the country, they soon became a useless mass of unemployed, whose presence would lead to social and political unrest.

A symptom of this economic decline is seen in the surviving census figures, which probably represent all adult male Roman citizens. After the great losses in man-power during the Hannibalic War, the figures steadily rose until 164 B.C., but thereafter they declined with equal regularity and had dropped by nearly 20,000 in 136 B.C. Nor was the fall in the population confined to the Romans themselves. The Latin authorities had on occasion to try to counter the drift of their population to Rome, while all the Italians found it increasingly difficult to meet the military demands of Rome. Both Appian and Plutarch stress the plight of the Italians at this time.

The development of the *latifundia* was accelerated not only by the plight of the small farmer, who was compelled to abandon his land, but also by the way in which the State had disposed of the public domain in the past. The *ager publicus populi Romani* was the land that Rome had acquired during her expansion in Italy: after a victorious war she normally confiscated about a third of the enemy's territory, leaving him in possession of the rest. This *ager publicus* had been used in various ways: for founding colonies, for distribution in allotments to individual Roman citizens, while some had been sold. The rest was leased out by the censors. The more fertile districts, as the *ager Campanus* in Campania, brought in a good revenue to the State, but large tracts were poor ground and the censors in Rome lacked an adequate staff to deal with this in a careful manner. In fact any Roman citizens (and, if there was enough land available, probably Italian allies as well) could occupy this land as squatters (*possessores*) in return for payment of a rent (*vectigal*): this was a poll-tax for graziers, but a fluctuating amount for others (a tithe on ploughland, and a fifth on vineyards and orchards). But to have enforced strict payment clearly would have involved creating a large fiscal machine which would not have justified itself financially. Instead, the rent was often overlooked and the squatters came to regard the land as their own, which they might even bequeath to their children.

There was, however, one proviso: the amount of *ager publicus* that any individual could hold was limited by law. This limitation had probably been imposed in 367 B.C., and two hundred years later the maximum amount that anyone could hold (Cato refers to it in a speech of 167 B.C.,) was 500 *iugera* (some 300 acres). But in practice this limitation had often been disregarded, and the State had turned a blind eye, partly perhaps because the senators themselves, as large landowners, would benefit, and partly because it was better that the land should be occupied rather than remain idle, while the rich would be able to develop it to better purpose. Thus the growth of large estates had gone on apace, though in so far as many men held public land in excess of the legal limit, it was always possible strictly to enforce the law and reclaim the excess land for the *populus Romanus*, its legal owners.[21]

II

THE GRACCHI[1]

1. ATTEMPTS AT REFORM

Thoughtful Romans began to realize the need to attempt some alleviation of the economic situation, if only because it affected Rome's military strength. The Roman army was a citizen militia: it consisted of men enrolled in five property *classes*, but if these men lost their farms and became urban paupers they would sink below the minimum property qualification and would be classed as *capitecensi* or *proletarii* who were not subject to conscription. The evidence suggests that the needs of recruitment had in fact led to some relaxation of the necessary requirement and that some such men had been enrolled in the armies which fought in Africa and Greece. This would produce further difficulty, because on demobilization men previously had a farm to which to return, whereas now some men might be left resourceless apart from any war-booty that they had won. If the strength of the army was to be kept up under the traditional system of recruitment, the peasant farmers of Italy must be restored to their old prosperity. This concern for the needs of the army might combine with distrust of recent developments in the countryside to induce some Romans to attempt some reform.

The first move came from Laelius, the close friend of Scipio Aemilianus who must certainly have been behind the proposal. At some date before or during his consulship in 140 Laelius raised the question of public land.[2] No details unfortunately are known about his scheme. It was possibly on the lines later followed by Tiberius Gracchus and envisaged that the State should reclaim all land held in excess of the legal limit of five hundred *iugera* and distribute this in allotments to the landless, but it may have been less thoroughgoing than the Gracchan plan (e.g. it might have dealt only with quite

recent seizures of land in excess of the legal amount). In view of the conclusion of the wars in Greece and Africa in 146 and the possible needs of some
of the troops, the allotments may have been designed for veterans as well
as the poor of Rome and Laelius perhaps made the proposal during his
praetorship in 145. But when the scheme was mooted, it met with such
severe opposition from the Senate and landowners that Laelius dropped it;
according to one tradition he gained the cognomen of Sapiens for this act of
political expediency.

Scipio also showed a similar moderation. The final fate of Carthage, which
he had witnessed at close quarters during the last six days of bitter street-
fighting, had impressed him with the impermanence of great empires, even
those with mixed constitutions as that of Carthage, and he may have begun to
harbour some fears for Rome's future. He wanted to maintain the existing
stability and the traditional balance of society. Thus in order to restore the
peasant-farmer he was willing to check the growing greed of the landowners,
but he would not push the issue to an open conflict when he realized the
strength of the opposition to Laelius' proposal.

After Laelius' failure, however, some senators continued to work for reform,
but so far from coming from Scipio's supporters they were in opposition to
the dominant Scipionic group. The political fortunes of the various groups
fluctuated at the elections during the next few years, when some important
reforms were carried: in 139 secret ballot was established for elections and
this principle was extended to the judicial assemblies of the People in 137.[3]
These measures would clearly give the People greater freedom from pressure
by the nobles. If Scipio's political power varied during these years, a series of
military disasters and scandals in Spain soon gave him a chance to win further
glory in war; a tried soldier was needed to bring the Spanish wars to a
decisive end, and the obvious man was the conqueror of Carthage. So in 134
Scipio became consul for a second time, after receiving from the People a
special dispensation from a law of 151 which prohibited such re-elections.
While he was absent in Spain, the reform party in Rome acted.[4]

2. TIBERIUS GRACCHUS

The lead was taken by Tiberius Sempronius Gracchus, one of the tribunes of
133 B.C. He belonged to a distinguished family. His grandfather, the elder
Scipio Africanus, had conquered Hannibal; his mother Cornelia,[5] Scipio's
daughter, was a lady of wide culture. His father, Ti. Sempronius Gracchus,
embodied many of the older Roman virtues: a good soldier and provincial
governor, he had brought a Celtiberian war to a successful end, established
peace there for a generation, and reduced Sardinia; twice consul (177; 163),
he had been censor in 169. After his death in 154 Cornelia refused an offer of

marriage from the reigning king of Egypt, Ptolemy Physcon, and devoted herself to the education of her children, Tiberius (born c. 163), Gaius (some ten years younger), and their elder sister Sempronia (who married Scipio Aemilianus, the adopted son of Publius, a son of the elder Africanus). An admirer of Greek culture, Cornelia employed Greek tutors for her children; one, an eminent rhetorician Diophanes, who was a political exile from Mitylene, taught the boys oratory, an art in which they soon excelled. Another formative influence on Tiberius' life was Blossius of Cumae, a Stoic philosopher and a member of a distinguished 'liberal' family which in earlier days had supported the democratic anti-Roman party at Capua.[6] In Rome, where he had settled as a guest (hospes) in the family of P. Mucius Scaevola, he won the friendship of Tiberius who will have been impressed by his family tradition of democracy and independence, perhaps even more than by his Stoicism.

Tiberius, who became an augur at the age of ten, served with distinction under his brother-in-law Aemilianus at the siege of Carthage (146) and married Claudia, daughter of the Princeps Senatus, Appius Claudius Pulcher. His quaestorship in 137, when he served under Hostilius Mancinus in Spain, had a twofold importance. It was while he was travelling through Etruria on his way to Spain that, seeing the large estates worked by slaves and noting the absence of free peasants, he realized the need for reform. After he had reached Spain he extricated a Roman army from disaster. When Mancinus' troops were cut off by the enemy near Numantia, the Spaniards allowed them to depart under terms for the fulfilment of which Tiberius made himself responsible since they trusted him for his father's sake. The Senate, however, later shamefully repudiated the treaty and made a scapegoat of Mancinus who was handed over to the Spaniards. His officers, including Tiberius, nearly suffered the same fate; though Tiberius escaped by the skin of his teeth, he may well have been embittered by this treatment. Even if the tradition that he turned demagogue because of the odium arising from this episode derives from the propaganda of his political opponents, at very least he will not have been encouraged to expect honourable conduct from the Senate in the future, while the fact that he had saved a Roman army in Spain will have enhanced his popularity.

It is difficult to be sure which were the dominant motives that turned him into a reformer. Knowledge of Greek political thought and practice, the effect of the Spanish episode, the contemporary slave-rising in Sicily, concern at the changing economic conditions with their impact on peasant husbandry and army recruiting, the consequent growth of unemployment at Rome, all these factors may have combined to urge a generous-hearted man to risk his own political future in an attempt to re-establish the peasants on small-holdings once again.[7] But he did not stand alone at first: his was not a voice crying in the wilderness, but one backed by a powerful group in the Senate. His father-in-law Appius Claudius Pulcher, who had been consul (143 B.C.) and censor (probably 136) was Princeps Senatus (i.e. his name now headed the senatorial roll). With them were linked by marriage two other influential men: P. Licinius Crassus Mucianus, a wealthy jurist and scholar (later to be consul in 131 and Pontifex Maximus), had married Pulcher's sister, Clodia, and their daughter Licinia married Gaius Gracchus. Crassus' brother P. Mucius Scaevola, one of the greatest jurists of the day, was holding the consulship in 133, the year of Tiberius' tribunate. Other outstanding supporters included M. Fulvius Flaccus (later consul in 125), C. Papirius Carbo (consul in 120) and C. Porcius Cato (consul, 114). With relations and friends of this weight behind him, Tiberius might at least hope for a fair hearing for his proposals, while even the Scipionic group, though politically hostile, could scarcely be expected to show unreserved opposition in view of Laelius' earlier attempt at land reform.[8]

3. THE LAND-BILL OF TIBERIUS GRACCHUS

Early in his tribunate Tiberius proposed a *lex agraria* to make land available for distribution in allotments. Everyone holding more *ager publicus* than the legal limit of 500 *iugera* (c. 300 acres) must give up the surplus, but should retain the 500 *iugera* (and possibly also 250 *iugera* for each son, up to a maximum of 1000 *iugera*) which should become the possessor's in perpetuity and should not be subject to rent (*vectigal*); probably no further compensation was offered. The fertile *ager Campanus* was not included in the scheme. The land so reclaimed by the State was to be distributed to Roman citizens in small allotments, with perhaps a maximum size of 30 *iugera*; the new holders were not allowed to alienate them and were to pay a small rent.[9]

As a short-term scheme the bill had great advantages. There could be no objection on the legal score to this resumption of land settlement: Tiberius' friend, the jurist Scaevola, would have seen to that. It would alleviate much distress, though if the terms of army-recruitment remained unaltered and overseas wars continued, it would scarcely prove a permanent solution to the problem as a whole. The existing occupiers of the public land had cause for both satisfaction and annoyance. Those who occupied a small amount could henceforth enjoy security of tenure, but those who had to surrender many acres had some reason to complain: for years, or even generations, they had regarded the land as their own, putting capital into it, building their homes and family tombs on it, using it as dowries for their daughters, perhaps mortgaging it. The majority of the large landowners, who had most to lose by the proposal, were of course senators, but Tiberius had friends in the Senate and if he had followed the normal procedure of bringing his bill to the Senate before taking it to the People, there is no justification for believing that it would not have been given a fair hearing. Vested interests would naturally have biased many senators, but others might have been willing to consider the good of the community first. Gracchus, however, decided to follow a hundred years old precedent, that of C. Flaminius who had carried a land-bill without consulting the Senate: he took his measure straight to the Popular Assembly. His motives are obscure: perhaps he thought that it might get bogged down in prolonged and futile discussion in the Senate, and so decided that, as he had only one year in which to act, shock-tactics would be better. But his impatience proved unwise. When with eloquent appeals he brought his bill to the Concilium Plebis, it was unexpectedly vetoed in the interests of the Senate by a fellow-tribune, M. Octavius, whom Gracchus may hitherto have considered as a friend. The Senate was unwilling to acquiesce in his blatant disregard of its traditional rights.

Undeterred, Tiberius pressed on. In his annoyance he may have withdrawn the concession that the 500 *iugera* retained by the *possessores* should become their private property and proposed that this should remain *ager publicus*, though still rent-free. He repeatedly urged Octavius to withdraw his veto; he may have tried to delay the transaction of public business until his bill was passed, even if he did not formally declare a *iustitium*; he was even persuaded to submit the question to the Senate for consideration at last, but this was useless, since his conduct had alienated much of the sympathy that he had enjoyed there.[10] Finally he summoned the People and after further vain appeals to Octavius to retract, he took a step of the utmost gravity: he proposed the formal deposition of Octavius from the tribunate (see p. 25 f.). The people voted the deposition, elected another tribune in his place and carried Tiberius' agrarian bill.[11]

The bill was passed but another hurdle remained: to secure its effective working. For this a commission independent of the Senate would be desirable, Tiberius accordingly proposed and the People established a triumviral agrarian commission, with judicial powers to settle disputes (*triumviri agris iudicandis adsignandis*), members probably being eligible for annual re-election.[12] The men chosen were a family group: Tiberius, his younger brother Gaius, and his father-in-law Appius Claudius Pulcher. The commission soon started work, but they needed money to help the settlers to stock their allotments, and public finance was controlled by the Senate which refused help and insulted Tiberius by offering him an allowance of about two shillings a day for his expenses. At this difficult moment news arrived that Attalus, king of Pergamum, had died and had made the Roman People his heir. Tiberius thereupon introduced a bill, or threatened to do so, to authorize the use of some of this wealth for his settlers, and said that he would bring the question of settling Attalus' kingdom before the People.[13] This was going too far: until now the Senate's control of finance and foreign affairs had been unchallenged, but Tiberius was interfering in both spheres. His action must have destroyed any sympathy that still remained for him in the Senate: his reliance on the People will have increased senatorial fears of his aims. He was reproved by Q. Metellus, and denounced by T. Annius, but he had got the funds for his settlers.

In the course of the summer the tribunician elections for the next year drew near, and Tiberius decided to stand for a second tribunate: his motive may have been to remain in office in order to safeguard the working of his agrarian bill, but his intention must have suggested to his opponents a dangerous personal ambition. Re-election was not illegal, but the last important case belonged to a period two hundred years earlier when the function of the tribunate was very different.[14] As harvest time prevented some country-voters from coming to Rome, Tiberius may have broadened his programme to appeal to more of the city population.[15] At first a dispute over which tribune should preside at the elections led to an adjournment. Next day Tiberius and his supporters gathered on the Capitol, where the Assembly met; during a discussion about his eligibility to stand a second time, he gave some signal which perhaps accidentally led to a brawl: the meeting broke up and the other tribunes fled. In the Senate, which met in the Temple of Fides, P. Mucius Scaevola was asked to save the State and destroy the tyrant, to which he replied that he would neither act illegally nor recognize any illegal act by the People. This was no answer for the Pontifex Maximus, P. Scipio Nasica, who resorted to force. Leading out those senators who would follow him, and joined on the way by other opponents of Gracchus, he rushed to the assembly where they clubbed and stoned to death three hundred Gracchans. Tiberius himself was struck down near the door of the Temple of Juppiter Capitolinus, close by the statues of the Kings. All the bodies were thrown into the Tiber by night. After nearly four hundred years blood had again been shed in Rome in civil strife.[16]

4. THE IMPORTANCE OF GRACCHUS' ATTEMPT

This unjustified recourse to force by part of the Senate was the result of much provocation by Tiberius. He had disregarded their customary prior right of discussing legislation, and he had interfered in finance and foreign affairs which he claimed should be handled by the People.[16a] Apart from any slight to their order, many senators much have had genuine misgivings about such conduct. True the Roman People was theoretically sovereign, but the Roman People could not be equated with the urban mob that thronged the assembly in Rome. This was becoming increasingly irresponsible and unrepresentative of the needs of the people as a whole. Further, since it clearly lacked the knowledge or skill to take over from the Senate the transacting of the complicated business of finance and foreign relations, Tiberius was unwise to encourage it to intervene on specific points. In thus transgressing traditional observance, he had not broken the law, but he had shown undue hastiness and folly.

His attitude to the tribunate was even more disquieting. Neither the deposition of Octavius nor his own attempt at re-election may have been formally illegal, but these acts must have suggested to the prudent some possibilities which may have escaped the consideration of the over-zealous reformer. The original function of the tribunes had been to protect the people against patrician domination, but this need had long passed and they had become useful agents for the nobility, often using their veto to check the popular assemblies. In urging the People to depose Octavius while he was still in office, on the ground perhaps that he was blocking the People's wishes, Tiberius was threatening to turn the tribunes into agents of the People's will, whereas constitutionally legislation could only result when magistrates co-operated with the People. To turn the tribunes into a mouthpiece of the People and to make their veto capable of being swept aside, would be to give the Concilium Plebis greater responsibility than it could properly wield. When, in addition, Tiberius sought reelection, the possibility of prolonged tribunates would open the way to demagogy: the result would not be democracy on the Athenian pattern, but mob-rule or dictatorship. Tiberius may not have been aware of the latent implications of his actions, but he does seem to have sought sufficient personal leadership in the interests of his land reform scheme, to render plausible, if not true, the charge of his opponents that he claimed that 'interempto senatu omnia per plebem agi debere'. To Rome's great loss the plebs were not capable of responding adequately to such a call. Instead, the Senate responded with force and thus set in motion the series of civil wars in which the Republic perished.

5. THE LAND COMMISSION, SCIPIO AEMILIANUS AND THE ALLIES

The Senate pressed home its advantage: it set up a court under the consul of 132, P. Popillius Laenas[17] and his more attractive colleague P. Rupilius, to punish more of Gracchus' surviving supporters. Many were condemned and executed: those that escaped were banished without trial. Of Tiberius' Greek friends Diophanes was killed and Blossius fled to join Aristonicus' revolt in Asia (p. 33). Despite this display of strength the Senate decided that, since Nasica's continued presence in Rome would remind men of his violation of the sacrosanctity of a tribune, he was better out of sight: he was therefore sent on a commission to Asia, where he soon died. The Senate, however, did not interfere with the working of the agrarian commission, a fact that demonstrates that its objection to Tiberius' bill was much weaker than its dislike of his methods. Tiberius' place on the commission was taken by Gaius Gracchus' father-in-law, P. Licinius Crassus, but as consul in 131 Crassus secured by intrigue a command in Asia, where he died in 130; Ap. Claudius, the other triumvir, also died. Their places were filled by M. Fulvius Flaccus and C. Papirius Carbo, who, together with Gaius Gracchus, remained in office until 122. As tribune in 131 (or 130) Carbo carried a measure to extend secret ballot (cf. p. 20) to legislative assemblies of the People and proposed one to legalize re-election to the tribunate. Scipio Aemilianus, who was back from Spain after sacking Numantia in 133, helped to defeat the proposal, though a similar measure possibly was carried soon after his death in 129.[18] The turbulence of the times was reflected during the censorship of 131, when this office was held by two plebeians for the first time in history; a disgruntled tribune tried to push the censor Q. Metellus Macedonicus over the Tarpeian Rock, from which condemned criminals were hurled. More memorable perhaps was Metellus' speech 'de prole augenda', an appeal to enforce marriage and thus increase the birth-rate; he was clearly conscious that Rome's economic difficulties required reform, though his solution was on different lines from that of Gracchus.

Meantime the commissioners were hard at work, asserting the State's claim to the extra *ager publicus* and distributing it to new settlers.[19] But difficulties arose, especially where the interests of the Latin and Italian allies were involved. Already exasperated by Rome's recent treatment of them, those allies who had been allowed to occupy *ager publicus* in the past would not now enjoy having to surrender any surplus they held in order to provide allotments for the unemployed from Rome, while disputes may have arisen with the commissioners over the title to borderland where land originally taken from the ally by Rome ran alongside land retained by the ally.[20] To air their grievances they sought the help in Rome of Scipio Aemilianus who as a soldier knew the true value of the allied contribution to Roman life. In 129 their new patron persuaded the Senate to warn the commissioners not to deal with disputes about land held by the allies; such cases should be transferred to the consul Tuditanus, who conveniently went off to Illyricum.[21] But the distribution of land went on: the census figures of 125 B.C. (about 395,000) were some 75,000 higher than those of 131 B.C., and this increase almost certainly reflects the progress of land settlement.[22]

Scipio's championship of the allies increased his unpopularity with the urban mob who had already disapproved of his opposition to Carbo's bill. One morning, when he was due to make a speech on the Italian question, he was found dead. His death remained an unsolved mystery. Although various people were blamed at the time or later (including Flaccus, C. Gracchus, Carbo, and even Sempronia or Cornelia), murder is not very likely; suicide is possible, but most probably he died a natural death (a heart-attack?).[23] Rome thus lost an upright soldier, who had exercised a moderating influence on her political and cultural life.

Many of the allies, now without their patron, began to come to Rome to agitate, but they met with a sharp rebuff: a tribune named Iunius Pennus (126) passed a law, despite the opposition of C. Gracchus, to prevent non-citizens settling in Rome and to expel those that had done so.[24] But the land commissioner Fulvius Flaccus won the consulship of 125 and tried to settle the whole Italian question in a most statesmanlike manner: he proposed that all the allies should receive Roman citizenship if they wished, or alternatively those who wanted should remain independent states and receive the right of appeal against Roman magistrates. If the Romans had accepted this generous and prudent proposal they would have solved a problem which embittered political life for the next generation and led to a terrible and 'unnecessary' war. But the Senate was too conservative: it responded to a timely appeal from Massilia for help against the Salluvii by assigning Gaul as a province to Flaccus, who was thus compelled to abandon his proposal.[25]

The allies were thwarted – all but the Latin colony of Fregellae in the Liris valley (modern Arce, not far from Monte Cassino). This hill-town, hitherto an outstandingly loyal ally, revolted. The attempt, unless based on a lively hope that its lead would be followed by others, was suicidal, but it demonstrates, as does nothing else, the bitterness felt towards Rome even by her old friends. Rome reacted sharply. Fregellae was besieged and then captured through internal treachery; the city was destroyed and the inhabitants were moved down to the plain where a colony was established at Fabrateria.[26] Thus a Social War was averted for another thirty-five years and the Senate had rounded a dangerous corner, just as internally it had survived the pressure of Tiberius and Flaccus. But a more powerful challenge was at hand.

6. THE LEGISLATION OF GAIUS GRACCHUS

Gaius Gracchus, who had served on the land commission since 133 when he was only twenty-one years old, became one of Rome's greatest orators.[27] He displayed his oratorical ability when he supported Carbo's proposal for re-election to the tribunate, opposed Pennus' alien-act, expressed approval of Flaccus' measure and defended himself against criticism by the censors for leaving Sardinia, where he served as quaestor in 126, when the command of his superior officer was prolonged; he also rebutted a charge of complicity in the revolt of Fregellae. Thus he was well known to the People who readily elected him tribune for 123, as one eager to continue and develop his brother's policy. Unlike Tiberius, who came to grief on this very issue, Gaius was easily elected to a second tribunate for 122 and thus gained a longer period in which to initiate reform. The exact order of his measures and their assignment to 123 or 122 cannot in many cases be established, but apparently after a preliminary warning to the Senate he acted with a certain restraint and only brought up his heavy guns later.[28] The Senate also showed moderation at first (unless its mildness arose from an inability to persuade any of Gaius' colleagues in 123 to oppose him), but during 122 it used a tribune, Drusus, to undermine his position.

His first proposal was to prohibit any magistrate or tribune who had been deposed by the people from holding any further office; this would make tribunes more chary of submitting to senatorial control, and would have thrown a cloak of legitimacy over Octavius' deposition, and in so far as it might suggest that the People could depose any magistrate who acted against their wishes it was potentially revolutionary. Since it also affected Octavius personally, Gaius was persuaded by his mother Cornelia to drop it. But he did not intend to be robbed of all revenge against Tiberius' opponents. He carried a measure that declared illegal all courts with powers of capital punishment that were not established by the People. This was aimed at such tribunals as that set up by the Senate under Popillius to try Tiberius' supporters. The measure was made retrospective: Popillius was impeached and driven into exile.

Gaius then turned to further economic reform. He re-enacted his brother's agrarian bill, removing whatever limitations Aemilianus had imposed on the working of the commission.[29] Since much of the land available had no doubt been distributed by this time, Gaius supplemented this bill with a plan to establish some colonies in Italy; though many of the colonists would be drawn from the very poor, some were to come from the middle classes in order to provide some capital for the promotion of industries in the colonies. Whereas the older Roman colonies had been primarily military centres and secondarily outlets for surplus population, now commercial motives were not overlooked. Two colonies were established in southern Italy, Minervia at Scolacium under the toe of Italy, and Neptunia near Tarentum; and others may have been planned. It is even possible that Gaius also thought of a colony on the site of Carthage as early as this (see below, p. 30). Stimulated partly perhaps by recent corn shortages in Africa and Sicily, he also carried a lex frumentaria. The State was to practice bulk-buying of corn, build warehouses to store it and then sell a monthly ration to any Roman citizen at a price slightly below the market-rate (at 6⅓ asses a modius). This would reduce the variation in price from year to year caused by good and bad harvests, and prevent private profiteering in lean years. It would also help those waiting to go to allotments or colonies or those for whom such relief could not be found. This was a novel idea at Rome, but many Greek States had been accustomed to control their own corn-trade. Later Roman moralists sharply criticized Gaius for 'demoralizing' the people, but unjustly: he was not responsible for subsequent perversions of this practice into a dole and a political bribe. Other popular measures included one to construct some secondary roads in Italy which would provide employment and improve communications, and another to make conditions in the army better by enacting that the State should provide clothing and that boys under seventeen should not be enlisted.

The relative value that Gaius set upon his various reforms cannot be determined, but the question of the allies was clearly close to his heart, and he possibly proposed in 123 to extend Roman franchise to the Latins; if so, the attempt failed. To handle this burning matter successfully, he clearly would need further political support. It was therefore perhaps with this in mind that he tried to win help from the Equites, or he may merely have felt that they could usefully be given more political influence in order to form a more serious counter-weight to the Senate. Whatever his primary motive, he carried two measures which greatly benefited them: he gave them control first of the taxation of Asia, and later of the jury courts at Rome.[30]

He enacted that the right to collect taxes of the new province of Asia (a tithe, together with some customs and pasture dues) should be auctioned by the censors at Rome. Since the successful contractor paid a lump sum to the State, and then recovered this and his profit from collecting the taxes, only rich Equites would have sufficient capital to accept the contract. The proposal was in line with previous Roman policy, by which private individuals had been utilized in order to avoid creating a professional body of financial officials. But the measure, while helping to protect provincials from rapacious governors, gave the Equites more than a chance for further wealth: those who gained the contracts could not be prosecuted for extortion (a crime which only senators could commit), while any governor who tried to check them could, on some trumped-up charge, be brought before the quaestio perpetua de repetundis, the court in Rome that tried provincial governors on charges of extortion. And here, after Gaius' second law in favour of the Equites, the jury would consist of members of that Order.

At first Gaius had probably mooted the idea of adding some 300 members of the equestrian order to the Senate and leaving the court in the hands of this enlarged Senate, but the suggestion was not accepted. Later, perhaps after the counter-attack by Drusus when the gulf between Gaius and the Senate had widened (p. 30), he sponsored a measure, which was moved probably by Acilius, to transfer the court from the Senate to the Equites.[31] This had very far-reaching political effects. It gave the Equites influence over senatorial provincial governors (this would have been avoided, if his first scheme had been accepted). However, if trust can be placed in Cicero's statement that the equestrian juries for some time did not succumb to the temptations that were open to them, Gracchus' measure may be regarded as good in so far as it gave the equestrian order a position in the State more consonant with its importance, but bad in so far as it antagonized relations between it and the Senate and made control of the lawcourts a bone of contention for the next fifty years.

Gracchus also carried a measure 'ne quis iudicio circumveniatur'. This has generally been regarded as a law against judicial corruption, making bribery of jurors a criminal offence and applying only to senators and not to Equites because it was passed before the court was transferred to the latter. But alternative interpretations are more probable.[32]

Another measure compelled the Senate, which decided to which provinces consuls should be sent (normally after their year of office in Rome), to fix the provinces before the consuls were elected instead of during their consulships. Thus the Senate could less easily reward its favourites with the best provinces, but since the provinces would now have to be allocated eighteen months in advance, the new arrangement would not make for efficiency. Gracchus may also have established some new dues (*portoria*) in Italian harbours, but, whatever his intentions, he probably did not alter the method of voting in the Comitia Centuriata.

7. THE OPPOSITION TO GAIUS GRACCHUS

During his second tribunate the Senate at last moved to the attack but at first by an indirect method. A tribune, M. Livius Drusus, was put up by the Senate to win over some of Gaius' supporters by offering a number of attractive proposals designed to show that the Senate also was not unconcerned about reform. He suggested twelve colonies, each to consist of 3000 men with no property qualification; all allotments distributed since 133 were to be relieved of rent; and no Latin was to be liable to scourging, even on military service, a measure which might satisfy the demands of some of the allies and at the same time save the Roman people from sharing their advantages more widely. A commission was set up to implement these *leges Liviae*, but apparently it did little.[33] The fact that the twelve colonies were not founded suggests that Drusus' purpose was primarily to undermine Gracchus' position rather than to accomplish genuine economic reform.

This opposition forced Gaius to more extreme measures. If he had not taken this action during his first tribunate, he now used a fellow-tribune named Rubrius to propose the foundation of a colony, to be called Junonia, on the site of Carthage, with allotments comprising up to 200 *iugera* for 6000 colonists with absolute ownership.[34] Hitherto colonization had been confined to Italy, but if overseas colonization was a Greek idea which might appear sinister to conservative Roman minds, the offer was attractive to the people: the allotments were large; the district, which had been ravaged by a plague, needed reclaiming; the actual site of Punic Carthage, which the Romans had laid under a curse, was probably not embraced in the scheme;

further, some Italians may have been included as colonists. Next (though the chronology and order of this and other measures must remain uncertain) Gaius probably carried his second law to help the Equites, described above (p. 29), and transferred the extortioncourt to them, a measure which may have been prompted by recent scandals when the juries were senatorial, but which had very serious effects. Finally, he decided to re-open the franchise question, this time on a wide basis: the Latins were to receive full Roman citizenship, and the rest of the allies Latin rights. Though helped by his fellow-tribune Fulvius Flaccus, who in his zeal for reform and the franchise question (p. 27) had not disdained to hold a tribunate after his consulship, Gaius was deserted by C. Fannius, whom he had helped to gain the consulship of 122.[35] Fannius repaid him by undermining the franchise bill through working on the selfish interests of the voters in Rome and their jealousy of the allies. To prevent agitation, all allies (except perhaps the Latins) were forbidden to come within five miles of Rome when the bill was to be decided. It was defeated, perhaps vetoed by Drusus: Gaius no longer enjoyed such popular support as had allowed Tiberius to secure the deposition of a fellow-tribune.[36]

At some point Gaius was away from Rome for over two months, supervising the foundation of Junonia, and his opponents exploited his absence by spreading fantastic rumours of setbacks there in order to discredit the scheme. In any case his popularity was fast waning with the fickle urban mob and when the tribunician elections for 121 were held, he failed to win election for a third period. Thus at the end of 122 he was without office, apart from his land-commissionership. A tribune of 121, Minucius Rufus, then opened the attack by proposing the repeal of the *lex Rubria*. Gaius rallied his followers to oppose this and unwisely formed a bodyguard of friends. In a minor disturbance one of the servants of the consul Opimius was killed. This was at most murder, not revolution, but Opimius, who was bitterly hostile to Gracchus and had shown his harsh character in crushing the revolt of Fregellae, made the most of his opportunity. The Senate was persuaded to pass a resolution for the first time in history that the consuls should see to it that the Republic suffered no harm. Such a motion, later called the *senatus consultum ultimum*, warned the magistrates that the Senate regarded the situation as critical and, although it did not increase their constitutional powers, it assured them of the Senate's moral support. Opimius then summoned to arms senators and Equites; even the latter responded, unmindful of Gracchus' past benefactions to them. Gaius was reluctantly compelled to accept Flaccus' determination to resist by force. The Gracchans occupied the Aventine: after vain negotiations they were soon defeated and killed. Opimius then rounded up and arrested 3000 survivors and supporters; these unfortunate men he executed without a trial. He is said to have rewarded men who brought him the heads of Gaius and Flaccus with their weight in gold. However that may be, he was ordered by the Senate to restore the Temple of Concord in the Forum at the foot of the Capitol which had been built by Camillus. The triumph of the Senate must have seemed complete.[37]

8. THE IMPORTANCE OF THE GRACCHI

The Gracchi were in a true sense martyrs: they had witnessed to their belief in the need for reform and they had suffered for their faith. Though not uninfluenced by Greek political ideas, they should not be regarded as would-be Greek tyrants, Fascist dictators or Marxist theorists. It is not certain, for instance, that Tiberius even objected to large estates as such, since his primary attack was upon the misuse of *ager publicus* for *latifundia*, while the reliance of the Gracchi on popular support does not prove that they aimed at prolonged personal predominance. They were later claimed as *Populares* but their motives were very different from many a later *popularis*. In fact their motives should be sharply distinguished from their methods. There is no good reason to deny that they aimed at disinterested social and economic reform. The wisdom they displayed in seeking this end is more open to question. It is impossible today to assess the situation in 133 with accuracy: it would appear that Tiberius' challenge to the Senate was unnecessarily provocative and ill-judged and that patience and negotiation might have achieved more, but we cannot really tell. But if Tiberius' conduct seems rash and shortsighted, the use of force by the Senate was still less justifiable. Gaius, who was temperamentally more aggressive than his brother, was obviously ready to go to greater lengths, but he was forced into his extreme position only by the uncompromising attitude of the Senate which had perhaps more reason to mistrust his ultimate motives in view of the breadth of his appeal. But clearly his death was due to the Senate's selfishness in refusing to face the urgent needs of the day, combined with the selfishness of the People who brought to nought his generous plans for Italy as a whole; and whatever may be thought of the Senate's appeal to force as such, nothing can excuse the barbarity of the methods which it condoned in the brutal agent whom it permitted to apply that force.

The Gracchi achieved some direct results. Though many of the economic difficulties remained, they at least helped to relieve, if not to solve, them. Many small farmers and colonists were set up, and to that extent the unemployment problem was alleviated. But the indirect results of their activities were the more important. The Italians were embittered, the Equites more self-conscious as a political force, the People had learned something of its powers, a new aspect of the tribunate was displayed, and above all the weakness of the Senate was revealed. This challenge to the traditional government of

Rome without the creation of any adequate alternative – since the Concilium Plebis was unfitted to form the organ of a true democracy – must lead to disaster. The tempo and temper of political life were heightened. Whether or not the Gracchi should be regarded as revolutionaries, without doubt they precipitated the revolution that overthrew the Republic.

9. FOREIGN AFFAIRS: ASIA AND GAUL

While the Senate was contending against the Gracchi, campaigns overseas resulted in the establishment of two new provinces: Asia and Gallia Transalpina or Narbonensis.

For many years the kingdom of Pergamum had lain under Rome's shadow, unable to take an independent line. Its king, Attalus III, who both lacked an heir and had to face some social unrest in his realm, tried to minimize the risk of political or social disturbances after his death by making the Roman people his heir. When he died in 133 Rome accepted the legacy and decided to take over this rich country which might prove profitable both to senatorial governors and Roman business-men. It was also highly opportune for Tiberius Gracchus, who proposed to appropriate some of the king's treasure in order to help finance his new settlers (p. 23). Before the end of 133 Rome had ratified the king's will and had sent out a commission of five senators under Scipio Nasica (p. 25), but any arrangements that they hoped to make were upset by a revolt led by Aristonicus, an illegitimate son of Attalus' predecessor Eumenes, against whom they could only summon help from the neighbouring rulers of Pontus, Bithynia, Paphlagonia and Cappadocia. At first Aristonicus appealed to the nationalistic longings of the Greek cities of Asia Minor and their desire for independence, but when this hope was disappointed he turned to the native population of the interior to whom he held out hopes of social betterment: he proposed to free serfs and slaves and to found a Utopian State called the City of the Sun, where all should be free and equal. He was joined by Blossius who had escaped from Rome after Tiberius' death. The first Roman army sent against him in 131 was led by Licinius Crassus (the father-in-law of Gaius Gracchus), who achieved little and was killed. His successor M. Perperna (cos. 130), however, secured the defeat and capture of Aristonicus, but did not live to complete the settlement which was arranged by Manius Aquilius (cos. 129) with a senatorial commission.

The main part of Attalus' kingdom was annexed as a new Roman province called Asia, and the road system was developed by Aquilius. Some of the less fertile eastern districts were handed back to local rulers (e.g. Lycaonia to the king of Cappadocia) but the fate of Greater Phrygia remained unsettled for over a decade when it was finally organized into a League. Within the new province some of the Greek cities, including Pergamum itself, were to be free (*liberae*), though the cities which had rebelled probably had to pay tribute. Gaius Gracchus, however, then re-organized the taxation-system and established a tithe on arable land and pasture dues: this he probably extended to all cities, subject and free (cf. p. 29). Many of the cities enjoyed local self-government, but for judicial purposes circuits (*conventus*) were established, and though Rome may not have interfered directly in the cities' internal affairs, these would tend gradually to conform with those of Rome.[38]

In the west, Rome's ally Massilia (Marseilles), which in the past had secured Roman help in repelling Ligurian raiders (e.g. in 154), appealed again in 125. The Senate, which would be glad to get the consul Fulvius Flaccus out of the way (see p. 27), sent him to help Massilia. He campaigned against the Saluvii, the Ligurians and the Vocontii (who lived between the Durance and Isère) in 125–4; when C. Sextius Calvinus (*cos.* 124) had captured the chief settlement of the Saluvii near Aquae Sextiae (Aix en Provence), a fort (*castellum*) of Roman veterans was established there to control the area.

Rome's advance into southern Gaul provoked the hostility of the Allobroges (between the Rhone and Isère) and the Arverni (west of the Rhone), though it is symptomatic of the lack of unity and of any national feeling among the Gallic tribes that the Aedui further north in Burgundy supported Rome. In 121 Cn. Domitius Ahenobarbus (*cos.* 122), with an army that included some elephants, defeated the Allobroges at Vindalium (between Orange and Avignon) and gained control of the area east of the Rhone. The Arverni under their king Bituitus then crossed over to the eastern bank, only to meet defeat, probably near Valence, at the hands of Q. Fabius Maximus (*cos.* 121) who had arrived with fresh troops. While Fabius returned to Rome where he received a triumph, took the *cognomen* Allobrogicus and built an Arch (Fornix Fabianus) in the Forum, Domitius captured Bituitus by treachery, gained control of the area between the Alps and Pyrenees, and proceeded to settle southern Gaul, which the Senate decided to annex as a province (Gallia Transalpina or, later, Narbonensis). Massilia remained an independent allied State within the province, the defeated Arverni were left outside it, and the Aedui were formally recognized as Rome's allies. Further, a secure road was needed to the Pyrenees and Spain, which Domitius now supplied; recently a milestone on this Via Domitia has been found, naming 'Cn. Domitius Cn. f. imperator' and providing the earliest known Latin inscription from Gaul.[39]

In 118 a proposal was made to establish a colony of Roman citizens at Narbo in the new province. This met with opposition in the Senate but was carried with the help of a young orator L. Crassus. He and Cn. Domitius, the son of the conqueror of the Allobroges, were appointed as commissioners (*duoviri*) for founding the colony and in this connexion they had struck a special issue of coins (serrated *denarii*), depicting Bituitus in a chariot with Gallic arms and trumpet. Though Narbo would provide good agricultural land for allotments, it also offered commercial possibilities, as a focus for the trade of southern Gaul and of Spain as well, and in particular as the terminus of a new route which was designed to bring tin from Britain via the Bay of Biscay and Burdigala (Bordeaux). The fact that it was named Narbo Martius calls to mind the Gracchan colonies that were placed under divine protection (Junonia, Neptunia). Thus while the establishment of Roman control was in line with normal senatorial policy (it was by chance that Gracchus' friend Flaccus happened to be consul in the year when Massilia appealed to Rome), the planning of Narbo may represent pressure from the Equites. In this they may have had the support of some senators who believed in the value of another outpost against Gallic aggression and the need to provide land for veterans; but other senators will have doubted the wisdom of a move which might complicate defence problems and will also have wished to avoid giving the Equites fresh opportunities for enrichment. The co-operation, however, of some senators with the Equites may have helped to develop the trend of policy started by Gaius Gracchus.[40]

In line with this, action was taken to secure the sea-routes to Spain. Trouble in Sardinia was suppressed in 126 (for Gracchus' service there see p. 27), and the piratical activities of the Balearic islanders were checked by Q. Metellus in 123. But with these military considerations were linked commercial interests. Two colonies of Roman citizens were established at Palma and Pollentia in Majorca, where many Roman or Italian emigrants from Spain joined the settlement. The islands were place under a prefect appointed by the governor of Hispania Citerior, and Metellus returned to Rome to receive a triumph and the cognomen Balearicus (121).[41]

III

THE RISE AND FALL OF MARIUS[1]

1. THE SENATORIAL SETTLEMENT

The supporters of Gaius Gracchus who had survived the slaughter and the subsequent assizes held by Opimius, were eager to avenge their leader and friends. By 120 B.C., they had gathered sufficient strength to challenge both the chief persecutor and the implications of the *senatus consultum ultimum*: Opimius was brought to trial 'apud populum' by a tribune named Decius Subulo.[2] A fundamental question of law was at stake: what latitude might be allowed to a magistrate in the exercise of his *imperium* at a time of internal disturbance, especially when he was backed by the moral authority of the Senate? Granted that the 'salus populi' must be the 'suprema lex', was he justified in disregarding the *ius provocationis* which Roman citizens had enjoyed for nearly 400 years, and in putting them to death without trial or appeal? It would seem that if men had actually raised arms against their country, they automatically became *hostes* and ceased to enjoy the rights of citizens: thus a strong case could be made for Opimius in his suppression of the Gracchans who fought on the Aventine. But it was very different when men had been disarmed or arrested later: many of these had not been granted any form of trial and those who secured the doubtful privilege of being hauled before Opimius' assize had been summarily executed without opportunity to exercise their right of appeal and in defiance of Gracchus' law 'ne quis iniussu populi Romani capite damnetur'. Here Opimius' action must have been illegal, but nevertheless he was acquitted.[3] One of his stoutest supporters at the trial was C. Carbo, who had deserted the Gracchan cause and had been rewarded with the consulship of 120. This renegade even went so far as to claim that Gaius had been justly killed, but in the following year he was himself prosecuted on some charge by the young orator L. Crassus and committed suicide. Thus by the acquittal of Opimius the authority of the Senate and its agent was vindicated; it received further backing when the People was persuaded by a tribune, L. Calpurnius Bestia (120, or possibly 121), to recall Popillius Laenas, who had been forced into exile by Gaius Gracchus for the part that he had played in the suppression of the followers of Tiberius (p. 27).[4]

The Senate did not, however, exercise its regained power in an entirely irresponsible manner: so far from attempting to secure the abrogation of Gaius' legislation, it allowed the colonists of Junonia to retain their land despite the repeal of the lex Rubria, and it did not oppose, so far as is known, the series of agrarian bills that was passed during the next few years. A law (probably of 121) allowed any Gracchan settler to dispose of his allotment if he wished: this was a sensible idea, since if after a number of years men had failed to make good farmers it was better to let them transfer their land to others; further, since the maximum amount of ager publicus allowed to any individual still remained fixed at 500 iugera, the transferred properties will normally have gone to other small farmers and not to swell the latifundia, though of course some men may have made money by speculative buying and selling. In 119 a second land-bill ended the further distribution of public land, by abolishing the commission,[5] granted perpetual tenancy to all occupiers of public land (i.e. those holding up to the maximum of 500 iugera) and re-imposed rent on such land; this revenue was to be used to benefit the people in some way (for the corn supply?). Eight years later in 111 another tribune, probably Sp. Thorius, carried a third agrarian bill, of which part still survives inscribed on a bronze tablet. By it all ager publicus dealt with by the commissioners, whether used for individual allotments or for colonies or left to the possessores, was converted into private property; the system of squatting (possessio) was abolished and rent was cancelled. The general effect was to consolidate and maintain the work of the Gracchi, but one result was that there was little ager publicus now left in Italy for further distribution.[6]

2. THE METELLI AND MARIUS

During the decade or so when these agrarian bills were carried, foreign affairs claimed some attention and on occasion led to a clash of policies. The proposal to found the colony at Narbo had caused political dissensions (p. 35), which were intensified when Jugurtha's conduct in N. Africa called for Roman intervention by diplomacy or war (see below, p. 39). There was also need to guard the northern frontiers of Macedonia against attacks by the Scordisci, a Thracian tribe on the lower Save. Here a Roman defeat was retrieved in 119 by L. Metellus who gained the cognomen Delmaticus.[6a] Four years later M. Aemilius Scaurus led Roman forces against the Taurisci, south of the Drave, but the Scordisci defeated one of the consuls of 114 and even penetrated into Greece as far south as Delphi. In 113 another danger threatened: Germanic tribes, the Cimbri and Teutones, were on the move. The consul Cn. Carbo, who was sent to ward them off, met with a resounding defeat at Noreia, but most fortunately for Rome, they moved off westwards through Switzerland instead of threatening the northern frontier of Italy (see p. 44). In the Balkans the Scordisci were gradually reduced by C. Metellus Caprarius (113–112), Livius Drusus, the tribune of 122 and consul in 112 (112–111), and M. Minucius Rufus (110–107). M. Caecilius Metellus (consul 115) was busy establishing law and order in Sardinia and Corsica from 115 to 112.

Thus the Caecilii Metelli were very prominent at this time: Metellus Balearicus gained the censorship in 119 and his cousin Delmaticus in 115, and they or their relations held one of the consulships in each of the alternate years from 119 to 109. They were in fact the dominant family and often showed more sympathy to the Equites than to the Die-Hard senators.[7] Their group was joined by M. Aemilius Scaurus who married the daughter of Delmaticus (later this Caecilia Metella became Sulla's wife). Scaurus belonged to a Patrician family which he lifted from the obscurity into which it had sunk in recent years: after hesitating between commerce and politics, he finally turned to the latter with such success that he became consul and princeps senatus in 115 and censor in 109.[8] This group of progressive men largely dominated the political scene, but they were later overshadowed by one whose early career they had helped to promote, Gaius Marius.

Marius came of a good municipal family from near the hill-town of Arpinum, some sixty miles south-east of Rome. After serving with distinction under Scipio Aemilianus at Numantia (133), he was helped to a political career by the Metelli and reached the tribunate in 119. As tribune, he showed some independence which may have cost him the support of the Metelli: he forced through a bill to limit undue influence at the Comitia (e.g. to check the intimidation of voters, by making narrower the 'bridges' over which they passed to record their votes). When the Senate, which Marius had perhaps failed to consult first, summoned him to explain, he swept aside the opposition of the consuls, Cotta and Metellus Delmaticus, and even threatened, it is said, to arrest them. On the other hand he took an unpopular line about corn-distribution: Gaius Gracchus' measure had been modified by a certain M. Octavius (not the tribune of 133) and Marius now opposed some scheme to extend the distributions.[8a] Thus the fact that he sponsored one measure that the Senate liked and the People disliked and another that appealed to the People and not to the Senate suggests that he had sought political support where he could find it. After failing to win the aedileship, he secured a praetorship for 115 although he was at the bottom of the list of successful candidates, and that perhaps only with the help of bribery: at any rate he was accused of this and was only just acquitted, the voting being equal. As praetor, or more probably as a promagistrate in 114, he served in Spain. Thereafter, since he had contacts with the Equites, he may have devoted his attention to business interests. Also at some time (perhaps c. 111) he married a Julia (an aunt of Julius Caesar): as a *novus homo* outside the governing class, he would find this link with a noble family most useful. Though he will hardly have reached a full reconciliation with the nobility, the Metelli may possibly have forgiven his conduct in 119, since he served later as legate to Metellus Numidicus in Africa. His purpose at this point was perhaps not so much to challenge the power of the Senate as to win an influential place within it. His methods are uncertain: one tradition represents him as energetic, courageous and dogged, another as a 'slick' betrayer of his friend Metellus.[9]

During these years of the pre-eminence of the Metelli, life became somewhat strained, especially as the shadow of Jugurtha lengthened, and at times superstitious fears seemed to sweep over the masses. The censors of 115 removed no less than 32 members from the Senate and 'censored' the stage. Scaurus (consul in 115) carried a law to limit the voting power of freedmen.[10] In 114, when two of three Vestal Virgins who were tried for unchastity were acquitted by the Pontiffs, the People were not satisfied and a tribune demanded the establishment of a secular court to try them. This was presided over by a former censor, L. Cassius Longinus, notorious for his severity and his use of the question 'Cui bono?'; he secured their condemnation.[11] Nevertheless popular unrest demanded that the Sibylline oracles be consulted, and they ordered that two Greeks and two Gauls should be buried alive, as in the grim days of the Hannibalic War a hundred years before. But even this enormity, which was not typical of Roman ritual (sixteen years later a decree of the Senate specifically forbade human-sacrifice), did not avail to avert all signs of divine displeasure: in 111 much of the city was devastated by fire.

3. THE OUTBREAK OF WAR AGAINST JUGURTHA

After the destruction of Carthage and the creation of the Roman province of Africa in 146, trade soon followed the flag, and businessmen from Italy began to develop interests in the province and the neighbouring client-kingdom of Numidia. Under King Micipsa (148–118 B.C.) Numidia flourished until his death when he bequeathed his realm jointly to his two sons and his nephew Jugurtha whom he had adopted as a son. The difficulties of a triple or tripartite rule were reduced when Jugurtha murdered one of his 'brothers' and defeated the other, Adherbal, who fled to the Roman province and then to Rome itself, seeking help to regain his rightful share of the kingdom. But Jugurtha also sent to Rome where he had 'friends at court': he had previously served with some Numidian troops under the command of Scipio Aemilianus at Numantia (134–133), where he had gained the friendship of many Romans. In the Senate Aemilius Scaurus advocated supporting Adherbal by force of arms, but the majority decided to send a commission under Opimius to divide Numidia between the two claimants (c. 116). Adherbal was given the more civilized eastern half including the capital named Cirta (modern Constantine in Algeria),[12] and Jugurtha received the less fertile western part.

Unwilling to accept this as a permanent settlement, Jugurtha later (112) drove Adherbal into Cirta and besieged him there. In response to Adherbal's appeals the Senate first reprimanded Jugurtha and then sent another commission, this time with Scaurus in charge, which achieved little. Finally the unfortunate Adherbal was persuaded by the Italian merchants resident in Cirta to surrender on condition that his life should be spared. But in vain: when Cirta was occupied by Jugurtha's troops, Adherbal was put to death by torture. Many Italian merchants were also killed: this was an irretrievable error by Jugurtha, whose troops may well have exceeded his orders. It provoked a political flare-up in Rome, where the Equites and People demanded action. At long last war was declared on Jugurtha and a Roman army was sent to Africa under the command of L. Calpurnius Bestia, consul in 111, who soon persuaded Jugurtha to make a formal surrender in return for the retention of the Numidian throne.

What did all this mean? The historian Sallust at any rate had no doubt: the whole series of Roman officials who had been sent to Africa had been successively bribed by Jugurtha.[13] And worse was to follow. Led by the tribune Memmius, the Roman People demanded an enquiry: under promise of safe-conduct Jugurtha should be summoned to Rome to disclose the names of the nobles whom he was alleged to have corrupted. When he arrived, however, at the end of 111, he is said to have bribed a tribune to exercise his veto and forbid him to make a public statement. He then murdered a cousin of his in Italy, named Massiva, a potential rival for the Numidian throne whom some senators were beginning to consider a possible substitute; Jugurtha then smuggled out of Italy the man that he had employed to commit the crime. Such conduct destroyed all hopes of reaching any agreement with the Senate, which, however, honoured its pledge and sent Jugurtha back to Africa. He, if any one, should know what truth lay behind his famous parting remark that Rome was 'urbem venalem et mature perituram, si emptorem invenerit'.

The war continued. The consul Spurius Albinus achieved little (110), but when he had returned to Rome to hold the elections his brother Aulus, whom he had left in command, was defeated by Jugurtha near Suthul and the Roman army was humiliated by having to march under a yoke of spears and to evacuate Numidia. Soon (probably early in 109) a tribune C. Mamilius carried a bill by which the People established a commission, a *quaestio* of

Equites, to get to the bottom of these scandals. Scaurus somehow managed to become one of the chairmen, and the commission acted with vigour, though not necessarily with justice: Opimius, Bestia, Sp. Albinus and others were condemned and went into exile. At length the conduct of the war was to be raised above personal and political considerations, and an upright and efficient commander, Q. Caecilius Metellus, was sent out to Africa.[14]

Rome was at last committed to full-scale war. The motives behind her recent policy, however, are by no means clear. She had been under no legal necessity to intervene in N. Africa and she might well have been able to check Jugurtha by other means short of war. Further, the German movements beyond her northern frontier and Carbo's defeat in 113 (p. 38) might make her slow to tie up troops in Africa, and she certainly did not go to war to extend her territory there. Thus many senators may genuinely have felt that diplomacy was preferable to war, and not all the charges of corruption levelled against them by Sallust may be justified. But as time went on more may have come to the conclusion that war was necessary and others that it might be profitable to themselves. Yet even so, some may have thought only of a short war to check Jugurtha; he could then be left on the throne, since peace without honour might be better than a prolonged and difficult campaign. More urgent than the senators, however, were the Equites. Their friends had been butchered in Cirta, their interests in Africa threatened, and their hopes of future development there aroused. The People, also were ready to use any stick with which to beat the Senate. Thus pressure from Equites and People at last forced the Senate to more decisive action against the wily Jugurtha who would probably have been only too glad to avoid war if he could have secured Numidia without it.[15]

4. THE DEFEAT OF JUGURTHA

In Africa Metellus,[16] who had Marius on his staff, restored discipline in his army, distrusted an offer by Jugurtha to surrender, and advanced westwards to the river Muthul where he fought an indecisive engagement. Avoiding further pitched battles, he then tried to wear down Jugurtha's strength by attacking various strong-points: Marius, for instance, was sent to seize Sicca, and though Metellus failed to capture Zama Regia, in the following year (108) when his command had been prolonged he recovered Vaga, where there had been a rising in Jugurtha's favour.[17] After another engagement Jugurtha fled westwards and Metellus captured Thala. Jugurtha, however, raised fresh troops and persuaded his father-in-law Bocchus, the king of Mauretania, to join him in an advance eastwards to Cirta, but Metellus avoided battle, Thus after two years of campaigning Metellus had begun to develop what was probably the best strategy to defeat a mobile enemy in the vast and often barren spaces of N. Africa, though lack of troops prevented its full realization. His methods, as elaborated by Marius later, have been compared with those used in the Boer War by Lord Kitchener, who wore down his opponents by planting block-houses ever further in enemy territory. But though Metellus' success might go far to restore the somewhat tarnished military reputation of the Senate, it was true that Jugurtha, although driven farther westwards, was still at large. An attempt by Metellus to secure his betrayal by treachery had failed, and only his capture or death in battle could end the war: this, rather than the occupation of Numidia, was the primary objective.

Metellus, however, had trouble nearer to hand. Marius began to press for leave to return to Rome to stand for the consulship, only to be told by Metellus that he should wait until he could stand with Metellus' own son who was then only about twenty years old. After this insult, or perhaps rather before it, as the anti-Marian tradition suggests, Marius began to stir up trouble in the army and to agitate through the Roman traders in Africa and through his friends in Rome, claiming that Metellus from incompetence or ambition was unnecessarily spinning out the war. At last Marius got his way and returned to Rome where by boastful demagogy he secured sufficient popular and Equestrian support to carry a novus homo into the consulship of 107; further, the People disregarded the Senate's decision to prolong Metellus' command and appointed Marius to succeed him in Africa. This intervention by the People in the Senate's traditional right to allocate the provincial commands established a very dangerous example which was later followed to exalt Pompey and Caesar to extraordinary commands to the great detriment of the Republic. Further, Marius intended to make sure of victory in Africa by taking out more troops. To raise these he disregarded the rule that the army should be recruited only from men enrolled in the five classes, and appealed for volunteers from the capite censi or proletarii, men who lacked the necessary property qualification. This innovation also had far-reaching political effects and paved the way for the later military dictatorships. At the moment it merely provided Marius with an enthusiastic army.

With these troops Marius sailed to Africa, leaving behind in Italy his quaestor, L. Cornelius Sulla, to raise a large force of cavalry. After spending much of the summer (107) in training his troops and in skirmishes with the enemy, Marius adopted the strategy of attacking fortified cities. Apart from a spectacular march through the desert to seize Capsa which would have good propaganda value, at first he achieved little; since his command was prolonged, he turned during the winter and the first part of 106 to a systematic reduction of Jugurtha's fortresses throughout Numidia in an area as large as peninsular Italy. At some point Sulla's cavalry joined him and in the autumn of 106 he launched a successful attack on a fortress near the river Muluccha, some 500 miles west of Cirta, where Jugurtha kept some of his treasure. This loss compelled Jugurtha to secure Bocchus' support by a promise to cede western Numidia to him, and the two kings were forced to consider risking a pitched battle. Marius, however, had not the forces to hold so large an area and could not winter so far west. On his return march he beat off attacks by Jugurtha and Bocchus, and when he was near Cirta (which may temporarily have been lost to the Romans) he decisively defeated the two kings in a final battle in which he snatched victory from defeat either through the sudden arrival of Sulla at a critical moment (Sallust) or because of an unexpected storm (the Livian tradition). When Bocchus applied to Rome for terms, he was told by the Senate that he must 'work his passage'. This later involved negotiations with Sulla who went to Bocchus' camp, uncertain whether he was walking into a trap; by his superior diplomacy, however, he persuaded Bocchus to betray Jugurtha to him instead of himself becoming Jugurtha's prisoner (105). Thus the war ended – only just in time in view of the menace on Rome's northern frontier – and Jugurtha, after gracing Marius' triumph at the beginning of 104, died in the State prison, the Tullianum.

Rome's settlement of N. Africa gained her no territorial advantage: the province of Africa was not enlarged. Eastern Numidia was given to a half-brother of Jugurtha, named Gauda, and Bocchus was rewarded for his treachery towards Jugurtha by receiving western Numidia in addition to retaining the throne of Mauretania. With peace re-established the Senate was satisfied to leave the whole area west of the Roman province in the hands of native rulers. If any Romans benefited from the settlement it was the Equites who could now resume their trade in Africa in safety.

The war had shown that despite weaknesses in the Roman army, such as lack of cavalry and an initial failure to cope with guerrilla warfare, yet the Roman legions could still win through. But more important than the war itself were its political effects. By provoking suspicions of senatorial corruption, it had exacerbated the relations of the Senate with the People and Equites, already aggravated by the Gracchi. It had increased interference by the last two groups in foreign policy and had elevated a 'popular' general to potentially dangerous heights. Metellus might be given a triumph and the *cognomen* Numidicus, and Sulla might claim solid credit for the final capture of Jugurtha, but it was not the senatorial generals who were regarded as the architects of victory or chosen to face the new menace in the North. Seeds of rivalry were sown between Marius and Sulla, champions of Populares and Optimates, and the influence of the army in political life was foreshadowed.

5. THE NORTHERN MENACE AND ITS POLITICAL REPERCUSSIONS

Meantime a much more serious menace had been developing in the North. The Cimbri and Teutones, two Germanic tribes, had started a mass movement from their homes somewhere in the Jutland area, and advanced southwards, taking with them their wives and children in their wagons. Checked by the Scordisci near Belgrade, they turned westwards. To meet this potential threat to her northern frontier Rome sent Cn. Carbo in 113 to head them off, but though they were willing to respond, Carbo insisted on fighting and met with disaster at Noreia near Ljubjana (see p. 38). To Rome's great good fortune the Germans decided to continue trekking westwards. On the way they were joined by the Tigurini and other Celtic tribes, and reached Gaul by 110 where they could threaten the new Roman province; to protect it the Romans sent out an army under M. Iunius Silanus, consul of 109. When the Senate rejected as too hazardous a proposal from the tribes that they should be allowed to settle on the frontiers, they defeated Silanus somewhere in the valley of the Rhone. The Cimbri, however, turned northwards, while the Tigurini continued to the west where Rome's allies the Volcae around Tolosa (Toulouse) revolted. Though L. Cassius Longinus, consul in 107, drove them back, he was routed and killed in an ambush in the Garonne valley and the survivors had to march under the yoke. A consul of 106, Q. Servilius Caepio, however, managed to recover Tolosa, but was then faced by the return of the Cimbri. His command was prolonged and he received reinforcements under Cn. Mallius, consul of 105, who was a *novus homo*. As proconsul, Caepio was subordinate to Mallius, but he was reluctant to obey or co-operate, though finally he joined Mallius east of the Rhone. The result was Rome's greatest defeat since Cannae, a hundred years before: at Arausio (modern Orange) the two commanders were thrust back against the river and defeated in detail, with a reported loss of 80,000 men. Italy was threatened with invasion, and Mallius' colleague P. Rutilius Rufus decreed that no man under thirty-five should leave the country.

These events abroad naturally had repercussions at home, where Caepio, who was a good senatorial, had earlier celebrated a triumph for victories over the Lusitani in Spain, and had been elected consul for 106, the year in which Metellus Numidicus received a triumph for his services in Africa. Before he had gone off to Tolosa, Caepio had secured the passing of a *lex iudiciaria* which deprived the Equites of some control of all *quaestiones*, both standing and special: it is hardly likely that he was able to transfer them back to the Senate alone, but more probably all were now to be empanelled from both Equites and senators.[18] The law-courts in fact increasingly became the battle-ground for political disputes. C. Popillius Laenas, who had accepted unworthy terms from the Tigurini when his commander Cassius had been killed in the Garonne valley, was prosecuted for *perduellio* by a tribune C. Coelius Caldus, who also introduced a bill to extend secret ballot to such cases. Caepio's turn was soon to come: as a preliminary move after his defeat as proconsul at Arausio, the People deprived him of his command.

Meanwhile in view of the menace in the North, Marius, the People's hero, was elected to a second consulship, for 104, in his absence. On his return from Africa he celebrated his triumph over Jugurtha on 1 January and was given the command in Gaul against the Cimbri and Teutones by the People, who again disregarded both the Senate's traditional claim to make such appointments (cf. p. 42) and the interval of ten years that was prescribed by law between the holding of two consulships. Marius, who then went off to train and organize a new army, was in fact elected consul again each year until his sixth consulship in 100; the People thus flouted the *lex Annalis* and refused to give the Senate the option of prolonging his command by prorogation. This rising tide of popular feeling soon helped to modify Caepio's judiciary law: a tribune, C. Servilius Glaucia (probably in 104) carried a measure to restore the extortion court (*quaestio de repetundis*) to the Equites.[19] The People and Equites were obviously beginning again to exert more pressure upon the Senate, and the unfortunate Caepio became the target for further attacks. Blamed for the disaster at Arausio, he lost his seat in the Senate when a tribune carried a bill expelling from the Senate all who had been deprived of their *imperium* by the People. Further, the treasure which Caepio had taken at Tolosa (p. 44) had mysteriously disappeared while being transported to Massilia in 106. A special commission of enquiry was appointed to investigate the loss, but Caepio may have succeeded in escaping serious penalty in this court.[20] His final trial followed later (p. 46).

Meantime a tribune, Cn. Domitius Ahenobarbus, was hitting out in many directions. He was unsuccessful in two prosecutions, one against Silanus (*cos.* 109) on a charge of misconduct on his campaign against the Cimbri, and the second against M. Aemilius Scaurus whom he accused of neglecting his sacral duties: he had a grudge against Scaurus for not having co-opted him as a Pontiff to succeed his father, the consul of 122. He then carried a law to transfer to the People the selection of priests, who were to be chosen by 17 of the 35 tribes; this was a very serious encroachment upon the privileges of the senatorial class. Further, Cn. Pompeius Strabo, a quaestor of 104 and the father of Pompey the Great, shocked public opinion by attempting to take part in the prosecution of his own commanding officer, a governor of Sardinia.[21]

Rome found time for all these political bickerings because the German threat was still hanging fire, although other trouble flared up nearer home. An outbreak of slaves at Capua was crushed, but a more serious slave-rising developed in Sicily. Thanks to the settlement by Rupilius after the First Servile War (pp. 11–12), conditions in Sicily may have improved somewhat, with a decrease of *latifundia* and an increase of smaller farms devoted to the production of corn, wine and oil, but the basic evil of slavery remained, and if the new uprising did not involve such large numbers as the earlier one, it at least spread more widely over the island. The immediate cause was that the Roman governor in 104, under pressure from the slave-owning landlords, failed to implement fully a decree passed by the Senate that provincial governors should seek out and release all citizens of allied states that were being kept as slaves, many of them having been reduced to slavery by the activities of the pirates. When a certain Salvius, who led a revolt in the south part of the island and styled himself King Tryphon, joined hands with a Cilician named Athenion in the west, the situation became grave for the Romans in view of the concurrent threat to their northern frontier. The commanders sent against the slaves achieved little in 103 and 102, but finally a lieutenant of Marius, Manius Aquilius (*cos.* 101), brought the war to an end.

6. L. APPULEIUS SATURNINUS

Another scandal of 104 was that the Senate used a rise in cornprices as an excuse to install M. Aemilius Scaurus in place of L. Appuleius Saturninus as the *quaestor Ostiensis* who looked after the corn that arrived at the port of Ostia. Saturninus not unnaturally was embittered and turned *popularis*. He was elected tribune for 103 and soon showed what he could do as a *popularis*, though since he was tribune again in 100 there is some doubt about dating his measures. Supported by his colleague C. Norbanus in 103, he launched an attack on Caepio and Mallius for their responsibility for the disaster at Arausio. He proposed a plebiscite to send Mallius to exile, and Norbanus prosecuted Caepio before the People. After disturbances, in which two opposing tribunes were driven off by force and the Princeps Senatus, Scaurus, was hit on the head with a stone, Caepio was convicted and imprisoned, but later was allowed to go into exile at Smyrna.[22] Saturninus also secured by a *lex Appuleia de maiestate* the establishment of a court to try cases of treason, that is offences against the *maiestas* of the Roman People, a crime which now began to replace the earlier charge of *perduellio*.[23] While no doubt the existence of the new court would tend to make generals more careful in the future, Saturninus' immediate object will have been political: the court would prove a useful weapon against senatorial commanders, and since the jurors were Equites it would win him further support in Rome. He also proposed a corn-law, which possibly went no further than to revive the provisions of Gracchus' law which had been modified by Octavius (p. 39).[24] At any rate the Senate objected, and when Saturninus disregarded the veto of two colleagues, the son of Caepio who was now quaestor forcibly broke up the Concilium; when this led to a prosecution for *maiestas minuta*, he was acquitted. The fate of the corn-bill remains uncertain. Saturninus also promoted Marius' interests: in addition to helping him to win his fourth consulship, he carried, despite tribunician opposition, a measure to provide allotments of 100 *iugera* in Africa for Marius' veterans. Thus Saturninus, who might appear as a *popularis* in the Gracchan tradition,[25] had secured the backing of Marius, People and Equites in his struggle against the Optimates.

Saturninus was clearly dangerous, but Metellus Numidicus, who was censor with his cousin Caprarius in 102, was unwise to try to omit the names of Saturninus and Glaucia from the list of senators. This provoked a riot in which Numidicus was forced to seek refuge on the Capitol; the more conciliatory counsels of Caprarius then prevailed. Saturninus' friends, the Equites, were no doubt gratified when the Senate decided to set up a special command to cope with the menace of piracy in the eastern Mediterranean which interfered with their trading interests, but the praetor and famous orator, M. Antonius, who was sent out with proconsular *imperium* in 102 to secure bases on the coasts of Pamphylia and W. Cilicia, achieved little even though he held his command until 100. Saturninus meanwhile continued on the path of violence. In 101 he insulted an embassy from Mithridates, king of Pontus, and was in consequence prosecuted on a capital charge, but he secured acquittal by calling on the mob to break up proceedings. Then after the murder of a competitor he gained a second tribunate for 100, and his friend Glaucia was elected praetor. Marius, now victorious over the Germanic tribes, returned to Rome to hold a triumph and to stand for a sixth consulship for 100. This would be the testing year.

7. MARIUS' VICTORY OVER THE GERMANS

Marius owed his victories largely to his military reforms, which helped to convert a citizen-militia into a semi-professional army. True, the Roman armies of this period were very different from those of the early Republic when men were eager to hasten back to their homes and farms after each annual campaign, and probably in practice many men not enrolled in the five property classes (i.e. the *capitecensi*) had been recruited,[26] but it was Marius who officially opened the army to them as a career (cf. p. 42). One far-reaching effect of recruiting these landless volunteers was that they would look to their commanders to provide spoils and to help them after demobilization. As the State did not step in with any scheme of pensions, the men tended increasingly to expect their generals to provide allotments for them by securing the passing of a *lex agraria*. This spelt danger: these semi-professionalized soldiers, bound to their commanders by ties of personal interest, made possible the rise of a series of military dictators who in the end overthrew the Republic.

Marius also introduced far-reaching tactical changes in the army. The legions had normally fought in a formation based on three separate lines which differed in age and equipment; these were now abolished and all the infantry were armed alike. For some time the sections (maniples), into which a legion was divided, had on occasion been grouped into threes in a unit known as a cohort. Marius now made the cohort the standard tactical unit (the battalion) of the legion, which henceforth consisted of ten cohorts of 600 men, each of which was subdivided into six centuries. At the same time each legion was given a silver eagle as its standard, and the men began to develop a 'regimental' loyalty to their legion. The legionaries' chief arms were the sword and a long javelin (the *pilum*). Marius, following the example set by Rutilius Rufus (*cos.* 105), gave his men a thorough training in arms-drill by methods based on those of the gladiatorial schools, and provided the *pilum* with a wooden rivet to help fasten the metal head to the wooden shaft; on impact this rivet would break and thus made it impossible for the enemy to throw the *pilum* back.[27] When on the move, Roman armies built a camp each night for protection and for this purpose had depended on baggage trains. Marius made the army more mobile and independent by making the men carry their own entrenching tools and other equipment: consequently they became known as Marius' mules (*muli Mariani*). But an efficient army is lost without efficient officers. The commanding officer was normally a consul, who had under him six military tribunes[28] and sixty centurions for each legion; and it was these centurions, seasoned and experienced veterans, six to each cohort, that provided firm leadership for the rank-and-file. Thus by his military reforms Marius partly gave final shape to earlier developments and partly introduced real innovations. The Roman army owed him much and became one of the finest fighting machines of antiquity.

Rome was exceedingly fortunate in that the rambling movements of the German tribes allowed Marius time to shape his army into a first-class force. In fact he had so much time that he employed his men in digging a new channel at the mouth of the Rhone to by-pass the estuary which tended to silt-up. This new waterway, the *fossa Mariana*, which ran from near modern Fos to Arles (Arelate), allowed shipping to get to the Rhone in safety, facilitated the supply-line of Marius' army, promoted the commercial prosperity of Arelate and of S. Gaul in general, pleased the Equites, and fore-shadowed the similar use of the imperial army on public works.[29] In 102, however, Marius, who had been elected to his fourth consulship in Rome with Saturninus' help, received news that brought him post-haste back to Gaul. The barbarians were planning a converging attack on Italy: the Teutones were hoping to advance along the coast from the west, the Cimbri over the Brenner Pass from the north, and the Tigurini over the Julian Alps from the north-east. This division may have weakened the strength of the attack, but it also forced the Romans to divide their armies. While his colleague Q. Lutatius Catulus stood guard in N. Italy, Marius at first refused battle in S. Gaul (probably near Tarascon), allowed the Teutones to march past him, and then managed to work his way round in front of them before they reached Aquae Sextiae (modern Aix). Here in a valley surrounded by hills he cut to pieces the Ambrones who arrived first, and then engaged the Teutones in a tough struggle; a detachment of 3000 Romans concealed in reserve suddenly threatened the enemy's rear and helped to achieve a complete victory. The western invasion was smashed and Narbonese Gaul was safe. Meanwhile Catulus had foolishly advanced up the Adige to meet the Cimbri in the hilly country near Tridentum (Trento), but his army managed to extricate itself, though at the cost of abandoning Transpadane Gaul to the invaders. Nevertheless his command was prolonged for 101 when he was joined by Marius, now consul for the fifth time. Together they advanced with some 55,000 men over the Po and finally in the heat of the midsummer met the enemy at Campi Raudii near Vercellae. Here the rout of the Cimbri was no less decisive than that of the Teutones at Aquae Sextiae. The Tigurini found safety by retreating to Switzerland, hastened on their way by Sulla.[30]

The northern peril was ended. Both Marius and Catulus received triumphs, but though some senators might try to believe that their man Catulus deserved his, the People's hero Marius clearly was the real saviour of Rome. Memories of the sack of the city by the Gauls in 390 B.C., combined with the series of recent defeats that had culminated at Arausio, had justifiably aroused Rome's fears and now increased her gratitude towards her preserver. Many Romans may have been thinking that disciplined legions must in the end have succeeded in defeating the barbarians, despite their numbers, but that would not have been possible without outstanding leadership. Marius in his army reforms, tactics and strategy had proved himself to be a general of great ability, if not of genius. The future was soon to show whether he could rival his military achievements when he turned to the battleground of politics.

8. MARIUS' SIXTH CONSULSHIP (100 B.C.)

After his triumph Marius enjoyed such prestige and *auctoritas* that, had he so wished, he might have achieved a great measure of social reform, but there is little to suggest that his mind ever moved on such lines except in so far as the interests of his veterans were involved. They needed land and they should have it, but of statesmanship to match his generalship he showed not a spark. So far from taking any personal lead, he merely used Saturninus for his immediate purpose. Saturninus, glad of the chance to increase his own popularity, sponsored measures to provide allotments in Transalpine Gaul and colonies in Sicily, Achaea, Macedonia, Cercina (an island off the coast of N. Africa), Africa (now or earlier), and perhaps in Corsica. A land commission (*decemviri agris dandis attribuendis iudicandis*), on the lines of the Gracchan commission, was set up, and it perhaps dealt with the colonies as well; one of the members was the father of Julius Caesar (he became praetor in 91). Though few of these ambitious plans were implemented, at least the settlements in Africa, which had been voted if not actually started in 103 (p. 46), were considerable. One feature of the scheme shows insight: some at any rate of the colonies were to be Latin not Roman. Since not many Romans would be willing to sacrifice their citizenship by joining them, the colonists presumably must have been drawn largely from the Latins and allies. It was only fair that their share in the joint repulse of the northern invaders should be rewarded, but unfortunately the experience of Gaius Gracchus had shown that the selfish Roman plebs was reluctant to share any of its privileges and so in fact this generous feature of the proposal alienated some of the popular support which Saturninus enjoyed in Rome.[31]

A law had been passed a little earlier (probably December 101) to supplement the efforts of M. Antonius against the pirates in the eastern Mediterranean (p. 47). It was designed to mobilize resources for a drive against them, and closed all harbours of the empire and of allied states to their ships. Its real purpose was scarcely to create an extra-ordinary command in Asia for Marius, as has been suggested, though he was probably becoming anxious about his future; nor can it definitely be associated with Saturninus, though he might well favour a measure which would promote the interests of the Equites.[32] The law contained a *sanctio* which bound magistrates to take an oath to observe its provisions. This was not necessarily an unusual feature, but Saturninus broke new ground when he tried to anticipate senatorial opposition to his *lex agraria* by inserting into it a *sanctio* under which all senators, on pain of exile, must swear to abide by it. This gave great offence. The urban plebs were already displeased because of his attitude to the allies, but by bringing some of Marius' veterans into the Forum Saturninus routed his opponents in a fracas and got his measures carried. After some hesitation the senators followed the lead of Marius who took the oath, but subject to the validity of the law; Metellus Numidicus alone refused and preferred exile.[33]

At the elections for 99 Saturninus secured a third tribunate. Glaucia, though holding a praetorship, illegally stood for the consulship; his chief rival, C. Memmius (tribune in 111) was murdered or killed in a riot. This was too much for Marius, who had a strong sense of law and order and must have been increasingly uncomfortable about the wisdom of his political alliance with these demagogues and perhaps also about their ultimate political aims. When the Senate passed the *senatus consultum ultimum* and summoned him to see to the safety of the state, he deserted his allies, who with their followers had seized the Capitol. By cutting off their water-supply he soon compelled them to surrender, and in order to save them from lynching at the hands of the mob he shut them up in the Senate House, but the crowd broke through the roof and pelted them to death with the tiles.

The Senate possibly declared that Saturninus' legislation, or at any rate the measures carried in 100, was invalid, since it had been carried by force (per vim). Marius' lack of political principle was exposed. No longer feared by the Senate or respected by the People, he was in a weak position; after a vain protest against a measure to recall Metellus from exile, in 98 he went off to Asia and obscurity.[34] This conduct at least showed his loyalty to the constitution: unusually close ties had bound him to his army, and the support of the People had secured him six consulships. These, however, he had held primarily because of the military needs of the day and he had not attempted to use them as stepping stones to a personal predominance. The use of his soldiers in the Forum in 100 was a disquieting precedent, but Marius' own lack of political ability or ambition, combined with his innate sense of law and order, limited the possible development of the evil. Danger to the State would arise only when military need elevated men of greater political insight who were prepared to use the army for their own personal advancement. In the meantime the authority of the nobility had prevailed over the turbulent demagogues and over the novus homo who became an army commander.

IV

THE RISE AND FALL OF SULLA[1]

1. THE NINETIES

The end of the second century had witnessed stirring events both at home and abroad. By contrast the first few years of the next century were relatively peaceful in both spheres, though in fact they were to prove merely an uneasy lull before even greater storms. Pacification abroad was symbolized in a series of triumphs by victorious generals: the joint triumph of Marius and Catulus over the Teutones and Cimbri was followed by those of M. Antonius over the pirates (100), T. Didius over the Scordisci, and Dolabella over the Lusitanians (98), while Manius Aquilius celebrated an *ovatio* for his reduction of the Sicilian slave-war. While these public spectacles assured the people of Rome that the frontiers of the empire were safe, the domestic scene was also enlivened by a number of political trials, in which several men alleged to have been sympathizers of Saturninus were condemned.[2] Both Senate and Equites were breathing more freely and in their common desire to avoid such upheavals as had disfigured the year 100 they achieved a state of co-existence, if not of harmonious co-operation. The Senate in particular failed to express by more generous action any relief it may have felt at having rounded a dangerous corner. Rather, it attempted to strengthen its position: the consuls of 98 carried a lex *Caecilia-Didia*, which (*a*) by forbidding 'tacking' various measures together in omnibus-bills guarded the Senate against possible coalitions, e.g. between Equites and People, and (*b*) by enacting that a regular interval must elapse between the promulgation of a measure and its voting in the Assembly, guarded the Senate against suprise attacks.

Of far greater moment, however, was the Senate's criminally short-sighted attitude to the Italian allies, many of whom had come to Rome during the recent upheavals. By a *lex Licinia-Mucia* the consuls of 95 set up a *quaestio* on aliens who were claiming to be citizens.[2a] This action, though quite legal, was incredibly foolish, but before its full consequences were felt the mutual toleration between Senate and Equites received a rude shock. An equestrian jury condemned on a charge of extortion P. Rutilius Rufus (*cos.* 105) who had served in Asia as a legate of Mucius Scaevola: so far from being guilty of oppression, he had helped to draft an exemplary edict for the administration of the province and had protected the provincials from the exactions of the equestrian tax-gathers.[3] The Equites now had their revenge: despite the dignity of his defence, Rufus was condemned and retired to live in exile at Smyrna among the very provincials that he was alleged to have oppressed. Though he was a *novus homo* (and therefore an easier target than Scaevola), the Senate must have felt this affront to their Order very bitterly, while the political bias of the 'Gracchan' juries was patent.

2. THE YOUNGER DRUSUS

Conscious of the personal risk that he was taking, a leader at long last came forward, bold enough to follow in the footsteps of Gaius Gracchus and to tackle the twin problems of the law-courts and the Italians. Ironically enough he was the son of Drusus who had opposed C. Gracchus. Elected tribune for 91, the younger M. Livius Drusus was not prepared to stand by and let the State drift into disaster. Aristocratic, wealthy and somewhat severe in manner, he sponsored a more generous senatorial policy and gradually worked towards his ultimate aim of gaining franchise for the Italian allies. In the Senate he had many friends who included the Princeps Senatus, Scaurus, and the great orator Crassus, but he needed wider support and so he turned to the People. He carried a bill to provide allotments, and served on the decemviral commission which it established, as well as being one of the five members of another such commission set up by a law of his tribunician colleague Saufeius. He also made arrangements for the distribution of cheap corn and sponsored a colonial bill, perhaps to implement the scheme started by his father (p. 31). After having gained, as he hoped, popular support he then turned to the thorny question of the law-courts. He probably proposed (the evidence is contradictory) that they should be shared between the two Orders, i.e. 'mixed' juries of senators and Equites should be established, and that all members should be subject to a law against judicial corruption, based on an adaptation of Gracchus' legislation (p. 30). Or he may have proposed to add 300 Equites to the Senate which would then provide the *iudices*.[4]

Relations between the two Orders, however, were too strained to permit of compromise: Drusus found that he had pleased neither, but had fallen between two stools. Some public disturbances ensued, in one of which

Drusus' brother-in-law Caepio, with whom he had quarrelled, was in danger of being hurled from the Tarpeian Rock. In the Senate the opposition to Drusus was led by one of the consuls, L. Marcius Philippus, whose following gradually increased despite the help that Drusus received from the oratory of Crassus. The scales began to tilt against him when it became known that he was contemplating a bill to give Roman franchise to the Italians, many of whom came to Rome to support him. He was known to have entertained the Marsic leader, Q. Poppaedius Silo, in his home, and men who feared that the Italians were now so restless that they might turn to force in order to secure their demands, began to doubt his loyalty. The fact that he warned Philippus of a plot to murder him showed that such doubts were unfounded, but it also revealed his knowledge of the allies' plans.[5] His position was thus quickly undermined: he lost the support of the Senate, of the Equites, of the People who continued selfishly to refuse to contemplate extending their privileges to the Italians, and lastly even of some of the Italians themselves who feared that their land might be threatened under his agrarian and colonial schemes. Philippus then persuaded the Senate to declare all Drusus' legislation invalid, because it infringed the lex Caecilia-Didia, probably on the technical ground that some of the measures (e.g. the agrarian and colonial plans) had been 'tacked' together. Disappointed, disillusioned and deserted on all sides, Drusus had to admit himself beaten, since he was not prepared to lead the Italians against Rome as some of his political enemies may have feared. Soon afterwards he was murdered by an unknown assassin. Nor were his friends left in peace: early in the year 90 a tribune, Q. Varius Hybrida, disregarded the veto of his colleagues and carried a law that established a court with equestrian jurors to try anyone suspected of collusion with the allies. Those who fell victims to this enquiry included many famous men (though in the next year Varius was hoisted on his own petard and condemned under his own law).[6] Thus Drusus' attempt at reform had failed. He may not have shown great wisdom in his methods, which combined with his proud manner may have aroused fears that he was seeking too much personal power, but at least his aims were the aims of a statesmen, and his death was the signal for war.

3. THE OUTBREAK OF THE ITALIAN OR SOCIAL WAR

Fearing widespread discontent in Italy, the Senate had already sent Roman agents to various districts to watch developments. At Asculum in Picenum the people, thinking that their plans were revealed, turned on a visiting Roman praetor who had behaved rashly: they promptly killed him and all other Romans in the city. A deputation of allies went to Rome to protest at Rome's past treatment of them, but the Senate refused to listen unless they made restitution for the massacre at Asculum. Feelings ran too high for compromise. The highlanders of Picenum and Samnium were determined to fight for their independence, and both sides spent the winter of 91/90 preparing for war.

The ensuing struggle is sometimes called the Social War (the war of the *socii*), but the title is misleading because it obscures a fact of the highest importance: the Latin allies did not join in, but every one, with the single exception of Venusia, remained loyal to Rome.[7] If therefore the more privileged Latin allies abstained, what drove the rest of the Italici to such extreme measures?[8] They had many grievances as has been seen, but why did they so eagerly want Roman citizenship? If they got it, few of them would have been able to go all the way to Rome to vote, and fewer still could ever have hoped to win their way into the exclusive circle of Roman nobles and magistrates. At first in the days of the Gracchi they apparently wanted the protection that citizenship would give them against oppression and exploitation by Roman magistrates and they might even have been satisfied if granted the *ius provocationis* (cf. p. 27). But as time went on and their hopes were continually shattered they became more sensitive to their social and political inequality. Rome could never have won her present position without their help: why should they not be treated as Romans? Thus Roman disregard of their legitimate complaints (about the effect of Roman agrarian laws and other matters) hurt their spirits even more than their material interests: frustrated and cheated of proper recognition, their patience suddenly snapped. Denied equality, they would fight for independence. The violence of the war that ensued testifies to the depth of the feeling involved.

The highlanders of the glens and hills of central Italy formed the heart of the uprising, and comprised two groups, the Marsic in the North (the whole war is sometimes named the Marsic War) and the Samnite in the South. Eight warriors, who are depicted on a coin taking an oath, probably represent the Marsi, Picentines, Paeligni, Marrucini, Vestini, Frentani, Samnites and Hirpini. They obtained no support at first in Etruria or Umbria; Latium and northern Campania remained loyal to Rome; Calabria was not affected, nor Bruttium at first; but they soon won help in southern Campania, Lucania and Apulia. Their first need was a headquarters and military organization. For the former they chose a good centre at Corfinium, which lies in a plain girdled by magnificent mountains in the territory of the Paeligni. But they at once showed that they were not mere rebels banded together to destroy Rome; rather, they sought to found an independent nation. Corfinium was proudly renamed Italia and the organization of the new confederacy may have outrun the needs of a purely military machine. Officers (two consuls and twelve praetors) and a Senate were established, but unfortunately the details are obscure: some suppose that the constitution was modelled on that of Rome, others that the council was a federal body of allied delegates, and others again that the organization was a binary league based on the two main cantonal groups of Marsi and Samnites.[9] Soon no less than 100,000 men were ready for battle: Poppaedius Silo commanded the Marsic group, Papius Mutilus the Samnite, each commander having six divisional officers under him. To pay the troops special issues of coins were minted, which both helped to unify the cause and advertise its ideals: on them we see groups of warriors taking oaths of loyalty, Italia personified, the Italian bull goring the Roman wolf, and the names of the commanders in Latin or Oscan. The men themselves were sturdy fighters and many of them had served alongside Roman armies in the past. Rome now found that her selfish policy had unleashed a veritable whirlwind of potential destruction.

4. THE ITALIAN OR SOCIAL WAR[10]

In the hour of their self-imposed danger the Romans did not lose courage. If they could weather the first onslaught, they might hope to survive, since they mustered some 150,000 men and through their control of the sea they might get further help from the provinces or client kings. The fighting flared up in two main theatres of war, each of which was entrusted to one of the consuls of 90 B.C., supported by more experienced men serving as *legati*. In the North P. Rutilius Lupus had Marius and Cn. Pompeius Strabo (the father of Pompey) on his staff; L. Iulius Caesar in the South had Sulla and T. Didius. In the North the Italians hoped to extend the revolt outwards from Picenum and at the same time to thrust westwards from Corfinium along the Via Valeria, which led across the peninsula to Rome itself, sweeping past the loyal colonies at Alba Fucens and Carseoli.[11] To meet these threats Strabo, who had large estates in Picenum, was sent there against Asculum, and after some misadventures he was able to start to besiege the city. In their attempts to rescue Alba, the Romans were less successful. Rutilius was defeated and killed in the Tolenus valley, and Caepio was destroyed by Poppaedius Silo; Marius, however, who had managed to retrieve the positions after these defeats, was now left in sole command and defeated the Marsi and Marrucini, though the fate of Alba remains uncertain. Meantime in the South the Italians gained successes in three areas: (*a*) they turned against Aesernia, a key fortress which covered their communications between the northern and southern areas; after twice defeating the consul Caesar, they forced Aesernia to surrender after a grim siege; (*b*) Papius Mutilus with the Samnites burst into southern Campania and won over many towns until he was defeated at Acerrae by Caesar; and (*c*) other Italian commanders led successful raids into Apulia and Lucania. Despite these losses, however, the Romans managed to survive the first year of the revolt and wisely made political concessions (see below) to prevent it spreading farther, for instance to Etruria which was becoming restless.

In 89 both consuls, Strabo and L. Porcius Cato, went to the northern front, while Sulla took command of the forces in Campania; Marius was curiously neglected. When Cato was defeated and killed near the Fucine Lake, Strabo was left in command of operations in the northern theatre, where he pressed on with the siege of Asculum. In a decisive engagement he defeated an Italian army of 60,000 men, who were hastening to its relief and no doubt hoped ultimately to break through to Umbria and Etruria. After this success he forced Asculum to surrender before the end of the year,[12] and the revolt in the North began to peter out: Poppaedius Silo fled to Samnium, and Italia, the confederate capital, was abandoned. Meantime in the South Sulla had moved over to the offensive: he defeated a Samnite army which was trying to relieve Pompeii, recovered some of the Campanian cities, advanced into the hills of southern Samnium where he took Aeclanum and Compsa, forced Papius to seek cover in Aesernia, and finally captured Bovianum Vetus, the Italian head-quarters. With good hopes might Sulla then return to Rome to stand for the consulship of 88. Italian resistance was now concentrated among the Samnites, Rome's old enemies, with new headquarters at Aesernia, where Silo bravely tried to build up fresh forces. He even succeeded in recapturing Bovianum, and in desperation appealed for help to Mithridates, king of Pontus, but he was soon defeated (88), while other centres of resistance in Apulia and the South were crushed: a few, as Aesernia and Nola, held out a little longer, but the war was essentially over.

The war would not have ended so quickly in the field, if Rome had not given ground on the political front and conceded the issue on which the Italians were fighting: Roman citizenship. During 90 the consul Caesar carried a *lex Iulia* which granted Roman citizenship to Latin and Italian communities, possibly only to those that had not yet revolted, but more probably also to any who laid down their arms; it further allowed generals to grant citizenship to individuals for service in battle.[13] All communities that accepted this offer would then become self-governing *municipia* instead of independent sovereign states, and probably some general law was passed later (the *lex Calpurnia?*) which arranged details of the municipal re-organization.[14] This wise measure would clearly confirm the support of the loyal and check the spread of the revolt. Early in 89 two tribunes carried a *lex Plautia-Papiria*, a supplementary measure under which, according to the older interpretation, individual members of allied states could obtain Roman citizenship by appearing within two months before the praetor peregrinus in Rome, that is individuals whose states had not accepted the offer under the *lex Iulia* and presumably any individuals whose states were still at war. This should be rejected: the *lex Plautia-Papiria* did not introduce a new principle of dealing with individuals as opposed to communities, but was designed partly to make good some detailed omission in the *lex Iulia*.[15] Another supplementary measure, the lex Pompeia carried by Strabo in 89, dealt with Cisalpine Gaul and granted Latin status to the Transpadanes.[16] Thus full Roman citizenship was potentially extended to all peoples south of the river Po. Those rebels who did not accept the offer in 90 or 89 became dediticii when they did finally submit, and were probably enfranchised during the struggle between Cinna and Octavius in 87.[17] But although Rome's conduct may seem generous, even if dictated by expediency, the newly enfranchised citizens still had a grievance: they were not at first distributed fairly throughout the thirty-five tribes with the result that their voting power was restricted in relation to that of the older citizens.[18]

The war was over, but at a terrible cost in human lives and suffering; its economic repercussions were serious[19] and the importance of the army cast its shadow over civil life. Nevertheless the political unification of Italy was an immense step forward: Romans and Italians could now grow into a nation, and men learn to reconcile their local loyalties with a wider national citizenship. A man could now remain a loyal son of the town in which he was born and lived and yet enjoy the benefits of membership of a large sovereign state. Without destroying the extraordinarily varied individual pattern of life in the different parts of Italy, Rome now made it possible for all to belong to a single society, membership of which was guaranteed by the civitas Romana. Within a few years all the city-states and tribal areas were organized as municipia with quattuorviri as magistrates: semi-Celtic settlements in the north, old and proud Etruscan cities, Umbrian tribesmen, Samnite highlanders, Oscan dalesman, the old cities of Latium, the Greek cities of the South, and the wilder Bruttian tribesmen, all now found in Rome their communis patria. As Cicero said (de legibus, 2. 2. 5): 'omnibus municipalibus duas esse censeo patrias, unam naturae, alteram civitatis'.

5. SULPICIUS' TRIBUNATE AND SULLA'S CAPTURE OF ROME

Sulla was rewarded for his services in the war by election to the consulship of 88; later he was granted the province of Asia and the command against Mithridates who was on the war-path in the East. Sulla's colleague in the consulship was an Optimate of no great distinction, Q. Pompeius Rufus. A more dominant figure however, was one of the tribunes, Publius Sulpicius,[20] a former friend of the younger Drusus and a great orator, whose main object was apparently to secure fair play for the newly enfranchised Italians, whom (together with all freedmen) he was ultimately to propose to distribute over the thirty-five tribes. Such a statesmanlike measure was bound to provoke the opposition of the Optimates which in turn provoked Sulpicius to collect some armed bands in his support (even though the story that he had an escort of 600 young Equites who were called 'anti-senators' may be doubtful). He then turned for co-operation to Marius with whom he had already collaborated in opposing the consular candidature (for 88) for Caesar Strabo. Marius' support would be valuable because it would swing the Equites behind Sulpicius, but it was dangerous: Marius had been curiously neglected since 90 and was now embittered; Sulpicius therefore agreed to secure the transference of the Mithridatic command from Sulla to Marius. Such a proposal was constitutionally improper and was not justified on military grounds since Marius was now nearly seventy and Sulla's war-record was quite creditable. Marius, however, had long hankered for such a command (he had visited Asia Minor after his sixth consulship, partly in order to investigate the eastern situation). With this backing Sulpicius could now proceed with his programme which included lesser measures: to recall exiles and to expel from the Senate all members who owed more than 2000 *denarii* (this would please the Equites). When the consuls tried to check the tribune's work by proclaiming a suspension of public business (*iustitium*), Sulpicius declared this to be illegal. An armed clash took place in the Forum, in which Pompeius Rufus' son was killed and Sulla was forced to seek refuge in the house of Marius. After this indignity Sulla called off the *iustitium* and joined his army that was mustering for the Mithridatic war at Nola.

Now master in Rome Sulpicius secured the passing of all his laws, including the transference of the Eastern command. Had Marius hastened to Campania, he might possibly have won over the army; instead he stopped in Rome and allowed Sulla the initiative. Sulla promptly appealed to the troops, and they stoned Sulpicius' envoys. Then a momentous event in Rome's history took place. At the head of six legions Sulla marched on Rome which he captured after a few hours of street-fighting since Marius and Sulpicius had no troops available. They fled, leaving Sulla in undisputed control of the city.

With an army at his call Sulla easily persuaded the Senate and Comitia to implement his wishes. Marius, Sulpicius and their followers, though unheard and untried, were declared outlaws. Sulpicius, a tribune in office, was hunted down and killed. Marius was luckier: after many adventures which included hiding in the marshes of Minturnae, he escaped to Africa where many of his old soldiers were settled.[21] Sulpicius' laws were then declared invalid, as carried *per vim*. Sulla, however, did not intend to forgo his Mithridatic command and so he passed some measures through the Comitia to strengthen the Senate until his return. It was enacted that all business brought before the People must go to the more conservative Comitia Centuriata (as tribunes could not present bills to the Populus but only to the Plebs, their activities were thus skilfully curtailed) and at the same time no business that had not previously received the Senate's approval was to be brought before the

People. If Sulla thought of adding 300 new members to the Senate, this plan was certainly not implemented, but he did carry an emergency measure to relieve debt. He allowed the consular elections to take their course, though his own nephew failed and one of the successful candidates was L. Cornelius Cinna on whose support he could hardly count; he perhaps made Cinna swear not to interfere with his arrangements. The other consul-elect, Cn. Octavius, was a loyal Optimate. Finally, in order to check Strabo, who still had an army in central Italy, Sulla transferred this command to his own colleague, Pompeius Rufus, though in fact the troops preferred Strabo and later murdered Rufus in a disturbance in which Strabo himself clearly was not disinterested if not involved. Sulla and his army then left Italy.

6. CINNA

Scarcely was Sulla's back turned when Cinna, oblivious of his oath, proposed to re-introduce Sulpicius' measure for the new citizens. After some violence in the Forum Cinna was driven from Rome by his colleague Octavius and was declared a public enemy by the Senate. He then won over a legion which Sulla had left besieging Nola and he was soon joined by many disgruntled ex-allies and others. Meantime Marius had returned from Africa and was raising troops in Etruria. The Senate, thus threatened from north and south, was in a perilous position since it lacked an army on the spot; it hastily summoned Strabo from Picenum and levies from Transpadane Gaul, but the latter were intercepted by Cinnan troops. Strabo responded, but slowly. Finally under the weak protection of Strabo and Octavius, Rome was attacked by Marius, who reached the Janiculum after seizing Ostia, and by three divisions of Cinna's forces, led by himself, Q. Sertorius and Cn. Carbo. Strabo died of disease, a man who had shown a certain moderation and willingness to compromise though the Optimate tradition regarded him as 'dis ac nobilitati perinvisum'.[22] Before the end of the year (87) Rome had fallen: Marius and Cinna controlled its fate.

That fate proved terrible. Marius, maddened by hate, allowed his troops and slaves to loot and murder. Although official executions may have been limited, they included Octavius, the orator M. Antonius and Q. Catulus (cos. 102). After five days even Cinna was disgusted and ended the bloodbath by force. Marius and Cinna were then declared consuls for 86, Sulla was formally exiled and his laws repealed, but a few days after entering upon his seventh consulship Marius died, and Rome breathed more freely.[23]

For the next three years Cinna was in control: he managed to secure his re-election to the consulship each year without undue regard to the formalities, and took as his colleagues L. Valerius Flaccus for 86 and Cn. Carbo for 85–84. Some attempt was made to improve economic conditions. Flaccus carried a measure which cancelled three-quarters of all outstanding debts. The Equites would be more pleased with a currency reform announced in the edict of a praetor, Marius Gratidianus, which re-asserted the old official exchange rates of silver and bronze.[24] But the greatest achievement of these years of Cinna's *dominatio* was the final settlement of the citizenship question. Censors were appointed for 86 to carry out the registration of the new citizens, and some progress was made. At last too the new citizens received justice: they were distributed throughout the thirty-five tribes, though perhaps not until 84 B.C.[25]

But if these years were peaceful at home, over all loomed the shadow of Sulla. In 86 Flaccus had been sent with a force to the East against Mithridates (cf. p. 64), but neither he nor his legate Fimbria who soon murdered him could win the co-operation of Sulla in joint operations. It then became clear that Sulla's campaign against Mithridates was ending in victory and that he would soon seek to return. In a despatch at the end of 85 he complained of his treatment, reminded the Senate of his past services and perhaps guaranteed to respect the rights of the new citizens. The Senate tried to open negotiations with him by offering an amnesty. But meantime Cinna had to prepare for the risk of war and possibly he took a bold decision: he would, if necessary, face Sulla in Greece and spare Italy further civil war at home. He shipped some troops across the Adriatic, but other men waiting to embark at Ancona, mutinied and killed him (84). The government was left in the hands of Carbo, who with considerable skill averted the election of a colleague and remained sole consul. Resistance to Sulla must now be built up in Italy, the more so as a further defiant message proclaimed that Sulla would not be reconciled with his enemies, nor disband his loyal troops, but would see to his own safety. In 83 while Carbo as proconsul took up a strong position in Cisalpine Gaul, the two consuls, L. Scipio and C. Norbanus, advanced to Campania. Soon afterwards Sulla landed with some 40,000 men at Brundisium.[26]

7. MITHRIDATES, KING OF PONTUS

Sulla's opponent, Mithridates, was no common man. His kingdom lay in central Asia Minor, south of the Black Sea.[27] Formed some two hundred years before, it was rich in natural resources, especially metals. It remained largely a country of villages, studded with royal castles, in a feudal state of development. Essentially the population was oriental in outlook, though the royal house, which was descended from the nobles of Persia, had acquired a considerable tincture of Hellenistic civilization, the official language being Greek. There were in fact a few Greek cities on the northern coast, but their cultural influence did not spread far inland, and the Greek and Iranian elements in the civilization of Pontus never really fused together. Under Mithridates V (150–121 B.C.) relations with Rome had been friendly and he had lent some help against Aristonicus (p. 33). His son, who secured sole rule by imprisoning his mother and murdering his brother, reigned as Mithridates VI Eupator. He was a man of exceptional physical strength and force of character, of whose energy and exploits many a tale was told. Imbued with a real admiration for Greek culture and art, he yet retained beneath the surface some of the attributes of an oriental despot. His ambitions were great, so that he readily responded to an appeal from the Greek cities of Bosporus and Chersonesus in the Crimea (S. Russia) to help them against the pressure from Scythian and Sarmatian tribes in the north. Posing as a champion of Greeks against barbarians, Mithridates sent the help and as a result became master of the whole north coast of the Black Sea, with a capital for this new Pontic empire at Panticapaeum. This conquest, together with an advance east from his kingdom to Colchis and the Caucasus, provided him with immense supplies of corn, money and men which enabled him to build up and support a large army and navy. Thus within a few years he became one of the most powerful rulers in Asia.

His ambition, however, reached farther. He sought a large Anatolian Empire in addition to his Pontic realm. Though expansion would bring him into conflict with neighbouring rulers who were friends of Rome, such a thought did not dismay him, especially as at this time Rome had Jugurtha and the Northern menace on her hands. Rather, he may even have dreamed of posing as a champion of the Asiatic Greeks and of sweeping the Roman foreigners right out of Asia Minor. Whether or not his thoughts were yet running on so far, he did not shrink from a clash with Rome, but at first he played his cards with shrewd caution.

Nicomedes II king of Bithynia, though a 'friend and ally' of Rome, had little reason to love the Romans because Bithynia was being exploited by Roman money-lenders; he was thus ready to fall in with Mithridates' suggestion that they should seize Galatia and Paphlagonia (104). This was done; at Rome only Saturninus raised a protest which was quickly smothered with bribes. The two kings then turned against Cappadocia but soon quarrelled over its control. Marius, who had failed to secure a command in the East as war with Mithridates had been averted, was in the East on his own business in 98 and warned Mithridates to take care; a year or two later the Senate decided to support the claim of Ariobarzanes to Cappadocia. The task of installing the new king was given to Sulla, who was proconsul of Cilicia in 96. He had clashed with some troops of Tigranes of Armenia, and went on to the Euphrates where he accepted an offer of friendship from a Parthian envoy: thus Rome made official contact with the great Parthian Empire which was to cause her so much trouble in the future. Mithridates was thus checked, but he soon secured Tigranes as a son-in-law; he was biding his time, and he did not have to wait long.[28]

8. THE FIRST MITHRIDATIC WAR

As soon as Rome was busy with the Social War Mithridates, helped by Tigranes, seized Bithynia and Cappadocia (90). The Romans, however, sent out Manius Aquilius and a commission to act with the governor of Asia in restoring Nicomedes to the Bithynian throne. Feeling perhaps that a real settlement could be reached only if he made more drastic demands than those of Sulla, Aquilius ordered Mithridates to withdraw from the two king-doms, which he did, and to supply troops, which he refused (89)[29]; Aquilius then persuaded Nicomedes to attack Pontus. Careful as he had so far been to avoid responsibility for starting a war, Mithridates now acted and again invaded Cappadocia. In 88 the Romans, who had only one legion in Asia, sent forward the unfortunate Nicomedes, who was defeated, and divided their own forces into three; all were beaten and Aquilius was ultimately captured and cruelly killed. Mithridates then swept through the province of Asia, promising freedom to the Greek cities and cancelling debts; he was received with much enthusiasm, though some cities resisted him and had to stand siege. His victorious fleet sailed into the Aegean, where Rhodes however managed to resist his attack. Hailed as a deliverer, he was then faced with the problem of what to do with the large number of Roman and Italian business men in the province. His solution was simple, but terrible. He ordered that on a fixed day all men, women and children, should be massacred: the victims numbered some 80,000. All the Asiatic cities who complied with his order were thus irrevocably bound to the cause of the enemy of Rome. Lord of Asia, Mithridates now looked westwards to Europe.

He soon received an invitation from the democratic party in Athens to cross over and liberate Greece. The ambassador, named Aristion, who had brought the message, on his return home managed to become tyrant of Athens and murdered members of the aristocratic party. Mithridates there-fore in the autumn of 88 sent a force across the Aegean under the command of Archelaus, who plundered Delos on the way. Rome had few troops in Greece, but a legate, whom the governor of Macedonia hastily sent south-wards, managed to save northern Greece and forced Archelaus back into Attica. Then in 87 Sulla landed with five legions in Epirus and marched hurriedly to Athens, where he besieged Aristion and penned up Archelaus in the Peiraeus. But his position was dangerous. Another Pontic army, on its way to Greece through Macedonia, might arrive from the north, and without command of the sea he could not reduce the Peiraeus. He therefore sent Lucullus to collect a fleet, while he plundered the treasuries of Delphi and

Olympia for funds. At last early in 86 he carried Athens by assault; Peiraeus fell soon after and Archelaus embarked his troops to join the Pontic army which had now reached Thessaly.[29a]

Sulla met these combined forces, which outnumbered his own men perhaps by three to one, at Chaeronea in a set battle.[30] By skilful tactics, speed of movement and personal intervention at critical points, Sulla routed the enemy despite their numbers and scythe-chariots. Mithridates, however, made a further effort. Another Pontic army was sent by sea to Euboea, where it joined Archelaus' defeated survivors. Sulla met them again in Boeotia, at Orchomenus. After digging trenches to cover his flanks against their superior cavalry, he succeeded in driving their chariots back on their phalanx, and thus won his second victory. Archelaus fled to Euboea; the invasion of Greece was ended, and before the end of the year Sulla met Archelaus on the coast of Boeotia to begin negotiating a settlement.

Sulla, however, had other pre-occupations. Not only had he been declared an enemy of the Roman People by the government in Rome, but Flaccus had been sent out by Cinna against Mithridates (rather than against Sulla, as the latter afterwards claimed).[31] Flaccus with his two legions marched straight to his province of Asia. Here he, and then his lieutenant Fimbria who succeeded to his command by murdering him, found great distress. Many of the Greek cities, discontented with Mithridates the Liberator, were in revolt against him and during a reign of terror were discovering in him an Oriental tyrant. They were indeed between the devil and the deep sea because Fimbria also did not hesitate to plunder many of them as he marched to defeat an army that Mithridates managed to put into the field on the banks of the Rhyndacus. He might even have captured Mithridates himself, if Lucullus, who was coasting by with his fleet, had been willing to co-operate.

At last Mithridates was ready to come to terms. Having in vain tried to play off Fimbria against Sulla, he met Sulla in the summer of 85 at Dardanus near Troy, where he accepted the terms already discussed by Archelaus, who now enjoyed the title of 'friend and ally' of the Roman People. Mithridates agreed to surrender seventy ships, evacuate all territory that he had conquered in Asia Minor and pay an indemnity of 2000 talents: in return he was recognized as King of Pontus and ally of Rome. He might well thank his lucky stars that Sulla had business in the west – else he would scarcely have received such lenient terms. Sulla then made short work of Fimbria, who soon afterwards fell on his sword.

The settlement that Sulla imposed on the unhappy province was bitter. It was now conquered territory, and even the free cities that had been Rome's allies had, by receiving the enemy, lost their former rights and independence; any privileges they now received were granted by the grace of Sulla and the Senate. Cities that had remained loyal to Rome (e.g. Rhodes) were rewarded, but those that had received the enemy (e.g. Pergamum, Ephesus, Miletus) now lost their freedom and became liable to the regular taxes collected by the *publicani*; many were plundered and had their walls razed. Sulla imposed on the province an indemnity of 20,000 talents (the cost of the war and five years arrears of taxation) and through the winter of 85/4 he billeted his troops on the unfortunate provincials who had to pay, feed and clothe them.[32] Unable fully to meet their obligations, they had to borrow and thus became the victims of heartless exploitation by Roman business-men. A further cause of trouble was the increasing raids of the pirates who were now becoming the scourage of the eastern Mediterranean: they even carried off 1000 talents' worth of booty from Samothrace, while Sulla himself was staying on the island. Thus when he sailed for Greece in 84, Sulla left debt and despair behind him in Asia.

Asia even had to endure some further fighting, which has been dignified with the title of the Second Mithridatic War (83–82). Though Nicomedes and Ariobarzanes were restored to their thrones, Mithridates remained quiet until he was stung into action by the aggressions of L. Licinius Murena, whom Sulla had left in the province in command of the two legions that he had taken over from Fimbria. Alleging that Mithridates was rearming, Murena attacked him and continued to raid his territory despite a warning from the Senate. Only after he had been beaten in battle by the king, did he finally obey an order from Sulla to desist. Sulla, now dictator in Rome, had other matters on hand.

9. CIVIL WAR

When Sulla landed at Brundisium in 83, he was soon joined by many of the younger generation who thought that he would win. M. Licinius Crassus, whose father (*cos.* 97) had perished in the Marian terror, came from Spain; Metellus Pius, son of Numidicus, arrived in Italy from Africa; and above all, Strabo's son, young Cn. Pompeius, raised a force in Picenum and, outmanœuvring the opposing armies, reached Sulla with three legions. This mustering of support from the provinces, and still more the raising of a private army, augured ill for the future of the Republic. Sulla greeted Pompey with honour, perhaps even saluting him as *imperator*, appointed him as his legate, and soon gave him his step-daughter, Aemilia, in marriage. On his march northwards Sulla met no serious opposition until he faced the two consular armies in Campania (p. 61). He made short work of these: he defeated Norbanus near Capua, and then the fox in him triumphing over the lion, he negotiated with Scipio near Teanum, while Scipio's army began to go over to him. He then disarmed another potential source of opposition by proclaiming that he would respect the rights of the new citizens. During the winter he built up his forces, while his opponents also increased theirs by winning over some of the Samnite tribes against whom Sulla had fought during the Social War.[33]

The consuls of 82 were Carbo and the (? adoptive) son of Marius. While the former consolidated in the north, young Marius was to hold Rome. Sulla, however, soon brushed him aside; after defeating him at Sacriportus near Signia, he drove him into Praeneste where he was besieged. Sulla then entered Rome where he found that many leading senators, including the Pontifex Maximus Scaevola, had been massacred on the orders of young Marius. Hastening on northwards, where his lieutenants Pompey and Metellus had been harrying Carbo, he managed to hem in Carbo near Clusium. When news reached Carbo that Norbanus, who had replaced him in the north, had been defeated by Metellus at Faventia, that Cisalpine Gaul was lost to the Marian cause, and that Marius was faring ill at Praeneste, he threw up the sponge and fled to Africa. In fact three attempts to relieve Marius had already been thwarted, partly because of 'The Narrows' which in the absence of any corresponding natural features at Praeneste were probably some blockading lines which Sulla had constructed.[34] In a final attempt to save the besieged, the Marian forces, which with their Samnite allies numbered some 70,000 men, made a sudden dash on Rome. Sulla raced there in the nick of time: on the afternoon of 1 November he met them outside the Colline Gate. It was a terrific struggle: at one moment Sulla himself on the left wing was at the point of defeat, but Crassus on the right turned the tide. Losses on both sides were heavy, while those Samnites that survived the battle were butchered in cold blood by Sulla's order. Soon afterwards Praeneste fell: Marius committed suicide and most of the survivors were massacred. A few cities still resisted, Nola until 80 and Volterrae a year longer, but Sulla was clearly undisputed master of Italy.

A few 'Marian' governors in the provinces still remained to be dealt with. Q. Sertorius (p. 60), who had gone out as governor of Nearer Spain, was pushed out of the peninsula by Annius; and Sardinia was secured. To Sicily and Africa, where Carbo and Perperna were organizing resistance, young Pompey, aged twenty-four, was sent, first as Sulla's legate and then with a senatorial grant of extraordinary propraetorian imperium. He quickly cleared Sicily and put Carbo to death: Pompey might be called 'adulescentulus carnifex', but this epithet belied his normally moderate temperament and he may well have acted on Sulla's orders. Then, leaving his brother-in-law Memmius in charge of Sicily, he crossed to Africa with strong forces and defeated Cinna's son-in-law Domitius Ahenobarbus who was supported by a Numidian pretender name Iarbas; Pompey restored the throne to Hiempsal. For this speedy and striking victory Pompey, whose troops had hailed him as imperator, hoped for a triumph, but at first his claim met with opposition perhaps rather from Sulla than from the Senate. Sulla, however, finally yielded and even, though perhaps with a touch of sarcasm, called Pompey Magnus, a title which Pompey did not use as a *cognomen* for some time.[35]

10. SULLANUM REGNUM

In Italy Sulla's butchery continued, against both individuals and communities. He was grimly determined to eliminate all potential political opposition and, despite the wealth he must have collected in the East, he needed money for land for his veterans and followers. After a period of indiscriminate murders, he was persuaded to post up proscription lists of his victims, by which they were outlawed with a price on their heads; these at first numbered 40 senators and 1600 Equites but no doubt the final figures were much larger (one author, Orosius, goes as high as 9000): the equestrian order suffered particularly severely. Besides confiscating his victims' property, Sulla permanently debarred their sons and grandsons from office and the Senate. As a further safeguard he freed 10,000 of their slaves and turned them into an unofficial bodyguard, the Cornelii. He then wreaked his vengeance on those parts of Italy that had opposed him: the towns of Etruria, Samnium and central Italy suffered most. He needed land for his veterans and the vicious nexus between an army and its commander, which Marius' career had first demonstrated, now began to get its stranglehold on Roman life. At least twenty-three legions had to be demobilized and Sulla ultimately secured land for over ten colonies for some 120,000 men. This naturally involved a major social and economic upheaval, but though the new colonists vastly increased the *clientela* of their new patron and would form a reserve of military strength on which Sulla could call in an hour of need, they did not necessarily all make good farmers and many tended to become restless.[36]

When Sulla re-entered Rome, his *imperium* technically lapsed, but the Senate, which proceeded obsequiously to confirm all his past acts as consul and proconsul, may have allowed him to retain it. It also decreed the erection of an equestrian statue to 'Cornelius Sulla Imperator Felix' facing the Rostra in the forum.[37] As both consuls were dead, the Senate appointed an *interrex*, the Princeps Senatus L. Valerius Flaccus (*cos.* 100). So far that was normal procedure, but Valerius instead of nominating *consules suffecti* followed Sulla's hint and introduced a bill into the Comitia (*lex Valeria*) which appointed Sulla 'dictator legibus scribundis et reipublicae constituendae'. Thus Sulla received full powers from the hands of the People to reorganize the constitution as dictator, an office which had lapsed since the Hannibalic War.[37a] But apart from the name, Sulla's office had little in common with the emergency magistrates whom the consuls used to name for periods of six months: Sulla held supreme authority as long as he wished, though it should be noted that since he was not vested with the office in perpetuity, he was free to resign when and if he liked. The new dictator received twenty-four lictors, who attended him in the city where he was unhampered by such checks as the veto or right of appeal that curbed ordinary magistrates. Soon after this, he celebrated his triumph over Mithridates in January 81 and turned to his legislative reforms.

Sulla's earlier career had not been that of an orthodox Optimate. Though he belonged to an old patrician family, it had long lived in obscurity and poverty. A legacy from his step-mother and another from a mistress helped him, somewhat late, to a public career. As Marius' quaestor he had captured Jugurtha and won the royal friendship of Bocchus. During the Teutonic wars he had transferred from Marius' staff to that of the aristocratic Catulus. He failed in 99 to win a praetorship, but secured one for 97, and after service in Cilicia, he rendered such a good account of himself in the Social War that he won the consulship for 88. Up to this point he may not have identified himself closely with the Optimates, but his marriage to Metella (the widow of Scaurus) brought him nearer to the nobility, while the attempt of the popular party and Marius to deprive him of the Mithridatic command forced his hand. As army-commander and dictator he could act with greater independence. He may not therefore always have been the fervent champion of the Senate that he has sometimes been depicted, but he probably came to realize that only if the Senate regained something of its old authority could Rome hope for peace and order.

That he had an innate desire for order and efficiency in public life can hardly be doubted, though it accorded ill with the disorderliness of his private life. His personality reflected a strange mixture, like his blotched face which was compared with a mulberry sprinkled with flour. A cynic, yet superstitious, self-indulgent yet energetic, scrupulous on occasion yet on others heartlessly cruel, fox and lion combined, he was forced to go on if only to secure his own personal safety. The only path that he saw led him through civil war to absolute power: a restoration of orderly government might follow, and then he could return to ease and private pleasures.

11. SULLA'S REFORMS

In carrying through his reforms Sulla observed constitutional procedure and passed them through the Comitia in a normal manner. He allowed consuls to be elected for 81, though they were in fact of little note. One candidate, Q. Ofella (or Afella) whom Sulla had put in charge of the siege of Praeneste, was not qualified to stand since he had not held even a quaestorship; when he went on canvassing against Sulla's orders, Sulla promptly had him killed. In the summer of 81 the proscription lists were at length closed.[38] While continuing to hold the dictatorship Sulla allowed himself to be elected consul (a rare, but apparently legitimate combination of offices) with Metellus Pius for 80, but he refused re-election for 79. Early in his dictatorship he started his work of reconstruction.

If the Senate was to resume firm control and become an effective governing body once again, Sulla's first task was clearly to increase its numbers, which through war and the massacres of Marius and Sulla had dropped to some 150 members. The new senators would naturally include Sulla's own supporters, both men of senatorial families and others who had rendered him good service during the wars, but he also included 300 Equites. This appears surprising when it is recalled how bitterly hostile he had been towards the Knights in Rome. Many of those chosen, however, may have belonged to the eighteen equestrian centuries in which younger members of noble families were enrolled, but others probably came from the ordo equester in a wider sense and included some of the local aristocracy of the cities of Italy which had recently been enfranchised. Whether Sulla's motive was to attempt to heal the breach between the two Orders or to blunt the opposition of the Equites by winning over some of their leaders, is not clear. One reason for the increase in numbers will have been to ensure an adequate supply of jurors for the law-courts which he intended to reorganize and to hand back to the Senate. The political result, however, was clear enough: in a new Senate of 500 or 600 members the majority would owe their position and allegiance to the dictator.[39]

Sulla also arranged for the automatic recruitment of the Senate in the future: the number of quaestors was raised from twelve to twenty and all ex-quaestors were to enter the Senate. This had two consequences: since quaestors were elected by the People, the Senate itself in the future would be indirectly elected by the People. Also the censors were deprived of one of their most important functions, the lectio senatus. Further, it is known that consuls handled some contracts (censoriae locationes) in 80 and again after a five-year interval in 75. It thus appears that Sulla was suspicious of the censorship and while not going so far as to abolish it, arranged to manage without it.[40]

Since the tribunate of Tiberius Gracchus this office had increasingly become a powerful weapon in the armoury of the opponents of the Senate. Sulla decided to change that. Henceforth tribunes could not propose legislation to the People (except perhaps measures already sanctioned by the Senate); they were deprived of their judicial powers (the new senatorial quaestiones replacing tribunician impeachments); their right of veto was limited, perhaps being taken away in criminal cases; and above all, tribunes were made ineligible for any other office. Thus the tribunate was disarmed and all ambitious young men would tend to avoid this political dead-end.[41]

Sulla determined to curb the regular magistrates also. Although perhaps he did not make it obligatory for all magistrates (besides the tribunes) to secure the *patrum auctoritas* before presenting legislation to the People, since it was from the tribunes rather than from the consuls that he feared possible attacks on the constitution, he nevertheless decided to prevent young men gaining high office and political power too quickly. He therefore redrafted the lex *Villia Annalis* of 180 B.C.: the *cursus honorum* was rigidly enforced, and no man was to become quaestor before the age of thirty, praetor before thirty-nine and consul before forty-two; further, no man was to hold the same office twice within ten years.[42] At the same time the number of quaestors was raised to twenty, and of praetors to eight. The principle of co-optation was restored to the college of pontiffs and augurs (cf. p. 45) and the membership of each body was increased to fifteen.

Magistrates at home were easier to control than magistrates abroad, and no one had demonstrated more clearly than Sulla himself what danger might threaten a government in Rome from a provincial proconsul backed by a loyal army. There were now ten provinces: Sicily, Sardinia and Corsica, the two Spains, Macedonia, Africa, Asia, Cilicia, Gallia Narbonensis, and Cisalpine Gaul.[43] Since the praetors had been increased to eight, they provided, with the two consuls, ten higher magistrates each year. Sulla probably did not establish by legislation a cut-and-dried scheme, but hoped that it would become normal practice for the magistrates of the year to remain in Rome or Italy and then as promagistrates to go out to govern provinces and command armies. The Senate would decide which provinces were to go to proconsuls and which to propraetors, and thus could partly control potentially dangerous men. Tenure of a province would normally be for one year only. Sulla also passed a lex *de maiestate*, a treason law which regulated the conduct of a promagistrate in his province, e.g. that he should not on his own initiative start a war, march his troops beyond the frontiers, or leave his province. By such measures Sulla hoped that magistrates both at home and abroad would be brought under the general control of the Senate.[44]

Other measures included the abolition of the corn distributions, some sumptuary laws and a forced levy on the empire, but by far the most lasting of his reforms was his handling of criminal justice. Since the establishment of the first standing court in 149 to try cases of extortion, some other similar courts may have been created. Sulla now undertook to increase and organize this method of trial, which was replacing trials before the People. Seven permanent *quaestiones* were organized in order to cover all major crimes: murder and poisoning, forgery, extortion, treason, electoral bribery, peculation and assault.[45] Penalties were fixed and from the verdicts of these *iudicia publica* there was no appeal. The empanelling of them, which had become a burning political issue since they had been handed over by Gaius Gracchus to the Equites, was now decided in favour of the Senate, who were given the exclusive right to supply the juries. Though the jury question remained controversial for the next ten years, the main system established by Sulla endured throughout the Republic into the Principate.

12. SULLA'S RETIREMENT

In 79 Sulla, no longer consul, resigned his dictatorship (now, if not earlier) and became a private citizen. He soon retired to his country estate in Campania, where he spent the rest of his life with Valeria, a young divorcée whom he married; there he wrote his autobiography, hunted, fished and, according to his enemies, indulged in less reputable pleasures. When against his wishes Aemilius Lepidus was elected consul for 78, Sulla did not bestir himself. He died aged sixty in 78 and the public funeral accorded to him in Rome was of unparalleled magnificence. His epitaph recorded that no friend ever surpassed him in kindness, and no enemy in ill-doing.

His abdication has puzzled posterity: Julius Caesar is alleged to have said that Sulla did not know his political ABC: 'Sullam nescisse litteras qui dictaturam deposuerit'. One solution offered by a modern historian is that Sulla's action was forced on him: he really hoped to become monarch, and thus he lost the support of Pompey, the Metelli and the rest of the nobility, who combined against him and forced him into retirement since he was unwilling to appeal to arms again.[46] This view, which well illustrates that Sulla was neither a mere reactionary nor at first a mere tool of the nobles and that the trend of events was carrying Rome towards autocratic rule, cannot be accepted. It may be that there is a tendency to regard events, with Caesar, too exclusively in the light of later history: to some of Sulla's contemporaries his retirement may have seemed tardy rather than premature. It is improbable that he saw a solution to Rome's problems in monarchy: it required thirty years more of political unrest and military menace to make that answer practical and another twenty to make it palatable. The pill was too bitter for a sickening but still strong patient to swallow voluntarily; later it was sugared by Augustus.

Sulla's solution was apparently to give the Senate another chance and to make the government more effective by curbing those forces that threatened it: tribunes, censors and magistrates, especially the army commanders. He realized that the People, meeting in the Concilium Plebis, was an unrepresentative and irresponsible body unworthy to govern, but he largely failed to infuse a new sense of responsibility into the Senate. Nor did he make an effective attempt fully to utilize the talent of the new citizens from the

Italian municipalities. Above all, arrangements to control the use or abuse of proconsular imperium, the threat from which his own career had so nakedly demonstrated, were clearly inadequate against men of determined ambition. It would have required, however, more prescience than Sulla or perhaps any of his contemporaries possessed to have foreseen that within ten years two of his own lieutenants, backed by military force, would have overthrown his constitution. He may well have thought that he had made reasonable and efficient arrangements which could be worked by men of good will. If the senatorial nobility should fail Rome, that was their responsibility: Sulla probably cynically shrugged his shoulders and with that cool and ruthless detachment that had not deserted him in war or peace, he resolved to enjoy in felicity the remaining span of life that fate should allow to him.

V

THE RISE OF POMPEY[1]

1. THE COUNTER-REVOLUTION OF LEPIDUS

Any hope that Sulla's settlement after the grim years of civil war might usher in a period of tranquillity was rudely shattered by the ambitions of M. Aemilius Lepidus. This noble, who had rallied against Saturninus (probably his father-in-law) in 100, soon afterwards abandoned the Optimate cause. He enriched himself during Sulla's proscriptions and his own propraetorship in Sicily (80). In 79 he stood for the consulship, supported by Pompey and advocating a policy hostile to Sulla's constitution. As Sulla did not trouble to intervene, he was elected for 78, but with a conservative colleague, Q. Lutatius Catulus, son of the consul of 102.[2] His programme included proposals to renew the sale of cheap corn, to give back confiscated lands to the dispossessed, to recall the Marian exiles, and to restore its old powers to the tribunate.[3]

He soon found a chance to promote trouble. Some dispossessed farmers at Faesulae in Etruria had attacked the Sullan colonists. Both consuls were sent there, but Lepidus soon fell out with Catulus, and the Senate made them both swear to avoid civil war. Whether or not Lepidus made a demonstration march on Rome now, he managed to secure Transalpine and probably Cisalpine Gaul as his province. His legate, M. Iunius Brutus, began to raise troops for him in Cisalpina where Lepidus had strong family connexions. When early in 77 Lepidus was reported to be marching on Rome, L. Marcius Philippus (*cos.* 91) persuaded the Senate to pass the *senatus consultum ultimum* and to declare him a public enemy. Catulus, as proconsul, met and repelled Lepidus at the Mulvian Bridge, while Pompey, to whom the Senate had rashly given a special grant of propraetorian *imperium*, went north against Brutus, whom he besieged in Mutina; after Brutus had surrendered, Pompey had him put to death, perhaps being uncertain whether to treat him as a citizen or enemy. Pompey then defeated Lepidus at Cosa in Etruria. Lepidus managed to slip away to Sardinia, but he soon died, and the survivors of his army, led by Perperna, joined Sertorius in Spain.

Lepidus' rising had been crushed without much difficulty, but not without granting a special command to a young man who had held no magistracy, an action of the kind that Sulla had wished to make impossible. Any senators who began to feel that in making this appointment they had unwisely given way to nervous fears, soon had further cause to regret their action. When ordered by Catulus to disband his army, Pompey delayed and suggested that he should be sent to help Metellus in his struggle against Sertorius in Spain. The Senate capitulated, and Pompey was given a proconsular command which made him a colleague, not a legate, of Metellus: Philippus wrily observed that Pompey was being sent 'non pro consule, sed pro consulibus'. The reason for the Senate's action is not clear. It is said that no senator was willing to go to Spain, and the consuls of 77 possibly hesitated either on grounds of military inexperience or for political reasons (they may not have wished to act against Sulla's intentions, but significantly they were a Lepidus and a Brutus). But even if there was a real lack of competent generals, to invest a young man who was not yet even a senator with proconsular imperium was a disastrous blow to Sulla's intentions, and in the event proved suicidal to the Senate that sanctioned the grant.

2. Q. SERTORIUS[4]

Action was certainly demanded in Spain, where Sertorius had built up a widespread and independent power. This Sabine-born leader was a man of remarkable ability who had served under Marius against the northern barbarians (102–1), under Didius against the Celtiberians (95), and in the Social War when he lost an eye. Thwarted by Sulla in an attempt to win the tribunate in 88, Sertorius turned to the Marians. In 87 he fled and returned with Cinna, defeating Strabo and putting an end to Marius' massacres. As praetor in 83 he helped the consuls against Sulla, and then withdrew to Etruria and from there went to his province of Hither Spain. During these years of civil war he had shown great moderation: 'inter arma civilia aequi bonique famam petit' (Sallust).

In Spain he began to win the support of the natives and to build up an army and ships, until Sulla sent two legions against him under Annius Luscus, who forced him out of the peninsula (81). With his followers Sertorius sailed out into the Atlantic and thought of settling first in the Islands of the Blessed (Madeira or Canaries) and then in Tingis (Tangier). Envoys from Lusitania, however, begged him to return to Spain to help them against Rome. This he did. His sympathetic approach to the Spaniards, combined with a skilful exploitation of their superstitions (he had a white fawn that was alleged to reveal the future), enabled him to build up a formidable army with which he defeated Fufidius the governor of Further Spain in 80. In undertaking this resistance and appealing to the Romans and Italians in Spain (the Hispanienses), he claimed to be fighting against Sulla's illegal government in Rome, not against Rome itself. Indeed to his Roman supporters he was no rebel, but a truer representative of Rome.

As the threat in Spain increased, the government in Rome decided to send out Sulla's colleague in the consulship of 80, Q. Caecilius Metellus Pius, as governor of Further Spain. In an attempt to reduce, the south-west, Metellus established headquarters at Metellinum (modern Medellin) from which he struck out in different directions: northwards to Castra Caecilia (modern Carceres, near which a camp of his still survives), westwards to Dipo and Caeciliana (near Lisbon), and south-west to attack Lacobriga (near Cape Saint Vincent) where he was thwarted by Sertorius (79–8). Meantime Sertorius' lieutenant Hirtuleius had defeated the governor of Nearer Spain, Domitius Calvinus, at Consabura (south of Toledo) and then crossed the Ebro to defeat the governor of Narbonese Gaul who was coming to help his colleagues. In 77 Sertorius advanced through central Spain to the middle Ebro where he was joined by Perperna, who brought from Sardinia the remains of Lepidus' army and built up a force of some 20,000 men. Not far away, at Osca, Sertorius set up a school for the sons of Celtiberian chiefs, who thus showed their enthusiasm for his cause and at the same time unintentionally provided him with hostages. On the Mediterranean coast, of which he controlled the greater part, he was able to get in touch with the pirates and co-operate with them. Thus in some four years he had defeated or held in check all the Roman forces which had been sent against him and he had built up a really formidable power which embraced the greater part of the peninsula. Well might the Senate fear that a second Hannibal might come from Spain, and decide that at all cost a competent general must be sent to help Metellus, even if it meant giving in to young Pompey's claims. A few years earlier Pompey is alleged to have told Sulla, who was opposing his request for a triumph, that more men worship the rising than the setting sun. The Senate, now blinded by his audacity, failed to see the political consequences of their concession.

On his arrival in Spain in 76 Pompey's first objective was to win control of the eastern coast road, especially the area around Valentia. He forced his way down as far as Saguntum, sweeping aside Sertorius' lieutenants, but Sertorius himself, who was in a reserve position on the upper Ebro, came down to the coast and thrust Pompey back northwards over the Ebro. Meantime, however, in the south Sertorius' lieutenant Hirtuleius foolishly got involved in a battle with Metellus at Italica and was defeated. It was perhaps during the following winter (76/5) that Sertorius negotiated with Mithridates for help: in return for money and ships he would recognize the king's claims to Bithynia and Cappadocia, but scarcely to the Roman province of Asia as the tradition hostile to Sertorius asserts. In fact the treaty had little practical result, except that knowledge of Mithridates' support would increase Sertorius' prestige, not least with the pirates, just as it would alienate sympathy in Italy.

The next year, 75, was critical. Pompey again reached the area of Valentia, but was checked on the Sucro by Sertorius. However, a decisive battle was fought at Segovia, in central Spain, where Metellus again defeated Hirtuleius and was enabled to join Pompey. Near Saguntum Sertorius then fought an even engagement against their united forces, and they withdrew slowly to the Pyrenees for the winter. Pompey was in fact getting desperately short of supplies and warned the Senate in a despatch that unless he received reinforcements the whole war might sweep into Italy itself. He obtained two legions and in 74 turned away from the coast to attack the highlands of Celtiberia, whence Sertorius drew much of his strength; he met with varying fortune, including a joint defeat with Metellus at Calagurris. But Sertorius' forces were gradually declining: his Spanish allies were beginning to tire and it is alleged that his own character was degenerating under the strain and that he was becoming more cruel. However that may be, Perperna turned against him and treacherously murdered him in 72. This usurpation of leadership did Perperna little good, since he was quickly defeated and killed by Pompey, who brought the war to an end by 71. His settlement was liberal and humane. By virtue of a consular law of 72 (lex Gellia-Cornelia) he granted Roman citizenship to many Spaniards, including Balbus of Gades, who had supported the Roman cause; and instead of massacring some of the obstinate, he transferred them to a new settlement north of the Pyrenees, Lugdunum Convenarum.

Though Sertorius is sometimes depicted in too romantic a light, he was certainly one of Rome's greatest sons. His military genius is undisputed: he gave to the guerilla warfare, which he imposed on his opponents and which the nature of the country demanded, a leadership and understanding seldom equalled. Self-restrained and humane, he appreciated the needs of the provincials and won their loyalty, as had Scipio Africanus earlier. Had he been able to devote his gifts to peace rather than to war, he might have served his country with great distinction. It may be that if the Senate had had the foresight to attempt to negotiate with him after the death of Sulla, his personal enemy, instead of raising up Pompey against him, a reconciliation might have been achieved. But though Sertorius' military genius did not ultimately prevail against the oligarchical government in Rome, it nevertheless by a tragic paradox indirectly created the stepping-stone by means of which Pompey gained a political ascendancy that rested on military power and thus overthrew Sulla's constitution. The influence of the army commanders now dominated Roman life.

3. THE SENATE'S ADMINISTRATION

The Senate, whose hand Sulla had tried to strengthen, had successfully coped with Lepidus and by utilizing Pompey had taken steps to suppress Sertorius, but as the seventies advanced its difficulties increased and its weakness became more apparent. Foreign affairs also occasioned increasing anxiety. Further efforts which had to be made against the pirates, were tolerably successful at first (78–75), but less effective later (74–72). In Macedonia the governors were kept busy repelling the Thracian tribes that attacked the frontiers (78–74) until M. Terentius Varro, brother of Lucullus, advanced to the Danube, defeating the Bessi and Dardani and even plundering the Greek cities on the western coast of the Black Sea. Rome also took action in Cyrene, which had been bequeathed to her on the death of its ruler in 96: for over twenty years she had been content to leave the government in the hands of the local Greek cities, but in 74 as part of her drive against the pirates she decided to annex Cyrene as a province.[5] But the greatest upheaval was in the East. The king of Bithynia died in 75/4 and bequeathed his kingdom to Rome. The Senate decided to accept, although this would obviously upset the status quo and balance of power in Asia. Mithridates was quick to act. He advanced into Bithynia, and Rome had a Third Mithridatic War on her hands. This war and the campaigns against the pirates, which are discussed more fully below, seriously increased the problems with which the Senate had to wrestle at this time.

At home also the Senate ran into stormy weather, though it is not now easy to distinguish the cross-current of feelings and pressures that determined its policy. Besides the interests of the Optimates, Populares and Equites, there had now been injected into the State a large body of new citizens, the enfranchised Italians, some of whom must have been exerting fresh influences, even if we cannot now easily detect or analyse them. Some members of the municipal aristocracies entered the Roman Senate and even if they were typified by the 'homo novus parvusque senator', they will have contributed their quota.

The main political issue was the question of the restoration of the powers of the tribunes. When a tribune of 76, Cn. Sicinius, began to agitate for this, he was checked by one of the consuls, but a successor in 75, Q. Opimius, kept up the pressure. This was followed by a remarkable success: one of the consuls, C. Aurelius Cotta, who had been a friend of the younger Drusus, took up the cause and carried a measure which allowed tribunes to hold further office. If the Senate was in a more liberal mood, this was only passing: in 74, although this law of Cotta was allowed to stand, another of his measures was repealed and Opimius was prosecuted for misuse of his veto. The agitation for complete restoration of tribunes' powers was continued by L. Quinctius in 74 and the annalist C. Licinius Macer in 73.

Quinctius was also active in another field where the conduct of senators was being discredited: the law-courts. He defended Oppianicus who was accused of poisoning his step-son A. Cluentius; the bribery at the trial was scandalous and did much to bring the senatorial juries into disrepute (after the trial Quinctius in fact secured the condemnation of the *iudex quaestionis* and of one of the jurors).[6] At two other trials a young nobleman, who had just returned from serving in the East and had wisely kept clear of the revolt of Lepidus, C. Iulius Caesar, gained some publicity. In 77 he unsuccessfully prosecuted Dolabella, proconsul of Macedonia, on a charge of extortion, and in 76 he was equally unsuccessful in his prosecution of an agent of Sulla, C. Antonius Hybrida (later consul in 63) on a charge of plundering some Greeks. A certain Terentius Varro was accused twice (in 75 and 74) of extortion in Asia: his acquittal, secured with the help of the oratory of Hortensius and marked ballots, added a further scandal to the series, which exposed the unscrupulousness of some senators in the provinces as well as the corruption of senatorial juries at home.

Foreign affairs led to fresh appointments of significance. The new struggle against Mithridates meant that the consuls of 74 were sent to the East: M. Aurelius Cotta was assigned to Bithynia, while his colleague L. Licinius Lucullus, by luck and intrigue, secured Cilicia, the command against Mithridates and probably also the province of Asia. If Sulla had hoped that consuls would remain in Italy and without armies (p. 70), his expectations did not long outlive him. Worse still, M. Antonius (later Creticus) was invested by the Senate with a special proconsular *imperium infinitum* to deal with the pirates (74).[7] In 73 the consuls carried a corn law (*lex Terentia Cassia frumentaria*): the demands of war and the activities of the pirates had been making corn scarce and expensive. This law aimed at speeding up the delivery of corn from Sicily and prescribed the distribution of five *modii* a month to perhaps 40,000 recipients at the Gracchan price of 6⅓ *asses* a *modius*.[8] In the following year the situation abroad was improving: Sertorius was murdered, Mithridates was driven out of Pontus, and the position beyond the frontiers of Macedonia was better. But in Italy matters were far worse: the slave revolt of Spartacus (see below), which had broken out in 73, had assumed such alarming proportions that a special proconsular command was entrusted to Crassus, who had probably held a praetorship in 73. Thus a proconsul was in command of an army in Italy itself, the very thing that Sulla had hoped to prevent at all costs. Worse still for the Senate, in 71 a second army arrived in Italy, that of Pompey back from Spain after his victory over the Sertorians. But before this double threat to the Sullan constitution and the Senate's pre-dominance is discussed, the fate of Spartacus must be considered.

4. SPARTACUS[9]

War and piracy had kept up the supply of slaves in Italy. Though no very large scale rising had taken place in sympathy with either of the two Servile Wars in Sicily (pp. 11 and 46), there was much potential unrest. Further, the Romans had developed a greater taste for blood, and gladiatorial shows (*munera*) at both public and private funerals became more common and elaborate. One of the gladiators in a training school at Capua was a Thracian-born slave named Spartacus, who at one time had served as an auxiliary in the Roman army. In 73 he managed to escape with a handful of companions and seized Mount Vesuvius (which was not an active volcano until A.D. 79). Joined by runaway slaves and herdsmen, he quickly built up a considerable force with which he overran Campania and Lucania and defeated the forces that Rome sent against him. Realizing perhaps that he could not hope to secure complete or permanent control of Italy, Spartacus wisely wanted to withdraw north of the Alps so that his followers could scatter to their original homelands; but the Gauls and Germans refused and preferred to stay in Italy to plunder, so that Spartacus had to withdraw to S. Italy for the winter.

As his forces now numbered some 70,000, the Senate at last realized the gravity of the threat and sent both consuls of 72 against him. They were, however, defeated first separately and then united. Again Spartacus moved north and defeated the proconsul of Cisalpine Gaul at Mutina; but once again his men would not leave Italy and he was again forced to march south, perhaps with the good plan of crossing to Sicily. The Senate then turned to Crassus, whom they appointed commander-in-chief with six legions. After Spartacus had broken through some lines by which Crassus hoped to bar him in the toe of Italy, the People voted that Pompey, who had just returned from Spain, should be associated with Crassus in the command. Crassus, however, wanted to win his own war. In this he was helped by M. Lucullus, who landed at Brundisium on his way back from Thrace and drove Spartacus back on Crassus. As Spartacus' forces insisted on dividing, Crassus was able to crush them in three successive engagements. Spartacus was killed and 6000 of his followers were crucified along the Appian Way. Some fugitives, who managed to escape northwards, were intercepted in Etruria by Pompey, who thus claimed credit for finishing the war. This boastful claim, which he made in an official despatch to the Senate, would not endear him to Crassus.

The revolt of Spartacus appears tragic, because the odds were too heavy against him. He was relatively humane and able. His achievement in creating, disciplining and arming from scratch forces that could defeat consular armies was little short of a miracle. But he could not always impose his will on them. On occasion they naturally turned to pillage and savage vengeance, dissensions arose among their various leaders, and complete unity of command eluded him. Idealized by Marxist historians as the champion of the revolutionary masses, he was rather the product of local conditions and scattered support: he made no appeal to the slaves in the towns, but drew his strength from the downtrodden and unsettled elements in the countryside. He was not a political theorist going into action, but a courageous individual who fought for the personal liberty that was denied him by the ghastly conditions of his place and time. The revolt caused much loss and destruction to the country, but it may have taught some of the large landowners to treat their slaves with less inhumanity; some began to make greater use of free tenants (coloni). Beside this social and economic aspect, the political repercussions were startling.

5. THE CONSULSHIP OF POMPEY AND CRASSUS (70 B.C.)

The administration of the Senate, both at home and abroad, had brought it little credit, so that its stock was low when the armies of Pompey and Crassus approached the city. It might well have tried to play off one of these commanders against the other in view of their mutual jealousies, but they decided to work together and they prevailed. Both wanted the consulship of 70. The claim of Crassus was reasonable enough: he had held the praetorship, defeated a dangerous enemy, and through his great wealth was a representative of the business interests of Rome. But Pompey was not qualified: he was six years too young and had held none of the requisite offices. He also wanted a triumph, and made that an excuse for keeping his army together near Rome. Under these circumstances the Senate gave way: Pompey was granted legal dispensation from the requirements of the lex Annalis of Sulla, and was allowed his triumph. He also enjoyed wide popular support, since he had made it known as early as 73 that he favoured the restoration of tribunician powers and he may have been known to approve of some equestrian participation in the law-courts: in any case the Equites would support him as a political ally of Crassus. Thus both men were elected. Pompey celebrated his triumph (Metellus Pius also received a triumph for his share in the defeat of Sertorius, and M. Lucullus for victory in Macedonia), but Crassus had to be content with the lesser honour of an ovatio. Political amicitia, however, did not always involve personal friendship, and the coolness between the two consuls was such that each hesitated to disarm. Further, as long as their armies remained in being (and the exact duration is uncertain),[10] they will have enjoyed an additional visible means of coercing the Senate. Finally, however, they staged a public reconciliation and disbanded their forces.

Pompey and Crassus, who had both been lieutenants of Sulla, now pro-ceeded to sweep away much that remained of his constitution. First they carried a measure which restored to the tribunate all the powers it had enjoyed before it had been muzzled by Sulla; whether Pompey could have had any idea that the restored tribunate might prove a means by which his own career might later be advanced, cannot of course be known. Then they revived the dormant censorship: the censors elected were the two consuls of 72, whose claim to fame was their defeat by Spartacus: they promptly ejected 64 members from the Senate.

Before the third main measure of the year was carried, Rome was shaken by a grave scandal: the prosecution of C. Verres, who had plundered and mis-governed his province of Sicily (73–1) on a shocking scale. Though Verres' victims included some of Pompey's Sicilian clients, he had many powerful friends in Rome, among them the orator Hortensius and three members of the Metellus family. In their need the unfortunate Sicilians turned for a prosecutor to the man who had dared to stand up to Sulla's agent some ten years before (p. 69, n. 38), M. Tullius Cicero. This young man, who came from the muni-cipal aristocracy of Arpinum, was seeking political advancement through the bar rather than the army, and he had reached the quaestorship in 75 when he served in Sicily. He now undertook their request to prosecute Verres. After various intrigues by his opponents, Cicero defeated in his Actio Prima an attempt to postpone the trial till 69 when two of Verres' friends would be consuls, and a third would preside over the court. In view of the damning evidence that Cicero produced, Verres' counsel Hortensius abandoned his brief and Verres went into exile. Cicero then published the Actio Secunda, which he had not had opportunity to deliver; it formed a terrible indictment of senatorial government in the provinces. Cicero thus became Rome's foremost advocate, but he had also incidentally paved the way for further reform.[10a]

This was undertaken, not by Pompey and Crassus in their own names, but by a praetor, L. Aurelius Cotta, a brother of the liberal consul of 75. By the lex Aurelia the Senatorial monopoly of the law-courts, which Sulla had enacted, came to an end, and in future they were to be empanelled in equal numbers from three groups: senators, Equites and tribuni aerarii.[11] As this last group had similar interests to the Equites, the new arrangement was a political victory for the Equites, who would control some two-thirds of each jury. Thus within ten years of his retirement the essential parts of Sulla's reforms had been swept away: little remained but his reorganization of the courts them-selves. His attempts to check tribunes and army commanders alike had failed, but although the restored tribunate might chastise the Optimates with whips, the military dictators chastised them with scorpions. The Senate had failed to rise to the opportunity that Sulla had given it, and the ultimate result was further civil wars in which the Republic perished.

6. POMPEY'S COMMANDS

For the moment there was a lull. Neither Pompey nor Crassus took a pro-consular command, but both retired into private life after their consulship and apparently made no effort to get any of their supporters into the consul-ship for the next years. Thus Optimate control, despite the weakening of Sulla's work, might appear to be re-established, though the *populares* were not silent: in the funeral oration which Julius Caesar delivered at the death of his aunt Julia, the widow of Marius, when the *imagines* of Marius were displayed, he emphasized his connections with this group. He also drew attention to his family's alleged descent from the kings of Rome (from Ancus Marcius) and the gods (from Venus, through Iulus, Aeneas' son).

Caesar's early life had not been uneventful. When he refused Sulla's order to divorce his wife Cornelia, Cinna's daughter, he was forced to flee from Rome. Later he was pardoned by Sulla and then served in the East (80–78), where he gained the civic crown (a decoration like the V.C.) for saving the life of a soldier in the assault of Mytilene. After his return to Rome, where he displayed his oratorical gifts in the courts, he left (75/4) to study rhetoric at Rhodes. He was captured by pirates, and, according to the anecdote, after his ransom he returned to fulfil the promise that he had made to them during his captivity that one day he would crucify all his captors. He then helped some communities in Asia to remain loyal against the appeal of Mithridates (74), and received news that he had been chosen a member of the college of pontiffs. On his return to Rome he drew closer to the *populares*: he backed the agitation for restoring tribunician power, held a military tribunate (71?) and supported the *lex Plotia de reditu Lepidanorum* by which citizenship was restored to the followers of Lepidus who had joined Sertorius (possibly in 70). He served as quaestor in Spain (69 or 68) and on his way home he extended his political *clientela* by interesting himself in the desire of the Transpadanes for full citizenship (cf. p. 58). Then in 67 he lent his support to Pompey.[12]

In 67 two tribunes became very active. C. Cornelius sponsored some measures to improve the administration of justice,[13] and A. Gabinius pro-posed that drastic action should be taken against the pirates whose raids were affecting the corn-supply of Rome itself. He moved that a man of consular rank, obviously Pompey was meant, should be given for three years an *imperium infinitum* by sea throughout the Mediterranean, and authority equal to that of all provincial governors for fifty miles inland, together with vast supplies of men, ships and money.[14] This proposal provoked a storm of protest in the Senate, where it was denounced by Optimate leaders such as Catulus and Hortensius and where Julius Caesar alone supported it. The Senate found two tribunes to resist Gabinius: Roscius Otho urged that Pompey should have a colleague, and Tribellius vetoed the bill. Gabinius, however, had recourse to the tactics of Tiberius Gracchus when faced by Octavius, and threatened to depose Trebellius. Amid scenes of great disorder the *lex Gabinia* was passed, but with increased supplies for Pompey which now included 6000 talents, 500 ships, 120,000 infantry and the right to appoint 24 legates.

Meantime the conduct of the Mithridatic War by Lucullus had caused discontent in Rome. His enemies alleged that he was needlessly prolonging the war for his own glory, and his just settlement of the financial affairs of Asia angered the Equites. In 69 therefore the province of Asia was withdrawn from him, in 68 Cilicia likewise, and in 67 Gabinius carried a law to assign Bithynia and Pontus to the consul Acilius Glabrio. Then in 66, as Pompey had finished off his pirate campaign with lightning speed, a tribune C. Manilius proposed that Cilicia, Bithynia and Pontus and the command against Mithridates should be entrusted to Pompey, who should still retain the command and forces granted to him by the *lex Gabinia*. In view of Pompey's spectacular success against the pirates, the Optimates could hardly prevail against Manilius when they had failed against Gabinius. Caesar supported the bill and Cicero, now praetor, gained further favour with the populace and Equites by delivering a speech (*Pro lege Manilia* or *De imperio Cn. Pompeii*) in which he advocated the appointment and lauded Pompey's past achievements.[14a] Thus Pompey received unprecedented powers and was little short of a monarch in the East. How he would use this power when he returned to Rome was a question that men began to ask before long with increasing anxiety, but in the meantime it was clear that the ramparts which Sulla had attempted to erect around the Senate were breached irrevocably by such action as the People had taken under the stimulus of the unfettered tribunes. Pompey might or might not remain loyal to the constitution, but even if he did, other tribunes might be used to elevate less scrupulous army commanders to positions of unassailable power.

7. THE PIRATES

One hundred years before the *lex Gabinia* Rome had dealt so harshly with Rhodes that this island-Republic lost its power to keep the eastern Mediterranean free of piracy: the increasing weakness of Egypt and Syria also helped the pirates. Rome made some half-hearted efforts against them between 102 and 100 B.C. (see pp. 47 and 49 f.), and Sulla possibly intended further action, but little was done until P. Servilius Vatia (*cos.* 79) was sent out to reduce Cilicia which was their main lair.[15] After a naval battle off the Lycian coast (77) he reduced Lycia and Pamphylia (76) and then by over-running Isaurica he opened up the way for an attack by land from the north on Cilicia Tracheia (75); but the outbreak of the Third Mithridatic War (74) halted these operations. In 74 the Senate tried to shut the pirates out of Cyrene by declaring it a province (p. 77) and conferred a special command on M. Antonius (son of the man who had campaigned against the pirates in 102); after long preparations Antonius decided to concentrate on Crete, where he did little except suffer a defeat at sea. The pirates gained a few years' respite when Rome devoted her attention to Mithridates, who was in alliance with them. This they used both to increase their organization and strength which was said to have reached 1000 ships, and to extend the range of their operations which now included the coasts of Italy itself. Then Q. Caecilius Metellus (*cos.* 69) was sent with three legions to reduce Crete, which he did with such cruelty (68–7) that the Cretans preferred to surrender to an officer sent by Pompey. After a tussle Metellus asserted himself and Crete was declared a Roman province.

Pompey's appointment under the lex *Gabinia* created such confidence that the price of corn in Rome dropped immediately, and he was quick to justify the trust he inspired.[16] He divided the Mediterranean and Euxine into thirteen sections under legates, and took command of a mobile squadron of 60 ships. Cutting the area into halves at the 'Sicilian Narrows' between Sicily and Africa, he dealt first with the western area, which he swept clear in forty days by driving detachments of the enemy into the arms of the section commanders. He then turned to the eastern half: after a naval victory off Coracesium in Cilicia and the capture of the pirates' mountain stronghold there, he brought the whole campaign to a victorious end within three months, and crowned his achievement by the moderation of his settlement. He settled many of these desperate and ruined men in Cilicia and elsewhere: the old man, whom Virgil (*Georgics* 4, 125 ff.) described as passing the evening of his days keeping bees in an idyllic setting near Tarentum, has long been thought to be one of these ex-pirates from Cilician Corycus.

8. THE THIRD MITHRIDATIC WAR: LUCULLUS

Although Mithridates had received lenient terms from Sulla under the Treaty of Dardanus (p. 64 f.), this treaty had not been formally ratified by the Senate, despite a direct request from the king in 79, partly because of the confusion that followed Sulla's death. Mithridates' suspicions were naturally aroused and he began to build up his resources. He recovered control of the Crimea, intrigued with the Thracians, negotiated with Sertorius and the pirates, established good relations with Egypt and Cyprus, and supported his son-in-law Tigranes, who had built a grand new capital for Armenia at Tigranocerta, and had annexed part of Syria and Cappadocia. Mithridates' forces were said to number some 100,000–150,000 men and 400 ships, and he had received help in training them from a former Roman quaestor sent to him by Sertorius. All this must have appeared to Rome to portend action.

When Nicomedes III of Bithynia bequeathed his kingdom to Rome (75/4) and Rome declared it a province,[17] Mithridates was unwilling to see control of the entrance to the Black Sea pass to Rome or to accept the changed balance of power in Asia Minor. He therefore invaded Bithynia. Of the two consuls of 74 M. Aurelius Cotta was assigned to the new province of Bithynia, while his colleague L. Licinius Lucullus, a former friend of Sulla, by intrigue secured Cilicia and Asia.[18] Lucullus raised five legions and advanced through Phrygia on Mithridates' flank, while Cotta, based on Bithynia, conducted naval operations. Eager to win the war himself, Cotta rushed into action and after defeat by land and sea he was besieged at Chalcedon.[19] Mithridates then advanced to Cyzicus, which he started to besiege, but Lucullus arrived and managed to cut off the king's supplies. As the siege dragged on Mithridates in desperation sent away his cavalry and then during the winter was compelled to withdraw his army: Lucullus defeated both forces and in the following spring (73) beat some naval forces that had got into the Aegean. Mithridates escaped with difficulty to the Euxine, where he suffered further losses by storm, and retired to Pontus. Thus within two years his immense expeditionary force was shattered, with the loss of perhaps 100,000 men.

Each leader then took a resolute decision: Mithridates to continue resistance despite past disasters, and Lucullus not to attempt a compromise, such as Sulla had reached, but to invade Pontus and drive the king out. This he did in some three years of systematic warfare. Behind the screen of his fortress towns (Amisus, Themiscyra, Eupatoria and Amasia) Mithridates tried to build up new forces at Cabeira, but Lucullus advanced, besieged Amisus, took Eupatoria and defeated the king at Cabeira (72). As his troops panicked, Mithridates was forced to flee and took refuge with Tigranes. The other fortress soon fell to Lucullus, who also reduced Armenia Minor: by 70 he was master in Pontus. He was, however, angered by the fact that his troops had disobeyed his orders and plundered the Greek city of Amisus when it was captured. While waiting for the return of Appius Claudius, whom he had sent to Tigranes to demand the surrender of Mithridates, Lucullus overhauled the finances of Asia which was still reeling under Sulla's settlement (cf. p. 64). He reduced the rate of interest to 12 per cent, cancelled arrears of interest that exceeded the principal, allowed no more than a quarter of a debtor's annual income to be seized by a creditor, and met the indemnity by a 25 per cent levy and some taxes. These measures cleared the province of debt within four years and many grateful cities established festivals called Lucullea in his honour. But he had antagonized the Equites, who began to work for his suppression by alleging that he was prolonging the war for his own glory.

Once again Lucullus decided that Asia would never remain at peace while Mithridates was still at large. When Tigranes refused to hand over his father-in-law, Lucullus resolved to invade Armenia, a policy which might commend itself to him more readily than to his troops, who were wearying of the long and gruelling campaigns, or to the Senate, which had not authorized such an advance. It also provided the Equites with ammunition against the man who had dared to protect the provincials from their exactions, and it encouraged the demagogues to denounce the ambition of the Optimates. Thus, as has been seen (pp. 82–83), his provinces were gradually taken from him until he was recalled home. His invasion of Armenia, however, started well. Reaching the upper Tigris he advanced to Tigranocerta, defeated Tigranes by skilful tactics in a decisive victory and captured Tigranocerta (69), though Tigranes himself managed to escape and was joined by Mithridates in the heart of Armenia. Undismayed, Lucullus in 68 advanced into the highland plateau, threatened Artaxata, the old capital, and defeated the two kings in battle. His men, however, long restless, now refused to go farther and thus compelled him to turn south where he captured Nisibis and wintered. Meanwhile Mithridates had managed to return to Pontus, where a ding-dong struggle ensued with the Roman troops there until in the spring of 67 Triarius was defeated at Zela by Mithridates with the loss of 7000 men. When Lucullus finally arrived, he could do little, since his successor, Glabrio, refused to leave Bithynia, and Lucullus found his troops taken from him. By a stroke of irony a senatorial commission, which included his brother, arrived to help him organize the province of Pontus, but Rome was no longer in control: Mithridates had regained his old kingdom, and Tigranes, the King of Kings, was attacking Cappadocia. Lucullus lingered on in Asia until the arrival of Pompey with whom he had a stormy interview. On his return to Rome he ultimately secured a well-deserved triumph, after which he retired into private life, devoting his time to cultural pursuits and the luxurious living for which he became notorious.

Lucullus had failed to bring the war to an end by capturing Mithridates, but for that the blame must go in part to his political opponents, but not entirely. Despite brilliant strategy and tactics, despite courage and a high sense of discipline, he was too aloof and lost touch with his men, who resented his ban on unrestricted plundering and failed to respond to his appeals to go ever farther into the unknown East. But he had saved Roman Asia from conquest by Mithridates and exploitation by the Equites, and though the final phase of his service in the East was an anticlimax, yet there can be no doubt that he had broken the real strength of the two kings and that Pompey merely arrived to give the final push to an already crumbling edifice.[20]

9. POMPEY'S VICTORY

Pompey was in Cilicia when news reached him of his appointment under the lex Manilia. He succeeded in persuading the Parthian king Phraates to invade

Armenia and thus distract Tigranes, while he himself marched into Pontus against Mithridates. Unlike Lucullus in 74, who was outnumbered by five to one, Pompey had some 20,000 more men than Mithridates, whom he defeated near Dasteira (which was later named Nicopolis, the City of Victory). This time Tigranes, who had driven back the Parthians, was unwilling to receive Mithridates, who was forced to flee northwards. Indomitable as ever, Mithridates succeeded in wresting his Russian possessions from his treacherous son Machares (whom Lucullus had recognized in 70) and raised fresh troops (65–63) with which he was alleged to be planning an invasion of Italy via the Danube. But he was pushing his subjects too hard; revolts followed, and even Pharnaces, another son, turned against him and drove him into the citadel of Panticapaeum. There the old king, now sixty-eight, ordered one of his Celtic bodyguards to kill him (63).

It was Mithridates' tragedy to fall between two worlds. He championed the Greek world like a Hellenistic monarch, and yet he could not entirely divest himself of the role of Oriental despot: the western and eastern elements in his culture and character never really fused. He showed extraordinary powers of mind and body, of generalship and diplomacy, but he failed to win the whole-hearted devotion of his supporters: the magic touch of an Alexander or Caesar eluded him. But it he had failed to free the Hellenistic world from Rome, his career demonstrated the unity of that world, which must come under one rule: Rome's political horizon must now reach the Euphrates, beyond which lay the great Parthian Empire. Thus he both opened up new problems of foreign policy for Rome and at the same time by his stubborn resistance he had forced Rome to entrust unusual powers to ambitious men for long periods of time and in consequence hastened the downfall of the Republic.

Meantime Pompey had advanced into Armenia, where he received the surrender of Tigranes, who was allowed to keep his throne and Armenia, though deprived of all his foreign acquisitions. Pompey then turned north to the Caucasus area, where he crossed swords with the Albanians and, in 65, with the Iberians (in modern Georgia), and advanced nearly to the Caspian.[21] He also made further diplomatic contacts with Parthia, but foolishly took a stronger line after the defeat of Tigranes: by refusing to allow Phraates to occupy Gordyene and Nisibis which he had previously promised to the king, he broke his word and thereby laid up trouble for Rome in the future. In 64, judging that Mithridates could be left to the effect of Roman naval pressure, Pompey went to Amisus and thence to Syria, which was in a state of great disorder.

Since 67 Palestine had seen civil war between two sons of Jannaeus, Hyrcanus and Aristobulus. Pompey's legate Gabinius settled the struggle in favour of Aristobulus, who was being besieged in Jerusalem. But Pompey himself after settling Syria and receiving deputations from the two Jewish princes at Damascus, decided to reverse Gabinius' decision and to favour

Hyrcanus (63). Though Aristobulus reluctantly submitted to this order, his followers refused and fortified themselves in the Temple quarters of Jerusalem. Pompey soon arrived and occupied the lower town, but only after three months' siege did he break the stubborn resistance; he then entered the Holy of Holies in the Temple but did not touch the treasures within. Hyrcanus was recognized as High Priest and ruler, though not king, of Judaea.[22] This flare-up in Jerusalem had diverted Pompey from an expedition which he had planned to the caravan-city of the Nabataean Arabs, Petra: he may have had commercial gain in mind, but he also wished to carry Roman arms to the Red Sea. In the event he sent his quaestor Aemilius Scaurus, who retired when the Nabataean king Aretas bribed him and made a show of submission.[23] It was while he was near Jerusalem that Pompey received a messenger, bearing a laurel-bound spear, who reported that Mithridates was dead. He could now turn to the task of reconstruction.

10. POMPEY'S SETTLEMENT OF THE EAST

Unaided by the customary decemviral commission of senators, Pompey redrew the map of Anatolia in the way which he considered would best secure the peace and security of this vast area.[24] His scheme was to have a continuous line of Roman provinces around the coast of Asia, from Pontus on the Black Sea in the north to Syria in the south (apart from the small strip of Lycia). These were Bithynia et Pontus (i.e. Bithynia extended to embrace the western part of Pontus), Asia, Cilicia, which was enlarged, and Syria which Pompey annexed as a new province: there would be outposts at Crete and (later, in 58) Cyprus. The eastern frontiers of these provinces were guarded by a large number of client kings, i.e. native rulers left in control of their own lands as friends or allies of Rome whom they must consult on all matters of foreign policy; in return, they received peace and considerable internal independence. The chief client kingdoms were Galatia (under Deiotarus, who received eastern Pontus), East Galatia (under Brogitarus), Paphlagonia (under Attalus and Pylaemenes), Cappadocia (under Ariobarzanes), Armenia Minor (perhaps granted to Deiotarus), Commagene (under Antiochus I), part of eastern Cilicia (under Tarcondimotus); in the north Bosporus (under Pharnaces, who had betrayed his father Mithridates); east of the Euphrates an Arab sheikh Abgar received Osrhoene, while Tigranes retained Gordyene (around Nisibis); east of Syria were Sampsiceramus of Emesa and Ptolemy of Chalcis, while the Nabataeans regained Damascus. Beyond all these states loomed the Parthian Empire. Thus Rome was forced to advance her strategic frontier, though not the sphere of her direct administration, to the Euphrates and Syrian desert. As long as Armenia remained friendly to Rome and hostile to Parthia, and Commagene continued to safeguard the crossings of the upper

Euphrates in Rome's interests, Pompey might feel that the western empire was well protected by this shield of provinces and its cushion of buffer states beyond.

It was necessary for Rome that this whole block of country should be made to face westwards away from the Parthian east, and Pompey helped to achieve this by developing one feature that was characteristic of the Hellenistic culture that united all this region, namely the city-state. Like Alexander and the Hellenistic monarchs he therefore founded or restored a large number of cities with Greek institutions, thirty-nine in Asia and Syria, and eleven in Bithynia and Pontus. One of his main motives may have been administrative convenience: in Bithynia and Pontus in particular, where the centralized bureaucracies were too complicated to be worked by existing Roman methods, administration had largely to devolve on local authorities; these therefore had to be created. But that is not to say that Pompey will have been blind to the wider benefits that such a system would create, even if his primary purpose was not cultural or civilizing. There was a further consideration: the cities might enjoy considerable autonomy, but few were immune from taxation, in the form of tithes, and the provincial revenues were collected by Roman *publicani*. Not only did Pompey distribute vast sums to his soldiers and pay 480 million sesterces into the Roman Treasury, but his reorganization of the East raised the annual revenue of Rome from tribute from 200 million to 340 million sesterces. In return for its taxes the East received a considerable measure of peace, security and the possibility of economic prosperity. The proof of the pudding is in the eating: when Civil War developed between Pompey and Caesar, the East supported Pompey as its benefactor. In the meantime it was no little gain to Pompey in the political field when he returned to Rome that he had added this vast array of eastern peoples to his *clientela*. Though it is partly true that in the military field he had reaped what Lucullus had sown, he had nevertheless shown himself a competent soldier and an outstanding administrator: what he would achieve at home among his peers, time would soon reveal.

VI

POMPEY AND CAESAR[1]

1. CRASSUS AND CAESAR

Since their joint consulship of 70 B.C. Crassus must have become increasingly jealous of Pompey's spectacular career. True, he had very considerable political influence, which he owed in part to a skilful, if not an over-scrupulous, use of his vast wealth, but the hero of the battle of the Colline Gate and the conqueror of Spartacus was overshadowed by the military triumphs of Pompey. A certain apprehension began to mingle with his jealousy. Pompey would return all-powerful: how would he use that power? might he become a second Sulla, and if so how would Crassus stand? He therefore attempted to build up his political power during Pompey's absence in a series of intrigues, in which he was supported by Caesar, who after his quaestorship in Spain gained the aedileship for 65, helped no doubt by Crassus' wealth. Caesar was more friendly to Pompey than Crassus was, but he may have found in Crassus a useful stepping-stone to advancement. The Optimate leaders (men like Catulus, the Metelli, the two Luculli and Hortensius) must have been even more apprehensive about Pompey's return, but despite a common fear they made no overtures to Crassus or the Populares.

The opening shots in the political tussle were fired in the so-called First Catilinarian Conspiracy. The consuls elected for 65, P. Autronius Paetus and P. Cornelius Sulla (probably the dictator's nephew), were condemned for electoral bribery (under the law of 67) and a second election was held, at which L. Sergius Catilina wanted to stand. Catiline, who was a member of an impoverished patrician family, had served under Sulla in the Civil Wars, but was awaiting trial for extortion committed during his propraetorship in Africa (67–6). The consul, who was to preside at the election, refused to accept Catiline's candidature, and two Optimates were elected. A plot was then formed to murder the new consuls on 1 January 65 and to replace them with Autronius and either Sulla or Catiline. The scheme miscarried and the whole scandal was hushed up. Much remains mysterious, but probably Crassus favoured the original election of Autronius and Sulla; though not backing the conspiracy, he may have decided to turn it to profit by using his wealth and his power as censor (an office he held in 65) to smooth things over: a grateful Catiline might prove a useful tool in the future.[2]

Crassus tried to gain power abroad as well: in Spain, Transpadane Gaul and Egypt. Calpurnius Piso, who had been involved in the plot, was sent to Spain as *quaestor propraetore*, but as he was soon killed there this plan was nipped in the bud. Then Crassus, as censor, proposed to grant full citizenship to the Transpadanes; he doubtless anticipated the opposition from his Optimate colleague Catulus that led to stalemate and their resignation from office, but he had at any rate won the support of these people, to whom Caesar had already shown sympathy (p. 82): they would provide good troops if the need arose.

In Egypt also there was a chance to intervene. When king Ptolemy IX, Lathyrus, died in 80, Sulla supported his nephew, who was proclaimed as Ptolemy XI Alexander II but soon was lynched by the Alexandrians; they then installed an illegitimate son of Lathyrus as Ptolemy XII, nicknamed the Fluteplayer (Auletes) and father of Cleopatra. His claim to the throne was rendered more doubtful when an alleged will of Ptolemy X or XI was produced in Rome, in which the latter had bequeathed his realm to Rome. The will may possibly have been genuine; slowness by the Senate to act upon it is no argument against its validity, as the case of Cyrene shows (p. 77).[3] Crassus then put up a tribune to propose the annexation of Egypt, and he perhaps hoped to get Caesar sent out to organize at least the financial side. It is not necessary to assume that Crassus was trying to seize Egypt as a military base against Pompey or to anticipate action by him there, but an attempt to open up the treasures and corn of Egypt would appeal to Equites and people alike, and would give Crassus popularity and a political asset of great potential value. The Optimates, led by Catulus, rallied their forces against the proposal, and Cicero, who was protecting Pompey's interests in Rome, delivered a speech 'De Rege Alexandrino'; the proposal was defeated, and Crassus was again thwarted.

Meanwhile Catiline had been tried and, through influence, acquitted on the charge of extortion. He was now preparing to stand at the consular elections in the summer of 64 for office in 63, together with another disreputable competitor, C. Antonius (brother of Marcus who had been defeated by the Cretan pirates); he was backed by Crassus and his financial interests.[4] The Optimates clearly wanted to secure the defeat of this pair, but had no obvious candidate to run against them. There was, however, the aspiring

Cicero: though he did not come from a consular family but represented the gentry of the Italian towns, and though he was a supporter of Pompey and enjoyed Equestrian backing, he must have appeared to the nobility a safer man than his competitors. In a speech to the Senate (*Oratio in Toga Candida*: candidates wore specially whitened togas) Cicero denounced his rivals and hinted that there were secret powers behind Catiline. Thus Cicero, the *novus homo*, secured the consulship for 63, with Antonius as colleague; Catiline was defeated.[5]

Crassus, however, still continued his intrigues. At the end of 64 a tribune, P. Servilius Rullus, was put up to propose an agrarian bill: a commission of ten was to be set up, for five years, with *imperium*, to allocate land and establish colonies in Italy and the provinces; for the purchase of this land the commissioners could use public funds and war-booty and they were empowered to sell any land in Italy or outside that had become public property since 88 B.C. The political purpose of this move must remain obscure in detail, because knowledge of the proposal derives from the speeches which Cicero delivered against it, in which he greatly exaggerated the powers to be granted to the commissioners. Whether or not Crassus, having failed to get control of Egypt one way, was now trying in another (on the assumption that all Egyptian crown-land might fall within the scope of the *decemviri*), he was clearly trying to get control of all available land, knowing that Pompey on his return would need land for his veterans; thus he would be in a strong bargaining position. Cicero's oratory, however, was triumphant and Rullus withdrew his measure. Once again Crassus was checked, and this time he took no further action.[6]

Caesar, however, who had been supporting Crassus in the background, now came more into the open. As aedile in 65 he had staged magnificent Games, with the financial help of Crassus, and in the next year, when acting as chairman of the *quaestio de sicariis*, managed to secure the ultimate acquittal of Catiline, who had been brought before the court for his activities during the Sullan proscriptions. In 63 Caesar was elected Pontifex Maximus, defeating two very senior candidates, Catulus (*cos.* 78) and Servilius Isauricus (*cos.* 78): Crassus' money again helped. The bill of a tribune, T. Labienus (later his lieutenant in Gaul), to re-establish the *lex Domitia* of 104 (cf. p. 45) probably did not affect the Pontifex Maximus. Caesar also brought to trial, at first making use of an archaic procedure, a certain C. Rabirius, who was alleged to have helped in killing Saturninus 37 years earlier after the Senate had passed the *senatus consultum ultimum*. Cicero, who defended Rabirius, suggested that Caesar was attacking the validity of the S.C.U., whereas in fact he was probably merely criticizing its misuse. However, before a verdict was reached, the court was dissolved (on Caesar's instructions?) by reverting to an obsolete practice: a red flag, which flew on the Janiculum, was lowered, an action which in the early Republic had warned of an Etruscan attack and ordered the immediate break-up of all public meetings.[7] Caesar also prosecuted C. Piso (*cos.* 67) for having executed a Transpadane when governor of Gaul, and sponsored a measure to restore full political rights to the children of men proscribed by Sulla (cf. p. 67). In both these moves Caesar failed because of the opposition of Cicero, but he will have won further friends.

2. CATILINE'S CONSPIRACY

Catiline determined to try his luck again at the consular elections of 63, but he needed further support and therefore came forward with a proposal to cancel all debts (*novae tabulae*). This would obviously make a strong appeal to all the discontented in Italy (e.g. any of Sulla's veterans that had failed as farmers) and especially to many spendthrift nobles, like Catiline himself, who were in debt, but it would antagonize the bulk of the Senate, the Equites, and the small shopkeepers and workers. He also made some unwise and threatening remarks, so that on election-day Cicero appeared with an unofficial bodyguard and ostentatiously wore a breastplate. The consuls elected were L. Licinius Murena and D. Iunius Silanus, not Catiline.

Hitherto Catiline had sought power by normal and legitimate means, but he now turned to more desperate action.[8] Together with some of his noble followers (who included P. Cornelius Lentulus, the consul of 71, who had been expelled from the Senate in 70), he planned an uprising in Rome for 28 October, small risings in other parts of Italy and a major one, led by L. Manlius, in Etruria to appeal to the veteran colonists. Cicero got wind of this, but not until 21 October was he able to convince the Senate of the danger. At last it recognized that a crisis was brewing and passed the S.C.U., which gave moral backing to the consul Cicero without increasing his legal powers; Cicero then took some military precautions in Italy.

At a meeting in the house of one of the conspirators in the Street of the Sickle-makers, on the night of 6 November, it was decided that as the first plan had failed, more drastic action must be taken: as a preliminary step Cicero was to be murdered early the next morning; later the city was to be set on fire and slaves called upon to loot; throughout Italy gladiators, herdsmen and discontented peasants were to take to arms; and the force being raised in Etruria was to march on Rome. Cicero, who was warned, escaped assassination and summoned the Senate, where he delivered his First Catilinarian Oration, denouncing him to his face, since Catiline attended the meeting in a spirit of bravado and bluff. That night Catiline hurried off to join Manlius and before long the Senate declared both these leaders and their men (who soon numbered some 10,000, though ill-armed) public enemies.[9]

Cicero then had to try to deal with the conspirators who still remained in Rome. As he could not obtain any written evidence against them, he was in a very delicate position, since as consul he was responsible for the maintenance of law and order. But before long they took a false step: they got in touch with some envoys from the Allobroges, who happened to be in Rome, with a view to getting Gallic help for Catiline, and postponed the rising till 17 December. These envoys reported this approach to Cicero, who persuaded them to trick the conspirators into giving them signed treasonable letters. At last having got documentary evidence, Cicero arrested the five ringleaders in Rome, and consulted the Senate about their fate on 5 December. In this famous debate the first sixteen speakers all favoured their death; then Caesar swung many over by a proposal that they should be imprisoned for life. There were in fact rumours that Caesar and Crassus were behind Catiline, but they had long ago severed any connection: they did not want a revolution and had even provided Cicero with some evidence of Catiline's plans. But Caesar's proposal, whatever its motive, did not win the day. The Senate was rallied to the death-penalty by the great-grandson of Cato the Censor, M. Porcius Cato. Reinforced by this expression of opinion (it was no more, because the Senate was not a Court of Law) Cicero went out and had the five conspirators killed; to the crowds in the Forum he announced laconically 'Vixerunt'. Within a month Catiline's forces in Etruria were brought to battle near Pistoria, and Catiline fell fighting.

Cicero had clearly saved his country from revolution. There is little to suggest that Catiline had the interests of the down-trodden poor at heart, but whatever be thought of his earlier moves, his final efforts, if successful, would have led to widespread destruction and suffering, not least among the poor. Nor could any success have been more than temporary: there would have been Pompey and his army to reckon with, and revolution would merely have been followed by a civil war of which the issue could not be in doubt. Thus genuine feelings of relief and gratitude prompted the hailing of Cicero in the Senate as Parens Patriae: his satisfaction was unbounded. But as the crisis receded, Cicero's execution-order, rather than his resolution and courage, was remembered, and the legality of his action was called into question. Had not the conspirators the right to a trial? The answer is ambiguous and depends partly on whether they could still be regarded as Roman citizens, or whether their own actions were so treasonable that they had, as it were, turned themselves into hostes. Was the gravity of the situation such that the consul ought to follow the precedent set by Opimius which had been justified by his acquital in 120 (cf. p. 36), and in the public interest to ignore the normal limitations imposed on his imperium and act on the principle 'salus populi suprema lex esto'? It may be that Cicero was over-hasty, but his first duty was to preserve society, and in that he succeeded; on the larger issue therefore, if not in regard to the strict letter of the law, he had good reason to feel that he had done his duty.[10]

3. THE RETURN OF POMPEY

Even before Catiline had died, the shadow of Pompey fell across the political scene. A tribune, Q. Metellus Nepos, acting for him in Rome, attacked Cicero and proposed a bill to summon Pompey home to take command against Catiline (whose army was already hemmed in: January 62) and to allow him to stand for the consulship in *absentia*. Despite the veto of his colleague Cato, Metellus pushed his bill with such energy that rioting ensued and the Senate again passed the *senatus consultum ultimum*; Metellus then hurried off to Pompey. But this proved to be only a passing squall and most of the year was peaceful.[11]

During this breathing space, Cicero was able to reflect on the state of the Republic and he evolved a constructive idea which shone out bravely amid the gloomy struggle between Optimates and Populares, so few of whom were striving for anything other than personal power: mostly they were devoid of higher motives, and if on occasion they appealed to certain aspects of *libertas* and constitutional principles, it was for their personal ends rather than for the preservation of the commonwealth.[12] Cicero, however, had been deeply impressed by the way in which the saner elements of society had closed ranks and allied against Catiline. He now began to dream of healing the breach between the Senate and Equites in a *concordia ordinum*, which later he came to envisage as a coalition of all 'Good Men' (*consensus omnium bonorum*). But he was a *novus homo*, without sufficient family connexions, and he had not been an army commander; he thus lacked an adequate *clientela*, and he could not build up a faction to support his political leadership: he depended too much upon the goodwill of the Optimates, who had accepted him with some reluctance. He had also to consider Pompey, to whom he turned hopefully, not realizing how annoying it was for Pompey to have been anticipated in saving Rome from Catiline. In a somewhat naïve letter Cicero urged him to co-operate in fostering the newly established harmony. In answer to Pompey's somewhat disappointing reply Cicero, who was hurt that Pompey had not adequately appreciated the way in which he had saved his country in 63, suggested an association like that between Scipio Africanus and Laelius, the soldier and the statesman. With one to guard, and the other to guide, the State, with the Senate and Equites allied against the *improbi*, all might yet be well. What Rome needed was a period of peace and tranquillity, of *otium cum dignitate*,[13] which a moderate conservative government might hope to achieve.

At the end of 62 Pompey finally reached Brundisium, and Rome must have had held its breath. Then he merely dismissed his troops to their homes. His motive was not fear, but probably the lack of desire to take control; he was at heart a constitutionalist, and though a great administrator, he lacked experience of political life at Rome. He wanted recognition of his greatness more than the hazards of a dictator's life. When he reached Rome he made a speech in the Senate that fell very flat. To the astonishment of many Pompeius Magnus sank back into private life, though he emerged later in 61 to celebrate his third triumph, unprecedented both in splendour and because his captives were spared the customary fate of execution.

Cicero, who found Pompey outwardly friendly but not very forthcoming, suffered a sharp setback in his hopes for a continuance of the *concordia ordinum*, thanks to the repercussions of a notorious scandal. A young noble, P. Clodius Pulcher, disguised as a woman, had penetrated into the festival of Bona Dea, which it was sacrilege for men to see; it was held in the house of the praetor urbanus, Caesar, with whose wife Clodius was alleged to be having an intrigue. Caesar divorced Pompeia, because 'Caesar's wife must be above suspicion', and after much wrangling about the nature of the court, Clodius was brought to trial for sacrilege. The bribery of the jurors was shocking ('there was never a viler crew round a table in a gambling hell', wrote Cicero) and Clodius was acquitted despite the fact that Cicero in court had disproved an *alibi* that Clodius had advanced, and thus incidentally incurred Clodius' lasting enmity. This result was a shock to the Optimates, many of whom had made too much of the affair, and it seriously weakened the *concordia*.[13a]

4. THE FIRST TRIUMVIRATE

The *concordia ordinum*, a little shaken, was soon shattered into smithereens. The cause was in large measure the demands of Pompey, Caesar and Crassus, which were by no means outrageous, and the short-sighted reaction of the Die-Hard Optimates. Crassus supported a request from a company of tax-gatherers that the Senate should adjust a bad bargain which they had made in contracting for the taxes of Asia.[14] Cicero, who regarded the claim as disgraceful, nevertheless supported it in order to prevent the breach between Senate and Equites from widening, but under Cato's leadership it was finally rejected (early 60). Meantime Pompey had been rebuffed by the Optimates in both his private and public life. Cato rejected a suggestion that Pompey should marry one of his relations, but of greater importance was Pompey's double request that his eastern settlement should be ratified by the Senate and that land should be provided for his veterans. Both demands were perfectly reasonable, and Pompey hoped that they would be put through by L. Afranius, whose election to the consulate of 60 he had secured by bribery. When however the Optimates under the leadership of men like Metellus Creticus, Lucullus and Cato began to obstruct and quibble over details, and Afranius proved ineffective, Pompey turned to the *populares* and the services of a tribune Flavius to bring a land-bill before the People. The senatorial opposition to this was led by the other consul, Metellus Celer, who at one point was even hauled off to prison by Flavius, but it prevailed in the end.

Finally, Caesar was back from Spain. After his praetorship (62) he had been enabled to take up the governorship of Further Spain thanks to Crassus who helped him to satisfy his creditors before leaving. In his province he campaigned in the west, acquired money and the friendship of Cornelius Balbus of Gades (who was to prove a most useful personal agent), and tried to improve economic conditions. On his return he wanted a triumph and the consulship, but since he could not as a commander enter the city to stand for election, he asked the Senate for permission to stand in *absentia*. Though there were precedents, the Senate refused. Caesar abandoned his triumph and entered Rome as an ordinary candidate. Any wild hope that Cicero might have had of winning him over to support the *concordia* was now lost.

The policy of the Senate was unrealistic, and even Cicero complained that Cato talked as if he were in the Republic of Plato, not in the sink of Romulus. By uncompromising refusal to meet the demands of Pompey, Caesar and Crassus the Senate naturally drove them into each other's arms. The three men agreed to form a political *amicitia*, which modern writers have called the First Triumvirate, but which was described by the ancients in less flattering terms, as 'potentiae societas', 'coniuratio' or 'dominatio'. It was essentially a private, and at first a secret, agreement to work together for their mutual political advantage.

Its formation was a turning point in the history of the Free State, and it was, as both Cicero and Cato recognized, the ultimate origin of the Civil War of 49 B.C. This truth was underlined when the historian Asinius Pollio, a supporter of Caesar and M. Antony, started his history of the great civil war with the year 60, the consulship of Metellus and Afranius. Three men, backed by armed force, by the urban populace and by many of the Equites, imposed their will on the State and destroyed the power of the Senate. Henceforth Cicero felt that he had lost freedom of speech, *auctoritas* and *dignitas*: 'tenemur undique neque iam quominus serviamus recusamus', he wrote in 59. The State and constitution were now at the mercy of dynasts, *principes*, who strove for *potentia* and *dignitas*. It was for these values that the leaders were to fight in the coming civil war.[15]

5. CAESAR'S FIRST CONSULSHIP (59 B.C.)

All this was to become plain only with the passage of time. At first men did not realize the existence of this compact and were in consequence puzzled by the way events developed: the masters who pulled the strings were hidden. If anything further was needed to stimulate Caesar to work with Pompey it was that the Senate, anticipating Caesar's election to the consulship, established as a proconsular province for 58 B.C. the *silvae callesque* of Italy, a kind of forestry commission, instead of an overseas command.[16] At the elections Caesar was

duly chosen consul for 59, though the Senate managed to push in a conservative, M. Calpurnius Bibulus, as his colleague by means of bribery to which
even Cato agreed 'in the interests of the Republic'. The strengthening of the
coalition was contemplated. Crassus, who first had to be reconciled with
Pompey, had come in because of the influence of his wealth. Respectability
would be gained if Cicero could be won over, but he stuck to his constitutional principles and rejected the triumvirs' attractive overtures. Before
long, however, the two leading members cemented their agreement with a
marriage alliance: Pompey married Caesar's daughter Julia.

When he entered office Caesar at once began to honour the promises that
he must have given to Pompey and Crassus. The most urgent matter was to
find land for Pompey's impatient veterans. Caesar therefore brought an agrarian bill before the Senate, by which a commission should be set up to acquire
and distribute land to the veterans and to some of the city poor. Despite the
need, the moderation of the measure, and the fact that Caesar had consulted
the Senate rather than the People, the Senators most foolishly allowed Cato
to persuade them to reject it. In disgust Caesar took his bill to the Comitia,
disregarding the obstruction of his colleague, Bibulus, and to make doubly
sure he brought some of Pompey's veterans into the Forum: the bill was
carried. Soon afterwards he found it necessary to introduce a supplementary
measure, the lex Campana, by which the already occupied ager Campanus was to
be redistributed to some veterans and fathers of large families. Unlike the first
bill, this was most harsh: it dealt a serious blow to an industrious peasantry
and deprived the Roman Treasury of its revenues from these lands. This
over-riding of civilian by military needs was in part the legacy of Marius.[17]

His other obligation to Pompey was settled by Caesar through a tribune,
P. Vatinius, who carried a bill by which Pompey's eastern acta were confirmed
en bloc.[18] He also paid Caesar's debt to Crassus by a measure which remitted
one-third of their contract to the Asian tax-collectors. Since the Senate had
refused help, Caesar thus turned to the People. After satisfying his two friends,
he next had to think of his own future, since he would clearly not be fobbed
off with the silvae callesque. Accordingly Vatinius carried a bill which gave
Caesar Cisalpine Gaul and Illyricum for five years (till the end of February
54?) with three legions and the right to appoint his own legates and to found
colonies. When the governor-elect of Transalpine Gaul suddenly died, on
Pompey's proposal the Senate made a virtue of necessity and added this
province and an extra legion to Caesar's command. At this time the German
chieftain Ariovistus asked to be recognized as a Friend of the Roman People,
and Caesar supported the appeal, perhaps hoping to keep him in play until he
himself was ready to drive the king out of Gaul. The triumvirs also secured
the recognition of Ptolemy Auletes as king of Egypt (cf. p. 91) in return for
a promise of 6000 talents. But in addition to these somewhat questionable

actions Caesar also carried some more statesman-like measures. He moved an excellent *lex Iulia de repetundis* which defined the powers of provincial governors (e.g. limiting the acceptance of gifts and requisitionings, and regulating the keeping of accounts). Another measure provided for the publication of senatorial resolutions and important news.

When in the course of 59 the existence of the triumvirate became clear, it met with considerable public criticism, including a pamphlet written by Varro which he entitled *The Three-headed Monster*, but attacks did not go much further than demonstrations in the theatre; abuse from Bibulus was disregarded. True, a professional informer named Vettius alleged that the Optimates were plotting to murder Pompey, but the charge was not substantiated.[19] The triumvirs, however, needed agents and Caesar planned to secure a friendly tribune to replace Vatinius in 58. He chose the young patrician, P. Clodius, who by a process known as *transitio ad plebem* became a plebeian in order to stand for the tribunate of the plebs. Caesar would find him useful for checking the Optimates, and also for keeping an eye on Pompey while he himself was away in Gaul. The triumvirs also secured co-operative consuls for the next year, L. Calpurnius Piso and A. Gabinius, and did not neglect, with the help of Clodius, to get important provinces for them, namely Macedonia and Syria.

6. CLODIUS[20]

Clodius, on entering his tribunate of 58, quickly moved four laws: (*a*) censors should expel senators only when both were in agreement and after judicial inquiry (in fact no censors were elected between 61 and 50); (*b*) no magistrates (tribunes were not included) should stop public businesses by observing ill-omens (this was the method that Bibulus had tried to employ against Caesar); (*c*) corn was to be distributed free to citizens; this removal of any price turned earlier schemes for cheap corn, such as that of C. Gracchus, into an unashamed dole and hastened the demoralization of the people, besides enhancing Clodius' own popularity; and (*d*) *collegia* (that is all associations apart from a few genuine old trade-guilds), which had been suppressed six years before, were to be legalized. This, like the corn law, was to have pernicious results: by forming political clubs, leaders could organize gangs of roughs, who increasingly dominated the political scene in Rome and disrupted order and security.

The triumvirs next used Clodius to remove from Rome two men whose presence was embarrassing: Cicero and Cato. Caesar first tried to spare Cicero by offering him a post on his staff in Gaul or abroad, but on Cicero's refusal he let Clodius have his head. Ever since the Bona Dea trial (p. 96) Clodius had hated Cicero and he now proposed a bill to outlaw anyone who condemned a Roman citizen to death without a trial. This was obviously aimed at

Cicero for his conduct to the conspirators in 63. Despite wide appeals, which evoked much sympathy, Cicero failed to move Pompey or Caesar, and was compelled to leave Rome: on the same day a bill was passed which officially exiled him and confiscated his property. While he was travelling south, however, he learnt that the bill had been amended to allow him to live anywhere not less than 400 miles from Rome. He crossed over to Macedonia, and it is pleasant to note that several friends had risked their lives by giving him shelter during his journey.

Cato was removed more gently: he was sent as pro quaestore pro praetore to announce the annexation of Cyprus on the excuse that its king Ptolemy had helped the pirates and to sell the king's property whose estates enriched the Roman treasury by 7000 talents. There was no military resistance and Ptolemy committed suicide; Cyprus was added to the province of Cilicia. If Clodius in proposing Cato's appointment had any hope that Cato might have lined his own pocket in the process and thus exposed himself to prosecution on his return, he was disappointed.[21]

Another departure from Rome was that of Caesar, who went off to Gaul: his campaigns are described in the next chapter. Clodius then began a series of humiliating attacks upon Pompey, though whether he received encouragement (or orders) from Caesar or Crassus in uncertain. These assaults became so violent that Pompey withdrew to his house and for some months took little share in public life. In 56 he was forced to organize a rival band of supporters under the able leadership of T. Annius Milo, and clashes between the two gangs became frequent: Rome unfortunately lacked a police force to maintain order. Under this pressure Pompey began to regret the exile of Cicero, whose friends had been agitating for his return. At last in August 57, as a result of Pompey's help and widespread support from country-towns of Italy, the Comitia Centuriata passed a consular law to recall Cicero.

Cicero's journey through Italy was like a triumphal procession, but in Rome he had a long struggle to get adequate compensation for his house which Clodius had destroyed.[22] He showed his gratitude to Pompey by proposing that he should be put in charge of the corn supply, because there was a shortage at the moment. By a consular bill Pompey was to receive proconsular imperium for five years with fifteen legates. A tribune C. Messius, then proposed much wider powers for Pompey, including maius imperium and military forces, but the former bill was carried. Messius had probably acted on his own initiative, but if he had been put up by Pompey or Pompey's friends, the result showed that Pompey was not willing to challenge either the Senate or Caesar by pressing for dictatorial powers. He accepted the lesser commission and with his usual administrative efficiency he soon relieved the shortage. He showed a similar unwillingness to challenge his rivals in another episode. In 57 the Senate ordered one of the consuls, Lentulus Spinther, to restore Ptolemy Auletes to his throne from which his subjects had driven him. But in 56 the friends of both Pompey (whom the king wanted) and Crassus begun to agitate for the commission to be entrusted to the triumvir of their choice. Again Pompey did not press the matter, which was allowed to lapse, but he will have been annoyed with Crassus. This feeling developed, as Pompey was increasingly attacked by Clodius' gang, which he believed to be instigated by Crassus. He even went so far as to allege in the Senate that there was a plot against his life and to accuse Crassus.

The triumvirate appeared to be breaking apart, as Cicero had always hoped it might.[23] In order to widen the rift Cicero attacked the absent member by proposing that sometime Caesar's Campanian land law should be discussed, suggesting perhaps not its cancellation but its suspension until more funds were available. About the same time L. Domitius Ahenobarbus, a consular candidate for 55, flung down a direct challenge to Caesar by announcing that if he was elected he would propose the recall of Caesar from Gaul as soon as possible. In reply Caesar, who had not started his annual campaigning but was still at Ravenna, called Crassus to confer, and then together they moved to Luca to meet Pompey, if he would come; after a short delay Pompey decided to join them. Some 120 senators then toiled all the weary way to Luca to wait on their masters: Cicero and others remained with more dignity and apprehension in Rome.

7. THE RENEWAL AND BREAKDOWN OF THE TRIUMVIRATE

At the conference at Luca the triumvirs decided to continue to work together and to secure their own futures. Caesar in particular needed considerably more time to complete the reduction of Gaul. This was to be given him, while Pompey and Crassus were to be consuls in 55 and thereafter to have respectively as their provinces the two Spains and Syria. Further, Clodius was to be restrained, Cicero was to be checked, and the task of restoring Ptolemy was to be entrusted to Gabinius.[23a]

Cicero could resist no longer. In a letter to Pompey he recanted and 'sang his palinode'. Then in the summer he had to make a public statement: in a speech to the Senate *De provinciis consularibus* he supported Caesar's claim to continue in Gaul and praised his achievements there. In 54 he even suffered the mortification of having to defend Vatinius and Gabinius in the courts. For the next few years he virtually dropped out of politics.[24]

After some disturbances and postponement the elections for 55 were finally held, and Pompey and Crassus entered on their second joint consulship. They employed a tribune, C. Trebonius, to propose that the two Spains and Syria should be allotted to the consuls for five years with considerable military powers, and that Pompey should have the right to administer his

Spanish provinces through legates so that he himself could stay near Rome. Despite opposition from two tribunes and from Cato, whom Pompey by exercising his augural authority had prevented from standing for the praetorship, the bill was carried. In addition to some lesser legislation the two consuls sponsored a *lex Licinia Pompeia* to prolong Caesar's proconsular command in both Gauls and Illyricum for five years until late in 50 (November?) or early 49.[25] Also a measure probably was carried by five tribunes (*lex Mamilia Roscia*, etc.) to supplement Caesar's land law of 59 and to secure land for his troops when needed. Pompey gave some magnificent Games when his new stone theatre in the Campus Martius was dedicated, but these were too brutal and lavish for cultured minds, as Cicero told his friends. Then before the end of the year, amid tribunician obstruction, Crassus went off to Syria to seek military glory in a Parthian war (see below), while Pompey was left in control at Rome and could continue to attend to the corn supply.

Two events soon destroyed the triumvirate. In 54 one of the chief bonds between Pompey and Caesar snapped when Pompey's wife, Julia, of whom he was really fond, died. When Caesar offered to renew the marriage alliance, Pompey declined and in 53 married Cornelia. Worse followed: in this same year came news of the disaster at Carrhae and the death of Crassus: another bridge, or buffer, between the two remaining triumvirs was gone. During these years disorder and corruption increased, and the future seemed to offer either anarchy or dictatorship. When 53 ended without consular elections having been held, men began to turn to Pompey, the more so when the gang-warfare culminated in the murder of Clodius by Milo: in the subsequent rioting his followers burned his body in the Senate House, which itself was burned down. The Senate declared martial law and gave Pompey as proconsul charge of a special levy.

If Pompey was going to assume unusual authority, he must take Caesar into consideration and so it was arranged that all ten tribunes should sponsor a bill to enable Caesar to stand for the consulship *in absentia* in order that he might step straight from his Gallic command into a consulship in Rome. Bibulus then proposed a bill which Cato supported and the Senate passed, that Pompey should be sole consul, i.e. consul without a colleague. He therefore now had consular and proconsular *imperium*, though only for a short time. As the trial of Milo for the murder of Clodius was approaching, Pompey carried two measures *de vi* and *de ambitu* which were applied retrospectively; they were probably not an indirect method of attacking Caesar, but were designed to facilitate the condemnation of Milo. Pompey was not yet completely reconciled with the Optimates, many of whom wanted to save Milo, and he had not made his final choice between them and Caesar. Cicero, who was defending Milo, for once in his forensic life, failed his client, intimidated in part by the troops with which Pompey had surrounded the court in order to counter the demonstrations of Clodius' supporters. Milo was condemned and went into exile at Massilia. When Cicero sent him a copy of the speech that he had meant to deliver, Milo ironically replied that he was glad the speech had not been made, since otherwise he would not have been enjoying the mullets of Massilia.

Pompey next carried two other measures. A law de iure magistratuum enacted that all candidates must appear in person. This may have been aimed at Caesar, but more probably the privilegium granted to him by the law of the ten tribunes would be valid against it; however, to avoid misunderstanding, Pompey personally added a clause to except Caesar. Pompey's second measure confirmed a senatorial resolution of 53 and prescribed a five years' interval between a magistracy and a promagistracy. This law, which superseded that of Gaius Gracchus (p. 30), may have been designed to check ambition and promote efficiency rather than to embarrass Caesar. It did, however, embarrass Cicero; since there was a shortage of available governors and he had not already held a proconsulship, he was reluctantly sent to Cilicia.[25a] Nor did Pompey neglect his own interests: though in the course of the summer he took a consular colleague, his new father-in-law Metellus Scipio, he secured a continuation of his command in Spain for five years. As he took no corresponding action on Caesar's behalf, this was clearly not in the spirit of the provincial arrangements agreed upon at Luca.

Meantime during 52 Caesar had weathered the storm of the revolt of Vercingetorix in Gaul and his campaigns were drawing to a successful conclusion. This will have stimulated the jealousy of Pompey and the apprehensions of the Optimates. Many of the latter therefore, men like Cato, Domitius Ahenobarbus, M. Brutus, the Metelli, Claudii Marcelli and Cornelii Lentuli, decided to turn to Pompey, even if not all of them approved of him. One of the consuls of 51, M. Marcellus, then moved to the attack. After securing the rejection of a request by Caesar that his command should be extended to the end of 49, he proposed that the Senate should consider the question of superseding Caesar on the ground that the Gallic war was over, and he challenged the validity of the law of the ten tribunes, though he met with tribunician vetoes. He then insulted Caesar by flogging a senator of Novum Comum as a demonstration that the town did not enjoy Roman citizenship when Caesar had been treating the Transpadanes as full citizens. Finally, he persuaded the Senate to agree that the possibility of a successor to Caesar should be discussed on 1 March 50.

To meet such attacks Caesar needed an agent in Rome and he secured the support of one of the tribunes of 50, a bankrupt young nobleman named C. Scribonius Curio, who promptly exercised his veto on 1 March.[26] Not long afterwards, when news came of a Parthian threat to Syria, the Senate voted that Pompey and Caesar should each send a legion: Pompey weakened Caesar by contributing a legion that he had lent in 53 to Caesar, who thus lost two; nor were the troops sent out of Italy, since better news came from the East. During the summer the consul C. Marcellus (cousin of the consul of 51) failed to persuade the Senate to compel Curio to withdraw his veto. Pompey remained undecided and outwardly ambiguous, and the year dragged on amid increasing apprehension of war. Then on 1 December Curio forced the Senate to vote on his proposal that both Caesar and Pompey should give up their commands and disarm: the motion was carried by 370 to 22 (such was the longing for peace), but it was promptly vetoed. The extreme Optimates refused to capitulate, and on the next day Marcellus asked Pompey to save the Republic and assume command of all forces in Italy. At last Pompey was driven to a decision: he accepted the call.

Caesar, who was in winter quarters near Ravenna, made several attempts to reach a compromise. M. Antony (tribune in 49) forced the consuls on 1 January 49 to read an offer from Caesar to implement Curio's earlier disarmament proposal; the consuls, backed by Pompey, refused to allow a vote. Metellus Scipio proposed that Caesar should be declared a public enemy unless he laid down his arms before a certain day (this will have been 1 March, if that was the terminal date of his command; otherwise, if this had already gone by, e.g. 13 November 50, it will have been a date to be fixed); the proposal was passed but vetoed by Antony. Cicero, who had just arrived back from Cilicia, tried to negotiate, but in vain. On 7 January Antony and a fellow-tribune were warned to leave the Senate, which then passed the *senatus consultum ultimum*; they fled to Caesar. From Ravenna Caesar advanced to Ariminum: in doing so he cast his die, because between these cities flowed the Rubicon, a little stream that separated his province of Cisalpine Gaul from Italy. The Civil War had begun.

If the technical responsibility for war rested on the shoulders of Caesar, it was clearly desired neither by him (witness his negotiations), nor by Pompey (witness his vacillations), nor by the vast majority of senators (witness their vote of 1 December), and still less by the bulk of the population of Italy who showed no enthusiasm to rise in defence of the constitution. Caesar himself perhaps put his finger on the point when, surveying the Optimate dead on the battle-field of Pharsalus, he exclaimed, 'Hoc voluerunt'. It was the small Optimate clique, the twenty-two senators who voted against disarmament, that forced the issue. Caesar had been compelled either to resort to force or go to Rome as a private citizen which would lead at least to political extinction and possibly to physical danger. The Optimate rump claimed to represent legitimate authority against a traitor, but their violation of the tribunician veto mocked their claims to legality. The hands of none of the leaders were spotless: behind them all gleamed the corrupting influence of power. No real principles were at stake. That was the tragedy. It was a struggle for personal power, prestige and honour, without regard for the *libertas* of others. Caesar frankly admitted that 'his *dignitas* had ever been dearer to him than life itself'. Of Pompey it was written: 'occultior non melior'.[27]

8. CRASSUS AND PARTHIA

The Parthian kingdom had been formed by a semi-nomadic people who moved into the Seleucid satrapy of Parthia in the mid-third century and gradually extended their rule from the Euphrates to the Indus, from the Caspian to the Persian Gulf, with their capital at Ecbatana. In their eastern expansion they were able to roll back a vast nomadic movement which had started when the Yueh-chi (or Tochari), driven out of N.W. China, had displaced on their march various tribes that were collectively called the Sacae. While the Yueh-chi overthrew the Greek kingdom in Bactria (Afghanistan), the Sacae broke into the Parthian province of Seistan (c. 128), from which they were soon driven out and forced eastwards to India. With peace established, the Parthian king made contacts with west and east. His envoys met Sulla in 92 on the Euphrates (p. 62) and he received an embassy from the Chinese Han emperor which opened up for Parthia the caravan Silk Route from China through Chinese Turkestan. In overrunning Seleucid Babylonia, the Parthians became masters of a Greek kingdom, but though they took over Greek methods of administration and made use of Greek secretaries, Greek science, and the Greek language for trading purposes, they were not deeply affected by Greek culture. When they conquered these wide areas, the native population naturally remained basically the same: the Parthians formed a landowning aristocracy of king and feudal nobles. The language that they used was a form of Persian (Pahlavi), but they have left no literature behind, although Greek literature flourished in the East in the first century B.C.: a 'History of Parthia' was written by Apollodorus of Artemita in Parthia, and a description of the empire was given by Isodore of Charax in his 'Parthian Stations'. It was rather in the art of war that the Parthians made original contributions. They relied primarily on cavalry, of two kinds. They bred a strong charger, on which the nobles fought as cataphracts, heavily mailed knights with huge spears. Besides these predecessors of the medieval knights, they employed horse-archers who were mounted on light horses and were armed with an asymmetrical bow, which they used with great skill in the 'Parthian shot' fired over the crupper as they pretended to flee. But though they had perhaps 6000 cataphracts and 40,000 horse-archers, the legion-minded Romans did not appreciate their strength – before Crassus!

The earlier friendly relations of Parthia with Rome were undermined by the folly of Pompey (p. 87) and by Gabinius, who as proconsul of Syria in 55 gave temporary support to a rebel brother of King Orodes II who had just come to the throne. It was the Romans, however, that turned to war. Crassus wanted a military reputation to balance that of his triumviral colleagues. Leaving Rome before the end of his consular year, he advanced with seven legions into Mesopotamia in 54, where he gained some success. Hoping to get some cavalry from his Armenian ally Artavasdes, he returned to the attack in 53. Orodes himself covered Armenia, and entrusted the defence of Mesopotamia to a member of the noble Suren family, a general of no mean ability. When Crassus gathered that Suren (his personal name is unknown) was in the desert east of the Euphrates, he decided to leave the protection of the river and march against the Parthian force: for this move he has sometimes been blamed, but he has also been justified on the ground that if his objective was Seleucia, he would at some time have had to risk crossing open country.

After a hard march the Romans reached a tributary of the Euphrates near Carrhae when Crassus learnt that the Parthians were on them. He formed his men into a square, and sent out a covering force of Gallic cavalry which his son Publius had brought from Caesar in Gaul. But in vain: Publius' men were overwhelmed. Meantime the main body was trying to stand up to the showers of Parthian arrows, which were discharged both straight and low and 'lobbed' in from above, so that the legionaries soon discovered that a shield could not cover both body and head. Those that survived, endured patiently, knowing that the enemy's ammunition must soon run out. But here they reckoned without the genius of Suren, who had organized a special corps of 1000 Arabian camels, one for every ten men, which brought up almost limitless supplies of arrows. After dark Crassus, who failed to risk a night attack on the enemy and their tired horses, abandoned 4000 wounded and retired to Carrhae. Without adequate provisions and deserted by his quaestor Cassius (later Caesar's murderer), he was forced by his demoralized troops to treat with the enemy. Though he knew he was riding into a trap, he met the Parthians, only to be cut down. Some 10,000 survivors ultimately reached Syria, while a like number were settled as prisoners by the Parthians at Merv (Alexandria) in Margiane not far from the Oxus.

The Parthians advanced again to the Euphrates, but an attack on Syria was delayed by the fact that Orodes suspected that Suren might be dangerously successful and had him killed. When they did invade Syria (51), they were soon driven out by Cassius. At Rome civil war distracted attention from the East, and Parthia did not renew her attacks. She was content with the result of Carrhae and with the legionary eagles that she had captured and was to keep for thirty years.[28]

VII

THE DOMINATION OF CAESAR[1]

1. CONDITIONS IN GAUL

When by the lex *Vatinia* in 59 (p. 98) Caesar received the provinces of Cisalpine Gaul and Illyricum, he must have been well satisfied. Cisalpine Gaul provided a fine recruiting ground and it was near enough to Rome to allow him to keep in touch with political events. He had in fact to fight on two fronts: while campaigning in the north he must defend and consolidate his political standing in Rome against all attacks. Further, Illyricum offered him the prospect of campaigning against Burebistas, king of the Dacians (living in what is now Romania), who had created an extensive empire in the Danubian lands and threatened the frontiers of Macedonia.[2] Since Caesar concentrated three of his four legions at Aquileia he appears to have intended to deal with this potential menace to the north-east frontiers of the Roman empire, where he might possibly have anticipated the achievement of Augustus. But when the Senate suddenly added Transalpine Gaul to his other provinces, the direction of his interest turned rather to the north-west.

Since the defeat of the Teutones at Aquae Sextiae by Marius, conditions in Gallia Transalpina had not been very happy: Roman *publicani* and business-men followed the armies, and Cicero in the speech which he delivered in defence of M. Fonteius, who had been governor c. 76–74 after a revolt stimulated by Sertorius' successes, reveals how heavy was the burden of the unfortunate provincials: 'Not a single sesterce in Gaul ever changes hands without being entered in the account-books of Roman citizens.' The governorship of L. Murena (64–63), who had Clodius on his staff, was not a happier period, and so unsatisfactory was the Roman response to an appeal for relief from debt from the Allobroges, whose envoys had made contact with the Catilinarian conspirators, that they rebelled (61) but were reduced after the destruction of Valentia (Valence).

Outer Gaul, or Gallia Comata ('long-haired Gaul') as the Romans called it, was a vast country. Its population was mixed but predominantly Celtic;[3] there was a substratum of pre-Celtic Iberians and Ligurians, but the Celts, who had come in from over the Rhine (from c. 800 B.C.), occupied most of the land. The Belgae, another group of Celts (with some German admixture), settled north of the Seine and Marne about 200, and not very long before Caesar's day some of them had crossed the Channel and settled in S.E. Britain. The civilization of the Gauls was mixed, in some respects advanced, in others backward. They practised agriculture and stock-breeding, mining and metallurgy. They made use of the fine river system to develop commerce, stimulated at first no doubt by the example of the Greek colony of Massilia near the mouth of the Rhone; and for trade they used coinage, both Greek and native copies. Their predominant language was naturally Celtic, but they did not know writing, except the Druids who used a Greek script. They had developed some small town centres (e.g. Avaricum = Bourges; Cenabum = Orleans), but they were politically backward. Most of their clans (pagi) had united into tribes (civitates) which were often at war with one another. Tribal kings survived among the Belgae and in Britain, but elsewhere they had mostly been replaced by aristocracies with one or more annual magistrates. The bulk of the population was probably in a state of semi-serfdom.

The nobility to some extent shared political power and wealth with the Druids, a privileged religious hierarchy which was excused from taxation and military service.[4] These priests, who met annually under an arch-Druid in the district of the Carnutes, took a large part in the administration of justice, but they probably did not greatly help the political unification of the country because they may have been divided among themselves as were the nobles. Their religious views are obscure, but they believed in the immortality of the soul, indulged in human sacrifice, and worshipped their gods in groves without temples or images.

Since the Gauls lacked political unity, their military efforts were naturally weakened by lack of organization, by tribal rivalries, and by a desire to scatter after battle for plunder or to return home. Their main arm was cavalry, though the Helvetii and Nervii still relied much on infantry; the war-chariot had gone out of use in Gaul, though not in Britain. The serfs and retainers of the nobles were not well-trained or disciplined. Thus Caesar may have hoped for easy victory.

Roman intervention resulted from two tribal movements, those of the Germanic Suebi, led by Ariovistus, and of the Celtic Helvetii. These two peoples had long been in hostile contact. From about 400 B.C. the Helvetii had occupied an area south of the Maine and east of the Rhine (Baden,

Wurttemberg, and part of Bavaria) until at the end of the second century they had been driven southwards into Switzerland by the German Suebi who in their expansion south-west reached the Rhine. Even in their new home the Helvetii were subjected to constant German pressure from the north. Soon, however, the Suebi were offered a chance to advance into Gaul. The strongest tribe in central Gaul, the Aedui (south-west of Dijon), who were friends of Rome, were at logger-heads with their easterly neighbours, the Sequani. The latter short-sightedly invited the Suebic Ariovistus to come to their help from over the Rhine. Nothing loth, he came and assisted them to defeat the Aedui, but then he settled down in Alsace with large numbers of his German followers, and refused to budge despite pressure from the Sequani and Aedui whom this common threat now united. The Aedui then appealed to their Roman friends, but the Senate failed to follow up an initial promise of help, and two years later Ariovistus was even recognized as a Friend of the Roman People, perhaps as a temporizing measure. The second disturbance arose from the Helvetii (in Switzerland); feeling German pressure from Alsace and from over the Rhine, they decided to seek new homes in western Gaul by a mass migration. This was planned to start in 58 and to pass peacefully through Roman territory near Geneva.

2. THE REDUCTION OF GAUL (58–56 B.C.)[5]

In the spring of 58 news reached Caesar that the Helvetii had burned their homes and were on the move, their men, women and children numbering over a third of a million. With one legion he hastened to block their route just west of Geneva and thus forced them northwards through the territory of the Sequani. He followed, joined soon by five more legions. His motives in thus seeking war with the Helvetii must remain uncertain, whether the desire for personal military glory or a genuine conviction that only by such action could the future safety of the frontiers of the Roman province be safeguarded; at any rate he rejected any attempt at a purely diplomatic settlement, as for instance an effort to unite the Gallic tribes against Ariovistus and the Germans. His excuse might be the Helvetian attack on his troops near Geneva or that on the Aedui after they had crossed the Saône. However that may be, he followed them up until he had to turn aside for supplies to the Aeduan capital of Bibracte (near Autun). The Helvetii, who unexpectedly followed him there, were decisively beaten after a tense struggle, but for the most part they were allowed to return to their original country, where they would help to cover the Roman province against German pressure.

Caesar was now urged by the Gauls to eject Ariovistus, whose earlier request to become a Friend of the Roman People Caesar himself had supported. This may not have worried Caesar unduly, but in any case Ariovistus made hostilities easier when in an interview later he insulted Caesar with some home-truths, including a reminder that Caesar's death would rejoice many a noble in Rome. Caesar then occupied Vesontio (Besançon), where for a moment his men wavered until they were recalled to duty by his threat to advance alone with his crack legion, the Tenth; never again during his Gallic campaigns did his troops falter. Confidence restored, he advanced through the Belfort Gap and along the eastern slopes of the Vosges until he encountered Ariovistus' force (perhaps near Cernay). After a tough struggle, which was only saved when young P. Crassus on his own initiative threw in the reserves on the left wing at the decisive moment, the Germans fled defeated to the Rhine; Ariovistus died soon afterwards.

Caesar put his troops into winter quarters at Vesontio outside his own province, and returned to Cisalpine Gaul. He may have believed that a with-drawal would provoke a fresh German invasion: at any rate, he was clearly taking over responsibility for the Rhine frontier and virtual control of the lands of the Aedui and Sequani. When news reached him that the great confederacy of the Belgae in the north-east was making military prepar-ations, no doubt in anticipation of further Roman advances, he raised two more legions in Cisalpine Gaul and in 57 marched against them. He established a bridge-head over the Aisne, where he gained the support of the Remi, and the Belgae who despite their numbers failed to organize a full-scale assault on his position gradually dispersed. The Suessiones (near Soissons), Bellovaci (around Beauvais) and Ambiani (near Amiens) submit-ted, but the Nervii further north (at Hainault) resisted and nearly defeated Caesar on the Sambre: however, he snatched victory from defeat, 'that day he overcame the Nervii'. Meantime young Crassus had advanced through Normandy and Brittany without real opposition. Thus in two years the greater part of Gaul had been over-run, if not conquered, and Cicero in Rome well might move that a public thanksgiving (supplicatio) of 15 days, an unprecedented length, be decreed by the Senate for Caesar's achievements.

In 56 it became clear that Gaul was by no means conquered. Caesar himself had to hurry off to Luca, where he reached the agreement by which his command would be prolonged until at least the end of 50: he could now plan on wider lines. Meantime the Veneti (in Brittany) had repented of their submission, especially when they heard rumours that Caesar might invade Britain and thus interfere with their cross-Channel trade. The Morini (opposite Dover) and the Menapii (at the mouth of the Rhine) also were restless, and another German invasion was feared. Caesar sent Labienus to watch the Germans and Belgae, while Q. Sabinus overran Normandy, and P. Crassus reduced the Aquitani in the south-west between the Garonne and Pyrenees. Caesar himself moved against the Veneti, but could achieve nothing by land, since most of their settlements were on peninsulas. At last a fleet under Decimus Brutus was made ready. In a naval action in Quiberon Bay the lighter Roman ships were at a disadvantage against the heavy oaken ocean-going vessels of the Veneti, until they managed to cut the enemy's rigging with scythes fixed on long poles: entirely dependent on sail, the Venetic ships were then at the mercy of the Roman oared fleet. Caesar took savage deterrent action against the Veneti: their councillors were executed and the population sold into slavery. Then he advanced against the Morini in Flanders, but their marshes saved them.

3. GERMANY AND BRITAIN (55–54 B.C.)

Two tribes, the Usipetes and Tencteri, who had been driven westwards over the Rhine by the Suebi, formed Caesar's next victims. When they refused his offer of land on the east of the Rhine, he annihilated them, probably near Xanten, and barbarously massacred their women and children. In Rome Cato proposed that Caesar should be handed over to the Germans, but his moral indignation will have been reinforced by political motives, and he achieved nothing. Caesar's terrible warnings to the Germans that they must keep to their side of the Rhine was strengthened by a Roman demonstration on the east bank. Skilled engineers built a trestle bridge over the river (near Andernach or the Lorelei) in ten days, but the army that crossed over met no massed enemy and after ravaging the lands of the Sugambri, returned after eighteen days, destroying the bridge behind it.

Though it was late in the summer (55) Caesar launched his first attack across the Channel on Britain.[6] His excuse might be the help that British tribes had given to the Gauls, but he will not have been unmindful of the glory that Pompey gained from conquests on the fringe of the known world, nor of the mineral wealth of the island. The Belgic tribes in the south-east had made considerable material progress, and apart from the old trade in Cornish tin, the island was reputed to be rich in pearls and precious metals. The invasion was brief. In face of the Britons Caesar effected a landing (near Deal?) with two legions, and the tribal chiefs in Kent submitted, but a storm wrecked his ships which were drawn up on the open beach; yet he succeeded in holding off hostile attacks, refitted his fleet and reached Bologne just before the equinox.

In 54 he returned to Britain with five legions and 2000 Gallic cavalry. Marching inland he met and defeated the Kentish forces near Canterbury, but had to return to the coast where his fleet had again been wrecked: he had not discovered an adequate harbour nor learnt the lesson of the previous year. He now turned to meet the Belgic chiefs who united their forces under Cassivellaunus, king of the Catuvellauni in Hertfordshire. After forcing the Thames, Caesar received the submission of the Trinovantes in Essex, who were hostile to Cassivellaunus, and stormed the king's stronghold (at Wheathampstead). Cassivellaunus then gave in, but there is no evidence to show that he ever provided the hostages and tribute that he promised. Caesar returned to Gaul, knowing that with S.E. Britain in a state of nominal submission he had at least paved the way for future conquest in the island if that was desired, but other matters claimed his attention.

4. REVOLT AND RECONQUEST

Gaul was restless. Even before the second British expedition there had been trouble among the Treveri and the Aeduan leader Dumnorix had been killed for disloyalty. Caesar was therefore compelled to spread his forces over a wide area of N.E. Gaul for the coming winter (54/3). Ambiorix, king of the Eburones (in the Ardennes) struck first and after treacherously luring the troops under Sabinus and Cotta out of their camp at Atuatuca (near Liège) he destroyed them. The Nervii tried the same trick on Q. Cicero (the orator's brother), but he wisely stood siege in his camp until relieved by Caesar who hastened up from his headquarters at Samarobriva (Amiens). Labienus managed to suppress the Treveri. During the winter Caesar increased his force to ten legions by raising two new ones and borrowing another from Pompey. In the course of the year he reduced the disunited rebels, the Senones, Carnutes, Menapii and Eburones; he also crossed the Rhine again. By devastating the country of the Eburones and executing some other leaders he attempted to overawe all opposition, but he probably sensed that all was not well.

News of disturbances in Rome after the death of Clodius in 52 encouraged a vast rising in central Gaul, which at last found a true leader in the Arvernian chief Vercingetorix. Caesar hastened back from Cisalpine Gaul, where he had spent the winter, but he reached his army at Agedincum (Sens) only with difficulty, coming through the thick snows of the Cevennes and eluding Vercingetorix, who in vain tried to force a scorched-earth policy on his supporters. After attacking and finally storming Avaricum (Bourges), Caesar sent Labienus against the Senones and Parisii and himself marched against Gergovia (near Clermont-Ferrand), but in attempting to storm the fortress he met with his first real defeat at the hands of the Gauls. This encouraged the Aedui to join the revolt. Caesar linked up with Labienus, who had won a victory near Lutetia (Paris) and then moved south, but on the way, perhaps near Vix, he fell in with Vercingetorix whom he worsted and forced into the hill-town of Alesia. Around this isolated hill Caesar built a double ring of the earthworks, one to keep Vercingetorix in, the other facing outwards against the inevitable Gallic army of relief.[7] This finally arrived, a quarter of a million strong if Caesar is to be believed, but its attack on his lines failed; it then withdrew and Vercingetorix surrendered in an attempt to save his men. After six years in captivity this great champion of Gallic freedom was led in Caesar's triumph and then executed.

After this titanic struggle the Aedui and Arverni submitted, but some other tribes fought on, perhaps in the knowledge that Caesar's command would soon end. The Bellovaci were not conquered until in 51 Caesar moved up seven legions against them, while some survivors from a defeated force of tribes in the west took refuge in the almost impregnable hill of Uxellodunum (north of the Dordogne) where they held out until Caesar cut off their water supply. One of the Gallic guerrilla leaders was Commius, whom Caesar in 57 had made king of the Atrebates and thereafter had used as an agent especially in Britain; he now managed to escape and fled finally to Britain, where he established a dynasty of the British Atrebates in Hampshire. Caesar spent the rest of the year and the next (50) trying to heal the savage wounds that he had inflicted on Gaul: in this he proved as successful as in war. He imposed a moderate tribute, which he left to the Gauls themselves to collect, and he left their tribal institutions alone. This conciliatory policy, though parallel to the *clementia* that he later showed to his political enemies in Rome, doubtless derived some support from the consideration that he would need a contented Gaul if he were to cross swords with the senatorial government. And for this struggle, if it came, he had won a devoted army, wealth and a reputation in arms to equal Pompey.

Few men could have achieved Caesar's success, which was perhaps only made possible within so short a period by the disunity of the Gauls themselves and, until Vercingetorix arose, by the lack of an accepted leader. Even Caesar, in more than one engagement, saw victory almost slipping from his grasp, and the Gauls' last desperate effort at Alesia long trembled in the balance. By common consent he is one of the world's greatest soldiers, and clearly his qualities can not be fully appreciated in a brief sketch of his campaigns, whether his strategic and tactical brilliance, his famous *celeritas*, his organization of supplies, his use of engineering skills, or his drive and personal magnetism which inspired all ranks. All these he needed to enable the better-armed and disciplined legionaries to overcome brave men who were fighting for their liberty.

The Gauls fought for freedom, but freedom for what? There is little to suggest that, if left alone, they would have composed their internal rivalries and have given their land peace instead of warfare. Indeed, if Rome had not stepped in, the Germans would probably have done so; and they would have brought, not a higher civilization, but a retrogression to barbarism. Whether Caesar, who did not shrink from ruthlessness and atrocity when he regarded these as necessary, always judged the need aright, unbiased by personal considerations and ambition, cannot be said with confidence. Roman civilization might have infiltrated into Gaul more peacefully, but only if the Germans did not flood over the Rhine. As it was, a generation bled, suffered and died, but the succeeding one enjoyed peace, thanks to their predecessors' sacrifice and to the wisdom of their conqueror's final settlement. His conquest of Gaul represents a vital act in world history: central Europe was opened up to Mediterranean civilization, and on the Celtic foundation there grew up a peaceful Latin civilization; this was made possible by Rome's hold on the Rhine frontier and it became so deeply rooted that, when the frontier finally broke as the Roman Empire itself collapsed centuries later, it survived the Germanic flood that followed and France emerged into the modern world as a Latin country. In that sense Caesar was the founder of France.

5. CIVIL WAR IN ITALY, AFRICA AND SPAIN (49 B.C.)[8]

When Caesar crossed the Rubicon (p. 104) the scales must have seemed heavily weighted against him. He had with him only one legion, control of the Po valley and of Gaul, and some political support in Rome, whereas Pompey, backed by the Senate, had all the rest of Italy, Spain, all the eastern provinces, and control of the sea and the corn-supply. But he had only two legions in Italy, and since these were the two that he had taken from Caesar (p. 103) he dared not risk an attack until he had raised more troops. Caesar struck first, with his usual speed: though it was winter, he pressed down the east coast, seized the passes to Etruria, and overran Picenum. Thus menaced, the consuls and Senate left Rome for Capua, and Pompey aimed at building up his forces in Apulia. His scheme was wrecked by the obstinate folly of L. Domitius Ahenobarbus, who had been appointed governor of Transalpine Gaul in succession to Caesar and was thus not subordinate to Pompey. Domitius, despite Pompey's advice and pleas,[9] insisted on trying to hold out against Caesar at Corfinium, where after a short blockade he was forced to capitulate. The addition of Domitius' men to Caesar's forces tilted the balance of legions against Pompey, who was thus compelled to withdraw to Brundisium, where he very skilfully embarked his men in face of Caesar's hasty attempt to thwart him; he then sailed across to Greece, leaving Caesar master of Italy after some two months' campaigning.

During these months at least three attempts at conciliation had been made. When Caesar was still at Ariminum he received an official communication from the Senate and a private message from Pompey. Caesar's reply envisaged roughly a renewal of their alliance, in which of course he would inevitably predominate. Though Pompey accepted most of Caesar's suggestions, negotiations broke down when Pompey insisted that he should continue to levy troops for the present. After the fall of Corfinium Caesar made another attempt, but the terms of Pompey's reply are not known; and again at Brundisium Pompey refused to meet him.[10] From Brundisium Caesar returned to Rome after taking steps to secure Sicily and Sardinia. Already he had got a praetor, L. Roscius, to carry a bill to grant full franchise to the Transpadanes.[11] When he reached Rome, no proscriptions followed on the pattern of Marius and Sulla: he merely collected what senators he could and tried to persuade them to renew peace negotiations with Pompey, but nothing came of it. Since he needed money, he disregarded tribunician obstruction, broke into the Aerarium and helped himself. Then leaving Aemilius Lepidus in charge of Rome as *praefectus urbi*, an office that had lapsed since the time of the Kings, and M. Antony in charge of Italy, after a fortnight in the capital Caesar went off to face the Pompeians in Spain: he had not got a fleet, so Pompey himself must wait.

Soon after this Pompey was joined by Cicero, who had spent some anxious months, first exerting himself for peace, and then trying to make up his mind whether to remain neutral or join Pompey. He owed this freedom of choice to the generosity of Caesar who had a frank discussion with him at Formiae when on his way to Rome; having failed to persuade Cicero to attend the Senate-meeting, Caesar left him unharmed. Finally, although his letters reflect no high opinion of Pompey's conduct or aims, Cicero decided that past loyalties demanded that he went to him. Pompey also received another unenthusiastic supporter when Cato joined him. At the approach of Caesar's legates Cato, who was organizing the defence of Sicily, had left the island in order to avoid needless bloodshed: if Caesar is to be trusted, Cato publicly blamed Pompey for having let him down by rushing into a 'non necessarium bellum'.

Sicily was thus occupied by Curio, to whom Caesar had entrusted the task of seizing Africa from its Pompeian governor, P. Attius Varus and his three legions. The political skill that Curio had hitherto exercised in Caesar's interests was not matched in the military field, where he lacked experience. After crossing to Africa he gained some initial successes around Utica, for which his legions optimistically hailed him as *imperator*, but then he had to face the forces of the Numidian king, Juba I, who had come to support the Pompeian cause: Juba was a personal enemy of Caesar, who many years before in Rome had pulled the king's beard in the heat of a quarrel. Lured into a trap in the Bagradas valley, Curio was killed and his army was annihilated. Africa, and its corn, remained in Pompeian hands for the next two and a half years.

Meantime Caesar was fighting for supremacy in Spain. On his way there he encountered the hostility of Massilia, which at first wished to remain neutral, but on the arrival by sea of Domitius, the governor of Transalpine Gaul, the city declared for Pompey. Caesar left Trebonius to conduct the siege with three legions and Decimus Brutus to command the fleet, and pressed on with six legions to Spain. There he faced five legions under two competent commanders, L. Afranius who had fought against Sertorius and in the East, and

M. Petreius, who had defeated Catiline in Etruria; in western Spain there were two more legions under M. Terentius Varro, more noted as a writer than soldier. Caesar found Afranius and Petreius entrenched at Ilerda by the Sicoris, a tributary of the Ebro. In the operations that ensued at one moment he ran short of supplies and was dangerously cut off by the spring rise of the river, but he succeeded in turning the tables and forced his enemies into a position where, cut off from supplies, they were compelled to capitulate. Caesar showed great clemency, pardoning the commanders and disbanding the men. He then marched south, received the submission of Varro at Corduba, and settled the province, granting Roman citizenship to Gades. In less than three months by brilliant generalship he had mastered Spain. Meantime Massilia, hard pressed by the blockade, was ready to surrender to Caesar on his return from Spain. In view of the city's past history and glories, Caesar allowed it to retain its autonomy, but deprived it of most of its territories: though it remained a centre of Greek culture, it quickly declined.

While on his way home Caesar learnt that four legions, which he had sent on ahead to Placentia, were restless. On his arrival a mere threat to decimate the Ninth and the execution of a dozen ring-leaders sufficed to quell this incipient mutiny. Shortly before this he had heard that Lepidus, as praetor, had failed to get special permission to hold the consular elections for 48, and in default had carried a law appointing Caesar dictator. As Caesar's main need was to secure the consulship (this being the issue on which his dispute with the Senate had hinged), his dictatorship was perhaps more limited in scope than that of a 'dictator rei publicae constituendae' as Sulla, and may only have authorized him to hold the elections (*comitiorum habendorum causa*) and the Latin Festival: in the fourth and third centuries dictators had often been appointed for such special non-military duties. When he reached Rome he held the elections, at which he won his second consulship, celebrated the Festival, and then, relying perhaps on the *imperium maius* inherent in a dictator's office, he carried some necessary legislation, helping debtors (by methods which involved creditors in an average loss of a quarter of the principal), forbidding hoarding large sums of cash, and recalling exiles.[12] Then having held his first dictatorship for eleven days, he abdicated.

6. WAR IN GREECE, EGYPT AND ASIA (48–47 B.C.)

Meanwhile Pompey had gone to Thessalonica, and by drawing upon the resources of the eastern provinces and client kings he was able to build up a force of some 36,000 legionaries, together with at least 300 ships which were commanded by Bibulus. He had with him, however, some 200 senators, and although he had been chosen commander-in-chief, he found it difficult to impose unity of purpose on these Roman nobles. To prevent these forces increasing still further Caesar had to act quickly. He hastened to Brundisium and despite the risk of winter navigation he got seven legions across the Adriatic early in 48, but Bibulus attacked his transports on their return and blockaded Brundisium. Caesar had occupied Apollonia, but he was prevented from winning Dyrrhachium through the sudden appearance of Pompey who had been hastening to the west. He was in fact in a very difficult position, but at last in the early spring M. Antony managed to slip across with four more legions, eluded Pompey and joined forces with Caesar, who then took up a position just south of Dyrrhachium. Pompey, who had avoided a pitched battle, camped a little south of Caesar, and secured himself by establishing fortified lines on a semicircle of hills that ran behind the coast and thus enclosed his whole position. Caesar then built an outer line of fortifications some fifteen miles long; these cut Pompey completely off by land, but not by sea. As the weeks went by, Caesar found his own supplies diminishing, and after he had repulsed at heavy cost a full-scale attack by Pompey on his lines, he was compelled to try to break away. This he managed successfully; he reached Apollonia and then made eastwards for Thessaly and its corn-fields.

Pompey followed and when he camped on higher ground opposite Caesar near Pharsalus[13] he outnumbered his opponent very considerably. At first he declined to engage, but then decided to fight on the very day that Caesar determined to move off. He hoped that the superiority of his cavalry would give him the victory, but Caesar thwarted this by posting obliquely behind his own line a reserve of eight cohorts who used their *pila* as stabbing spears. Caesar then threw in his third line with devastating effect. Pompey quickly rode off the field: his losses numbered some 6000 dead and 24,000 captured. As Caesar surveyed the stricken field and the Optimate dead, he cried, 'They would have it thus' (*hoc voluerunt*).

Pompey fled with a few friends to Egypt, but as he stepped ashore he was murdered on Ptolemy's orders. His death at least smoothed the path of Caesar, who arrived three days later: it is unlikely that he would have felt able to show the same generosity to him as to lesser opponents or that, if he had, Pompey would have chosen to have survived as a living example of his conqueror's *clementia*. Pompey was widely mourned. Cicero, who had been so drawn to him and yet disappointed in him, wrote: 'non possum eius casum non dolere: hominem enim integrum et castum et gravem cognovi'. His private life commanded respect in a period of increasing licence, and he won the affection of Julia and Cornelia, whom he had married for political reasons. In political life he had shown lack of understanding and of sureness of touch: the puzzled frown seen on his portraits reflects a frequent hesitation, arising in part from an innate moderation. Ambitious he was, but he sought glory before power: the violence of his earlier days and his great military gifts secured for him immense authority, both official and private. This, at the moment of inescapable decision, he placed at the service of an unworthy Senate, whose control his own earlier career had done so much to weaken, in an attempt to uphold constitutionalism and his own *dignitas* alike. His gifts as soldier and administrator raised him high above his contemporaries and made him a worthy opponent of Caesar; he lacked only that final spark of genius that set Caesar apart.[14]

The political scene in Egypt was disturbed. Ptolemy Auletes, who had finally been restored to his throne by Gabinius at Pompey's instigation, had died in 51 and left his kingdom to his son Ptolemy, aged about ten, and his daughter Cleopatra, aged about eighteen, whom he commended to the care of the Roman People. Around the young joint-rulers, who married one another, gathered a motley crowd of advisors and adventurers, including some Roman troops whom Gabinius had left behind. One court faction soon succeeded in driving Cleopatra out of Alexandria, but she had just returned at the head of an army when news came of Pompey's approach: the young king's advisors bid for Caesar's support and treacherously effected Pompey's murder. Three days later Caesar arrived with a small force of some 4000 men. When he decided to settle Egypt and collect the money which Auletes had promised to pay the triumvirs for his recognition, his autocratic manner soon enabled Ptolemy's supporters to rouse the royal guard and the Alexandrian mob against him: he was besieged in the palace quarters of the city through the winter (48/7), while he awaited reinforcements from Asia. Meantime Cleopatra, who wanted to put her claims before the would-be Roman arbitrator, had been smuggled by a boatman into the city and palace. She was, like all the Ptolemies, a Macedonian not an Egyptian; of unbounded ambition and energy, she was highly cultured and amusing, charming rather than beautiful. Caesar was captivated, and Cleopatra stayed on in the palace as his mistress.

During the winter one legion reached Caesar, and there was some stiff fighting by sea in and around the harbours: at one moment Caesar had to swim for his life. But in the spring a force, which a certain Mithridates of Pergamum had raised for Caesar in Syria, arrived; Caesar managed to join hands with it and together they defeated the army of young Ptolemy in the Nile Delta. Ptolemy fell in battle, and his crown was transferred to a younger brother, Ptolemy XIV, but Cleopatra remained the effective ruler. Caesar is said to have spent the next two months with her on a tour up the Nile, but he had to hurry off to Asia Minor where Pharnaces, the son of Mithridates and ruler of the Bosporus, had overrun Cappadocia and Armenia Minor, defeated at Nicopolis Cn. Domitius Calvinus whom Caesar had sent against him, and then occupied Pontus.[15] Caesar left three legions in Egypt and set off to deal with Pharnaces, whom he defeated in a brilliantly swift campaign of five days at Zela, after the king had rashly launched an attack up-hill; later at his triumph in Rome Caesar displayed his famous message summing up the campaign: 'veni, vidi, vici' He rewarded Mithridates of Pergamum by granting him the eastern part of Galatia and the vacant realm of Bosporus, but in trying to occupy the latter Mithridates was killed. Now at last, in the course of the summer (47) Caesar was free to return to Italy.

7. THE END OF THE CIVIL WAR

Caesar was badly needed in Italy. In 48 B.C. attempts by the praetor Caelius Rufus to obstruct the working of Caesar's debt-law had caused such rioting that the consul Servilius, fortified by the senatus consultum ultimum, deposed him from office. Caelius was joined by Milo, who returned from exile, and both caused further disturbances in Italy until they were killed. Soon came the news of Pharsalus, and the return of Antony with some of the victorious troops. Servilius then named Caesar in his absence dictator for a second time, probably 'rei gerundae causa' and for a year from October 48; Antony was appointed his Magister Equitum.[16] No consuls were elected for 47. Antony's task was to keep order in Italy. This was made difficult by Cicero's unprincipled son-in-law, Cornelius Dolabella, who as tribune in 47 agitated against the debt-law with such virulence that the Senate empowered Antony to keep troops within the city. More serious was the dissatisfaction of some of Caesar's veterans in Italy who were awaiting his arrival for their rewards and discharge. They even marched on Rome, but Caesar was back just in time: he suddenly appeared on the tribunal in the Campus Martius and addressed them as 'Civilians' (Quirites, or 'citizens') unworthy any longer to serve under him. Rebuked, they returned to their allegiance.

Caesar then had much to do in a short time, short because the survivors of all the Pompeian forces were mustering in Africa in such menacing numbers that he must go there himself. Consuls were elected for the last three months of the year (47), Caesar's dictatorship probably ended in October, but he retained proconsular imperium (possibly maius), and he was elected to his third consulship for 46. To ease the tense economic situation he released tenants from the payment of small rents for a year and remitted interest that had accrued since the start of the war. He rewarded his followers, many of whom were made senators, and he pardoned many Pompeians who submitted. His generosity is illustrated by his first meeting with Cicero after his return: 'when Caesar saw him coming to meet him, he dismounted and embraced him and walked several furlongs talking with him alone. Thereafter he treated him consistently with respect and good will'. Cicero could now return in peace to his literary life. Caesar sailed for Africa.

The Pompeians who had held Africa since the defeat of Curio, had gathered ten legions, while king Juba brought four more; their cavalry numbered

15,000. The Roman forces were commanded by Pompey's father-in-law,
Q. Metellus Scipio, whose most competent legate was T. Labienus, the only
officer of the Gallic wars to have deserted Caesar for Pompey's camp.[17] So
urgent was the need to grapple with these forces that Caesar took the risk of
shipping his troops over by detachments during the winter (47/6). After
landing with the first group on the east coast of Tunisia, he was taken partly
off guard by Labienus and Petreius at Ruspina but saved the day by a bold
manoeuvre. When the rest of his troops arrived he had eight legions and was
ready to face the enemy. While he was besieging Thapsus, which lay on the
coast and was approached by two corridors of land on either side of a large
lagoon, he managed to tempt Scipio into the western corridor and force him
to stand and fight. Caesar quickly broke and rolled up his line, but in the
moment of victory his men got out of hand and spared none of the enemy.
Few escaped: Labienus and Pompey's son Sextus managed to reach Spain,
where his brother Gnaeus Pompeius was trying to establish himself. Cato,
who was holding Utica, on finding the position hopeless committed suicide:
'victrix causa deis placuit, sed victa Catoni'. His death symbolized the death
of the Republic, which he had loyally if short-sightedly sought to uphold
with unbridled vigour all his life: under the Principate he was idealized as the
martyr of Republican liberty and a paragon of Stoic virtues.[18]

When news of Thapsus reached Rome in the spring (46), fresh honours
were voted for Caesar. He was appointed praefectus morum for three years and
dictator (for the third time) for ten years (with perhaps a formal annual
designation), the dictatorship being more probably 'rei publicae constituendae' than 'rei gerundae causa'. On his return Caesar at last celebrated a
fourfold triumph of unparalleled magnificence over Gaul, Egypt, Pontus and
Africa. He gave cash bounties to his troops and 100 denarii to every citizen;
they were also entertained by feasts and shows. He pardoned more of
his enemies, including M. Marcellus (who had flogged the Transpadane:
cf. p. 103) and Q. Ligarius (who, already pardoned after Pharsalus, had again
fought against Caesar at Thapsus); Cicero spoke in public on behalf of both
men, praised Caesar's generosity and urged the need for social reform.[19] This
task Caesar now began to undertake: his measures are discussed in the following section. Less popular was his treatment of Cleopatra: he enrolled her
among the Friends of the Roman People, put her statue in the temple of
Venus Genetrix, and installed her with her infant son Caesarion (of whom he
was almost certainly the father) in his suburban house on the Janiculum. But
he could not continue uninterrupted with his measures of reconstruction:
one more campaign must be fought. Pompey's sons had built up a formidable force of thirteen legions in Spain and Caesar himself must now follow
the legates whom he had sent on ahead. He left Lepidus, who was both
his fellow-consul and his Magister Equitum, together with eight praetorian

prefects, to look after Italy, while his agents Balbus and Oppius kept an eye on affairs less officially. When finally Lepidus held the consular elections for 45, Caesar was elected consul, for the fourth time, without a colleague. Before the end of 46 he had left for Spain.

Although the Pompeians had the help of Labienus and were in control of most of the Baetis (Guadalquivir) valley, the campaign was brief. The decisive battle was fought at Munda, between Seville and Malaga, where the Pompeians had the advantage of a slope: it was touch-and-go during a long grim struggle until at last Caesar's Tenth legion pushed back the enemy's left wing, which was then assailed by the cavalry of the Mauretanian king, Bogud. The slaughter of the Pompeians was heavy: of the leaders only Sextus Pompeius escaped. After occupying Corduba, Hispalis (Seville) and Gades, Caesar punished severely the districts that had supported the Pompeians, and made some preliminary arrangements for the colonies that he planned to settle in Spain.

At news of Munda the Senate voted fresh honours to Caesar, including the title Liberator. On his return he celebrated another triumph. His dictatorship had been automatically renewed, but in October he resigned his (sole) consulship, and two of his nominees were elected *consules suffecti*. One of them, however, died on the last day of the year and Caesar gave offence to the nobles by having another suffect appointed for the day, thus cheapening the office. He now remained in Rome until his death. He was elected to his fifth consulship for 44, with Antony as his colleague; he received further excessive honours (see below); and finally, probably about mid-February 44 (perhaps when his ten-year dictatorship was due for its formal annual renewal), he was made instead Dictator Perpetuus. The Ides of March soon followed.

8. REFORM AND RECONSTRUCTION

Over thirty years earlier another dictator had tried his hand at reform after a civil war, but Caesar's task was easier in at least one respect: he had not to face recriminations arising from proscriptions or confiscations in Italy, but rather he had readily pardoned his enemies, both individual leaders and bodies of troops. All men were impressed by his clemency, and Cicero had openly urged him in 46 to restore the Republic to health by social reform, a plea that was re-echoed in a pamphlet attributed to Sallust.[20] Caesar responded to the need with restless energy in the intervals between his campaigns abroad: in view of the short time that he spent in Rome the amount and variety of legislation that he sponsored is amazing and its incompleteness understandable.

A whole series of measures was designed to improve administrative efficiency and to benefit Rome and Italy. One of the best-known was his reform (in 46) of the calendar, which kept getting out of gear with the solar year: this was both inconvenient and, because priests could intercalate months at will, often led to political trickery. With the advice of an Alexandrian astronomer Caesar added three (instead of the normal one) intercalary months to 46 B.C. and introduced a reformed calendar: this Julian calendar, with some slight adjustments by Pope Gregory XIII which were introduced into Britain in 1752, is still in use. Caesar carried a less effective sumptuary law to check extravagance. He suppressed all *collegia*, except genuine old trade guilds and the gatherings (synagogues) of the Jews who had helped him in Alexandria. He excluded the *tribuni aerarii* (p. 82) from the *quaestiones*, which were now shared equally by senators and Equites. He even planned to codify Roman civil law, a huge task not accomplished for 500 years. His measures to relieve debt have already been mentioned. He cut down the list of recipients of free corn from 320,000 to 150,000 because he was planning colonies for some of the surplus city population.[20a] He improved the city itself by new buildings, which included a new Forum (Forum Iulium) to relieve congestion and a basilica; he planned a public library in charge of Varro, together with schemes to prevent the Tiber flooding the city; in his new Forum he dedicated a temple to Venus Genetrix, the goddess from whom the Julian *gens* claimed descent. He also drafted measures to provide for the unkeep of roads, the regulation of traffic, and the use of open spaces. In Italy he planned to build a new road over the Apennines and to extend the area available for agriculture by draining the Pomptine Marshes and the Fucine Lake. To mitigate the danger of brigandage and to help unemployment he enacted that at least one-third of the *pastores* on the large ranches should be free men. He re-imposed harbour-dues (*portoria*) which had been abolished in 60 B.C., to help Italian industry. He planned to construct a harbour at Ostia to facilitate imports, especially corn. He introduced a new gold coinage, the first regular issue in this metal. Though he did not carry a general law to standardize the municipal administration of all Italy, he did draft some regulations that were carried a few months after his death by Antony. These established qualifications for local magistrates and membership of local senates: undesirables, such as gladiators or bankrupts, were excluded, but not apparently freedmen; municipal censuses were also regulated.[21]

During his first consulship in 59 Caesar had shown his regard for the provinces by his *lex de repetundis* (p. 98). He now saved some of them from the worst exactions of the tax-gatherers: he had fixed the tribute which Transalpine Gaul was to pay, and in 48 he abolished the tithe system in Asia for which he substituted a land-tax of fixed amount, thus eliminating the middlemen; the same system was also applied to Sicily. A measure, however, which limited proconsular governorships to two years and propraetorian to one year, may have had less regard for the interests of the provincials than for the potential danger arising from longer terms of office: Augustus later provided for longer governorships in the interests of the provincials.[22] More important, however, was the fact that by indirect methods Caesar began to break down the barriers between Italy and the provinces, through the number of Romans that he settled in the provinces and by his liberal grants of Roman citizenship to provincials.

To meet the needs of his veterans, who wanted to return to civilian life, and those of the superfluous proletariat in Rome, Caesar planned no less than twenty colonies which are reckoned to have provided new homes overseas for some 100,000 citizens: though Gaius Gracchus had first breached the older prejudice against overseas settlement, nothing on this scale had yet been thought of. In view of his military plans (see below) Caesar was not ready to disband all his troops: in fact in 44 B.C. he still had thirty-five legions under arms. But many veterans of the Gallic wars (perhaps 20,000) were settled, some in Africa and Corinth, men from the Sixth legion at Arelate in Gaul and from the Tenth at Narbo; for the rest land was found in Italy. The overseas settlements received the status of Roman or Latin colonies, some of them being planned at sites that offered commercial or industrial opportunities. Colonies founded or planned by Caesar include Carthage, Clupea and Cirta in Africa, Carthago Nova, Hispalis and Tarraco in Spain; not so many were sent to the Greek east, but these included Corinth and Sinope. Part of the charter of one of these colonies survives, that of Colonia Genetiva Iulia at Urso (modern Osuna) in Spain, and it illustrates their nature: perhaps the most important clause is that specifying the right of freedmen to hold the office of local senator (*decurio*) which reveals Caesar's generous policy to this class.[23]

One reason for sending these settlements overseas was that land was more readily available and was cheaper outside Italy, but Caesar must have been conscious that these settlers would help to spread Roman ways of life in the provinces. The other side to this policy was his extensive grant of Roman citizenship to provincials, both individuals and groups. He enfranchised the whole Legio Alaudae, which he had raised in Narbonese Gaul, and provided for the future enfranchisement of doctors and teachers in Rome. In the provinces he tended to grant citizenship to those areas where there had been a certain amount of Italian immigration, while he gave Latin rights to communities where the native element predominated. Thus Gades (Cadiz) and Olisipo (Lisbon) received citizenship, and towns such as Tolosa, Vienna (modern Vienne), Avenio (Avignon) and all the towns of Sicily were given Latin rights.[24]

9. POLICY AND ADMINISTRATION

Caesar's expenditure was lavish. His building programme and public works might give employment, but they cost money. So did his veteran settlement, and he virtually doubled the pay of the thirty-five legions that he retained. He had, however, raised large sums of money from the cities that had opposed him (thus, e.g., Thapsus and Utica had to pay large fines), and as the war went on he was less careful to spare the estates of stubborn Pompeians. He also looked after the Treasury when necessary: e.g. in 46 when no quaestors had been elected, he entrusted it to two of his prefects. The reduced corn-dole and the restored portoria would help, but economy was not indispensible: the Treasury contained 175 million denarii and Caesar's own estate was worth 25 million. There was enough for the moment; if need arose, excuse might be found to annex Egypt (and pacify Cleopatra), while further conquests would bring in yet more treasure.

Caesar was in fact planning further warfare. As far back as 58 he had been conscious of threats to the north-east frontier (p. 107). Ten years later he sent Gabinius to check the Delmatae (in Bosnia); Gabinius was defeated, but his successor Vatinius was somewhat more successful. More serious was the growth of the Dacian empire of Burebistas farther east. Caesar planned that in 44 he would march against him, as a preliminary to a great attack on Parthia. He expected to be away three years and in order to avoid a second Carrhae he strengthened his legions with 10,000 horsemen and a body of archers and proposed to advance through Armenia rather than Mesopotamia. His motives are uncertain. True, he had a slight excuse in that Caecilius Bassus, a Pompeian, who had been giving trouble in Syria, had received some help from Parthia. To avenge Crassus would be popular, to win further military glory would make Caesar's grip on Rome yet tighter. Before he left he made sure that the important provinces in the west and the eighteen legions in them were in the hands of governors that he could trust. Had he lived, he might well have anticipated Augustus in advancing the Roman frontier to the Danube, though the rumours that he intended to return through Russia and Germany may be exaggerations; how he would have settled the eastern frontier remains unknown.

Caesar no doubt intended that during his absence the Senate should continue to exercise its old functions: he could be more happy about this in view of its present composition. Depleted by civil war, it needed replenishing; further, if it was to provide half the iudices (p. 122), its numbers could well be increased. Caesar therefore raised its numbers to 900. He had come to power as a princeps, as a faction leader, whose party comprised senators, equites and centurions, businessmen and provincials, kings and dynasts. After his victory these required their suitable rewards, and for some this would be entry into the Senate. Thus the new senators would naturally be his adherents. A very few were centurions, freedmen or provincials: the stories of the trousered Gauls who did not know the way to the Senate-House merely parodies the fact that Caesar admitted a few notables from Gaul (who may indeed have been of Roman origin). A large number of the new senators will have been Roman knights, men of substance, many of them from the propertied classes of the Italian towns, men who had made their wealth from agriculture, industry or banking. In so far as they came from the parts of Italy enfranchised during the Social War, Caesar's policy will have helped to unite Italy – whether or not that was one of his conscious motives – and Cicero's phrase *tota Italia*, which the end of that war had made a theoretical reality, now began to be realized in fact.[25] This newly constituted Senate, in which a majority owed allegiance to Caesar, would obviously reflect his wishes despite a small surviving Optimate opposition. Further, he had taken care to gather into his own hands control of those functions that the Senate had in the past regarded as peculiarly its own: finance, foreign policy and the provincial commands. True, he often consulted it even here (e.g. the privileges that he had granted to the Jews were confirmed by a *senatus-consultum*), but at the other extreme Cicero once complained that his name had been added to a draft decree at a meeting which he had not even attended. With the bulk of the Senate acquiescent, Caesar must have felt that he could leave Rome with safety.

Caesar also controlled the magistrates. He increased their numbers, raising the praetors from 8 to 16, the aediles from 4 to 6, and the quaestors from 20 to 40, but he did not thereby increase their prestige.[25a] As dictator he was not subject to the tribunician veto and he had superior imperium to all other magistrates whom he could thus control. He was even offered the right to nominate some of the magistrates, but he preferred merely to control the elections. It may also be noted that he received the right to create new patricians and to grant priesthoods. Though he did not interfere directly with the consulship, his attitude towards it gave great offence to the older nobility. It has been seen that no consuls (nor any curule magistrates) were elected for 47 or for 45 until the last months of the year (pp. 119, 121), while in 46 he appointed eight prefects who helped the Master of the Horse, Lepidus, to manage affairs in Rome (probably starting in 45) during his own absence in Spain. Thus by overshadowing both magistrates and Senate, Caesar was becoming dangerously powerful.

10. CAESAR'S AUTOCRACY

In the last resort Caesar's power might rest on the support of his legions and veterans, but it had been vested in proper constitutional forms. Its basis was the dictatorship, which had been granted to him in varying forms and for varying periods, but which early in 44 he received 'for life'. Compared with this all his other offices were secondary. His consulships (in 48 and 46–44) had been useful in cloaking his rise to power in Republican form: even his sole consulship in 45 had a precedent in that of Pompey in 52. He had not sought the tribunate as a means either to win popularity or to introduce reform, though he knew how to use tribunes (as Trebonius or Curio) for his personal advantage. As a patrician he could not have held the office unless he had followed Clodius' example of becoming a plebeian, nor did he receive in 48 the authority of a tribune (*tribunicia potestas*) as the historian Dio Cassius records; but in 44 he was granted the personal inviolability of the tribunes (*sacrosanctitas*) and the right to sit with them on certain public occasions.[26] He had been Pontifex since 63 and augur since 47: he was thus well-placed to control the religious organization of the State. He could exercise censorial powers through the *praefectura morum* which he had received in 46. Like other victorious generals, he had been hailed by his troops as *imperator*, but he did not use this word as a title to describe his power, nor as a *praenomen*.[27] He needed neither additional titles nor the further powers (e.g. to declare war and make peace) that some later writers wrongly ascribe to him. The dictatorship, which raised him above the veto of tribunes and the *imperium* of all other magistrates, was enough. He could dominate Senate, magistrates and people: his patronage was all-pervasive.

Honours were heaped on him especially in the last few months of his life: some he welcomed as deserved, others merely reflected the empty flattery of an obsequious Senate. The month Quinctilis was renamed Iulius (July). After Munda he was named Parens Patriae, and in the games which celebrated the battle his statue was carried with that of Victory. His statue was placed in the temple of Quirinus (deified Romulus), another near those of the kings of Rome, and yet another showed him with a globe beneath his feet; his chariot was set up opposite the temple of Juppiter. As a *triumphator* he was granted the right to a gilded chair, a triumphal robe and a laurel crown on public occasions. In 44 his head appeared on Roman coins, a practice developed by Hellenistic kings but not despised two years later by so good a Republican as Brutus.[28] A temple was erected to his Clemency; a new college of priests, the Julian Luperci, was established (two other *gentes*, the Fabii and Quinctii, were already linked in this way with the Luperci); and a priest (*flamen*) was appointed, perhaps in Caesar's honour rather than for his worship. Antony was made the *flamen*, but it is not probable that Caesar was associated with Juppiter by the grant of a title Juppiter Julius, nor that a cult was created in his honour in Rome during his life-time. The evidence for such a view is confusing and confused, since soon after his death a cult of Divus Iulius was established. Whatever the truth, it is unlikely that Caesar himself deliberately sought divine worship for himself in Rome, though Roman generals in

Greece and the East had received divine honours for the last 150 years: in this Caesar was no exception when he was described in an inscription at Ephesus as 'god manifest and common saviour of the life of man'.

Caesar had acquired autocratic power, but whether he intended to use this authority to overthrow the Republic and become king remains uncertain. The meaning of several incidents early in 44 is ambiguous. Two tribunes, Flavus and Marullus, removed a diadem (the symbol of monarchy) which had been put on Caesar's statue, and said that he had threatened to punish anyone who spoke of him as king; they also prosecuted persons who hailed Caesar as Rex when he was returning from the Latin Festival (26 January); Caesar had replied that he was not King but Caesar ('non sum rex sed Caesar'; Rex was a Roman cognomen, just as King is an English surname). At the Lupercalia on 15 February he refused a diadem which was offered to him by M. Antony, his colleague in the consulship; he ordered it to be dedicated to Juppiter Capitolinus and an entry to be recorded in the Fasti that he had declined royalty. Then a Sibylline oracle was discovered, which was interpreted to mean that the Parthians could only be defeated by a king: and Caesar was preparing his Parthian expedition. Only rumours about this interpretation were known before it was officially reported to the Senate: how Caesar would then have tried to counter this move cannot be known. If it is believed that Caesar was seeking monarchy, all these incidents will be interpreted as his efforts to win it: for instance, if when Antony offered him the crown the crowd had gone wild with enthusiasm, he would have accepted it. On the other hand they can be explained otherwise, some as attempts by Caesar to kill rumours that he wanted to become king and others as attempts by his political enemies to embarrass him.

Some have thought that Caesar sought to become a Roman rex, reviving the monarchy that had preceded the Republic five hundred years earlier, despite the hatred which the Romans had for the word rex. Others have believed that he found a model for his would-be monarchy in the Hellenistic kings, whom, one by one, Rome had overthrown. This view, that he wished to be Basileus not Rex, may find support in contemporary rumours that he intended to transfer the capital to Alexandria and to marry Cleopatra and legitimize their son Caesarion. But far more probably these rumours were set on foot by his political enemies in order to discredit him; nor is it likely that, although he had spent a winter in Alexandria, he thought highly of Hellenistic monarchy as a form of government. Monarchy suggests the need for dynastic planning. But although Caesar, who had no legitimate son, adopted his grand-nephew Octavian, there is no decisive evidence that he intended the young man to 'succeed' him. The idea that he named Octavian as his Magister Equitum belongs to the propaganda of his enemies, while a clause in his will, appointing guardians for any son that might be born to him, suggests that he thought his wife Calpurnia might yet bear a son. Others again believe that Caesar had not yet reached a final determination to destroy the form of the Republic. It is true that with realistic vision he regarded the Republic as 'appellatio sine corpore ac specie'. He had not fought his way to victory and power in order to let the world relapse into anarchy, and if he could brand Sulla's retirement from the dictatorship as political ineptitude, he scarcely would have repeated the mistake. He must have realized that some form of autocratic control was necessary, but since he was on the point of leaving for a three-years' campaign in the East, it is not likely that he had already formulated his ultimate plans in detail. Thus while the pattern of Hellenistic monarchy may safely be rejected, it was wiser to avoid too close an attribution to him of aims which he himself had perhaps not yet finally determined.[29]

Whatever his future plans may have been, his present power and conduct were sufficient to bring about his death. Many nobles were not reconciled to the overshadowing of their traditional powers in the Senate and resented his autocratic behaviour. They will have disliked the oath, by which the Senate bound itself to protect his life, while his dismissal of his personal bodyguard of Spanish horsemen enabled them to break it with greater ease. They naturally took offence at any lack of courtesy on his part, as when he failed to stand up to greet members of the Senate who went in a body to inform him of a grant of honours: he will have appeared to some as a patron receiving his clients. There is no reason to believe that illness undermined his physical or intellectual powers, but he was ageing and impatient: 'satis diu vel naturae vixi vel gloriae'. During his last months he showed a certain lack of responsibility which contrasts with the hopes he had inspired in men like Cicero in 46: his earlier geniality and humanity were overshadowed at times by bitterness and overbearing conduct (superbia). Whether this was superficial or was due to more deep-seated causes, arising from the corrupting influence of power, it was sufficient to emphasize his depotism and provoke his assassination.[30] His enemies tried to undermine his popularity by spreading wild rumours of his alleged intentions and then turned to more drastic action.

A conspiracy was formed and since many of the conspirators were men who had served Caesar faithfully and could expect further support from him, it must be assumed that their motives were not mean or petty. They regarded him as a tyrant and tyrannicide became a duty in the interest of Liberty and the Republic: they did not stop to consider a fact which Caesar himself is said to have remarked upon, namely that his removal would merely involve the Republic in further trouble and civil wars. Caesar must have suspected that his life might be in peril, but he disdained any precautions: 'It was better to die than to live in dread of death.' Despite the fact that there were at least sixty men involved in the conspiracy, the secret was well kept. The leader of the move was C. Cassius Longinus, praetor in 44, who had once described Caesar as his 'old and merciful master'. The figurehead was his colleague and brother-in-law, M. Iunius Brutus, who claimed descent from the Brutus who had killed Tarquinius Superbus, the last king of Rome in 510 B.C. A student and philosopher rather than a man of action, he was deeply attached to the Republican tradition. As a young mint-official in 60 or 59 he had issued coins with portraits of his ancestor and the inscription 'libertas', while the half-brother of his mother Servilia was Cato whose influence over him was so great as to lead him in the civil war to support Pompey, though the latter had in 77 been responsible for the death of Brutus' father. After Pharsalus Brutus had accepted pardon and office from Caesar, but he was not reconciled with him at heart, and his marriage with Cato's daughter Porcia in 45 renewed his links with the Republican tradition. Once he was persuaded where his duty lay, Brutus threw himself into the conspiracy with energy. Urged on by the prospect of Caesar's departure for the East, the conspirators decided to strike on the Ides (15th) of March.[31] Undeterred by the fears of his wife Calpurnia Caesar attended the fatal meeting of the Senate. Unarmed, he was surrounded by a group of conspirators who drew their hidden daggers and stabbed him to death: he fell at the foot of Pompey's statue.

Caesar's outstanding abilities are unquestioned.[32] One of the world's greatest soldiers, he was also a writer of great distinction and an orator of the first rank. Urbane, cultured and courteous, he possessed a will of steel and an intensity of intellect that may have been reflected in his tall spare figure, his clear complexion and his lively dark eyes. An aristocrat by birth and nature, he had a true Roman sense of the practical: clear in purpose and swift in decision, he could be ruthless and coldblooded, but was more often clement and generous. The charm, as well as the force, of his personality captivated the loyalty of his troops and supporters, but awareness of his genius engendered in him a certain aloofness. That spark of mysticism and idealism that burned in the heart of Alexander the Great was lacking in Caesar whose genius matched Alexander's in many ways: if Caesar worshipped a goddess it was Fortuna or Venus. His family connexions led him away from the Optimates; he became a *popularis* but no democrat. With immense skill he played the game of politics, using the weapons of his day to win power and pre-eminence. That he carried through so great a programme of reform in so short a time was due in part to his desire and flair for administrative efficiency which he perhaps valued more than the support of public opinion: in his last years he carried measures which would please some and displease other sections of the community. He made no attempt to bind Senators, Equites and people into a *concordia ordinum*: as long as the army was loyal, he could impose his will without courting all men. Whether his gifts as a politician were matched by his statesmanship is a question to which the Ides of March have obscured the answer. Caesar must have realized that the Republic could not be revived in its old form – Sulla's career and the fate of his constitution had shown that. A selfish oligarchy of nobles and capitalists, who exploited the provincials in the interests of themselves and of an idle urban mob, had failed to preserve law and peace, let alone to set their house in better order. The days of the city-state were over, and Rome must recognize her responsibilities to the non-political orders in Italy and the provinces. That Caesar's mind must have been moving towards some form of monarchy as the only practical solution of the constitutional problem is probable enough. But an outraged group of nobles, many of whom honestly but blindly identified the Republican government of their day with Liberty, prevented Caesar from revealing to the world the solution that he would have decided to apply to its ills.

VIII

THE SECOND TRIUMVIRATE[1]

1. THE RISE OF ANTONY

When the dictator was murdered the official heads of the State were the surviving consul, M. Antonius (Marc Antony), and the Magister Equitum, M. Aemilius Lepidus. Antony's family had not distinguished itself in recent years: his father's campaign against the pirates in 74 had been a fiasco. He himself had passed a dissipated youth: extravagant and boisterous, he was a popular and competent soldier, whom Caesar had employed and trusted in the civil war and had chosen as his consular colleague for 44. Cicero called him a gambler (*aleator*) and in the confusion that followed the murder he played his cards with considerable skill. The conspirators met with so cold a reception from the crowd that they hurriedly withdrew to the Capitol, where they were joined by Cicero; they soon had cause to regret that Cassius had failed to persuade Brutus that Antony should be killed together with Caesar. Antony, who had secured Caesar's papers and treasures from his widow Calpurnia, obtained the co-operation of Lepidus, who as governor of Narbonese Gaul and Hither Spain had some troops outside Rome; these he brought in, and thus with men and money Antony could negotiate from strength. He won over P. Dolabella by acquiescing in his assumption of the vacant consulship, and at a meeting of the Senate on Cicero's proposal a practical, though illogical, compromise was reached between the Caesarians and Republicans: Caesar's murderers were to receive an amnesty, while Caesar's will and acts were to be respected and his funeral was to be celebrated. Thus fresh fighting was averted and the wheels of constitutional government could start moving again. Brutus and Cassius dined on the Capitol with Antony and Lepidus.

Antony then published Caesar's will, the contents of which were a bitter personal disappointment to him in that Caesar's great-nephew Octavian had been preferred to him as the chief heir. But it also contained inflammatory material: Caesar had left his fine gardens beyond the Tiber to the Roman people and bequeathed 300 sesterces to every Roman citizen. This good news was followed by Caesar's funeral, at which, against Cassius' advice, Brutus allowed Antony to deliver the customary funeral oration (*laudatio funebris*); in this Antony succeeded in stirring up the fury of the people against the murderers of Caesar, whose blood-stained toga and corpse had already inflamed their emotions.[2] With the mob rioting, Brutus and Cassius were forced to flee from Rome less than a month after the murder. Antony, left in control, secured for Lepidus the office of Pontifex Maximus and authorized him to negotiate with Pompey's son, Sextus, who had six legions in Spain; he also appeased the Senate by proposing the permanent abolition of the dictatorship. Two of the conspirators were allowed to go to their provinces, Decimus Brutus to Cisalpine Gaul and Trebonius to Asia. The Senate allotted Macedonia to Antony and Syria to Dolabella. Following this conciliatory policy further, Antony secured a dispensation from their duties as praetors for Brutus and Cassius, carried an agrarian bill to provide land in Italy for Caesar's veterans, and scandalously attributed to Caesar's 'acts' some forged measures to benefit himself. Thus two months after Caesar's death Antony was in control, and Cicero could confide in his friend Atticus that Antony was so unprincipled that 'at times one could wish Caesar back'. The Liberators had shown too many scruples and too little policy: their naïve assumption that the Republican government would automatically regain full vigour once the dictator was removed had proved vain. The consul Antony was not a new dictator, but he had skilfully gathered into his hands great power.

2. THE RISE OF OCTAVIAN

Julius Caesar's great-nephew, C. Octavius, belonged to a municipal family of Velitrae, near Rome. Born in the year of Cicero's consulship (63), he had lost his father while a child and had been brought up by his mother Atia, a niece of Julius. Though delicate in health he attracted the notice of the dictator who must have formed a high opinion of his promise since, unknown to the boy, he decided to adopt him as his heir. When Caesar was murdered, Octavius was at Apollonia in Illyricum, getting some military training in preparation for the Parthian war. As soon as the news reached him young Octavius boldly decided to cross to Italy. Any hopes that he may have formed of trying to avenge Caesar must have been immensely strengthened when on landing at Brundisium he heard that Caesar in his will had adopted him and made him heir to three-quarters of his estate. Using the name

C. Iulius Caesar Octavianus, he reached Rome by the end of April, where he was welcomed by Caesar's friends and veterans. He naturally turned to Antony, Caesar's former colleague and supporter, but Antony was embittered that this youth should have been preferred by Caesar; nor was Antony prepared to relinquish Caesar's money which he had taken over and some of which he had already spent. Rebuffed by Antony, Octavian began to pay off Caesar's legacies from his own resources. Antony then strengthened his position by getting a law passed which transferred Cisalpine and Transalpine Gaul to himself for five years in place of Macedonia but which allowed him to retain command of the Macedonian legions. His quarrel with Octavian, however, was not yet allowed to grow too serious.

In the course of the summer Brutus and Cassius, who had been given responsibility for the Asian and Sicilian corn supply, decided to leave Italy, though they were not yet necessarily thinking of war; instead of going to Crete and Cyrene which had been assigned to them as provinces, they went off to Macedonia and Syria. By September Cicero had ventured to return to Rome and began to attack Antony in the first of a series of speeches, the Philippics. While Antony went to Cisalpine Gaul, which Decimus Brutus, the original governor for 44, refused to evacuate, Octavian was busy appealing to Caesar's veterans and by his own efforts without any legal authority raised a considerable force and even won over two of Antony's legions that were back from Macedonia: the magic of Caesar's name was Octavian's talisman. While Antony was besieging D. Brutus in Mutina, Cicero and the Senate were turning to Octavian. With great energy Cicero came forward as the champion of the Republic; gradually in his Philippics he persuaded the Senate and people that Antony was aiming at a dictatorship, that Octavian could be used as long as they needed his help ('laudandum adolescentem, ornandum, tollendum'), and that the young man should be made a senator and propraetor in order to co-operate, if need be, with Hirtius and Pansa, the consuls of 43, against Antony. At last Cicero's appeals that Decimus Brutus should be supported were successful, and the two consuls, together with Octavian were sent against Antony. Two battles were fought at Forum Gallorum between Mutina (Modena) and Bononia (Bologna): Antony was defeated and fled with difficulty to Transalpine Gaul, D. Brutus was relieved at Mutina, but the two consuls died, Hirtius in battle and Pansa of wounds. Octavian was thus left in sole command of the consular armies.

Thinking that Antony could be easily handled and that Octavian could be dispensed with, the Senate foolishly slighted the 'boy'. Antony was declared a public enemy, Brutus and Cassius were granted their commands in Macedonia and Syria and received *maius imperium* in the East, Sextus Pompeius was put in command of a fleet, and Decimus Brutus was given a triumph and the command of the consular armies. Octavian reacted sharply: he refused to co-operate with Decimus, one of Caesar's murderers, and, since he controlled eight legions, he demanded the consulship. Refusing to be fobbed off with the offer of a praetorship he marched on Rome, where he was elected consul suffectus together with an obscure relative Q. Pedius. Thus once again the Senate had to yield to a revolutionary leader with an army behind him. Having thus underestimated Octavian, it suffered a further blow in its policy towards Antony if it hoped that Lepidus could be used against him. With his seven legions in Narbonese Gaul, Lepidus decided, or was persuaded by his troops, to support Antony. Though Lepidus was declared a public enemy, two other former officers of Caesar soon followed his example and joined Antony: they were C. Asinius Pollio from Further Spain and L. Munatius Plancus from northern Gaul. When Antony re-entered Cisalpine Gaul, Decimus Brutus was deserted by his troops and forced to flee, but was overtaken on his way to Greece and was killed. The Republican cause in the west had collapsed. In Rome a *lex curiata* had been passed which formally confirmed Octavian's adoption by Julius Caesar and made legitimate his use of the name Caesar:[3] this was the name that he had been employing (he is called Octavian by modern writers to avoid confusion). Pedius then carried a measure which revoked the amnesty granted in 44 to Caesar's murderers and outlawed them: since Brutus and Cassius now commanded considerable forces in the East, this would lead to further civil war. Pedius also persuaded the Senate to revoke the decrees of outlawry against Antony and Lepidus, whom Octavian now decided to meet. Cicero's policy had tragically failed, and the Republic was again at the mercy of the men who commanded the loyalty of the legions.

3. THE SECOND TRIUMVIRATE AND PHILIPPI

By courage, skill and appreciation of political realities Octavian had used all the forces available to him to win power: as Caesar's heir he had appealed to the plebs and veterans, raised a private army and built up a faction of friends, men of ambition and ability, including three Roman knights, Q. Salvidienus Rufus, M. Vipsanius Agrippa and C. Maecenas. Thus he secured official recognition, which he was soon strong enough to flout. Consul before he was twenty, he must next face the rival army commanders.

Octavian met Antony and Lepidus on a small island in a river near Bononia: all three brought their legions with them. There they were reconciled and decided to have themselves appointed Triumviri Reipublicae Constituendae for five years with authority to make laws and to nominate magistrates and governors. Unlike the first triumvirate, which was merely a private agreement between Pompey, Caesar and Crassus to work together for their mutual benefit, the second triumvirate (which came into being on 27 November 43 by means of a bill carried through the Tribal Assembly by a tribune named

P. Titius) was a formal magistracy legally appointed which could dominate the Senate and state. In place of the dictator Caesar, there were now three dictators, although the title was carefully avoided. They then divided the western provinces: Antony retained Transalpine and Cisalpine Gaul, a strong position from which he could keep watch on Italy: Lepidus took the rest of Gaul and all Spain; Octavian had Africa, Sicily and Sardinia. In 42 Lepidus was to be consul, while Antony and Octavian attacked the republican armies in the East. To advertise their rule and the effective death of the Republic, they all three had coins issued bearing their portraits.

The triumvirs needed political security and money; they therefore forgot the example of Caesar and remembered Marius and Sulla. They carried out a ruthless proscription, in which they signed the death-warrant of some 300 senators and 2000 knights. Since they had forty-five legions behind them and their victims included so many knights, whose share in politics will often have been negligible, their dominant motive will have been the need to confiscate estates with which to pay their troops. All three must share the responsibility: Octavian cannot be excused as the junior partner. With the money they raised by these grim means and by imposing some special taxes, they satisfied their men, for whom they also got land from eighteen flourishing Italian municipalities (e.g. Capua, Venusia, Beneventum). Some of the proscribed managed to escape and to join Sextus Pompeius, who though deprived of his command as Praefectus Classis et Orae Maritimae by Octavian, still had over a hundred ships and was beginning a campaign to occupy Sicily. Many stirring tales were told of the heroism and treachery shown by individuals during the reign of terror.[4] The most famous victim, on whose death Antony insisted, was Cicero. Antony's agents overtook him at Formiae: he ordered his slaves to leave him and save themselves, and met his death with courage. Antony had his head and hands hung up on the Rostra in the Forum at Rome: such was the barbaric revenge that he took on the man who had dared to challenge him in the name of the Republic and had denounced his policy with such vigour in the Philippics.

Thus perished one of Rome's greatest sons.[5] Charged by some with irresolution or even cowardice, he showed neither failing in the first act of his public life when he stood up to the dictator Sulla in defence of Roscius, or in his final stand against Antony. His career had reached its zenith when he had thwarted Catiline during his consulship in 63. But he had no army to help him enforce his will, and as a *novus homo* he lacked the full backing of a faction; he therefore was unable to achieve his ideal of a *concordia ordinum* between senators and knights, which later he developed into a *consensus omnium bonorum* to include *tota Italia*. Conscious that the State needed a *rector*, he soon realized that Pompey could not fill that role, and amid the increasing pressure that the military *principes* were exerting upon the free state, Cicero withdrew from public life to ponder and write upon philosophic and political themes.[6] In his *De Republica*, published in 51, he saw the ideal statesman and constitution in the past, in the days of Scipio Aemilianus and a balanced constitution guided by a group of enlightened nobles. Then he turned to the *Laws*, and any hopes he may have had in Caesar soon gave way to disillusion. After the dictator's death he finished his *De officiis* in which he depicted the duties that a citizen owed to his country. But he did more than write: he took action. Though the chances of success may have been faint, he boldly struck one more blow in defence of that free state, where men would rule by persuasion and reason, and refused to admit that the choice lay only between tyranny and anarchy. His attempt to play off Octavian against Antony failed and the consequences of this policy were fatal to the Republic, but responsibility for that certainly does not rest on Cicero's shoulders alone. He may have come forward to fight for an ideal and to try to save a Commonwealth that was past saving, but he was willing to sacrifice his life in the attempt rather than to continue to live under a tyranny. Further, besides wrestling with these practical problems, he wrote works that have had a profound influence on the course of European civilization. In Cicero's *humanitas* Rome produced one of its most precious gems.

The death-sentence had been carried out against the Republicans in Italy by the proscription; in the East where Brutus and Cassius had built up power-ful armies it had to be executed by force of arms. Brutus had consolidated his strength in Macedonia, at first perhaps hoping for a compromise settle-ment with Antony. For a victory over a Thracian tribe, the Bessi, he was hailed by his troops as Imperator. He became increasingly independent and the chief Republican rallying-point: he issued coins which referred to the Ides of March and showed the daggers of the Liberators, together with the portrait of Brutus, now the living symbol of Republican Libertas. Then late in 43, instead of thinking of advancing to Italy to join Decimus Brutus, he moved against the advice of Cicero into Asia to meet Cassius and to raise money: he forced the Lycian cities to contribute and stormed Xanthus which refused. Meantime in Syria Cassius had defeated Dolabella (Antony's consular col-league of 44) who had been declared an outlaw for killing C. Trebonius, the governor of Asia. With twelve legions, and 700 talents which he had extorted from the Jews, Cassius then joined Brutus in overrunning Asia Minor, robbing Rhodes, Tarsus and other cities. After meeting at Sardes, the two commanders, with nineteen legions and a powerful fleet, reached the Hellespont by September 42.

In the west the triumvirs commanded forty-three legions. Octavian's pres-tige had now risen even higher: he had become the son of a god (*divi filius*), since on 1 January 42 the Senate recognized Julius Caesar as a god. He and Antony took twenty-eight legions against Brutus and Cassius, leaving Lepidus to keep order in Italy. They found their opponents entrenched in a strong position at Philippi on the Via Egnatia. A possible shortage of supplies compelled the Caesarians to force an action. In the first engagement Cassius, who was routed and wrongly thought that Brutus was faring ill, committed suicide. In a second battle about three weeks later Brutus was defeated; he too took his own life. Some of his supporters, as Valerius Messala and the poet Horace, surrendered to the triumvirs; others fled to join Sextus Pompeius or elsewhere; the Republican cause was irretrievably lost; and Julius Caesar's murder was avenged. If Brutus' rigidly doctrinaire outlook and slight air of superiority did not endear him to all his contemporaries, and if his notorious attempt to exact interest at 48 per cent from the unfortunate Salaminians of Cyprus does not easily square with his theoretical pursuit of virtue, at least his single-minded devotion to an ideal and the earnestness with which he followed it, afford some justification for the claim that he was 'the noblest Roman of them all'.[6a]

A fresh division of the western provinces followed: to avoid future misunderstandings this was recorded in a signed compact. Antony took all Gaul except Cisalpine which received no governor and became part of Italy. Lepidus, who was suspected of intriguing with Sextus Pompeius, was ignored. Octavian received Spain, Sardinia and Africa, though he was perhaps to hand over Africa to Lepidus if the latter proved satisfactory. The triumvirs disbanded all but eleven of their legions. For the veterans land must be found: this difficult task was entrusted to Octavian, together with that of dealing with Sextus Pompeius. Antony was to go to the East to raise the necessary funds and re-establish order there. Thus the stage was set for the subsequent division of the Roman world into a western half under Octavian and an eastern under Antony: only after Octavian's victory at Actium was it re-united in peace.

4. OCTAVIAN'S CONSOLIDATION OF THE WEST

Octavian, whose health had been bad during the campaign of Philippi, had to try to get land in Italy for some 100,000 veterans. If he gained their gratitude, he also incurred the hatred of the farmers whom he ejected from their holdings: not many, as the poet Virgil, were lucky enough to find compensation through a patron's help. A protest raised in Rome was backed by Antony's wife Fulvia and his brother L. Antonius (consul in 42), who managed by skilful propaganda to raise eight legions and occupy Rome. But they were soon forced out by Octavian, aided by his friends Salvidienus and Agrippa; they were driven into the hill-town of Perusia (Perugia), where after a grim siege starvation forced them to surrender at the end of the winter of 41/40. Octavian showed no mercy to the unfortunate city, though he was careful to spare L. Antonius whom he then made governor of Spain. All this will have strained his relations with M. Antony, who probably heard nothing of the episode until it was over. He then sent Salvidienus to occupy Gaul where Antony's legate had died, and Lepidus was given Africa.[6b]

In 40 Antony decided to return to the west, but he was refused admittance at Brundisium, as he thought by Octavian's orders. He thereupon began to overrun S. Italy until Octavian's forces arrived. Another civil war, which the soldiers of neither commander wanted, was imminent, but through the good offices of Maecenas and Asinius Pollio the leaders were reconciled. By an agreement, known as the Treaty of Brundisium (October 40), Antony retained the East, Octavian added Transalpine and Narbanese Gaul to his previous command, and Lepidus was confirmed in Africa. Antony also warned Octavian that Salvidienus was plotting against him; Salvidienus was called to Rome and killed. In order to secure their future the triumvirs nominated consuls for some years ahead. Further they followed the example of the First Triumvirate by arranging a marriage alliance: Antony, whose wife Fulvia had died, married Octavian's sister, Octavia. War had been averted and Italy breathed again. This relief and hope is probably reflected in Virgil's fourth Eclogue, which foretold the birth of a child who would usher in a Golden Age: the poet may have been thinking of a son that might be born to Antony and Octavia.[7]

The situation was soon complicated by the claims of another competitor for power, Sextus Pompeius, who had succeeded in occupying Sicily and Sardinia and had hoped for due recognition under the Treaty of Brundisium.[8] Disappointed in this, he increasingly interfered with the overseas corn-supply of Rome until the triumvirs decided to meet him near the promontory of Misenum (39) where they agreed that he should be given a proconsular command for five years in Sicily, Corsica, Sardinia and Achaea, and that thereafter he should hold the consulship: the exiles that had joined him (Republicans, men expropriated from their farms by Octavian and others) were to be restored. Though the treaty was deposited with the Vestal Virgins in Rome for safe-keeping, there was little prospect that it would long be honoured. A break came when Octavian accepted Sardinia, which Sextus' governor Menas treacherously offered to hand over to him, together with three legions. Octavian also divorced his wife Scribonia, a relative of Sextus, on the day on which she bore him a daughter, Julia. He had fallen in love with Livia, the wife of Ti. Claudius Nero who at the time of the Perusine war had fled with her and their child Tiberius (the future emperor) to join Sextus in Sicily. The elder Tiberius now complacently divorced the nineteen-year-old Livia whom Octavian then married and lived happily with for fifty years.

Faced with war against Sextus, Octavian asked for some help from Antony who had spent the winter of 39/8 in Greece where he was planning a campaign against the Parthians who had invaded Syria. But when Antony crossed to Brundisium to meet him, Octavian did not come in time and

THE SECOND TRIUMVIRATE 139

Antony did not wait. Octavian then advanced by sea against Sextus, but lost half his fleet in an engagement off the toe of Italy: Sextus proclaimed himself 'son of Neptune'. Octavian clearly needed a larger fleet and a better admiral. He turned to his friend Agrippa, who had just returned from a campaign in Gaul where he had secured the Rhine frontier and settled the Ubii on the site of Cologne. Agrippa undertook extensive constructions near Naples: joining lakes Avernus and Lucrinus to the sea, he built and trained a fleet in safety in this new Portus Julius.[9] Before it was ready for action Antony arrived in Italy again, at Tarentum, where he hoped to exchange some of his ships for some of Octavian's soldiers, but Octavian decided to rely on Agrippa's efforts and only the tactful intervention of Octavia averted an open rupture and the outbreak of war. At a conference at Tarentum (37) the armament exchange was arranged, and the triumvirate, which had technically lapsed at the end of 38, was renewed until the end of 33 by an agreement that perhaps was later confirmed by a legislative act.[10]

By 36 Octavian was ready to strike a decisive blow against Sextus by a converging attack on Sicily. While Statilius Taurus advanced from Tarentum with 120 ships which Antony had handed over, Lepidus was to land with large forces from Africa, and Octavian and Agrippa sailed southwards from Portus Julius. But although Lepidus managed to overrun western Sicily with twelve legions, the plan was disrupted because the other two squadrons encountered a tremendous storm and were driven back. When they attacked again a month later. Octavian was caught off his guard while landing troops in eastern Sicily and suffered another defeat at sea. Agrippa, however, who had got ashore in the north-east, managed to join up with the men that Octavian had landed. Sextus, seeing the island gradually slipping from his grasp, staked all on a naval engagement at Naulochus, near the Straits, where each side mustered some 300 ships. Thanks in part to the invention by Agrippa of the harpax (a grapnel shot from a catapult), only seventeen of Sextus' ships escaped.[11] Sextus himself fled to the East where he was soon put to death on Antony's order. He was not a great figure or an inspiring leader who might have given real life to a Republican rally. In fact the son of Pompey the Great, who had cleared the Mediterranean of pirates, was an adventurer who developed into something of a pirate-king: 'impetu strenuus . . . fide patri dissimillimus' (Velleius). In Sicily events then took an unexpected turn: Lepidus, who after receiving the submission of some Pompeian troops commanded twenty-two legions, claimed the island and ordered Octavian to leave. But the weary troops did not want further fighting and began to desert to Octavian, who finally spared Lepidus' life and allowed him to remain Pontifex Maximus, but deprived him of his triumviral powers: Lepidus' public career was ended. Octavian now commanded some forty legions: he disbanded 20,000 veterans, settled Sicily and returned to Rome.

Octavian was granted an *ovatio* and other honours, not the least important of which was the *sacrosanctitas* of a tribune,[12] a reminder of civilian life to the man who two years before had adopted the title 'Imperator Caesar'. The inscription on a golden statue set up in the Forum proclaimed that order had been restored by land and sea.[13] This was Italy's greatest need, and it was as a champion in the cause of security and prosperity for Italy and the West that Octavian appealed to his countrymen. He had a sincere respect for Italian tradition and thought, which grew deeper with the years and was sharpened by contrast with Antony's increasing leaning towards eastern traditions. He was fortunate therefore in being able to identify his own cause with that of his country, since he was in fact a revolutionary leader whose faction had steadily grown in Rome and Italy and was now beginning to appeal not only to ambitious new men but also to more aristocrats of the ancient families. But his very success was ominous: in eliminating his two colleagues and all rivals from the West, where he now controlled Sicily, Africa, Corsica, Sardinia, Gaul and Spain, he was splitting the Roman world into two. Further, as the First Triumvirate had been weakened by the deaths of Julia and Crassus, so now Antony's treatment of Octavia and the elimination of Lepidus thrust the surviving triumvirs farther apart.

In order to safeguard the north-eastern frontier of Italy and to bind the people of Italy still closer to himself by a military success to match Antony's eastern campaigns, Octavian under-took operations in Illyricum.[14] In 35 he advanced against the Iapudes who had been raiding Aquileia and Tergeste (Trieste), and reached Siscia on the Savus (Save); in 34–3 he reduced the Dalmatian coast and the interior up to the Dinaric Alps. In these campaigns he did not spare himself, and followed up victory with colonial settlement or resettlement at Pola and Emona. The Adriatic was cleared of piracy, the north-east frontier secured, and when he returned to Rome Octavian and his friends, as Agrippa, Maecenas and Statilius Taurus, began to adorn the city with new buildings, to provide good water and cheap food, and not least to remind men of Rome's earlier beliefs and traditions, by expelling astrologers and magicians, banning eastern rites, and repairing old shrines and temples. Octavian was looking beyond his imminent quarrel with Antony.

5. ANTONY IN THE EAST

After Philippi Antony had, in agreement with Octavian (p. 137), gone to the eastern provinces to raise money (41). The unfortunate cities of Asia Minor, who were still groaning from the extortions of Brutus and Cassius, now had to raise more funds for the man whom Ephesus worshipped as a new Dionysus. Antony made a half-hearted re-adjustment of some of the client-kingdoms, and when he reached Tarsus he summoned Cleopatra to meet him: the excuse was that she had given help to Cassius, the reason probably was Antony's need for the treasures of the Ptolemies. Antony must have seen her as a girl of fourteen when he had visited Alexandria, and again in Rome when she was living there as Caesar's mistress. After Caesar's death she had gone back to Alexandria, where she killed her young brother and consort, Ptolemy XIV. After her meeting with Antony on the Cydnus, which has been immortalized by Shakespeare, she became his mistress but probably did not yet really win his heart: his support would strengthen her rule in Egypt, not least when she persuaded him to kill her sister Arsinoe. She then returned to Egypt where Antony later joined her for the winter (41/40), but in the spring he had to leave, and he did not see her again for four years, nor the twins that she bore him.

Antony in fact found that he had two wars to cope with: the Parthians were invading Syria, and the Parthini (an Illyrian tribe, not to be confused with the Parthians) were invading Macedonia: he also had to negotiate terms with Octavian at Brundisium (p. 138). Making Athens his headquarters, where he lived with his new wife Octavia, he conducted his wars at first by deputy. By 39 C. Asinius Pollio had reduced the Parthini, but the Parthian menace was more serious. The Parthians possibly thought that Antony intended to carry out Julius Caesar's plan for an attack on their country. At any rate Parthian forces entered Syria, led by Pacorus, son of the king Orodes, and by Q. Labienus, son of Caesar's former general, who had been sent by Cassius to the Parthian court.[15] While Labienus swept into Asia Minor, Pacorus won most of Syria and was welcomed by Mattathias (Antigonus) at Jerusalem, where Hyrcanus was overthrown; Herod, Hyrcanus' vizier, managed to escape to Rome where the Senate proclaimed him king of Judaea. In 39 Antony sent out Ventidius with eleven legions who drove Labienus from Asia Minor and thrust the Parthians back over the Euphrates. When Pacorus attacked again in the next year he was defeated and killed by Ventidius at Mt. Gindarus (not far from Antioch): he had relied too much on cataphracts and too little on horse-archers. Later in the year Antony himself went east and took Samosata, though he was back in Greece for the winter. In 37 he sent C. Sosius with two legions to instal Herod as King of Judaea; after Jerusalem had been captured, Herod the Great started his reign.[16]

Antony had so far shown considerable forbearance towards Octavian, who had snubbed him twice at Brundisium (in 40 and 38) and again at Tarentum; nor had Antony received the troops which Octavian had promised in exchange for ships. Although relations had been patched up at Tarentum and the Triumvirate renewed (37), later in the year Antony sent Octavia back to Italy as she was expecting a child; he was joined in Antioch by Cleopatra. Whether he married her now or later in accordance with Macedonian or Egyptian law, is uncertain, but no such ceremony would have been valid under Roman law: to the Romans Antony's legal wife was still Octavia, who nobly continued to safeguard his interest in the west.[17] At any rate Antony formally acknowledged the children that Cleopatra had borne him and renamed them Alexander Helios (the Sun) and Cleopatra Selene (the Moon);[18] he also gave her control of Coele-Syria, Cyprus and part of Cilicia. As a precautionary measure before his Parthian campaign, he reorganized other client-kingdoms, setting up Amyntas in Galatia, an Archelaus in Cappadocia, and Polemo in an extended Pontus: all these men, together with Herod, served him well. In the spring of 36 he sent Cleopatra, who was expecting another child (Ptolemy Philadelphus), back to Egypt, and then launched his attack on Parthia.

With some 60,000 legionaries and other troops Antony advanced northwards through Armenia to the Median capital Phraaspa (near Tabriz), which he failed to capture because his artillery train had already been defeated. After an engagement with the Parthian forces, he was compelled to withdraw. For nearly a month he fought his way back to Armenia, amid great hardship and suffering, harassed continually by the enemy. Although he lost some 22,000 legionaries, the remainder owed their survival not least to Antony's courage, perseverance and leadership in the time of disaster. Both Cleopatra and Octavia had prepared supplies of food and clothing for his starving army: he accepted Cleopatra's gift, but not Octavia's. After reorganizing his forces, in 34 he invaded Armenia and captured the king Artavasdes, whom he blamed for the loss of his artillery two years before. Although Armenia became a Roman province for two years Carrhae had not been avenged, nor Julius Caesar's Parthian hopes realized: Parthia now held still more Roman 'eagles'.

Antony, who was now more dependent on Cleopatra's financial support, became increasingly dependent on her also as a woman: he was now in love with an exceptionally able, ruthless and ambitious woman, who probably drove him further than his instinct dictated. Whether or not Cleopatra had a great vision of world-rule and believed, as a nameless Greek oracle foretold, that she would overthrow Rome and then raise it up again in a partnership of East and West and inaugurate a golden age of peace and brotherhood, can hardly be determined.[19] Whether she hoped to use Antony and Roman troops to challenge Rome, she could at any rate count on his loyalty, if not on his infatuation, in her more immediate aim which must have been to extend her kingdom and revive the empire of the Ptolemies. Antony, foreseeing the possibility of a clash with Octavian, would be ready to create a source of power, which might even serve as a potential refuge if he failed to achieve overwhelming victory; but his problem would be to persuade troops, who might be ready to be led against Octavian, to fight for Cleopatra or an Antony who was king of Egypt.

On his return to Alexandria (autumn 34) Antony celebrated a 'triumph' for his Armenian victory and staged a pageant in the Gymnasium. This episode is known as the Donations of Alexandria. Antony and Cleopatra, the latter robed as the goddess Isis, sat on high golden thrones, together with their children. To the assembled people Antony proclaimed that Caesarion (Ptolemy Caesar) was the legitimate son of Julius Caesar (thus by implication the adopted son, Octavian, was a usurper).[20] This boy, now proclaimed King of Kings, and his mother Cleopatra, Queen of Kings, were hailed as joint monarchs of Egypt and Cyprus.[21] Under them Antony's children were to govern parts of the empire: Alexander Helios received Armenia, Parthia and Media, Ptolemy Philadelphus Syria and Cilicia, and Cleopatra Selene Cyrenaica and Libya. Although Antony avoided taking any royal title for himself, and announced these arrangements by virtue of his triumviral authority, this partition of Rome's eastern provinces under the new Queen of Kings must have aroused considerable mistrust in Rome.

6. THE FINAL BREAK AND WAR: ACTIUM

After news of Antony's actions had reached Rome in the spring of 33 much of the year was spent in a campaign of mutual slander by Octavian and Antony, during which Octavian drew the damaging picture of a demoralized Antony in the thrall of an eastern Fury (Horace's 'fatale monstrum') that has tended to persist thereafter: Octavian needed to win over public opinion for the struggle for which he was preparing. Antony's offer to lay aside his triumviral powers, if Octavian would do the same, met with no response. But at the end of 33 the Second Triumvirate came to its legal end. No official action was taken: Antony kept the title and acted as if still in office, but Octavian dropped the title, and presumably the powers; since he was already sacrosanct and would be consul in 31, he was prepared to take the risk and rely on his prestige, his *auctoritas*.[22]

The consuls of 32, C. Sosius and Cn. Domitius Ahenobarbus, were Antony's supporters but when they entered office they refrained in his interest from reading to the Senate his despatch in which he asked for ratification of his eastern *acta*. Sosius, however, tried to move a vote of censure on Octavian in the Senate, but was vetoed by a tribune. When Octavian defended himself at another meeting, and attacked Antony, the two consuls and over three hundred senators left Rome to join Antony. Thereafter Antony sent Octavia formal letters of divorce. Octavian reacted sharply: he seized Antony's will, which was deposited with the Vestal Virgins, and read it to the Senate. It acknowledged Caesarion, provided for Antony's own children by Cleopatra, and ordered that he should be buried at Cleopatra's side. This was grist to Octavian's mill: the report could now be spread that Antony hoped to transfer the capital to Alexandria. Amid increasing tension the communities of Italy, and then many through the western provinces, passed a vote of confidence in Octavian: largely spontaneously, though doubtless encouraged by his agents here and there, they took an oath of allegiance (*coniuratio*) to him personally, thereby becoming the *clientela* of an individual party-leader; personal allegiance to a *dux* was replacing loyalty to the constitutional forms of a departed Republic. Octavian later described his personal mandate to proceed against Antony: 'Iuravit in mea verba tota Italia sponte sua et me belli quo vici ad Actium ducem depoposcit.'[23] Antony, who had crossed with Cleopatra and his forces to Greece, was deprived of his powers and prospective consulship for 31, and Octavian formally proclaimed a *iustum bellum* on Cleopatra. In 31 Octavian, who was holding his third consulship, also advanced to Greece.

Antony had a strong following, and the adhesion of the two consuls and so many senators suggested that he was more than a mere adventurer: many of his supporters were men of principle, former followers of Caesar, Republicans and Pompeians. But they lacked a cause to unite them: personal loyalty to Antony was not always sufficient, and the presence of Cleopatra alienated some: desertions began, but Cleopatra must stay since she was providing so much of the finance. In military strength the opponents were not ill-matched: Antony had some thirty legions, but he also had some 500 ships to Octavian's 400. With these forces he took up a defensive position in Greece: he dared not advance on Italy because the presence of Cleopatra would have ruined his cause. By abandoning the Via Egnatia and moving to the south-west, with headquarters at Patrae and his fleet and army centred on the promontory of Actium on the Gulf of Ambracia, Antony was able to entice Octavian to come to meet him, perhaps hoping in the first instance for a land rather than a naval engagement.

When Octavian crossed to Greece he left Maecenas in Rome and took with him most of the senators still in Italy. His army managed to occupy a position just north of Actium, while his fleet, commanded by Agrippa, captured Leucas, Patrae and Corinth and thus cut Antony off from the Peloponnese and began to interfere with his supplies by sea. When Antony failed to dislodge Octavian's army, he abandoned land operations, and his situation quickly deteriorated: he was short of supplies, desertions increased, and his men became restless. Rejecting a suggestion that he should retire to Macedonia and fight by land, he followed Cleopatra's advice to use the fleet. His real purpose is not clear: probably he hoped to fight a full-scale action, with the secondary plan of trying to break through to Egypt if this failed. Others believe that he was merely trying to escape from the blockade.[24] However that may be, on 2 September Antony drew up his fleet off Actium in three squadrons, facing to sea westwards, with Cleopatra's squadron behind nearer the shore. On his right wing Antony tried to turn Agrippa's squadron opposite him, but at this point for some reason his centre and left wing began to retire.

Antony was thus forced to signal to Cleopatra, who had the war-chest aboard, to escape. He broke off the engagement and managed to join her with forty ships. As they sailed off to Egypt, the rest of his fleet was captured or surrendered. A week later his land forces also capitulated. Octavian was undisputed master of the Roman world after an engagement which, as far as the actual fighting went, was something of an anticlimax in view of the vast forces assembled on each side. However it was the decisive battle and it was soon portrayed by Virgil and others as the victory of West over East.

Octavian at once began to disband part of his vast forces, and promptly sent some veterans back to Italy. Agrippa also had to be sent back to deal with a plot by the son of Lepidus. More serious was the restlessness of the veterans who wanted pay and settlement, so that Octavian himself had to go to Italy before following Antony. In the summer of 30 he reached Egypt and occupied Alexandria, which Antony could not defend: his remaining troops had deserted. Hearing a rumour that Cleopatra was dead, Antony stabbed himself but survived long enough to die in her arms. Cleopatra was taken prisoner and when she found she could not retain her kingdom for her children, she too died, at the bite of the asp which the Egyptians believed deified its victim.[25] Octavian had secured what he most needed: the treasure of the Ptolemies. He was relieved at her death, at which he may have connived, since he did not wish to take her to Rome to grace his triumph. Towards Antony's Roman followers Octavian was lenient. Towards the children of Antony and Cleopatra he was merciful and they were later brought up by Octavia (Selene ultimately married Juba II of Mauretania); but he killed Antony's elder son by Fulvia, Antyllus, and Caesarion: he could not allow a potential rival to survive. Egypt was annexed, but not as an ordinary Roman province: it became the private possession of the Roman emperor, administered by his agent, the first Prefect being the knight C. Cornelius Gallus. The Donations of Alexandria were naturally cancelled, and Octavian spent some time re-establishing the old provinces and client-kingdoms in the East, but he made few serious changes in Antony's arrangements in Asia Minor and he was content not to interfere beyond the Euphrates. On 11 January 29 the Temple of Janus in Rome was closed, a symbol of restored peace. In the summer Octavian returned to Italy and celebrated in Rome a triple triumph for his victories in Illyricum, at Actium and over Egypt. The century of civil wars that had started with the murder of Tiberius Gracchus was ended. The Republic and liberty had gone; men turned gratefully to their new saviour.

IX

ECONOMIC AND SOCIAL LIFE IN ITALY AND THE PROVINCES IN THE LATE REPUBLIC

1. AGRICULTURE, INDUSTRY AND TRADE[1]

During the sixty years between the Social War and the battle of Actium Italy had been the scene of proscriptions and confiscations, of devastation and casualties, in one civil war after another, so that its whole economic and social life might well have been undermined. But despite all the suffering and loss she did not succumb and in fact remained surprisingly prosperous, thanks partly of course to the wealth that she drew from the provinces. The problem that had faced the Gracchi had been to arrest the spread of *latifundia* and to restore to prosperity the small farmer. In this they had achieved considerable success, and much land had been returned to the peasant farmer. When this process came to a standstill, other causes began to operate which led to its continuation in another form: the needs of the soldiers. Sulla, Caesar and Octavian all had to find land in Italy or abroad for allotments or colonies, and it has been estimated that during these fifty years half a million men received new holdings in Italy. This huge transference in the tenure of land and the resultant moving around of people in Italy naturally had far-reaching social consequences and helped to spread Roman culture and ways of life, including the use of the Latin language; the political unification of Italy, achieved by the Italian War, was thus followed by the slower process of its romanization. But these changes also meant that the small farmer survived and that the process of breaking up the large estates continued.

Thus some large estates were sacrificed to the needs of land-hungry veterans, but very many more survived intact: civil war might on occasion lead to a change in ownership, but the nobility and the rich business-men still controlled affairs and retained their possessions. Some of the new soldier-farmers would soon tire of country life and be willing to sell out to their richer neighbours; others might leave tenants on their land and go off to the cities, thus turning peasant-holdings into the country estates of city residents. On the larger estates slave-labour still predominated, though under Caesar's law it was limited to two-thirds, while the great landowners were tending to let out their land in leasehold to free peasants, *coloni*; Caesar's opponent, Domitius Ahenobarbus, for instance, had thousands of such tenant-farmers on his vast estates. On the whole slaves tended to receive better treatment, as can be seen from contrasting the evidence given by Varro in his book on farming with that of the elder Cato. But the landowners, living in the cities, often displayed little personal interest in agriculture as such: some regarded their estates as mere profit-making machines, others as country residences for their personal delectation; details of farming and administration could be left to mere bailiffs.

Thus the civil wars did not destroy the prosperity of Italy, which Varro could even describe enthusiastically as 'one large orchard'. Advances were made in horticulture and market-gardening in the more fertile parts, where oil, wine, vegetables, fruit, poultry and stock would be produced. Around the towns also, especially inland where there was less competition from cheaper transport by sea, corn was still grown and traditional methods continued. Rome itself was increasingly becoming a cosmopolitan centre which supported its vast growing population by means of corn imported from abroad and raised the standard of luxurious living for its upper classes by means of the wealth that it drew from the provinces and foreign wars. Thus Italy as a whole was able to support its population which with the inclusion of Cisalpine Gaul may at the end of the Republic have numbered nearly 14 million (including slaves), but more probably nearer half that number.[2]

But without the provinces Italy might not have withstood the strain. Apart from the fact that Roman capitalists were acquiring large amounts of land in Sicily, Spain and Africa and that the business-men of Italy were swarming around the Mediterranean, the provinces offered a means of official relief when the limits were reached in Italy. Thus Gaius Gracchus' Junonia had been followed by the foundation of Narbo and the settlement of Marius' veterans in Africa and elsewhere. During his first consulship in 59 Caesar might seek land for his veterans and for poor families in Italy (including the hitherto sacrosanct *ager Campanus*), but later the problem grew so big that, rather than risk a repetition of the disturbances that had followed Sulla's seizure of land in Italy, he turned to the provinces where he found new homes for 80,000 Roman citizens.[3]

The growth of industrial and commercial life in Italy was naturally affected by the civil wars, but it continued to develop on traditional lines. Agriculture remained the chief way of life for a large part of the population, but the equipment and tools of everyday life had to be provided and industry produced these for the home markets. Rome had been slow to turn to industry; the larger manufacturing centres in Italy were in Campania and Etruria, and much of the production was in the hands of people of non-Roman stock. The Campanian industry in bronze and silver ware and furniture doubtless continued to flourish, and a few 'factories', establishments specializing in spinning and weaving, began to appear. Arretium in Etruria started to produce the famous red 'Samian Ware', which later was to spread all over the western provinces. But during this period we hear of no major developments in manufacturing industry. There was, however, much activity in building, both public and private, at Rome (see p. 153 f.) and elsewhere: the city, the suburbs and fashionable villa sites were all developed. The prosperity of the Italian towns is best illustrated by the growth of Pompeii, which entered upon a new phase of development from Gracchan times; this extended to the farm villas outside it. To the years between 120 and 90 B.C. belong some of its finest public buildings (e.g. the Basilica) and some of the best private houses (e.g. those of Pansa and of the 'Faun') of which some were built over the foundations of groups of earlier houses. The city suffered a sharp setback when it was captured by Sulla in 90 and was later colonized, but it soon recovered and prospered, as the fine new temple of Capitoline Juppiter in the Forum testifies.[3a]

Before the time of Ti. Gracchus the Romans had not been much interested in commerce, although many of their Italian allies, especially the Greek cities of S. Italy, indulged in widespread trading activities. As the Romans began to exploit the provinces, the publicani and their agents naturally stimulated and even took part in private business ventures. There is considerable evidence for the activities of Italian business-men (who after 90 B.C. of course became Romans) at Delos, which became one of the chief markets for commerce in the Eastern Mediterranean especially after the destruction of Carthage and Corinth in 146. Here, as elsewhere, these resident merchants, Italici, formed clubs (collegia) for social and business purposes.[4] Italians were attracted by trade to Greece, Asia Minor, Sicily, Africa, Narbonese Gaul and Spain in increasing numbers: it is said that no less than 80,000 were massacred by Mithridates in Asia in 88, and there were sufficient in Cirta during the Jugurthine war to organize the defence of the city. Their activities, however, were hampered by the increasing scourge of piracy until the Romans allowed Pompey to make a final successful effort to sweep the seas clear. Thus Delos, which had been sacked by Mithridates in 88, suffered again from the pirates in 69, and never really recovered. The later civil wars also naturally interfered with commerce.

While Italy exported a certain amount of pottery, hardware, wine and oil, and Rome received much corn and raw materials for her military needs from her provincial tribute, the demand for luxuries increased: statues and other works of art, jewellery (e.g. pearls), rare table-woods, tapestries, purple-dyed wools, rare marbles for building, animals from Africa for the arena, linen, glass and papyrus from Egypt, all found a ready market in Rome. Examples of the cargo of some ships that were lost on their way to Rome can be seen in that recovered in 1907 from a vessel wrecked off the African coast at Mahdia (c. 85 B.C.) and those found in recent years off the Ligurian and French Riviera.[5]

2. THE ARISTOCRACY

During the years from 133 to 31 standards of public and social life changed considerably, but it would be wrong to project too far back into the century the picture of a lax society that may seem, in part at any rate, to represent the end of the period. It has been seen (p. 10 f.) that wealth and luxury began to undermine earlier standards of public and private conduct, but the process did not gain its full impetus until the civil wars which followed the Social War. And even then it is easy to exaggerate the extent of the evil. Many Roman nobles retained a high standard of public duty and of personal culture and lived in comparative simplicity. Where personal integrity was lacking, custom might still win outward respect for an Optimate senator, who was marked out from his fellow men by the very dress that he wore. But corruption and provincial maladministration increased as a more luxurious and ostentatious standard was set by fashion. Generals and governors needed more and more to line their pockets and secure their futures. In the scramble for position and prestige many of the lesser nobles fell into debt and ruin. Others turned to business activities: these were forbidden to senators by law, but they could do much behind a screen of agents. Apart from ordinary commercial enterprises, moneylending could be very profitable, as M. Brutus, 'the noblest Roman of them all', appreciated when he made a loan to some unfortunate Cypriots at 48 per cent in place of the more normal 12 per cent and sought military help to enable his agent to collect the debt. In times of civil wars and commotions fortunes could be quickly made as well as lost. The triumvir M. Crassus, the richest man of his day, had inherited a fortune of 300 talents from his father, but by 55 B.C. his property was worth over 7000: among other methods he had skilfully cashed in on the miseries of civil war by buying property cheap during Sulla's proscriptions and selling it later when prices had risen after Sulla's settlement. He would have found no difficulty in maintaining from his income that legion which he said every wealthy man should be able to support: nor would Pompey, whose final fortune was not much less. Even men with more scruples could amass considerable wealth: Cicero started life with a modest patrimony, but his career at the bar won him many legacies and presents from grateful clients, and his governorship of Cilicia, where he tried to check maladministration, was by no means without profit to him. But men of wealth formed a tiny fraction of the community and the consequent mal-distribution of property involved political danger as well as social injustice.

Luxury, display and extravagance were seen particularly in the houses of many nobles. Besides a town house in a fashionable quarter (e.g. on the Palatine), they had numerous villas on country estates, by the seaside or in the hills (even Cicero had more than eight): Baiae and the Bay of Naples were an especially favoured area for holiday resorts. But occasional relaxation out of town did not necessarily imply a love of the country; rather, many nobles were thoroughly urbanized, and even Cicero could write to young Caelius, 'The city, the city is what you must make the object of your devotion.' There society had its heart: politics, often violent, in Forum or Senate House, and social pleasures and duties from morning to night, from the early morning *salutatio* when clients waited upon their noble patron to pay their respects or seek his advice or aid, to the dinner-parties at night.

In this hectic atmosphere family life declined. Wives did not necessarily come under the authority (*manus*) of their husbands as in older days, and consequently gained greater independence since they were able to control their own properties which they had acquired by dowry or legacy. The Roman matron had always held a respected place in society and indeed often exercised considerable indirect influence on public affairs. Many continued to do this: Brutus, for instance, paid much heed to the advice of his mother Servilia and his wife Porcia. Other women gained their ends by their charms, for instance Clodia, the sister of P. Clodius, wife of Q. Metellus, and lover of the poet Catullus until he was ousted by Caelius and others, was the notorious leader of a fast set. Further, political friendships had often been strengthened by marriage alliances, as when Pompey married Julia, and these would not always lead to enduring marriages. Divorce and re-marriage were common: Sulla and Pompey had five wives and Caesar four. Thus there was a steady decline of morality in part of the governing class. But this must not be exaggerated: despite much immorality and extravagance, the aristocracy was not entirely decadent. Many men lived honourable and moderate lives and turned to cultured living rather than to vulgar luxury. Wider intellectual interests and appreciation of literature and art, combined often with greater humaneness and finer taste, led to a new *humanitas* in society. Cicero, despite his many failings, is not a bad example of this cultured and urbane society.[6]

3. THE KNIGHTS[7]

Since the possession of at least 400,000 sesterces was the minimum qualification for membership of the Equestrian Order, the Knights should be included in the upper classes: they were the moneyed as opposed to the landed aristocracy (though most probably were landowners and many wealthier than some of the poorer senators), nor was the social distinction between the two orders always very great (see above, p. 8). Rather it was a political gulf that separated them: the Knights preferred to remain outside politics, but especially after Gaius Gracchus gave them control of the Courts they could exercise an increasing pressure on policy, as has been seen in their attitude to the founding of Narbo or the Jugurthine War. Thereafter their relations with the Senate varied in degree: often hostile, they were at times prepared to co-operate, especially in the face of serious dangers that might threaten their financial interests. These interests were ever extending, not least through the action of Gaius in giving to the Knights the right to farm the taxes of Asia (p. 29). These men helped the government to collect taxes and harbourdues, to work the provincial mines and to undertake public buildings; organized in companies, in private partnerships or as individuals they engaged in industry, trade, banking and money-lending throughout the Roman world. With the decline in standards of morality the *publicani*, their agents and the moneylenders began callously to exploit the unhappy provincials. They received a set-back when Sulla proscribed 1600 knights and confiscated their property, but they soon recovered and flourished until Julius Caesar deprived them of the tithecollecting of Asia (p. 122); thereafter their operations were more carefully watched.

But as not every provincial governor was a Verres, so the unscrupulous transactions of many of these men should not blind us to the useful functions performed by others. Cicero himself belonged to this class by birth and though he was the first member of it to reach the consulship for a generation he retained a strong regard for it and sought by a *concordia ordinum* to bring it into harmony with the Senate. His great friend and correspondent, T. Pomponius Atticus, who as an Epicurean avoided political life, provides a good example of a cultured, popular, and successful business man. His wealth was based on his estates in Epirus and he pursued varied business activities from banking to publishing: discreet, urbane and sympathetic, he won the friendship of many, of Optimates and Caesarians alike.[8]

4. OTHER CLASSES

The rest of the city population comprised many groups. There were the clients of the nobles and knights, established by their patrons in various pursuits. Another section was formed by those who were self-supporting, small business-men, shopkeepers and workmen, an increasing number of whom were sons of freedmen or even freedmen themselves. Then there was the urban proletariat which relied in varying degrees on public support: since this consisted only of the corn dole, most of them must have found some means of supplementing it by some kind of work, even though it was not regular. One thing, however, they had for sale, their votes: hence particularly in the last half-century of the Republic they became more clamant as violence and corruption in politics increased. They must have lived in great squalor in blocks of high tenements (*insulae*) in narrow streets in such districts as the Subura. Other sections were formed by resident aliens and by the large number of slaves in the houses of the wealthy or employed in trade and industry.[9]

Many of these slaves were of foreign extraction, especially Greeks and easterners, and since the Romans were generous in their attitude towards manumission, large numbers of slaves had in fact been gaining freedom and citizenship during the last generation or two. This must obviously have had some effect on the racial stock of the population of Rome: the extent is debatable. Some historians have believed that the Italian element was swamped and that anything up to 85 per cent of the people employed in factories, shops and households were slaves or ex-slaves.[10] But even if this high figure were to be accepted, uncertainty about the origin of the slaves and about the birth-rate in freedmen families must render theories of radical racial change doubtful. A considerable foreign element clearly did infiltrate into the population, but it may have been largely assimilated by the Italian element which will therefore have been adulterated but not superseded (see also p. 196).

The cry for Panem et Circenses, for free food and entertainment, that rose so loudly during the Empire, was already heard in the late Republic. Since Clodius had changed Gracchus' corn-law into a free dole, the proletariat had claimed this as a right which no politician who needed their votes could refuse, until Caesar, who devised other means of relief, was able to limit the number of recipients (p. 122). As to Circenses, the number of public games was increased by the establishment of Ludi Sullanae victoriae and Ludi victoriae Caesaris in honour of Venus Genetrix. In addition to the regular festivals, individuals, especially candidates for office, staged gladiatorial combats and won votes by pandering to the cruelty and blood-lust of the mob. Animal-hunts (*venationes*) also increased in number and elaboration. An age which was apparently unmoved when 6000 of Spartacus' followers were crucified along the Appian Way, is not likely to have been affected by the sufferings of animals, but it is good to know that at least once some qualms were felt. When at the games which celebrated the dedication of Pompey's gift to Rome of her first stone theatre in 55 B.C., 500 lions and 17 elephants were slaughtered, Cicero wrote, 'What pleasure can it give to a cultured man to see a weak human being mangled by a powerful wild-beast or a splendid animal transfixed by a hunting-spear?' Pliny records that the spectators were so moved at the killing of the elephants that they rose as one man and cursed Pompey.[11] Unfortunately this feeling of pity was merely a passing mood, but the demonstration reminds us that the theatre could perform another important function: it served as a sounding-board for public opinion.

5. THE CITY

The city of Rome, whose population in the Ciceronian age may not have fallen a great deal short of a million, must have been steadily expanding, and during the period from Sulla to Caesar much systematic building and planning was undertaken in the centre.[12] Under Sulla the Forum, where the Senate-House (Curia) was restored and the Rostra probably rebuilt, was linked as an architectural unit with the Capitol by the construction of the Record Office (Tabularium) which was completed by Catulus in 78. This fine building overlooking the Forum with its arcaded façade and high Italic base (podium), its combination of Roman arch and Greek pilaster, is among the most striking examples of surviving Republican architecture. Sulla also restored the Capitoline Temple of Juppiter which had been burnt in 83. Pompey was responsible for a group of buildings in the Campus Martius, centred on his new theatre and portico. The next of the great principes, Caesar, started work on his new Forum (a colonnaded area with shops behind, which included a temple to Venus Genetrix) in order to relieve pressure on the crowded old Forum, where he built a magnificent new Basilica Iulia. He also planned to rebuild the Curia, burnt again in the rioting of 52, and a new voting-enclosure (Saepta Iulia). But much of his work was finished only by Augustus, who in turn, as Octavian, started his own great building schemes as early as 36 in his attempt to foster national pride (see below, p. 192).

Better building materials were coming into wider use. Older material, as wood, crude brick, and tufa, was being superseded in many richer buildings by the cream-coloured limestone from Tibur, now called Travertine; marbles from overseas were also employed, and from Caesar's day those of Carrara in N. Italy. From the second century onwards concrete was increasingly used for interior construction; it was faced with stone, at first with little irregular pieces (opus incertum) and later with square or lozenge-shaped bits arranged in a network pattern (opus reticulatum).

Thus Rome gained many fine buildings, her water-supply was improved by means of two new aqueducts (in 125 and 33), and the gardens of men like Lucullus, Sallust, Maecenas and Caesar, provided open spaces in the sub-urbs. But there was much squalor in the poor quarters, where rose the high and over-crowded tenements of the more humble. The city too was liable to fire and flooding, the streets were not lighted, and there was no police force. Though the well-to-do were safe enough at home, if they ventured out at night they might need an escort of slaves or clients. Such conditions naturally encouraged crime and violence.

Much building in other towns belongs to the Sullan period. That at Pompeii has already been mentioned (p. 148). Partially surviving monuments of this epoch include two temples at Cori, two others at Tibur (Tivoli), the great temple-complex of Juppiter Anxur on the hill above Terracina with its imposing surviving platform, and the enlarged sanctuary of Fortuna at Praeneste. Many villas also belong to this period, for instance an earlier one under Hadrian's Villa near Tivoli. Thus many of the towns of Italy, like Rome, began to assume a new appearance in the late Republic.

6. THE PROVINCES[13]

Before 133 B.C. Rome had acquired six provinces (cf. pp. 3 ff.), but gradually the number was increased: Asia (133–129), Gallia Narbonensis (between 121/20 and 100) to which the rest of Transalpine Gaul was added by Caesar's conquests (58–50), Cilicia (from c. 102), Bithynia (74) to which Pompey added parts of Pontus, Cyrenaica (74 or later), Crete (c. 67), Syria (64–3), Illyricum (from 53 or earlier), Cyprus (58), Egypt (30) and the somewhat anomalous Gallia Cisalpina (89, 81 or later). The inhabitants of all these provinces varied greatly in race and civilization; in the East the city-dwellers were mainly Greek or Hellenized, but in the West there was no predominant culture apart from that enjoyed by the Celtic peoples. The Romans had no clear-cut theoretical methods of administration that they wanted to force on the provincials; they preferred to leave local arrangements alone so far as these did not clash with their own interests. They therefore used for the basis of their rule the existing communities (civitates), either city-states or native tribes, though as they naturally found the more advanced cities easier to deal with, they tended where possible to promote the development of city life.

When a province was annexed by Rome the conditions of its administration might be defined in a charter (lex provinciae) which was drafted by a higher magistrate and a commission of ten senators. These charters, which were varied to suit local conditions, established the status of the communities within the province and laid down regulations about such questions as tribute and jurisdiction. Matters of detail which fell beyond the scope of the charter were announced by each succeeding governor in his edict, but since he would normally tend to follow his predecessor's principles, the provincial edicts tended to become standardized. Within each province there were two groups of especially favoured communities, the civitates foederatae and civitates *liberae*, the chief difference being that the status of the former was guaranteed by a permanent treaty, whereas that of the latter (which had been granted under the *lex provinciae* or by a special *lex rogata*) was revocable and could be revised by Rome. The *civitates liberae* were more numerous than the *civitates foederatae*, which in Sicily numbered only three out of a total of some sixty-five communities. Both types, however, enjoyed certain privileges in common: they could use their own laws, they normally remained outside the governor's jurisdiction, they sometimes were exempted from the obligation to quarter Roman troops, and, not least, all the *civitates foederatae* and probably most of the *civitates liberae* were exempt from taxation. In theory they might be liable to supply military help on demand, but Rome did not normally employ provincial levies, although on occasion she might summon contingents from the wilder tribes. The less favoured communities (*civitates stipendiariae*) were also normally allowed by the government a considerable degree of local self-government; although Rome usually required a property qualification for municipal office, she interfered as little as possible in local politics when her own interests were not threatened.[14]

The chief burden laid upon the provincials by Rome was taxation, but this, if judged by the standards of the time, was not generally exorbitant; the amount was arranged by Rome, and was not the governor's concern. Before the time of Caesar the provinces fall into two categories: the majority paid a fixed tax (*vectigal certum*), which from Caesar's time appears to have become universal; on the other hand a tithe (*decuma*) on agricultural land and a grazing-tax (*scriptura*) on pasture (reckoned according to the number of animals grazed) was paid by Sicily and Asia, by parts of Sardinia, and after Pompey's settlement possibly by Syria, Bithynia-Pontus, Cilicia and Cyprus. In addition to this *tributum soli*, tolls (*portoria*) were levied at a low rate (2–5 per cent) on goods entering or leaving a province.

The method of collecting the taxes differed in the two groups. Where the land tax was a fixed sum of silver, representing a proportion of the value of an average harvest, it was collected by the various local authorities (who might be helped by private contractors) and then handed over by them to the Roman quaestor. The tithes were either delivered in grain, as in Sicily and Sardinia, or commuted into a cash payment, as in Asia: in both these cases the right to collect it was put up to auction. In Sicily, where the Romans had taken over the system formerly used by king Hiero of Syracuse, the taxes were auctioned locally, with the result that a city could bid for its own tithes, and their collection was carefully controlled (6 per cent profit being allowed to the collector), so that the large Roman companies (*societates*) were not interested (except in the *portoria* and *scripturae* which were auctioned in Rome). But the tithes of Asia were, by Gracchus' law of 123, auctioned en bloc in Rome, so that they fell under the control of the Equestrian Order which supplied the shareholders (*socii*) and directors (*magistri*) of the *societates* of *publicani*. In addition to the taxes, provincials were liable for the upkeep of the governor's staff and soldiers, but conditions were carefully regulated and payment was made for the grain that he might require. In Sicily and Sardinia the Roman government also claimed the right of pre-emption of further corn, but not more in quantity than a second tithe. Further, since it is unlikely that rich men who happened not to own any land escaped taxation altogether, a property tax (*tributum capitis*) probably could be imposed, although not much is known about it before the Principate.

The provincial governor was normally a proconsul or propraetor, who had held a magistracy in Rome during the previous year (or five years previously according to Pompey's law of 52 B.C.). The Senate usually decided which provinces should be assigned to the consuls and which to the praetors (between 123 and 52 B.C. the consular provinces had to be named before the consuls were elected); they were then assigned to the prospective governors by lot. Governorships were theoretically annual, but through an insufficiency of senior magistrates they were often prolonged for a year or so. A governor's authority was almost unlimited over the provincials (except through the *lex provinciae* and treaties), but any Roman citizens in the provinces were entitled to use their right of appeal (*provocatio*).

His chief duties were defence, against both external attack and internal disorder, and jurisdiction. For the latter purpose a province was divided into a number of circuits (*conventus*) in which he would hold assizes to try cases of serious crime in accordance with the rules that he had laid down in his provincial edict. He kept the balance of any money that he handled in a provincial *fiscus*, and both he and his quaestor were liable to account, but only at the end of their term of office. By Caesar's *lex Julia* (59), however, financial arrangements were tightened up and a governor had to balance and publish his accounts before leaving his province. Each governor had a considerable staff. His right-hand man was his quaestor, allocated to him by lot, who was chiefly responsible for finance but who could be entrusted with other tasks such as jurisdiction and levying or even commanding troops. A consular governor usually had three *legati*, normally senators chosen by himself and approved by the Senate, while other friends or young relatives of semi-official status (*comites* or *contubernales*) helped to swell his suite; in addition he could appoint *praefecti* for specific tasks or to honorary *praefecturae*. Further, he had a large staff of subordinate officials (*apparitores*), who included a private secretary (*accensus*), clerks (*scribae*), lictors, *viatores, haruspices, praecones, medici* and the like.[15] He clearly had at his disposal a great amount of patronage, while, if unscrupulous, he could also show favour to the businessmen, the *publicani* and *negotiatores*.

The happiness of a province depended largely on the personal character of its governor. A man of integrity might withstand the temptations of office, but although few sank as low as Verres, many came to regard their year of office, which was unpaid, as an opportunity to recoup themselves for the great sums they had spent on winning office and to provide for future expenses; their staffs would no doubt follow their example. Among the commonest abuses were the sale of justice and of exemptions from requisitioning and a profitable commuting for money of a governor's right to demand corn for the maintenance of himself and his staff: he might, for instance, order it to be delivered at so distant a place that the farmer would be glad to make a cash deal to avoid the heavy costs of transport. Beside this semi-official plundering, a governor might co-operate with the *publicani*, or at any rate turn a blind eye to their exactions; Cicero once told his brother that it was dangerous to offend them, but that, if allowed, they would utterly ruin the provincials. These vultures flocked to all the provinces, especially in the Greek East and they did not lack spoil: the hatred that they inspired is shown by the eagerness with which the Asiatics, instigated by Mithridates, had massacred tens of thousands of them in 88 (p. 49). Governors who tried to protect the provincials from them, might suffer the fate that had overtaken Rutilius Rufus (p. 53) and Lucullus (p. 85). It is true that the jurors, whether senatorial or equestrian, were not always free from class loyalty or immune from bribery. On the other hand many corrupt governors were brought to book and, since it is the most scandalous cases that make the headlines, much straightforward and uneventful administration must have been accomplished: if standards in the first half of the last century of the Republic were not as high as those in the preceding century, they were probably better than those of the second half.

What benefits then did the provincials gain in return for their payment of tribute and the sufferings they endured? Theoretically perhaps peace was the greatest, although this was not fully realized until the Principate. Rome had unified the Mediterranean world and gave it some protection against barbarian invasions from beyond the frontiers. But she did not create a planned frontier system and failed to establish a professional army that could adequately guard the provinces, where the standing garrisons might be too small and the governors might lack the requisite military ability: thus, for instance, it was lucky for the Roman East that the Parthians did not renew their attacks when Cicero was governor of Cilicia in 51, because as he urgently reminded the Senate he lacked adequate troops to meet the threatening invasion. Further the provinces suffered from Rome's slow decision to eradicate piracy and also from the civil wars, which brought actual fighting to many and exactions to most (e.g. those of Brutus and Cassius in the East). Yet notwithstanding all this, the aim and direction of Roman policy was to establish peace in large areas where previously warfare had been normal.

Rome was also largely successful in securing peace within the *civitates* and suppressing class strife, an endemic disease in so many Greek cities. But here the cost was the overshadowing of democratic assemblies by Councils drawn from the propertied classes. In other areas, however, Rome's coming meant political advance, for instance to serfs in Asia Minor and especially in the more backward West, where oppression decreased, the status of the common man improved, and economic prosperity followed. It is noteworthy that Rome normally had never tried to restrict production in the provinces for her own benefit (e.g. by imposing preferential tariffs or arranging for commercial privileges in her treaties), but rather by establishing peace and security, and not least by her construction of roads, she provided conditions which naturally fostered economic development.

Another outstanding merit of Roman rule was its toleration of local differences, in culture, language, religion and law. Apart from encouraging urbanization as opposed to tribal organization, Rome interfered in local matters as little as was consistent with her security: she did not try to force her own civilization on others, and was in consequence slow to extend Roman citizenship to provincials until Julius Caesar adopted a more generous policy (her reluctance is not surprising in view of the fact that it was not until 90 B.C. and only as the result of a bitter war, that she extended her citizenship to the whole of Italy itself). Roman citizens in the provinces enjoyed few juridical privileges (except the right of *provocatio*) that were denied to the provincials themselves, but in practice they naturally had far greater influence and prestige and would receive more consideration from the governor. The abuse of this *de facto* privileged position naturally tended to make Roman rule unpopular where it was moderate, and hated where it was oppressive.

One of the most damning indictments of Roman maladministration comes from Cicero's prosecution of Verres, where he deliberately paints a dark picture but admits that 'lugent omnes provinciae . . . locus . . . nullus est . . . quo non . . . nostrorum hominum libido iniquitasque pervaserit'. Four years later he exclaimed 'difficile est dictu, Quirites, quanto in odio simus apud externas nationes'. Such hatred helps to explain the readiness of the lower classes to follow any leader who challenged Rome's power, such as Aristonicus or Mithridates. And if a Roman could be so outspoken as Cicero, clearly the sentiments of the provincials themselves must have been even more violent. They have not left many traces in the surviving literature, which is written mainly by Romans or from the Roman point of view, but they do find expression in some of the so-called Sibylline Oracles which hopefully prophesy the downfall of Rome and the coming reign of law and justice.[16] Yet in the event it was Rome herself that introduced the new era. The pressing need for reform was only too obvious, but at length Rome recognized her responsibility and although it was too late to save the Republic, Augustus at least saved the provinces.

X

ART, LITERATURE AND THOUGHT IN THE LATE REPUBLIC

1. GRAECO–ROMAN CULTURE

The blending of Greek and Roman culture was the result of a long process. Some five hundred years earlier Rome had first encountered Greek influences in her contacts with the Etruscans and with the Greek cities in Italy. Then in the third century her contacts became more personal: Roman soldiers, administrators and traders began to visit Greek lands, and under the stimulus of Greece Latin literature was born. The full impact came in the second century, when Greece itself and part of the Hellenistic East were included in Rome's empire, and we have already seen how Rome assimilated much without being overwhelmed and gave to what she received a Latin appearance (p. 9 ff.). In the next century Greek culture at Rome was no longer merely a foreign importation but had become 'naturalized' and civilization in the late Republic represented essentially the harmonious blending of the two backgrounds, a synthesis to which both traditions contributed, each enriching without destroying the other.

The share of each culture has been differently assessed at different times. In the eighteenth and early nineteenth centuries, with the romantic revival and the 'discovery' of Greek culture and art, many were dazzled by the glories of Greece, and tended to regard the Romans as mere borrowers and to attribute most of what was good in Graeco–Roman culture to the Greek side. But a more balanced appreciation suggests that whereas the technical forms which art and literature assumed in the late Republic were Greek, the spirit within was new. It is true that there were certain main differences between the natural endowments of Greek and Roman, which are summed up in Virgil's famous lines,

excudent alii spirantia mollius aera
(credo equidem), vivos ducent de marmore vultus,
orabunt causas melius, caelique meatus
describent radio et surgentia sidera dicent:
tu regere imperio populos, Romane, memento
(hae tibi erunt artes), pacisque imponere morem,
parcere subiectis et debellare superbos.

Romans had a more practical bent and showed their talent in law, administration and engineering: Greeks excelled in art and philosophy, and in this sphere the Roman was a learner and 'Graecia capta ferum victorem cepit'. But their gifts were complementary: Rome's slower artistic and philosophical development was stimulated by Greece, and Roman political wisdom finally united a world which all the genius of the Greeks had failed to bring together. Thus Greece provided much of the cultural impetus and example and Rome built up a framework in which it could flourish, but it would be wrong to regard Graeco–Roman culture merely as Greek civilization dressed up in Roman guise; Rome did more than preserve Greek culture for later generations: borrowing much she injected her own spirit into it. Latin writers might use Greek forms of verse, but they infused a fresh and individual feeling into them, and Cicero's thought, though largely derived from Greek thinkers, bore a distinctive Roman stamp and was clothed in a language which he had made sufficiently flexible to convey new ideas to his fellow-countrymen. It was this amalgam, hammered out in the hectic days of the late Republic, that was handed on to the more tranquil days of the Empire for men of genius, as Virgil or the sculptor of the Ara Pacis, to work further upon.

In creating this mixture the inspiration from Greece naturally came from varied elements in Greek culture, and its impact was not the same in all spheres and in all directions. Though educated Romans read and knew their Greek classics, in the late Republic they were even more conscious of the later Hellenistic world of the post-classical period. Thus Cicero owed more to Posidonius than to Plato; sculptors and architects looked to the Hellenistic cities of Pergamum and Alexandria rather than to the Athens of Pheidias and Ictinus; and whereas earlier Latin poets had turned to classical Greek poetry, Catullus and his friends found guidance in the learned poetry of Alexandria. The measure of Rome's debt varied also in different fields: in art her dependence was greatest, in science (as mathematics, medicine and the natural sciences) she showed most indifference, while in literature she responded best by producing fine work in which both Greek and native elements were harmoniously fused. So too the impact of Greece varied in intensity in the different strata of society. In early days it was the Roman aristocracy that had welcomed Greek ideas and ways, but at the same time Greek and Oriental slaves and freedmen had spread Greek manners at a lower level of society, while Roman soldiers had campaigned, and middle-class business men, had traded, in Greek lands. Thus while one class assimilated Greek philosophy and literature, others welcomed some of the more sensational cults and beliefs of the East. On the whole therefore Hellenistic ideas must have permeated widely through society in a Rome that by the end of the Republic had become a great cosmopolitan city and was overshadowing, not only in polit-ical power but also in economic and cultural life, the cities of the Hellenistic world. On the other hand many of the more remote country towns of central Italy must have retained a more untouched Italian way of life, and it was from this healtheir source, rather than from the older Hellenized aristocracy or urban mob in Rome that Augustus was to seek regenerative powers for Roman society. How this fusion of cultures was effected in art, literature and other cultural activities must now be briefly examined.

2. ART AND ARCHITECTURE[1]

In no sphere perhaps more than that of art was Rome's contribution for so long ignored in modern times, to the greater glory of Greece. This was due in part to the great influence of Winckelmann (eighteenth century) who believed that Rome made no individual contribution to an art which she inherited from Greece. And even when distinctively Roman elements were recognized, it was at first in the art of the Empire alone; only comparatively recently has the older Italic and Roman contribution to the art of the Republic been established. The nature and extent of Rome's particular contribution is still debatable in detail, but that she made such a contribution is more widely recognized. In sculpture Rome did not so much invent what was character-istic of herself as recognize in Greek and Hellenistic art those aspects which could best express her spirit, and these she developed or encouraged Greek artists to develop for her. Her chief contributions here were a realistic por-traiture, the creation of spatial depths in relief-sculpture and painting by means of illusionistic methods, and the development of Greek narrative art in historical reliefs with a 'continuous' manner of narration in which her feeling for history and imperial ideas could find expression. This last devel-opment is well illustrated in the 'altar of Ahenobarbus' (see chapter II, n. 40) and later in imperial reliefs from the Ara Pacis onwards.

One of the most striking developments in the first century B.C. is the extraordinary desire by Romans for works of art; since great artists cannot be produced to order, the Romans demanded copies of great originals. This demand was not confined to sculpture, but extended to most branches of art. In sculpture a response was made easier by the invention of a mechanical copying process, the so-called pointing method. Most of the sculptors were

Greeks, who either executed the commissions of wealthy Romans in their own cities or else settled in Rome. Thus a booming new industry grew up, in which Greek statues of all periods were reproduced or adapted (e.g. the statue of a Greek god might be copied and then given the features of a living Roman). A similar use of Greek prototypes was made for the copying of bronze statuettes, pottery with relief decoration, terracotta plaques, stucco reliefs, glassware, engraved gems and also probably painting. Since in the process the products came to reflect Roman taste, all this work may justly be called 'Graeco–Roman'.

Private and public Roman patronage also began to make requests that could not be answered by mere adaptation but evinced new conceptions. The desire for decoration on sepulchral monuments was met by adorning sarcophagi with sculpted scenes taken from mythology or later with battle-scenes. This new form is linked with the desire to commemorate public events, such as victories, and it gave rise to the historical reliefs which were to blossom out in their full glory during the Empire. Another striking development is found in portraiture: there was a widespread demand for portrait-busts, which displayed a dry realism (or verism) which contrasts strongly with the idealizing realism of Greek portraiture. This Roman realism may derive in spirit from Etruscan and early Italic art, but since most of the late Roman portraits were made by Greeks and since many Greeks of the Hellenistic period had turned to a veristic style (as the magnificent coin-portraits of the Greek kings of Bactria show), this fascinating development of first century portraiture may have arisen primarily from Greek artists responding to a demand from practical realistic Romans for 'photographic' portraits of themselves, warts and all.[2]

Art and portraiture are both well illustrated in the Roman silver coinage (chiefly *denarii*). Rome's earliest coin-dies had been cut by Greeks (the so-called Romano–Campanian coins) and no doubt the Roman mint, which was administered by young Roman nobles, continued to employ a preponderance of Greek workmen. Artistically many of the coins are excellent, particularly from the time of Sulla and especially from 68 to 55 B.C. Realistic portraiture on Roman coins started when the mint-official Coelius Caldus (c. 62) issued a coin portraying his grandfather, a tribune in 106. The portraits of living men commenced with the dictator Caesar and were followed by those of the triumvirs. In this, as in other forms of art, the way was paved for imperial developments.

In architecture again the debt of Rome to Greece was immense, but Rome's individual development of Greek ideas is at once apparent if one visualizes for a moment the Acropolis of Athens and the Fora of Imperial Rome. Rome displayed here her great gift of borrowing what she needed from others and adapting the loan in accord with her own national genius: in the process something new was created. The qualities perhaps most associated with Roman architecture are magnificence of conception and solidity of construction. Something has already been said (p. 154) about developments in the late Republic in Rome and Italy, due in part to the use of new building materials. Here it is necessary only to recall the fact that throughout Italy and the Roman world characteristically Roman buildings, many of which made skilful use of the arch, were constantly being constructed: temples, basilicas, bridges, aqueducts, drains, triumphal arches, city-walls, tombs, baths, theatres, amphitheatres, town and country houses. Nor should the work of the engineer who co-operated with the architect be forgotten; not least his genius in the construction of those thousands of miles of roads which bound the Roman world together and made the economic and administrative life of the empire possible.

3. THE POETS[3]

Early Latin literature had been born under the inspiration of Greek, starting with translation from the Greek classics, then imitating them, and finally, still under their spell, developing into a national literature. The pioneers in epic, tragedy and comedy had been Livius Andronicus (who died in 204), Naevius (d. 199), Q. Ennius (d. 169), M. Pacuvius (d. 130), Plautus (d. 184) and Terence (d. 159), all of whom owed an immense debt to Greece. But in one branch the Romans 'had it all their own way', which is what Quintillian in a famous comparison of Greek and Roman literature seems to mean when he said 'satura tota nostra est'. Early satire, which means a 'medley', was probably a form of Variety produced on the stage, but it developed into a literary genre, in poetry, and also in prose and verse intermixed. Ennius was the first to write a poetic miscellany of this kind, but its full potentialities were first realized by C. Lucilius (c. 180–102), a Latin from Suessa Aurunca who settled in Rome and became a friend of Scipio Aemilianus; starting to write about 131 B.C., in all he composed thirty books of satires in hexameter verse, of which less than 1300 lines survive. Turning for his subject-matter to the society in which he moved, he exposed its vices and follies in satiric verses. His connexion with the Scipionic circle brought him into close touch with Roman politics, personalities and life. If he could be harsh (and he did not spare the political opponents of Aemilanus), he could also show wit and grace as he ranged over many events of everday life; his language was colloquial. His writings formed the model for Horace's satires later and, if they had survived, would have thrown a flood of light on the social and political life of his generation.[4]

Epic poetry at Rome reached its peaks with Ennius and Virgil: the century or more which lay between these two giants produced no great epics, and those who attempted the task are now little more than names. By the Gracchan age drama was passing its zenith, both in tragedy and comedy, but a few notable figures emerged.[5] L. Accius (c. 170–c. 85) became a very popular tragedian. We have the titles of over forty of his tragedies which were based on Greek drama (fabulae palliatae) and of two historical dramas (praetextae): his treatment was melodramatic and he preferred violent plots, but his work was highly esteemed not only by his contemporaries but also by Cicero, Horace and Quintillian. The practice of adapting Greek comedies for the Roman stage, which Plautus and Terence had followed with such skill, came to an end with the death in 103 of a writer named Turpilius. A more popular form of comedy emerged in the fabulae togatae, 'comedies in native dress', which portrayed domestic life in Italian towns and villages. The pioneer here was Titinius, who was perhaps slightly junior to Terence. T. Quinctius Atta (who died in 77) excelled in his women characters; the titles of eleven of his plays survive. More important was L. Afranius (born about 150), of whose works we have forty-four titles; though he retained an Italian background, he admired Menander and other New Comedy Greek poets. This turning again to Greece suggests that the native inspiration was weakening; at any rate Afranius found no successor to rival his achievements in this field. But if Rome gradually ceased to produce new dramatists of talent (and men tended to write plays as mere literary exercises rather than for production), the earlier plays remained popular in the days of Cicero. Old tragedies and comedies were revived, and stage stars, such as Aesopus and Roscius, enhanced their reputations by their performances in plays by Accius and Plautus. At the same time the theatres were made more attractive and the performance more spectacular and lavish.

Many theatre-goers, however, demanded less intellectual fare: the farce and mime were the answer. A primitive form of rustic farce had grown up in Campania, whence it had spread to Rome ('Oscan' or 'Atellan' farce). It had a few traditional clownish characters (like Punch and Judy) and much of the dialogue was probably impromptu, crude in jest and language. It was given a more literary form during the Sullan period by two writers, L. Pomponius and Novius, who retained the rustic crudeness and stock characters, but extended the range and even introduced some of the conventional characters of Greek New Comedy. Thereafter the Atellane drama probably reverted to its less literary semi-improvised form and in this guise it continued to enjoy great popularity during the Roman Empire.

The mime, well known in Greek South Italy in early days, was performed by groups of strolling players, who with simple stage and curtain put on a plain show, the chief actor or actress using one or two others as foils to their wit and banter, unrestrained by any sense of decency. This shapeless and varied performance was given literary status by a Roman knight, Decimus

Laberius (c. 115–43), but although the names of 43 of his mimes survive, little is known about their form or nature, apart from their frequent indecency in subject and language. No less popular was a slave from Syria, Publilius Syrus, whose ability soon won for him patronage and freedom. In a general challenge to all rivals at the ludi *Caesaris* in 46 or 45, he defeated even Laberius. Later a collection was made of the moral sayings of his characters, which shows that mimes could provide ethical maxims as well as much indecency. Like the farce, the mime continued in undiminished popularity during the Empire.

At the other extreme from these sub-literary, or non-literary, forms of entertainment stand the literary circles and above all the two splendid poets that emerged in the late Republic, Lucretius and Catullus. Many cultured men tried their hands at poetry for their own or their friends' amusement, and there seems to have been a guild or college for professional poets which met in the temple of Minerva on the Aventine; at one time Accius was its head. Private literary circles did not necessarily cease with the death of Scipio Aemilianus' various friends. Lutatius Catulus (*cos.* 102) had contacts with other literary men even if he did not form a 'circle' in the way that Aemilianus had done; he thus helped to form a link with Cicero and his contemporaries. In the late Republic a coterie of younger poets, the Neoterici, turned away from earlier Greek poetry for their inspiration to the school of Alexandria, which was marked by great and often pedantic learning; it sought fresh material, not before handled in verse, and often the poet's own emotions were given more rein. Members of this group in Rome included C. Licinius Calvus (son of the annalist Licinius Macer), of whose poems only a few fragments survive, Cinna (possibly C. Helvius Cinna the unfortunate tribune of 44 B.C.), and their friend C. Valerius Catullus.[6]

Catullus[7] (c. 84–c. 54) was born in Cisalpine Gaul at Verona, the son of a wealthy family, and went to Rome about 62. He became infatuated with the Lesbia of his poems, whose real name was Clodia; she was one of the sisters of the tribune of 58, P. Clodius, probably the wife of Metellus Celer (*cos.* 60). Later he was supplanted in her affections by other lovers, including Caelius, presumably Cicero's young friend M. Caelius Rufus. If these traditional identifications are correct, as they most likely are, Catullus will have fallen in love with one of the most profligate women of Roman society and the leader of a fast set. In 57 he served on the staff of the propraetor Memmius in Bithynia, and probably after his return he composed a final bitter farewell to Lesbia (poem 11). He also directed some stinging lampoons against Caesar and the Caesarians. His poems, of which 116 survive, comprise short lyrics on a variety of subjects, a few longer pieces, and a group in elegiac metre. Though he owed much to Alexandrine influence, he also turned to the older Greek poets, especially Sappho. With her, he may be reckoned among the greatest lyric poets of ancient, and indeed, all times. His success he owed partly to his love of nature and to the sincerity and depths of the personal feelings that he expressed, which contrasted strongly with earlier Roman conceptions of *gravitas* and yet reflected a *simplicitas* alien to the sophisticated society in which he lived.

Titus Lucretius Carus[8] (c. 94–55), the slightly older contemporary of Catullus, is an obscure figure: it is even uncertain whether he was a member or only a dependant of the aristocratic family of the Lucretii. He dedicated his poem to C. Memmius, a son-in-law of Sulla and praetor in 58, who had befriended Catullus and Cinna: whether Memmius was primarily his friend or patron cannot be said. Nor can the famous story that he was poisoned by a love-philtre, suffered bouts of insanity and committed suicide be confirmed. As an Epicurean, he took no part in public life. His poem De Rerum Natura, in six books, is didactic in purpose: it expounds the materialism and atomic theory of his master Epicurus, in an attempt to free man from superstitious fears by proving that the human soul does not survive death (which should therefore not be feared) and that the gods do not intervene in mundane affairs; these are governed by mechanical laws which control the movement of the atoms of which the universe is made, though owing to a postulated spontaneous swerve in the motion of the atoms, man is allowed free-will in this otherwise deterministic system. If he had merely succeeded in putting Epicurus' philosophy before Roman readers (and this is what Lucretius himself regarded as his main achievement), his great technical skill in handling such material in verse would have been noteworthy, but that was not all, because he happened to be a great poet also. He brought to this unpromising theme such intensity of feeling that his poems are shot through with passages of great majesty, eloquence and splendour, and on the strength of these tokens of a powerful and vivid imagination he is reckoned by some critics worthy to be classed with Virgil himself.

4. HISTORICAL WRITING[9]

The earliest Romans to write histories were some senators who lived during the Hannibalic War. Somewhat surprisingly they composed their works in Greek, not Latin: this was partly because they wanted to justify and explain Roman policy to the Greek world. Though they found some imitators in the second century, Cato the Censor set the example of writing in Latin when he composed an account of Rome's origins and history down to his own day. Other writers then began to treat Roman history in a year-by-year 'annalistic' manner: one of the earliest of them was L. Calpurnius Piso, the consul of 133, whose work ran from the origins of Rome down to his own day. An important development took place c. 123 when the Pontifex Maximus published in eighty books the Annales Maximi. This was a systematic arrangement of the material provided by the Tabulae Pontificum, which had for centuries been set up annually in the Regia and gave the names of the magistrates (*fasti*) and other matters of public interest. The publication of this material in convenient and 'standard' form stimulated other writers. In Gracchan times Cn. Gellius wrote Annales on a fuller scale than his predecessors, and the son-in-law of Laelius, C. Fannius (*cos.* 122), was the author of an authoritative history, perhaps from the origins, but probably of his own times. Three later annalists of the Sullan age, Valerius Antias, Claudius Quadrigarius and C. Licinius Macer (tribune in 73) wrote on an extended scale (Valerius in at least seventy-five books) and elaborated their material. By literary devices and rhetorical skill they heightened the interest of their works, but their facts were often less reliable than those of their more sober predecessors. Valerius in particular confused and misrepresented much, partly under the political and family influences of his own day. The works of these three writers are particularly important because they were later extensively used by Livy who gave the annalistic tradition of Roman history its classic form.

Beside the strictly annalistic tradition another method of historical presentation developed, partly from the example of the earlier senators who had written in Greek and from the more discursive work of Cato, but chiefly under the impact of the Universal History of Polybius, the Greek statesman who had been interned in Italy and had won the friendship of Scipio Aemilianus (p. 11). He wrote to show how and why Rome had united the world and how her empire was bringing material and moral advantages to its members. The same idea and viewpoint also inspired the *Histories* of Posidonius, a Greek philosopher (*c.* 135–51/50 B.C.), who continued the history of Rome and the eastern and western peoples with whom she same into contact from the point where Polybius' work had ended (146 B.C.) down to Sulla's dictatorship. He wrote from the standpoint of the Roman nobility, while his personal contacts with Marius and Pompey led him to dislike the former and admire the latter. The works of Polybius and Posidonius, with their justification of Roman imperialism, their wider interest in mankind as a whole, and their historical accuracy, made a tremendous impact on Roman thought. One of the immediate effects was that Sempronius Asellio (military tribune at Numantia in 133) wrote a history of his time (down to at least 91 B.C.), following Polybius' more pragmatic attitude. Although Posidonius' *Histories* do not survive, they influenced Roman historians as Sallust, Caesar and Tacitus, and Greek writers as Plutarch and Diodorus: the last, who lived at the end of the Republic, wrote a Universal History down to 54 B.C. in forty books.

In an age when the individual began to count more in public life men naturally turned to composing their autobiographies or Memoirs: Aemilius Scaurus, Rutilius Rufus, Q. Catulus and Sulla all did so, and though their works are lost they are reflected in the use made of them by Plutarch for his *Lives*. Biography is represented by the *De Viris Illustribus*, written by Cicero's friend Cornelius Nepos who came to Rome from Cisalpine Gaul: in this book of Lives he compared famous Greeks and Romans. He also wrote some longer biographies, e.g. of Cato the Censor and Cicero, together with a universal history in three books. In his surviving work, a small part of *de Vir. Ill.*, his value as a historian is not great. Another friend of Cicero, Atticus, provided some material for historians when he produced a *Liber Annalis*, a chronological table of Roman history, and drew up pedigrees of some famous families as the Fabii and Aemilii. He also wrote a Greek monograph on Cicero's consulship. The historical monograph had been introduced at Rome by Coelius Antipater, who composed after 121 B.C. an account of the Second Punic War in seven books. Written in Latin with vividness and literary skill and based on Carthaginian as well as Roman sources, this work set a new fashion in addition to providing a standard history of its period. The example was followed by Caesar and Sallust.

Caesar's *Commentaries* on the Gallic and Civil Wars (the former based on his annual despatches to the Senate) provided material for future historians rather than claimed to be in themselves *historia* in the Roman sense of the word; they have already been briefly discussed (chapter VII, n. 5). Although their publication no doubt had a political purpose and the author was not free from a natural desire to establish the rightness of his conduct, they bear the stamp of essential truth: the simple and vigorous style, the lucidity of language and exposition, the unobtrusiveness of the writer, and the candour with which he lets the facts speak for themselves, all this suggests a basic honesty rather than a sinister manipulation of the facts. Some implicit self-justification there may have been, but scarcely deliberate tendentious distortion. The *Commentaries* cannot but show events as Caesar himself saw them and Caesar was both a general and a politician, fighting first for position, then for *dignitas* and survival.

The eighth book *De Bello Gallico* was written by A. Hirtius (*cos.* 43), an officer of Caesar, who lacked Caesar's military experience. Hirtius was also probably the author of a continuation of Caesar's *Civil War*, the *Bellum Alexandrinum*, though he did not take part in that war himself; this book includes Caesar's campaign at Zela. Two other works deal with Caesar's campaigns: the *Bellum Africum* (of 47–6 B.C.), written by a competent soldier who was not a staff officer, and the *Bellum Hispaniense* (campaign of Munda), written in awkward Latin by an eye-witness.

Something has also already been said about the historical works of Caesar's supporter, C. Sallustius Crispus,[10] who after serving him in the civil war, was appointed governor of Africa (p. 47; chapter III, n. 13; VI, n. 4; VII, n. 20). Thereafter he was accused of extortion, but avoided trouble and spent his remaining days in his famous Gardens (*Horti Sallustiani*) in Rome. In 43 he published his account of the Catilinarian Conspiracy (*Bellum Catilinae*) and his *Bellum Iugurthinum* some two years later. After 39 B.C. he turned from monographs to a full *History* of Rome, beginning from 78 B.C. where an earlier writer, L. Cornelius Sisenna (who had started from the Social War) had left off, and continuing the story down to 67 B.C. But whereas Sisenna had written from the conservative point of view, the five books of Sallust's *Historiae* and his monographs champion the popular cause. Both the *Catiline* and the *Jugurtha* denounce the degeneracy and corruption of the Optimates, and the former also defends Caesar from the charge that he was involved in Catiline's conspiracy; both therefore are political pamphlets rather than impartial and detailed accounts of their subject-matter. In style Sallust followed Thucydides and developed a terse, archaic manner which was epigrammatic, vivid and effective, but he fell woefully short of his master in objectivity of matter. Yet despite his bias, he by no means always exalts his hero Marius (partly because he made use of Sulla's *Memoirs*), and his vivid character sketches, even of politicians of the other side, are not always unfair. Unfortunately only a few fragments of his chief work survive. Two *Letters to Caesar* and an *Invective against Cicero* are also attributed to Sallust, but their genuineness is very doubtful (see chapter VII, n. 20). Sallust was much concerned with the corrupting effects of power, ambition and avarice on character, but his views are not original and he should not be claimed as a great thinker. As a critical historian he cannot be placed among the great, but his literary skill raises him high among the writers of Rome.

5. ORATORY[11]

Oratorical skill became of increasing value to its possessors, whether displayed in the Senate House, lawcourts or Assemblies. Distinction in oratory or law, it was said, ranked with nobility of birth and military service as one of the three claims to the consulship. It was owing to his powerful oratorical gifts that Cicero won his way to the consulship and into the ranks of the nobility. Increasing numbers of young Romans studied the technique of public speech, whether at Rome or at the Greek rhetorical schools in the East. In Cicero's opinion Roman achievement first equalled that of Greece in the oratory of Gaius Gracchus and his successors, many of whom published their speeches after delivery. Two masters of the next generation whom Cicero admired were M. Antonius (*cos.* 99), grandfather of the triumvir, and L. Crassus (*cos.* 95). When Cicero himself began to practise, the chief figure at the Roman bar was Q. Hortensius Hortalus (114–50), who favoured the Asiatic school of oratory which was more floral and ornamental than the simpler and more restrained Attic style that was cultivated by many, including young Caesar. Cicero himself followed a style midway between these two extreme schools, and with such success that when he triumphed over Hortensius at the trial of Verres he gained the first place, which he retained for the rest of his life.

In his speeches Cicero raised Latin prose to its highest point in this sphere. A rich vocabulary, amplitude of expression and great attention to the rhythm of his clauses produced a sonorous and majestic style, which might be varied with subtle strokes of irony, wit, or bitter invective. This result was not reached by mere natural talent; oratory was now a skilled and technical art, and Cicero not only studied the theory, but also wrote upon it. The most important of his rhetorical treatises are the three books of the *De Oratore*, the *Brutus* and the *Orator*.

In Cicero the culture of the later Republic is seen at its best. Unsurpassed in the field of oratory, he also turned his hand to works on political theory (p. 135 f.) and philosophy (p. 173), to translations of Greek authors, and to poetry; his most famous poem was the one he composed on his own consulship (*de consulatu meo*) in which he appears to have shown a lack of skill surprising in such a master of prose-rhythms. Not the least of his contributions were his private letters which he wrote to his friends without any idea of later publication. They are among the most interesting legacies of antiquity, not only for the flood of light that they throw upon the Roman world of his day, but also for the revelation of his own thought and personality. Through them we have a more intimate knowledge of Cicero than of almost any other figure of antiquity. There he stands revealed, in all his strength and weakness, and, taken all in all, few other statesmen of his day, had their private thoughts been thus recorded, would have provided so worthy an example of the culture and humanity of the age.

6. EDUCATION AND LEARNING

During the Ciceronian period Roman education was organized on similar lines to that in the Hellenistic world.[12] Apart from children who were educated at home by private tutors, boys and girls went to a primary school where they learned to read, write and count at the instruction of a *magister ludi*, whose profession was despised. Many a Roman, beside Horace, in later life remembered his cane if not his flogging. Those who were fortunate enough to proceed to a secondary education went to a school presided over by a *grammaticus*, who was generally badly paid. There they would make some acquaintance with the works of Livius Andronicus, Ennius and the comic poets, and with such texts as the Twelve Tables: when through Varro (see below) Latin grammar was studied scientifically, it too would be included in the curriculum. But Latin was not the only language: many young Romans learnt Greek at home from Greek slaves and education became bilingual. Higher education consisted chiefly of rhetorical studies. Greek rhetoricians held classes in Rome, and many young Romans went to study at Greek university towns, as Athens; Cicero and Caesar both studied rhetoric at Rhodes. In 93 the first school for the study of Latin rhetoric was opened at Rome by a supporter of Marius, but it was closed the next year by the aristocratic censors. Political motives may have operated: the Optimates may not have wished to make it easier for Populares to gain oratorical skill. Further, a *Manual of Rhetoric* dedicated to Herennius and written in the 80s B.C., suggested as themes for declamation not only traditional Greek subjects but also topical questions about the Gracchi, Saturninus, Drusus and Sulpicius; the unknown author seems to have been favourable to the popular party, although not suppressing arguments on the other side: such topics might prove inflammable.[13] Cicero through his rhetorical writings (p. 170) helped to promote the teaching of Latin eloquence, but it does not seem to have gained a real foothold in Rome until the time of Augustus.

The growth of scholarship is illustrated by L. Aelius Stilo, who was born at Lanuvium about 150 B.C. Of equestrian rank and a Stoic in belief, he wrote on many subjects, including grammar, etymology and literary criticism, and produced critical editions of Ennius and Lucilius. His pupils included Cicero and Varro. The life of M. Terentius Varro (116–27), who became one of Rome's greatest scholars, was not one of unbroken academic calm. A supporter of Pompey, he was pardoned by Caesar who appointed him keeper of his intended public library; he was then outlawed by Antony, but settled down peacefully after the Civil War. His writings were encyclopaedic in range. Among those that survive in part are a treatise on Latin grammar and vocabulary (*De lingua Latina*; 25 books) and the three books on agriculture. His *Antiquitates rerum humanarum et divinarum*, in 41 books, is a great loss. Other works included 15 books on famous Greeks and Romans, dialogues, an encyclopaedia of *artes liberales*, and 150 books on Menippean satires; in all he published some 620 volumes.

7. LAW[14]

Roman legal science, no less than other branches of Roman thought, was compelled during this period to come to terms with Hellenism, but as its roots went down deep into Italian soil, it was not overwhelmed by Greek influences: rather, it accepted or rejected at will. Roman sacred law had originally been exclusively in the hands of priests, especially the college of pontiffs, who had gradually encroached into the realm of private law. During the third century secular jurisconsults increasingly helped in the development of private law alongside the pontifical jurists, and before the end of the

Republic laymen were beginning to concern themselves with sacral law. But all this is less surprising when it is realized that all these men enjoyed the same social background: they were all members of the governing nobility, and many of the priests held public magistracies. But although the three famous members of the Mucian *gens* who all held the office of Pontifex Maximus, P. Mucius Scaevola, P. Crassus Mucianus and Q. Mucius Scaevola the 'Pontifex' (p. 22), all acted as consultants in private law, after their time the pontiffs began to withdraw from this activity. Later in the Ciceronian age the jurisconsults began to come from a different social class; some were of equestrian stock, others of even humbler origin, while a few men even broke off a public career to dedicate themselves to the law.

In addition to their practice some legal experts turned to writing. The publication of the Annales Maximi by the Pontifex Maximus P. Scaevola (p. 167), provided much material for legal, religious and secular history, and his son Q. Scaevola (*cos.* 95) published the first systematic treatise on the Ius Civile, an exposition of the whole private law. Q. Fabius (*cos.* 142) had published a large work on pontifical law, and in the late Republic at least four augurs wrote on augural law. Cicero's friend Servius Sulpicius Rufus (*cos.* 51), who was a jurisconsult of the older traditional type, wrote on the praetorian edict and on sacral law.

Nothing can be said here about the content of Roman law, which was one of the finest achievements of the human mind, but it is noteworthy that in the last century or so of the Republic civil procedure was being adapted to new needs. The old stereotyped procedure (*legis actio*), by which the issues to be tried were settled before a praetor, had proved too rigid and was modified under a *lex Aebutia* (*c.* 150) by the introduction of an alternative formulary system under which the praetor could allow formulas that were drafted to meet the requirements of the specific case: the *legis actiones* virtually disappeared under Augustus. At the same time Rome's own *ius civile*, which had proved inadequate in dealing with foreigners, had been adapted for this purpose to the *ius gentium* (i.e. Roman law as applied to foreigners). Beside the old *ius civile* there also gradually grew up a whole body of law arising from the edicts of magistrates, especially praetors (*ius honorarium*); the two systems combined, much as common law and equity have united to make up the English legal system. With the growing mass of statutory provisions, actions and the interpretations often embodied in the *responsa* of jurisconsults, Q. Scaevola was clearly undertaking a very necessary task in publishing a systematic account of the *ius civile*. The main development in criminal law in the period was the establishment of various *quaestiones perpetuae* and their development by Sulla and Caesar. The different *leges* which created them, however, dealt with single crimes and little attempt was made to produce a coherent code of criminal law.

8. PHILOSOPHY AND RELIGION

The two philosophic systems that appealed most to educated Romans, and whose study in fact formed part of their education, were Stoicism and Epicureanism.[15] Something has already been said about the reception of the former at Rome by the Scipionic circle, which was joined by the Stoic Panaetius (p. 10 f.). His influence and that of his creed were profound; it was later reinforced by the teaching of Posidonius, whose contribution to historiography has been mentioned above (p. 167). Beside revising further the system of the early Stoics, he displayed wide scientific interests (e.g. he calculated the circumference of the earth), and through his natural philosophy Stoicism influenced many scientists (e.g. astronomers and the geographer Strabo). By identifying political and ethical activities, sanctioned by religious duty, he further enhanced the influence of his creed on Roman life; not least among its followers were Cato and M. Brutus. The rival creed of Epicureanism, proclaimed with such religious fervour by Lucretius, gave solace to many, but its impact on public life will have been negative in that it withdrew men from politics. Only once did some of its adherents desert their philosophic scruples and turn to action: it was the tyranny of Caesar that stirred them. Though some Epicureans remained consistently loyal to the dictator, Cassius, who turned Epicurean in 46, and the majority of his fellow-philosophers decided that liberty and Republicanism demanded violent political action.

Between the claims of rival philosophies Cicero steered a middle course.[16] He was attracted on the theoretical level by the Scepticism of Carneades, the founder of the New Academy, and a visitor to Rome in 156/5, who disbelieved in the possibility of certain knowledge and argued that probability was the only guide. Disliking the inactivity of the Epicureans, Cicero was drawn to the practical morality of the Stoics, with their emphasis on humanity and the social virtues, though he would not go all the way with them. He was thus an eclectic, an interested inquirer rather than an original thinker. Yet his influence was profound, because as a distraction from the grief he felt at the death of his daughter Tullia in 45, he decided, as he says, to make philosophy accessible to his fellow-countrymen. This was almost pioneer work and in his task of adapting his Greek originals to his Latin medium he practically had to invent a vocabulary in which to express simply some of the Greek technical terms. The result was a series of works, written in lucid and graceful Latin which both enhanced Latin literature and popularized Greek thought. They include *De Officiis, De Finibus, Academica, Tusculanae Disputationes, De Natura Deorum, De Senectute* and *De Amicitia*. But Cicero did not enrich merely his fellow-countrymen: he put the whole world in his debt, Fathers of the Church, Italian humanists of the Renaissance, and French Revolutionaries alike.

The official cults had long been empty of any deep religious meaning for most of those that attended them: provided that their formal celebration maintained the pax deorum they need inspire no personal feelings, though they would offer at least a spectacle, if not a belief, to the poor. While some priesthoods were less regarded, membership of the great priestly colleges was increasingly sought for political ends. No doubt the simple worship of the household continued to retain real meaning for the more old-fashioned, and in the countryside the older cults must have flourished. But if official cults meant little to the educated classes, it must not be supposed that Lucretius and the philosophers had caused them to abandon all superstition, which must also have been rampant among the poor. The teaching of Pythagoras, with its belief in the transmigration of souls, appeared in Rome in the first century, and the learned praetor of 58 B.C., P. Nigidius Figulus, was a follower of this Neopythagoreanism. He also wrote a treatise to expose astrology, which despite the expulsion of 'Chaldeans' from Rome in 139, had become popular.[17] The way had been paved by Posidonius, whom Augustine described as a 'philosopher-astrologer'. He regarded astrology as a branch of applied astronomy and believed that an all-embracing power ('sympatheia') linked up all the parts of the universe both large and small. This belief in cosmic sympathy and the linking of a fatalistic astrology to Stoicism helped to spread the doctrine widely among the upper classes. But beside rationalists, who found in astrology a link between human causality and the cosmic laws that governed the movement of the stars (and its exponents included Varro), many more were attracted by its emotional and mystic, rather than by its 'scientific' appeal. Such 'religious' believers in its powers of revelation practised various forms of star-cults. Despite the scepticism preached by men like Lucretius, Cicero and Caesar, astrological beliefs received something like official recognition when the comet that appeared during the games in honour of Caesar was thought to be his soul received in heaven and he was officially included among the gods of the State.

It is impossible to establish how widespread was belief in life after death. Among the philosophers it was denied by Academics and Epicureans and in any fully personal sense by the Stoics, but it seems to have revived somewhat in the first century. Cicero, for instance, who after the death of his beloved daughter, decided to erect to her not a tomb but a shrine (fanum) as for a divine being, seems to have had some intimations of immortality. To what extent the thunderings of Lucretius against popular fears of future punishments attest widespread belief in some kind of Hell can only be conjectured.

As an outlet for emotional and religious feelings the Romans had long turned to the more popular ceremonies and cults of Greece and the East.[18] The 'enthusiastic' cults of the Thracian Bacchus and the Phrygian Magna Mater, which gave rise to emotional frenzy through intoxication from wine and blood, had reached Italy with disastrous results, but their excesses were quickly curbed (see p. 8). The cult of Bacchus is not heard of again until the time of Caesar when it appears as a more respectable mystery-religion. The cult of the Great Mother Cybele was carefully regulated by the Roman authorities: Romans, for instance, must not serve as her priests or take part in her processions. If, however, Lucretius' famous description of these wild ecstatic processions reflects contemporary practice in the streets of Rome, the cult will have attracted Roman attention if not direct participation. Other eastern religions, as that of Cappadocian Ma and Persian Mithras reached Italy in the late Republic, but only gained importance later. From Egypt the worship of Isis and Sarapis had reached some cities of Italy by the second century, and traditionally was established at Rome by Sulla's day, no doubt at first as a private and secret cult. In 58 B.C. altars to Isis on the Capitol were destroyed by the consuls; though temporarily recognized by the triumvirs in 43, the cult was again suppressed by Augustus. Thus in the later Republic the authorities made constant attempts to regulate, restrain or expel these foreign religions, but in the long run, especially as the population of Rome was becoming more cosmopolitan, they failed. But before the eastern cults took deep root, the battle against them was to be fought by a doughty champion of the Italian tradition, Augustus. To this cause he was committed while he was still Octavian: were not Isis and the deities of Egypt ranged on the side of Antony and Cleopatra at Actium against the ancestral gods of Rome? 'Monstrous gods of every shape', wrote Virgil, 'and Anubis, the yelping dog, bear arms against Neptune and Venus and against Minerva.' The battle was on.

XI

THE AUGUSTAN PRINCIPATE[1]

1. OCTAVIAN'S PROBLEM

Octavian, who had emerged as the heir of Caesar and the leader of a faction, had successfully led his followers to a victory in a civil war that had eliminated all rivals: his faction could now be identified with the State. 'Per consensum universorum potitus rerum omnium': in these words he proclaimed his unchallenged and universal sovereignty, and the moral basis upon which he claimed that it rested.[2] As long as this *consensus* continued to include the loyal support of the armies, Octavian was secure. But now that peace was established, how was he to act? If, like Sulla, he retired, civil war would flare up once more; if he retained autocratic power, naked and unshamed, he might suffer the fate of Julius Caesar. He was thus faced with a most perplexing problem. In order to prevent the outbreak of internal disorders and to safeguard the empire against barbarian incursions, he must retain a unified military command in his own hands: to allow provincial commanders too much independence in the protection of the frontiers, would be to invite a repetition of the use that ambitious Republican proconsuls had made of their provincial commands to turn against the central government in Rome. Yet an autocratic military despotism would so outrage a five-hundred-year-old tradition of Republican government that it must lead ultimately to an explosion.

Faced by this dilemma, Octavian must seek a compromise. In the event he produced a solution so successful that it gave the world a large measure of peace and stable government for over two hundred years. But he did not sit down and draft an ideal solution on paper and then try to implement it. Rather, he proceeded by a slow process of trial and error, feeling his way forward with patient care; by thus testing and responding to public opinion he was enabled to create the Principate and establish it on a secure basis. In considering his achievement it is all too easy to concentrate on the result and to overlook the length of time devoted to it: a process that takes many years may appear as a sudden revolutionary adjustment in the eyes of later ages, but to men who lived through it year by year it may seem a far more gradual and natural development.

Until he moved to a new definition of his position in 27, Octavian was content to hold the consulship every year from 31 onwards while he attempted to ease the transition from war to peace and to restore confidence. While still absent from Rome in 30 B.C., he had been granted various honours (prayers and libations), and had also been offered *tribunicia potestas* (he had received tribunician sacrosanctity in 36), but he probably did not accept the offer; if he did, he made little practical use of this power before 23 B.C.[3] He was granted the right to create new patrician families, whose numbers had been depleted in the civil wars, and he officially used the *praenomen* Imperator which he had employed unofficially for some ten years. At the beginning of 29 all his *acta* were confirmed by the Senate.

By August of 29 Octavian was back in Rome and celebrated his triumph, at which his colleague and the other magistrates followed behind him instead of preceding him in the normal position. He used part of the treasures of Egypt to make lavish distributions of money to the people, for various shows and for starting a great building programme of public works. Thanks to some financial measures (e.g. the overlooking of some debts to the State) confidence was restored and the rate of interest dropped by two-thirds. The closing of the temple of Janus, which symbolized the re-establishment of peace, was followed by demobilization on a large scale: not only were there to be no proscriptions, but Octavian's military backing was to be significantly lessened. He reduced his sixty legions ultimately to twenty-eight, which he judged would suffice for purposes of defence. Some 100,000 veterans received gratuities and were settled in colonies, either old or new settlements, in Italy or in the provinces; twenty-eight were founded in Italy, while those abroad included Carthage, Pisidian Antioch and Berytus in Syria. As the land was bought, the settlement cost hundreds of millions of sesterces. Returning stability and normality were seen when Octavian held his sixth consulship in 28 with his friend Agrippa as colleague, and both consuls for the first time in twenty years remained in Rome throughout the year. They turned their hands to a necessary task, a census of the whole people (neglected since 70 B.C.) and a revision of the Senate. To have sought the censorship might have given offence to the nobility, and so they received a grant of *censoria potestas* (or else permission to act *qua* consuls); this would appear quite natural to any historically-minded Romans who might recall that in the fifth century before the institution of the censorship the consuls had exercised these functions.

Their *lectio* (perhaps in 29, before the census of 28) reduced the senators from 1000 to 800, and Octavian's name was placed at the head of the list as Princeps Senatus. Further, by edict he proclaimed an amnesty and annulled any illegal and unjust orders that he had given during the civil wars. In short, by all these means life was in many ways brought back to normal, and it was time for Octavian to make clearer his own position and intentions.

2. THE FIRST SETTLEMENT (27 B.C.)[4]

Although he was now probably ready for a settlement, Octavian was perhaps hurried to a decision by the sudden realization that time might otherwise confront him with rivals in the military field; at all cost this must be avoided. M. Licinius Crassus, the triumvir's grandson, had as proconsul of Macedonia pacified Thrace and defeated the Bastarnae: he required a triumph and the exceptional honour of the *spolia opima*, granted to only two Romans since Romulus, for having killed the enemy leader in single combat. Octavian demurred: Crassus was granted his triumph, but not the *spolia opima*, nor even the title of *imperator* which other proconsuls had received since Actium. Again C. Cornelius Gallus, the ambitious prefect of Egypt, lost Octavian's favour; recalled, perhaps in 28, he was prosecuted for high treason and committed suicide (27). His precise offence is not known, but he had set up at Philae a grandiloquent trilingual inscription, claiming to have led his victorious troops farther south in Egypt than any other Roman or ruler of Egypt.

After Octavian had doubtless consulted his friends and thus paved his way, in a meeting of the Senate on 13 January 27 B.C. he suddenly renounced all his powers and provinces and placed them at the free disposal of the Senate and Roman People. When this statement was greeted with cries of protest, he agreed with apparent reluctance to undertake the administration of a large *provincia*, comprising Spain, Gaul and Syria, for a period of ten years, possibly with proconsular authority.[5] He was also, and continued to be, consul in Rome, but that need cause no difficulty, since Pompey had been in a similar position in 52 (p. 103). The rest of the provinces would be governed by promagistrates, responsible to the Senate, as earlier. Three days later a grateful Senate voted him further honours. His doorposts were decorated with laurel and his door-lintel with oak because he had saved the lives of Roman citizens ('ob cives servatos', as the coins declared). A golden shield was set up in the Senate-house, commemorating his 'valour, clemency, justice and piety', and proclaiming the virtues of the ideal ruler, about which philosophers had long contended.[6] More important still, he was given the name Augustus, and the month Sextilis was also so renamed. Thus, to all appearances, a plain settlement was reached on traditional lines: Octavian became Augustus, the first citizen (*princeps*) because of his services to his country, and he was given a large province with no more theoretical powers than any other consul or proconsul, in a restored Republic.[7]

But was it all as simple as it seemed? What was the real meaning? The answer is by no means unambiguous. In the first place, however, it is clear that Augustus, though not made commander-in-chief of the armies, did in fact exercise a predominant military power and that the ultimate sanction of his authority was force, however much the fact was disguised. It is often said that in effect he and the Senate divided control of the provinces between them, Augustus taking the military ones where the armies were stationed, and the Senate retaining the more peaceful ones. As a general statement that may not be an unfair summary of the position later in his reign, but in 27 the situation was rather different. While he took over Spain, Gaul and Syria, three proconsuls with armies under their command still governed Illyricum, Macedonia and Africa; but he had under the settlement eliminated proconsuls from three large areas which he would administer through his own *legati*, who would be newer men loyal to himself. And whereas he commanded some twenty legions in his *provincia*, the three proconsuls had only some five or six. Thus, provided his officers remained loyal, his grip on the military position was secure: and that should mean peace in place of civil war.

A further break with the revolutionary past is indicated by his new name and title; Octavian, the former triumvir, is forgotten in the presence of Augustus the Princeps. The use of Princeps (First Citizen), which was not an official constitutional term but rather a general form of address, was a happy choice. The word had been applied to outstanding statesmen in the Republic (e.g. Pompey), and it was not strictly limited to Augustus; Horace could hail him as 'maxime principum'.[8] His new name Augustus, which was preferred to that of Romulus for the new founder of Rome, had semi-religious connotations, and many men would recall that Ennius had described how Romulus himself had originally founded Rome 'augusto augurio'. Another word that derived from the same root as *augustus* is *auctoritas*, and in a very famous passage of the *Res Gestae* Augustus claimed that 'post id tempus [i.e. 27 B.C.] auctoriate omnibus praestiti'. The precise meaning of his *auctoritas* has been the subject of prolonged discussion. In all probability it had no strict constitutional significance and did not provide any legal basis for his power; rather, it only meant that he had more prestige, more moral authority, than any other individual in the State; the *principes viri* of the Republic had enjoyed *auctoritas*, and it was only the method by which men had secured the carrying out of their wishes without having to resort to direct orders or the use of their *imperium*. And few would dispute that Augustus enjoyed that kind of prestige.[9]

In another well-known passage of the *Res Gestae* Augustus emphasized the link with the past: in his sixth and seventh consulships (28–27 B.C.) 'rempublicam ex mea potestate in senatus populique Romani arbitrium transtuli'. This was in fact the official version of the settlement, and such phrases as 'restituta republica' occur in other writers. It appeared to be true: the Republican machinery of government was working again after the civil wars, with Augustus holding successive consulships, which in fact gave him civil control in Rome and Italy; if this imperium was limited to Italy, then he enjoyed a proconsular authority in a group of provinces. But there was little trace of autocracy, and none of dictatorship or tyranny. Yet when a phrase as 'rem publicam restituit' appears in an official document (such as the Fasti from Praeneste) it would be better to say that he restored 'constitutional government' rather than 'the Republic'. Few men could doubt that they were overshadowed by a new master, who was in fact to develop into a constitutional monarch.

3. THE SECOND SETTLEMENT (23 B.C.)

For nearly three years Augustus absented himself from Rome, thinking perhaps that it would be wise to allow the New State time to settle down and adjust its outlook. About the middle of 27 he set off for his western provinces; from Gaul he passed to Spain where there was trouble in the north-west. In 26 he conducted a campaign against the Cantabrians, but was taken ill and had to leave others to finish it. His position at Rome in the meantime remained unshaken: he was duly elected consul again each year, and his colleagues in the city were loyal: his friend Agrippa in 27, and Statilius Taurus, who had supported him in many a campaign in the civil wars, in 26. Nevertheless, when he returned in 24, he soon ran into troubles and the following year proved of crucial importance. M. Primus, the governor of Macedonia and one of the independent proconsuls still left, was charged with having made war against Thrace without orders; Augustus denied in court that he had issued any such order and Primus was condemned for treason. More serious, a conspiracy was discovered, led by a Republican named Fannius Caepio; a Varro Murena, perhaps Augustus' colleague in the consulship, was implicated and was among the conspirators that were condemned in their absence and killed on capture.[10] This crisis was quickly followed by another: Augustus was taken seriously ill. He handed his signet-ring to Agrippa, and some state documents to his fellow-consul Piso, who had succeeded the unfortunate Murena: these gave little evidence of his hopes for the empire, which was not however to be left without his guidance. Thanks to some drastic cold-water treatment, prescribed by his doctor, he recovered.

It was clearly time for Augustus to make a fresh start. He resigned his consulship on 1 July. Whether Murena's plot or his own illness was the more important factor in this decision, the abandonment of the consulship had obvious advantages: it would relieve him of a certain amount of routine business; it would remove the opprobrium of keeping one of the nobles out of a consulship each year, and of holding an un-Republican series of consulships; at the same time it would increase the number of ex-consuls available for administration. By way of compensation the Senate voted that his *imperium* should be enhanced in two important ways: it should not lapse when he entered the *pomerium* (the sacred boundary of the city) as did that of any other proconsul, and secondly it should be *maius imperium proconsulare*. The fact that it was made greater than that of any other proconsul meant that if Augustus disagreed with the governor of any senatorial province, he could exercise his own over-riding *imperium* there, or in other words he had a potential *imperium* over the whole empire and could issue orders to any army. In practice however he was most restrained and tactful, and interfered outside his own province very seldom and only when asked.[11]

But this was not enough: he needed some compensation for the loss of the oversight of civilian affairs that the consulship had given him. In practice he might have found consuls and tribunes willing to implement his wishes (and many of his major laws were in fact sponsored by consuls), but he needed direct authority. This he obtained when he was given *tribunicia potestas*, probably for the first time, in 23 (p. 177). He made much display of this new power: he numbered the years of his reign by it, and Tacitus described it as 'summi fastigii vocabulum'. It was popular and it gave him such rights as bringing measures before the People, and exercising a veto (*intercessio*), together with the *iura* of *coercitio* and *auxilium*. He could also summon and consult the Senate, but here consuls and other magistrates took precedence over tribunes; he was therefore given a special additional right, the *ius primae relationis*, by which he could bring forward the first motion at any meeting. Though the initiative in granting these honours came from the Senate, all his powers were probably sanctioned by the People, who will have passed a *lex de imperio*.[12]

Thus the authority of Augustus was re-established on two foundations: *tribunicia potestas* which gave him civil authority in Rome itself, and proconsular *imperium maius* which gave him control of the armies and provinces. Of the two he discreetly kept the latter in the background (he did not even mention it in his *Res Gestae*), while he paraded the former before all men's eyes. And these two powers remained the constitutional basis of the Principate throughout its history.

4. CONSOLIDATION OF THE PRINCIPATE

For further help Augustus turned to Agrippa, to whom he entrusted *imperium*, which is more likely to have comprised general authority over all the provinces (senatorial as well as imperial) in the East; Agrippa is unlikely to have received *maius imperium*.[13] At any rate he was needed in the East and there he went before the end of 23. Since Augustus had recovered from his illness, there was less need to think of a successor: two possible 'candidates' were his nephew Marcellus or his friend Agrippa, but if there existed any tension between them, this was removed less by Agrippa's departure than by the death of Marcellus during the autumn.

The winter brought flood and famine. Rioting followed, and Augustus was urged to accept a dictatorship, an annual and perpetual consulship, or the censorship. He declined all these offers, but he did accept, like Pompey in 57, a *cura annonae* and helped to relieve the situation; he also secured the appointment of censors for 22, but they did little. Augustus then went to the East (22–19), while Agrippa, after a brief visit to Rome, went to Gaul and Spain where he ruthlessly established peace (20–19). While Augustus was away, the People wanted to elect him consul for 21 and when he refused they would not elect a second consul until Agrippa on his return finally induced them to do so. Even so at the elections for 19 they insisted on keeping a place vacant for Augustus. With the Princeps and Agrippa both away, the sole consul of 19, C. Sentius Saturninus, had to face a difficult situation when a certain Egnatius Rufus presented himself as a consular candidate, encouraged by the popularity that he had won a few years before when as aedile he had organized a private fire-brigade. Saturninus refused to accept Rufus' candidature; rioting followed and envoys were sent to beg Augustus to return, but before he arrived in October, Rufus had been accused of treason and executed. Augustus, whose return was celebrated by the erection of an altar to Fortuna Redux, was granted the right to sit between the consuls of the year and to have twelve lictors. Whether he received other consular powers is uncertain: the historian Dio Cassius says that he was granted consular powers for life. This must certainly be an exaggeration: it is just possible that Augustus' *imperium* was equated to that of the consuls and thus would be valid in Rome and Italy;[14] alternatively he may have received some other specific rights enjoyed by a consul, as that of appointing a Prefect of the City. Then in 18 B.C. his ten-year grant of proconsular *imperium* was renewed for another five years.

The needs of the provinces and frontiers had thus kept Augustus abroad for many years (27–24; 22–19; and again 16–13). The burden had to be shared, and he had turned to his friend Agrippa, who served in East (23–22) and West (20–19) and helped (though with what specific authority, if any, is unknown) to steady affairs in Rome in 21. Augustus then made him his son-in-law: Agrippa, who had to divorce his wife (Marcella the niece of Augustus), married Augustus' daughter Julia, the widow of Marcellus. In 18 Agrippa's *imperium* was enlarged: for five years he exercised proconsular *imperium maius* (like that of Augustus) and he received a grant of *tribunicia potestas.* Though he lacked some of the Princeps' specific powers and his *auctoritas*, he nevertheless was approaching the position of a co-regent. If anything happened to Augustus, he might hope to secure power; for the moment he was needed in the East and he did not return to Rome until 13.

Meanwhile Augustus was busy initiating reforms in Rome. He probably refused a 'cura legum morumque' which was voted him, and using his *tribunicia potestas* he carried some important social legislation (which is discussed below). He also remodelled the criminal code (including laws against electoral bribery and violence), and his right of appellate jurisdiction, that is of judging cases when Roman citizens, condemned on criminal charges, 'appealed to Caesar', was put on a sounder footing. He also conducted in 18 B.C. another revision of the Senate, by which its numbers were reduced to six hundred.[15] By 17 B.C. the general work of reconstruction, which is discussed in more detail below, had reached a point at which Augustus felt that the new age of peace and prosperity might be marked by a public ceremony. By a certain manipulation the staging of the Ludi Saeculares was arranged for 17 (a *saeculum* was fixed at 110 instead of 100 years). At this thanksgiving ceremony a chorus of youths and girls sang the *carmen saeculare*, which was composed by Horace, on the Capitol and Palatine to the older and newer gods of Rome, and Augustus and Agrippa offered sacrifice. 'Grant, o gods,' sang the choir, 'grant to the young a spirit to learn and righteous conduct, grant to the old peace and calm, grant to the race of Romulus wealth and offspring and all glory.'[16] This same year Julia bore Agrippa a second son, Lucius, who with his elder brother Gaius was adopted by Augustus, who had no son of his own. His stepsons, however, were advancing into public life: in 16 Tiberius held a praetorship and Drusus a quaestorship, after which they campaigned with success on the German front (see below). Meanwhile Augustus was away in the west for three years; this time he left Statilius Taurus, his old general and fellow-consul of 26, as Praefectus Urbi. On his return to Rome in 13, when Tiberius was consul, the only honour that he accepted was the erection on the Campus Martius of an Ara Pacis Augustae, one of the great monuments of the age. His proconsular *imperium* was renewed for another five years and Agrippa's *imperium* and *tribunicia potestas* were also renewed. Augustus carried out a third *lectio* of the Senate (probably in 11 rather than 13).

5. THE LAST TWENTY-FIVE YEARS OF AUGUSTUS' PRINCIPATE

In 12 B.C. Lepidus, the former triumvir, died; Augustus had allowed him to retain the position of Pontifex Maximus, but now he assumed it himself, thus becoming the official head of the priesthood. Another death had important consequences: Agrippa, who had been in Pannonia, returned to Italy and died before Augustus could reach him. The Princeps therefore had to adjust his thoughts about the future: no doubt he had anticipated that one of his grandsons would ultimately succeed to his position, but in the meantime Agrippa could have watched over their interests. Augustus therefore now turned to his stepsons, Tiberius and Drusus. Tiberius was compelled to divorce his wife Vipsania (daughter of Agrippa), whom he loved, and to marry the now widowed Julia. During the next two or three years the two brothers did good work on the northern frontier, but Drusus was killed in 9 B.C., so that Augustus had to rely more on Tiberius, for whom he had no great affection. In 8 B.C. Augustus received a renewal of his proconsular *imperium*, this time for ten years, and held a census 'consulari cum potestate'; perhaps he used this power in order to levy troops which were needed for the German wars, which he himself directed this year. In 5 B.C. and again in 2 B.C. he reverted to an office that he had not held since 23 B.C., the consul-ship. His primary object was to introduce his grandsons, Gaius and Lucius Caesar, to public life on the occasion of their assuming the *toga virilis* (their 'coming of age'). The young princes received the title of *principes inventutis*, and the Senate designated Gaius as consul for A.D. 1. Tiberius, who felt over-shadowed, retired to Rhodes for the next seven years. Besides holding his thirteenth, and last, consulship in 2 B.C., Augustus that year received the title of Pater Patriae, which brought the long list of his titles to an end; it did not of course add to his powers, but he might now be regarded as the father of the State, and Romans would recall the authority, the *patria potestas*, that a father exercised within his own family. In a sense the settlement, which basically had reached its final shape in 23 B.C. and has been consolidated in detail in the years that had followed, now reached its culmination.

The Principate was now running smoothly. The chief remaining prob-lem was to secure that it so continued when Augustus died. To this he gave much thought, but in his plans for a succession, he suffered grievous setbacks. In 2 B.C. he was forced to banish his own daughter Julia because her scandalous conduct contrasted too sharply with his attempts to improve family life; thus she could no longer be used in the furtherance of dynastic plans. Two further blows followed in quick succession: Lucius Caesar died in A.D. 2 and his brother Gaius, who in 1 B.C. had received proconsular *imperium* in the East, died in Lycia in A.D. 4. Reluctantly Augustus turned to Tiberius, who had come back to Rome in A.D. 2; in A.D. 4 he adopted him as his son (though he required Tiberius in turn to adopt his nephew Germanicus, the son of his brother Drusus).[17] Tiberius was again given *tribunicia potestas* for ten years and was sent off to the Rhine frontier with a special *imperium*. Defence problems soon caused increasing anxiety. In A.D. 6 a serious revolt broke out in Pannonia, and three years later when this was finally being crushed, Varus and three legions were destroyed in Germany. Augustus was badly shaken by this disaster and when in A.D. 13 he realized that his life was reaching its close, he elevated Tiberius to a position of virtual co-regency with himself: Tiberius' tribunician power was renewed and by a special enactment he received equal rights in provincial administration and the command of armies, and the authority to hold a census with Augustus. The *lustrum* was concluded in the spring of A.D. 14, but Tiberius had no sooner started for Illyricum than he was recalled by news that Augustus was ill; they met for one day before Augustus died.

Augustus had achieved a unique position. He had received at the hands of the Senate and Roman People a great variety of powers, many of which had precedents in the Republic, but his accumulation and long tenure of these, together with his personal *auctoritas*, raised the First Citizen far above the level of a magistrate and made him in effect seem not unlike a constitutional monarch. His authority both at home and abroad was unparalleled. He commanded the armies, who took an oath of allegiance to him in person, and he made provision for their retirement. Since he had received the right to make treaties, he virtually controlled foreign policy. He governed a large part of the Empire directly through his deputies, and all new provinces added to the empire likewise came under his administration; if need arose, he could even intervene in the provinces that were still left under senatorial government. The Senate frequently transferred to him various tasks of administration in Rome and Italy which his agents then undertook. He took an increasing part in financial, legislative and judicial matters. And behind all his official authority lay his unequalled powers of patronage. How he used, and to what extent he shared, these wide-ranging powers, must now be considered in greater detail.

6. PRINCEPS AND SENATE

The Augustan system was regarded by the great German historian, Mommsen, as a Dyarchy, a joint rule of Princeps and Senate, under which in effect the Emperor undertook the administration of one part of the Empire, and the Senate that of the other. This conception is not now generally regarded as valid, since whatever the appearance Augustus designed to create, it is clear that power was not divided: he carefully kept in his own control the ultimate sanction that was the army. On the other hand there was a division, but what was divided was work. In building up the administrative machinery necessary to run the Empire, Augustus carefully preserved all that he could from the shipwreck of the Republic and leaned heavily upon the Senate: tradition, common sense, need and his own inclination, all united to commend this policy, and he will not have been unmindful of Julius Caesar's cavalier attitude to Rome's most venerable Council. In order to purge it of unworthy members who had crept in during the civil wars, he had gradually reduced its numbers to 600 (pp. 178, 183), and, as will be seen, he carefully regulated conditions of entry into the senatorial Order. The Senate, together with the People, remained the sole permanent legal source of authority, as becomes clear on the death of a Princeps, but in practice it could not enforce its wishes in the last resort because it lacked military power. Augustus, however, treated it with great respect, and we must now see how the various functions of government were shared between the two.

In the sphere of legislation both the Princeps and Senate could take action. This is well illustrated in a phrase of Augustus in his first edict to Cyrene in which he suggests that governors there should follow a certain method when impanelling jurors 'until the Senate shall deliberate on this matter or I myself shall have found some better solution'. The Princeps could legislate in various ways: apart from presenting bills to the People by virtue of his *tribunicia potestas* (cf. the *leges Iuliae*, pp. 231), he could take more direct action by issuing legally-binding edicts (this right was specifically recognized about 19 B.C.), *decreta* (judicial decisions), *mandata* (instructions to officials) and *epistolae* or rescripts (replies to petitions). The Senate on the other hand ultimately gained the right to make law, i.e. its *senatus-consulta* became law, and although this right may not have been formally established before the reign of Antoninus Pius, even under Augustus the Senate's advisory capacity was recognized and some of its resolutions became law (e.g. the S.C. Silanianum proposed by Silanus, consul in A.D. 10). But though in practice the Senate increasingly developed into an active legislative assembly, the initiative and advice behind its activity may often have come from the emperor.

During the later Republic capital jurisdiction had resided in the *iudicia publica* (the *quaestiones* which Sulla had organized); these courts alone could condemn a Roman citizen to death, since a magistrate's *imperium* was limited by the right of *provocatio* which applied throughout Italy and the provinces, in war as in peace.[18] These courts continued to function, but they were supplemented in a novel manner: cases of treason and of political importance and those that involved senators or men of high rank were now generally brought before one of two new courts, either the emperor in council or the consuls in the Senate. Thus both emperor and Senate gained a primary jurisdiction against which there was no appeal to the People. Such senatorial trials were being held before A.D. 8, and although our knowledge of trials before Augustus personally derives mainly from undated anecdotes, such trials were well established at the beginning of Tiberius' reign. Further, as Roman citizenship spread more widely through the provinces, it became difficult to remit all criminal charges to Rome; as a result proconsuls, and perhaps all provincial governors, were granted limited criminal jurisdiction. But, by a grant in 30 B.C., Augustus was enabled to reverse a capital sentence passed by a magistrate using his *imperium*: thus *provocatio ad populum* was replaced by *appellatio ad Caesarem*, the most famous case of the latter being the appeal of St. Paul to Nero. Thus the judicial activities of both emperor and Senate increased, and in particular their two new high Courts of criminal justice emerged; these were quite independent, and there was no appeal from the verdict of one to the other.[19]

In the sphere of finance also both emperor and Senate were active, but the old view must be abandoned that there was a division on 'dyarchic' lines by which the emperor established a Fiscus at Rome for the revenues of the imperial provinces while those of the public provinces continued to be paid to the senatorial Aerarium. Rather, the Aerarium remained the chief Treasury, and its management was entrusted (from 23 B.C.) to two praetors in place of quaestors. Into it were paid the revenues of all the provinces and from it Augustus, like a Republican magistrate, was authorized by votes of the Senate to withdraw sums necessary for the discharge of his duties. In practice, however, it was unnecessary to move much of the actual cash to and from Rome, since the emperor kept departmental chests, *fisci*, in his provinces (as the governors of the public provinces also probably did); into these went the taxes of each province and from them the emperor would draw money for military and administrative purposes, so that in the main only accounts of balances would pass between each provincial *fiscus* and the Aerarium. As few provinces produced a surplus over local expenditure, not much money would go from them to Rome. In fact the Aerarium was often in financial difficulties, and Augustus made grants to it from his private funds. This he could do because he had great wealth, which came from inheritance, the civil wars, the imperial estates, and legacies. From this *patrimonium* (sometimes called *fiscus*, which may cause confusion) he paid to the Aerarium, to the Roman plebs and to discharged veterans no less than 600 million sesterces: he was comparatively poor when he died.[20]

It was not desirable that the financial burden of providing for retired soldiers should seem to depend on the private generosity of the emperor. In A.D. 6 therefore Augustus created a special fund for this purpose, the Aerarium Militare; he started it off with a gift of 170 million sesterces and arranged that in the future it should receive the yield of two new taxes that he instituted, a sales-tax (*centesima rerum venalium*) and death-duties (*vicesima hereditatum*). This was a very wise move, since it cut the personal link between a general and his men who had been forced to look to him to make provision for their future; if such a public fund had been established a hundred years earlier, in the days of Marius, the history of the later Republic would have been very different. This new treasury was administered by three expraetors. Thus in general while the Senate and magistrates had a fair share in the work of financial administration, the emperor was probably able to direct policy.

This is seen in the fact that he regularly published for information a general balance-sheet of the Empire (*rationes imperii*), a practice which his successors soon dropped.

The issuing of coinage was also a joint responsibility of Princeps and Senate, but not on equal terms. During the civil war the rival military *imperatores* had minted what they needed. Octavian, the war-lord, and Augustus, the Princeps, had issued plentiful gold and silver in Asia, Spain and, perhaps after 23, at Rome. But in 15 B.C. he established an imperial mint at Lugdunum in Gaul, which from 12 B.C. became the sole source of gold and silver. The senatorial mint in Rome, in the charge of *triumviri monetales*, was thus restricted to the output of bronze and copper. The Senate doggedly continued to proclaim its control of the *Aes* coinage almost as long as the Empire lasted, by putting on all the coins the letters S.C. (Senatus-consulto), but in the choice of types the Princeps soon exercised as efficient a control over the 'senatorial' bronze as over the 'imperial' gold and silver. This was important because the types were a deliberate reflexion of official policy, designed to provide world opinion with a commentary on this policy; in the twenty-five years after Actium the silver issues displayed no less than 400 types. In this aspect the views of the Princeps must prevail.[21]

The administration of Rome and Italy was the concern of the Senate and ordinary magistrates, and Augustus may well have intended that this should continue. At first he interfered very little, but the failure of the Senate to provide adequate public services led him gradually to take action, with the result that by the end of his reign most departments had come under the control of prefects or *curatores* nominated by him (pp. 193 ff.). In the wider sphere of provincial administration, as has been seen, the Princeps and Senate shared the task. The original settlement of 27 B.C. was modified later when for instance the Senate took over Gallia Narbonensis in 22 B.C. and the Princeps took Illyricum c. 11 B.C., while all the new provinces created after 23 came under his administration. The division between the two parties, however, remained clear-cut, although his *maius imperium* gave Augustus a potential right to intervene anywhere.[22]

Thus in all spheres of government and administration, other than military, the Senate retained some of its traditional activities, and co-operated with Augustus in running the Empire. He showed it respect and often consulted it, and in order that it should take its duties seriously he increased fines for non-attendance in 17 B.C. and again in 9 B.C. when he also established the quorum necessary for transacting various kinds of business. How he influenced its composition and tried to increase its sense of responsibility is discussed in the next section. In one important way he made the Senate more efficient and at the same time more amenable to his own wishes: he established (probably between 27 and 18 B.C.) a senatorial standing committee, consisting of himself, one or both consuls, one of each of the other magistrates, and fifteen other senators chosen by lot; some of the members changed every six months, and the whole committee (apart from the Princeps) every year. Its function was probouleutic, to prepare business for the full Senate; its usefulness is obvious, both in enabling Augustus to test senatorial reactions more privately and in expediting the conduct of business in the larger body. Near the end of his reign in A.D. 13 he changed its composition and thereby its nature: consuls-designate replaced the other magistrates; the ordinary members, now twenty and annual in tenure, were not perhaps chosen by lot; three powerful men were made permanent members (Tiberius, his son Drusus and nephew Germanicus); the emperor could co-opt; and above all, its decisions were given the validity of *senatus consulta*. This re-organization no doubt helped to smooth the transmission of power from Augustus to Tiberius, but it killed the probouleutic committee. Alongside the latter Augustus had throughout his principate consulted his friends for everyday political and administrative advice, and in particular for judicial matters he had turned to a council of advisers. These *amici principis* did not develop into an official permanent *consilium*, but they were publicly recognized as the men whom the emperor summoned to meet him in council for judicial or other business. They were soldiers, jurists, diplomats, men like Agrippa and Maecenas and their less famous successors; and since many of them survived from one reign into the next, they helped to give continuity to policy. The immediate effect, however, of the drafting by Augustus of some of his *amici* into the senatorial committee in A.D. 13 was so to change its basis that it never revived in its earlier form (Tiberius' *consilium*, though theoretically its continuation, consisted in fact of his *amici*, the *principes viri*) and thus the useful link between the Princeps and the average member of the Senate, which Augustus had originally designed, was destroyed.[23]

7. THE EXECUTIVE: MAGISTRATES AND OFFICIALS

The Senate as a whole was thus restored to a position of considerable prestige and influence, if not of power, but individual senators also were needed in large numbers for administrative duties, and they must be men of greater principle than many of the magistrates and provincial governors of the late Republic. Augustus therefore took steps to control entry into the Senate which was normally recruited from members of the Senatorial Order, that is men of senatorial birth, who wore a broad purple stripe on their tunics (the laticlave). He made membership of the Order, however, depend on more than birth: other necessary qualifications were normally the performance of a period of military service as a *tribunus militum* or *praefectus alae*, possession of a sum that was probably fixed at 1,000,000 sesterces, and above all personal integrity.[23a] But in practice entry to the Senate was not so restricted, since Augustus himself exercised the right to grant the *latus clavus* to young men of non-senatorial birth; by thus encouraging men of equestrian stock to turn to an official career, he infused some fresh blood into what was mainly a hereditary body. Men who were thus suitably qualified could then seek one of the minor offices known as the vigintivirate;[24] after that when they were twenty-five they could, if elected, become quaestors (who numbered twenty) and thus enter the Senate. After this apprenticeship the more efficient could then ascend the higher rungs of a senatorial career. All, except patricians, must hold either the tribunate of the plebs or aedileship (six in number); then, if they had reached thirty, they could stand for the praetorship (normally twelve posts). Since the regular minimum age for holding the consulship was forty-two, an interval followed in which many 'praetorian' posts were open: a man might become commander (*legatus*) of a legion, *legatus* on the staff of a provincial governor, governor of a lesser imperial province (*legatus Augusti pro praetore*) or proconsul of a senatorial province. Then for the successful came the consulship, to be followed for some by the governorship of a more important imperial province (as *legatus Augusti pro praetore*), a curatorship in Rome (e.g. *operum publicorum*) or even the Prefecture of the City or, if the appointment was senatorial rather than imperial, the proconsulship of Africa or Asia. The chances of a man reaching the consulship in fact slightly increased as Augustus' reign progressed, because the custom had been growing for consuls to retire before the end of their year of office to make room for *consules suffecti*. This practice was regularized in 5 B.C., the year in which Augustus had himself resumed the holding of a consulship, and later (probably in 2 B.C.) the office was specifically limited to six months, and the suffects took over on 1 July each year. The reason for this was to increase the number of consulars available for public service.

Augustus could also have regulated the quality of the higher officials through the elections, but in fact for many years he seems to have let the consular elections take a fairly normal course. He will naturally have exerted some influence on them, but he seems to have made little use of the powers of nominating or commending candidates (*nominatio* and *commendatio*) which were exercised by later emperors. The fact that he passed bribery laws in 18 and 8 B.C. shows that bribery was rife, and men do not spend money when an issue is a foregone conclusion. Moreover, the majority of consuls between 18 B.C. and A.D. 4 were *nobiles*, whereas after that until the end of the reign many more *novi homines* and members of recently ennobled families reached the consulship. Thus it appears that for a long time Augustus normally let the elections take their course, but later secured the election of candidates from a wider circle.[25] This is connected with the introduction of a system known as *destinatio*, by which candidates were 'destined' or recommended for office by a complicated preliminary voting procedure. This may have been introduced in 5 B.C. and have been in the hands of the Senate, but more probably it was set up by the *lex Valeria Cornelia* in A.D. 5, when the preliminary voting was entrusted to ten special centuries of senators and Equites, whose decision gave a strong lead to the Comitia Centuriata. As the Equites preponderated and many of them would be prosperous men from the Italian municipalities, namely the class of men that Augustus wanted to see elected to praetorships and consulships, he would favour this new machinery which would secure the election of this type of man without any direct interference in the elections by himself.[26]

Augustus, however, needed more than senators to help him in the task of administering the Empire. He turned therefore to the equestrian Order and by employing its members in the public service, from which they had largely been excluded during the Republic, he secured their loyalty to the State and helped to heal the breach that for so long separated them from the Senate. But public servants must be worthy, and so he re-organized the Order, for which the necessary qualifications became free birth, possession of a census rating of 400,000 sesterces, military service and good character. Membership gave the right to receive a public horse (*equus publicus*) and a gold ring, and to wear a narrow purple stripe on the tunic (*angustus clavus*). Augustus revived the annual parade and inspection of the Equites in Rome, at which he could expel any unworthy members. He could also add new members to the Order by granting the *equus publicus*: the most common source of recruitment comprised veteran senior centurions, the richer men from the country towns, and even some freedmen. The Order also included sons of senators until they reached the age of twenty-five. After the qualifying military service (perhaps as a *praefectus* or *tribunus* of an auxiliary cohort), the prospect of a good career opened up in a series of administrative posts. In view of the traditional business interests of the equestrian order, Augustus used them as financial agents (procurators) in his provinces, and also as governors (procurators) of the less important imperial provinces (e.g. Judaea).[27] After that the most successful could hope for one of the great Prefectures: the Fleet, the Watch (*vigiles*), the Corn Supply (*annona*), Egypt, or the Praetorian Guard.

By employing the services of the senatorial and equestrian Orders in this way Augustus laid the foundations of a Civil Service. For unlike the amateur magistrates of the Republic, these men became professionals, serving for long periods and receiving a salary. The majority were the servants of the emperor, and few of the smaller groups that were appointed by the Senate to serve in the senatorial provinces and posts would be likely to secure office unless the emperor approved. Thus an efficient system was established which was free from many of the weaknesses that had marked the administration of the late Republic and had often led to misgovernment and corruption. This aspect of the work of Augustus was not the most spectacular, but it was one of the most important: by preserving and adapting what was best in the Republican system and by supplementing it with new machinery, he avoided a revolutionary break with the past and at the same time created a means not only to hold the Empire together but also to promote its well-being.

The higher grades of the administrative service naturally required the help of what have been called the Clerical (*scribae*) and Sub-clerical grades. As under the Republic, magistrates and provincial governors needed secretaries, accountants, messengers and others. Augustus too, as controller of a vast administrative service required help of this nature, and for it he turned to his own household. Like any wealthy Roman he had many freedmen and slaves to keep his accounts and to manage his property, and many, even of the slaves, enjoyed a not intolerable social and economic status when they began to handle a great variety of public business for him. They were in fact indispensable and before long some of the freedmen secretaries attained great influence and prestige when they reached what may be regarded as the administrative grade.[28]

Thus in general the Senate, individual senators and the equestrian Order were ready to co-operate with the Princeps in establishing and working the 'new order'. What then of the People and its Assemblies? With the assumption of so many powers by Augustus and the increase in the functions of the Senate, the People were in fact almost squeezed out. They occasionally legislated, but were here subject to his tribunician authority. They formally elected the magistrates, but these had already in fact been chosen by 'destinatio' after A.D. 5. They conferred *tribunicia potestas* on the emperor, but this was a mere formality. They had lost their judicial powers. But the city mob was far too irresponsible to exercise political power: rather, it wanted 'panem et circenses'.[29] Thus, as no serious measures were taken to make it more representative of the Empire as a whole or infuse into it a new spirit, it was better that the functions that it had previously exercised should pass to other hands. But if the city plebs was a liability, the ordinary men of the Italian municipalities proved their worth by supplying the lower officers of the legions; these centurions provided the backbone of the armies, and many of them ultimately reached an equestrian career and further opportunities for public service.

8. ROME AND ITALY

The famous claim of Augustus that he found Rome brick and left it marble epitomizes his attempts to make the city a worthy capital of the restored Empire. The boast is not unjustified if applied to the monumental centre, but elsewhere high tenement houses (which Augustus did, however, limit to sixty feet) rose up in blocks (*insulae*) amid winding narrow streets. He did not plan any slum-clearance or town-planning for the city as a whole, but he did provide it with fine public buildings, baths, theatres, libraries, temples, granaries and warehouses, restoring old buildings (he gives the number of restored temples as 82) and constructing new ones. A large part of this immense expense was borne by himself and his friends and relatives, such as Agrippa and Tiberius. In the Forum there was much rebuilding, especially around the new temple to the deified Caesar, which Augustus dedicated in 29 B.C.; next to it arose the new Arch of Augustus, on the walls of which were engraved the Fasti, the lists of the chief magistrates and triumphant generals of the Roman Republic, an ever-present reminder of the men and families that had made Rome great. To the north of the old Forum and over against the new Forum of Caesar, which he completed, Augustus at great expense bought the site for a new Forum Augusti. In the centre of its back-wall stood the temple of Mars Ultor, vowed at Philippi where Caesar was avenged; and in niches in the semi-circular exedrae which flanked the temple stood statues of the past triumphatores, whose elogia proclaimed their careers and deeds. On the Palatine, where Augustus lived in a house of modest size, he built a temple to Apollo, which he had vowed in 36 B.C. In the Campus Martius building was undertaken on a lavish scale. In the south a Portico was named in honour of his sister Octavia, who added a library to it in memory of her son Marcellus. Near to it Augustus constructed the fine Theatre of Marcellus, which he dedicated to the memory of his nephew and son-in-law in 13 B.C. Agrippa, who laid out a park called the Campus Agrippae, built Baths and the Pantheon; the latter, put up in 27 B.C., was later destroyed, and the existing Pantheon with its rotunda is the work of Hadrian. This complex of buildings was balanced by the Mausoleum which Augustus began to build as early as 28 B.C. as a memorial for himself and members of his family. This circular construction, covered with a conical tumulus, would remind men more of the Etruscan past than of the splendours of Greek mausolea; in front of it later were set up the two bronze pillars on which were inscribed the Res Gestae of Augustus, a restrained, clear and proud document in which he rendered to his contemporaries and to posterity an official account of his stewardship. Not least of his achievements was peace, and this was commemorated in the noble monument that stood near the imperial Mausoleum, the Ara Pacis Augustae[30] (cf. p. 348 f.).

Public buildings require upkeep and some time after 11 B.C. Augustus transferred this responsibility to two praetorian or consular curatores operum publicorum. Under the Republic the Senate and magistrates had been responsible for all public services, but commitments overseas had led to much neglect at home, which Augustus began to repair, though he went about this very slowly and did not generally take action until some breakdown threatened. The water supply was at first improved by Agrippa who built two new aqueducts; as aedile in 33 he had not hesitated to make a personal inspection of Rome's main sewer, the Cloaca Maxima, by boat. On his death in 12 B.C. Augustus put Agrippa's staff of 240 trained slaves in the charge of three *curatores aquarum*, of whom the chief was a consular. Thus Rome gained a Metropolitan Water Board, which was maintained by the Senate with occasional help from the Princeps. Measures were also taken to prevent the Tiber flooding the city: a permanent board was set up later in A.D. 15, comprising five *curatores riparum Tiberis* under a consular. To maintain the food supply, Augustus was given a *cura annonae* in 22 B.C. after he had relieved a famine at his own expense. Further difficulties led to the appointment in A.D. 6 of two consulars, but a few years later a permanent food commissioner was established, the *praefectus annonae* of equestrian rank. Though Augustus at one time contemplated abolishing the corn dole, he limited himself to reducing the list of recipients to 200,000 (in 2 B.C.); the distribution since 22 B.C. had been in the hands of *praefecti frumenti dandi ex senatus consulto*.

Then the danger of fire must be faced, especially as the ambitious Egnatius Rufus had won popularity in 26 by organizing a private fire-brigade (cf. p. 182). At first Augustus put some public slaves under the command of the aediles (21 B.C.), but in A.D. 6 he established seven cohorts (each of 1000 freedmen) of Vigiles,[31] commanded by an equestrian *praefectus vigilum*. Each cohort assumed charge for two of the fourteen *regiones*, into which Augustus had divided the city in 7 B.C., when partly in order to help with fire-fighting he revived the *vicomagistri*, four of whom were elected by each of the 265 wards or parishes (*vici*). Another public service that the Republic had lacked, as men like Clodius and Milo knew only too well, was a police force. Augustus made good this deficiency by creating three *cohortes urbanae* (each a thousand strong), commanded ultimately by the *praefectus urbi* (an office which did not become permanent until perhaps A.D. 13). Unlike most other prefects who were equestrians, the Prefect of the City was a consular, who held office for long periods and exercised some powers of summary jurisdiction; later in the Empire this office became one of very great importance.[32] The Urban Cohorts were a semi-military body, and if they needed further support to keep order, the Praetorian Guard (see p. 205 f.) could be summond to help.

Thus the amateur system of the Republic was superseded by more permanent establishments and the municipal organization of Rome was set on a sounder basis. But Augustus did not neglect Italy. The numerous colonies of veterans that he had established on land which he, unlike his predecessors, had bought, would help to maintain law and order. Colonia Augusta Praetoria (Aosta), for instance, assisted in keeping the Alpine Salassi in check and the Alpine passes open. To reduce brigandage and promote easy travel for soldiers, civilians and merchandise, Augustus, who in 27 had repaired the Via

Flaminia and its bridges at his own expense, established in 20 B.C. a permanent board of senatorial *curatores viarum* of praetorian rank to maintain the main roads. The expense fell partly on the Aerarium and partly on roadside towns, which also had to provide relays of horses and carriages for the new state-post (*cursus publicus*) which Augustus established. Italy, which now included Cisalpine Gaul, had a large population, which has been put as high as ten million free inhabitants, and some 474 municipalities; it was divided into eleven administrative districts. After the turmoil of the civil wars it now entered on a period of peace, security and prosperity, and many more men from its leading municipal families began to enter the equestrian and senatorial orders in Rome. Thus the class that had contributed so largely to the support of Octavian the faction-leader received their reward: a *concordia ordinum* was achieved, and furthermore it was based upon a *consensus Italiae*. The Augustan revolution was both military and political, but it was also social, and the non-political class of Italy shared in its success.

9. SOCIAL REFORMS

If Italy was to be fully integrated into the Roman tradition, she must be made increasingly aware of and loyal to that tradition. But if she turned her eyes on the capital she would see much that was unworthy of Rome's past. It is easy to draw an unpleasant picture of the Roman aristocracy at the end of the Republic, of luxury, vulgar ostentation, money-grabbing, legacy-hunting, and the licence of women like Clodia or of young rakes like Caelius, but exaggeration must be avoided (cf. above pp. 150 ff.). Demoralization was largely limited to part of the governing class in Rome itself, while throughout most of Italy family life remained normal and healthy. But if Rome was to be a worthy leader of Italy, and still more if she felt that she had an imperial mission to the wider world, she must not only infuse fresh blood from Italy into the old Roman oligarchy, but also reform the heart of Roman society itself. Realizing therefore that only so could Rome fulfil the mission to which Augustus believed she was called, he attempted to regenerate society by social reform. For this task, despite his own alleged marital infidelities, he was not unsuited by temperament and birth: his family came from Velitrae, a small town in Latium whence he derived older ideas of family and religious duties.

A body of legislation, presented to the People by Augustus in person (*leges Iuliae*), was designed to stabilize and encourage marriage and to discourage childlessness.[33] A *lex Iulia de adulteriis coercendis*, probably of 18 B.C., by a striking innovation, made adultery a public crime as well as private offence. After divorcing his wife, a husband could prosecute both her and her lover; penalties were severe, including banishment to an island. In certain circumstances he might even kill the lover. A *lex Iulia de maritandis ordinibus* was passed about the same time; later, in A.D. 9 it was amended and supplemented by a *lex Papia Poppaea*. The former removed a barrier to marriage by recognizing the validity of marriages between free-born and freed, with the exception of senators and their sons who might not marry freedwomen. Disabilities, based on the assumption that it was the duty of men between twenty-five and sixty and women between twenty and fifty to marry, were imposed on those who failed to comply and on those who married but remained childless; the chief penalty was a varying limitation on the right to inherit. These disabilities were increasingly removed and exemption was correspondingly gained by marriage and the birth of children; the number of a man's children gave him precedence when he stood for office, and he could stand as many years before the legal minimum age as he had children (*ius liberorum*). Such measures naturally provoked opposition, and one of the modifications introduced by the *lex Papia Poppaea* was to remove the unfair lack of distinction between the childless and the unmarried, and also to allow women who had been divorced or widowed a longer unpenalized period before they remarried. The success of these measures is difficult to gauge. The census figures of A.D. 13 (probably all adult citizens) were a million higher than those of 28 B.C.; the return of peace and prosperity must have been the basic cause, but Augustus' legislation will have played its part within the area that it affected.

Augustus wished not only to increase the Italian element in the Roman citizen body, but also to limit the foreign element that was mixing with it, especially as a result of manumission (see p. 152). In order to evade the tax on manumission some masters had adopted an informal method of freeing their slaves who thereby gained neither legal freedom nor citizenship.[34] By a *lex Iunia* (probably in 17 B.C.) such freedmen were granted the intermediate status of 'Latins' which gave them statutory freedom but imposed some limitations (e.g. the inability to receive legacies or make a will). The children, however, of these Junian Latins were full Latins and so might look forward to Roman citizenship. Manumission was further checked by two laws: a *lex Fufia Caninia* of 2 B.C. limited the number of slaves that could be set free under the will of their master, and a *lex Aelia Sentia* of A.D. 4 restricted manumission during his lifetime by imposing some age limits, e.g. he must be twenty and the slave thirty. Freedmen, though Roman citizens, laboured under certain disabilities, e.g. they were debarred from holding office in Rome or the Italian municipalities and from serving in the legions, and in private life their social status was inferior, but Augustus was not unmindful of their needs. Some were absorbed into the administrative work of his own household, while in many Italian towns the richer freedmen were given an outlet for their social and local patriotism by the institution of the *Seviri Augustales*, a group of six, who were responsible for the cult of Augustus and some local entertainments. Another municipal institution, the *Iuvenes* or *Iuventus*, helped to unite Rome and

Italy and to promote loyalty to the new order. These were clubs of freeborn young men, organized for physical exercise, especially riding; the skill of the younger members was shown at a display known as the Lusus Troiae. They had antecedents in the Republic, but Augustus now encouraged them both at Rome and in the municipalities in order to invigorate the youth of Italy. His favour was shown when he chose as an honour for his grandsons Gaius and Lucius the title Princeps Iuventutis.

10. RELIGIOUS REFORMS

More than social legislation was needed to achieve a moral regeneration. While poets and writers proclaimed the ideals that Augustus wished to instil into the Roman people, he himself was busy reviving old religious rites and ceremonies which had fallen into neglect. It is true that Roman religious practice had very little influence on private morality, but there were certain old fundamental ideas which, if rekindled, might appeal to the conscience of the people. Chief among these was the primitive desire to ensure prosperity for man and beast, for farmer and city-dweller by securing the *pax deorum*; this could be achieved by due observation of the *ius divinum* and by the individual exercise of *pietas*. Despite widespread scepticism and rationalism, despite the exploitation of religion for political ends, despite the attraction of foreign cults, there still lurked in many a Roman heart the belief that Rome's success had been due to Rome's piety and that peril could be averted by propitiating the gods by means of the traditional ceremonies. Roman conservatism proclaimed that the Augustan peace must rest upon the *pax deorum*.

As early as 35 B.C. Horace could refer to Octavian as one who cared for 'Italy and the shrines of the gods' ('delubra deorum': *Sat.* 1.6.35), and during his fight for power Octavian had increasingly championed the traditions of the West against the religious beliefs of the East which were reflected in the threat from Antony and Cleopatra (cf. p. 175). After Actium, supported by the general enthusiasm for the restorer of peace, he was free to go further in his attempt to rebuild national faith. His restoration of old shrines and the building of many fine new temples have already been mentioned (p. 192). He himself became a member of the sacred colleges and orders of the pontiffs, augurs, fratres Arvales, fetiales, and others; on the death of Lepidus in 12 B.C. he became Pontifex Maximus. He increased the privileges of the Vestal Virgins and appointed a Flamen Dialis, a post that had been vacant since 87 B.C. because of the primitive taboos that hindered the incumbent. This policy found splendid outward expression in his celebration of the Ludi Saeculares in 17 (see p. 183) when emphasis was laid on the worship not of the underworld deities, Dis Pater and Proserpina (to whom the Games had earlier been sacred), but of Apollo and Diana. Following closely upon the social legislation of 18, this ceremony will have drawn together all the hopes for the new age and have reminded men that 'moribus antiquis stat res Romana'.

Among the cults that Augustus revived was that of the Lares, spirits that guarded crossroads as well as homes. The worship of the Lares compitales at shrines at crossroads was brought into relation with the vici and placed under the supervision of the vicomagistri (see p. 194).[35] One result was to provide a religious interest for the humbler population of the city, including freedmen; but, more important, the worship of the Lares was now linked to that of the Genius of Augustus, the divine spirit that guarded and promoted his family and fortunes. Thus the plebs of Rome, and many others as the cult of the Lares Augusti spread through Italy and the provinces, were encouraged, not to worship the emperor himself, but to regard him as their guardian.

To have sought worship for himself would have contradicted the nature of the Principate that he was trying to establish and to have created a cult would have accorded ill with the worship of the old gods of Rome that he was reviving.[36] But the matter was by no means simple: in gratitude for the restoration of peace and order Rome and Italy were eager to heap exceptional honours on their human benefactor, of whom Virgil could say 'deus nobis haec otia fecit', while the Empire included provinces in the East where the population was accustomed to emperor-worship. In one respect Octavian had long been unique: since 42 B.C. and the consecration of Divus Julius he had been the son of a god, 'Divi filius'. After Actium his birthday was celebrated as a public holiday; libations were poured in his honour at public and private banquets; from 29 B.C. his name was added to those of the gods in hymns; two years later he received the title of Augustus; his Genius, perhaps in 12 B.C., was inserted in official oaths between the names of Juppiter and the Di Penates; in A.D. 13 an altar was dedicated by Tiberius in Rome to the Numen Augusti; and, as has been said, his Genius had been linked with the worship of the Lares, and freedmen seviri Augustales had been established in Italian cities. But all this, although very near to deification, probably just fell short of it, and Augustus himself certainly deprecated any real worship of himself in Rome or Italy.

In the East Hellenistic kings had been deified while still living. This did not mean that all their subjects thought that they were in fact beings of an essentially different nature from themselves, but only that as an act of gratitude or homage, rather than of worship, the subjects were willing to accord to them in an official cult many of the honours that were normally given to gods. Thus when Roman generals had gone to the East and had then overthrown or circumscribed the power of a Hellenistic king, his subjects would not unnaturally tend to offer extravagant or even divine honours to his conqueror. As far back as 196 B.C. Flamininus, who had defeated Philip the king of Macedon and had proclaimed the freedom of Greece, had been hailed by the grateful Greeks as divine; Caesar, M. Antony and others had received similar honours. The cities of Greece and Asia had also begun to worship a personification of the Roman state, the goddess Roma, when she became obviously more powerful than their own rulers: thus Smyrna had erected a temple to Rome as early as 195. It was a natural development therefore when in 29 Pergamum and Nicomedia sought and received permission to dedicate temples to Roma and Augustus. Augustus encouraged such cults as an expression of loyalty, and most of the eastern provinces established one; they were maintained by Koina, groups of cities who sent delegates for this purpose to a common assembly, which came to play an important role in the life of the province. Such federations, formed for religious or social purposes, had long been common in the East, but they were unknown in the West. Augustus therefore, seeing in the imperial cult a valuable instrument to promote unity within a province and a bond of loyalty between the various provinces and himself, deliberately introduced the cult in the West. In 12 B.C. an altar to Roma and Augustus, built by sixty tribes from the three Gallic provinces at Lugdunum (Lyons), was dedicated by Drusus; the cult was to be administered by a *concilium Galliarum* comprising delegates sent annually by the three districts. Between 9 B.C. and A.D. 4 a similar altar was built at Oppidum Ubiorum (Cologne) to form a centre for the projected new province of Germany.

Thus while deprecating worship of himself alone, Augustus welcomed the cult of *Roma et Augustus* when it emerged spontaneously in the East, and he encouraged its spread to the West. All this of course involved his official sanction, but when individuals, groups or towns, both in the East and in Italy, began voluntarily to worship him or his Genius, it was less easy to check them. His official attitude was to discourage any move by Roman citizens in this direction: he was their fellow-citizen, not a king, and still less a Hellenistic Basileus or a god. But nevertheless municipal cults developed, though less in the West than the East, and they could scarcely be denied when Horace could imagine Augustus as being Mercury (*Carm.* 1. 2) or write (*Carm.* 3. 4)

> praesens divus habebitur
> Augustus adiectis Britannis
> imperio gravibusque Persis.

11. VIRGIL, HORACE AND LIVY[37]

Patronage, a pervasive element in Roman life, had cast its mantle over literature from early days. It was natural therefore that Augustus and some of his friends should be patrons of writers, and no less natural that he should gradually gather these, as so many other, threads into his own hand, because even in Augustan Rome, without printed books and the broadcast word, writers could exercise great influence on public opinion. He wished to spread abroad the ideals and hopes of the new age. He might command the pens of publicists, but he was in fact most fortunate in winning the loyal and enthusiastic support of three writers who proved to be among the greatest that the world has known. Virgil and Horace started indeed as poets of the revolutionary triumviral period but they became the evangelists of the settlement. That their co-operation with Augustus was advantageous does not mean that it was insincere. Both men had suffered enough from the civil war to relish the restoration of peace and both loved Italy. Little can be said here about the greatness of their poetry; it can only be touched upon.

P. Vergilius Maro was born in 70 B.C. near Mantua, a district that suffered severely from the land confiscations in 41. Educated at Cremona, Milan and Rome, he had won the patronage of Asinius Pollio and then of Augustus' great friend and adviser C. Maecenas. Though he lost his paternal farm, he later recovered it or received greater compensation from Octavian. These early difficulties are echoed in some of his *Eclogues*, pastoral sketches written between 42 and 37; though modelled on the poems of the Sicilian Greek Theocritus, they breathe a genuine delight in the countryside, while one at least (the fourth: cf. p. 162) reflects some of the hopes of a troubled age. During the next seven years, when latterly Virgil was living in Naples, he composed the *Georgics* at the suggestion of Maecenas. This was a didactic poem, influenced by Hesiod's *Works and Days* and giving practical advice to farmers on the cultivation of crops, fruit-trees and vines and on stock-breeding and bee-keeping. In the attempt to reestablish Italian agriculture after the long years of civil war, such advice would not come amiss, but the *Georgics* were far more than this. They are imbued with Virgil's intense sympathy with nature and the Italian countryside, and they reveal the deep satisfaction that a man may win from unremitting labour on his native soil.

Virgil recited the *Georgics* to Octavian after his return from the East in 29 and was encouraged by him to compose an epic poem. Work on this was not completed when in 19 B.C. he was taken ill in Greece where he had met Augustus; together they returned to Italy but Virgil died at Brundisium and was buried at Naples. In the *Aeneid*, as in his other poems, Virgil owed much to earlier poets, both Greek (here especially Homer) and Roman, and fructified by these various influences that worked upon his natural genius he produced a national epic that unfolded the origin and achievements of the Romans, who now embraced all Italy, and that looked forward also to the culminating achievement, the rebirth of Rome under Augustus. Virgil adopted the legend that Rome's origins went back to the Trojan hero Aeneas. The first six books describe the wanderings of Aeneas and his followers after the sack of Troy, and not least how duty led him to desert Dido the queen of Carthage in order that he might sail on to Italy and fulfil his destiny of founding the Roman people. The last six books portray the arrival of the Trojans at the Tiber, the betrothal of Aeneas to Lavinia, daughter of king Latinus, and the subsequent struggle by which he asserted his settlement in Latium against the hostile clans: 'tantae molis erat Romanam condere gentem'. And many of Virgil's readers might reflect on the weight of the task that the new founder of Rome was shouldering, though it was a task that was lightened by Virgil's co-operation. The poet's pride in Rome's past, his faith in the peoples of Italy and his confidence in Rome's future sprang from deep conviction. He might write of wars but he had no love of fighting: rather, he had a profound compassion for mankind's sufferings ('sunt lacrimae rerum et mentem mortalia tangunt'), and it was this tenderness, love of nature and a natural piety, rather than his belief in Rome's majestic imperial mission that led many later to feel that Virgil was the most 'Christian' of the pagan poets. Written in 'the stateliest measure ever moulded by the lips of man', the *Aeneid* won immediate recognition and ever since has continued to exercise a profound influence on the Roman and the later world.

Q. Horatius Flaccus was a friend of Virgil and another protégé of Maecenas. Like Virgil also, he was not of Roman origin but the son of a freedman of Venusia in Apulia. He had, however, been sent to school at Rome and had continued his studies at Athens. There he was caught up in the civil war and served in the army of M. Brutus at Philippi. Back in Italy in 42 he found that his father's farm had been confiscated, but his poverty was relieved by Maecenas to whom Virgil had introduced him. As the friend of Maecenas, Horace now entered Roman society and swung over to support Octavian, whose forces he had faced at Philippi. With the gift of a Sabine farm about 33 B.C., his financial position was assured and he devoted much of his time to writing poetry: in the years between Virgil's death in 19 and his own in 8 B.C., he was Rome's outstanding poet. His earliest poems were the *Epodes*, written between 41 and 31 B.C., and two books of *Satires* or miscellanies, published c. 35 and c. 30 B.C. Here Horace was developing the tradition of Lucilius (p. 163), but with more genial wit and less personal invective. In subject-matter they range far, autobiographical and moralistic, and cast a bright light on varied aspects of contemporary life and human nature in general. In his lyrical *Odes* (*Carmina*) he rose on occasion to greater heights; three books were published in 23 B.C. and a fourth in 13. In the first six odes of the third book in particular, the so-called 'Roman Odes', he expounded the traditional virtues of the race and nobly reflected Augustus' policy of social regeneration; though an Epicurean, he applauded frugality and the simple life. Other themes are less solemn, such as love and wine, but all are clothed in unparalleled economy and charm of language. There followed the *carmen saeculare* (see p. 183), two books of *Epistles*, further mellow comments on life and literature, and a discussion of poetry, the *Ars Poetica*. The wide appeal of his attractive and balanced personality, the shrewdness, if not the depths, of his comments on human nature, and the skill of metre and diction in which they were clothed, have alike combined to ensure his perennial attraction.

A third great writer, who did much to shape Rome's thought about the past and to bring it into line with Augustus' hopes for the present and future, was Titus Livius (59 B.C.–A.D. 17). Little is known about his life. He was born at Patavium (Padua); later at Rome he gained the friendship of Augustus who called him Pompeianus, meaning perhaps not a republican so much as an admirer of Pompey, who had represented a wider Italian background than some of the Roman aristocrats. Livy also taught the future emperor Claudius whom he encouraged in historical studies. Livy set himself the task of composing an epic account in prose of Rome's history that would balance Virgil's epic in verse and emphasize some of the same moral qualities. It was a pageant of the Roman state from its beginnings down to Livy's own day and stressed the men and their virtues that had made Rome great in the past and which if revived could make her great again. His whole work therefore was infused with a moral purpose. His history (*ab urbe condita libri*) was written in 142 books, of which only 35 survive, but we have summaries (*Periochae*) of the missing books which dealt with the years between the battle of Pydna (167) and the death of Drusus (9 B.C.). He followed the annalistic tradition of historiography and for the earlier periods made great use of the Sullan annalists Valerius Antias and Quadrigarius (p. 167); for later years he turned to Caesar and the *Memoirs* of Augustus among other works. If he is judged by the standards of modern historical scholarship, it is easy to point to some of his shortcomings, such as an insufficiently critical use of his sources, but much of such criticism is beside the point in relation to his purposes. He is sincere and aimed at the truth, which no doubt became easier to ascertain as he approached his own times. His powers of historical reconstruction and imagination are great. Rhetorical in manner, he presents a vivid and living narrative, varying the style to suit the events: he displayed 'clarissimus candor' and 'lactea ubertas'. The work was an immediate success, but since it was perhaps three times the length of Gibbon's *Decline and Fall*, there was soon a demand for epitomes of his new 'classic' which were widely read. All earlier histories of Rome were overshadowed, and later writers (as Florus, Licinianus, Orosius, Obsequens) made great use of it. Asinius Pollio might mock Livy's 'Patavinitas', which probably refers not to any supposed provincialisms of style or even to his personal accent, but to Livy's moral and romantic approach to history. But this is just what was needed: an account of the *mos maiorum* and the exploits of their ancestors that through its imaginative appeal might stir contemporary Romans to action and imitation. Seldom can any statesman-reformer have been as fortunate as Augustus when he gained the friendship and sympathetic support of three such men of genius as Livy, Horace and Virgil.

12. OTHER WRITERS OF THE AUGUSTAN AGE

The principate of Augustus was rich in literary production, even apart from the giant figures, and Maecenas was not the only patron. There was for instance a literary circle around M. Valerius Messalla Corvinus, who had distinguished himself in the civil war and had been Octavian's consular colleague in 31. It included Tibullus (c. 48–19 B.C.), an elegiac poet, of equestrian stock, whose main themes were his loves and country life, full of much quiet charm and reflecting the restored peaceful conditions of rural Italy. A man of stronger feeling was Sextus Propertius, an Umbrian from Asisium (Assisi), whose first book of elegiacs, dealing mainly with his mistress Hostia whom he called Cynthia, brought him to the notice of Maecenas who encouraged him to express the patriotism that he felt. Propertius, however, though praising Augustus, was unable to adopt a more heroic style, and love remained the chief but not the sole subject of his next two books (c. 28–22 B.C.). In his fourth book (c. 16 B.C.) love has been largely replaced by antiquarian interests in poems of a more Alexandrian manner.[38]

P. Ovidius Naso (43 B.C.–c. A.D. 17), born at Sulmo amid the hills of central Italy, was of equestrian rank and was educated at Rome where he abandoned any thought of a public career and devoted himself to social life and literature. He was independent of patronage, and became the friend of Propertius and Tibullus; Virgil he only saw. His early frivolous love poems, the *Amores* (published c. 16 B.C.), were a great success, and were later followed by his *Ars Amatoria* and *Remedium Amoris* (c. A.D. 1). He might argue that these poems were not immoral on the ground that he had in mind only loose women and not respectable Roman matrons, but they gave offence to Augustus who was striving to reform public morals. A few years later in A.D. 8 Ovid was involved in some scandal that affected the imperial house (the whole episode remains a mystery) and he was banished from Rome to Tomis (modern Constanza) on the Black Sea where he remained until his death, composing pathetic pleas for his pardon (*Tristia* and *Epistulae ex Ponto*). Other works included the *Heroides*, the *Metamorphoses*, which had an immense influence on the Middle Ages and later writers, and six books of *Fasti*, a metrical calendar of half the Roman year, full of religious and historical material. Thus in part at least Ovid's life ran counter to the current of official policy and he reflected the carelessness and immorality of high society that Augustus was trying to reform. Of his brilliant poetic talent there can be no question. An incomparable story-teller, vivacious, witty and urbane, he wrote with great lucidity, ease and charm.

While Livy devoted himself to the great theme of Rome's growth from its foundation, others turned to more detailed aspects. C. Asinius Pollio (76 B.C.–A.D. 5) consul of 40 B.C., who had fought in the civil wars for Caesar and Antony, retired from public life after the failure of the treaty of Brundisium and turned to literature, as writer and patron; he encouraged the custom of semi-public recitations of his own works by an author, as a means of preliminary 'publication'. His most important work was a history from the year 60 B.C. down to, perhaps, the battle of Philippi; it was much used by Plutarch and Appian, but does not survive.[39] Pompeius Trogus, another historian, wrote a *Universal History* in forty-four books, dealing with the peoples outside Italy, of which a surviving epitome was made later by Justin. Among memoirs and biographies our greatest loss is that of the thirteen books of Augustus' autobiography, which probably went down to the year 25 B.C. Augustus was in fact a man of culture who composed much both in verse and prose, e.g. a biography of Drusus, a poem on Sicily and epigrams. His chief surviving work is the simple and dignified account of his own *Res Gestae*. Maecenas and Messala both tried their hands at writing as well as encouraging others.

Finally, three Greek writers of the Augustan age may be mentioned here. Nicolaus of Damascus, the secretary of Herod the Great, wrote a *Universal History* in 144 books and also a panegyrical account of Augustus' youth, of which some fragments survive. Timagenes of Alexandria, who taught rhetoric in Rome, attacked Augustus, whose favour he lost, and found refuge with Asinius Pollio; his *Histories* may be the source of much of the scandalous gossip about Augustus that is found in later writers as Suetonius. Strabo from Amasia was both historian and geographer; his historical work is lost, but the seventeen books of his *Geography* are a mine of information about the world of the early Principate.

XII

FRONTIERS AND PROVINCES

1. IMPERIAL PROBLEMS

It was not enough to try to restore better social and political conditions in Rome and Italy, not enough even to extend an adequate administrative system to the provinces: the heart and body of the empire must be shielded from attack from beyond its frontiers. This involved two problems: the establishment and maintenance of suitable frontiers and the ability to man them. The last requirement involved yet another problem: an adequate army must be created on a professional basis, and its loyalty to the central government must be guaranteed. One reason for the collapse of the Republic had been the challenge that had arisen from successful provincial governors, backed by their armies: the Principate must not be allowed to go the same way to destruction. Thus Augustus was faced with an awkward problem. The safety of the empire demanded that he should push the frontiers well back, but distant frontiers involved entrusting armies to men far from the eye of the Princeps, and long frontiers required more men and expense. Augustus therefore tried to establish as economical a frontier system as was consistent with safety, and at the same time to create an army that would guard it adequately while remaining loyal to himself. We must therefore look first at his army reforms and then at the various provinces and the problems that their defence involved.

2. THE ARMY

Realizing the weakness and dangers inherent in the army system of the Republic, Augustus created from the armies of the triumviral period a professional standing force, loyal to State and Princeps. Under the later Republic generals had normally kept a bodyguard (*cohors praetoria*). Augustus, besides keeping a select body of German troops as a personal bodyguard, developed the praetorian cohorts as a special corps: the Guard comprised nine infantry cohorts each one thousand strong with a cavalry squadron and commanded by a tribune.[1] It was commanded by prefects, usually two in number, who were of equestrian rank; in the course of time they often became extremely influential since they tended to be entrusted with a variety of duties and to serve the emperor as general aides-de-camp. Under Augustus normally only three cohorts were stationed in Rome, the other six being quartered in various Italian towns. The Guard did not usually undertake active service unless the emperor or a member of his family took the field, and its members enjoyed privileged conditions as compared with the legionaries: they served for only sixteen years, were paid 2 *denarii* a day, and received a bonus of 5000 *denarii* on discharge.

The first task of Augustus was to reduce the swollen number of forces (over sixty legions) that were under arms at the end of the civil war, and then to retain what he regarded as the necessary minimum.[2] For those that were discharged he found land, which he claimed to have purchased and not confiscated. After 13 B.C. not more than twenty-eight legions were retained and these were reduced to 25 by the disaster in Germany in A.D. 9. The legions were now permanent units, each with its number and title and comprising 5500 infantry (divided into ten cohorts) and 120 cavalry. As under the Republic, they were recruited from Roman citizens; this meant that they came primarily from Italy and the western provinces, and any non-citizens that might be admitted thereby received citizenship (as happened more frequently in the east than in the west). Though conscription could be applied if necessary, numbers were normally maintained by voluntary enlistment, since conditions were not unattractive: good pay (225 *denarii* a year), occasional bonuses (*donativa*), and a pension in the form of money or land after twenty years' service (3000 *denarii*). Prospects of promotion were reasonable; there were 60 centurions in each legion, and the senior centurions (*primi ordines*, and especially the *primus pilus*) were men of considerable authority. Most of them had risen from the ranks and after retirement they might look forward to other useful forms of employment; a *primus pilus* received equestrian rank on leaving his legion. As under the Republic the higher positions were reserved for men of senatorial or equestrian rank: the legion was commanded by a senatorial *legatus* (new as a regular title, though Caesar had assigned parts of his army to *legati*); they were exquaestors, and later normally ex-praetors, and usually did not hold their commands for more than two or three years. Under the *legatus* were *tribuni militum*, young men who were starting a senatorial or equestrian career and who had received little technical military training apart from their experience in the clubs of *Iuvenes* (p. 196);

they were concerned largely with administrative duties on the legate's staff. Any lack of military experience in tribunes or legates was counter-balanced by that of the centurions and men like the regular *praefecti castrorum* (quarter-masters) and *praefecti fabrum* (chief engineers).

The second main branch of the army consisted of the Auxilia.[3] Their units came under the command of the legionary legate and were brigaded with a legion, but they are to be sharply distinguished from the legions. They numbered perhaps some 150,000 men, roughly the same strength, so that the total number of the regular army was about 300,000 men. Like the legions, the auxiliaries bore titles (often geographical) and numbers. They comprised infantry cohorts (normally 500 men) commanded by *praefecti cohortis*, and cavalry *alae* under *praefecti equitum*; the prefects were often tribal chiefs or legionary *primipili*. The *auxilia* were recruited from non-citizens in the less Romanized (i.e. the imperial) provinces. Their period of service was, later, twenty-five years, and on discharge they received Roman citizenship. This use by Augustus of the manpower of the provinces was not only a wise measure of economy, but involved much more. Under the Republic the provinces had not been seriously drawn upon for their own defence: now Augustus by showing confidence in their trustworthiness fostered their loyalty to the empire and they felt that they had a share in defending civilization against the barbarians beyond the pale.

The army was permanently stationed in the provinces where it was most needed, and in relation to the length of the frontiers to be guarded, it was none too large. Wars often involved moving troops from one front to another, especially under Augustus: under his Julio-Claudian successors the normal distribution was to keep three legions in Spain, eight on the Rhine, seven on the Danube, four in Syria, two in Egypt and one in Africa. In peace-time the army would be engaged on many tasks, as building roads and frontier-fortifications, bridges, aqueducts and canals. Living in their permanent camps, the legionaries would gain efficiency through knowledge of local conditions. They would attract traders, whose settlements (*canabae*) outside the camps often developed into small towns where the retired soldiers might themselves settle. Further, as the troops naturally brought their own language and customs with them, they automatically became centres of Romanization from which Roman ways of life spread to the more remote parts of the empire. Men also often developed a pride in their local units: excellent as this was, there was a risk that their links with Rome might weaken, that they might gain an unhealthy local patriotism and that rivalry might grow up between the different armies. But these were dangers that developed slowly.

Under the Republic the navy had always been the junior service, and so it remained.[4] Augustus, however, had learned its importance in his war with

Sextus Pompeius and at Actium, and resolved to maintain a regular force with naval bases at Misenum, Ravenna, Forum Iulii (modern Fréjus; in Gallia Narbonensis),[5] Alexandria, and probably Seleuceia in Syria, and with river flotillas on the Rhine and Danube. Thus the seas could be kept free from piracy, and troops and supplies could be moved with ease and safety. During the stress of the civil war both Sextus and Octavian had enrolled slaves in their fleets (though Octavian freed his), but in the more settled times that followed the crews were raised from freeborn provincials, though at first with a certain admixture of freedmen. The two fleets in the Tyrrhenian and Adriatic Seas were commanded by equestrian prefects, or on occasion during the Julio-Claudian period by imperial freedmen. In general, conditions of service resembled those of the Auxilia. A ship's company was organized as a *centuria* under a naval centurion, and the majority of the ships were triremes.

By this reorganization of the army and navy, provided always that Augustus could rely upon the continued co-operation of the commanders, the *pax Romana* was secured. One of the compliments that Augustus justly deserved and valued most was given to him just before his death when some sailors in a ship off Puteoli thanked him: 'per illum se vivere, per illum navigare, libertate atque fortunis per illum frui'.

3. THE EASTERN FRONTIER[6]

The importance of eastern problems is shown by the presence of Augustus himself in the East after Actium in 30–29 and again in 22–19 and by the eastern commands granted to Agrippa in 23–21 and again in 16–13.[7] The basic question was to reach a *modus vivendi* with Parthia, the one power that might seriously threaten any settlement by Rome in Asia Minor. Here were three Roman provinces, Asia, Bithynia and Cilicia; the rest of the area was occupied by native rulers who were client-kings of Rome. One of the greatest of them was Amyntas who ruled over Galatia and neighbouring districts. When he died in 25 B.C., Augustus decided to annex his kingdom as a Roman province: this, after it had been reduced in size five years later, consisted of Galatia, Pisidia, Isauria, western Lycaonia, and Pamphylia, but no legions were stationed in the new province. Part of Cilicia was incorporated in the province of Syria, and part transferred to Archelaus, king of Cappadocia. Just to the north there lived a wild tribe, the Homanades, whom Amyntas had been trying to pacify when he was killed. Between 12 B.C. and A.D. 1 they gave further trouble until they were crushed by P. Sulpicius Quirinius, who was appointed governor of Galatia and Pamphylia and was given troops from Syria and Egypt.[8] In order to maintain order in this area, five colonies of veterans were settled: three in Pisidia and two (including Lystra) in Lycaonia, while some years before (19 B.C.) a colony had been established at Pisidian Antioch (Colonia Caesarea). The construction of roads also helped to spread Roman influence.

In northern Asia Minor Pontus was ruled by a vassal-king, Polemo, while across the Black Sea in southern Russia the Bosporan kingdom remained in the hands of Rome's 'friend' Asander until his death in 17 B.C. Disturbances followed, and it was not in Rome's interests that neighbouring Scythian or Sarmatian tribes should benefit or that trade in the Black Sea should be threatened. Agrippa therefore used Polemo to intervene and granted the kingdom to him. Polemo then married Dynamis, the widow of Asander, but they soon quarrelled and in 8 B.C. Polemo was killed. Augustus, however, decided to accept the situation and Dynamis was left in control and remained a loyal friend of Rome until her death (A.D. 7–8). Thus the northern flank of Asia Minor was covered.

The key to the whole eastern question however was the native kingdom of Armenia, because geographically it looked both east and west; it is attached to the plateau of Asia Minor and to the Iranian plateau. It was thus a potential bone of contention between Rome and Parthia.[9] After his conquest of Egypt, Augustus might have turned against Parthia in order to avenge the defeats of Crassus and Antony: in fact public opinion expected that he would. But he judged that the two Empires could live at peace, with the Euphrates as a limit of their spheres of interest. To have attempted to overthrow Parthia would have been expensive in men and money, and if successful would have upset the whole balance of the Roman empire which was based on the Mediterranean. Further, Rome needed peace, not more wars, and conditions were such that it could be attained. The Parthian king, Phraates, was involved with a pretender named Tiridates; and Rome, who was holding as hostages the brothers of the Armenian king Artaxes, also established an enemy of his called Artavasdes on the throne of Armenia Minor. Thus Augustus was ready to welcome envoys from Phraates and postponed the issue for ten years.

An opportunity then occurred for Augustus to deal with both Parthia and Armenia. The pretender Tiridates had fled to Augustus with the kidnapped son of Phraates, who requested his surrender. At the same time there was a demand in Armenia that Artaxes should be replaced by his younger brother Tigranes who had spent ten years in Rome. Augustus decided to go to the East and ordered Tiberius to advance from Macedonia through Armenia to join him. In face of this show of force Phraates decided not to fight, but agreed to surrender to Augustus the Roman standards that he had captured from Crassus and Antony. In Armenia Artaxes was murdered and Tiberius crowned Tigranes as a client-king (20 B.C.). Augustus regarded this diplomatic triumph over Parthia as one of the great achievements of his reign: coins depicted the handing over of the standards with the legend 'signis receptis', the scene adorned the centre of his breastplate on a famous statue, and he was acclaimed Imperator IX; other coins showed a kneeling Armenia ('Armenia capta'). Thus Parthia acquiesced in Roman control of Armenia, and peace was established; it was strengthened a few years later when Phraates sent his four sons to live in Rome. After the death of Tigranes (c. 6 B.C.) struggles in Armenia enhanced Parthian influence there, so that later Augustus decided to send out his grandson, the young prince Gaius Caesar. When Gaius in A.D. 1 met Phraataces, the new king of Parthia who had succeeded his father Phraates, on the Euphrates, agreement was once more reached between the two Powers, and Roman influence in Armenia was again recognized. But internal dynastic troubles developed in Parthia and in Armenia where Roman influence was weakened. If Augustus thus failed to establish stable Roman control over Armenia by these indirect means, he had at any rate pursued a prudent policy: considerations of prestige precluded the complete abandonment of Armenia, while its annexation would have involved further advance eastwards and fresh commitments, and at the same time it would have provoked Parthia. In his Parthian policy he had achieved a diplomatic success sufficient to silence the earlier Roman demands for war and to provide security for the eastern provinces. When the recovered Roman standards were placed in the new temple of Mars Ultor, dedicated in 2 B.C. in his new Forum, Augustus may well have felt that a policy of compromise had been justified.

The military defence of the East, on which all these diplomatic moves rested, was based on the province of Syria, to which eastern Cilicia had been added. Its governorship ranked highest of all the imperial provinces. Its normal garrison was four legions, stationed in the northern part, whence they could turn to the Euphrates, Armenia or Asia Minor; the south of the province could be watched by client-rulers in Emesa, Ituraea and Judaea. As the legions were quartered in or near cities rather than in more remote fortresses, discipline tended to suffer. The towns of Syria, as Tyre, Berytus (where there was a colony of veterans) and Antioch (a legionary centre), were wealthy and prosperous.

Judaea was left in the hands of Herod the Great who had started his reign in 37 B.C. (see p. 141).[10] On the material level he did much for his country, which thanks to the continued favour of Augustus was enlarged by the inclusion of Ituraea and other districts (23 and 20 B.C.). He enforced order, developed the economic resources, built a new port (named Caesarea in the emperor's honour), refortified Jerusalem and started rebuilding the Temple, refounded several cities including Samaria-Sebaste, and in general tried to enhance the standing of his country at home and abroad. But by behaving as a Hellenistic monarch and by promoting the hellenization of his realm he won the bitter hatred of the orthodox Jews (he himself was a dissenting Jew, an Idumaean). He had therefore to impose his rule by force, by crushing the old nobility, by employing secret police and mercenary troops, by building a chain of dominating fortresses, and by developing a centralized bureaucracy. Further, he offended not only the religious but also the nationalistic feelings of many of his subjects: he was 'Philocaesar', the friend of the Roman oppressor. This friendship, however, was later jeopardized by the cruelty which he showed in his domestic quarrels; this offended Augustus, who was further annoyed when in 9 B.C. Herod attacked the Nabataeans.

When Herod died in 4 B.C. his kingdom was divided between his three sons. Philip received outlying parts in the north-east (Batanea, Gaulonitis, etc.) which he ruled for 37 years; Herod Antipas ('that fox') got Galilee and Peraea, which he held until A.D. 39; and Archelaus was given Judaea itself and Idumaea. Archelaus, however, ruled so badly that the Jews and Samaritans for once united in a request to Rome that the monarchy should be abolished. In A.D. 6 therefore Archelaus was banished and Judaea was made into a Roman province, governed by an imperial procurator with judicial authority (ius gladii); he commanded a small body of local troops and resided at Caesarea, not in Jerusalem. This last arrangement was typical of the tact that Augustus showed to the Jews, to all of whom (those in Palestine and the Dispersion) he continued the privileges already granted by Julius Caesar: freedom of worship, exemption from military service, the right to send their annual temple-tax to Jerusalem, and money coined without the emperor's head or any 'image'. Though the Jews were not very popular in Roman eyes, their importance (and potential restlessness) in the eastern provinces was very considerable. Augustus must therefore choose between protecting or suppressing them: he chose the more generous policy.

One other area in the East claimed the attention of Augustus: Arabia. Deviating from his general policy of non-aggression in the East, Augustus ordered Aelius Gallus, who had been Prefect of Egypt, to lead an expedition against the Sabaean kingdom (Sheba) in Arabia Felix, the south-west corner of the Arabian peninsula (the Yemen, behind Aden).[11] His purpose may have been mainly economic: the district exported frankincense, myrrh, gold and gems, but even more important the Sabaeans acted as intermediaries in the trade between India and the Mediterranean, with a centre at Eudaemon Arabia (Aden) whence merchandise from the East could be transshipped up the Red Sea, either to the African coast and Egypt or to Leuke Kome on the Arabian coast and then on by the caravan routes to Syria, Egypt and the Mediterranean. The expedition was launched in 26 B.C. and amounted to some 10,000 men, but too little was understood about climatic and geographical conditions. After reaching Leuke Kome, the men suffered much from scurvy and palsy, and in the next year endured a gruelling march through the desert, only to have to turn back at a place called Mariba, which possibly is the Sabaean capital Mariba (modern Marib). Despite this failure the Sabaeans had been impressed with the might of Rome; they appear to have accepted *amicitia* and to have abandoned their monopolistic control of the Straits of Bab-el-Mandeb. Further, interest in trade with India (see p. 278 f.) led Augustus to receive at least two embassies from Indian rajahs (26 and 20 B.C.).

4. AFRICA, SPAIN AND GAUL

When Augustus annexed Egypt after the death of Cleopatra, it became something between a normal province and his personal domain.[12] It was administered for him by a Prefect of equestrian, not senatorial, rank who commanded a legionary army; and no senator was allowed to enter the country without the emperor's express permission. It was an area of such potential value that he determined to allow no loophole for the ambitions of others. Further, his own position there was unique. As the successor of the Pharoahs and Ptolemies he received divine honours, and to his Egyptian subjects he was an absolute monarch. The Prefect, who represented him, was therefore a viceroy and was given royal honours: no wonder that the head of the unfortunate first Prefect, Cornelius Gallus, was turned (p. 197). How Augustus took over and adapted the complicated bureaucratic and monopolistic system of administration that the Ptolemies had developed, cannot be described here, but Egypt was made to continue to produce corn and wealth for her new ruler. Throughout the countryside the peasants toiled in semi-serfdom, while the Greek cities, as Alexandria, flourished as centres of commerce and intellectual life.

Geographical conditions made the defence of Egypt relatively simple: protected by the sea in the north and by desert each side of the Nile valley, it was thus exposed only in the south, where it was subject to raids from the Ethiopian realm centred on Meroe. Cornelius Gallus advanced the southern frontier to the First Cataract, and agreed with the Ethiopians to leave the area between it and the Second Cataract as a buffer state. An Ethiopian raid, however, in 25 B.C. led the Prefect C. Petronius to launch a punitive expedition into Ethiopia against the Queen (Candace: a title perhaps, rather than a personal name). This was successful and after a little further trouble the Ethiopians sent an embassy which received terms from Augustus (21/20 B.C.).[13] For the defence of Egypt the Prefect had under his command at first three legions and a corresponding force of auxilia, but one legion was withdrawn after c. A.D. 7. The remaining legions were based one in the suburbs of Alexandria and the other probably at Thebes or Coptos, but small detachments of troops were established at posts throughout the country and a river patrol was kept on the Nile.

The province of Africa was another of the chief granaries of Rome. Its defence was important and therefore, although it was a senatorial province, its governor (a proconsul of consular rank) was allowed an army; after A.D. 6 the one legion was stationed probably at Ammaedara near Theveste. The province itself was peaceful enough, with Carthage, restored as a colony, as its chief city; Roman civilization continued to spread through an area already permeated with Berber and Punic influences. But its frontiers needed watching. On the east and south there was much intermittent fighting. L. Cornelius Balbus (a nephew of Julius Caesar's agent) campaigned in 19 B.C. against the Garamantes in Fezzan south of Tripolitania, and perhaps a little later P. Sulpicius Quirinius dealt with the Marmaridae to the south of the province of Cyrene. In A.D. 5–6 Cossus Cornelius Lentulus defeated the Gaetulians in the west, south of Mauretania. Thus raiding tribes were kept well back from the provincial frontiers. Mauretania itself was entrusted in 25 B.C. to a native ruler Juba (son of Juba, the last king of Numidia), who had been brought up in Italy and had married Cleopatra Selene, the daughter of Antony and Cleopatra.

Spain was one of Rome's oldest provinces, but the wilder tribes of the north-west, the Gallaeci, Astures and Cantabri, were far from pacified, and the mountainous nature of the country made their subjection difficult. Augustus himself took the field against the Cantabrians in 26 B.C., but illness forced him to leave the reduction of Asturia and Gallaecia to Antistius and Carisius the following year.[14] The war, however, soon flared up again and was only brought to an end by the ruthless methods of Agrippa in 19 B.C. Conquest was followed as usual by settlement: hill-tribes were moved down from their mountain strongholds to the valleys; new towns were developed in the north-west at Bracaraugusta (Braga), Lucus Asturum (Lugo) and Asturica Augusta (Astorga), and veterans were settled at Emerita (Merida) and Caesaraugusta (Saragossa). The permanent garrison of Spain was gradually reduced to three legions, stationed in the north and west. Further Spain was divided into two provinces (perhaps in 16–13, or possibly in 27): the more civilized Baetica in the south was handed over to senatorial administration, while Lusitania in the west became an imperial province; some time later Asturia and Gallaecia were transferred to Nearer Spain (Tarraconensis) which was also imperial. This reorganization was adapted to the varying levels of Spanish civilization. Urbanization, new roads, the spread of trade, all helped the Romanization of the peninsula, which provided valuable minerals, corn, oil and not least fighting men for the Auxilia.

Gaul had been conquered by Julius Caesar, but complete pacification was not attained without a few risings even as late as 12 B.C. The basic task of Augustus here, however, was organization.[15] Gallia Narbonensis, the most urbanized and Romanized area which had been a province for nearly a century, was handed over to the Senate. Here there were five military colonies, and many native towns enjoyed Latin rights. The rest of Gaul was divided into three districts, Aquitania, Lugdunensis and Belgica, which during Augustus' reign were administered by one governor with a subordinate legate in each of these Tres Galliae. Here the existing cantonal system was preserved and sixty-four *civitates* were recognized. Each of these had its chief village which might develop into a town, but tribal sentiment remained so strong that it is the names of the tribes rather than of the towns that tended to survive: thus Lutetia, the centre of the Parisii, is now called Paris. As early as 27 B.C. Augustus went to Gaul to superintend the taking of a census, which would form the basis of the assessment of tribute. A great road-system, centred on Lugdunum (Lyons), was developed by Agrippa. This city, at the junction of the Rhone and Saône, became the commercial and political capital of the Three Gauls, and here in 12 B.C. was erected an Ara Romae et Augusti, built by the sixty-four tribes as a cult centre and administered by a Concilium Galliarum. The future defence of this now tranquil land was entrusted to the legions which, as will be described, were stationed along the Rhine. Gaul might be threatened from the east, but Augustus judged that no serious danger would arise from the British chiefs across the Channel. When he was in Gaul in 27 B.C. rumour attributed to him the intention of invading Britain, but he probably harboured no such thought. Nor did he change his policy when later two British princes fled to him. Though trade across the Channel increased and Londinium began to develop as a port, Augustus was content to leave Britain outside the Empire.

5. THE NORTHERN FRONTIER

In the north Roman occupation stopped at the Alps. In order to secure Cisalpine Gaul Augustus decided that it was necessary to conquer the whole Alpine range and by reducing the districts of Raetia and Noricum (roughly eastern Switzerland, the Tyrol and Austria) to advance the frontier to the Danube from Lake Constance to Vienna. He further judged that the southern Balkans would never be secure unless the Romans advanced northwards there also to the Danube. He thus planned a large-scale advance to the whole length of the Danube from Lake Constance to the Black Sea, with the establishment of new provinces in the conquered land of Raetia, Noricum, Pannonia and Moesia. The northern frontier of the Empire could thus be guarded by the Rhine and Danube. But communications would be shortened and the awkward re-entrant angle between the sources of the Rhine and Danube (in the Black Forest area) would be eliminated if the frontier was advanced eastwards over the Rhine to another river such as the Elbe and if this new frontier was joined to the Danube frontier near Vienna. This great plan would involve the conquest of western Germany and the reduction of the Marcomanni who lived in what is now Bohemia. We must now see in more detail how this vast scheme to advance to the Danube was successfully carried out and how various events induced Augustus to abandon his policy of advancing beyond the Rhine after it had been initiated with considerable success.

Communications over the Alps between North Italy and Transalpine Gaul required safeguarding, especially in the neighbourhood of the Great and Little St. Bernard Passes which were subject to raids by the tribe of the Salassi. Earlier indecisive campaigns (35–34 B.C.) were followed by more drastic action in 25 B.C. when Terentius Varro ruthlessly crushed the Salassi, while M. Vinicius was probably defeating the tribes further north in the Vallis Poenina (modern Valais). To guard the roads over the St. Bernard Passes a military colony was established at Augusta Praetoria (modern Aosta). Further south the Cottian Alps and the Pass of Mont Genèvre were left in the hands of a native ruler M. Julius Cottius with the rank of a Roman prefect; a few Roman troops were posted at Segusio (modern Susa). Still further south the Ligurian tribes were checked by the establishment in 14 B.C. of a small province called Alpes Maritimae, governed by a military prefect. When P. Silius Nerva had cleared the valleys from Como to Lake Garda and the Upper Adige (17/16), Augustus entrusted the great advance to the Danube to his two stepsons. Tiberius, advancing from Gaul, defeated the Vindelici near Lake Constance, while his brother Drusus moved up from the south over the Resia and Brenner Passes to the valley of the Inn; together they swept forward to the Danube (15 B.C.). These victories were commemorated by Horace, who renewed his earlier songs of triumph, and by the erection of the Trophy of Augustus, naming forty-six subdued Alpine and Raetian tribes, which still survives at La Turbie, above Monaco.[16]

The conquered area south of the Danube comprised two districts, Raetia and Noricum. The former was established as a new imperial province, administered at first by the governor of Gaul and subsequently by an equestrian prefect or procurator. At first two legions were kept near Augusta Vindelicorum (Augsburg), but after A.D. 9 it remained without legions until the reign of M. Aurelius; the commander of the armies of the Rhine was responsible for peace in Raetia and little attempt was made to Romanize the province. Noricum (roughly Austria) was incorporated in the Empire about 16 B.C., but it was not organized as a province until later (probably under Claudius); the governor of Pannonia to the east was responsible for its security.[16a]

Thus Rome had gained control of the territory up to the Danube from Vienna westwards. With the Alps and Spain now pacified, Augustus could turn to the crucial question of the northern frontier of the Balkans. In his earlier Illyrian campaigns (35–33) he had penetrated to Siscia on the Save in Pannonia and had defeated the Iapudes, Pannonii and Dalmatians (p. 140).

Thus in 27 it had been possible to make Illyricum a senatorial province; at the same time further south Achaea was detached from Macedonia, as a separate province, both being entrusted to senatorial administration. But the Pannonians were not really subdued. Fighting started again in 13, and this time Augustus determined that it should be decisive: first Agrippa (in 13) and then Tiberius conducted a series of campaigns (12–9) by which all Pannonia up to the Danube was brought under Roman rule: it was added to Illyricum, which since c. 12 had again become imperial. Further to the east other tribes were turbulent. In 29 Licinius Crassus, the governor of Macedonia, had ejected the Bastarnae from Thrace, reduced the Moesi and captured Serdica (modern Sofia). The Moesians were incorporated in Macedonia, but the Thracian tribes were left under their own rulers. Intermittent disturbances were followed by a general rising in Thrace which was crushed by L. Calpurnius Piso only after three years of hard fighting (c. 11–9); the loyal kingdom of the Odrysian Thracians was extended. Some time later, probably in A.D. 6, Moesia was established as a province, though Thrace to its south remained under native rulers. Thus Roman control was established up to the Danube along its whole length from Switzerland to the Black Sea.[17]

Before this frontier was finally settled it had to endure what may reasonably be called the Great Rebellion. In A.D. 6, while Tiberius was engaged on critical operations in Germany (see below), Dalmatia and Pannonia both rose in revolt, each led by a chief called Bato; Roman residents were massacred and if the enemy had united they might even have threatened the frontier of Italy itself. But Sirmium, a key position on the Save, was held by the legate of Moesia, and the Dalmatians wasted time attacking coastal cities; thus Tiberius was enabled to fight his way to Siscia which he held with five legions. The efficiency of the whole Augustan military system was now at stake, and the absence of a strong central reserve of troops nearly proved fatal: Augustus had reduced the forces of the Empire to a dangerously low level. When at last, however, some legions from the East reached Tiberius, he was able with an army of some 100,000 men to take the offensive and to crush the Pannonians in two campaigns (A.D. 7–8). The Pannonian Bato turned traitor, but was soon killed by his namesake who fought on. The following year (9) Tiberius planned a converging attack on Dalmatia, in which his nephew Germanicus won his spurs. The revolt was thus crushed. Pannonia was established as a separate imperial province, under a *legatus Augusti pro praetore*, and Illyricum was soon renamed Dalmatia. Tiberius had shown great military ability, but he could not rest on his laurels: news came of an overwhelming disaster to Roman forces in Germany.

The Rhine frontier had remained fairly quiet. German tribes had launched raids across it in 29 and 17 B.C., but these were not in themselves sufficient to lead Augustus to change his policy, though they would afford him an excuse if he so decided. However, the general pacification that had been attained by about 13 B.C. enabled him, as already has been seen, to think of further advance. Thus when in 12 B.C. he ordered a move over the Rhine which led Roman arms to the Elbe, it is not unreasonable to suppose that he had decided upon the permanent conquest of western Germany and the substitution of an Elbe-Danube frontier for one based upon the Rhine and Danube. This task was entrusted to his stepson Drusus, who made annual thrusts eastwards beyond the Rhine and brought a fleet from the Rhine to the North Sea through a canal which he made through the lakes of Holland; he thus secured the support of the Batavians and won that of the Frisii, who in return for supplying auxiliary troops became Rome's allies. In 11 B.C. Drusus advanced from Vetera (Xanthen) to the Visurgis (Weser), subduing the Usipetes, north of the Lippe; the next year he attacked the Chatti from his base at Moguntiacum (Mainz); in 9 B.C. he attacked the Marcomanni, advanced through the territory of the Cherusci and reached the Elbe, but he died as the result of an accident. His elder brother Tiberius was given proconsular authority and was put in control of the Tres Galliae and the Rhine armies; he carried on the task of pacification until recalled in 7. Other commanders continued to operate in the area, though on a lesser scale: for instance L. Domitius Ahenobarbus advanced from the Danube to the Elbe along the river Saale, a tributary of the Elbe; he also built a causeway (*pontes longi*) over marshy land between the Rhine and Ems.

In A.D. 4 Tiberius returned to the German front. In the next year his fleet and army combined in an advance to the Elbe, while some ships were despatched to explore the coast of Jutland. The stage was now set for the next big move: the conquest of the Marcomanni in Bohemia. If they were reduced the defence of the Elbe could be linked with that of the Danube, and a new frontier be established along the line of the modern cities of Hamburg, Leipzig, Prague and Vienna and thence along the Danube to the Black Sea. The Marcomanni had recently moved from the valley of the Main to Bohemia where their leader Maroboduus had built up a strong kingdom, but Roman diplomacy and arms had limited its expansion: the Hermanduri to its west and the Semnones (east of the Elbe) to its north were friendly to Rome, while the Dacians to its east (in modern Romania, north of the Danube) had recently been defeated by the Romans as a reprisal for Dacian raids. In A.D. 6 therefore Tiberius was ready to launch a great converging attack with twelve legions on Maroboduus, but as the Roman troops were advancing and the net was closing around him Maroboduus was dramatically saved. News came of the great revolt in Pannonia (p. 216 f.). Tiberius prudently broke off operations, reached an agreement with Maroboduus by which he was recognized as king and a friend of the Roman people, and hastened off to save Illyricum from disaster. This done, Tiberius was not free to give further thought to the

Marcomanni since a fresh calamity in Germany demanded his presence. His military services to the Empire were indeed of a high order.

Roman armies had overrun the country from Rhine to Elbe, but the conquest had not yet been consolidated by the construction of permanent forts or roads, and regular patrolling was still needed.[17a] About 9 B.C. an altar to *Roma et Augustus* had been established at the tribal capital of the Ubii (later Cologne), whom Agrippa had earlier at their own request settled on the west bank of the Rhine; and in 2 B.C. Domitius had erected another altar on the Elbe. But the country between the rivers lacked cities and clearly was not yet ripe for conversion into a normal Roman province. Tribal unrest found a leader in Arminius and an opportunity in the arrival of Quinctilius Varus. Arminius, chief of the Cherusci, had obtained Roman citizenship, served in the Roman auxilia, and gained equestrian rank; he now plotted rebellion with neighbouring tribes. Varus, who had married the grandniece of Augustus, owed his appointment as legate of the Rhine armies in A.D. 9 to the emperor's favour. His earlier governorship of Syria had been successful, but he appears to have misjudged conditions in his new command, where he is said to have tried to introduce unpopular methods of taxation and jurisdiction. At any rate he unsuspectingly entertained Arminius in his camp on the Visurgis and when winter approached he began to withdraw his three legions westwards to their winter quarters. But as he was marching through the dense Teutoburgian Forest, he was treacherously attacked by Arminius: the three legions were virtually annihilated and Varus committed suicide.[18]

Tiberius hurried to the spot, and although Rome lost all east of the Rhine, there was little fear that Arminius, who failed to win the co-operation of Maroboduus, would threaten Gaul itself. With eight legions Tiberius and his nephew Germanicus, who took over the chief command in A.D. 12, successfully reorganized the defence of the river and conducted some reprisals beyond it. Had Augustus so decided, the lost ground presumably could have been recovered, but he was old and shaken: he would cry out to the spirit of the man whom he himself had appointed, 'Quinctili Vare, legiones redde', and he wore deep mourning on each anniversary of the *clades Variana*. The loss involved a serious diminution of the narrow margin of military man-power, and the standing army was reduced from twenty-eight to twenty-five legions; the moral effects might be more widespread. What policy Augustus would have adopted, if he had enjoyed the prospect of a long life before him, cannot be known, but in the circumstances he appears to have abandoned all thought of any frontier beyond the Rhine. A narrow area along the river was divided into two districts, Upper (southern) and Lower (northern) Germany, with the division near Coblenz. Each received a permanent garrison of four legions, commanded by consular military legates: they were military zones, not provinces, and their civil administration was the responsibility of the governor of Belgica. The legions were quartered in permanent camps at Vetera (Xanten; a double camp), Novaesium (Neuss), Bonna (Bonne), Moguntiacum (Mainz; double), Argentorate (Strassburg) and Vindonissa (Windisch in Switzerland).[19]

The Varian disaster no less than the Pannonian revolt was a dark shadow, but none the less Augustus had in general achieved a lasting success. He had secured the Danube frontier by the organization of Raetia, Noricum, Pannonia and Moesia, backed by seven legions; and the Rhine was firmly held by its eight. Four in Syria, two in Egypt, one in Africa and three in Spain, aided by oceans, deserts and rivers, co-operated in holding back all assailants on those frontiers which Augustus had chosen with care and deliberation for the Empire. The pattern was complete and must not lightly be altered. In the *Brevarium totius imperii*, which he wrote in his own hand, he added as a final clause a piece of advice: 'consilium coercendi intra terminos imperii'.

6. PROVINCIAL ADMINISTRATION

Many aspects of the ways in which Augustus improved upon the provincial administration of the Republic have already been noticed, but it will be well to draw some of them together here. The provinces fell into two groups, senatorial and imperial, which corresponded roughly with the 'unarmed provinces' and those in which legionary troops were stationed. The former were governed by proconsuls of consular or praetorian standing, the latter by ex-consuls or ex-praetors who bore the title of *legati Augusti pro praetore* or else by equestrian procurators. Though the proconsuls normally held their provinces only for a year, they were nevertheless very different from their Republican predecessors owing to the reorganization of the senatorial Order on a professional basis by Augustus. The senatorial and equestrian governors of the imperial provinces held office for longer periods. The employment of Equites in this way was a complete break with Republican traditions, especially in that such governorships were dissociated from the magistracy. It is true that equestrian officials in general were more concerned with the civil side of administration, but the procurators who governed provinces might command *auxilia* (while the equestrian Prefect of Egypt even commanded legions). Thus Augustus succeeded in building up an efficient body of salaried professional administrators: all of them indirectly depended on his favour, and a large proportion were directly appointed by him and responsible to him alone.[20]

The provinces provided a very large proportion of the revenue of the Roman state, but even under the late Republic in normal conditions the provincials would perhaps not have found the burden of taxation unduly heavy or irksome, if its collection had been properly controlled: the system was less open to criticism than the abuses to which it was too often subjected. Here was a field in which Augustus made one of his most valuable and enduring contributions. In order to secure a more equitable distribution of the burden he surveyed the resources of the Empire by means of censuses, which would clearly be easier to hold in the more urbanized provinces. Roman towns had to hold a census every five years which was conducted by local magistrates called quinquennales. It is not probable that a simultaneous census was taken of all the provinces, but gradually the resources of the whole Empire would be revealed. In Gaul, for instance, censuses are mentioned in 27 and 12 B.C., and again in A.D. 14 just after Augustus' death, while the assessment by Quirinius of Judaea on its annexation in A.D. 6 is famous. Such surveys would provide information about the extent and ownership of land and about other forms of wealth: how detailed such information might be is shown by one of the edicts of Cyrene.

Such returns provided the basis for fair taxation. Direct taxes comprised tributum soli, levied on all occupiers of land, and tributum capitis, levied on other forms of property (not a poll-tax except in backward regions, as Egypt). All provincials, including Roman citizens and the liberae civitates, had to pay the land-tax, with the sole exception of the very few towns that enjoyed the Ius Italicum (i.e. the exemption enjoyed by Italy itself); those that had immunitas were perhaps exempt from the tributum capitis. Freedom from taxation could of course be granted to specific communities or individuals by Augustus. Indirect taxes included portoria (dues up to 5 per cent on goods that crossed certain frontiers; cf. p. 155);[21] the tax on manumission and on the sale of slaves (to which the Italians were liable; but only Roman citizens in the provinces paid death-duties, vicesima hereditatum: p. 188); grain for the governor and his staff (p. 155); and aurum coronarium, a gift paid later at the accession of an emperor. Revenue from provincial estates (e.g. saltus) that had become the emperor's private property either by confiscation or bequest, was naturally paid into his patrimonium. Such estates would be managed by procurators, often freedmen; other imperial procurators were in charge of the mines, which they let out to contractors (conductores) to work.[22]

'Where the publicani are, there is no respect for public law and no freedom for the allies', Livy had written of Republican times; it was by his control of these subordinates that Augustus rendered such valuable service to the provinces. In the imperial provinces the direct taxes were collected by an imperial procurator of equestrian status, who was largely independent of the governor: there might often be friction or enmity between the two men. The indirect taxes were still let out to contractors, but these publicani were carefully supervised. In the senatorial provinces the quaestor was responsible for finance, but publicani continued to act as middlemen in some of them; further, imperial procurators, who officially had authority only in connexion with any of the emperor's private property in a senatorial province, could keep an eye open for abuses. Unable immediately to dispense altogether with the help of *publicani*, Augustus subjected all financial operations to careful control and scrutiny.

Besides this immense boon of improved financial administration, the provinces gained many other solid advantages compared with Republican days, not least greater care in the choice and control of the governors, now salaried professionals whose prospects of promotion depended upon their efficiency. Naturally all misgovernment and corruption did not disappear: Valerius Messalla, proconsul of Asia, was alleged to have executed three hundred people on one day, and the exactions of the freedman Licinus, imperial financial procurator in Gaul, were notorious. But in general retribution was swifter and surer: imperial officials would be recalled and punished by the emperor; offenders in the senatorial provinces, possibly more numerous than in the imperial ones, were brought to trial before the Senate. Further, the improvement of communications made it easier for the emperor to keep in touch with and if necessary to restrain his officials: the road systems in the provinces were improved, and the imperial post, the *cursus publicus* (see p. 194), was extended to them. Though the local authorities who were responsible for the cost of this system might grumble, messages could be sent at an average speed of fifty miles a day in the imperial provinces. Governors could also be checked by means of the provincial Councils that grew up to promote the imperial cult (see p. 198). These assemblies of representatives from different parts of a province, meeting together annually, would naturally discuss their common interests as well as transact the business for which they had met. Since they lacked legislative powers, they could not develop into provincial parliaments, but they could voice any grievances and from the time of Tiberius they were authorized to approach the Princeps or Senate direct without the intervention of the governor, and to complain about, and even initiate the prosecution of, governors guilty of maladministration.[23]

Augustus continued the Republican method of working through existing provincial communities, whether cities or tribes (p. 154).[24] Without an adequate basis of local self-government the administrative system that Rome imposed on the provinces would have collapsed: the officials had to rely on the co-operation of the provincials. Rome naturally encouraged city-life where there were communities with organized magistrates and senates. Where these did not exist (as in Gaul, and later in Britain), she used the tribal system, but before long the tribe (*civitas*) often borrowed the titles used in Roman cities and had its own *duoviri* and senate (the *ordo*). Rome did not enforce a policy of urbanization, but she encouraged it where she thought it feasible. Towns also served as centres to which large surrounding areas of territory were attached ('attributed') for administrative purposes; when these became more civilized, municipal privileges might be extended to them. One of the chief ways in which city-life spread was the settlement of veterans in the provinces: to the forty or so colonies established in the triumviral period Augustus added at least a similar number: the majority were placed in peaceful areas in the west (as Narbonensis, Spain and Africa), but others were planted in the east (as those in Asia Minor, which ringed off the rebellious Homanades: p. 247).[25]

The status of the cities in the provinces varied greatly, from colonies and municipia to 'Latin' cities and the great bulk of the 'stipendiary' cities. The most privileged were not, as under the Republic, civitates foederatae (though some of these survived), but those that had Roman citizenship, i.e. colonies and municipia. Before the time of Julius Caesar the idea of establishing Roman towns outside Italy was not popular, and Narbo was the only example: Roman citizenship was given to individuals in the provinces but not normally to cities. Caesar broke away from this narrow convention with his numerous overseas colonies for veterans and the poor, and Augustus, though less liberal in his ideas of the wisdom of widespread grants of franchise, followed Caesar's colonizing policy. At the top of the hierarchy of cities stood the colonies: some of them were immunes and probably did not pay tributum capitis, and a few had the privilege of Ius Italicum which excused them from the land tax. Next came the municipia which were existing cities that had been given Roman citizenship, not settlements of immigrant Romans: thus Gades received the title and privileges from Caesar. In practice one chief difference between municipia and colonies was not that the magistracies in the former were less uniform, but that the prestige of the latter was higher; the municipia gradually (but more especially in the second century) began to seek the status and title of colony. They spread through the western provinces, especially in Mediterranean regions, but this status is not found in the east until much later. Below the municipia come the 'Latin' cities, which enjoyed a status partway between citizenship and non-citizenship, like the cities of Latium in relation to Rome in the earlier days of the Republic; the most important aspect was that their local magistrates became Roman citizens. These 'Latin' rights were usually given to cities before they were granted Roman citizenship and became municipia, and thus formed a valuable stepping-stone to greater reward. Lastly were the 'stipendiary' cities, which formed the majority in most provinces; a few of them had been 'free' or 'federate' cities under the Republic, but this status no longer exempted them from taxation, though perhaps they might expect less attention from the governor.

Thus Roman control in the provinces was to a large extent indirect and rested upon the support and loyalty of self-governing communities. The internal municipal constitutions of these cities naturally varied: those comprising Roman citizens, as colonies, would obviously tend to adopt a Roman pattern, but even those that did not possess Roman rights tended to model their constitutions on that of Republican Rome, with popular assemblies, senates and magistrates, while the Greek cities of the East had enjoyed well-developed constitutions often for centuries. Local assemblies of burgesses elected local magistrates and accepted or rejected proposals put before them; gradually inhabitants of the *territorium* 'attributed' to the town might receive limited voting rights. But influence tended to rest with the propertied classes who controlled the local senate (*ordo* or *decuriones*). This usually numbered one hundred; its members held office for life and consisted largely of ex-magistrates. The magistrates, as in Rome, were chosen on a collegial and annual basis: usually they consisted of *duoviri iure dicundo*, two aediles, and two quaestors. The *duoviri* exercised judicial powers, presided over meetings of the senate and assembly, were responsible for local Games and festivals, and every fifth year served as censors (*quinquennales*) when they filled up vacancies in the senate. As they received no salary and their office involved heavy expenses (gradually it became customary even to pay an 'entrance fee'), the magistrates would naturally be drawn from the wealthier classes. Many men were extremely generous to their towns, and provided baths, theatres and other local amenities. The motive may often have been personal pride, but it was also often a genuine affection for their cities. Thus an active spirit of local patriotism fostered healthy municipal life, which was made possible by the degree of civic liberty that the Romans with wisdom and generosity accorded to the provinces.

An improved administrative system and the encouragement of local co-operation and responsibility were not by themselves enough. Their success depended in turn upon the maintenance of the greatest benefaction of Augustus to the Roman world, the *pax Romana*. His personal interest in the provinces, exemplified in his early tours of inspection, and his development of a consistent frontier policy to replace the somewhat haphazard development under the Republic, together with the creation of a standing army to hold the frontiers against barbarian attacks, helped to restore confidence and to open up for the provinces a prospect of increasing security and prosperity.

7. AUGUSTUS

The long life of Augustus falls into three phases. The revolutionary faction leader, fighting his way to power, developed into a constructive statesman who with the help of loyal friends achieved a remarkable constitutional reform; then, stability won, he spent the last twenty or so years of his life in a period of quieter development that was, however, not unmarked by personal and national anxieties. Unlike his immediate successors, he turned not from better to worse but from worse to better: the youth, whom many

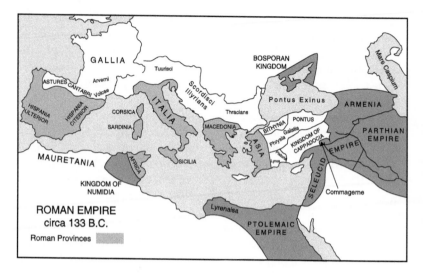

ROMAN EMPIRE
circa 133 B.C.

Roman Provinces

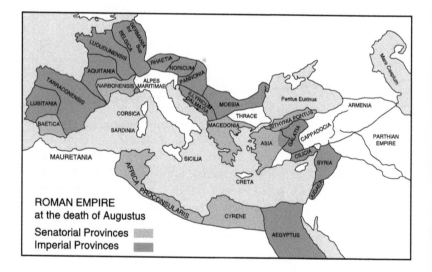

ROMAN EMPIRE
at the death of Augustus

Senatorial Provinces
Imperial Provinces

contemporaries may have branded as another 'adulescentulus carnifex', grew into a balanced and revered Pater Patriae. But behind all outward change the sources of his power continued unaltered. His personal character remains somewhat enigmatic. If he was superstitious, this did not deflect his judgement. Cautious and shrewd, in his private life he could be friendly and even homely, always preferring simplicity to luxury. Though he lacked the personal magnetism of Julius Caesar, he yet secured the enduring loyalty of his friends whose qualities supplemented some of his defects. The ruthlessness of youth was replaced by an unshakable sense of duty and a determination to achieve what he believed to be in the interests of his country, despite many a setback and ill-health; proceeding by trial and error, he succeeded where a more doctrinaire approach would have led to disaster. He thus exemplifies the common-sense practical point of view of an Italian of the upper middle-class from the countryside from which his family stock derived. He may have lacked deep spiritual insight and have regarded the attainment of law and order as a higher ideal than the promotion of human liberties, and he clearly was not a man of genius in the sense that Julius Caesar had been, but his talents matched the desperate needs of his day. However Rome might develop in the future, her immediate need was peace without which there might be no future for the Roman world. That peace he secured, and with it he laid the foundations for the romanization of western Europe, which is his most enduring monument. His hope was not in vain: 'Ita mihi salvam ac sospitem rem publicam sistere in sua sede liceat atque eius rei fructum percipere quem peto, ut optimi status auctor dicar et moriens ut feram mecum spem, mansura in vestigio suo fundamenta rei publicae quae iecero' (Suetonius, *Augustus*, 28). 'So may I be allowed to establish the State in a safe and secure position and gather from that act the fruit that I seek, that I may be called the author of the best government, and carry with me the hope, when I die, that the foundations which I have laid for the State will remain unmoved'.[26]

XIII

TIBERIUS AND GAIUS

1. THE ACCESSION OF TIBERIUS[1]

Tiberius, the son born in 42 B.C. to Ti. Claudius Nero and Livia, had lived through many changes of fortune. First, he became the stepson of Octavian who had married his mother after her divorce from Claudius in 38. With his younger brother Drusus he had been granted many privileges by Augustus whom he had accompanied on journeys both to the West and East; in 20 he had received the lost standards from the Parthians. He then served with distinction on the northern frontier, and held the consulship first in 13 and again in 7 B.C. But he had been compelled to divorce his wife Vipsania Agrippina (daughter of Agrippa and the mother of his son Drusus) whom he loved, in order to marry Augustus' daughter Julia (Agrippa's widow) in 11 B.C.; this marriage was not successful. He was given *tribunicia potestas* for five years in 6 B.C. and was offered a diplomatic mission in the East, but to Augustus' annoyance Tiberius preferred to retire to Rhodes where he passed eight years in virtual exile; dislike of his wife and a growing realization that he had been forced to marry her only in order to protect the interests of her children, the princes Gaius and Lucius, will have contributed to his decision. He enjoyed the cultural life of the island, until through Livia's help he was enabled to return to Rome, though not to the favour of Augustus, in A.D. 2. Two years later the scene had changed dramatically: the two heirs apparent were dead, and once again Augustus' plans had been brought to nought. He therefore turned again, though with reluctance, to his stepson Tiberius, who was adopted as his son, received *tribunicia potestas* for ten years, and was granted a special command (proconsular *imperium*) on the northern frontier; but even so he was compelled to adopt his nephew Germanicus as his son, though he already had a son of his own, Drusus. Then came years of fine military service which put the Roman world deeply in his debt, when he crushed the revolts in Pannonia and Illyricum and then saved the situation on the German front after the disaster to Varus. After his return to Rome he triumphed in A.D. 12, and in the following year his tribunician power was prolonged and he received proconsular *imperium* like that held by the emperor: he became in fact almost a co-regent, though he lacked above all the *auctoritas* of Augustus.

He might therefore appear an ideal successor: he had shown skill in diplomacy and brilliance in war; he was popular with the army, the first and indispensable need for any successor; nor did he lack experience of civil administration. But his character was not well adapted to his task. Silent and reserved by nature, often obscure and ambiguous in expression, he appeared severe and suspicious to many. His innate diffidence and his family pride (the Claudii had an ancient reputation for *superbia*) were aggravated by his experience of having been set aside by Augustus and adopted by him only as a last resort. Thus when he became Princeps, he was already disillusioned, soured and embittered.

The life-work of Augustus might easily have been undone if his powers could not be transmitted smoothly to another: there must be no long dispute that would open again the flood-gates of civil war. He had not, it is true, attempted to establish any law of succession (this would have offended the nobility too deeply), but his more circuitous method in practice worked out well. The only conceivable rivals to Tiberius were Agrippa Postumus, whom Augustus had adopted in A.D. 4, and Germanicus. The latter, as will be seen, was easily controlled; Postumus, whom Augustus himself had exiled because of his depraved character, was killed immediately after the death of Augustus. This was perhaps done on the order of Augustus and even without the knowledge of Tiberius, though Tacitus blamed Tiberius.

Augustus died on 19 August A.D. 14, but Tiberius allowed no constitutional adjustment until after the funeral, at which an eagle was released from the burning pyre to denote the flight of Augustus' spirit to join the gods. On 17 September the Senate met: Augustus was deified as Divus Augustus, with a temple and priests; Livia, who under Augustus' will became by adoption Julia Augusta, was voted honours; and it was proposed that Tiberius should keep his tribunican power and proconsular *imperium* for life, together with such other powers as Augustus had enjoyed. This last offer Tiberius at first declined (according to Velleius, he preferred to be an 'aequalis civis' rather than an 'eminens princeps'), but his apparent reluctance was at length overborn; by accepting, he became Princeps.[2] In the description of this scene painted by Tacitus the hesitation of Tiberius is attributed to hypocrisy, but it may well have been genuine. He was fifty-five years old, and rule would involve heavy responsibilities if not dangers. He was to show himself a loyal follower of the example of Augustus, and so he may have been mindful that Augustus himself in 27 B.C. had hesitated before accepting full control. The fact that he was a member of the Claudian and not the Julian *gens* by birth may not have affected his popularity very deeply,[3] but he would be glad if his accession should be seen to derive from the pressure of the Senate. Further, he may have felt that he lacked the necessary tact and adaptability to maintain the delicate balance between Princeps and Senate. And even when accepting, Tiberius added the hope that he might be relieved of the task in his old age. But if he hesitated before the Senate, even though already fortified by an oath of loyalty which the consuls had taken and had administered to the Senate, Equites and People, he nevertheless acted firmly within the sphere of his proconsular *imperium*: he issued orders to the Praetorian Guard and informed provincial governors that he was their new superior. Thus by a mixture of firmness and tact the dangerous corner was rounded.

2. GERMANICUS

Although all was quiet on the home front, two mutinies broke out among the troops on the Danube and the Rhine. These arose from grievances about terms of service (more pay, shorter terms of service and less bullying by officers were demanded); they were aggravated by the fact that in the emergencies of the Pannonian revolt and Varian disaster many ex-slaves had been drafted into the legions. Their political significance, if any, was slight, since they were not protests against Tiberius personally. The mutiny in Pannonia was crushed by Tiberius' own son, Drusus, who was enabled by a convenient eclipse of the moon to work on the superstitions of the rebels. The Rhine frontier was the responsibility of Germanicus, who was governor of the three Gauls and commander of the armies on the Rhine. The revolt was confined to the army group in Lower Germany, but there was a risk that these men might try to thrust Germanicus on the throne. He remained, however, loyal to Tiberius and after some rather theatrical efforts he succeeded in quelling the mutiny.

Germanicus, the son of Tiberius' popular brother Drusus, was himself well-liked. Young and handsome (he was now twenty-eight), he was quite ready to emulate his father's exploits on the northern front; he may also have felt that the best remedy for the recent discontents would be a series of campaigns. However that may be, he led his troops over the Rhine at first without direct authorization from Tiberius and proceded to re-conquer the territory between it and the Elbe. In A.D. 14 he advanced from Vetera along the Lippe against a tribe called the Marsi. In 15 he advanced from Moguntiacum against the Chatti, rescued the pro-Roman chieftain Segestes from his hostile son-in-law Arminius, and executed a converging move to the Amisia (Ems), where he himself brought four legions by sea. He then visited the

Teutoburgian Forest and buried the remains of Varus' troops, but as he with-drew for the winter he suffered losses in men and still more in stores from floodtides in the North Sea, while the army of his lieutenant Caecina further south was harassed by Arminius. He then prepared a great fleet for the cam-paign of 16 when he sailed through the lakes of Holland to the Amisia; advancing thence to the Visurgis (Weser), he fought Arminius at Idistaviso (probably near Minden) but even a second engagement led to no decisive result, and his fleet suffered loss on its return.

Despite his attempts to overcome transport difficulties, Germanicus had in three campaigns advanced and then retreated: he had failed to create condi-tions which would have enabled him to remain in Germany throughout the year. At this point Tiberius recalled him, not unreasonably. To Tacitus, who admired Germanicus and disliked Tiberius, this action was due to Tiberius' jealousy, but more probably it was based on a sound appreciation of the position. Germanicus had restored Roman prestige and thereby strength-ened the Rhine frontier, and this was probably the reason why Tiberius had allowed the campaigns so far. To have attempted once again to establish the frontier on the Elbe would have involved disregarding the policy (*consilium*) of Augustus which Tiberius regarded as a *praeceptum*, together with great expense and the reduction of Maroboduus. Further, Tiberius saw that it was unneces-sary, since internal dissensions beyond the Rhine would keep the district weak, as in fact came about: the Chatti and Cherusci were continually quarrel-ling, and Arminius warred with Maroboduus until the latter was driven into exile (A.D. 19); Arminius himself was assassinated in 21. Thus Tiberius' decision was justified, and Germanicus can have had little real ground for complaint when he was accorded a magnificent triumph in A.D. 17, given *maius imperium* over all the eastern provinces, and granted a consulship with Tiberius in 18.[4]

Unrest in the East, where amongst other changes the Parthian king had expelled the Roman nominee from the throne of Armenia (p. 209), required firm handling by a high official. Thus Germanicus' appointment was no empty compliment. At the same time Tiberius sent out a new governor to Syria, a certain Cn. Calpurnius Piso who had been consul with him in 7 B.C., in place of a friend of Germanicus: it would do no harm for Germanicus to be watched by a man of independent spirit even though of inferior status. Tiberius did not want ambition for military glory to lead Germanicus to start another war with Parthia. When he reached the East Germanicus reduced Cappadocia and Commagene to provinces and installed a new king in Armenia. He then went on to Egypt, thereby acting illegally since no senator was allowed to enter the country without the emperor's permission. His purpose may have been the harmless one of visiting the antiquities, but his conduct was tactless. He relieved a famine in Alexandria by releasing some reserve stores and advertised his popular reception by issuing an edict in which he deprecated the warmth of his welcome.[5] On his return to Syria where he found that Piso had tried to cancel some of his arrangements, he ordered him to leave the province. No sooner had Piso left than Germanicus died (A.D. 19), firmly believing that he had been poisoned by Piso. After Germanicus' widow Agrippina had sailed with his ashes to Rome, Piso unwisely re-entered Syria, but was forced to leave by the acting legate.

Back in Rome Piso was brought to trial, and since the alleged crime related to the adopted son of the Princeps, another court than the ordinary *quaestio de veneficis* was appropriate. Tiberius referred it to the Senate, where Piso had to face his peers on the double charge of murder and of re-entering his province by force; on the former he cleared himself, but knowing that he could not refute the latter he committed suicide. This episode seriously increased Tiberius' unpopularity. Rumour alleged that not only had Piso in fact murdered Germanicus but that he had acted on behalf of Tiberius, who wanted his own son Drusus to succeed him. It is true that Tiberius deprecated the fuss that the people had made at the funeral of their hero,[6] and neither he nor his mother Livia had attended; further, Livia protected Piso's wife Plancina from the hostility of Germanicus' widow Agrippina, whose hatred was now directed against Tiberius. But rumour was clearly false.

3. THE CIVIL GOVERNMENT OF TIBERIUS

During the earlier part of Tiberius' reign the civil administration was, by general consent, excellent. Even his most biting critic, Tacitus, delivers what is almost a panegyric on the years down to the death of Drusus in A.D. 23 (*Annals*, iv, 6); the only aspects that he can find to criticize are Tiberius' own ungracious manner and the law of treason. The advantages to which he draws attention include: all public business transacted in the Senate; freedom of debate; sycophancy checked; appointments by merit; dignity of magistrates maintained; laws, except that of treason, well administered; men of character appointed to imperial posts and long maintained in them; protection of provincials; corporal punishment and confiscations unknown; Tiberius' estates in Italy few, his slaves modest; any disputes that he had with private citizens were decided in the law courts. And it would not be unreasonable to extend these 'mitia tempora' until A.D. 26 when Tiberius left Rome for Capreae.

In his relations with the Senate Tiberius followed the example of Augustus: he genuinely tried to co-operate with it and even extended its administrative duties. He attended its meetings, often consulted it on matters that he might well have settled by himself, took part in debates as an ordinary senator and tried to respect liberty of discussion; he maintained that 'bonum et salutarem principem senatui servire debere', and he showed respect to the consuls by rising in their presence and giving way to them in the streets. Such a partnership in government, however, required more than goodwill on both sides: extraordinary tact was needed to hold the delicate balance, and though at first the Senate showed some real independence it soon realized the risk of encroaching too far. Thus the force of circumstances was too heavy for each side to withstand; Tiberius' early hopes gradually diminished and growing weary he could exclaim, 'O homines ad servitutem paratos!' This was not the least of the tragedies of his reign.

In various spheres the activities of the Senate were enlarged. According to the literary sources the elections were transferred from the People to the Senate in A.D. 14: how in detail this change fitted in with the system of *destinatio* established by Augustus (p. 193) is uncertain, but some time during Tiberius' reign any participation by People or Equites in the elections must have been eliminated and the Senate have been left in control.[7] The Senate's choice, however, was in part preconditioned by the emperor's power to commend or nominate candidates. Candidates who enjoyed his *commendatio* were elected automatically. Tiberius did not commend more than four men for the twelve praetorships, and *commendatio* was not at first employed for the consulship though it was extended to this office before the end of Nero's reign. The emperor could also 'nominate' candidates and thus give them more prestige though no legal backing. He apparently nominated twelve candidates for the praetorship, but since four places were already virtually filled by his commendation, this left the Senate free to choose eight from among the twelve, or from among more if other nominations had been accepted by the presiding magistrate. Though it is unlikely that men of whom the emperor disapproved would be elected, these new elections in the Senate were genuine contests, especially for the consulship, and they eliminated the potential scandal and corruption of elections in the Comitia.

The judicial functions of the Senate (cf. p. 187) developed further under Tiberius and it gradually became the chief court for treason and criminal offences committed by its members and by prominent equestrians. This had many advantages, not least that the Senate could exercise jurisdiction over the administrators in its own provinces, without the emperor having to intervene directly. Under Tiberius also the Senate passed many *senatus consulta*. He consulted it often, sometimes even on matters outside its ambit (e.g. the discharge of soldiers) and not least on religious matters, in which he showed an old-fashioned objection to Oriental cults. For instance, a scandal in 19 allowed him to have the image of Isis thrown into the Tiber and her convicted priests crucified; another scandal in the same year led him to persuade the Senate to expel the Jews from Rome and to send four thousand of them on military duty to Sardinia. His dislike of public Games caused the Senate to expel actors from Italy in 23; the number of gladiators to be exhibited was also limited. Tiberius himself of course continued the practice of Augustus in consulting a judicial council and his amici (p. 188 f.), but he displayed great moderation in style: he did not use Imperator as a praenomen, he twice refused the title of Pater Patriae, and above all he avoided the consulship which he held only three times (in 18, 21 and 31), on each occasion to honour his colleague (respectively Germanicus, Drusus and Sejanus).

To Tacitus and later writers a sinister feature of Tiberius' reign was the increase in the number of treason-trials and of the informers (delatores) who were ready to bring charges of treason against prominent men in the hope of reward, since, if successful, they received at least a quarter of the confiscated property of the condemned. But Tacitus had lived through and suffered from the period of delation and judicial murders with which the reign of Domitian ended, so that his account of how the reign of Tiberius degenerated through the application of the law of treason can hardly be accepted uncritically at its face-value. The evil arose partly because Rome had no public prosecutor, but left it to private individuals to bring abuses to official notice, and partly because of the incompleteness of the definition of the crime of maiestas. This had meant any offence against the State, but was now used to protect the emperor against treachery or even insult.

Many early cases of alleged slander or libel, often based on flimsy evidence, were dismissed by Tiberius with the contempt they deserved; some of them in fact may only have been brought as test cases in order to establish precedents. One of the early spectacular trials was that of a young noble, Scribonius Libo Drusus, in A.D. 16. He was charged before the Senate with plotting against Tiberius, Germanicus and Drusus (some mysterious marks were found against their names in his notebook) and also with magical practices; he committed suicide before the end of the trial. Tiberius was not involved in the matter personally and Libo probably was guilty of 'nefaria consilia' as the Fasti recorded. It is not possible here to refer to the numerous cases mentioned by Tacitus, but it may safely be asserted that at any rate until A.D. 26 Tiberius showed good sense and moderation in face of a growing evil.[8]

4. SEJANUS

The death of Germanicus had conveniently opened up the path to the principate for Tiberius' own son Drusus who hitherto had been loyally willing to play second fiddle to his cousin Germanicus whom he liked. Although allegedly cruel, Drusus was competent as his handling of the Pannonian mutiny had shown. He held a consulship in 15, and again in 21 with Tiberius; in the next year he received tribunicia potestas. Further, not only his own, but the future succession seemed secured, since in 19 his wife Livilla (the sister of Germanicus) had borne him twin sons.[9]

Soon, however, the bright hopes of Drusus were overcast by the sinister shadow of Sejanus. L. Aelius Seianus was the son of a knight of Etruscan descent, L. Seius Strabo, Prefect of the Praetorian Guard. An able administrator, he quickly won the approval and then the personal friendship of Tiberius, who appointed him first joint Praetorian Prefect with his father (in 14) and then sole Prefect (16 or 17). His influence was immensely increased when (between 21 and 23) he was permitted to concentrate the Guard in permanent barracks near one of the gates of Rome. The confidence that Tiberius reposed in Sejanus whom he named the 'socius laborum', angered Drusus, who on one occasion even struck him in the face. But the rivalry soon ended in 23; Drusus suddenly died. It was later suspected that he had been poisoned by his wife whom Sejanus had seduced, but of such foul play Tiberius had no suspicion, and even without it the shock of his son's death was grievous enough. However, he still had his friend Sejanus to rely upon, and since Drusus' child was too young (the other twin died), he decided to adopt the sons of Germanicus namely Nero (not the future emperor) and (a third) Drusus, whose mother Agrippina still survived.

The influence of Sejanus grew steadily and he began to plot to secure the succession for himself. Though Tiberius refused his request to be allowed to marry Livilla in 25 after divorcing his wife, he made skilful use of the treason law to strike down a number of potential enemies and began to implant in Tiberius' mind jealous fears of Agrippina, her children and friends. Though these became his victims, it is uncertain how far they were innocent victims. There was little love lost between Tiberius and Agrippina, and her hostility was potentially dangerous since, as the widow of Germanicus, she was popular with the army, but whether she actually plotted against him remains obscure. Sejanus' path was further cleared when he persuaded Tiberius to leave Rome (26) and retire to Capreae (27); the emperor's faith in him was strengthened since on the way there Sejanus saved his life when the roof of a grotto in which they were dining collapsed.[9a] Tiberius' motives in leaving Rome were probably mixed: he was 67 and tired of the responsibilities of office, he had been saddened by Drusus' death, he may have found his mother Livia trying, and he may even have thought that he would be safer away from Rome. But although he still attended to public business, his retirement had serious constitutional repercussions: it was one thing for the Senate to debate matters in the emperor's presence, and another to have to seek his views by correspondence and await the replies of one who was their *princeps* but not in law their *dominus*.

The influence of Sejanus was increased not only by Tiberius' retirement but also by the death in 29 of the empress-mother at the age of eighty-six; Livia, whose help to her husband Augustus in earlier days had been great, more recently had exercised some restraint at court.[10] In this very year

Tiberius denounced Agrippina and her son Nero, and the Senate banished them; in 30 Sejanus persuaded Tiberius to send the other boy Drusus to Rome, where he was promptly imprisoned. Having thus eliminated possible successors to Tiberius, Sejanus now moved to bolder action. He secured the commands of some of the provincial armies for his friends, he at last obtained Tiberius' permission to marry a member of the imperial family (presumably Livilla), and he was nominated as joint consul with Tiberius for 31: he was clearly to be the successor. But Tiberius' suspicions were at long last aroused when he received a message from Antonia (the widow of his brother Drusus and the mother of Germanicus) that made him doubt Sejanus' loyalty. Yet he acted slowly and with caution. He summoned to Capreae and safety Gaius (the future emperor Caligula and the youngest son of Germanicus) who had hitherto been allowed to survive in Rome in neglect. It was soon learnt that his brother Nero was dead, thanks no doubt to Sejanus. When he entered his consulship in 31 Sejanus is said to have received proconsular *imperium*, but when Tiberius resigned his consulship in May Sejanus had to do the same. Neither man could wait indefinitely, but while Sejanus was maturing his plot Tiberius struck first. He appointed Sutorius Macro to succeed Sejanus as Praetorian Prefect and secured the allegiance of the Vigiles. On 18 October Sejanus, unsuspecting, attended the Senate to hear the consul read a despatch from Tiberius in which he expected that he would be given tribunician *potestas*: but as the content of this 'verbosa et grandis epistula' gradually unfolded, Sejanus found himself tricked: it ended not with honours for Sejanus but by denouncing him as a traitor. The Senate then condemned him; he was strangled in prison and his body was torn to pieces by the mob. His children and many of his partisans were illegally put to death by the Senate and the mob in Rome. Later Tiberius took further vengeance, though the reign of terror depicted by Tacitus is probably exaggerated; as late as A.D. 33 Tiberius ordered the death of twenty of Sejanus' followers who were still in prison, but he then granted a kind of amnesty to the survivors. This dramatic rise and fall of an emperor's favourite has powerfully impressed the imagination of later generations.[11]

5. PROVINCIAL AFFAIRS UNDER TIBERIUS[12]

In general Tiberius remained loyal to Augustus' 'consilium coercendi intra terminos imperii', and made only those changes that security demanded. The main provincial alterations affected the East, where the client-kings of Cappadocia, Commagene and Cilicia died. Cappadocia, whose king Archelaus had died in Rome where he had been summoned on suspicion of treason, and Commagene were made Roman provinces; Cilicia was incorporated in the province of Syria. While this reorganization was carried out by his legates,

Germanicus was, with the acquiescence of the Parthian king, installing a ruler on the Armenian throne. This arrangement gave peace until c. A.D. 34 when the death of the Armenian king stimulated Artabanus III of Parthia to intervene, but after meeting L. Vitellius, legate of Syria from 35 to 37, on the Euphrates, he agreed to accept the Roman settlement of a certain Mithridates on the Armenian throne.[13] Vitellius did good work also in Judaea, where the governor Pontius Pilate (26–36) had committed a series of blunders which culminated in the unnecessary massacre of some Samaritans on Mt. Gerizim. After despatching Pilate to Rome to stand trial Vitellius conciliated Jewish feelings by restoring the High Priest's vestments and by sending his troops on a detour to avoid bringing their standards onto Jewish soil. Few contemporaries, however, can have realized that the most important event for the future of the Roman empire as well as for the later world, that took place in the reign of Tiberius, was the life and teaching of Jesus Christ in Palestine under the procuratorship of Pilate who, yielding to the hatred of the Jews, ordered his crucifixion (p. 307 f.).

Little change was made on the Rhine-Danube frontier after Tiberius had decided not allow Germanicus to continue with his plan to advance to the Elbe (see p. 228 f.). In fact when the Frisii revolted in A.D. 28 against oppressive taxation, Tiberius did not attempt to reduce them. On the Danube he made an interesting experiment of a type which was developed only by his successors in the second century; he settled on the north bank of the river (in Czecho-Slovakia) some Suebi and Marcomanni under a native ruler called Vannius to form a breakwater against invasion. He also tried to strengthen the frontier in S.E. Europe by combining the senatorial provinces of Achaea and Macedonia with the imperial province of Moesia, thus putting the whole of the Balkans under one command; this was held by C. Poppaeus Sabinus already governor of Moesia (A.D. 11–15), for an extremely long period (A.D. 15–35) and the arrangement remained in force until 44.

Three small wars occurred during the reign: in Thrace, Gaul and Africa. In Thrace, which Augustus had divided between two native rulers, one king murdered the other in 19. Rome intervened by force, deposed the survivor, entrusted his realm to Rhoemetalces II, and installed a resident Roman officer in what had been the eastern kingdom of Cotys. Native Thracian risings were crushed in 21 and 25. Tiberius established a settlement called Tiberia, perhaps a new foundation at Philippopolis.

A rising took place in Gaul in A.D. 21, led by two Romanized Gallic nobles, Julius Florus and Julius Sacrovir. The chief cause may have been economic distress, arising from the demands of the campaigns of Germanicus and from exactions of Roman businessmen, but another potent factor was Druidism, which Augustus and Tiberius disliked, partly because of its potentially dangerous nationalist and anti-Roman influence, and partly perhaps because they disapproved of the human sacrifice and cruelties which were alleged to have formed part of the worship (although such ritual murders by this time may have become less common in Gaul than in Britain).[14] Augustus had forbidden Roman citizens to take part in the cult, and Tiberius took some measures against it, possibly suppressing the Druidical priesthood. The revolt, which was chiefly supported by the Aedui and Treveri, was crushed without difficulty when the legions of Upper Germany, commanded by C. Silius, were brought up to help the urban cohort stationed at Lugdunum (the only Roman troops in the vast area of the Gauls). Silius, however, abused his victory and three years later was exiled by Tiberius for extortion.

The third rising was that of the Musalamii in Africa, led by a Numidian named Tacfarinas who had deserted from the Roman army and raided Roman territory from the south (A.D. 17).[15] Africa was a senatorial province, but the commanders that the Senate sent to deal with Tacfarinas were not very successful in guerrilla warfare. On Tiberius' advice Junius Blaesus, the Pannonian commander and uncle of Sejanus, was sent out in 20; after some victories for which he was hailed as *imperator*, he was succeeded by P. Cornelius Dolabella who finally trapped and killed Tacfarinas (24). With peace restored, Africa quickly settled down to a period of prosperity, as shown by the public buildings that were constructed during Tiberius' reign at such places as Thugga and Bulla Regia, and it continued to be one of the main granaries of the Empire.

These disturbances should not obscure the fact that in general the provinces enjoyed peace and increasing prosperity under Tiberius' administration. He told a governor who had collected more than the legal amount of taxation that 'you should shear my sheep, not flay them', and in the main the governors that he chose were good: L. Vitellius is an excellent example, while Pontius Pilate was far below the average. Governors were made responsible for their wives' misdoings, and Tiberius was harsh to bad governors, some of whom preferred to commit suicide rather than face a trial for extortion. At the time of disaster he could be liberal: for instance after Asia had suffered severely from an earthquake in A.D. 17, he advised the Senate to excuse the city's taxes for five years, and he himself gave Sardes ten million sesterces. Asia showed its gratitude by voting a temple to Tiberius, Livia and the Senate, which was erected at Smyrna. But Tiberius did not encourage any widespread growth of emperor-worship, since he refused a similar request from Spain: he told the Senate that he was satisfied to be human, to perform human duties, and to occupy the first place (*principem*) among men.[16]

6. TIBERIUS' LAST YEARS

Tiberius, proud and lonely in spirit, suffered a severe shock when he realized that the friend that he had trusted for so many years had proved disloyal, but his grief and disillusionment will have been sharply intensified when he was suddenly made aware that this treachery was no recent development. The widow of Sejanus, before committing suicide, revealed in a letter to Tiberius that eight years earlier Sejanus had seduced Livilla and that they had poisoned Tiberius' own son Drusus. For nine months the emperor refused to leave his villa; he suffered a severe nervous breakdown and spent most of the rest of his life at Capreae, never again entering Rome. Malicious stories arose that he passed his time on this secluded island in debauchery and vice, but they are substantiated by no first-century evidence, and are not made more plausible by the fact that he lived to be seventy-seven and that he is known to have enjoyed the company of scholars, jurists and men of letters as well as of astrologers. A more serious aspect of his absence was the continued dependence of the Senate in Rome upon him. Old and weary, he was not prepared to submit again to the formal duties of earlier days, and disinclination will have been strengthened by the knowledge that he was safer in Capreae from risk of a conspirator's knife. But he in no way disregarded his duty to the empire as a whole, and he carried on his work on its behalf.

He doubtless became more suspicious and morose, and a certain natural indecision increased, but the view that he developed into a sinister tyrant whose rule ended in a reign of terror must not be accepted without some reservations. To the supporters of Sejanus he proved implacable and ruthless, but he did not strike down his victims without inquiry: in A.D. 32 seven people who were accused were saved, and of the nine who perished Tacitus implies that only two were innocent. The number of well-known persons accused of treason throughout the whole twenty-two years of his reign has been put at sixty-three, and although this indicates no very healthy state of affairs it scarcely suggests indiscriminate murder. Tiberius' victims certainly included young Drusus, the son of Germanicus, and possibly also the boy's mother, Agrippina who is said to have starved herself to death on the island to which she had been banished. Her third son Gaius was kept at Capreae, practically a prisoner.

Tiberius still devoted care to public affairs. He alleviated a financial crisis in 33 due to shortage of currency by establishing a loan-fund of one hundred million sesterces from which debtors could borrow without interest.[16a] Three years later he made a similar princely gift for relief after a fire on the Aventine. Where possible he practised economy: he spent little on public shows or buildings, or on the upkeep of a lavish court, so that he was enabled to reduce the unpopular sales-tax from one per cent to one-half per cent, and to leave 2700 million sesterces in the treasury when he died.

Since Tiberius was 'solus et senex', the question of the succession became increasingly urgent. His own grandson Gemellus (the son of Drusus) was as yet too young, his nephew Claudius was regarded as too foolish, and so he turned to his grand-nephew Gaius, despite his evil promise, but the issue was by no means certain, since in 35 Tiberius made Gaius and Gemellus his joint-heirs: perhaps he hoped to live until Gemellus was of full age when Gaius might be set aside. At any rate though Gaius, who would be popular because of his Julian connexion, was allowed to hold a quaestorship in 33, Tiberius did nothing to train him for greater responsibility. However, the Praetorian Prefect, Macro, began to seek Gaius' favour, and both men were rumoured to have hastened Tiberius' end when he lay ill near Misenum in March 37. The news of Tiberius' death was received in Rome with joy: the people, long deprived of public amusements could cry 'To the Tiber with Tiberius' while the Senate refused to accord divine honours to the man whom many had increasingly come to suspect and fear.

If Tiberius had died shortly before or shortly after his accession, he would have been judged very differently by later generations. As it is, his years of competent and even outstanding service as soldier and administrator have been overlaid by the hatred which his last years engendered. Further, it is difficult to modify the impression that must remain on the mind of all readers of Tacitus' masterly portrait of Tiberius, even when they recognize that it is coloured by the historian's own experiences under Domitian: the work of genius may be spell-binding. Yet even though Tiberius did not lack his admirers, such as the soldier historian Velleius Paterculus (who significantly published his work in A.D. 30 before the last excesses), it is true that Seneca and the elder Pliny, who lived through the reign, both condemn Tiberius and contrast the later with the earlier years. In general Tiberius' wise continuation of the policy of Augustus, even if it lacked brilliance, provided a valuable period of stability for the young Principate. His administrative and foreign policy was good: if he failed at home to win the full co-operation of the Senate, that was partly their responsibility and partly because the task was too delicate for a man of his temperament. He honestly tried, but he failed and his failure was made irremediable by his retirement to Capreae. That he sometimes hid his real feelings behind ambiguous phrases may argue an attempt by a man who lacked his brother's affability ('civile ingenium') to allow freedom of discussion to the Senate rather than a sinister natural hypocrisy. And few will believe that he maintained a mask of virtue for nearly seventy years and rejoiced when he could throw it aside and emerge as a bloodthirsty tyrant. It was his tragedy that, while trying to do his duty as he saw it, he was plunged into a position that he had not sought and that demanded other talents than he possessed and that he increasingly realized this: 'tristissimus homo'.

7. GAIUS (CALIGULA)[17]

Gaius, the sole surviving son of Germanicus and Agrippina born in A.D. 12, was descended through his mother from Julia and through his father from Antony. Brought up among the armies on the Rhine which his father had commanded, he was nicknamed Caligula (Little Boots) from the military dress that he used to wear as a small boy. After his father's death his life cannot have been happy, since his mother and brothers had been persecuted by Tiberius; after living with his grandmother Antonia, he had finally to join the gloomy Tiberius at Capreae. Though not trained for full responsibility, he was popular with the army and his Julian connexion would commend him to all who hated or feared the Claudians. Supported by Macro, he was acclaimed emperor in March 37 and received all Tiberius' property since the Senate declared the latter's will to be invalid. After the years of Tiberius' oppression hopes now ran high and the young emperor was welcomed with enthusiasm both at Rome and in the provinces.[18] He adopted Tiberius Gemellus and named him Princeps Iuventutis; he made his uncle Claudius his colleague in the consulship; he checked delation and treason-trials; recalled political exiles and allowed the publication of some suppressed works; abolished the sales-tax; gave shows and distributed largess.

But Rome did not breathe this freer air for long. In October Gaius had a serious illness and when he recovered he emerged, according to tradition, a monster of lust and diabolical cruelty. The balance of his mind was to some degree upset and he developed into a megalomaniac and tyrant: whether he was mad is a matter of definition and in the absence of a clinical-pathological report of the type which some modern writers attempt to establish for such historical figures from somewhat inadequate evidence, the question can hardly be settled. The possibilities of power went to the head of this inexperienced young man and he acted with increasing irresponsibility. He ignored or humiliated the Senate and struck several blows at the 'diarchic' ideals of Augustus. Thus he held the consulship each year except in 38; he moved the imperial mint from Lugdunum to Rome; he handed back the elections from the Senate to the People; he transferred the command of the legion in Africa from the senatorial proconsul to an imperial legate; once he smashed the *fasces* of two consuls and deprived them of office. A charge that may be taken less seriously than these is the famous rumour that he intended to make his favourite horse Incitatus consul. Beside these attacks on senatorial privilege, he killed many individuals or drove them to their deaths, including Tiberius Gemellus and Macro. He now encouraged delation and revived treason-trials, which (unlike Tiberius) he used as a method of personal enrichment. He needed money, since with wild prodigality he wasted the large sums that Tiberius had accumulated: he thus did not hesitate to impose new taxes on the people.[18a]

In contrast to his two predecessors, Gaius sought and accepted honours which hardly fell short of deification, and he perhaps intended to turn the Principate into an absolute monarchy, on Hellenistic or Oriental lines. He may have imbibed ideas about the East from his friend Herod Agrippa, and while some Hellenistic monarchs (the Ptolemies) married their sisters, Gaius committed incest with his sister Drusilla; after her death in 38, which removed a restraining influence from him, he ordered her deification. He appeared in public in the dress and with the insignia of various gods and established a special temple for his own divinity. Hardly less offensive, to the nobility at any rate, must have been the way in which he anticipated Nero by performing as a charioteer, gladiator and singer, while one of his most spectacular appearances was when he drove, wearing the breastplate of Alexander the Great, over a bridge of boats which he had constructed across the Bay of Naples from Baiae to Puteoli.

Folly at home, reinforced by folly in foreign affairs that drove Judaea and Mauretania to the point of rebellion (see below), increased the hatred of Senate and people for Gaius and engendered conspiracies; the opposition would become yet more serious if it spread to the armies. The first conspiracy arose in fact in the camp of Cn. Cornelius Gaetulicus, the popular legate of Upper Germany. One of the ringleaders, who was perhaps himself hoping to supplant Gaius, was Aemilius Lepidus, the widower of Gaius' sister Drusilla and the lover of another sister Agrippina. Gaius hastened to the scene and restored order by his prompt action (39). Lepidus and Gaetulicus were executed, and Gaius' sisters Agrippina and Julia Livilla, were banished. Gaetulicus was replaced by the future emperor Galba; Gaius had received help also from another future emperor, the praetor Vespasian. To give his troops some employment Gaius directed their attention to Germany and Britain.

Gaius' tyranny and oppression were intensified by this episode: senators and army-commanders, Stoics and philosophers, jurists and men of letters, were alike threatened, and other conspiracies naturally followed. Even Herod and Gaius' freedman Callistus began to turn from him. Finally a Praetorian tribune named Cassius Chaerea decided to avenge the insults that he had received from the emperor. The two Prefects of the Guard (Gaius had appointed two after Macro's death and had raised the number of cohorts to twelve) were privy to the plot, and in January 41 Gaius was struck down in his Palace and was despatched with thirty wounds. Few will have wept.

8. THE PROVINCIAL POLICY OF GAIUS

The half-hearted actions that Gaius took in regard to Germany and Britain are most puzzling: were they the irresponsible antics of a madman or did some sound strategic purpose lie behind them? Whether or not he was contemplating going to Germany in any case in order to make himself known to some of his troops, his hurried departure thither was caused by the conspiracy of Gaetulicus. After this was crushed, Gaius conducted some raids across the Rhine into Germany. Fantastic stories circulated about this campaign: for his 'triumph' he used slaves who had to dye their long hair red and even learn some German. It is possible that some serious manoeuvres, which he planned in order to restore discipline in the Roman army or to overawe German tribes, have been misunderstood and distorted by a tradition hostile to him. He then spent the winter (39/40) in Gaul, where he received a congratulatory embassy from the Senate, led by his uncle Claudius, whom according to 'rumour' he ducked in the Rhone; at Lyons he auctioned some imperial property at fantastic prices, and also held a contest in Greek and Latin eloquence with humiliating punishments for the losers.

In the spring of A.D. 40 Gaius drew up his troops on the English Channel, preparatory to an invasion of Britain; here he was joined by Amminius, the exiled son of the British ruler Cunobelinus (Cymbeline), who promised submission. Gaius then suddenly cancelled the expedition, using Amminius' action as an excuse. His real motive is uncertain; possibly the troops were restless and mutinous or Gaius may suddenly have feared to go so far from Rome. He is said to have ordered his soldiers to pick up sea-shells (musculi), 'the spoils of Ocean'; whether this anecdote arose from a misinterpretation of an order to his engineers to pack up their huts (musculi) or reflects the wildness of Gaius' mind must remain uncertain. Thus it is possible to believe that he planned some serious movements against Germany and Britain or that he merely indulged in some fantastic parades. At any rate he compromised Roman prestige to the extent that his successor resolved upon the conquest of Britain.[19]

Gaius made some unwise changes among the client-kingdoms, partly in order to reward his own friends. Commagene, which Tiberius had organized as a province, was given to the son of its former king. Gaius found kingdoms (Lesser Armenia, Pontus and part of Thrace) for the three sons of the Thracian ruler Cotys who had been brought up at Rome with him. By dethroning the king of Armenia Gaius created a vacuum into which Parthia was drawn. His friend Herod Agrippa was given the tetrarchies of his uncles, Philip and Herod Antipas (Ituraea and Galilee). Ptolemy, the king of Mauretania, who had been summoned to Rome, was ordered to kill himself: Gaius intended to annex his kingdom, but it resisted by force.[19a]

Gaius' policy towards the Jews was no less disastrous. The persistent requests by the large Jewish community in Alexandria for local citizenship which was denied them by the Alexandrine Greeks, often led to disturbances and anti-Semitic riots. The situation in the city was complicated further by the grievances of the Greeks against Rome; they were jealous that the Jews were allowed their ethnarch and Senate, while their own municipal rights were limited (they perhaps lacked a Senate).[20] Thus nationalist leaders, as Isodorus and Lampon, arose who in their opposition to Rome were ready to face martyrdom if need be. This anti-Roman movement developed a literature of its own, which is also often anti-Semitic, the so-called 'acts of the Pagan Martyrs'; it survives only in fragmentary papyri.[21] One of the anti-Jewish pogroms flared up in A.D. 38 when Agrippa on his way to the East called in at Alexandria which he had left hastily two or three years before because of his debts.[22] It was aided by the Prefect of Egypt, Avillius Flaccus, who accepted the demand of the Greeks that statues of the emperor should be placed in the Jewish synagogues. Gaius was glad of the excuse to recall Flaccus, who had been the friend of Tiberius Gemellus and Macro; Flaccus was later put to death.[23] Meantime both Jews and Greeks in Alexandria sent deputations to Gaius, that of the Jews being led by the philosopher and theologian Philo.

When the deputations reached Italy they heard that Gaius had ordered that a statue of himself should be set up in the temple at Jerusalem: this was his reply to an incident in Jamnia in Palestine where the Jews had pulled down an altar which the Greeks had erected to Gaius. Philo has left a vivid account of how his deputation had to chase Gaius from room to room and obtained no greater concession than the remark that 'men who think me no god are more unfortunate than criminal'. Gaius' intended action in Palestine was more serious. The governor of Syria, P. Petronius, who had to enforce the order, knew that it would provoke widespread resistance and so he wisely 'went slow', while Agrippa bravely persuaded Gaius to revoke it. Soon, however, the emperor changed his mind, ordered the statue for Jerusalem to be made in Rome and instructed Petronius to commit suicide. Only news of Gaius' death prevented revolt in Palestine. Petronius also was saved because the news reached him before the death-warrant.[24]

With Judaea on the point of revolt and Mauretania in open rebellion, Gaius' death did not come too soon. With disorder abroad and autocracy at home, the Augustan system was subjected to a severe strain which fortunately was not prolonged to breaking point. But these years, short though they were, left their mark, not least upon the Senate and nobility who realized that behind a Princeps might lurk a despot.

XIV

CLAUDIUS AND NERO

1. THE ACCESSION OF CLAUDIUS[1]

In the confusion that followed the murder of Gaius a soldier of the Praetorian Guard found Claudius hiding behind a curtain in the palace on the Palatine and rushed him off to the camp of the Guard. At first uncertain whether he was going to be killed or made emperor Claudius soon found that the Praetorians realized that their own interest demanded the continuance of the Principate and that a son of Drusus and a brother of Germanicus, even if not a soldier himself, had at least a family tradition to commend him. Meantime the Senators were debating whether the Republic might be restored or, if not, who among them might be made Princeps, but, in Gibbon's famous words, 'While the Senate deliberated, the Praetorian Guards had resolved.' Their resolution was in fact fortified by a promise from Claudius to give a donative of 15,000 sesterces to each man; this attempt to reward, if not to buy, the loyalty of troops, though not without precedent, did not provide a healthy example for future emperors.[2] After Claudius had rejected a demand from the Senate to submit, his friend Herod Agrippa negotiated for him, and the Senate, which lost the support of the Urban Cohorts, was compelled to give in: on 25 January A.D. 41 it accepted Claudius as the new Princeps, on whom the titles and powers of his predecessors were then conferred.

The Senate might be pardoned for having forgotten the claims of Claudius, since he had deliberately been kept in the background by his own family throughout his fifty years. This was due in part to his physical infirmities, which resulted perhaps from a form of infantile paralysis: he had weak legs, a shambling walk, a slobbery mouth and a shaky head, though Suetonius admitted that when standing still or seated he 'possessed majesty and dignity of appearance'. His own mother Antonia disliked him and clearly he would not follow in the soldierly footsteps of his father, the elder Drusus, or his brother Germanicus. Augustus, although not unconscious of his intelligence, had not considered him suitable for public office, and Tiberius had followed this lead; Claudius had not even been admitted to the Senate. Gaius had brought him more into the open, with a consulship in 37, but chiefly as a butt for his own malicious wit. Scorned or neglected, Claudius is alleged to have become a glutton, a drunkard and a gambler (vices that he shared with many another Roman noble), but, more important, he developed a love of history and his country's past. Encouraged by Livy, he had started a History of the Civil War from the death of Julius Caesar, but after he had written two books his friends persuaded him to move to a less controversial period and he composed forty-one books on Augustus whom he much admired, covering probably the forty-one years from 27 B.C. to A.D. 14. He also wrote a defence of Cicero, an autobiography in eight books, a History of the Etruscans in twenty books and a History of the Carthaginians in eight (these last two works were written in Greek); another work was on the Latin Alphabet, to which he wished to add three new letters.[3] His historical studies will have exercised an important influence on his thought and action: his youthful enthusiasm for the Republic developed into a wider appreciation of the past and above all of the fact that Rome's greatness owed much to her ability to introduce change and reform while still preserving essential traditions. He thus looked back, past Tiberius' years of attempted conformity, to the more creative period when Augustus tried to reconcile Republic and Principate, and even beyond him back to the masterful developments initiated by Julius Caesar.

Proud of his country's past, Claudius wanted to rule well, and in many respects he achieved his desire. Yet the main trend of the surviving literary tradition about his rule is contemptuous when it is not hostile, and depicts him as the victim of unscrupulous exploitation by his ambitious freedmen and scheming wives, particularly his third wife Messalina, who was put to death in 48, and her successor Agrippina the younger. But luckily sufficient imperial enactments survive in inscriptions or upon papyri to reveal the thought of Claudius himself and these, though sometimes tortuous in manner, show that he possessed great administrative common sense. He not only showed skill in his choice of efficient freedmen-servants and outstanding generals (as Corbulo, Galba, Vespasian, Hosidius Geta and Suetonius Paulinus), but he also impressed his own mind and policy upon public affairs. In the last few years of his reign, however, his powers began to fail and the traditional view of him as a pawn in the hands of more determined men and women approximates more closely to the truth.

Like many another emperor, he started off well. Since he could hardly overlook the murder of a Caesar, he punished Chaerea and a few conspirators but not any senators who were suspected. He cancelled Gaius' 'acts' and allowed a return of exiles under a general amnesty, including Gaius' two sisters; nor did he hesitate to refer to Gaius as a madman in a public document. By assuming the name of Caesar he identified himself with the Julian family. He showed respect to the Senate and magistrates, dropped treason trials in the Senate and enhanced his popularity by giving gladiatorial shows and abolishing Gaius' new taxes. Long honoured by the Equestrian Order, which more than once had chosen him as its representative, he now had the support of the Praetorians, and he was accepted by the armies whose interests he cultivated; during his principate he was saluted as Imperator by the army no less than twenty-seven times. In A.D. 42 Furius Camillus Scribonianus, the legate of Dalmatia, was persuaded by some senators to revolt, but his two legions would not support him for more than four days, and the revolt did not spread; Claudius rewarded these loyal legions with the titles of Claudia Pia Fidelis. It was chiefly the Senate that Claudius had to watch.

2. CLAUDIUS AND THE SENATE[4]

Claudius reacted sharply from Gaius' autocracy and sincerely tried to co-operate with the Senate on Augustan lines. Gaius may have restored the elections to it, but Claudius made frequent use of *senatus consulta*; he held the consulship only four times: he tried to maintain the social position of senators and developed Augustus' provision of the best seats in the Circus for them; he restored Achaea and Macedonia to the Senate in 44; he shared the new provinces acquired during his principate between senatorial and equestrian legates, the former receiving Britain and Lycia. He showed the Senate outward respect and assiduously attended its meetings. But his revival of the office of censor which he held himself in A.D. 47–8, gave offence, since one of his objects will have been to adjust membership of the Senate by means of *adlectio*. Besides expelling some old members he added a number of provincials, including some Gallic chiefs (see p. 251); his creation of new patricians will also have been designed to infuse new blood into the aristocracy.

Claudius further insisted that the Senate should work with efficiency. He thus enforced attendance. In an interesting fragment from a speech he delivered on procedure in trials, which is preserved on papyrus, he put forward proposals designed to break 'the tyranny of the accusers' and urged the Senate to vote honestly on them: 'If you disapprove, find another solution, but here and now . . . it is unbecoming to the majesty of this assembly that one man alone, the consul-designate, should repeat the remarks of the consuls word for word as his opinion and that the rest of you utter only one word, "I agree" and then when you leave say, "We debated".'[5] This denunciation of 'yesmen' reveals the increasing inadequacy of the Senate, and it was this, not a desire to humiliate it, that led Claudius to encroach on its activities in various ways. Chief among these was his creation of a centralized administrative machine, staffed by freedmen, which is described below, but a few other specific examples may be mentioned. Thus he abolished the senatorial *quaestores classici* because the prefects of the fleets at Misenum and Ravenna could do their work; an imperial 'procurator portus Ostiensis' replaced the quaestor Ostiensis; in 44 Claudius himself nominated two quaestors to administer the Aerarium for three years; imperial officials relieved the quaestors of the care of the roads in Rome: Claudius may on occasion have interfered in the appointment of governors to senatorial provinces; and in 53 powers of jurisdiction in financial questions in senatorial provinces were transferred from the proconsul to imperial procurators.[6] He may also have made some adjustments in the distribution of corn.[7] All changes of this kind were no doubt made by him in an attempt to secure greater administrative efficiency, and in part the Senate may have had only itself to blame for its losses, but clearly such measures would increase the difficulty of friendly co-operation between the Princeps and Senate. In fact by infringing senatorial administrative duties, by interfering with the composition of the Senate, and by his attacks on individual senators (Claudius is said to have executed thirty or thirty-five during his reign), he alienated still further a body with which he wished to be on good terms. He perhaps underestimated the resentment of some of the older aristocratic families when they found their members being turned, through his drive for efficient administration, from independent officers of state into officials of an emperor.

To some extent the Equestrian Order benefited from Claudius' policy towards the Senate and from his provincial policy: there were more posts for equestrian officials. But although his outward relations with them continued to be friendly and he was careful to preserve the integrity of the Order (his reorganization of their *cursus honorum* was short-lived), they too found themselves often overshadowed by him, even in commercial activities, and they were increasingly becoming merely his agents. Their discontent sometimes resulted in conspiracies, and Claudius is said to have put to death up to three hundred Equites.

3. CLAUDIUS' CENTRALIZED ADMINISTRATION

One of the fundamental causes of Claudius' difficulties with the Senate and the Equestrian Order was that beside making them more dependent on himself he was at the same time becoming more independent of them through the creation of a private secretariat. Augustus, following the normal Roman practice, had used the freedmen and slaves of his own household as secretaries and clerks, and his successors had perhaps slightly increased their staff. But it was Claudius who first developed a centralized bureaucracy by creating specialized departments, each under a freedman, which were miniature Ministries and formed the basis of an Imperial Civil Service, which was independent of the older authorities, the Senate and Knights. Further, this chancery was staffed with men, mostly of non-Italian origin, who were not imbued with the Roman tradition and who owed loyalty to the Princeps alone. Thus in the interest of more efficient administration Claudius unwittingly sowed the seeds from which was to spring that gigantic bureaucratic machine which two or three centuries later began to choke the free life of the whole Roman world.

The immediate cause of this development was the growing complexity of the business which the emperor had to handle, arising in part from the great increase of imperial property and estates and the addition of new provinces. The new departments and their freedmen heads were: Narcissus, the chief secretary (*praepositus ab epistulis*), through whose office all official correspondence must have passed; Pallas, the financial secretary (*a rationibus*);[8] Callistus, a secretary (*a libellis*) who dealt with petitions to the emperor and also (unless this was the work of a separate department) with judicial inquiries (*cognitiones*); and Polybius (*a studiis*) whose functions probably included those of librarian and literary adviser. The new imperial freedmen, by fair means or foul, gained great wealth and power, but during most of the reign they remained essentially the servants of the master who appointed them. Their existence caused continual annoyance to the old senatorial aristocracy and at the same time greatly increased the personal power of the Princeps. Greater efficiency in administration was thus obtained at a high cost.

Finance in particular was closely concentrated in the hands of Claudius and his servants. It is perhaps not likely that he established a centralized Fiscus in Rome (in the sense of a Treasury where he kept public money), but the development of the office of *a rationibus* (which had existed under Tiberius, and probably even under Augustus) will have led to a closer organization of the imperial provincial *fisci* (see p. 187). The emperor also had a vast private fortune, and this was contained in a treasury known as a *fiscus*; the accounts of these personal monies (the *ratio patrimonii*) were kept by a *procurator a patrimonio*, a post perhaps first created by Claudius. He also established an official *procurator vicesimarum hereditatum* to control the inheritance tax, while the procurators secured more financial authority in senatorial provinces (p. 245). He himself gained greater control over the Aerarium when he received the right to appoint quaestors to administer it (p. 245), and in practice he would presumably not be held accountable for monies that he drew from it, because any formal vote of funds to the emperor would be made without a time limit, since all emperors from Tiberius onwards at their accession were given their powers for life (and not for specific periods, as with Augustus).

A similar desire for efficiency is shown in Claudius' judicial administration. He had so great a personal interests in jurisdiction that he was mocked for the time that he spent in the courts, but he set right many abuses in the judicial system, not least by expediting the transaction of business (cf. his speech mentioned on p. 291). Here as elsewhere his actions were inspired by a spirit of equity. A less pleasant aspect was that he himself often judged criminal cases such as his predecessors might have remitted to the Senate. The hearing of such trials intra cubiculum principis became unpopular, especially when it was thought that they were used by Claudius' freedmen or wives as a means of getting rid of their personal enemies by playing upon his fears of conspiracy: sometimes uncertainty of himself, combined with a touch of naïveté, may have misled him into acts of cruelty. But his essential sense of justice is shown in a considerable body of minor legislation for which he was responsible. Details cannot be given here, but two examples may illustrate its humanity and equity: usurers were forbidden to lend money to a son in expectation of a father's death; and sick slaves, for whom Roman masters sometimes callously disclaimed responsibility by exposing them in the temple of Aesculapius, were, if they recovered, to obtain their freedom.

Claudius was not backward in his public help and works. An S. C. Hosidianum punished those who purchased and demolished buildings for profit; the bill aimed especially at preventing the destruction of farms and the consequent reversion of the farmland to grazing. Claudius helped the corn supply by insuring ships and cargoes against damage by storm, and by granting privileges to aliens who built ships. At Ostia, the port of Rome, where the Tiber mouth was silting up, he built a harbour some two miles to the north, linked to the Tiber by canal, and constructed moles, a lighthouse and granaries.[9] He completed two aqueducts for Rome which Gaius had started: remains of the Aqua Claudia still stride across the countryside outside the city. Thirty thousand men, working for eleven years, tunnelled a three-mile long emissarium which drained the Fucine Lake into the river Liris and reclaimed a large area in central Italy for agriculture, though this was later partly lost again through the choking of the channel. Both in this work and in his harbour works at Ostia, Claudius was following earlier schemes of Julius Caesar. He built roads in Italy (continuing the Via Valeria as the Via Valeria Claudia to the Adriatic) and in Alpine districts (e.g. the Via Claudia Augusta from Altinum to the Danube). And, as will be seen, he was no less concerned about the well-being of the provinces.

In his religious policy Claudius, though conservative by nature and antiquarian in interest, did not avoid all novelty. He did much to restore the old religion of the State, e.g. he reorganized the college of haruspices, and in 47 he managed to celebrate the Secular Games by reckoning their start from 613 B.C. instead of 666 B.C., the date used by Augustus; the Games were thus made to coincide with the eight-hundredth anniversary of the foundation of Rome. In another ceremony in 49 he extended the old sacred boundary of Rome (the *pomerium*) to include the Aventine and part of the Campus Martius; this privilege belonged to generals who had extended the imperial frontiers, within which Claudius had brought Britain, Mauretania and Thrace. Towards emperor-worship, in reaction against the wild extravagances of Gaius, Claudius reverted to the sensible attitude of Tiberius. In the famous letter that he wrote to the Alexandrians in 41 he said that he did not want a high priest or temples, 'for I do not wish to be offensive to my contemporaries', but naturally he did not in general receive less honours than had Tiberius. Towards foreign religions he was tolerant where he regarded them as harmless to older Roman ideas. Thus he thought of transferring the Eleusinian Mysteries to Rome, but he expelled astrologers from Italy. Towards Druidism he went further than his predeccessors (see p. 235): if Tiberius had not already done so, Claudius decreed its complete suppression. Towards the Jews he reverted to the more generous attitude prevailing before Gaius, and restored to them throughout the Empire freedom of worship and exemption from the imperial-cult. But in Rome he was more severe. Though Tiberius' expulsion order had not been revoked, a large Jewish colony had re-established itself in Rome: in 41 Claudius denied them the right to hold meetings (other than those of the individual synagogues?), presumably to stop them proselytizing and perhaps as the result of some disturbance; at any rate in this same year he wrote angrily to the Alexandrine Jews, accusing them of 'fomenting a universal plague'.[10] In 49 there was a further clash with the Jews in Rome, and they were apparently expelled; whether the emerging new religion of Christianity had nay influence on these events is uncertain, but Suetonius says that a riot was provoked 'impulsore Chresto'.[11] Claudius also admitted the festival of Attis into the Roman calendar and reorganized its priestly colleges: the cult was robbed of some of its wilder features and was 'romanized'; the chief priest, the *archigallus*, now had to be a Roman citizen and not an eastern eunuch.

4. THE PROVINCIAL POLICY OF CLAUDIUS

Undeterred by the advice of Augustus that the Empire should be kept with the limits that he had established for it, Claudius added no less than five provinces: Mauretania (two provinces), Britain, Thrace and Lycia. This policy arose partly from the legacy that he had received from Gaius of a Mauretania in revolt and of a Britain proclaimed as ripe for annexation, but also in part from his belief that the time had come to advance and to replace client-states by direct rule in some areas.

The revolt of Mauretania, which followed the murder of its ruler Ptolemy by Gaius (see p. 241), was led by one of his freedmen Aedemon, but it could not last long. The conquest of the country was begun by C. Suetonius Paulinus (41–2), who in a bold march became the first Roman to cross the Atlas mountains and reach the Sahara; it was completed by Cn. Hosidius Geta by 44. Two provinces were created, Mauretania Caesariensis and Tingitana with capitals at Caesarea (Cherchell) and Tingis (Tangiers) respectively; both towns, together with Tipasa and Lixus, received colonies of Roman veterans.[11a] The conquest of Britain is described below (pp. 252 ff.): in 43 Claudius hastened to join his general Aulus Plautius, who had forced the Thames, and witnessed the defeat of Caratacus. South-east Britain became a Roman province with a colony of veterans established at Camulodunum (Colchester) and its frontiers guarded by client-kings. Claudius himself, who returned to Rome to celebrate a triumph in 44, named his young son Britannicus. In Thrace, which had long been restless, the reigning king was murdered by his wife, and Claudius decided that the time had come to annex it (46). Lycia, which also had been disturbed, was made a province in 43.

In Gaul, where some whole tribes received Latin rights and many individuals were given Roman citizenship, there was much development. The legate of Lower Germany, Cn. Domitius Corbulo showed his military efficiency be reducing the Frisii who were again restless (47) and by checking raids of the Chauci who were organizing piracy in the North Sea under the leadership of Gannascus who had served formerly in the Roman Auxilia. After killing Gannascus and destroying his ships Corbulo was ordered by Claudius to withdraw westwards over the Rhine: the emperor had no intention of adopting a new policy towards Germany and the Rhine frontier. A colony was established at Cologne, named Colonia Agrippinensis in honour of Claudius' wife, and colonial status was given to Augusta Treverorum (modern Trier or Treves), an important centre in the Moselle valley between the Rhineland and Gaul. The administration of Noricum was entrusted to an equestrian procurator in place of the *praefectus* whom Augustus had employed, while control of Achaea and Macedonia was given back to the Senate.

In the East also, especially in Asia Minor, road-building and other development proceeded apace. Claudius rewarded his friend Herod Agrippa for his past services (see p. 243) by installing him as ruler of Judaea, which since A.D. 6 had been a Roman province. But when Agrippa died in 44, Claudius judged that it might be too risky to leave such a key position under any other native ruler, and so Judaea reverted to provincial status, governed again by procurators. But Agrippa's brother, Herod, who had been installed in the little principality of Chalcis, received the right to nominate the High Priests and to supervise the Temple of Jerusalem and its funds. Commagene was restored in 41 to its king Antiochus IV, whom Gaius had first installed and then deposed;

Antiochus reigned until 72 when Vespasian incorporated Commagene into the province of Syria. Towards Parthia Claudius at first showed a firmer hand than Gaius had done and managed to gain some control over Armenia owing to the dynastic dissensions in Parthia, but near the end of his reign a new king, Vologeses I, established himself on the throne of Parthia and his brother Tiridates on that of Armenia (52–4); thus it was left to Nero to tackle the Armenian question once again.

In some respects Claudius' line of thought followed Julius Caesar rather than Augustus. He set less store on the privileges of Rome and Italy and tried to raise the status of the provinces by generous grants of Roman citizenship and municipal rights, not least in the less romanized parts of the Empire. This policy is well illustrated by his treatment of Volubilis in Mauretania, which is known to us from an inscription.[12] This town, which had helped Rome during the war, received Roman citizenship, municipal status and exemption from taxation for ten years; further, the native tribes (incolae) living within the territory of the municipium were 'attributed' to it. By this wise provision the more backward inhabitants of an area could be introduced to the responsibilities of city life by gradual stages: in this case, the incolae were probably given the right to vote for the municipal magistrates but not to hold office themselves. Rome thus gave citizenships to those who were ripe for it and trained the less civilized peoples of the empire in the responsibilities of citizenship before they were raised to this status. The colonies that Claudius established in Mauretania, Britain, Gaul and Germany have already been mentioned; there were others in Thrace, Cappadocia and Syria.

Claudius' generous attitude to Roman citizenship, which is summed up in Seneca's gibe that 'constituerat enim omnes Graecos, Gallos, Hispanos, Britannos togatos videre', is illustrated in another inscription containing an edict of Claudius granting citizenship to the Anauni and some other Alpine tribes.[13] Difficulty had arisen because these peoples had been assuming citizen rights in the belief that they were members of the municipium of Tridentum (modern Trento), whereas an enquiry showed that some of them were only 'attributed' to the municipium and others had not even this status. When Claudius found that many of them had made good use of their supposed citizenship (some were serving in the Praetorian Guard, others as centurions), he wisely granted them citizenship and thus showed that he believed this should be the reward given for service to those who had attained an adequate degree of Romanization. The extent to which in practice he granted citizenship to communities or individuals must not be exaggerated: what is important is that he realized that the Empire had now had time to settle down, that Latin culture was being more widely assimilated, and that further extension of rights was desirable.

The possession of Roman citizenship by a provincial gave him many social and economic advantages, but it also enabled him, in theory, to stand for office in Rome and seek entry into the Senate: prejudice, rather than law, stood in his way. This issue became alive when some Gallic chieftains sought admission. During his censorship (47–8) Claudius outlined his policy in a speech to the Senate which is partly preserved in an inscription (the so-called Lyons Tablet found at Lugdunum) and also in the version given by Tacitus in the *Annals*.[14] Drawing on his knowledge of Rome's history Claudius emphasized that the Republic had flourished because it had welcomed foreign elements into the citizen body and because it had adjusted the constitution to meet each fresh need. Thus he persuaded a reluctant Senate to proclaim the right of all Roman citizens in Gallia Comata to stand for office in Rome. At the same time as censor he probably added some of the nobles of the Aedui to the Senate by virtue of his right of *adlectio*, thus saving them from the need to go through the minor qualifying offices. This was a great step forward: under Augustus the Senate had become more representative of *tota Italia*, and now Claudius opened the way to the Senate House for more provincials, though at the cost of alienating some of the older senatorial families.

Thus in general Claudius developed an imaginative provincial policy in line with Rome's better traditions. He extended the frontiers, where he judged this advisable; he promoted good administration (a procurator like Felix in Judaea fell below the average); he suppressed disorders; and by extending citizen and municipal rights he began to raise the provinces nearer to equality with Italy.

5. THE CONQUEST OF BRITAIN

Almost a century passed between Caesar's invasion of Britain in 55 B.C. and the Claudian conquest in A.D. 43, and during these years the face of Britain had changed somewhat.[15] The south-east had been united within the kingdom of the successors of Caesar's opponent Cassivellaunus, who had moved his capital to Prae Wood above Verulamium (St Albans) and had reigned peacefully until c. 15 B.C. Later Cunobelinus (Cymbeline) overran the territory of the Trinovantes in Essex (whom Julius Caesar had protected against the Catuvellauni), parts of Kent and the middle Thames valley; he thus dominated the south-east. About A.D. 10 he moved his capital to Camulodunum ('the fortress of Camulos', the war-god, at Colchester) where it sprawled over some twelve square miles surrounded by dykes. Though essentially an agricultural community, as the corn-ear on the coinage proclaimed, the kingdom of Cunobelinus began to absorb Mediterranean influences. In art an interesting blending of Celtic and classical styles took place, while the British nobles began to demand luxury imports from the Roman world: jewellery, glass, fine pottery, metal-work and wine. These imports were paid for by exports which in the time of Augustus included, so Strabo records, wheat, cattle, hides, slaves, hunting-dogs, gold, silver and iron; of these the metals must have come from beyond the borders of Cunobelinus' kingdom. The import of goods from Italy and Gaul helped to stimulate the growth of a trading-post on the north bank of the Thames at Londinium. On the death of Cunobelinus his realm was divided between his sons Caratacus and Togodumnus (40–3).

West of this kingdom were rival tribes. Commius, king of the Gallic Atrebates, had deserted Julius Caesar and settled with his followers in Surrey and Kent (see p. 113). Other Gauls had followed his example, settling in Dorset and Hampshire amid peoples of their own culture. Such immigrants gave the name Belgae to the tribe in Wiltshire; they defended their settlements with great ramparts and ditches. Out of these warring tribes there emerged in Surrey and Sussex the realm of a descendant of Commius, named Verica (c. A.D. 10) who maintained himself for thirty years until he was driven out by Cunobelinus and his sons: he fled to Rome to seek help from Claudius, thus following in the steps of the exiled Amminius who had appealed to Gaius two or three years before (see p. 241). The fact that Verica had used the Latin title rex on his coinage suggests that he had had some contact with Rome earlier, even if he fell short of having become a client-king.

This appeal, though not determining Claudius' policy, will have been timely, since he was already probably contemplating action against Britain, partly in order to restore prestige after Gaius' fiasco, but primarily no doubt because he wanted and needed military success: the Praetorian Guard had helped him to the throne, but the armies as a whole would like to see the son of the elder Drusus in the field, extending the Empire and reviving Rome's martial traditions. Lesser motives may have contributed to his decision, as the desire to stamp out Druidism (cf. p. 255) and to acquire wealth from the island. Further, the fact that the Britons replied to Rome's refusal to extradite some refugees by causing disturbances on the coast of Gaul will have encouraged Claudius to act at once rather than to allow a British 'question' to develop in the future, the more so since the thought of annexing the island had been 'in the air' from the time of Augustus.

In A.D. 43 four legions were mustered under the command of Aulus Plautius: II Augusta, XIV Gemina and XX Valeria Victrix from the Rhine armies and IX Hispana from Pannonia. Together with their auxiliary troops they numbered some 40,000 men. Unwillingness to leave the quarters they knew led to a temporary refusal to embark, but at last they sailed in three divisions, and finally the main force landed in the safe harbour of Rutupiae (Richborough), where traces of their defensive works still survive. Their first real battle was fought against Caratacus on the Medway, where in a two-days' engagement Vespasian, commander of the Second Legion, and Hosidius Geta contributed manfully to a decisive victory; Caratacus fled west, while the troops of his dead brother Togidumnus retreated northwards. Plautius then halted the advance at the Thames and waited until Claudius could arrive and lead his troops to a final victory north of the river. Claudius then entered Camulodunum, the old capital of Cunobelinus, established it as the capital of the new province of Britannia, and received the submission of other tribes: Cogidumnus, King of the Regni, whose capital was at Noviomagus (Chichester in Sussex), received Roman citizenship and the title of 'rex et legatus Augusti'; Prasutagus, king of the Iceni in Norfolk, was also accorded Rome's friendship. With its flanks thus protected by client-kings, the new province was left to the care of its first governor Plautius, and Claudius returned to Rome where he celebrated a triumph, set up a commemorative arch in the Campus Martius and named his son Britannicus.

Since Caratacus was still at large, building up his strength in Wales, Plautius decided on a threefold advance. The Ninth Legion, acting as the right wing, advanced northwards towards Lindum (Lincoln) and established peaceful relations with Cartimandua, queen of the Brigantes, who occupied a large part of northern England. A central column marched through the Midlands. Vespasian, who led the Second Legion westwards, reduced Vectis (the Isle of Wight), over twenty native fortresses (*oppida*), and 'two powerful tribes', who will be the Durotriges and Belgae in Dorset and Wiltshire. Archaeological evidence has revealed the grimness of the struggle when the Romans stormed the great fortress of Maiden Castle and has shown how after capturing another fort on Hod Hill (near Blandford) they established a camp of their own on it for legionary detachments and cavalry. Soon the Severn estuary and the Wash had been reached, and it was perhaps Plautius rather than his successor P. Ostorius Scapula (47–52) who created a military frontier line (*limes*) based on the Fosse Way from Exeter to Lincoln with supporting forts, thus protecting S.E. England. Disturbances among the Silures of S. Wales and the Brigantes, however convinced Ostorius that to hold the lowlands required further advance. He therefore decided to disarm all tribes south of the Fosse Way and to advance beyond it into the gap between the headwaters of the Severn and Trent. He intervened against the Brigantes, and attacked the Deceangli of Flintshire (49), tribes that were perhaps acting together; he probably advanced his Midland troops to Uriconium (Wroxeter) for this campaign. He then turned to the Silures, with whom Caratacus had taken refuge, and established a legionary base at Glevum (Gloucester). But Caratacus, who had no intention of being caught like a rat in a trap, moved to the district of the Ordovices in N. Wales. Here, however, he was defeated in a pitched battle (perhaps near Caersws), and although he escaped to Cartimandua, the Brigantian queen handed him over to the Romans (51). Claudius, however, treated him well and kept him in honourable confinement in Rome. Thus Ostorius had done much to advance and strengthen the new province. He also established a colony of veterans at Camulodunum, where the city was being developed on Roman lines as a worthy capital, with a temple of Claudius as the centre of the imperial-cult. This was the first colony in the province; it is uncertain whether Claudius gave the charter of a municipium to Verulamium. Thus Rome had gained firm control of S.E. England, with legions at Gloucester and (soon) at Lincoln to cover the Trent-Severn frontier, within which the autonomous client-kingdoms of the Regni and Iceni were allowed to exist. The whole area was now opened up to the peaceful penetration of Roman influences.[16]

6. COURT HISTORY UNDER CLAUDIUS

These various achievements of Claudius are of far greater importance than the palace intrigues to which Tacitus and lesser writers devote much attention. Yet his domestic background, even if he was not dominated by it as a hostile tradition suggests, was not without influence in the shaping of events. The extent to which his freedmen and wives influenced imperial policy may be doubtful, but they certainly wielded great power. Freedmen like Pallas and Callistus started as paupers and ended as millionaires, and Roman dignity was seriously affronted when Claudius could send an ex-slave Narcissus to try to quell an incipient mutiny among the legions that were mustering for the invasion of Britain: not thus had Julius Caesar dealt with mutineers. But however offensive the freedmen may have been, at least they rendered much good service to emperor and State. This could scarcely be said of Claudius' last two wives. Messalina, his wife at the time of his accession, bore him a daughter Octavia and a son whom he surnamed Britannicus (born A.D. 41). A woman of unbridled licentiousness and cruelty, she may well have played on Claudius' fears of conspiracy which will have been sharpened by the plot of Scribonianus in 42 (see p. 245) and other lesser threats. He ignored her infidelities until in 48 she had the audacity to go through a form of marriage in public with her lover, the handsome consul-designate C. Silius. Behind this strange affair there probably lurked treason and a serious senatorial conspiracy: Silius may well have been plotting to replace Claudius and he appears to have won over the Prefect of the Vigiles and the head of the imperial gladiatorial school. While Claudius remained confused at this revelation, Narcissus acted and persuaded him to order the deaths of Messalina and Silius.

In choosing another wife Claudius followed the advice, so it is said, of the freedman Pallas who supported the claims of the younger Agrippina, though she was Claudius' own niece. Daughter of Germanicus and great-granddaughter of Augustus, this dominating woman had already had two husbands; by the first of these she had a son, L. Domitius Ahenobarbus (Nero). She married Claudius in 48, was greeted as Augusta, and began to play the role of empress in the grand manner. In 50 she persuaded Claudius to adopt her son Nero and began to intrigue for his succession in place of Claudius' own son Britannicus who was five years younger. Ambitious and unscrupulous, Agrippina struck down a series of victims: no man or woman was safe if she suspected rivalry or desired their wealth. Her weapons were poison or a trumped-up charge, often of magic; delation and treason-trials revived, but the trials were held in the privacy of the palace. Though Narcissus remained loyal to the claims of Britannicus, she secured the support of Pallas, and of Seneca who was recalled from banishment to become young Nero's tutor; in 51 Afranius Burrus, on whom she could rely, was made Praetorian Prefect. Nero was quickly advanced. Adopted by Claudius ostensibly to act as the guardian of Britannicus, at the age of thirteen in 51 he assumed the *toga virilis* (i.e. 'came of age') and received the title of Princeps Iuventutis, together with a grant of proconsular *imperium* outside Rome. Two years later he made his first speech in the Senate and married Claudius' daughter Octavia. In 54 Claudius suddenly died after eating a dish of mushrooms: it is not difficult to credit the belief that he had been poisoned by Agrippina. Even if she felt that the ultimate succession of her son Nero was secure, she may have wished to see him on the throne while he was still young enough to follow her advice and will.

With all his faults, and they may have increased during the last few years of his reign, Claudius had served his country well. This was publicly recognized when he was accorded divine honours after his death. Seneca might give pleasure to some of the senatorial aristocracy through the parody that he wrote on Divus Claudius, which he called the Pumpkinification instead of the Deification of the emperor, but Claudius was the first emperor to be thus consecrated since Augustus, and the provinces had not been slow to honour a man that had worked for their well-being. But both his drive for efficiency at home and abroad and his attempt to raise the provinces closer to the level of Italy had potentially dangerous consequences: they involved the further undermining of the old governing class and the greater centralization of power in the hands of one man. Though Claudius revered Augustus, the effect of his well-intentioned principate was to disturb further the delicate balance of the Augustan settlement.

7. NERO'S FIRST YEARS[17]

A remark attributed to the emperor Trajan has often been interpreted as recording his belief that a 'quinquennium Neronis' was a period in which Nero's rule excelled the government of all other emperors. Trajan, however, if he ever made the observation, may in fact have been referring only to Nero's building activities in the later part of his reign and not to the general administration of his first five years. But whatever the application of the remark, it at least accords with the undoubted fact that his reign commenced well.[18]

Agrippina with unscrupulous skill had so prepared the way for her sixteen-year-old son that the transference of power from Claudius to Nero was smooth: the great-great-grandson of Augustus was generally acceptable. He had the support of the Praetorian Prefect, Burrus, and confirmed the loyalty of the Guard by a donative of 15,000 sesterces a man. He was also welcomed by the Senate which he addressed in a speech composed for him by his tutor Seneca: he promised to follow the Augustan model in his principate, to end all secret trials *intra cubiculum*, to have done with the corruption of court favourites and freedmen, and above all to respect the privileges of the Senate and individual senators. The evils of the last years of Claudius were thus renounced, though Claudius was deified, and Nero, now *divi filius*, pronounced the oration at the state funeral. *Clementia*, a word that Seneca chose as the title of a work that he dedicated to Nero in 55, was to be the ruling quality of the new administration, and at first Nero responded. He modestly refused the title *pater patriae*, he opposed the first charge of *maiestas*, he exempted his fellow-consul in 55 from swearing the usual oath *in acta principis*, he avoided using *imperator* as a *praenomen*, he employed as a coin type the civic crown of oak which was a symbol of liberty, and he restored to the Senate the right to issue gold and silver coinage which now was issued 'EX S.C.' This good start and the hopes for a happier age were mirrored in the *Bucolics* of the poet Calpurnius Siculus and in the first book of Lucan's *Pharsalia*.

Agrippina now meant to rule through her son. She murdered or drove to suicide potential foes: Domitia Lepida, Nero's aunt; M. Iunius Silanus, proconsul of Asia and a great-grandson of Augustus; and the freedman Narcissus. Her power was advertised on the coinage which bore confronting busts of herself and Nero on the obverse, with the legend 'Agripp(ina) Aug(usta) divi Claud(ii uxor) Neronis Caes(aris) mater'; Nero's name and titles were banished to the reverse. Seneca and Burrus, however, although they owed their positions to her, had little love for petticoat government, while Nero himself would be glad to free himself from the role of puppet-king, if only to have time for indulging his artistic fancies and sensual passions. First they struck at her supporter, the financial secretary Pallas, who was deprived of his office and fortune; he was replaced by another freedman, probably Phaon, who would be more amenable to their direction (55). Agrippina, who received a public rebuff when she tried to sit alongside Nero at a reception of some Armenian ambassadors, then began to show affection for Britannicus. This could not be endured and Britannicus was poisoned (55): Nero clearly was guilty, though the extent of the complicity of Seneca and Burrus in the crime remains uncertain. Agrippina then showed interest in Britannicus' sister Octavia, Nero's wife, whom he was neglecting for a freedwoman named

Acte. This new move by Agrippina was less dangerous politically, but it was equally obnoxious to Nero and led to her fall. Nero ordered her to leave the palace, and her influence was broken. The struggle for the regency was over: Seneca and Burrus had won.[19]

Nero continued to fear and hate his mother even in her retirement though on one occasion she boldly disproved a charge of treason. His hatred was encouraged by his new mistress Poppaea Sabina, whose husband, his friend Otho (the future emperor), was sent off to Lusitania as governor. Finally Nero decided to murder his mother. First he devised a collapsible boat which might crush or drown her when after dining with him at Baiae he put her on board to go home, but the attempt miscarried and Agrippina swam to shore. Having gone so far, Nero now must go further; alleging that her messenger who came to report her 'escape from an accident', had tried to murder him, he ordered Anicetus, the freedman prefect of the fleet at Misenum, to assassinate her: some sailors then battered her to death. Whether or nor Seneca and Burrus had knowledge of the crime beforehand, they helped to smooth over Nero's return to Rome six months later: the crime had shocked the world, but his explanation was officially accepted, if not believed, and the Senate passed extravagant votes of gratitude for the 'deliverance' of the matricide. According to the popular account Nero, like Orestes pursued by the Furies, was haunted by his mother's ghost: whether his conscience was in fact stirred we do not know. At any rate he was free from her dominance.

8. THE ADMINISTRATION OF SENECA AND BURRUS

During these years the general administration was good. Though he held a consulship in 55, 57 and 58, Nero declined a perpetual consulship in 58 and did not obtrude himself. When personal action by him is recorded (e.g. part of a letter that he wrote to Rhodes in 55 survives), it cannot be certain how far he was merely following the advice of Seneca, who with Burrus was the power behind the throne after Agrippina's decline. Together these two men were responsible for the administration, but although Seneca may have had the interests of the Senate at heart he also had to give the appearance that all was being done by Nero's beneficence. Thus while outwardly the relations between Princeps and Senate might seem cordial, in fact the emperor's autocracy was no less than it had been in the past, since upon it in the last resort the power of Seneca and Burrus rested. They aimed, however, at promoting the wellbeing of the Empire, and not least its economic prosperity. Seneca himself had wide financial interests.

Financial administration was improved, and the emperor's influence over it was increased, when in 56 two imperial prefects (ex-praetors) replaced quaestors at the Aerarium, to which in the next year Nero transferred forty million sesterces. Measures were taken to make the prosecution of extortion-ate governors easier, and to preserve the agrarian wellbeing in Cyrene. The food-supply of Rome was safeguarded by the appointment of an efficient Praefectus Annonae, Faenius Rufus, and by the completion of Claudius' har-bour works at Ostia, which Nero advertised on his coinage.[19a] He distributed *congiaria* of 400 sesterces per head to the people of Rome on two occasions. To meet the needs of the army and as a measure to check the increasing depopulation of Italy, several colonies of veterans were established in Italy, e.g. at Capua and Nuceria (57), Puteoli, Tarentum and Antium in 60 (the last, Nero's birthplace, received a colony of Praetorians), and Pompeii after the earthquake of 63. Finally, there was the famous scheme for free trade, spon-sored if not originated by Nero himself in 58, that all indirect taxes should be abolished in the expectation that the consequent increase in trade would improve the amount derived from the direct taxes. The suggestion was dropped in face of the practical difficulties involved, but it at least showed interest in promoting the economic life of the Empire.

9. NERO THE ARTIST[20]

Vicious and vain, cruel and lustful, Nero nevertheless had genuine artistic leanings. He wrote poetry, including a poem on 'The Sack of Troy': the few surviving fragments do not suggest total lack of merit. He took great trouble to improve his somewhat husky voice ('vox exigua et fusca'), by lying with heavy lead sheets on his chest in order to strengthen his diaphragm, and by dieting and purging. He studied the playing of the harp with great determin-ation. That he should appear in private performances as singer, artist, actor or poet was harmless enough, as also was his passion for horsemanship. But unfortunately he gained an exaggerated idea of his abilities and craved wider audiences, and here he met opposition from the aristocracy; for an emperor to perform in public shocked Roman sentiment. Further, he had a genuine interest in Greek art, and wanted to introduce Greek Games into Rome, including athletic contests, chariot driving, and competitions in poetry, music and oratory. It may be that one of the causes of his quarrel with his mother was her opposition to the development of these interests. Certain it is that after her death he gave full rein to them.

In 57 he had forbidden gladiatorial combats to be fought to the death, presumably not from humaneness but because such games were unHellenic. In 59 he held Ludi Iuvenales, gymnastic and artistic competitions, in his own gardens, at which a special body of young aristocrats, the Augustiani, took part: citizens had taken part in the games of Greece, and Nero intended senators and knights to follow this example. In 60 he established quinquen-nial Neronia, based on the Olympic games. He himself appeared as singer, harpist and charioteer: one of the functions of the Augustiani was to act as his claque.[21] In 61 he built a gymnasium and Baths (the Thermae Neronianae). In 64 he appeared on the stage at Greek Naples. When he presided at these games, men might wonder whether he did not resemble a Hellenistic king rather than a Roman emperor.

Having thrown off all restraint in this field, Nero was encouraged to indulge his less reputable desires and rid himself of any who stood in his way: in 62 treason trials started again. When Burrus died, possibly a natural death, Nero appointed two Praetorian Prefects, Faenius Rufus and a vicious Sicilian Ofonius Tigellinus who had managed to become Prefect of the Vigiles.[21a] Without Burrus and unable any longer to rely on the Praetorian Guard, Seneca was powerless and was forced into retirement. While Tigellinus pandered to Nero's vices, Poppaea persuaded him to divorce Octavia and marry her. Octavia was banished, but a false rumour that she was going to be re-instated led to public demonstrations in her favour. Nero acted promptly: he accused her of adultery with Anicetus and treason. She was put to death and Anicetus, an awkward accomplice of Nero in the murder of Agrippina, was neatly banished. Nor did Nero spare the aristocracy: he forced the deaths of a grandson of Tiberius, Rubellius Plautus, and of a son-in-law of Claudius, Cornelius Sulla. The greater freedom that the Senate had enjoyed thanks to Seneca in the early part of the reign was now lost, and Nero was being corrupted by unbridled power. To the hatred of the Senate was next added that of the people of Rome.

10. THE GATHERING STORM

On the night of 18 July 64, when the sky was bright with a full moon, a fire broke out in Rome which raged for over a week; it destroyed at least ten of the fourteen Augustan regions, three of them being totally gutted. Nero, who was at Antium when the disaster started, hurried back to Rome, helped to direct the firefighting and undertook energetic measures to relieve the home-less. He then used the opportunity to benefit both Rome and himself. The re-building of the city was planned on more scientific lines compared with its earlier haphazard growth, with a rectangular street system and blocks of skyscrapers (insulae). For himself Nero started to build on the ground between the Esquiline and Caelian hills (where later the Colosseum was built) his vast Golden Palace (Domus Aurea) with its parks, lakes, colonnades and a colossal 120-foot-high statue of Nero himself, together with statues and works of art for which his agents ransacked Greece. Here he could indulge his artistic sense and his mania for the grandiose, while wits might declare that his expropriations not only engulfed the city but would soon embrace Veii, ten miles distant.[22]

In their loss and misery the city populace turned against Nero and accused him of having started the fire, while rumour added that he had watched the burning city from the Tower of Maecenas and had sung as an aria over it his own 'Sack of Troy'. Neither charge can be taken seriously: if he had wished to destroy Rome he would hardly have chosen a bright moonlit summer night when the movement of his fire-raisers would have been hard to hide. But he was suspected and in order to divert suspicion from himself he sought a scapegoat. He might have turned to the Jews, who were always unpopular with the mob, but his wife Poppaea was interested in Judaism and her interest may have saved them.[23] Instead there was the new sect of the Christians that was now growing up in Rome, about which little was known except that it was popularly credited with 'humani generis odium'. It is one of the anomalies of history that a sect, which on the human plane, apart from its theological claims, was preaching the brotherhood of man, should have been so misunderstood, but the secrecy of the meetings helped to give rise to such ideas that the Christians practised cannibalism, an idea based probably on a misunderstanding of the Lord's Supper. Here were suitable victims, and Nero took savage action. In so far as Christians were charged with incendiarism the charge must normally have broken down (and it is only Tacitus that connects the persecution with the fire), and they will have been persecuted as Christians.[24] There is little evidence for any persecution outside Rome, but here their punishment was terrible: some were thrown to the beasts in the amphitheatre, and others were smeared with pitch and used by Nero as living torches to light the games he held by night in the imperial gardens and Vatican circus; the victims included, according to tradition, Saints Peter and Paul.[25] This attempt to divert hostility from himself, however, recoiled on Nero's own head, because the ruthlessness of the punishment excited pity for the victims, who were regarded as sacrificed to one man's cruelty rather than to the national interest.

The rebuilding of Rome required money, and so did Nero's luxurious life, not to mention a grandiose scheme to link Ostia with Lake Avernus by canal in order to improve access to Rome for sea-borne goods. He therefore imposed forced contributions on Italy and the provinces and seized what he could, not stopping short of putting to death six landowners in Africa who owned half the estates there, in order to appropriate their land. He also tried to ease the position by debasing the coinage. He added an alloy to the silver and reduced the metal content of both gold and silver by a tenth or less, and thus brought them into a better ratio with one another and with the fine new series of aes coinage that he proceeded to strike: he also opened a subsidiary mint at Lugdunum. This depreciation was not a good precedent and it certainly did not increase Nero's popularity, but it was less serious than the steady drain of precious metals to the East in payment for luxury goods.

The growing hatred of the Senate for Nero was aggravated by the increasing number of freedmen, Greeks and Orientals that he employed in high office (e.g. Balbillus, the Prefect of Egypt, 55–59, who is probably the Alexandrine astrologer mentioned on p. 360, or Felix the procurator of Judaea). In 65 it burst into flame in a conspiracy that had been smouldering since 62 and involved at least five eminent senators and as many knights: it was supported by Faenius Rufus, one of the Praetorian Prefects. All the conspirators were united in their intent to kill Nero, but the next step was less clear. The majority probably wished to enthrone the noble C. Calpurnius Piso (after whom the plot is generally named), but others may have thought of Seneca, while a few may even have played with Republican ideas. The plot, however, was betrayed and Nero took savage revenge: trials intra cubiculum principis were revived, and his senatorial victims included Piso, Seneca and his nephew the poet Lucan. In the first flush some nineteen persons including Faenius were killed and thirteen exiled.

Frightened by the narrowness of his escape Nero became a ruthless tyrant, employing more spies and the surviving Praetorian Prefect, Tigellinus, to hunt down all suspects. His victims included the son of Ostorius Scapula, the former governor of Britain, and C. Petronius, Nero's elegantiae arbiter, who when dying smashed his precious vases which he knew Nero wanted. Another group of people to taste Nero's wrath were some Stoic philosophers, headed by Thrasea Paetus, an ex-consul who had shown considerable independence of action. From 63 he had absented himself from the Senate as a protest against injustice and flattery, and he had been angry when the deification of Poppaea was voted (Nero had killed her by a kick in 65, and then married Statilia Messalina in 66); he had also failed to applaud Nero's 'divine voice'. The Senate meekly condemned him for setting a bad example, since there was no evidence that he had shared in the conspiracy. His son-in-law Helvidius Priscus was banished and another leading Stoic, Barea Soranus, was executed. These Stoics, Republicans in spirit who used to celebrate the birthdays of Brutus and Cassius, objected to tyranny, if not to monarchy, and they showed a bold and obstinate opposition to Nero's rule, without resorting to actual treason or conspiracy. Another plot was detected in 66 at Beneventum, led by Annius Vinicianus who perhaps hoped to replace Nero with his own father-in-law Corbulo. This was crushed, but Nero's position would be vitally endangered if discontent spread to the armies, as might well happen since he had not shared any of their campaigns or troubled to visit their camps. Disloyalty among the army commanders, suspected or real, soon revealed itself. When he had gone to Greece in 66–7 Nero summoned Corbulo and the commanders of Upper and Lower Germany, Scribonius Rufus and Scribonius Proculus, to join him: on arrival they received his order to kill themselves, and obeyed.

In Rome Nero's autocracy and megalomania increased. He identified himself with various gods (Hercules, Apollo or Helios) and coins depicted him wearing a radiate crown. The month of April was renamed Neroneus and Rome itself might even be called Neropolis. A climax of glory was reached in a magnificent ceremony in 66 when Tiridates came to Rome to be crowned king of Armenia by Nero and to worship him as Mithras. Then Nero the philhellene decided that the Greeks were really the only people who deserved to hear his art: he would go to Greece and compete in the national festivals. This he did with such success that he returned with 1808 first prizes; at Olympia he had fallen out of his ten-horse-team chariot, but was put back and received the crown just the same. It is difficult to reconcile this clowning and levity with his earnest belief in his art. He spent nearly a year in Greece, where he took up Gaius' plan to cut a canal through the Isthmus of Corinth: at a solemn ceremony he cut the first sod with a golden trowel. An even more spectacular occasion was his special convocation of the Isthmian Games, at which in 196 B.C. Flamininus had proclaimed the freedom of Greece; now Nero proclaimed a second liberation. This in practice meant immunity from taxation and the kind of freedom from the governor of Macedonia that free federate cities enjoyed.[26] The Senate was given Sardinia as compensation for this loss of revenue. Nero's action evoked great enthusiasm and his grand tour was a fine success, but in a more profound sense than in the rumour of 64, he was fiddling while Rome was burning: amid his artistic triumphs and joys he failed to heed the fact the Judaea was in revolt and, more serious still, that the whole basis of his power in the west was threatened. He must return to Rome without delay.

11. THE PROVINCES AND FOREIGN AFFAIRS

Throughout a large part of the Empire during most of Nero's reign life was normal and prosperous. He himself, unlike his predecessor, appears to have shown little personal interest in the provinces apart from Greece. The Alpes Cottiae were turned into a small procuratorial province c. 58, Latin rights were given to the inhabitants of the Alpes Maritimae, and Pontus was annexed c. 64. Nero is said to have had ambitious schemes for campaigns in the Caucasus area and in Africa (p. 266 f.), but they did not mature. In three places, however, danger and even disaster threatened: in Britain, in Armenia and in Judaea.

While the new province of south-east Britain continued to develop peacefully, its frontiers were still threatened by the tribes beyond. The Silures had to be checked by Ostorius and by his successor A. Didius (52–7); the latter also had to intervene in Brigantia in order to re-instate Rome's friend Queen Cartimandua who had been deposed by her consort Venutius. The next advance was made when in 59 Suetonius Paulinus, the conqueror of

Mauretania, was sent out as governor. He decided to strike at Mona (the island of Anglesey), which formed a supply base and refuge for Rome's enemies in Britain. It was a centre of the Druids, who since Claudius' proscription of their cult must have been Rome's bitter foes. The discovery of the great hoard of objects at Llyn Cerrig Bach, which were thrown into a lake at this time either by the Druids to save them or to appease their gods or by the avenging Romans, demonstrates, through the variety and source of these objects, from how wide an area in Britain the Druids could claim offerings or seize booty. This dramatic illustration of the power of the Druid community helps to explain the purpose of Paulinus.[27] In 61, though his troops at first wavered in face of the defenders backed by their priests and supposed supernatural powers, he forced the Menai Strait. Then while he was busy felling the sacred groves and settling the island, news came of the revolt of Boudicca in the south.

In East Anglia the Iceni were suffering from the exactions of Roman tax-collectors, such as the procurator Catus Decianus, and from Roman money-lenders who included the financier Seneca. In 60/61 their king Prasutagus died, leaving half his wealth to Nero and half to his two daughters. He had no son, and Roman experience with Cartimandua may have suggested that it might be wiser not to recognize his widow Boudicca (Boadicea), but to absorb the area into the Roman province. When Roman officials began to seize for the emperor land which Claudius had granted to tribal nobles and when finally Boudicca was scourged and her daughters were violated, the whole tribe rose in revolt. The Iceni were joined by the neighbouring Trinovantes who were smarting from both the confiscation of some of their land for the Roman colonists settled at Camulodunum and from the cost of the upkeep of Claudius' temple and cult, which was a symbol of their subjection, the hated 'arx aeternae dominationis'.

The first move was against Camulodunum: it was unwalled, and the nearest Roman legions were over a hundred miles away. In two days it was overwhelmed and all Roman survivors, men, women and children were butchered. The Ninth Legion, hastening to the rescue from Lindum, was defeated; only its commander Petilius Cerialis and the cavalry escaped. Meantime Suetonius Paulinus decided to hasten to London ahead of his main troops. But when neither his own legions nor the Second Legion which he had summoned from the south-west arrived, he was forced to abandon both London and Verulamium to Boudicca's fury: 70,000 people are said to have perished in the sack of the three towns. Withdrawing along Watling Street, Suetonius finally decided to fight although he found that the commander of the Second had disobeyed orders and was not coming. Although heavily outnumbered, he fought on ground of his own choosing, perhaps not far from Lichfield; Boudicca and her forces were utterly routed thanks to superior Roman discipline; she took poison. Suetonius then began to take savage reprisals, but the new procurator, Iulius Classicianus, who could report direct to the emperor, urged that Suetonius should be checked and a more lenient policy be adopted.[28] After a commission had reported, Nero decided to send out a new governor, C. Petronius Turpillianus who was more conciliatory, and Britain settled down to a period of peace so that in 67 Nero was able to withdraw one of the legions, the Fourteenth, for service in the East.

When news reached Nero near the beginning of his reign that the Parthian king Vologeses had established his own brother Tiridates on the throne of Armenia (p. 251)[29] Nero prepared for action. Cn. Domitius Corbulo, who had shown his ability on the Lower Rhine under Claudius, was appointed to Cappadocia and Galatia and was empowered to take over two legions and auxiliaries from the governor of Syria. But troops stationed in Syria tended to become slack (p. 210) and Corbulo, a stern disciplinarian, had first to toughen up his men (A.D. 55): he was given the chance because Vologeses was embarrassed by a rebel son and by a revolt in Hyrcania. After wintering (57/8) in northern Armenia amid snow and ice (Armenia is a land of great climatic extremes), Corbulo advanced against Tiridates who refused terms; he then captured the Armenian capital, Artaxata (probably 58). As Tiridates had fled, Corbulo in 59 marched 300 miles south-west to capture Tigranocerta. This victory, as the previous one, was celebrated by Nero being saluted as *imperator*. After a vain attempt by Tiridates to get back to Armenia, the Roman government decided to establish a Romanized prince on the Armenian throne and chose a certain Tigranes, a great-grandson of Herod the Great and of the former Cappadocian king Archelaus. After this settlement, which did not please the Armenians, Corbulo retired to Syria, of which he was appointed governor.

Tigranes, however, soon provoked Parthia by attacking Adiabene; Corbulo, who feared a Parthian attack on Syria, could only spare two legions to help Tigranes and urged Nero to send out a separate commander to aid Armenia. Nero chose one of the consuls of 61, L. Caesennius Paetus who arrived in Cappadocia in 62. It is usually supposed from the boastful words that Tacitus put in Paetus' mouth that this move represents a change in imperial policy and that Nero had determined to annex Armenia at last: it is just possible, however, that Paetus was only instructed to defend Armenia. But whatever his purpose, he proved incompetent. In an advance towards Tigranocerta, he encamped at Rhandeia for the winter. When the Parthian army appeared he sent for help to Corbulo who did not hurry, perhaps because he thought that Paetus' forces were sufficient to withstand any attack on their camp. Paetus, however, panicked and surrendered to the Parthians when Corbulo was less than fifty miles away. Rhandeia was not so serious a loss as Carrhae, but the disgrace was even greater: cowardice had combined with incompetence. Corbulo then reached an agreement with the Parthians that he would withdraw west of the Euphrates, if they would withdraw from Armenia. When negotiations for a final settlement were protracted, Rome decided on a great show of force. Paetus had been recalled and Corbulo was entrusted with a *maius imperium* over all the Roman forces in the East. After he had demonstrated beyond the Euphrates he agreed to meet the Parthians at Rhandeia. Here a final settlement was negotiated: Rome agreed to recognize the Parthian Tiridates as king of Armenia, and he in turn agreed to go to Rome to receive his diadem from Nero. This coronation ceremony was held with great splendour in 66. Thus friendly relations were established between Rome and the two eastern kingdoms which, helped by some readjustments made later by Vespasian, lasted half a century. In Armenia Artaxata was, temporarily, renamed Neroneia, while in Rome the temple of Janus was closed and the coinage that advertised the fact *urbi et orbi* proclaimed 'pace populi Romani terra marique parta Ianum clausit'.

The incorporation of eastern Pontus into the province of Galatia, which has already been mentioned, was occasioned by the retirement, nominally voluntary, of the King Polemo II. At the same time Rome took over the royal fleet and kept a squadron of some forty ships, based on Trapezus, on patrol in the Black Sea. Nero also planned an expedition in the Caucasus area towards the Caspian Sea, perhaps a drive to hold back Sarmatian tribes (the Alani) from advancing to the Danube or to occupy the country of the Iberians in the Caucasus, thus following in Pompey's footsteps. But these further plans to strengthen Rome's hold in the East were not carried out.[30] Nero also had some plans for Africa, though their exact nature is uncertain. In 61–3 a detachment of praetorian soldiers was sent up the Nile past Meroe to the marshes of the White Nile. This was perhaps a scientific expedition, designed to discover the source of the Nile, or it may have been a reconnaissance for a campaign against the king of Axum (Abyssinia). In any case no Ethiopian war ensued: on military and probably on economic grounds it was unnecessary, though a victory in such distant and mysterious lands might have appealed to Nero's vanity.[31]

The great revolt that flared up in Palestine in 66 was the result of old grievances and protracted disturbances. It was not a happy land. It suffered from internal stresses, both economic and religious: there was tension between rich and poor, between Sadducee and Pharisee, between Jew and Samaritan, between Jew and non-Jew, especially Greek, and between Jew and Christian. Little wonder that some men had turned to a less complicated life like that of the Essenes and, a landmark in history, established the monastic community at Qumran on the Dead Sea, whose scriptures now partially survive, the famous Dead Sea Scrolls.[32] Above all, there was a common hatred of Rome, although this was moderated among the upper class which looked to Rome to protect its interests. This sentiment naturally was nationalistic in aim and sought to throw off the yoke of the unclean and idolatrous Gentile. Feelings were often further aggravated by Roman lack of tact, since Roman policy towards the Jews in general had tended to fluctuate between great generosity or undue harshness (see pp. 121, 211, 234, 241, 247). True, there had been no religious persecution as such, and the Jews had been granted freedom of worship and association. The mad folly of Gaius had been counteracted by Claudius' re-establishment of a native ruler, but the reversion to provincial status after Agrippa's brief rule (41–44) will have re-emphasized Judaea's dependence on Rome. His son, Agrippa II, was well treated by Rome: in 50 he was given Chalcis, the kingdom of his uncle Herod who had died (p. 251), and in 53 he received in exchange for Chalcis, Philip's tetrarchy (Trachonitis, Gaulanitis, etc.) and that of Lysanias (Abilene), to which Nero added part of Galilee and Peraea.

The Roman procurators obviously had no easy task with so recalcitrant a people, but they were too often incompetent. Cuspius Fadus in 44 had killed a prophet and agitator named Theudas; his successor, Tiberius Alexander, was a renegade Jew;[33] and his successor, Ventidius Cumanus (48–52), crushed some fighting between Jews and Samaritans with such rigour that he himself was later court-martialled and exiled. The next procurator was Antonius Felix (52–60), brother of the freedman Pallas and husband of a Jewess Drusilla, the sister of Agrippa II. He had to face increasing social unrest, from bands of fanatical robbers (Sicarii or 'Men of the Knife') who plundered the rich and pro-Romans, and also from a violent group of Zealots, led by Eleazar, son of the High Priest. He had to deal with rioting between Greeks and Jews in Caesarea and it was he who tried St. Paul whom he kept in confinement as he judged that release would be politically dangerous. Like other governors, he had only some 3000 local troops at his disposal, although in grave difficulty he could appeal to the governor of Syria for legionary help. The next governor, Porcius Festus (60–2), was relieved of the problem of St. Paul when the latter 'appealed to Caesar', but he had other difficulties. When Festus died and before his successor Albinus arrived, the Sadducee High Priest took the chance to crush some opponents, including James, the brother of Jesus, who was stoned to death. Finally, under Gessius Florus (64–6) the storm broke.

The immediate cause was some rioting at Caesarea and in Jerusalem where the High Priest refused to sacrifice to Jehovah on behalf of the emperor and where, despite the intervention of Agrippa, the small Roman garrison was massacred. Faced with a spread of disorder, Florus called in the legate of Syria who arrived with some 30,000 men but winter was approaching and he dared not assault Jerusalem but withdrew (66). As the rebellion was extending to the whole of Palestine, Nero appointed a new governor of Syria, C. Licinius Mucianus, and put a tried soldier, T. Flavius Vespasianus, in command of the expedition against Judaea. Vespasian's plan was to use his three legions to reduce Palestine district by district and thus isolate Jerusalem before the final attack. In 67 he reduced Galilee which was defended by Josephus, a philo-Roman Pharisee who managed to survive and to pass over to the winning side: he gained pardon and friendship from Vespasian, whose elevation to the throne he prophesied. In 68 Vespasian reduced Samaria and Idumaea, but when news came of the death of Nero he slowed down operations. During all this time Palestine had been far from united in its opposition to the Romans and there had been much fighting between Jews and Gentiles, while Jerusalem became the scene of bitter fighting between three Jewish factions. Thus when Vespasian went off to seek the Principate and left his son Titus to conduct the final siege of Jerusalem, Titus invested a city divided against itself. Nevertheless the resistance was fanatically heroic, but in August 70 the city fell and was sacked. The sequel is soon told. The temple was destroyed, the Sanhedrin and High Priesthood were abolished, the annual contribution paid by every pious Jew to the temple was diverted to Juppiter Capitolinus. The Jewish State ceased to exist as a political entity, but Judaism as a religion continued and was even protected as in the past, its followers being allowed their Sabbath, freedom from military service and exemption from the Imperial cult. Judaea remained a Roman province but the equestrian procurator now became the subordinate to a senatorial legate who commanded the Tenth Legion which henceforth garrisoned Jerusalem. When after the reign and death of Titus (81) a commemorative arch was erected in his honour, all Rome was reminded by its sculptures of the end of Jerusalem.[34]

12. THE STORM BREAKS

The course of events in Palestine and reports of growing discontent in the West persuaded Nero to listen to the appeals of Helius, the freedman whom he had left in charge at Rome, that he should return from Greece. He left reluctantly and reached the city early in 68. Here he found the populace angry because of a cornshortage; the aristocracy hated him, and the armies were becoming restless at his lack of interest and angered through his murder of commanders like Corbulo and those of the Rhine armies. His reception befitted an opera star more than a Roman emperor: the victor of the sacred games of Greece hung up his 1808 crowns for the public to admire. But he still longed for a Greek setting and so by March he had gone to Naples. Here news reached him that C. Julius Vindex, the governor of Gallia Lugdunensis, was in revolt.

The objectives of Vindex, a Romanized Gaul, are uncertain, beyond that of getting rid of Nero: he probably had no intention of restoring republican authority nor is it clear how far he may have championed a Gallic nationalist movement which sought autonomy, or at least more freedom, for Gaul. He probably merely wanted a better emperor. He won the support of some Gallic tribes, but others opposed him; Vienna in the Rhone valley declared for him, but Lugdunum remained loyal to Nero. Nevertheless Vindex raised a force said to number 100,000 men. All would depend on the reaction of the army commanders in the West, with whom he got into touch. Servius Sulpicius Galba, the governor of Hispania Tarraconensis, responded and proclaimed himself the 'legatus senatus populique Romani', that is, presumably, no longer a servant of Nero. In Spain he was supported by M. Salvius Otho, governor of Lusitania, and by A. Caecina, the quaestor of Baetica. L. Clodius Macer, the legate in Africa, also revolted. He, Galba and Vindex all issued propagandist coins and began to build up their forces.

The attitude of the armies on the Rhine was critical. The legate of Upper Germany, L. Verginius Rufus, advanced against Vindex and the armies met at Vesontio (Besançon). What happened is obscure: the two leaders conferred, but Verginius' men are said to have insisted on fighting; possibly they regarded the Gauls as dangerous nationalists. In the battle that followed Vindex was defeated and committed suicide. Verginius Rufus was immediately offered the principate by his victorious troops, but he refused, perhaps less out of loyalty to Nero than because he was of equestrian origin. Meantime Galba in Spain was left in a dangerous position and even thought of taking his life, but in June a message reached him that Nero was dead and that the Senate and Praetorians had chosen him as emperor. In two famous phrases of Tacitus, 'a secret of empire was revealed that an emperor could be made elsewhere than at Rome', and Rome gained a ruler who was 'omnium consensu capax imperii nisi imperasset'.[35]

Resolution in this crisis might have yet saved Nero; the Praetorians were loyal and he still had troops on whom he could rely. But he hesitated and beyond making himself sole consul he did little. Tigellinus fled, and the other Praetorian Prefect, Nymphidius Sabinus, bribed the Guard with 30,000 sesterces a head to support the Senate and proclaim Galba emperor. Nero, who was hiding in the villa of his freedman Phaon near Rome, heard the news that he had been proclaimed a public enemy by the Senate. While steeling himself to strike the fatal blow he is said to have bemoaned the loss to the world of such an artist ('qualis artifex pereo'), and when his pursuers were at last on him his freedman Epaphroditus helped him thrust his sword home. So died the last of the Julio-Claudian dynasty on 9 June 68, aged thirty.

The promise of his early years had been unfulfilled, and on his way to open absolutism and tyranny Nero had incurred great hatred in the West. In the East, however, he had been popular, except with Jews and Christians who regarded him as the anti-Christ; indeed two pretenders who emerged in the East in 69 and 79, claiming to be Nero, easily gained some temporary following. But his death did not immediately solve all problems: the lack of an heir

GENEALOGICAL TREE OF THE CHIEF MEMBERS OF THE JULIO-CLAUDIAN DYNASTY

Genealogical tree of the chief members of the Julio-Claudian dynasty undermined the hereditary principle of succession. This was decided by the army groups in mutual rivalry. In 69, the 'year of the four emperors', Galba, Otho, Vitellius and Vespasian succeeded each other in quick succession, but in the end the will of the armies of the East and of the Danube prevailed and Vespasian's claims were vindicated. Since he had two sons, Titus and Domitian, Rome might look forward to a period of peace in which the succession would not again be contested in bitter civil war, and in fact the new dynasty of the three Flavian emperors served Rome well. Though the principate advanced a little farther along the path to absolutism, stable government and sound administration were again established and Rome could once more believe in herself and her future: she was given a new lease of life. Not without hope could the legend of a coin of Vespasian proclaim the promise of 'The Eternity of the Roman People'.

XV

ECONOMIC AND SOCIAL LIFE IN THE EARLY EMPIRE

1. AGRICULTURE

Economic life in the early Empire did not differ essentially from that under the late Republic.[1] Augustus neither introduced a new economic policy nor sought to establish State controls or monopolies: the old *laissez-faire* continued. Taxation was not used as a direct means of controlling trade or industry and its incidence was not heavy enough to hamper private enterprise. As earlier, there was little competition between the State and the individual, but rather competition was allowed to develop freely between all those who interested themselves in industry or trade. The essential difference was the establishment of the *pax Romana*: no longer were wars or civil strife to be allowed to strike crippling blows at the economic life of the community. By developing the political unity of the Mediterranean world, Augustus thereby created the conditions for its economic unification. Given peace, the economic prosperity of the Empire would take care of itself.

Italy became increasingly prosperous and dominated the economic life of the Empire. In agriculture no sudden changes took place. *Latifundia* continued and perhaps even increased in some parts, as Etruria, S. Italy, and in parts of Latium and Campania, but medium-sized farms held their own. Some of the latter in central Italy, as Horace's famous Sabine farm, would be owned by city-dwellers, run by bailiffs, and worked in part by slaves but in part leased out in plots to tenants (*coloni*: a term that only later came to mean renters tied to the soil, or serfs). In Campania, in the farms around Vesuvius at Pompeii, Herculaneum and Stabiae, a higher proportion of owners lived on their estates which were worked by slaves rather than by *coloni*; many owners, however, probably a majority, also had town-houses. The main changes were in labour and produce: the independent peasant farmer was tending to disappear and to be transformed into a tenant, while wine and oil became the main products. Since grain came as tribute from Egypt and Africa, the cereal culture of Latium declined, but provincial grain probably did not seriously affect corn-production in the rest of Italy. The population of Italy was increasing and therefore much wheat must have been grown: if its production declined, this will probably have been because viticulture often proved more profitable.

Features which became more noticeable as time passed, included the declining number of slaves, provincial competition, and the concentration of land in fewer hands. The cessation of wars and piracy naturally caused a diminution of slaves. This was offset to some extent by an increase in the number of home-bred slaves and by better treatment. Columella, the agricultural expert of Nero's day, shows that the work of slavewomen was lightened in proportion to the number of their children and that the mother of three was entitled to her freedom. Though he implies that slaves were often bound, Pliny a little later says that he never used chained slaves. Whether farm slaves received the customary five *denarii* a month that was given to town slaves remains uncertain. More humane treatment might increase efficiency to some extent and thus help to compensate for the difficulty of obtaining slaves, but Columella gives the impression that efficiency was rare without constant vigilance. Another aspect of the Julio-Claudian period was that marketing conditions were changing: the economic development of the western provinces was progressing; Gaul, Spain and Africa were producing more wine and oil. Again, during the reigns from Tiberius to Nero imperial confiscations of land, both in Italy and the provinces, increased, while the emperor received much property by inheritance. He thus became the greatest landowner, and in general there was a tendency to concentrate land among fewer owners (Seneca, for instance, secured great estates after the murder of Britannicus), but this does not prove the truth of Pliny's famous observation that 'latifundia Italiam perdidere'. Some of the medium-sized and smaller estates may have been absorbed while in face of changing conditions an increasing number of large landowners may have let out more land to tenants and turned more over to cereal production. But there is enough evidence to show that the concentration of land to which Roman satirists and moralists often refer, did not occur everywhere: many small farmers in the central Apennines continued to work their own plots, and estates of moderate size flourished in Campania.

2. INDUSTRY AND TRADE

This diveristy of development in different parts of Italy, ranging from small farm to great ranch, finds a parallel in the industrial development.

Farm-households in early days naturally tended to a 'house-economy' and self-sufficiency; as much food, clothing and equipment as possible would be home-produced. But as towns developed, their needs would be met by the growth of industry on a small scale: cobblers, smiths and others would use their special skills for the community and establish their small workroom-shops employing one or two free or servile hands, but not seeking to provide for more than their own immediate neighbourhood. But as men became more wealthy and demanded more luxuries, they created a wider market that was satisfied by the increase of commerce and of specialized lines of industrial production. Division of labour increased and something like a factory system emerged for the production of certain goods on a large scale and for wide distribution.

Thus industry ranged from home-production through the artisan-shop to the specialized factory. The first, with such activities as spinning and weaving, needs no description. The work of the small shop-factory, which might represent more than half the output in the early empire, is illustrated from the remains at Pompeii. Residential blocks, built around a central courtyard, often had their street-frontages lined with small rooms which were self-contained, i.e. they did not connect with the main block but merely opened on the street. Here worked the small manufacturer: in the front he might have a counter to display his wares, and behind was his workshop with its bench, forge or furnace where he made his cutlery, shoes or leather-work. Such retail trade conducted on the spot would be supplemented by the peddling of hawkers and street-fairs.[2]

Specialization in larger factories, worked by slave labour and aiming at mass production for wider distribution or even export, increased, but really large-scale development was hampered by the cost of transport by land and by the ubiquity of slavery: not only did many wealthy men employ their own slaves on industrial work that otherwise might have fallen to the open market, but the supply of cheap labour did not encourage inventiveness in labour-saving devices that might have stimulated fresh developments. One of the most striking aspects of 'big industry' was the production of a red-glazed table ware, Arretine *terra sigillata* (the so-called Samian ware). This was manufactured at Arretium (Arezzo) and one or two other centres in Italy (especially Puteoli and perhaps in Rome) and gained such popularity that it was exported widely to nearly all parts of the Roman world except the south-east. The scale of production is illustrated by the fact that one mixing-basin at Arretium had a capacity of 10,000 gallons; the largest known single work-shop employed 58 slaves. Since most of the decorated pieces are stamped with the maker's name, much can be learned about the organization of the trade. The reason for the popularity of this particular ware is not of course that it was a patented trade-process (such methods were unknown) but perhaps because of its technical excellence; the process of red-glazing may have been a trade-secret and the necessary fine clay was localized. This particular trade not only provides the best example of a factory-system producing for an 'international' market, but its fate illustrates another tendency. Production at Arretium began about 30 B.C., but some fifty years later the ware was being manufactured in the provinces, especially in Gaul: in order to reduce cost of transport producers apparently found it profitable either to migrate or to establish branch-factories. So flourishing did the potteries in southern Gaul become that the Arretine factories declined and virtually ceased business in the Flavian period. This change illustrates how the extreme prosperity of Italy in the early years of the Empire was gradually overshadowed in some spheres by provincial competition.

Another specialized industry was the production of glassware, which received a great impetus from the invention in Sidon of the process of glass-blowing; previously glass-paste had been poured into a mould, and a new mould had been needed for each article. Skilled workers migrated from the East to Italy and suitable sand was found on the Volturnus river in Campania. Here factories were established and specialists produced fine translucent glassware, usually signed by the maker, for export. Metal industries developed on various lines. Much ironware continued to be made by the smith at the forge in his small shop, but there was also a concentration of the iron trade at Puteoli where pig-iron was shipped from Elba and manufactured in quantity. This did not involve the bringing together of specialized skills, since each man worked much as he could have done in his own shop (and it was not until the fourth century A.D. that the invention of valved bellows improved smelting to a point where cast iron could be made), but Puteoli could provide wood for the furnaces and was an excellent distributing centre. The production of copper and bronze utensils, however, led to a truer factory system, since more varied processes and artistic skills were brought together. This was centred at Capua, which had an old tradition of metalwork; large factories employed hundreds of men, and the products were exported as far north as Germany and Britain, while nearer home much of the fine metal furniture and *objects d'art* of Pompeii came from the Capuan factories. They also produced much of the splendid silver plate that has been found at Pompeii and neighbourhood (e.g. the treasure from Boscoreale). Jewellery and goldwork on the other hand continued to be made and sold in small shops.

Bricks, though used in North Italy, were not widely used in Rome before the time of Claudius apart from roof-tiles. Thereafter brickfaced concrete became more common and after its superiority to travertine as heat-resisting had been demonstrated during the fire in Nero's reign, it was widely used in the rebuilding of Rome and thereafter. Brickyards helped to make the fortunes of Domitius Afer who came to Rome under Tiberius a poor man and died in 58; his descendants, using the opportunity created by the fire, almost gained control of the industry in the city, and few buildings did not contain bricks bearing the name of Afer. The business ultimately passed by inheritance to Marcus Aurelius and imperial possession, but the making of bricks had always been regarded more as part of agriculture than industry and was therefore regarded as a reasonably 'respectable' source of wealth.

The public and private water supply of Rome required the production of large quantities of standard lead pipes, but curiously this need did not result in the growth of factories. Two groups of imperial slaves were responsible for the aqueducts, one inherited by Augustus from Agrippa and the other created by Claudius; they had to make and lay the pipes. The water supply to private buildings and houses was provided by individuals who bought from the authorities the right to tap the public water-mains and who then laid down the pipes. The names of the makers that are stamped on these pipes indicate that they were made in small shops and not large factories. Thus here Roman conservatism preserved older methods at the expense of more efficient organization: the plumber and manufacturer were rolled into one.

During the Republic most clothing was produced at home and men wore homespun: the small shop system therefore was less needed in this industry. But the processing of such homespun woollen cloth (e.g. the elimination of the oil) was not easy and in the early Empire at latest the task was often transferred to skilled fullers. At Pompeii, for instance, there are remains of many fulleries which in addition to laundry and dyeing services helped to process cloth for individual use; a fullers' hall on one side of the Forum suggests that they may also have bought the rough cloth and after treating it have displayed and sold it there. In some centres both in North and South Italy, however, there were some large slave-run factories for the production of finer clothing fabrics. Other materials were imported, as silk from the Far East and linen from the state factories of Egypt which Augustus inherited from the Ptolemies.

The Augustan peace naturally enabled the provinces also to improve their economic conditions. In general there is a distinction between the newer provinces of the West, which tended to supply the raw materials, and those of the East with their much older traditions of trade and industry. All produced what they could for their own needs, but most also managed to provide a little more, both of natural products and manufactured articles, for export. The products of Egypt found a wide market; they included corn (sufficient it is said to feed the population of Rome for four months), papyrus (of which Egypt enjoyed a monopoly), glass, textiles, metalware, stones and jewels. Syria supplied wine, dried fruits, spices, drugs, glass and textiles (her dye-works were famous); and she also benefited from her position astride some of the eastern caravan routes, and from the old Phoenician carrying trade. Asia Minor exported oil, wine, fruits, salted fish, wood, copper, precious stones and also textiles (including woollens from Miletus, goat-hair coats from Cilicia, silks from Cos, and carpets and rugs). Greece was rather poor but managed to send abroad some wine and oil and art bronzes. Sicily continued in its old role as an exporter of corn. The western provinces began to enter on a period of great prosperity. Gaul exported wine and oil from the south and corn from the north. It produced much crude metal but probably did not export much of it or of the objects manufactured from it. But it did export textiles, and, as has been seen, from about A.D. 20 began to develop its pottery industry, of which a centre was at La Graufesenque in the south; by the end of the century production was moving to the north (e.g. at Lezoux). Glass also was produced from the middle of the century at Lugdunum which had become a most prosperous trade centre. Spain, rich in minerals, was also very productive and exported gold, silver, copper, lead, tin, iron. It also sent overseas corn, oil and wine, and some specialities as pickled fish, *garum*-sauce and esparto-grass for rope-making. The discarded pottery-containers of the wine and oil were thrown on to a heap in Rome, which in the course of time became a great mound (the Monte Testaccio). The exports of Britain have already been mentioned (p. 252). Africa exported corn, oil, animals for the arena, citron wood and precious stones. The Danube lands despatched some agricultural produce and much iron (some of it manufactured) and gold. This trade passed through Aquileia in N. Italy, which became a great commercial city, balancing the harbour of Puteoli in the south.

3. TRADE BEYOND THE EMPIRE[3]

Such a cursory survey thus shows that, while the countryside would supply basic local needs, a considerable interchange of goods took place within each province and a brisk trade developed between various provinces; further, this interprovincial trade was not confined to luxuries. But trade also developed between the Empire and the peoples beyond the frontiers. It had in fact sometimes preceded the flag: thus for more than half a century before the Claudian conquest, there had been much interchange of goods between Britain and the Roman world. With 'free' Germany and the lands to the North trade steadily increased, though not all the objects found beyond the Rhine reached there through trade. Thus the famous silver dinner-service found at Hildesheim near Hanover may be loot taken from a Roman commander; much of the equipment of Varus' legions must have passed into German hands (this may be the origin of a remarkable concentration of Augustan gold coins found between the Ems and Weser). Diplomatic gifts to native chiefs may explain the origin of other finds, such as that discovered at Hoby on the Danish island of Laaland: of approximately Augustan date, this hoard consisted of a fine table-service of silver and bronze; since one of the silver cups, which represents a scene from the story of Philoctetes, bears the name 'Silius' scratched on its base, it may once have been owned by C. Silius the legate of Upper Germany from A.D. 14 to 21. But the volume of regular trade with the North increased. Most of the goods in the first century A.D. came from Italy and passed by road to the Danube at Carnuntum. Thence in the early part of the century they moved on to Bohemia, where the Marcomanni were for a time both customers and also acted as middlemen for distribution further north, but after the death of Maroboduus their importance decreased. Under Nero a new trade-route was brought under Roman control, the so-called 'amber route' from Carnuntum to the eastern Baltic. This was due to the enterprise of a knight who pioneered the route and brought back a great quantity of amber. All this northern trade stimulated the prosperity of Aquileia, the nodal point through which it passed; and beside acting as middlemen, Aquileia itself manufactured amber for export. The operation of Roman warships in the North Sea (p. 250) will have helped to open up the sea routes to Jutland and Scandinavia, but most of the carrier trade probably remained in the hands of the Frisii of the Dutch coast, and few Roman goods reached Norway or Sweden before the third century.

A few trading stations on the coast of East Africa are known, from the mouth of the Red Sea to Zanzibar. From this region exports to the Roman world included ivory, rhinoceros-horn, tortoiseshell, palm-oil, cinnamon, frankincense and slaves. At the southern exit from the Red Sea Augustus seems to have broken the monopoly of the Arabs who had acted as middle-men for goods coming from the East (see p. 211). Till this time any trade with India involved a long coast-wise journey from Aden, along the shore of southern Arabia, and thence to the mouth of the Indus and the west coast of India. But a great discovery was made, probably under Augustus (less probably earlier), by a sea-captain named Hippalus who found that it was possible to establish a direct sea-route from Aden to India by making use of the regularity of the monsoons. The summer monsoon would take ships safely to the mouth of the Indus and the anti-trade winds of winter would take them back; by Nero's time an even more southerly direct route was taken to Muziris in South India.[4] This discovery revolutionized trade with India. The actual shipping was probably in the hands of Alexandrine and other Greeks, but Rome was the chief customer. Strabo records that 120 merchantmen would sail from the Red Sea harbour of Myos Hormos to India in a year, and the extent of the trade has recently been strikingly demonstrated by excavation at Podouke (modern Pondicherry) on the east coast of India, where quantities of Arretine ware manufactured in Italy between 30 B.C. and A.D. 45 have been found. To reach the east coast involved sailing round the treacherous southern tip at Cape Comorin, which was not attempted until near the end of the first century (this explains Rome's comparative ignorance of Ceylon, Taprobane, at this earlier date). In consequence goods were landed on the west coast and were carried over the tip by land via Coimbatore: this trade route is marked by the survival of many hoards of first-century Roman coins. The main exports from India were pepper, spices, jewels and muslin. These luxury goods were paid for by Rome very largely in gold and silver coins (which the Indians would treat as bullion; they therefore preferred coins minted before A.D. 64 when Nero depreciated the metal content). This Indian trade is said to have resulted in an annual adverse balance for Rome of 60 million sesterces in Nero's day, and the effect of draining away so much precious metal to the East became serious. That this commerce was desired by India as well as by Rome is shown by the Indian embassies that were sent to the West: two at least, possibly four, visited Augustus.

Northern India produced less of what Rome required, but it played an important role as middleman in forwarding to the West other luxury goods from farther Asia as silk from China, turquoise and lapis lazuli. The normal trade route, the so-called Silk Route, ran from China to Bactra in Afghanistan and thence across Iran to Syria.[5] But in Iran lay a political barrier, the Parthians. Hence some goods were diverted when they reached Bactra and were sent on south-eastwards through Begram and Taxila (where most interesting finds have been made) to Barygaza (modern Broach) south of the Indus; here they could be picked up by the regular sea routes and brought to the West.

4. GENERAL ECONOMIC CONDITIONS

This healthy state of economic life was largely a spontaneous growth and the result of private enterprise. The State interfered as little as possible, and in Egypt, where Augustus inherited a highly centralized economic system, State ownership and monopolies were decreased. Certain internal customs barriers existed within the empire, but these indirect taxes (*portoria*) were imposed merely for purposes of revenue and not for 'protection' or to keep provincial goods out of Italian markets. The frontiers, at which a fixed percentage of the value of the goods that crossed was exacted, enclosed larger units than the individual provinces: thus the three Gauls formed a customs district that paid 2½ per cent, 'Illyricum' (i.e. all the Balkan provinces) paid 5 per cent, Spain paid 2 per cent. At certain points within these districts, at bridges or ferries, transit tolls were collected. There is little evidence to suggest that these taxes, the collection of which was let out to *publicani*, proved a serious burden to trade.[6] Goods that came into the Empire from outside also paid duty: thus, for example, luxuries from the East were subject to a 25 per cent tax at Leuke Kome. Some individual cities also might impose local octrois and transit tolls to help their municipal revenues: thus there is later evidence for elaborate tariffs at the caravan city of Palmyra under Hadrian.

Though the emperors might avoid direct interference, they kept a watchful eye on some activities and gave indirect encouragement. In particular they were concerned about the corn-supply and the feeding of Rome, the supply of metals for the coinage, and all the needs of the army. Thus Claudius took measures to improve the harbour and warehouse facilities at Ostia and to encourage the corn merchants (see p. 248). The operation of mines during the Republic had been let to companies of publicans, but under the Empire the mines of precious metals and quarries came under imperial ownership or control: there must be no shortage of gold and silver for the currency, iron and lead for the army, stone and marble for roads and buildings. Another indirect stimulus to trade that came from the emperor was the provision of a sound currency which won the confidence of traders throughout the provinces. Yet another was the existence and upkeep of the great road system of the Empire: designed first mainly for military purposes, it also served the ends of peace. The arterial roads, the rivers, and the sea-routes, all carried a rising quantity of merchandise which was reasonably free from risk of attack by robber or pirate. In a world at peace there was an unceasing movement of goods from one end of the Empire to the other along a network of communications. Men could move freely, without passport and unhampered in the main by racial prejudice or colour bar. Though sea voyages were avoided in the winter, during most of the year travellers could normally rely on finding a passage from the great ports. But journeys, though reasonably safe, were slow by modern standards. On land the imperial post service covered some fifty miles a day, but ordinary commercial traffic would be slower. Ships, up to 1000 tons, might carry some 600 persons, but ordinary freighters were probably only about 200 tons or less. The journey from Ostia to Gades took over a week, to Alexandria nearly three weeks, and to Berytus about a month. If transport by land was dear, it was cheaper by sea, but there were still many risks and difficulties to be encountered at sea, as the story of St. Paul's journey to Rome, recounted so vividly in *Acts* 28, illustrates. St. Paul's adventures, as he travelled freely on his missionary journeys to the cities of Asia Minor, Macedonia and Greece, provide a classic example of the liberty of movement allowed to all citizens and non-citizens alike. The traders were men of all races and status: many, of whom a great number were of freedman origin, went forth from Italy to East and West, and even more orientals, Syrians and Alexandrians, found their way to the West. The class of *negotiatores* included importers and distributors of foreign goods (such as the Italian merchants in

Gaul, mentioned by Diodorus, who in exchange for slaves distributed wine by river or land transport), together with travelling merchants, both salesmen and buyers, who went from town to town with their goods. In the same way independent shipowners 'tramped' their cargoes from port to port; partnerships might be formed, but these seem to have been generally limited and not to have worked with more than four or five ships. Foreign merchants might rent an office (*statio*), perhaps with warehouse facilities and dock space, in another country, as those of the Nabataean Arabs and of the Tyrians at Puteoli which are attested for a later period. At Ostia a large portico (Piazzale delle Corporazioni) behind the theatre was set aside as a chamber of commerce for foreign shippers. This represents an attempt by the government not to control trade, but merely to provide facilities for encouraging the corn-supply that was so vital to Rome's needs; although the famous mosaics that adorn this building belong to a much later period, offices in the portico probably existed in the early Principate. Thus organization and distribution generally continued on a small scale, though a kind of co-operative society may have developed for the distribution of the mass output of *terra sigillata* by the Gallic factories at La Graufesenque, and the shippers may have acted as salesmen as well as mere distributors.

The capital behind all this commercial activity came largely, so far as the Romans were concerned, from the Equites who now enjoyed less opportunity for exploiting the provinces and turned therefore from tax-farming to trade. Roman aristocrats may have used their freedmen and agents to promote business interests but they did not break with tradition so far as to come out into the open as business-men, while men who enriched themselves through trade would retire to country villas if they wanted to gain any social standing. An example of the wealthy retired businessmen living on country estates is the portrait or caricature that Petronius has drawn of Trimalchio, a slave from Asia Minor who was set free by his master from whom he inherited some wealth. Then as he told his guests at his famous banquet, he went into business: he built five ships and loaded them with wine, but every ship was wrecked; not losing heart, he built more ships, larger and better ones, which he filled with wine, pork, beans, perfumes and slaves. As a result of this voyage, so he boasted, he made ten million sesterces; he then, significantly, bought up all his former master's farms and went in for cattle-raising. When he was wealthier than all his fellow-citizens put together, he retired from active business, made his freedmen agents, and built a palatial home on his Campanian estate. But if such a vulgar parvenu was a suitable subject for satire, the emergence of other more thrifty freedmen craftsmen, shopkeepers and agents will have contributed to the common good.

The quickening of economic life was linked with the increase in the number of cities and of the prosperity of the bourgeoisie living in them. In the third century B.C. as a result of the policy of Alexander the Great, the Near and Middle East had been studded with Greek cities; many of these began as military colonies, but they soon attracted Greek civilians and developed into self-governing cities, with a Greek bourgeoisie which helped to spread Greek culture as far as the Indus. It was the work of the early Principate and of the Italian bourgeoisie to parallel this achievement in the west, where city life was promoted not only in the already partly urbanized areas but also through much of the tribal areas in Spain, Northern Gaul and Britain. Urbanization thus led to the Romanization of the interior of the provinces, and the presence of Roman troops had a similar effect on many of the frontier areas. Thus the middle-class town-dwellers of Italy and the provinces fulfilled both a cultural and an economic role, and the urbanizing policy of Augustus and his successors had far-reaching effects. As many of the older senatorial families were dying out (a process hastened by the reigns of terror under Tiberius and his successors), a new class more easily came to the fore, whose main interests lay in industry and trade, and whose energy increased the prosperity of the towns and of the whole Empire. Old and newer towns alike flourished: in Italy, Puteoli and other cities of Campania, Ostia, Aquileia and Patavium; in the East, Corinth, Ephesus, Antioch, Palmyra and Alexandria; in Africa, Carthage and Utica; in Spain, Gades (the second city of the Empire; the number of its capitalists were equalled by Patavium alone, according to Strabo); in Gaul, Arelate and Lugdunum; in Britain, Londinium; and a host of others.

While the Roman world pulsated with activity, really large-scale industry and large-scale commerce may have been limited to a comparatively small number of towns, and the perennial importance of land should not be forgotten.[7] In Italy it was still the main source of senatorial incomes; and the governing aristocracy in the majority of the towns of the Empire consisted of a group of local landowners who lived in the town, although it would be increasingly recruited from the sons of men who had made money in trade or industry and had invested it in land. Nor did such town councils show much interest in promoting or protecting local trade: the imperial policy of laissez faire was reflected at this lower stage also. They did of course generally provide a market and encourage the adornment of their cities with fine buildings but the motive will have been civic pride more than economic development. The construction of baths, theatres and (though less in the east than west) amphitheatres was designed to provide public games and entertainments worthy of a city's local patriotism, and if possible better than those of its neighbours: only incidentally were the economic benefits considered. It is also noteworthy that although great individual fortunes could still be made, they were often soon dissipated: upstart freedmen, nouveaux riches, and reckless luxury were features of social life under Nero; thereafter wealth was used with greater moderation and wisdom and more of it was diverted from luxuries into productive industry and commerce, while the really large fortunes were made more easily in the provinces than in Italy.

A wealthy aristocracy and a prosperous middle-class were not balanced by any great improvement in the condition of the labouring class which consisted largely of freedmen and slaves. Skilled slaves would normally receive reasonable treatment, if only because of their economic value, and their conditions tended to improve (p. 273). The life of the freeborn labourer was more precarious and must often have been grim; competition by slave labour will have depressed his living standard and many men must have been near to bare subsistence. He could be kept from actual starvation by the corn-dole, and the State also supplied free amusements and free public baths where he could meet his friends. There existed also societies of craftsmen and traders, but these were not real guilds or unions which bargained for better wages or working conditions. They were rather social clubs or friendly societies, and membership of such a *collegium* was not rigidly limited to followers of a particular trade. Most of them, whatever other purpose they served, were 'burial clubs' which beside providing companionship in life also assured a member a decent burial. When judged by modern standards conditions must often have been bad, but they tended to get better: thus even in the mines, worked generally by slaves and convicts, arrangements improved, since regulations for the mining settlement at Vispasca (in southern Portugal) show that under Hadrian the children of the workers had schools and teachers and that the pit-head baths were open from 2 to 8 p.m. Many free workers must have shared in the general affluence of Italy, while some of the less fortunate may have found a better life by joining the army or emigrating to the provinces where free labour predominated and where a rising tide of prosperity led to the extraordinary flowering of municipal life that was one of the great achievements of the Empire.

5. THE SENATORIAL CLASS

Economic, social and political factors had brought about a profound change in the composition and outlook of the senatorial nobility by the end of Nero's reign.[8] The downfall of the Republic with its civil wars and proscription had wrought havoc in the ranks of the nobles, and many of those that survived had little sympathy for the new emerging régime which provided less scope for the free exercise of their ambitions and talents. The names of members of old families, as the Scipios, Metelli and Claudii Marcelli, were disappearing from the consulship under Augustus; the Porcii, Luculli, Lutatii, Hortensii, Servilii Caepiones and Calpurnii Bibuli produced no more consuls;

the last Scipio and the last Appius Claudius Pulcher perished in the scandal that ruined Julia in 2 B.C., while the Sempronii Gracchi survived only a little longer. The Claudii and Domitii endured, to provide emperors, but Nero was to prove the last of the Domitii Ahenobarbi who had given Rome eight consuls in the previous eight generations. The names of Sulla, Cinna, Crassus, Pompeius, and Cornelius Lentulus still managed to appear in the consular fasti of the Julio-Claudian period, but not thereafter. While so many of the older nobility were sinking into obscurity or extinction, many of the newer men that had emerged in the revolutionary period fared little better: the younger Cicero, Vatinius, Trebonius, Gabinius, and Ventidius had no consular descendants. Some too of the new families whom Augustus had ennobled for their services failed to perpetuate their lines: Quirinius had no children, and consulars bearing the names of Statilius Taurus, Sentius Saturninus and Vinicius are not found after the reign of Claudius. And few of the Republican, or even of the Augustan, nobles, who did survive to hold the consulship, received army commands: the legates who controlled the armies in the imperial provinces increasingly were drawn from men of less social distinction, sons or grandsons of Roman knights some of them coming even from Narbonese Gaul. Thus a new nobility was gradually replacing the older aristocracy.

Whence came these newer men to dilute and then to supersede the older blood in the Senate? It has already been seen that the enfranchisement of Italy during the Social War opened up a new reservoir of supply, which Sulla may not have totally neglected when he added some 300 knights to the Senate (p. 69). Caesar's new senators included many more of these Roman knights from Italy, men of substance and property; the freedmen, centurions or provincials that he admitted were few in number (p. 125). Under Augustus the Senate received yet more of the 'flower of Italy', wealthy men from the colonies and municipalities, not only from central parts but from all Italy from the foothills of the Alps down to Bruttium and Apulia. The civilized regions of the West also began slowly to supply their contingent. Caesar had pointed the way, with a handful from Cisalpine and Narbonese Gaul and from Spain: the younger Balbus of Gades had become quaestor in 44 B.C. Under Augustus and Tiberius the Senate will have been largely limited to the *senatores Italici*; but under Tiberius in 35 a consul came from Narbonensis, with a second in Gaius' principate: Claudius then opened the doors of the Senate-House wider for the Gauls (p. 251); soon Seneca, from Spanish Corduba, and Burrus, from Gallic Vasio, had gathered great powers into their hands, and provincial senators became more common. But under Nero they still came mainly from Italian families abroad: the senators who were descendants of native provincials belong to the succeeding period.

6. SOCIAL LIFE

It is clearly impossible to describe adequately in a few lines the rich and varied social life of the age.[9] Various aspects of it, not least the economic background, have already received some mention, but it may be well to glance at some others. As already seen, Roman society was somewhat sharply divided into classes, ranging from aristocrats to slaves. The nobles and senators devoted much time to public administration and law, both at home and abroad, but how did they pass the rest of their lives? Let us see briefly how a member of the upper class might spend a day.

After getting up early, probably about dawn, he would spend only a few minutes dressing, washing and eating: his main bath and meal came later in the day. Since he did not wear special night-clothes, he would already have on his *subligaculum* (a kind of loin-cloth) and, if it was cold, his tunic, which was a long shirt of wool or linen; in winter he might put on another one for warmth. Before going out, and for any formal business in the house, he would put on his toga, the carefully arranged cloak that every Roman citizen had to wear in public (naturally the ordinary Roman working on his land or at his bench did not wear his toga, but he had to put it on if he went to any public gathering). The broad stripe of purple on his tunic and the crescent ornament on his shoes would mark out the senator from other classes. If he had a private barber (*tonsor*), he might be shaved at home; otherwise he would later go to a barber's shop, which was often a social centre for exchanging gossip and news. Shaving must have been a painful and often bloody business, but at this period it was *de rigueur*. Meantime his wife might be giving similar time to her make-up and to her hair-dressing which from the time of Messalina became increasingly elaborate; in these tasks she would be helped by her *ornatrices*, slaves who attended their mistress while others were waiting on their master.

The first duty of the day would be to receive formally the clients who had called to pay their respects to their patron and were waiting in his ante-room. To these *salutatores*, who came wearing their togas (*togati*), he would distribute food or money (*sportula*); the whole proceedings were governed by strict rules of etiquette. As most Romans owed *obsequium* to some superior, our senator might himself in turn have to go to pay his respects to some one more elevated, perhaps the emperor himself. After holding his own levée he might then take a stroll, accompanied by some of his clients, perhaps to the Forum, the heart of Rome's life. Here he might attend a court, from interest if not officially, or perform some social duty for a friend; he might go to the public *recitatio* of the latest work of a writer that he knew, though the wiser authors would not start their 'readings' before the afternoon. If he went home for lunch (*prandium*), it would be a light meal, which his wife and children might take with him; while the parents reclined, the children were seated at table. After a siesta or some time spent in reading, he might visit the Baths, the theatre, the races in the Circus, or the Games in the amphitheatre. Then followed dinner (*cena*), the main meal of the day; not all Romans were gourmands, and many men must often have dined quietly and simply with a few friends. A *synthesis* would be worn in place of the toga, and the company, often nine in number, reclined on benches arranged to form three sides of a square (*triclinium*), the fourth side being left open to give the servers access to the table which was placed in the centre. Since knives and spoons but not forks were used, slaves frequently attended the diners with ewers of water and towels for their hands. The talk might be on social or literary topics; politics would usually be avoided. On occasions a man would entertain his clients, and would normally show them more courtesy, it may be hoped, than those hosts who did not offer all their guests the same fare. At times larger banquets might be given, and though not all the disgust expressed by the satirists need be taken at its full value and not every dinner was an orgy, gluttonous over-eating, and over-drinking must often have ensued. Such feasts, however, tended to last many hours, which provided opportunities between the courses for professional entertainment, whether music, poetry or dancing-girls. While a Nero or Trimalchio might prolong the feast till midnight or after, the more temperate host after bidding his guests good-night might read, or be read to by a slave, before retiring to his often austerely furnished bedroom and to his bed of which the frame and fittings might be a work of art but which, with mattress and bolster resting on strips of webbing, might not provide excessive comfort.

The manifold business interests of the rich Equites and the multifarious activities of the middle and lower classes in field and farm, in city shop or factory, defy description, but one difference from our own society may be noted. Physicians, surgeons, and teachers, whom we regard as members of the professional classes, were recruited mainly from Greeks or other foreigners who were freedmen or slaves. For the population in the city there were three outstanding centres of attraction: the Baths, 'Bread and Circuses'. The Baths, though not without their corrupting influences, were of great physical benefit. Attached to them was a *palaestra*, where sports, ball-games, gymnastics and athletics could be practised; after exercise a man could enter a *sudatorium*, then the *caldarium* where he cleansed himself with hot water and a scraper (strigil); next he cooled off in the *tepidarium*, and finally took a cold plunge in the *frigidarium*. Many Baths had existed in the later Republic, built for profit or given by the wealthy; in a census taken by Agrippa in 33 B.C. there were 170. Soon afterwards he built the first great public Bath; it bore his name and entrance was free. The next benefaction came from Nero, and later emperors followed suit. Further, these Baths served an important social function: they were centres where men (and women) could meet and talk and stroll, and if a few bathers were ennervated by over-indulgence, the majority including the poor, gained much good from these fine health-giving centres.

'The people that once bestowed commands, consulships, legions and all else, now meddles no more and eagerly longs for just two things, *panem et circenses*.' That Juvenal's well-known observation was more than the rhetoric of a satirist is shown by a more sober remark in a letter from Fronto to Marcus Aurelius, but in the Julio-Claudian period the evil had not yet assumed such threatening proportions.[10] Julius Caesar had cut down the list of recipients of free corn to 150,000, but this may represent roughly the male citizen population of Rome in his day (with women and children, some 600,000; in addition there were the foreigners and slaves). In any case most citizens came to feel that they had a claim on the State for free corn. In 2 B.C. Augustus had reviewed the list and increased the recipients to 200,000 possibly including some boys from the age of ten. Each recipient had a ticket (*tessera*) which he exchanged every month at the Porticus Minucia for his ration; later the *tessera* was used simply as an identification disk. The process of distribution was improved by Claudius. Another form of benefit that the privileged citizens of the capital enjoyed was the distribution of money (*congiaria*) that emperors made as their personal gifts on occasions. Augustus made at least seven such distributions (a normal amount being 75 *denarii*, which in his day equalled the pay of a legionary for four months), and his successors followed his example; the distributions may have been made in the Atrium Libertatis behind the Senate-House. Non-citizens in Rome could not share in these benefactions and had to be content with *missilia*, tickets that were thrown to spectators at the Games which entitled them to presents.

The Romans had no seventh day of rest, but they had a remarkable number of days in the year that were available for holidays and games, days marked *dies nefasti* in the calendar when public business was suspended. The calendars record 45 *feriae publicae*, old surviving religious festivals (as the Saturnalia and Lupercalia) which might be accompanied by spectacles, as the footraces at the Robigalia. There were also six old Games (Ludi Romani, Plebei, Apollinares, Ceriales, Megalenses and Florales) which together lasted at least 59 days. Sulla and Caesar added their Victory Games, Augustus his Ludi Fortunae Reducis (11 B.C.) and Livia established Ludi Palatini in Augustus' memory. Another type of holiday was created when the Senate decreed the commemoration of an important event in an emperor's life, such as his birthday: eighteen holidays celebrated events connected with the life or memory of Augustus. In all, by Claudius' reign, there were 159 holidays a year, on 93 of which games were given at public expense. Thus nearly half the year consisted of official holidays, although naturally not everyone could afford to take so much time off from his work.

The chief amusements were four, each with its appropriate building: the theatre for acting, the stadium for athletics, the circus for horse-racing, and the amphitheatre for gladiatorial and animal contests. Romans had a choice of three theatres, those of Pompey, Balbus and Marcellus, which together may have seated some 50,000 people; each of them was thus far larger than a modern theatre. The decline of tragedy and comedy at the expense of farce and mime has already been noted (p. 164 f.). Tragedy developed into a mixture of opera, ballet and music-hall, comedy into the mime which illustrated the seamy side of life. A form of entertainment, which became popular from the time of Augustus was that of the pantomimus, a dancer who was accompanied by music and chorus and who in dumb show represented various themes of tragedy or comedy. Two such actors, Pylades and Bathyllus, displayed great skill and achieved immense popularity under Augustus. So popular were such actors that under Tiberius the mob rioted over their rival merits and caused the death of several soldiers.

Attempts had been made as early as the early second century B.C. to introduce Greek athletic games and musical contests into Rome, but they had met with an unenthusiastic response. Augustus fared little better; he founded the Actiaca which were to be celebrated every four years in Rome and Actium, but they are not heard of after A.D. 16. Nero's Greek Games (p. 259) met with little success after his death, though soon afterwards the emperor Domitian achieved a better result with his Capitoline Games.

The chief Games, however, were the chariot-races held in the Circuses, the old Circus Maximus, that of Flaminius, and Caligula's new one on the Vatican. The Maximus, in the hollow between the Aventine and Palatine hills, was gradually improved: Augustus decorated the spina (the axial wall around which the chariots raced) with the obelisk of Rameses II from Egypt (now in the Piazza del Popolo) and with a 'box' (pulvinar) for himself and friends on the Palatine side above the cavea, the seats. Stone seats were introduced for senators by Claudius, and for Equites by Nero. In all it seated some 150,000 spectators. In it various games might be staged (athletics, races on horseback, the Trojan Game for nobles' sons), but the chief feature was the chariot-races. These might last up to fifteen days, with as many as twenty-four races a day; each race comprised seven laps of the course by teams of two (bigae) or generally four horses (quadrigae). Four teams would race at a time, representing the factions of the Whites, Greens, Blues and Reds. These 'sides' were supported with great fervour by their followers (Caligula and Nero both backed the Greens) and gambling was heavy. Racing involved great skill by the charioteers, and risk to limb or life for man and beast was severe, especially when the two turning-posts (metae) were being rounded. Pedigree horses won great fame: one that achieved a hundred victories was then called a centenarius. Not less renowned were the star charioteers, such as Scirtus of the

Whites under Tiberius. But the excitement of the race was not the only attraction: here Sulla met his last wife Valeria when she pulled a thread from his toga, and Ovid, the poet of love, could point out the opportunities provided by the Circus for flirtation and gallantry.[10a]

More brutal was the carnage that went on in the amphitheatre. The first permanent one in Rome was built by Statilius Taurus in 29 B.C. Here were staged the gladiatorial combats which were the responsibility (*munera*) of magistrates, praetors under Augustus and quaestors under Claudius. Under the Julio-Claudians the number of gladiators was limited to 120 a time, less perhaps for humane reasons than to check the popularity of the magistrate. The emperors gradually assumed chief responsibility; Augustus gave eight special shows, and built a flooded arena near the Janiculum where mock sea-fights (*naumachiae*) could be staged. From Rome the practice spread widely through Italy and the western provinces; few cities of note would lack an amphitheatre, and before long Rome gained the greatest of them all, the Amphitheatrum Flavium, dedicated in A.D. 80 and better known as the Colosseum. The Greek East was less receptive to this barbarous practice, but cosmopolitan Corinth and gradually Greek cities in Asia Minor succumbed.[11]

Gladiators, who were recruited from condemned criminals and prisoners of war, were trained in schools (*ludi*) and were classified according to their equipment as Samnites, Thracians, *murmilliones, retiarii* (armed with net and trident), *laquearii* and others. When successful, a gladiator might receive great rewards and become a popular idol (the Thracian Celadus is described on a *grafitto* at Pompeii as 'decus puellarum, suspirium puellarum'), but his hour of fame was likely to be brief and he would have to survive many a further combat before he could hope for his *rudis*, the wooden sword that symbolized his discharge. Courage and skill might occasionally save a man, but even more pitiful and degrading for the spectators were the *munera sine missione*, butcheries from which no one might survive, and also the practice of exposing unarmed victims *ad bestias*, to the mercy of the lions.

Gladiatorial combats in the amphitheatre might be supplemented with *venationes*, animal fights or hunts, or even only exhibitions. Men pitted against animals, *bestiarii*, were not gladiators but at first condemned criminals and later specially trained men; they too could become stars who prided themselves on their scars and bites. More pleasant was the exhibition of trained animals, as elephants which danced and dined and even, under Tiberius, walked a tight-rope; a race of chariots drawn by camels was staged by Claudius. Augustus exhibited in the arena or elsewhere an Indian rhinoceros, a white elephant from Siam, and a large snake, probably a python; under Nero a polar-bear made its appearance. The vast numbers of animals, as elephants, lions, tigers, leopards, panthers and hippopotami, that had to be shipped to Rome to gratify Roman cruelty gave rise to a large-scale trade in wild-beasts.

Italy

These ghastly displays, with their degrading influence on the spectators, lasted for centuries. The *ludi bestiarii* persisted until the sixth century, but the Christian emperors gradually took action against gladiatorial combats: in 326 Constantine forbade condemnation *ad bestias*, and in 404 after the monk Telemachus had been torn to pieces by the angry spectators when he had jumped into the arena to separate the combatants, Honorius suppressed by edict gladiatorial combats in the West.

XVI

ART, LITERATURE AND RELIGION IN THE JULIO-CLAUDIAN PERIOD

1. ARCHITECTURE AND ART

The demand for theatres, amphitheatres, circuses, baths and other public buildings naturally stimulated architecture. The establishment of colonies and the development of older towns throughout the provinces, and especially in the less urbanized west, gave employment to workmen and architects alike, and each municipality strove to outdo its neighbour in the splendour of its public buildings. In Gaul, for instance, there was tremendous building activity under Augustus. Arelate, Nemausus, Forum Julii, Vienna, Lugdunum and Augustodunum (Autun) all had Augustan walls (incidentally if Londinium and Verulamium had enjoyed the same privilege, accorded to Roman colonies and those with Latin rights in Gaul, they would not have succumbed so easily to Boudicca's attack). Other famous Augustan monuments in Gaul included the Maison Carrée, a temple built by Agrippa, at Nîmes; possibly the famous Pont du Gard which majestically carried an aqueduct over the river to bring water to Nîmes (though it may be later); and the temple at Vienne. In Spain and Africa also similar development took place, and although these were all lands where city life had long been known, their external appearance must have been changed considerably during the early principate.

The great architectural changes that Augustus had brought about in Rome have already been mentioned (pp. 192 ff.). The contribution of Tiberius included a temple to Divus Augustus, barracks for the Praetorian Guard (Castra Praetoria: traces of the brick and concrete walls survive), and a sumptuous palace on the Palatine, which contrasted with the modest house of Augustus; Tiberius also developed Augustus' villa at Capri into a large estate.

Gaius constructed a private Circus on the far side of the Tiber, where the first Christian martyrs were to suffer. Claudius was much concerned with engineering, and endowed Rome with two new aqueducts, while the triumphal arch which celebrated his conquest of Britain was a transformation of an existing aqueduct-arch where it crossed a main road. The reconstruction of the city by Nero after the Great Fire has already been mentioned (p. 261). His Domus Aurea is interesting not only for the scale of its conceptions, but also for its wall-paintings (which influenced artists of the early Renaissance in a building which still survives under the later Baths of Trajan) and for its circular dining-room with a revolving ceiling. This probably had no religious significance (the conception was not, as has been suggested, that of a sacred palace for the Sun-god, borrowed from the Parthians) but it illustrates the love of Nero ('incredibilium cupitor') for mechanical marvels. More important is the purely architectural significance of this room since it is probably an early example of a new use of the shape of space within a building at the expense of the function of the masonry masses that contained it: this conception was to become increasingly fruitful in the architecture of the later Empire.[1] Another interesting building which looks to the future and in its arrangement anticipates in some respects the later Christian basilica, is the underground hypogeum near the Porta Maggiore. Probably of Claudian date, it is a vaulted and arched hall, with stucco decorations that suggest that it may have formed the meeting-place for a mystery religion, perhaps Neopythagorean. Augustan architecture had in the main followed the Greek classical tradition: it had added the use of fresh materials (coloured stone and veined marble from Numidia, Phrygia and Euboea), but with all its excellence it was following a conventional Greek pattern. Under Nero, however, Augustan classicism began to be complemented by bolder developments which led on to the amazing buildings of the Flavian emperors and their successors.

Domestic architecture also received a stimulus in the rebuilding of Rome after the fire. Space was valuable and the tendency was to build upwards. The houses known to us from excavation at Ostia reveal the type of building at Rome: a high block built around a central arcaded court, with shops, windows and balconies facing outwards on to the streets, now often laid out on a grid-system; the rooms would be let as flats. At Pompeii, on the other hand, where an earthquake in A.D. 63 led to much rebuilding, the richer inhabitants continued to live in the more old-fashioned rambling houses of one or two storeys only, built around atrium and peristyle. The heating of some houses was improved in the Augustan period by the adaptation to private dwellings of the system, used in baths, of heating a floor by a furnace underneath (hypocaust); this was extended during the first century by the use of box-tiles in the walls to circulate the heat.

In wealthier houses it was customary to have mural paintings.[2] Many survive at Pompeii, and these have been classified in four styles. The earliest Incrustation style was followed in the first century B.C. by the so-called Architectural style which lasted until the end of Augustus' reign. Here the wall-surface was broken into a number of architectural features designed to produce an illusion of space; the panels were often filled with pictures which were not 'pictures on the wall' but designed to show, as it were, the open country beyond the wall. Examples of this style are the scenes from the *Odyssey* from the Esquiline, the smaller landscapes in the house of Livia (probably the home of Augustus) on the Palatine, the lovely garden scene, with shrubs, birds, flowers and butterflies, which create the illusion of a real garden, from the villa of the empress Livia at Prima Porta, and the ritual scenes from the House of the Mysteries (Villa Item) at Pompeii. This style overlapped with the Third or Ornate style (from c. 20 B.C.), in which the painted architecture becomes more elaborate and the painted groups become more like panel-pictures. The fourth or Intricate style from c. A.D. 50 to the destruction of Pompeii showed pictures, often impressionistic, set in fantastic architecture: examples are the paintings in the House of the Vettii and the shop-front sign of Venus Pompeiana in a car drawn by elephants, both at Pompeii, and those of the Domus Aurea at Rome.

Many of the achievements of the Augustan age must have been commemorated in paintings, as they were in sculpture and other arts, but such paintings have all perished. An impression of their style, however, can be gleaned from some cameos, whose composition is essentially pictorial. Two of the most famous, themselves exquisite works of art, are the sardonyx 'Gemma Augustea' in Vienna which depicts one of the German triumphs of Tiberius (7 B.C. or A.D. 12), and the 'Grand Camée de France', a composition grouped around the figures of Tiberius and Livia.[3]

Portraiture is represented by a few paintings from Pompeii and in the continuation of the tradition in sculpture that flourished in the late Republic (p. 161 f.). It was desirable that the appearance of Augustus, the founder of the new age, should be made known to as many of his grateful subjects as possible. His portrait was most widely diffused by means of the coinage, but numerous statues and busts also were set up in Italy and the provinces. They show great variety and various aspects of his personality, and their style tended to be reflected in portraits of Agrippa, Tiberius and Gaius. The individuality, and indeed the dignity of Claudius is brought out in most of his portraits. With Nero, and increasingly under his successors, a great blending can be observed between the classical plastic style, which emphasized the essential character of the subject, and the more realistic Roman emphasis. The coinage also presents a fine portrait-gallery from Augustus to Nero, including the more important members of the imperial family; while the reverses blazoned forth the imperial achievements in a way which even the illiterate could understand, the obverses revealed the ruler who was thus speaking to his subjects. And he was revealed in portraits made by artists of great skill; many of the die-cutters were Greeks, and it is appropriate that Nero with his Greek interests should have been served so well in this respect: his portraits artistically rank very high.

Among the most important products of Augustan art are the reliefs of the Ara Pacis (p. 193).[4] The altar itself stood in a precinct of which the internal walls were decorated with sculptured festoons; the external walls had a lower frieze of foliage and above, on the longer sides a processional frieze, on the shorter ends four panels with allegorical scenes of Empire. Of the last the most famous is Terra Mater, seated amid a pastoral scene of great fertility and beauty; another depicts the Arrival of Aeneas in Latium; another Romulus and Remus. The processional frieze shows Augustus offering libation, followed by the priests, members of his family and a long file of senators. Instinct with serenity and religious feeling, this great reminder of the majesty of Rome is yet a very human document (as the child clinging to the cloak of the pontifex shows); it is also a historical document, depicting the actual consecration of the altar in 13 B.C. and skilfully showing the *princeps* as *primus inter pares*, a figure sharing in the common ceremony, yet by the slightest emphasis subtly marked off from the rest. It is also, both in subject and style, a work in which Greek and Roman elements are skilfully harmonized and embodies Augustan art at its highest.

Emphasis on one outstanding work should not obscure the rich profusion of the Augustan and Julio-Claudian age, of which a few examples may be named. The two silver cups from Boscoreale near Pompeii, with reliefs depicting Augustus as world-ruler, and Tiberius' triumph; the gilt-bronze plaque of a sword-sheath, showing Tiberius enthroned; the fierce bronze wolf-heads from Gaius' ships recovered from Lake Nemi; the bronze gladiatorial helmet from Pompeii with scenes in relief from the Trojan War; the bronze horses, now on St Mark's in Venice; cameos, gems, portraits, statues and other works, all deserve mention, if space allowed. Thus, in art and architecture the great creative activity of the Augustan period was followed up in the succeeding years. In literature, however, there was a much sharper falling off from the golden age of Virgil, Horace and Livy: the silver age was at hand.

2. POST-AUGUSTAN LITERATURE[5]

Literature might have been expected to flourish under the Julio-Claudians since the emperors themselves were writers. Tiberius wrote a poem on the death of Lucius Caesar, an autobiography, letters and speeches; he was a student of Greek literature and rhetoric and composed poems in Greek; he also liked the society of learned men. Gaius, if not a writer, was an effective speaker, and his criticism of Seneca as 'sand without lime' suggests no lack of judgement. The wide literary and historical interests of Claudius have already been mentioned (p. 244), together with Nero's artistic abilities and his encouragement of public competitions (p. 259 f.). Germanicus also composed a competent verse paraphrase of Aratus' poem on astronomical matters, a task already attempted by Cicero. His daughter, the younger Agrippina who was Nero's mother, wrote her autobiography.

But there is another side to the picture. Under a rule that was tending towards autocracy, freedom of expression became more hazardous, and Tacitus attributed the decline in literature as well as the corruption of oratory to political causes. Tiberius suppressed some works: he is said to have killed two minor poets for attacks on him in their poems, and at Sejanus' instigation Cremutius Cordus, an elderly senator, was prosecuted for treason and his History was publicly burned (A.D. 25). This was a work on the Civil Wars down to at least 18 B.C., in which Cassius was described as 'the last of the Romans' and Augustus was not praised. Gaius allowed suppressed works to be published, and Cremutius' History, of which copies had been saved by his daughter, re-appeared, and was used by later writers as the elder Pliny and Seneca. Under Nero the suppression of Piso's conspiracy involved the death of the writers Lucan and Seneca; Petronius was another of his victims.

But in addition to political considerations, more technical reasons led to the decline of literary achievement: the influence of rhetoric and too close an imitation of the past. The introduction of the teaching of rhetoric in Rome had not met with a ready welcome (see p. 171), but under the early Empire it was all-pervasive. Declamation was a regular method of instruction in the schools, and boys learnt to speak on a thesis whether deliberative (*suasoria*) or argumentative (*controversia*).[6] The themes were often stock-subjects remote from real life, such as, according to the criticism of Petronius, pirates and tyrants who ordered sons to chop off their fathers' heads. This rhetorical training was the culmination of a boy's education, to which preparatory linguistic and literary studies had led up; basically it may have been a valuable training but it was too often carried to extremes. Further, it was not confined to the classroom, and declamation became a fashionable social activity, while from the time of Augustus it became common for authors to recite their new works to an audience before publication. This whole approach to literature led to a competitive spirit in which authors tended to try to outdo each other in mere cleverness, in striving for epigrammatic effect, unusual collocations of words and a heightened colouring: the *sententia* (an epigram or pointed saying) became the ideal, and the bane, of literature. The tendency was for prose to become more artificial and often poetic in diction (few writers approached the skill of Tacitus in brilliantly making rhetoric his servant), while poetry became more prosy. The effect of rhetoric on poetry is seen at its best in Ovid, who thus forms a link between the earlier Augustan poets and those of the Silver Age.

Another check on creative work was an undue attempt to imitate the immediate past. This appreciation of the values of the Augustan poets was in itself no bad thing, nor was the following of great models: the Augustans themselves had been inspired by Greek models. But veneration for the past, and in particular for Virgil, was carried to excess; lacking his genius, his admirers might have been wiser to have struck out more boldly on lines of their own. There was much genuine love of poetry, but it could not shake itself free from the stranglehold of rhetoric: much good work was produced, but it was second-rate when compared with that of the Augustan age, silver rather than gold.

3. THE WRITERS

Astrology was the theme of a poem by M. Manilius, who lived under Augustus and Nero; though not great poetry, it is composed in hexameters with considerable ease, but the subject, though popular, was treated in too technical a manner to secure many readers. Phaedrus, a freedman from Macedonia who incurred the hostility of Sejanus, wrote fables, beast-tales based on Aesop, in iambic senarii and in a simple style which contrasts pleasantly with the contemporary rhetoric. A later prose paraphrase, though not the original poems, had considerable influence in the Middle Ages.

Much light is thrown on the rhetorical schools by the writings of L. Annaeus Seneca, the elder or Rhetor as he is called to distinguish him from his son, the Philosopher. He came to Rome from Corduba in Spain, made a good deal of money, but did not hold public office in Rome; he died between A.D. 37 and 41. He and his wife Helvia had three distinguished sons: the elder, Annaeus Novatus, became by adoption L. Iunius Gallio, the proconsul of Achaea (c. A.D. 52) who dismissed the Jews' case against St. Paul; the second was the philospoher, Nero's minister; the third, M. Annaeus Mela, was an *eques* and the father of Lucan. In his old age Seneca recorded his memories of rhetoricians that he had known: of these works five books of *controversiae* and one of *suasoriae* survive. They are full of interest and reveal their author as an old-fashioned Roman who admired tradition and Cicero.

The younger Seneca was born at Corduba, but was brought up as a child in Rome by an aunt. There he studied rhetoric and started upon an official career. In A.D. 41, when he was about forty-five, Messalina secured his banishment to Corsica on a charge of adultery with Gaius' sister, Julia Livilla. He was recalled in 49 through the influence of Agrippina who made him tutor to her son Nero. His subsequent rise to power until his fall in 62 and death in 65 have already been recounted. He was one of the most important writers of his day, both in prose and verse. Ten books survive of what are miscalled *Dialogi*; they are not dialogues but ethical essays, on subjects such as anger, the constancy of the Stoic sage, and tranquillity of mind. Three of them are 'consolationes' to the bereaved: that to Claudius' freedman Polybius on the loss of his brother, written during Seneca's exile, is full of flattery of both Polybius and the emperor; that addressed to his mother Helvia is more pleasant in tone. He presented to Nero, early in his reign, a treatise *De Clementia*, recommending this quality to the autocrat (Shakespeare may have had it in mind when composing Portia's great speech on the quality of mercy); he also wrote *De Beneficiis* in seven books. His eight books on physical science, the *Naturales Quaestiones*, achieved great popularity. This work was addressed to C. Lucilius, who held various equestrian procuratorships. So also were the *Epistulae Morales*, of which 124 survive; they give philosophical and ethical advice to his friend. Some of these essays were probably real letters, but they were prepared for publication and they abound in *sententiae*. Lastly the *Apocolocyntosis*, almost certainly by Seneca, written as a Menippean satire in prose and verse, is an amusing but bitter skit on the deification of Claudius; it redounds to Seneca's credit as a writer but not as a man, since he owed his recall from banishment and much else to the emperor whom he mocked. Seneca also wrote nine tragedies on Greek mythological subjects, designed to be read or recited rather than acted. They are often forceful and rhetorical, sensational, melodramatic and violent. They had an influence on Elizabethan tragedy in England out of all proportion to their merits. A tenth tragedy, the *Octavia*, is probably not by Seneca, but was written soon after Nero's death, and it is interesting as the only surviving example of a historical drama (*praetexta*) and as a fine criticism of Nero's tyranny; the subject is Octavia's helplessness after her divorce from Nero in 62, and the characters include Seneca and Agrippina's ghost.

Seneca's moral writings had great influence and gained the respect of later Christian writers; so much so that before A.D. 400 a forged correspondence between him and St. Paul had been composed. This was natural enough in view of his broad humanitarian outlook. He was a Stoic and shared the Stoic cosmopolitan view of life, but in many ways he was in advance of his contemporaries. He denounced the false values established by wealth, the cruelty of the Games, the stupidity of much in the official religion; he showed compassion for slaves; he believed that the spirit of God dwelt in every man; and on occasion he rebuked the tyranny of princes. But between Seneca's teaching and his life there seems such discrepancy that to some he appears as unduly morally complacent and to others as a loathsome hypocrite. How could the millionaire who flattered Polybius, showed such spite to the dead Claudius and drafted Nero's justification for the murder of his mother, at the same time preach virtue and the simple life? The explanation is hardly to be found in his ill-health or even neurosis, but rather perhaps in his circumstances which proved too strong. He reluctantly accepted the principate since Republican *libertas* could not be restored, and as Nero's tutor he hoped to turn the young prince to true virtue: in the *De Clementia* he urged the ruler voluntarily to limit his autocratic powers. But as Nero became more wilful, Seneca's influence over him waned and he weakly condoned one excess after another, perhaps still hoping to prevent worse; ultimately he was defeated and retired, and like Cicero in retirement, he devoted himself to philosophic writing, the *Moral Epistles*, seeking inner freedom of spirit and the virtue that led to it. Whether like Cicero he also emerged from retirement in order to strike a blow for freedom cannot be determined, since his complicity in Piso's conspiracy is uncertain; at any rate he suffered from Nero's suspicion and faced his enforced suicide with tranquillity and courage.[7]

Seneca's nephew M. Annaeus Lucanus, born at corduba (A.D. 39), was brought as an infant to Rome where he received a normal rhetorical and philosophical training, studying under the Stoic Cornutus, a freedman of Seneca. After further studies at Athens, he gained Nero's favour and held the quaestorship. In 62 or 63 he published three books of his epic on the Civil War, but, whether or not from artistic jealousy, he lost Nero's support and then joined Piso's conspiracy and was compelled to commit suicide; the allegation that he sought pardon by revealing the names of other conspirators, including his own mother, may or may not be true. The unfinished poem in ten books, the *Bellum Civile* (or *Pharsalia*), deals with the struggle between Pompey and Caesar, culminating in the battle of Pharsalus where the Republic and freedom of speech perished: 'To us, born after that battle, Fortune gave a master; she should have given us also the chance to fight for freedom.' Pompey and Cato, the Republican Stoic, were the heroes, and Caesar, or what he stood for, the arch-enemy. If his Republican feelings were sincere, Lucan, like Seneca, must have felt that acquiescence in the Principate was the only way to preserve any internal freedom of spirit; then when Nero's tyranny increased, he attempted to overthrow him. The poem itself contains some magnificent rhetoric: whether it is great poetry must depend on the definition of what poetry is. Though it has many faults (exaggerations, paradoxes, unduly horrible details of wounds and battles), it must be remembered that Lucan was still a young man; at times it rises to real eloquence and nobility, and many of its great lines, as 'victrix causa deis placuit sed victa Catoni' or 'nihil actum credens cum quid superesset agendum', still ring down the centuries and stir the imagination.[7a]

Another poet to come under the influence of Cornutus was Aulus Persius Flaccus, a rich but modest young man from Etruria. Persius knew Lucan and members of the Stoic 'opposition' to the Principate: he died young

(A.D. 34–62), but not before writing six satires, obscure and difficult in style, but earnest in thought; these Stoic sermons are critical of contemporary conditions without direct reference to Nero himself. A very different member of the court circle was C. Petronius who had been governor of Bithynia and became Nero's *arbiter elegantiae*, a kind of Master of the Revels, until he incurred Tigellinus' enmity and was forced to commit suicide on suspicion of complicity in Piso's plot; when dying he sent to Nero not a flattering will and a large legacy but a detailed denunciation of all the emperor's vices. He is almost certainly the author of a novel called *Saturae* (popularly the *Satyricon*) in 'Menippean' form, prose interspersed with verse. Only parts of books 15 and 16 survive, which recount the adventures of three disreputable freedmen, including their visit to Trimalchio's banquet. This racy work throws a lurid light on low life in south Italy and on economic and social conditions; it is also a most valuable source of everyday Latin as spoken in the street or gutter as contrasted with literary language in which most of the extant literature is written. A writer more appreciative of the Neronian age was the poet Calpurnius Siculus, who wrote *Bucolics* in the tradition of Theocritus and Virgil. He foretells the advent of a Golden Age with young Nero's accession: it is not known whether he lived long enough to change his mind. He is not very probably the author of an anonymous *Laus Pisonis*, a panegyric on a Piso, probably the Neronian conspirator.[7b]

A general history of Rome down to A.D. 30 in two books was written by a retired officer, Velleius Paterculus who had served under Tiberius for eight years on the northern front; the second book expands in scope for the period of Velleius' own lifetime. It is a useful source for the northern campaigns of A.D. 4–12 and it is interesting in being, unlike most of the sources, favourable and even enthusiastic towards Tiberius and also Sejanus. Though not a critical historian, Velleius shows interest in personalities. Another Tiberian, Valerius Maximus, produced nine books of noteworthy doings and sayings, as a useful source-book for rhetoricians. He flattered Tiberius, to whom he dedicated the work, but denounced Sejanus, presumably after his fall from power. The style is bad and Valerius is quite uncritical, but his work contains some useful scraps of information and it was much read in the Middle Ages. Curtius Rufus, writing under Claudius, avoided a Roman theme and composed a history of Alexander the Great, which followed the more romantic and less accurate tradition about him and thus helped to hand on the 'Alexander legend' to the Middle Ages.

The *History* by Cremutius Cordus has already been mentioned (p. 295). Other lost historical works, which had important influence on the formation of the tradition and were used by Tacitus, include the *History* of Aufidius Bassus, which began about 44 B.C. and continued to A.D. 31, 37 or even 50; Bassus, who lived into Nero's reign, also wrote on the German War (probably

A.D. 4–16).[8] Cluvius Rufus, consul before A.D. 41, enjoyed Nero's favour and later took part in the Civil Wars of 68–70. His *History* perhaps began with Gaius and ended in 70; in it he showed a moderate attitude to the Principate. The elder Pliny (C. Plinius Secundus: A.D. 23/4–79), who came to Rome from Comum, served as a cavalry officer in Germany (45–57) and as a pleader in Rome; later under Vespasian with whom he was friendly he held various procuratorships. His great interest was reading and writing (p. 302) and his historical works included a *History* of his own times in thirty-one books from the point where Aufidius Bassus left off down to 70. Corbulo wrote an account of his eastern campaigns and Suetonius Paulinus one on his fighting in Mauretania. Thrasea Paetus, Nero's victim, wrote a *Life* of Cato Uticensis, whose Stoic and Republican ideals he admired. Thus it will be seen that the extant tradition for this period is but a fragment of all the work that was one written about it.

The more technical writers may now be mentioned. A. Cornelius Celsus, writing under Tiberius, composed an encyclopaedia of wide range; only the books on medicine survive, which include a valuable history of medicine before his time. The eight books show good sense and had considerable influence in the Renaissance. Scribonius Largus, a Roman doctor, went with Claudius on the expedition to Britain and dedicated to his patron Callistus his work on Prescriptions (*Compositiones*).[9] Agriculture is represented by an authoritative work in twelve books by L. Iunius Columella, a Spaniard from Gades who settled in Rome and wrote in a clear style under Nero. This practical handbook covered the main topics *De Re Rustica*. A similarly useful and comprehensive work on architecture and engineering had been written by Vitruvius Pollio under Augustus. The two most important contributions to geography at this time came from M. Agrippa, the friend of Augustus, and Pomponius Mela, who wrote under Gaius or Claudius. The former, who set up in Rome a large map of the Roman Empire, wrote a geographical commentary on it, using the results of Greek knowledge; the Roman road-system would supply the skeleton for map and description. Mela's work was a popular survey, not based on personal research.

The tradition of scholarship (see p. 121) was continued by C. Iulius Hyginus, whom Augustus appointed librarian of the Palatine Library, and by Verrius Flaccus, whose important work *De significatu verborum*, has survived only in an incomplete epitome by Festus (late second century); he set up in his native Praeneste a stone calendar with explanations of the festivals (the so-called Fasti Praenestini). Q. Asconius Pedianus, in Nero's reign, wrote a commentary on Cicero' speeches, of which a fragment survives. Pliny the elder, whose historical work has been mentioned, wrote 102 volumes but only 37 survive, those of his *Naturalis Historia*, based more on reading than on scientific observation (though he was to lose his life by approaching too close to Vesuvius to investigate the eruption in 79): he said that its composition had involved reading 2000 books. This survey of the natural world, though not profound, contains much valuable information; for instance, the books on minerals explain how they were used in the arts and therefore give a valuable history of painting and sculpture.

The two chief legal writers under Augustus were M. Antistius Labeo and C. Ateius Capito. Both legally and politically they were opposed to each other. Labeo, a man of tremendous learning (he wrote 400 volumes), was an independent innovator, but refused a consulship which Augustus offered him. Capito, more conservative in his legal beliefs, was more willing to co-operate with the new régime and held a consulship in A.D. 5; he was particularly interested in sacral law, ius pontificum. Their differences led to the development of two schools, the Sabinians and Proculians. Masurius Sabinus was a pupil of Capito and wrote on the ius civile; the Sabinians were also known as Cassians, after the jurist C. Cassius Longinus, legate of Syria (45–49), who was exiled by Nero (65), but recalled by Vespasian. The other school followed Proculus, who both taught and wrote under the Julio-Claudians.

Thus beside the more purely literary writers of this age, there was an immense output of works by professional men, scientists, doctors and lawyers. If genius was lacking, there was no shortage of solid and useful achievement. It is noteworthy also that the western provinces were beginning to make their contribution to Roman culture. As earlier northern Italy had provided Catullus and Virgil, so now from Spain came the Senecas, Lucan and Columella, soon to be followed by Quintillian and Martial. Thus in the course of time it was not only the Greek East that helped to enrich the cultural life of the Roman world. But these men were so Romanized that their works do not sound a distinctively provincial note: that comes later with writers like Apuleius and Tertullian from Africa and Ausonius from Gaul, at a time when the provinces were providing even emperors for Rome.

4. PHILOSOPHY AND RELIGION

The various schools of philosophy continued to make their appeal to an intellectual aristocracy and to win fresh followers in each generation. The Epicureans attempted to simplify life by removing fear of death. The Stoics were increasingly concerned with social ethics and with finding the way to virtue by living according to nature: as external circumstances which cannot be controlled become harder, so the controllable internal opinions, impulses and desires must be disciplined. The Cynics preached the attainment of independence by the renunciation of worldly goods and obligations: some became itinerant beggars who preached anarchy and denounced all rulers.

Meantime other men turned to the more mystical approach of Neopythago-reanism and hoped in a common cult to purify the soul by prayer and discipline and to free it, in part even in this life, from the burden of the body. Philosophy was thus now less concerned with creative thought and metaphysical enquiry than with providing a way of life and a shield against the oppressions of the world around.

Two exponents of Stoicism in Rome at this time were C. Musonius Rufus and L. Cornutus, the freedman whose pupils included Lucan and Persius (p. 299 f.); his contact with men of this group led to his exile in 66. Musonius Rufus, who came from a good family in Etruria, in A.D. 60 followed Rubellius Rufus, whom Nero had banished, to Asia Minor, but after Rubellius' enforced death he returned to Rome, was involved in the Pisonian conspiracy and himself suffered exile, though he returned after Nero's death. His teaching was humane and advanced: he condemned war and gladiatorial games, advocated equality and education for women, opposed infanticide, urged sympathy for slaves, and preached respect for manual labour. This stalwart philosopher, whose deeds matched his words, had considerable influence and numbered Epictetus among his pupils.[10] Seneca was not a creative thinker, but rather something of an eclectic willing to accept a good moral teaching where he could find it; yet he had great influence in spreading Stoic doctrines in a form which a weary world might accept.

Thus Stoicism was the creed of many of the men who joined Piso in his attempt to kill Nero, and it was linked with practical politics: a group of Stoics formed an 'opposition' to Nero's increasing tyranny. Stoics did not in principle object to monarchy, provided that it aimed at the benefit of the ruled, but they did resent the autocracy of Nero and the moral decay of the court. Their heroes were men like Cato and Brutus, but although there may have been some talk of Republicanism, in practice they probably only sought a better emperor (cf. p. 261). Stoic opposition became more vocal under the Flavians, though with less reason, but it was confined to a small and obstinate group, whose excesses offended the majority of senators; Tacitus and the younger Pliny might admire their courage but not their conduct.

Philosophy, although it was becoming more 'religious', could appeal to only a limited circle. The imperial-cult, which became a kind of communal thanksgiving ceremony to a benefactor, would at times attract widespread interest. In this matter Tiberius followed the example of Augustus (see pp. 191 ff.). The cult of *divus Augustus* was established both in Rome and in the provinces, where it superseded that of *Roma et Augustus*, but Tiberius depre-cated worship of himself (see p. 236) and did not encourage foreign cults, as demonstrated by his destruction of the temple of Isis in A.D. 19, his expul-sion of the Jews (p. 231), his attitude to the Druids (p. 249), and his driving out Chaldaean astrologers early in his reign. Gaius' wild demand for worship was fortunately ended by his early death but it revealed dangerous possibilities; it was followed by the saner policy of Claudius (p. 174), who perhaps deserved his deification after death, but not Seneca's parody of it. Nero, who allowed a temple to Divus Claudius on the Caelian hill, later had it destroyed. As his megalomania increased, the tendency to worship him as ruler of the world became stronger, and in Rome his features appeared on the colossus of the Sun near the Golden House, while his head was represented on the coinage with a radiate crown. Members of the imperial house also began to receive unheard of honours: under Claudius, Messalina's birthday was celebrated and Agrippina appeared in sumptuous robes, while Nero deified his child by Poppaea and Poppaea herself after their deaths. All this was far removed from the modest attitude of Augustus.

The ordinary man may have enjoyed watching the official cults of the State but he is unlikely to have derived much spiritual comfort from them beyond the feeling that they helped to secure the well-being of the Roman world. But the individual lived also in a much smaller private world which was often terrifying or disheartening, and he needed help and strength. While the educated might turn to Stoicism, the more humble could seek refuge in the older gods of the household or countryside, but if these did not suffice then he could turn either to magic or one of the eastern religions. Common forms of superstitious belief, as charms, amulets and fortune-telling, were naturally widespread. Curses and imprecations against private enemies, inscribed on lead, had long been used. Necromancy, sorcery and the darker forms of magic attracted some, and astrology retained its hold (see pp. 174 f.).

Although on occasion astrologers were expelled from Rome or Italy (in A.D. 16, 52, and perhaps 66 and 68) generally on the ground that they caused unrest, most of the emperors were interested and Tiberius was himself a practitioner. Further, two astrologers, probably father and son, gained great influence at court. The first was the Alexandrine scholar Thrasyllus, a man of wide interests, whom Tiberius met when in semi-exile in Rhodes; after his return to Rome in A.D. 2 Tiberius secured Roman citizenship for his friend, on whose judgement and companionship he leaned until Thrasyllus' death in 36. The latter's son, Ti. Claudius Balbillus, shared his father's astrological lore and had won the friendship of Claudius when he was young. On Tiberius' death he had retired to Alexandria, but at the accession of Claudius he returned to Rome and to honour: he accompanied Claudius on the British expedition and later probably became Prefect of Egypt (55–9) in the Principate of Nero whose confidence he enjoyed at least until 64/5. Another astrologer was Chaeremon, a Stoic from Alexandria, whom Agrippina chose as one of young Nero's tutors; he was perhaps suggested to her by Balbillus who at one time was in charge of the library in Alexandria. The influence of these men on the various emperors was very considerable, but how far they strengthened the ties of natural friendship still further by using their astrological skill must be uncertain. Clearly, however, both in high and low society this pseudo-science had a great vogue, and men sought to know their Fate even if there was no escape from it, since it had been determined by what star was in the ascendant at the moment of a man's birth. Fear and uncertainty thus drove even practical people like the Romans to a superstition which the columns of some newspapers show to be still far from dead today.[11]

Despite any attempt to warm up the innate fatalism of astrology by approaching it in a spirit of faith and religion rather than of science, many must have found but cold comfort in the stars and have turned to other cults that also came from the East, particularly those that by initiation and worship provided a lively hope of personal immortality. Beside the officially author-ized cults (*religiones licitae*), many small groups of semi-secret and unregistered (*illicitae*) worships must have flourished in Italy. The Porta Maggiore chapel (p. 293), with stuccos depicting symbolically the carrying-off of the soul to a higher life, was the centre of one such sect, whether Neopythagorean or not, which appears to have been quickly suppressed. Since the chapel lay in the gardens of the Statilii, the sect may have had some connection with Statilius Taurus, one of Agrippina's victims who when charged with magical practices in A.D. 53 committed suicide.[12] Another cult was celebrated at the so-called Villa of the Mysteries (Villa Item) at Pompeii: its walls are decorated with a series of frescoes, connected with Dionysus and some initiation-rites.[13] These examples illustrate obviously wealthy sects, but many of the small authorized clubs of the humbler folk may well have had religious as well as purely social interests.

Of the spread in Italy of some of the better-known eastern cults something has already been said (p. 174).[14] The most attractive of these was perhaps that of Isis which had made good headway in Italy in the late Republic until it was naturally checked by Octavian's war on Cleopatra and the gods of Egypt. Gaius, however, welcomed the cult and erected a temple to her in the Campus Martius (c. A.D. 38). Though an Egyptian goddess Isis was becoming a universal deity, partly through a process of syncretism which identified various deities. She was the true mother-goddess, the principle of all life, whom other nations might worship under other names. She claimed to be stronger than Fate, to be the giver of law and order, of justice and mercy, and through the sufferings, which according to Egyptian legend she had endured, to sympathize with suffering humanity. The immemorial antiquity of her cult, with its professional white-robed clergy, made a wide appeal: its demands were not heavy, involving initiation and occasional abstinence. Further, its worshippers, men and women alike, actually took part in the cult instead of watching a ceremonial performance by others. Very different was the cult of the Phrygian Mother-goddess Cybele with its eunuch priests, the Galli, and her young consort Attis, in origin a vegetation spirit who was born and died with the plants each year. Although Claudius in admitting this cult into the Roman calendar (see p. 249) checked some of its grosser features, it remained a very un-Roman worship which appealed to the cosmopolitan population of the capital. It involved a belief in immortality, but the ceremony of the taurobolium (blood-bath) did not develop until the second century, when Attis also became a solar deity. Ma, the Mother-goddess of Cappadocia, was no serious rival to Cybele, but she had her devotees, who in frenzied dances slashed themselves with swords. Introduced into Italy by the soldiers of Sulla, who favoured it because an adherent had prophesied his victory over Marius, this cult continued under the Empire, Ma being identified with the Roman war-goddess Bellona. Its priests, as those of Cybele, were often referred to as fanatici, the 'people of the shrine'. The cult of the Persian god Mithras, which was to become so important later, though spreading in the eastern provinces, had scarcely affected Italy or the Roman armies in this period.

5. JUDAISM AND CHRISTIANITY

Very different were two other beliefs that came from the East and still live while their rivals perished: 'ex Oriente lux'. As the Jews of the Dispersion had scattered through the Mediterranean world, they had naturally taken their religious beliefs with them, together with their Scriptures of which the non-Jewish world had needed a Greek translation (the Septuagint). The traditional Roman attitude to foreign cults was essentially tolerant, as any polytheistic belief should be, but it required a degree of reciprocity, and this it could naturally not gain from any people holding a monotheistic faith. Hence in order to avoid head-on collisions with the Jews Rome had made exceptional concessions to them in the matter of their worship, as has been seen. Local disturbances had on occasion resulted in Roman repressive meas-ures, as expulsions of Jews from Rome or Italy, or the re-establishment of order in Alexandria. Further, the Jews of Palestine had not succeeded in reconciling their nationalistic longings and their internal dissensions with Roman rule and this finally led to the tragedy of the revolt and consequent destruction of Jerusalem. But in the religious sphere the Jews, who actively attempted to proselytize, met with some success. In a world of lowered standards, the lofty moral code and monotheism of Judaism would interest many better minds, even if some ceremonial features were less attractive. Conversion might be less than complete: full proselytes became naturalized Jews, but a group called the Sebomenoi only attended the synagogue and observed the commandments, while the Hypsistarioi were still less strict.

An interest in Jewish beliefs may even have become 'fashionable' in Rome for a short time: at any rate Poppaea Sabina showed an interest in them, though Josephus does not call her a convert.[15]

For some time the Romans failed to distinguish Christianity from Judaism: this is not surprising, since it began as a Jewish sect and, although the ordinary Roman will not have realized this, it was characteristic of Judaism in the last century B.C. to split up into sects. These voluntary communities within the larger body of the Jews in Palestine included the Pharisees and Scribes (not quite identical), the aristocratic and worldly Sadducees who despised the more pious and democratic Pharisees, the Apocalyptists (less a party than representatives of a way of thought), the ascetic Essenes, and, unless they are to be identified with the Essenes, the Qumran community by the Dead Sea, whose monastic life is revealed by their Scrolls, which it may be remarked throw much light on religious thought and conditions in Palestine at this time, but have provided no evidence to connect Jesus or primitive Christianity with this sect.[16] With this national tendency for the community to break up into smaller groups, the establishment of new groups by the disciples first of John the Baptist and then of Jesus was a natural development. In various forms and in varied degree the Jews continued to look forward to the appearance of a Messiah, a Saviour, a king in David's line who would 'restore again the kingdom to Israel' and cause the world to acknowledge the kingdom of God. Religious stirrings were felt when about A.D. 27 John the Baptist emerged in the desert by the Jordan, a successor to the Old Testament prophets, calling his people to repentance and foretelling that he would be succeeded by a 'mightier one'. He was imprisoned by Herod Antipas and later executed through the intrigues of Herodias and her daughter Salome.

These long-cherished Messianic hopes were at last realized, in the belief of his followers, in the person and life of Jesus, son of a carpenter of Nazareth in Galilee.[17] There is a margin of uncertainty about the precise dates of his birth (probably before the death of Herod the Great, which occurred in 4 B.C.), his ministry of not less than two years, and the Crucifixion (probably A.D. 29, 30 or 33).[18] This is because his disciples were at first less concerned with recording historical detail or writing a full life of their Master than with proclaiming that his life was the supreme intervention of God in human history, recalling stories of his life and teaching, and emphazing the central fact of his life and resurrection. This proclamation of the crucified and risen Messiah was the keynote of the apostolic preaching (kerugma); by the middle of the first century it had probably been put into some recorded form (in Aramaic) and was then expanded by the authors of the first three Gospels from their own knowledge and that of the disciples. Thus Luke in the preface to his version of the Gospel mentions other attempts to record the earliest traditions and set his hand to the same task of collecting, sifting and arranging the written and oral tradition.

This is not the place to discuss the content of the teaching of Jesus nor the theological implication of his assertion that he was the Son of God, a belief shared by his disciples and members of the Christian Church ever since. It is sufficient here to record the indisputable fact that what he said and did in the two or three years of his ministry changed the whole course of human history. At first he received baptism from John the Baptist, but his conception of the kingdom of God and the Messiah soon outran that of John: the former was to be no earthly kingdom nor the Messiah a secular ruler. Rather, he gathered round him a small group of followers to whom he explained the true nature of the kingdom and God's purpose of salvation for man. His personality and teaching, however, combined with a ministry of healing, drew large numbers of ordinary people to him (5000 in one part of Galilee on one occasion), and their enthusiasm led Herod to fear political trouble. Jesus became equally suspect to the Jewish religious authorities who resented the interpretation of the Mosaic law by the new prophet. A turning-point came when Jesus made clear to his disciples who had recognized him as the Messiah that he would not fulfil Jewish hopes of an earthly kingdom, still less by force attempt to throw off the Roman yoke ('Render unto Caesar the things that are Caesar's); rather, he would continue his ministry come what might. After his entry into Jerusalem, tension with the Jewish authorities increased until finally after a preliminary investigation by the Jewish supreme court of the Sanhedrin on a charge of blasphemy he was then handed over by them to the Roman procurator on a charge that he was a rival to Caesar and was seeking the throne of David as 'king of the Jews'. Pilate, who 'found no cause of death in him', was willing to release him but, fearing a mob-rising and its political repercussions, weakly gave in to the hatred of the Jews who cried out for the crucifixion of Jesus.[19]

If that had been the end, there would have been no Christian Church.[20] But his sad and disillusioned disciples, who must have felt that all their hopes had been thwarted, suddenly gained a new assurance: Christ's death was followed by his resurrection. However the accounts of the empty tomb and the various appearances of their Risen Lord to different groups of his followers are to be explained, it is quite clear that these disheartened men suddenly became completely convinced that Jesus had 'risen from the dead' and was actively guiding and commissioning them to continue to spread his teaching 'both in Jerusalem, and in all Judaea, and in Samaria, and unto the uttermost part of the earth'. To this task they pledged themselves when they gathered in an upper room in Jerusalem. 'The number of names together were about an hundred and twenty'; these quickly increased, first to 3000, and then to 5000. Under the leadership of Peter they continued to observe the Jewish law and to attend the Temple services, but a less rigidly orthodox element was injected into their number when they converted some of the Jews of the

Dispersion who had come to Jerusalem for the feast of Pentecost. Now the Jewish authorities, who had been responsible for the death of Jesus, were not likely to be tender-hearted towards his followers who instead of melting away began to consolidate into a new sect, especially when some of its members began to argue that it should release itself from the bonds of strict Judaism in order to appeal to the Gentile world. Thus persecution started and the persecutors were Jews not Romans.

Their first victim was Stephen, the leader of the Hellenist Christians who advocated a more liberal Judaism for propagation among the Gentiles. He was condemned by the Sanhedrin and was stoned to death. Then followed systematic persecution of the Christian leaders who were driven out of Jerusalem, some as far afield as Syrian Antioch, where they and their follow-ers first received the name of Christians.[21] One of the fiercest persecutors was a strict Pharisee, Saul from Tarsus, who acted with the blessing of the High Priest – until his astounding conversion to Christianity when he was journey-ing on the road to Damascus in order to persecute the Christians there. Using his Latin name Paul (he was a Roman citizen), the persecutor now became the defender of the faith and of the faithful, and a leader of the stature of Peter.[22] At first the scattered Christians preached only to Jews, but they then began to baptize Gentiles, Samaritans, an Ethiopian and the Roman centurion Cornelius. This created a new and difficult question: must Gentile converts accept Jewish customs in full? The problem was solved when Peter was finally convinced that the more liberal policy of Paul was right. Paul, the Apostle of the Gentiles, could now carry the Christian message throughout the Roman world, freed from the narrower shackles of Judaism.

The account in *Acts* of the missionary journeys that Paul made through Asia Minor and Greece throws much light on conditions there; he won many converts, mostly in the humbler walks of life, but met with much opposition and persecution from the local Jewish communities. His journeys were facilitated by the *pax Romana*, and his preaching by the *koine*, the common Greek dialect that was widespread in the East: his life was saved by his posses-sion of Roman citizenship. His presence often led to disturbances, provoked by Jews who trumped up charges against him or by people with vested interests in pagan cults who feared for their livelihood (as at Philippi and Ephesus). Thus he came for investigation or trial before various authorities: Gallio, the proconsul of Achaea, Claudius Lysias, the military tribune in command of the cohort at Jerusalem, Felix and Festus, the procurators of Judaea, and king Herod Agrippa II (pp. 266 f.). These men in general did not find him guilty of any offence against Roman law, and regarded the issues at stake as internal religious matters that concerned only the Jews themselves (p. 266). Finally, when accused of treason, Paul appealed to Caesar, and Festus sent him to Rome, which he reached after shipwreck and other adventures.

There he was kept for two years in some kind of free custody; whether he was tried and acquitted is not known since the book of *Acts* breaks off at this point. There is a strong tradition, which may well be true, that he perished with other Christian martyrs in the Neronian persecution.

At the time of his arrival in Rome, a Christian community was established there, consisting probably of some Gentiles as well as Jews. The Jews, expelled under Claudius' order (p. 249), will have soon returned. Membership of this community was probably largely confined to the poorer classes; some adherents were found in the service of the emperor, but it is not certain whether the *externa superstitio*, with which a noblewoman Pomponia Graecina was charged in A.D. 57, was Christianity. At first to the man in the street the Christians were probably not distinguished from the rest of the Jewish community, but then came the fire and Nero's savage onslaught. Thereafter they will have been known as a sect apart, suspect and liable to persecution. But the blood of the martyrs proved the seed of the Church. Few who witnessed their sufferings under Nero would have believed that in two hundred and fifty years Christianity would have triumphed, that the Roman Empire would have accepted it as an official religion and that a Christian emperor, Constantine, would be sitting on the throne of the Caesars.

ABBREVIATIONS

AJArch.	*American Journal of Archaeology.*
AJP	*American Journal of Philology.*
Aufstieg	*Aufstieg und Niedergang der römischen Welt* (ed. H. Temporini, 1972–).
Badian, For. Cl.	E. Badian, *Foreign Clientelae*, 264–70 B.C. (1958).
Badian, Studies	E. Badian, *Studies in Greek and Roman History* (1964).
Broughton, MRR	T. R. S. Broughton, *The Magistrates of the Roman Republic.*
CAH	*Cambridge Ancient History.*
CIL	*Corpus Inscriptionum Latinarum.*
Cl. Ph.	*Classical Philology.*
Cl. Qu.	*Classical Quarterly.*
Cl. Rev.	*Classical Review.*
Crawford, RRC	M. H. Crawford, *Roman Republican Coinage* (1974).
Dessau, ILS	H. Dessau, *Inscriptiones Latinae Selectae.*
Ehrenberg and	V. Ehrenberg and A. H. M. Jones,
Jones, Documents	*Documents illustrating the Reigns of Augustus and Tiberius* (2nd. ed. 1955).
Gabba, RR, Army	E. Gabba, *Republican Rome, the Army and the Allies* (1976).
Gr. and R.	*Greece and Rome.*
Greenidge, Sources²	A. H. J. Greenidge and A. M. Clay, *Sources for Roman History*, 133–70 B.C. (2nd ed. by E. W. Gray, 1960).
Gruen, Rom. Pol.	E. S. Gruen, *Roman Politics and the Criminal Courts*, 149–70 B.C. (1968).
Inscr. Ital.	*Inscriptiones Italiae.*
Jacoby, Fr. Gr. Hist.	F. Jacoby, *Die Fragmente der Griechischen Historiker.*
Jones, CERP	A. H. M. Jones, *The Cities of the Eastern Roman Provinces.*

JRS	Journal of Roman Studies.
Lewis and Reinhold, Rn.Civ	N. Lewis, and M. Reinhold, Roman Civilization.
Magie, RRAM	D. Magie, Roman Rule in Asia Minor.
Malcovati ORF	H. Malcovati, Oratorum Romanorum Fragmenta (2nd ed. 1955).
Num. Chron.	Numismatic Chronicle.
OCD	Oxford Classical Dictionary^2 (1970).
OGIS	G. Dittenberger, Orientis Graeci Inscriptiones Selectae.
Rice Holmes, RR	T. Rice Holmes, The Roman Republic.
Riccobono, FIRA	S. Riccobono, Fontes Iuris Romani Antejustiniani, I.
Seager, Crisis	R. Seager (ed.), The Crisis of the Roman Republic (1969).
Sydenham, CRR	E. A. Sydenham, The Coinage of the Roman Republic (1952).
Sylloge	G. Dittenberger, Sylloge Inscriptionum Graecarum (3rd ed. 1915).
TAPA	Transactions of the American Philogical Association.
Warmington, ROL	E. H. Warmington, Remains of Old Latin, IV.

NOTES

The text reference is given thus [p. 76] at the end of each note.

CHAPTER I

1 THE DOWNFALL OF THE REPUBLIC. This subject has been treated in a lecture by R. Syme entitled *A Roman Post-mortem* (Sydney 1950 = *Roman Papers*, 1979, i, 205 ff.), in ch. x of *The Theory of the Mixed Constitution in Antiquity* by K. von Fritz (1954) and in a book by R. E. Smith on *The Failure of the Roman Republic* (1955). Smith attributes the failure largely to the Gracchi and believes that the senatorial class, if left to itself, would have worked out a satisfactory system; this view has not gained wide support. The topic is handled now by Christian Meier in *Res Publica Amissa. Eine Studie zu Verfassung und Geschichte der späten römischen Republik* (1966; 2nd ed. 1980, with long new introduction), who regards the late Republic as a reasonably contented community which was upset by the problems arising from the excessive extension of the territory of the State, and not least from the decline in moral standards among the powerful individuals who found themselves supported by professional armies as the result of exceptional crises; since, in his view, the political classes were reasonably satisfied, there was not sufficient pressure to adapt old institutions to meet the threat from the military *principes*. For a discussion of this book see P.A. Brunt, *JRS*, 1968, 229ff., and E. W. Gray, *Cl. Rev.*, 1969, 325 ff. In 'The Army and the Land in the Roman Revolution', *JRS*, 1962, 69 ff., P. A. Brunt has emphasized the continuing need of the poor for land as a major factor in the revolution which transformed an oligarchic Republic into the Principate of Augustus. E. S. Gruen (whose book, *The Last Generation of the Roman Republic* (1974), provides a valuable survey of the political history of the last decades of the Republic) believes that modern historians have tended to regard the 'downfall' with too much hindsight: the oligarchical government was stronger than often envisaged and civil war was not anticipated by contemporaries until it was almost upon them; the breakdown was relatively sudden rather than gradual. [p. 1]

2 ROME'S ITALIAN CONFEDERACY. See Tenney Frank, *Roman Imperialism* (1914), chs. i–v; A. J. Toynbee, *Hannibal's Legacy* (1965), i; H. H. Scullard, *History of the Roman

World, 753–146 BC[4] (1980); E. T. Salmon, *The Making of Roman Italy* (1982). On *ius fetiale* see Frank, *op.cit.*, R. Ogilvie, *Commentary on Livy books i–v* (1965), 110 ff., 127 ff., and V. Ilari, *L'interpretazione storica del diritto de guerra romana* (1981), ch. i. [p. 2]

3 ROMAN IMPERIALISM. The earlier view of Rome as Dryden's 'old unquestioned pirate of the land' has long been largely superseded by the idea that Rome's creation of a Mediterranean empire resulted essentially from a policy of defensive imperialism (see, e.g., Tenney Frank, *op.cit. supra*, and M. Holleaux in *CAH*). This interpretation in turn has recently been challenged by W. V. Harris, *War and Imperialism in Republican Rome, 327–70 BC* (1979), who attributes to Rome a much more aggressive policy (but this reaction may be too strong: see, e.g., A. N. Sherwin-White, *JRS*, 1980, 177 ff.). Some aspects of Roman Imperialism are discussed in *Imperialism in the Ancient World*, ed. R. D. A. Garnsey and C. R. Whittaker (1978), while K. Hopkins, *Conquerors and Slaves*, i (1978), considers the impact of empire on the political economy of Italy. See also the important study by E. Badian, *Roman Imperialism in the Late Republic*[2] (1968). [p. 5]

4 THE NOBLES. The true nature of the Roman nobility was revealed in an epoch-making little book by M. Gelzer, *Die Nobilität der römischen Republik* (1912), of which an English translation is now available: *The Roman Nobility* (1969). For some of the ideas and ideals which inspired the nobles see D. Earl, *The Moral and Political Tradition of Rome* (1967), who writes (p. 21), '*Virtus*, for the Republican noble, consisted in the winning of personal preeminence and glory by the commission of great deeds in the service of the Roman state.' In the late Republic men struggled for *fama, gloria, auctoritas* and above all *dignitas:* it was in defence of his *dignitas*, which he asserted to be more important than life itself, that Caesar crossed the Rubicon and marched on Rome. On the *novi homines* see T. P. Wiseman, *New Men in the Roman Senate, 139 BC–14 A.D.* (1971). See also L. Schatzman, *Senatorial Wealth and Roman Politics* (1975). [p. 6]

5 GROUP POLITICS. On the nature of political life in the Roman Republic in general see R. Syme, *The Roman Revolution* (1939); L. R. Taylor, *Party Politics in the Age of Caesar* (1949); H. H. Scullard, *Roman Politics, 220–150 BC.* (1951, 2nd ed. 1973); E. Badian, *Foreign Clientelae, 264–70 BC* (1958); A. E. Astin, *Politics and Policies in the Roman Republic* (Belfast, 1968), a lecture; E. S. Gruen, *Roman Politics and the Criminal Courts, 139–70 BC* (1968); and a balanced assessment by T. R. S. Broughton, 'Senate and Senators of the Roman Republic: The Prosopographical Approach', *Aufstieg*, I, i, 250 ff. (with relevant bibliography). See also R. Seager on *factio, JRS*, 1972, 53 ff. Much of this modern work stems from F. Münzer's study of Roman aristocratic parties and families, *Römische Adelsparteien und Adelsfamilien* (1920), which in turn developed some of Gelzer's ideas (though not all in a way acceptable to Gelzer himself) and thus gave rise to the 'prosopographical' interpretation of Roman politics. While most historians would now agree on the essentially personal nature of Roman political life and on the absence of anything like modern political parties, they remain divided on the extent to which groups, based on family connexions, formed around outstanding individuals, and above all on how permanent such groupings, which were held together by ties of family and *amicitia* (political alliance), might be. An extreme view of the essential unimportance of such coteries is advanced by Chr. Meier, *Res Publica Amissa* (see above n. 1), who believes that in the late Republic senators were divided into coteries only on everday matters in general (though occasionally on greater issues) and that conflicting interests led to constant changes in such groups which must be regarded not as enduring family alliances but as ephemeral kaleidoscopic entities. E. S. Gruen (*op.cit. supra.*) on the other hand, though cautious, finds 'a strikingly consistent structure of political alliances for the 140s and 130s . . . the factional

structure of senatorial politics admits of no doubt' (p. 25. See further below ch. II, n. 8). [p. 6]

6 OPTIMATES AND POPULARES. See Ch. Wirszubski, *Libertas as a Political Idea at Rome* (1950), ch. 2. On the Populares see Chr. Meier, Pauly-Wissowa, *Realencyclopaedie*, Suppl. x, 550 ff., and *Res Publica Amissa*, 116–50 on 'the methods of the populares and the great political themes of the late Republic'; also R. Seager, *Cl. Qu.*, 1972, 328 ff., on Cicero's use of *popularis* and on Livy's use *Cl. Qu.*, 1977, 377 ff. On the *Optimates* see H. Strasburger, Pauly-Wissowa, xviii, 773 ff. [p. 6]

7 THE TRIBUNATE. There had been exceptions to the general docility of the tribunes, especially in the two decades before the Gracchi. One cause of trouble was a widespread dissatisfaction with the military levy, especially for service in Spain, which on appeal was sometimes voiced by tribunes on behalf of the dissentients. On two occasions, in 151 and 138, feelings reached such a pitch that the tribunes had temporarily thrown the consuls into prison. This was open sedition, even if of brief duration (cf. p. 14). It is against the background of such 'forerunners of the Gracchi' as they have been dubbed in an article with that title by L. R. Taylor (*JRS*, 1962, 19 ff.) that the revolutionary use of the tribunate by the Gracchi should be seen. On the tribunate see J. Bleiken, *Das Tribunat der klassischen Republik* (1955).

On the relationship of the Roman citizens to the structure of the State in the second and first centuries B.C. see the detailed study by C. Nicolet, *The World of the Citizen in Republican Rome* (1980). [p. 7]

8 THE MIXED CONSTITUTION. See K. von Fritz, *op. cit.*, n. 1, and C. O. Brink and F. W. Walbank, *Cl. Qu.*, 1954, 97 ff. [p. 7]

9 THE EQUITES. On the history of the Equestrian Order during the Republic see H. Hill, *The Roman Middle Class* (1952); 'The establishment of the *equester ordo*' by M. I. Henderson (*JRS*, 1963, 61 ff. = Seager, *Crisis*, 69 ff.); C. Nicolet, *L'ordre équestre à l'époque republicaine*, i (1966), ii (1974); and P. A. Brunt, 'The Equites in the late Republic' in *Deuxième conférence internationale d'histoire économique, Aix-en-Provence, 1962*, i (1965), 117 ff. (= Seager, *Crisis* 83 ff.); E. Badian, *OCD*[2] s.v. Equites, *Roman Imperialism in the late Rep.* (1968), vii ff. and especially *Publicans and Sinners* (1972).

The Equites were not of course a monolithic block: the most prominent in Rome were naturally those *publicani* who helped in the public finances, as described above (see p. 8), and indeed the business men and traders in general, but in addition there were the country gentry of the towns of Italy who preferred the interests of their landed estates and the affairs of their local communities to both the glamour of political life in Rome and the risks of business. It is the publicans, described by Cicero as the 'flower of the equestrian order' who in the main began to clash with the Senate in the political arena. See further below p. 177 f. and n. 7. [p. 8]

10 GREEK INFLUENCES ON ROME. *Rome et la Grèce* by G. Colin (1905) is a most useful collection of material for the period from 200 to 146 B.C. See also N. K. Petrolochos, *Roman Attitudes to the Greeks* (Athens, 1974). [p. 9]

11 THE BACCHANALIA. See A. H. McDonald, *JRS*, 1944, 26 ff. [p. 9 f.]

12 STOICISM. See E. V. Arnold, *Roman Stoicism* (1911); M. Pohlenz, *Die Stoa*, 2 vols. (1948); J. Rist, *Stoic Philosophy* (1969); F. H. Sandbach, *The Stoics* (1975). [p. 10]

13 THE SCIPIONIC CIRCLE. On this so-called coterie see A. E. Astin, *Scipio Aemilianus* (1967), 294 ff. H. Strasburger, *Hermes*, 1966, 60 ff., argues that Polybius does not mention any member of the 'circle' and implies that Scipio's interest in philosophy was more moral than intellectual; he believes therefore that the 'circle' is an invention of Cicero. This would seem to be going rather far, though perhaps the links between the members of the alleged group were less communal, if not weaker, than is sometimes

supposed. See also E. Rawson, 'Scipio, Laelius and the ancestral Religion', *JRS*, 1973, 161 ff. and 'Religion and Politics in the late second century B.C. at Rome', *Phoenix*, 1974, 193 ff. (the Optimates used the official religion for political propaganda; the Populares used less official cults). [p. 11]

14 SLAVERY. See W. L. Westermann, *The Slave Systems of Greek and Roman Antiquity* (1955), 57 ff. Cf. P. A. Brunt, *JRS*, 1958, 164 ff., and eleven papers on various aspects, entitled *Slavery in Classical Antiquity* (1960), edited by M. I. Finley; J. Vogt, *Ancient Slavery and the Ideal of Man* (1975); K. Hopkins, *Conquerors and Slaves*, i (1978); *Greek and Roman Slavery* (1981) by T. Wiedermann contains a translation of a large number of passages dealing with slavery from the ancient sources. [p. 11]

15 SICILIAN SLAVE WAR. Two interesting documents survive: the little bronze coin, struck at Enna, on which Eunus styles himself King Antiochus (cf. *CAH*, Plates IV, p. 2), and the sling-bullets found there bearing the name of Piso (Greenidge, *Sources²*, p. 10). J. Vogt, *Struktur d. ant. Sklavenkriege* (1957); P. Green, *Past and Present*, 1961, 10 ff. (reprinted in *The Shadow of the Parthenon* (1972), 192 ff.); W. Forrest, *ibid.*, 1962, 87 ff. [p. 12]

16 PROVINCIAL ADMINISTRATION. The references are Polybius, vi, 56, 14, and Cicero, *In Verr.* ii, i, 2. In general see G. H. Stevenson, *Roman Provincial Administration* (1939) and E. Badian, *Publicans and Sinners* (1972). On the lex Calpurnia see E. S. Gruen, *Rom. Pol.*, 13 ff., who does not believe that the motive in establishing the new court was concern for the provincials; 'politics provided a decisive impetus', i.e, senatorial interests. E. Badian on the other hand (*Roman Imperialism in the late Republic²* (1968),9) thinks that the Senate was taking its responsibilities towards the provincials seriously. On the ways in which the Romans, through ties of patronage or friendship, relied on local rulers beyond the frontiers of the empire to help maintain peace see P. C. Sandys, *The Client Princes of the Roman Empire under the Republic* (1908) and M. R. Cimma, *Reges socii et amici populi Romani* (1976). [p. 13]

16a ALLIED TROOPS. On the method by which Rome called up allied troops (*formula togatorum*) and the numbers in relation to those of the Romans see P. A. Brunt, *Italian Manpower* (1971), 545 ff., 677 ff.; on their pay see C. Nicolet, *Papers Brit. Sch. Rome*, 1978, i ff. [p. 14]

17 ALLIES AND CITIZENSHIP. On Rome's reations with her allies in the first half of the second century see A. H. McDonald, *Cambr. Hist. J.*, 1939, 124 ff., and briefly, H. H. Scullard, *Roman Politics*, 145 ff. On citizenship see A. N. Sherwin-White, *The Roman Citizenship²* (1973). On the date (c. 124 B.C.?) of granting Roman citizenship to Latin magistrates see below, ch. IV, n. 7. On Rome's relations with her allies in general see A. J. Toynbee's important contribution in *Hannibal's Legacy* (1965) and on her relations with the Latin colonies see E. T. Salmon, *Roman Colonization* (1969). See also H. Galstaren, *Herrschaft und Verwaltung im republikanischen Italien* (1976) and E. T. Salmon, *The Making of Roman Italy* (1982). [p. 15]

18 AGRICULTURE. In general see K. D. White, *Roman Farming* (1970), and for the agricultural regions of Italy and their resources, see ch. 2; also *Farm Equipment of the Roman World* (1975). See also J. M. Frayn, *Subsistence Farming in Roman Italy* (1979); E. Gabba and M. Pasquinucci, *Strutture agrarie e allevamento transumante nell 'Italia romana (iii–i sec.a.C.)* (1979). – The devastating effects of the Hannibalic War on Italian agriculture are judged to have been less severe by P. A. Brunt, *Italian Manpower* (1971), 269 ff. than by A. J. Toynbee, *Hannibal's Legacy* (1965), ii, 10 ff. [p. 16]

19 EFFECT OF SICILIAN GRAIN. See Tenney Frank, *Economic Survey of Ancient Rome*, I, 158 ff. On the effects of overseas conquest on the economy and the growth of slavery see K. Hopkins, *Conquerors and Slaves*, i (1978), 1–132. On the corn supply see in general G. Rickman, *The Corn Supply of Ancient Rome* (1980). [p. 16]

20 MULTIPLE HOLDINGS AND LATIFUNDIA. Further, richer men could hold several farms of considerable size either adjacent to one another or even in different parts of Italy. Thus not all *latifundia* (great estates) need have been unified areas (cf. C. A. Yeo, *Finanzarchiv*, 1952, 459 f. and P. A. Brunt, *Gnomon*, 1964, 189 and *Italian Manpower, 225 BC–A.D. 14* (1971), 352, 365).

Recent archaeological investigation, based on field-work and the evidence of pottery, suggests that large estates were less widespread in the second century than has been generally assumed and that smaller farms, at any rate in some areas, were holding their own. Thus in South Etruria, at Veii, Sutrium and Capena, the work of members of the British School at Rome has shown that at this period small farms formed the majority of the individual sites identified in the area. Further, around Luceria in Apulia air-photography has revealed a pattern of small individual farms, each of some ten *iugera*, which provided oil and wine (remains of olive trunks and trenches for vines can still be seen). They appear to date from *c.* 120 or a little earlier and it is tempting to connect them with the settlement work of the Gracchi. For S. Etruria see *Papers Brit. Sch. Rome*, 1958, 1961, 1963, 1968; for Luceria (pending the publication of the work of G. B. D. Jones) see A. J. Toynbee, *Hannibal's Legacy*, II, 536. For a general assessment see M. W. Frederiksen, 'The Contribution of Archaeology to the Agrarian Problem in the Gracchan Period', *Dialoghi di Archeologia*, IV–V (1970–71), 330 ff.) [p. 17]

21 AGER PUBLICUS. See the full discussion by G. Tibiletti, *Athenaeum*, 1948, 1 ff., 1949, 67 ff., 1950, 183 ff., and the resumptive account by D. Stockton, *The Gracchi* (1979), 206 ff. [p. 18]

CHAPTER II

1. SOURCES FOR THE GRACCHAN PERIOD. The more important passages are collected in A. H. J. Greenidge, A. M. Clay and E. W. Gray, *Sources for Roman History BC 133–70* (2nd ed. 1960). Since most of the work of contemporary writers is now lost, we depend for our knowledge of this period very largely upon late writers such as Appian and Plutarch (see below).

The development of historical writing at Rome is discussed on pp. 196 ff., where it is seen that this period was dealt with by contemporary historians such as Calpurnius Piso (*cos.* 133), C. Fannius (*cos.* 122), Sempronius Asellio (mil. trib. 133) and the Greek Posidonius, whose works are now lost. Speeches of men like the Gracchi circulated in antiquity, but do not survive: for the remaining fragments see H. Malcovati, *Oratorum Romanorum Fragmenta* (2nd ed. 1955). The more important surviving inscriptions are mentioned in the following notes, e.g. the 'Popillius' inscription, some boundary-stones of the agrarian commissioners, and the *lex iudiciaria*.

Thus we have to depend very largely upon later writers. One of the most important of these is Cicero who as a young man studied the earlier orators and whose writings abound in references back to this period; on his attitude to the Gracchi see R. J. Murray, *TAPA*, 1966, 291 ff. and J. Béranger, *Aufstieg*, I, i, 732 ff. Historical writers fall into three groups. First, Livy and the writers that made use of him. His history (see p. 202 f.) of these years survives only in the Epitomes. It was used by Velleius Paterculus (p. 300), Valerius Maximus (p. 300), Florus (who wrote in the second century A.D. an account of Rome's wars), Eutropius (who wrote in the fourth century), Orosius (fifth century) and Obsequens (who compiled from Livy a list of prodigies). With these may be mentioned the Greek writer Cassius Dio Cocceianus who held the consulship with the emperor Severus Alexander in A.D. 229, and wrote a general history of Rome down to his own day. Of books 24–35 (which covered the years 133 to 69 B.C.) only a few fragments survive; books 36–54 (68–10 B.C.) are preserved in full, and books 55–63 (9 B.C.–A.D. 69) in abbreviation but fairly fully till A.D. 46. See further, Fergus Millar, *A Study of Cassius Dio* (1964).

Secondly, Plutarch, who was born in Boeotia in the principate of Claudius, wrote in Greek *Parallel Lives* of famous Greeks and Romans. These were conceived as moral biographies rather than as critical histories, and should be judged as such. They are written without prejudice or deliberate falsification, and their historical value depends largely on what sources Plutarch happened to be using for any particular passage. He is interested in men and their behaviour and although he had no profound know-ledge of the historical background of the lives of many of his subjects, he has provided much valuable and fascinating material. His *Lives* of the two Gracchi are among his best; he made use of the Roman annalistic tradition and also of the main source used by Appian (on this see n. 10 below). For general accounts of Plutarch see R. H. Barrow, *Plutarch and his Times* (1967), C. P. Jones, *Plutarch and Rome* (1971) and D. A. Russell, *Plutarch* (1973).

Thirdly, Appian, an Alexandrine Greek (c. A.D. 95–165), who went to Rome where he gained a place in the imperial civil service under Antoninus Pius. He wrote 24 books of *Romaika*, dealing largely with wars on an ethnographic arrangement; thus, e.g. book 12 described the wars against Mithridates. Books 13–17 covered the Civil Wars and are usually numbered separately; his sources are discussed by E. Gabba, *Appiano e la storia delle guerre civile* (1956). Book I of the *Civil Wars* (of which there is an edition by J. L. Strachan-Davidson, 1902; and also one in Italian by E. Gabba, 1967) covers the years 133 to 70 B.C. For the Gracchi Appian has followed an excellent source which goes back to the tradition of the contemporary annalists (e.g. Fannius). Though he understood the empire of his own day, Appian had little accurate personal knowledge of the Republican constitution and therefore on occasion may have misunderstood his source, but in general his account of the Gracchi is first-rate.

Finally Diodorus Siculus should be mentioned. He wrote at the end of the Republic a World History from earliest times to 54 B.C. in 40 books, of which those dealing with the later Republic are lost apart from some fragments. Those from books 34 and 36 dealing with the Sicilian Slave Wars are valuable and derive from the account by Posidonius; these are now conveniently available in the Loeb Diodorus, vol. xii (1967) by R. M. Geer. See below p. 302 f.

The sources for one of the largest areas of Republican history, namely magisterial activities, are conveniently listed in T. R. S. Broughton's indispensable work, *The Magistrates of the Roman Republic*, 2 vols and Suppl. (1951–60).

Modern works. Chapters I and II of *CAH*, IX (1932) by H. Last are fundamental. See also A. H. J. Greenidge, *A History of Rome BC 133–104* (1904); ingenious essays by J. Carcopino, entitled *Autour des Gracques*[2] (1967); H. C. Boren, *The Gracchi* (1968); K. Richardson, *Daggers in the Forum* (1976), a popular treatment; D. Stockton, *The Gracchi* (1979), a useful survey and assessment of recent views. On Tiberius Gracchus see D. C. Earl, *Tiberius Gracchus. A Study in Politics* (1963), A. E. Astin, *Scipio Aemilianus* (1967), esp. pp. 190–226, a valuable critical discussion by E. Badian, *Aufstieg*, I, i, 668 ff. and A. H. Bernstein, *Tiberius Sempronius Gracchus* (1978). Badian also has an extremely useful survey of work done on the period from the Gracchi to Sulla in the years 1940–1959 in *Historia*, 1962, 197 ff. = Seager, *Crisis*, 3 ff.). J. M. Riddle, *Tiberius Gracchus* (1970), provides a selection of interpretations of Gracchus (cf. C. Nicolet, *Les Gracques* (1968). [p. 19]

2 LAELIUS' REFORM. See Plutarch, *Tib. Gracchus*, 8. 4. Cf. H. H. Scullard, *JRS*, 1960, 62 ff.;

L. R. Taylor, *JRS*, 1962, 24 ff.; A. E. Astin, *Scipio Aemilianus* (1967), 307 ff. Astin inclines to follow Plutarch's view that Laelius' main concern was with the problem of manpower available for military service rather than to forestall a potentially revolutionary situation: he believes that the economic and social problems were much less severe even as late as 140 and that they increased sharply in the 130s. [p. 19]

3   SECRET BALLOT. See Cicero, *De legibus*, 3. 15 ff. [p. 20]

4   SCIPIO'S POLITICS. See H. H. Scullard, *JRS*, 1960, 59 ff., and in general, including a discussion of some of these views, A. E. Astin, *Scipio Aemilianus* (1967). For a detailed analysis of Scipio's political friends and enemies and the political developments during the decade preceding 133, see Astin, pp. 81 ff., and Gruen, *Rom. Pol.*, ch. i, 'Politics in the Age of Scipio Aemilianus'. [p. 20]

5   CORNELIA'S FAMILY. See J. Carcopino, *Autour des Gracques*, ch. 2. [p. 20]

6   BLOSSIUS. See D. R. Dudley, *JRS*, 1941, 94 ff. On Greek influences on Tiberius see T. S. Brown, *Cl. Journal*, 1947, 471 ff. J. B. Becker, 'The Influence of Roman Stoicism upon the Gracchan economic land Reforms' (*La Parola del Passato*, 1964, 126 ff.), argues that Stoicism created a generally favourable 'humane' background in the Scipionic Circle, but this received a set-back with Laelius' failure. (On *humanitas* see A. E. Astin, *Scipio Aemilianus*, 302 ff.) But whatever influence Blossius and Diophanes may have had on the development of Tiberius' thought, the tradition that they actively incited him to reform may be dismissed: they will have been supporters rather than promoters. M. Gelzer rather surprisingly attaches more importance to the influence of Diophanes than to that of Blossius (*Kleine Schriften*, II (1963), 77 f.). [p. 21]

7   TIBERIUS' MOTIVES. Both Appian and Plutarch stress that his chief motive was to relieve the economically distressed (cf. Appian, *Bell. Civ.* 1. II. 43: οὐκ ἐς εὐπορίαν ἀλλ' ἐς εὐανδρίαν), namely to resettle the poor on small farms, with the incidental advantage of reducing the amount of slave labour on the land. The repopulation of the countryside and the consequent diminution of the unemployed in Rome are two sides of the same problem. A factor in the urban crisis has been emphasized by H. C. Boren (*Amer. Hist. Rev.*, 1958, 890 ff. = Seager, *Crisis*, 54 ff.), who indicates that government expenditure was high in the 140s (on building, coinage, etc.) but declined in the 130s, thus leading to a depression: Tiberius' aim will have been to relieve the crowded city and help those whom the boom had attracted to it. It need scarcely be doubted however that the country came first in his thought. But as has been seen (above p. 20) there was a close connexion between agricultural distress and military service (in general see P. A. Brunt, 'The Army and the Land', *JRS*, 1962, 69 ff.), and there can be little doubt that one of Tiberius' motives (as it certainly was a result of his legislation) was to make more citizens liable to military service by increasing the number of independent peasant farmers. But that is not necessarily to accept one of D. Earl's main contentions (*Tiberius Gracchus* (1963)) that the crisis lay primarily in the recruitment for the legions rather than in the agricultural, economic or social sphere which he minimizes. Badian (*Aufstieg*, I, i, 684 ff.), however, emphasizes, with Earl, the military crisis. See also Y. Shochet, *Recruitment and the Programme of Tiberius Gracchus* (1980). The impact of the Numantine affair on Tiberius has again been stressed by M. G. Morgan and J. A. Walsh, *Cl. Ph.*, 1978, 200 ff., while F. Coarelli, *Papers Brit. School Rome*, 1978, 1 ff., has underlined the building activity in Rome in the Gracchan period and consequently the low level of unemployment among the urban plebs. [p. 22]

8   TIBERIUS' FRIENDS. See Cicero *De Rep.*, 1. 19; Plut., *Ti. Gr.* 9.1. There can be no doubt that these men supported Tiberius, though P. Scaevola's support was less open than that of his brother Crassus Mucianus (Cic. *Acad, Prior.* 2. 13): this may be due to his earlier support of Scipio Aemilianus (as late as 136); he will have moved towards

Gracchus and Appius Claudius under his brother's influence (cf. E. Gruen, *Athenaeum*, 1965, 321 ff.). The extent to which Tiberius' supporters were united in any other sense is controversial. Those who deny the functioning of 'group-politics' would say, with P. A. Brunt (*Gnomon*, 1964, 191), 'there is no evidence for the existence of a powerful noble faction behind Gracchus, only that a few isolated nobles sought *vindicare plebem in libertatem*'. But this is surely too extreme a reaction from, e.g., the view of D. Earl (*Tiberius Gracchus*) who argues that the Claudii Pulchri, Sempronii Gracchi and Mucii Scaevolae formed 'a political group of the classic Roman type . . . a *factio* with bonds of *amicitia* strengthened by those of marriage' (p. 12). The power and hopes of these men were too deeply rooted in the oligarchical system and its spoils to provoke a wish to destroy it: 'whatever was contemplated in 133, it was not revolution'. The opposition of the other nobles will have been provoked by the potential increase to the *clientela* of the Claudian gens, combined with the powerful *clientela* which Tiberius inherited from his father in Rome, Italy and the provinces. Whether or not Earl is right in seeing the connexion between the Claudii and Sempronii as a continuation of old traditional links, and whatever the motives of the different members of the group, E. S. Gruen at any rate has no doubt about the background: 'the factional nature of this struggle cannot be gainsaid . . . Meier, *Res Pub.*, 98, in defiance of the evidence, denies all factional considerations to the Gracchan program. Few will follow him' (*Rom Pol.*, 53 and n. 41). On the career of P. Mucius Scaevola, see now A. L. Bernstein, *Cl. Ph.*, 1972, 42 ff. and R. A. Bauman, *Revue internat. des droits de l'antiquité*, 1978, 223 ff. The political supporters and opponents of Tiberius are discussed by J. Briscoe, *JRS*, 1974, 125 ff., while E. Gabba considers the economic motives in the opposition to the agrarian law (*Polis and Imperium*, ed. J. A. S. Evans, 1974, 129 ff). [p. 22]

9   THE LEX AGRARIA. The idea of compensation depends on a remark by Plutarch (*Ti. Gr.* 9. 2) which is probably a misunderstanding of what was recorded by the source of Appian, *Bell Civ.* 1. 11. 5. Since neither the amount of land available nor the number of claimants would be known in advance, no standard size for allotments is likely to have been fixed in the bill; a reference to thirty *iugera* in the *lex agraria* of 111 B.C. might suggest a possible maximum. The evidence that rent was charged is that it was abolished by Drusus in 122. The prohibition on selling was probably not meant to be permanent: allotments could be passed by inheritance. The view, based on Appian, that Italian allies as well as citizens might benefit under the bill, has once again been refuted by E. Badian, *For. Cl.*, 169 ff. It has however again been revived, and D. Stockton, *The Gracchi* (1979), 42, seems inclined to accept it: Bernstein, *Tiberius Gracchus* (1978), 137 ff., believes that it was Tiberius' original intention to include the Italians but that he later changed his mind, while J. S. Richardson, *JRS*, 1980, 1 ff., argues that Tiberius did include in his measure Italians who thereby received both Roman citizenship and land. Badian has also given a salutary warning (*Historia*, 1962, 210, n. 52) that the supposed 500 extra *iugera* granted for two sons is in fact only a modern suggestion, based on references in the sources to 500 and 1000 *iugera*; in any case demographic policy and later parallels would suggest three children rather than two sons. He is, however, inclined to think (*Aufstieg*, 702 f.) that the law, as finally passed, imposed an absolute limit of 500 *iugera*, without any extra for children. [p. 22]

10 CLASH BETWEEN TIBERIUS AND OCTAVIUS. One of the chief problems of historical criticism for this period is to determine what historical value should be given to those episodes which are recorded by Plutarch and not by Appian. They are rejected by Carcopino (*op. cit.*, ch. i) but for a criticism of Carcopino and a defence of Plutarch see R. M. Geer, *Classical and Medieval Studies presented to E. K. Rand* (1938), 105 ff. Cf. also A. E. Astin, *Scipio Aemilianus*, 332 ff. Thus the historicity of Plutarch's account of

Tiberius' redrafting of his law and declaration of a *iustitium* is uncertain. Appian (*BC*, 1. 12) describes three meetings of the People when (*a*) Octavius vetoed, (*b*) Octavius repeated his veto, and (*c*) Tiberius carried Octavius' deposition. He implies that they were held on consecutive days, but the probability that there is a gap in the text and the possibility that in his description of the adjournment of the first meeting the phrase εἰϕ τὴν ἐπιοῦσαν ἀγοράν may mean 'to the next meeting' rather than 'to the following day' (i.e. to the next comitial day, not the next day in the calendar) suggest an interval in which may be placed some of the episodes recounted by Plutarch and not by Appian. D. C. Earl has argued (*Latomus*, 1960, 657 ff.) that an alliance of Octavii, Popillii and Cornelii Scipiones, formed earlier in the century, was operating against Tiberius in 133 and that Octavius was known as a political opponent. Cf. also A. E. Astin, *Scipio Aemilianus*, 346. Octavius himself maintained that the vote deposing him was invalid and refused to leave the tribunal, but was forced away by part of the crowd. In a sense this was a resort to open violence, but it was 'a brawl rather than a riot' (Astin, 209) in which Tiberius himself probably tried to shield Octavius. Nevertheless by Octavius and his supporters it would be represented as forcible violation of a tribune's sacrosanctity. Badian (*Aufstieg*, 706 ff.) emphasizes the role of Octavius, through whose persistence (*patientia*) the conflict came about. 'The veto – or at least its persistence – could not have been expected: it was nothing less than a breach of all constitutional custom.' M. G. Morgan and J. A. Walsh, *Cl. Ph.*, 1978, 200 ff., stress the deposition of Octavius as Tiberius' crucial mistake. [p. 23]

11 DATE OF THE LEX AGRARIA. This was probably passed either in Feb. or April. Tiberius perhaps waited until after March when the consul Calpurnius Piso went off to Sicily; the other consul, Scaevola, was friendly. Also a lull in agricultural work in April may have made it easier for the peasants to come to Rome to vote. D. C. Earl has suggested that, contrary to the usual belief, Calpurnius Piso was not hostile to Tiberius: at worst he showed a benevolent neutrality (see *Athenaeum*, 1960, 283 ff.). But he later opposed Gaius Gracchus (*Cic. Tusc. Disp.* 3–48). [p. 23]

12 THE AGRARIAN COMMISSION. A law of uncertain date prohibited anyone who proposed a commission from becoming a member of it. If the law was pre-Gracchan, Tiberius' action will have contravened it: if slightly post-Gracchan, his action will have been unprecedented though not technically illegal. Appian's phrase αἱρετοὺς ἄνδρας ἐναλλασομένους κατ' ἔτος (1. 9. 37) is generally interpreted as in the text, since the personnel in fact changed only when vacancies were caused by death. Carcopino argued (*op. cit.*, 149 ff.) that the phrase refers to an internal change of an acting president with two 'sleeping partners'; this view, if not acceptable in full, at least emphasizes the fact that at given times some commissioners were more actively engaged on this work than at others. On the commissioners see J. Seihert, *Rivista Storica Antica*, I (1972). R. A. Bauman, *Historia*, 1979, 384 ff., argues that the commission was illegal (contrary to an earlier *lex Licinia*, he supposes), received its judicial powers under a subsequent law, and had *imperium*. [p. 23]

13 TIBERIUS AND ATTALUS. E. Badian has suggested (*For. Cl.*, 173 f.) that Tiberius was able to anticipate senatorial action on Attalus' will because he heard about it before the Senate did: because of the personal connexions of Tiberius' father with the Attalid house, the Pergamene envoy who brought the will to Rome would naturally stay at the home of his Roman patrons, the Gracchi. [p. 23]

14 RE-ELECTION TO THE TRIBUNATE. Despite Appian *Bell. Civ.* I.14 (which is supported by L. R. Taylor, *Athenaeum*, 1963, 56 f., and A. E. Astin, *Scipio Aemilianus*, 351 f.), it is unlikely that re-election was technically illegal (cf. A. H. M. Jones, *Proc. Cambr. Philological Soc.*, 1960, 35 ff.; Earl, *Ti. Gracchus*, 103 f.); if it had been, anti-Gracchan

sources would surely have left stronger traces in the tradition that Tiberius was acting illegally. But if not illegal, it certainly was excluded by custom (*mos maiorum*), and some genuine contemporary uncertainty or confusion may have existed arising from the fact that though the tribunate was not technically a magistracy, in practice tribunes had for long been treated as magistrates. But Tiberius' decision to stand again, though shocking to many, was not entirely 'out of tune with the times' (Astin, 216) since Scipio Aemilianus and Scipio Nasica had held a second consulship within the forbidden period of ten years and thus accepted constitutional practice was subordinated to immediate political interests.

L. R. Taylor, believing that re-election was illegal, goes further and argues that the last Assembly meeting, which led to Tiberius' death, was in fact not electoral (i.e. called to elect new tribunes) but legislative, i.e. to vote on a proposal to legalize his candidature. Although Appian clearly indicates (*BC*, 1. 14) that the Assembly was electoral, she prefers the indications of Plutarch and the Livian tradition (Plut., *Ti. Gr.* 16; Obsequens, 27a; Ampelius, 26. 1; and, if taken quite literally, even another passage of Appian, viz. 1. 2. 4) that it was legislative. One of her arguments is that since Appian describes the tribes giving their votes successively, this indicates the procedure of a legislative Assembly because at elections the tribes voted simultaneously: this latter point however has been denied as valid for 133 by U. Hall ('Voting Procedure', *Historia*, 1964, 288 f.), while even if valid, the actual *renuntiatio pro tribu* would have to be proclaimed in order of tribes successively and thus Appian might still be describing an electoral meeting. Miss Taylor's arguments have been rejected by D. Earl, *Athenaeum*, 1965, 95 ff., to which Miss Taylor has replied in *Athenaeum*, 1966, 238 ff., and by Badian, *Aufstieg*, 720 f. He also argues (716 ff.) that it was fear of a successful prosecution when he became a *privatus*, rather than fear that his programme might suffer if he retired, that led Tiberius to seek re-election. [p. 23]

15 TIBERIUS' NEW PROGRAMME. Plutarch (*Ti. Gr.* 16) attributes to him proposals to shorten the period of military service, to allow *provocatio* against judicial decisions by senatorial commissions, and to constitute the jurors of the *quaestio repetundarum* equally from senators and Equites instead of from senators alone. It is uncertain whether these proposals were in fact put forward by Tiberius or may have been falsely transferred to him from his brother's programme; if any go back to Tiberius, the military service proposal is perhaps the most probable. Fears among some of Tiberius' opponents that he might be approximating to the revolutionary pattern set by the Spartan social reformer, Cleomenes, will, according to H. C. Boren (*AJP*, 1961, 358 ff.) have increased their hostility. According to Dio Cassius (fr. 83. 7 f.) not only was Tiberius to stand for a second tribunate, but his young brother was also to be a candidate and his father-in-law Appius Claudius (already consul in 143) was to stand for a second consulship. This tradition may derive from anti-Gracchan sources. Yet it could be reliable, at least as regards Claudius if not Gaius Gracchus, and if so, the Gracchan threat to the opposition might indeed appear strong, if not even sinister.

D. B. Nagle (*Athenaeum*, 1970, 372 ff. and 1971, 111 ff.) believes that Tiberius' main support came from men still living in the countryside rather than from those that had drifted to Rome (incidentally a considerable part of the commissioners' work would therefore be to resettle men who were still in the districts where they had lost their farms). An important result was that as Tiberius' attempt to implement his programme dragged on in Rome, it became increasingly difficult for him to get his country supporters to stay on in Rome or return to it; hence he later had to appeal more to urban dwelling voters. [p. 24]

16 VIOLENCE. Differences in the surviving sources about the events of Tiberius' last day

make it impossible to reconstruct the details of the tragedy, still less the motives of the opposed factions. Since both sides had to improvise weapons, neither group apparently had come with the cold-blooded intention of initiating violence (though they might accuse each other of such intentions): cf. Astin, *Scipio Aemilianus*, 219 ff., who, in general minimizes the revolutionary aspects of Tiberius. A. W. Lintott, *Violence in Republican Rome* (1968), 68, 221, argues that 'there was at least mental preparation on both sides to use violence in self-defence or to protect supposed rights'. Much depends on the interpretation of Nasica's words and acts: did he really call on Scaevola to 'put down the tyrant', or is the phrase a *post eventum* intrusion (cf. Astin, 223, n. 1)? When Nasica, the Pontifex Maximus, covered his head with his toga, was his action meant to convey that he was about to offer a sacrifice, namely to kill Gracchus to save the State (cf. Earl *Ti. Gracchus*, 118 f.) or was the gesture that of a consul when declaring a *tumultus* and calling the citizens to arms (the phrase in which Nasica is said to have called upon his fellow-senators, 'let all who wish to save the State, follow me', is that used by a consul in proclaiming an emergency levy. Thus Lintott, 91, 183, 221)? While the absence of cold steel and the use of sticks and stones does suggest that Nasica did not start the day with the intention to kill, it is impossible to say how precisely his purposes developed, especially when what started as a brawl began to escalate. The fact remains that a private citizen had led others to kill their fellow-citizens untried. The casualties, 200 or 300, may be exaggerated or else be the result in part of panic and confusion as well as deliberate clubbing to death. On the topography of the events see B. Bilinski, *Helikon*, 1961, 264 ff. [p. 24]

16a CONSTITUTIONAL OFFENCE. Badian (*Aufstieg*, 694 ff.) rejects the common assumption that it was outrageous and unheard of for a tribunician bill to be put to the People without the Senate 's approval; rather it was Octavius' persistence in his use of his veto that offended against constitutional custom. [p. 24]

17 THE POPILLIUS INSCRIPTION. A famous inscription from Polla in Lucania (Greenidge, *Sources*², 14) records that a magistrate built a military road from Rhegium to Capua, rounded up some 900 fugitives when he was praetor in Sicily, was the first man to bring it about 'ut de agro poblico aratoribus cederent paastores', and built a forum. The man's name is missing, but he is usually assumed to be Popillius, who will thus have co-operated in carrying out the Gracchan land-bill, though a political enemy. A suggestion by E. Bracco (*Rendiconti dell' Acc. di Napoli*, 1955, 5 ff., and 1960, 149 ff.), that the man may be an Annius (either the consul of 153 or of 128), is strengthened by the discovery of a mile-stone near Catanzaro: 'cclx T. Annius T. f. pr(aetor)'. But more probably the road was started by Popillius as consul in 132 in connexion with the slave-war and completed by Annius as praetor in 131. See A. Degrassi, *Philologus*, 1955, 259 ff.; *Inscript. Latinae Lib. Rei Publicae* (1957) n. 454. P. T. Wiseman, however, has argued (*Papers Brit. Sch. Rome*, 1964, 21 ff.) for equating the road-builder of the inscription with Annius in 131. For F. T. Hinrichs ('Der römische Strassenbau zur Zeit der Gracchen', *Historia*, 1967, 162 ff.) the matter is settled because he apparently believes (quite wrongly) that Popillius' name actually survives in the inscription. G. Radke (Pauly-Wissowa, *RE*, Suppl. and XIII, 1971, 1509 f.) would assign the Via Annia to the consul of 153, and the Via Popillia to the consul of 132, while G. P. Verbrugghe, *Cl. Ph.*, 1973, 25 ff., believes the author of the Elogium to have been Appius Claudius Pulcher (*cos.* 143).

More important is the claim of the author of the inscription (and both Popillius and Annius were opponents of the Gracchi) to have been the first man to make the shepherds give place to the ploughmen, an apparent link with the Gracchan agrarian scheme. If the link is valid, it would appear that the opponents of the Gracchi were making a virtue of necessity and trying to claim some credit for the reform. However, it is just possible that the magistrate is referring to local action to help the inhabitants of his Forum or to his activities in Sicily (cf. P. Fraccaro, *Opuscula*, II, 55 ff.; Astin, *Scipio Aemilianus*, 354). [p. 25]

18 RE-ELECTION TO THE TRIBUNATE. It is difficult to decide from Appian's confused account (*BC*, 1, 21) whether re-election was formally legalized or not. See Jones, *op. cit.* in n. 14 above. Carbo's proposal does not necessarily involve the assumption that re-election had hitherto been illegal: it was aimed at removing the ambiguity which had clouded the issue in 133. The matter was apparently soon settled: at any rate we hear of no agitation when Gaius Gracchus stood for a second tribunate in 123. [p. 26]

19 WORKING OF LAND-COMMISSION. Nine boundary-stones (*cippi*) established by the *triumviri* survive: they give the names of the men, and come from Campania, Lucania, Apulia and Picenum, but it is hazardous to try to establish the developing geographical patterns of the whole distribution from so few stones. See A. Degrassi, *Inscriptiones Latinae Liberae Rei Publicae* (1957), p. 269 ff. and Greenidge, *Sources*[2], 14, for the stones. On the carrying-through of the agrarian reform see J. Molthagen, *Historia*, 1973, 423 ff. Another stone, recently found in Apulia (see M. Panni, *Ist. Lombardo Acad.*, 1977; Stockton, *The Gracchi* (1979), 60), names only Flaccus and C. Gracchus (i.e. it dates to the period after Crassus' death and Carbo's appointment). On the need for caution in relating these stones to the developing plan of settlement and surviving centuriation see M. Frederiksen, *Dial. de arch.*, 1970–71, 330 ff. [p. 26]

20 ALLIED GRIEVANCES. It is not very likely, though possible, that the commissioners would call into question *ager publicus* which had been granted to Latin communities as corporations and of which the leases would be guaranteed by treaty. For a suggestion that the Latins possibly held comparatively more *ager publicus* than the other Italian allies see E. Badian, *Dialoghi di Archeologia* IV–V (1970–71), 398. [p. 26]

21 SCIPIO AND THE LAND-COMMISSION. Appian (*BC*, 1, 19, 2) who describes Scipio's action is not very clear. It is sometimes argued that the judicial powers of the commissioners were transferred to an inactive consul and thus the whole effective work of the commission was hamstrung. Thus again recently R. A. Bauman, *Historia*, 1979, 384 ff., argues that they were so transferred to the consul who could delegate to the triumvirs as long as he remained in Italy. This view is less probable than that given in the text: see H. Last, *CAH*, IX, 42 f. and more briefly F. B. Marsh, *History of the Roman World 146–31 BC*, 3rd. ed., p. 409, n. to p. 48. [p. 26]

22 CENSUS FIGURES. The precise interpretation of the figures given by Livy and others is very debatable: probably in theory they represent all adult male citizens, though in practice some men may have failed to register. A. H. M. Jones (*Ancient Economic History*, p. 6) believes that though they are not reliable for demographic purposes, yet the rise in 125 B.C. does reflect the effect of Tiberius' land bill. An alternative is to suppose that the rise in 125 was due to the censors having generously enrolled a number of Italians. See also ch. III, n. 26. On the Roman census figures in general see P. A. Brunt, *Italian Manpower, 225 BC–A.D. 14* (1971), and 77 ff. for the census of the Gracchan period. [p. 26]

23 SCIPIO'S DEATH. For a lively discussion of 'Whodunnit' see J. Carcopino, *op. cit.*, ch. iii. A fragment from Laelius' funeral oration for Scipio *may* suggest a natural death: Malcovati, *ORF*[2], p. 121; cf. E. Badian, *JRS*, 1956, 220. [p. 27]

24 PENNUS' EDICT. E. Badian has pointed out (*For. Cl.*, 177) that Pennus' bill must fall in the early months of 126 (not 125), since it was attacked by Gaius Gracchus who left Rome in 126 for a two-years' quaestorship in Sardinia. Attempts, which have been made to link this measure with Flaccus' citizenship bill of 126, are viewed with caution by D. Stockton, *The Gracchi* (1979), 94 f. [p. 27]

25 FLACCUS. It is often said that the People, unwilling to share their advantages with the allies, failed to support Flaccus, who was thus more easily persuaded by the Senate to go to Gaul. But E. Badian (*For. Cl.*, 178) accepts Appian's statement that the Roman People supported Flaccus and believes that their opposition to Italian enfranchise-ment was not yet strongly developed. See also Badian, *Dialoghi di Archeologia* IV–V (1970–71), 391 ff. On Flaccus' motives see U. Hall, *Athenaeum*, 1977, 280 ff.; on his career see W. L. Reiter, *Athenaeum*, 1978, 125 ff. [p. 27]

26 FREGELLAE. For the possibility that Fregellae was not popular with other Latin states see E. Badian, *Cl. Rev.*, 1955, 23 (but contrast E. Malcovati, *Athenaeum*, 1955, 137 ff.). Many Samnites and Paelignians, who spoke Oscan, had migrated to Fregellae in the second century. Since the Romans disliked 'Oscans', this may help to explain their ruthlessness: cf. E. T. Salmon, *Phoenix*, 1962, 110. E. Badian (*Dialoghi di Archeologia* IV–V (1970–71), 389 ff.) regards the revolt of Fregellae as due to special local causes and not a symptom of a widespread discontent among the Latins. It was probably at this time (cf. G. Tibiletti, *Rend. dell'Istituto Lomb.* 1953, 57 f.) that a measure was passed which granted Roman citizenship to all magistrates in Latin colonies (cf. p. 17), thus strengthening the loyalty of the local governing class to Rome. [p. 27]

27 GAIUS' SPEECHES. For the surviving fragments see H. Malcovati, *Oratorum Romanorum Fragmenta*, 2nd ed. 1955. [p. 27]

28 GAIUS' LEGISLATION. On the chronology see H. Last, *CAH*, IX, 49 ff. and n. 34 below; also D. Stockton, *The Gracchi* (1979), 226 ff. Confusion may have arisen because Appian has put into Gaius' second tribunate some of the measures that may really belong to that part of his first tribunate that fell after his *election* to his second term, i.e. July to Dec. 123. Cf. Badian (*For. Cl.*, 181): the year 123 'produces the impression of a lull'. On the other hand P. A. Brunt (in Seager, *Crisis*, 146 ff.) argues, against Last's view, that Gracchus' judiciary law and indeed most of his legislation should be placed in the first half of 123, i.e. he 'tried to consolidate support among all classes outside the Senate at the very beginning of his tribunician career, and his projects of reform apart from his *rogatio de sociis* (which, as he must have known, was more likely to alienate than secure goodwill), were launched at once'. U. Hall, *Athenaeum*, 1972, 2 ff., believes that no law to legalize the re-election of tribunes can be assigned to the Gracchans and that in 123 Gaius at first did not consider himself as a candidate for re-election. If so, he may have tried to push through much legislation early in 123. On his re-election see also D. Stockton, *The Gracchi* (1979), 169 ff. [p. 28]

29 LEX AGRARIA. The statement of a writer on field-surveying (*gromaticus*) of unknown date, named Siculus Flaccus, that Gaius enacted that no one should possess more than 200 *iugera* in Italy, can scarcely mean that Gaius reduced the 500 to 200 *iugera*, nor is Carcopino's view likely that the size of the allotments was raised from 30 to 200 *iugera*. Possibly the reference is to allotments in colonies. See A. R. Hands, *Mnemosyne*, 1976, 176 ff. D. Stockton, *The Gracchi* (1979), 132 ff., argues that Gaius' law empowered the commissioners to dispose of public land outside Italy as well as within and envisaged founding colonies as well as viritim assignments. [p. 28]

30 THE EQUITES. Cf. R. J. Rowlands, 'C. Gracchus and the Equites', *TAPA*, 1965, 361 ff., who believes that Gracchus deliberately aimed at weakening the Senate and strength-ening the Equites (and helping the lower classes) and thus hoped to reform the constitution on the lines of the Polybian mixed constitution. Rowlands has also argued (*Phoenix*, 1969, 372 ff.) that in 123 Gaius had the support in the Senate not only of the old followers of his brother but also some of Aemilianus' old associates, but the latter abandoned him when in 122 he proceeded to more extreme measures. [p. 29].

31 GRACCHUS' LEX IUDICIARIA. The view that Gracchus' legislation on the juries in the

quaestio de rebus repetundis fell into two stages (as, e.g., H. Last in *CAH*, X) has recently been upheld by A. H. M. Jones (*Proc. Cambr. Philological Soc.*, 1960, 39 ff.). Although he rejects two of the arguments on which this view rested, he has strengthened the third; he believes that the curious figure of 450 jurors, mentioned in the Naples Tablet (see below), was taken over from a previous law. This cannot have been the *lex Calpurnia* of 149, but will have been Gracchus' first proposal (to add Equites to the Senate) and should be identified with a mysterious *lex Iunia* which will have been promulgated or passed in 123 B.C. As to the main law, carried in 122, a large part of a *lex de rebus repetundis* survives on a bronze tablet from Naples (sometimes referred to as the Tabula Bembina because of its association with Cardinal Bembo) and there can be little reasonable doubt that it is part of Gracchus' law. (Text in Riccobono, *Fontes Iuris Romani AnteJustiniani*, i. 94 ff., E. H. Warmington, *Remains of Old Latin*, iv, 317 ff.; E. G. Hardy, *Six Roman Laws*, 1 ff.) The attempt by J. Carcopino to identify it with the law of Glaucia (on which see below) has been adequately rejected by J. P. V. D. Balsdon in a valuable paper (*Papers Brit. Sch. Rome*, 1938, 98 ff. = Seager, *Crisis*, 132 ff.) on the history of the extortion-court. In two passages Cicero (1 *Verr.* 51; 2 *Verr.* i, 26) refers to a *Lex Acilia Repetundarum*, which has generally been identified with Gracchus' law (e.g. by Mommsen and Last). In a discussion of the *leges de repetundis* G. Tibiletti (*Athenaeum*, 1953, pp. 5 ff.) denied this and, though accepting the identification of the Naples inscription with the law of Gracchus, has supposed the *lex Acilia* to be a measure of lesser importance of *c.* III B.C. E. Badian, however, has successfully defended the identification of the *lex Acilia* with the inscription (*AJP*, 1954, 374 ff. and 1975, 67 ff.).

The debate continues. E. S. Gruen, who accepts the identification of the Naples tablet with the Lex Acilia as part of Gracchus' legislation, has rejected Jones' view of the Lex Iunia (*Rom. Pol.*, 293 f.) and also the attempt by A. R. Hands (*Latomus*, 1965, 225 ff.) to represent the lex Acilia as an anti-Gracchan measure. The interpretation of C. Nicolet (*L'Ordre Équestre* (1966), 109 ff., 482 ff.) is precisely opposite to that of Hands: Gracchus sponsored the lex repetundarum but his enemies proposed enrolling Equites in the Senate; see against this Gruen, 295 f. Finally, P. A. Brunt (see Seager, *Crisis*, 107 ff.) argues that Gracchus' legislation covered more than the *quaestio de repetundis* and deprived Senators of other judicial functions: all the latter, both civil and criminal, were to be dealt with by a mixed panel of senators and Equites. The evidence, however, for the existence of permanent *quaestiones*, other than the *de repetundis*, at the time of Gracchus is frail (but see also Brunt, *Tijdschrift voor Rechtsgeschiedenis*, 1964, 444 ff. in an important review of W. Kunkel, *Untersuchungen zur Entwicklung des röm. Kriminalverfahrens in vorsullanischer Zeit*). Brunt also would date the judiciary legislation to the first half of 123 (cf. above n. 28). See now also D. Stockton, *The Gracchi* (1979), 138 ff., 230 ff., who believes that Gaius passed a general *lex iudiciaria* as well as a *lex de pecuniis repetundis* (and that the inscription is the *repetundae* law of Gaius and more likely than not is a *lex Acilia*).

H. B. Mattingly, *JRS*, 1969, 129 ff., has attempted to rearrange the fragments of Tabula Bembina and to relate them to the fragmentary law from Tarentum (on which see ch. III, n. 18). In *JRS*, 1970, 154 ff. and *Cl. Qu.*, 1974, 255 ff., he adduces some complicated arguments to suggest that the Tabula Bembina is not the law of Gaius Gracchus but is identical with the law of the Tabula Tarentina and is likely to have been the law of Servilius Glaucia (on which see ch. III, n. 19). This view is refuted by A. N. Sherwin-White (*JRS*, 1972, 83 ff.) who reaffirms the usual view that the Tabula Bembina *is* the Gracchan law.

In the inscription unfortunately the passage that should give the positive qualifications of the jurors is missing, but the law contains many interesting details about procedure in the court. On procedure see M. I. Henderson, *JRS*, 1951, 71 ff. and A. N. Sherwin-White, *JRS*, 1952, 43 ff. The law fixed (though possibly not for the first time: cf. Nicolet, *op. cit.*, 47 ff.) the equestrian census, i.e. the minimum qualification for enrolment in the Ordo; the figure was probably 400,000 sesterces. On the Equites see above p. 8 f. and the literature cited in ch. I, n. 9. The jurors were first known as *iudices*, but apparently soon (sometime between 122 and 88) they claimed or acquired the title Equites. The use of Equites in Cicero's day is obscure; in general terms it meant all freeborn Roman citizens who were not senators and who were worth at least 400,000 sesterces. The equestrian jurors were either distinct from the equestrian centuries which were still limited to 1800 *iuniores* or else, as argued by M. I. Henderson (*JRS*, 1963, 61 ff. = Seager, *Crisis*, 69 ff.), the equestrian centuries no longer were limited to 1800 members and the mere census qualification allowed a citizen to call himself an *eques Romanus*. Cf. also E. Badian's remarks (*Roman Imperialism in the Late Republic*[2] (1968), vii ff.). [p. 29]

32 NE QUIS IUDICIO CIRCUMVENIATUR. N. J. Miners has argued (*Cl. Qu.*, 1958, 241 ff.) that this law was directed against senators who conspired to secure a false condemnation of a Roman citizen on a capital charge. U. Ewins (*JRS*, 1960, 94 ff.) also dissociates it from the extortion court: rather, it was designed to prevent unfair use of judicial powers by senators against the people; although similar in object to the *lex Sempronia de provocatione* (Miners, following Mommsen, would identify the two laws), it will have been a separate law. (It will also have been adapted by the younger Drusus in 91 to cover bribery by Equites.) See also A. H. M. Jones, *op. cit.* in n. 31. The provision which excluded Equites from the ambit of the bill makes better sense if the bill was directed not against the *quaestio de repetundis*, which Gracchus at some point handed over to the Equites, but against the special tribunals which his *Lex Sempronia de provocatione* established: though such courts could now be set up only on the authority of the People, they would be manned by members of the senatorial class and 'Gracchus, from the experience of 132, was worried about senators, not *equites*' (Gruen, *Rom. Pol.*, 86). [p. 30]

33 DRUSUS' LEGISLATION. A passage of Sallust (*Iug.* 69. 4) has often been taken (see H. Last, *CAH*, X, 72) as implying that Drusus' measure protecting the Latins was carried out. But see E. Badian, *For. Cl.*, 190 and below ch. III n. 17. [p. 30]

34 LEX RUBRIA. References in Livy, Plutarch and Appian suggest that Rubrius was tribune in 122, though other writers assign his tribunate to 123. In support of 122 see H. Last, *CAH*, IX, 891. One of the strongest arguments for 122 has been a reference in an inscription from Astypalaea (Greenidge, *Sources*[2], 84) to a *lex Rubria Acilia* (thus if Acilius was tribune in 122, cf. n. 31 above, then Rubrius must have been also). But Tibiletti (*op. cit.*) has argued that the phrase κατᾶτόν νόμον ετόν τε͂ 'Ρόβριον καὶ τόν' Ακίλιον in the inscription must refer not to a joint law but to two laws, one carried by Rubrius and the other by Acilius, and that therefore the men were tribunes in different years. If this argument is accepted (as it is by Badian, *op. cit.*) and the possibility is excluded that they carried two laws in the same year, and if Acilius belongs to 122, then Rubrius' law to found Junonia would belong to 123. See E. Badian, *For. Cl.* 300 f., but he now (*Historia*, 1962, 206, n. 31 = Seager, *Crisis*, 12) doubts the identity of the Rubrius of the inscription with the founder of Junonia. A large area in N.E. Tunisia still shows traces of the division of the land into units (*centuriae*) of 200 *iugera* each; part of this may represent allotments at Junonia: see J. Bradford, *Ancient Landscapes* (1957), 197 ff. and pl. 48; R. Chevallier, *Mélanges d'arch.*, 1958, 61 ff.; K. Johannsen, *Die lex agraria des Jahres 111 v. Chr.* (Munich Dissertation, 1971), 341 ff. On the rural centuriation by Gaius and the urban grid system of the Augustan colony of Carthage, see E. M. Wightman, *New Light on ancient Carthage* (1980, ed. by J. G. Pedley), 34 ff. [p. 30]

35 FANNIUS. E. S. Gruen (*Rom. Pol.*, 93) thinks that Fannius was never closely attached to the Gracchi: his earlier connexions were with the Scipionic group. C. Gracchus supported his candidature for 122 only in default of better candidates (L. Opimius was certainly worse). [p. 31]

36 THE FRANCHISE BILL. E. Badian (*For. Cl.*, 185 ff., 299 ff.) has argued that Gracchus proposed only one *lex de sociis*, which was vetoed by Drusus (Dec. 123–Jan. 122); Gracchus then left for Africa. With the help of the renegade consul Fannius, Drusus developed his programme, which was to stir up the Roman people (hitherto not much concerned by proposals in favour of the allies) against the Italians, and secondly to split the Italians by setting the Latins against the rest. Thus when Gracchus on his return to Rome promulgated his bill, it was defeated. K. Meister, *Chiron*, 1976, 113 ff., argues for a *rogatio* of Gaius (mid 122) which granted Roman rights to Latins, but only voting rights (not Latin rights) to the other allies. [p. 31]

37 FAMILY FORTUNES. E. S. Gruen (*Rom. Pol.*, 98) writes: 'The slaughter of the Gracchani entailed the final demise of the old Claudio-Fulvian group . . . The Sempronii Gracchi vanish from the pages of Republican history. The Fulvii never again held curule office in Rome. The proud patrician Claudii turn up again only as hangers-on of a more power- ful political group.' [p. 32]

38 ASIA AND ARISTONICUS. On Aristonicus see F. C. Thomes, *La rivolta di Aristonico e le origini della provincia Romana d'Asia* (1969); Z. Rubinsohn, *Rendiconti dell'Ist. Lomb.*, 1973. 546 ff.; C. Delplace, *Athenaeum*, 1978, 20 ff.; J. Hopp, *Untersuchungen zur Geschichte des letzen Attaliden* (1977); on the commission under Scipio Nasica in 133–2 see B. Schleussner, *Chiron*, 1976, 97 ff. For Asia under the Romans see D. Magie, *The Roman Rule in Asia Minor* (1950); for the settlement of the province A. H. M. Jones, *Cities of the Eastern Roman Provinces* (1971), 57 ff.; see also A. N. Sherwin-White, *JRS*, 1977, 62 ff. for Roman involvement in Asia Minor from 167 to 88 B.C. (66 ff. for the inheritance of Attalus). Details of the terms of Attalus' will are obscure. The city of Pergamum itself and probably some of the Greek cities on the coast were to be free. Translations of three inscriptions relating to Rome's settlement will be found in Lewis and Reinhold, *Roman Civilization*, I, 321 ff. One (*OGIS*, 338; Greenidge, *Sources²*, p. 9) is a decree of Pergamum passed before Rome had ratified the will; another (*OGIS* 435, Sherk, *Roman Documents from the Greek East* (1969), n. 11; cf. T. Drew-Bear, *Historia*, 1972, 75 ff.) confirms an earlier decree of the Senate, probably of 133, regarding the settlement (cf. Sherwin-White, *JRS*, 1977, 68; and a third (Dittenberger, *Sylloge* 694) is a decree celebrating the grant of the status of Rome's ally to a city, probably Pergamum, for its help against Aristonicus. Mithridates of Pontus later claimed that the Romans had forged Attalus' will (Sallust, *Hist.* iv, 69M), but wrongly, as is shown by *OGIS* 338. We also have two fragmentary copies of a *Senatus Consultum de agro Perga- meno* (Sherk, n. 2; Greenidge and Clay, p. 278) which is usually dated to 129 B.C. (though see H. Mattingly, *AJP*, 1972, 412 ff.): the consuls and a large advisory body heard a dispute between some *publicani* and Pergamum concerning some boundaries, presumably when the *publicani* tried to collect some of the taxes on the public land which had been sold by the censors of 131. The Pergamenes apparently won their case. Cf. E. Badian, *Publicans and Sinners* (1972), 60, 132. – The attempt by Carcopino to show that Attalus died *after* Tiberius and therefore to disprove the account (not recorded by Appian) of Tiberius' use of the legacy, has generally been rejected – Aristonicus' revolt is likely to have started on a serious scale only late in 133 or in 132. The extent of his initial successes is doubtful: probably southwards to Mysia but not to Caria, and possibly northwards to Cyzicus. – A small group of Pergamene coins (cistophori), which bear the title 'King', are to be referred to the pretender Aristonicus and illustrate his claim to be

heir of the Attalids (cf. the coinage of Eunus in Sicily: ch. I, n. 15): see E. S. G. Robinson, *Numismatic Chronicle*, 1954, pp. 1 ff. On further problems arising from the coinage see E. Badian, *JRS*, 1980, 202; J. P. Adams, *Historia*, 1981, 302 ff. – Greater Phrygia was claimed by the kings of Pontus and Bithynia. Aquilius, who is alleged to have received the larger bribe from the former, was granted a triumph but was later tried before the senatorial *quaestio de repetundis*; but he was acquitted, and Gaius Gracchus cited this scandal in justification for transferring the court to the Equites. [p. 33]

39 GAUL. Contradictions in the sources make many details of the campaigns in Gaul uncertain. See C. Jullian, *Histoire de la Gaule*, III, 1 ff.; J. Carcopino, *Histoire Romaine*, II, 275 ff.; C. H. Benedict, 'The Romans in southern Gaul', *AJP*, 1942, 38 ff., and *A History of Narbo* (1941), ch. i. For the milestone see Degrassi, *Inscr. Lat. Lib. Rei Publ.* n. 460a; Greenidge, *Sources²*, 49: this suggests the possibility that Domitius continued as proconsul till 118 and that his triumph was delayed till then. An inscription from Olympia records men from Achaean cities serving under Cn. Domitius Ahenobarbus against Galatae; almost certainly in these campaigns: see J. Reynolds, *JRS*, 1966, 118. E. Badian has argued (*For. Cl.*, 264, n. 3, and 287 f., and more fully in *Melanges Piganiol* (1966), 901 ff.) that Gaul was not established as a province (i.e. formally became a sphere to which a Roman magistrate was annually appointed as governor) until near the end of the century after Marius' victories over the Germans. C. Ebel, *Transalpine Gaul: the Emergence of the Roman Province* (1976), argues for a Roman protectorate and virtual *de facto* province in southern Gaul from the early second century, but see J. Richardson, *JRS*, 1979, 157 f. On the continuing interest in, and patronage of, Gaul by the Domitii and Licinii see E. Badian, *For. Cl.*, 264 f. [p. 34]

40 NARBO. The date of the foundation is uncertain. Velleius i. 15.5 dates it to 118, and this seemed to be supported by the coinage when the latter was also assigned to the same date (cf. H. Mattingly, *JRS*, 1922, 230 ff.). Evidence from the hoards led E. A. Sydenham (*CRR*, 64 f.) to date the coins *c.* 112–109, and H. B. Mattingly (*Hommages Grenier* (1962), 1159 ff.) to date the foundation to 110, but this interpretation has been doubted by C. A. Hersch, *Num. Chron.*, 1966, 71 ff., and M. Crawford believes the coins are nearer to 118 than Mattingly thought (cf. Badian, *Roman Imperialism²* (1968), 98, who himself would date the colony as late as 115, *op. cit.*, 24). H. B. Mattingly now accepts (*Num. Chron.*, 1969, 95 ff.) 114 for Narbo. B. Levick, *Cl. Qu.*, 1971, 170 ff., supports 118 for the foundation, but concedes that the coins might be a later commemorative issue of 114–13. M. Crawford, *RRC*, 71 ff., after discussion dates both foundation and issue to 118. – The founding of Narbo has been seen depicted on an altar dedicated to Neptune supposedly by a descendant of Domitius (the consul of 32 B.C.?): see *CAH*, Plates iv, p. 86; but other interpretations are more probable (e.g. enrolment of soldiers rather than of colonists; census, as R. M. Ogilvie, *JRS*, 1961, 37). – Neither Brunt in Seager (*Crisis*, 97) nor Badian (*Rom. Imp.²*, 24) admit equestrian interests behind Narbo's foundation. Cf. also E. T. Salmon, *Roman Colonization* (1969), 121 f. [p. 35]

41 THE BALEARIC ISLANDS. M. G. Morgan, who discusses Roman motives for intervention in the Balearic Islands (*California Studies in Classical Antiquity*, 1969, 217 ff.) notes a recent influx of pirates from Sardinia and Gaul into them. [p. 35]

CHAPTER III

1 SOURCES FOR 121–100 B.C. These are in the main the same authors as those mentioned in ch. II, n. 1. See Greenidge and Clay, *op. cit.* Appian's narrative (*BC*, I, 27–32) is very brief. Plutarch's *Life of Marius* and in part that of *Sulla* are valuable; for his

account of Marius' northern campaigns Plutarch drew on Posidonius (on these see also the fragments of Appian's *Celtica* and the geographer Strabo, VII, 293). For the African campaign Sall'ist's *Bellum Iugurthinum* is the chief source: see below, n. 13. Some scraps of Granius Licinianus, who lived in the second century A.D., deal with the year 105 B.C.; his work is in the Livian tradition. A number of important inscriptions are mentioned in the following notes. Coinage becomes a more useful source since the types on the *denarii* begin to show considerable variety from about 120 B.C.: see E. A. Sydenham, *CRR* and M. H. Crawford, *RRC*.

For a general survey of the period of Marius and Sulla in the light of work done in the decade or two before 1970 see E. Gabba, *Aufstieg*, I, i (1972), 764 f. [p. 36]

2 P. DECIUS SUBULO. He was subsequently prosecuted in 119 in the interests of the Optimates, on a charge of *repetundarum*, but he was acquitted by the equestrian jury. His importance has been emphasized by E. Badian (*JRS*, 1956, 91 ff.). Decius rallied equestrian strength against the Optimates, and his acquittal was in the same year that Carbo was prosecuted and Marius became tribune, helped by the Metelli. The year 119 thus saw mounting pressure by the class that now controlled the law courts, conscious of its powers and supported by useful allies (cf. *Historia*, 1962, 215. = Seager, *Crisis*, 21). On Decius' trial see also Gruen (*Rom. Pol.*, 109 ff.) who doubts that the charge was *de repetundis*, and consequently the jury may not have been equestrian; in any case Gruen believes it to be unwise to refer to the Equites as if they were a compact unit with a consistent policy and to suppose that any *factio*, as the Metelli, could win the support of the *equester ordo* for any length of time. [p. 36]

3 OPIMIUS AND THE SCU. For the arguments used see Cicero, *de orat.* 2. 132; *part. orat.* 104. For a fundamental discussion of the questions at issue see H. Last, *CAH*, IX, 85 ff. For further discussion of the *SCU* see A. W. Lintott, *Violence in Republican Rome* (1968), 149 ff. [p. 36]

4 PINPRICKS TO THE SENATE. Valerius Maximus records (5. 3. 2) that the elderly Princeps Senatus, P. Lentulus, who had helped to storm the Aventine with Opimius' men, was forced by public opinion to withdraw to Sicily; if this is true, the Optimates did not have it all their own way. Further, Q. Mucius Scaevola the Augur, who may have shared his family's sympathy towards the Gracchi (p. 22), was acquitted when accused by T. Albucius of extortion in Asia (119). The satirist Lucilius parodied this trial in his second book. For Scaevola and his trial see Gruen (*Rom. Pol.*, 112 ff.), who doubts his earlier Gracchan sympathies. For other trials in this decade see Gruen, ch. iv. [p. 37]

5 THE LAND COMMISSIONERS. An inscription from Carthage refers to three commissioners, Galba, Papirius Carbo and Calpurnius Bestia (*ILS*, 28; Greenidge, *Sources²*, 51). These men may have formed a special African commission If, however, Carbo is C. Carbo the Gracchan renegade (and not one of his brothers), the inscription must be earlier than his death in 119 and the men may have been the Gracchan land-commissioners with Galba and Bestia replacing C. Gracchus and Fulvius Flaccus: if so, the commission will have had an anti-Gracchan bias, since only Galba was pro-Gracchan. See also H. Chantraine, *Untersuch, z. röm. Geschichte* (1959), 15 ff. [p. 37]

6 THE AGRARIAN LAWS. These are recorded by Appian (*BC*, 1. 27), who (probably incorrectly) ascribes the second law to Thorius (cf. Cicero, *Brut.* 36. 136. For another view see Broughton, *MRR*, I, 542). For the law of 111 see E. G. Hardy, *Six Roman Laws*, 35 ff.; Warmington, *ROL*, iv, 370; it also granted all colonies and *municipia* security of *ager publicus*, and dealt with the sale of land in Africa and at Corinth (to provide funds for the war against Jugurtha?). An agrarian law, *lex Mamilia Roscia*, probably belongs to 55 B.C. rather than to 109 (cf. p. 38). Recent views on the *ager publicus* and on

Appian's three agrarian laws are assessed by E. Badian (*Historia*, 1962, 209 ff. = Seager, *Crisis*, 15 ff.; cf. Badian, *Studies*, 235 ff. on lex Thoria). His own conclusion is that Appian's second law (the *lex Thoria*) is the *lex agraria* of 111 and that there was another law c. 109. See further K. Johannsen, *Die lex agraria des Jahres 111 v. Chr.* (Munich Dissertation, 1971) with text, and commentary and discussion of agrarian bills. K. Meister, *Historia*, 1974, 86 ff., argues that the Lex Thoria was the second of Appian's laws and belonged to 119/8 B.C. [p. 37]

6a METELLUS AND ILLYRIA. On the campaigns in Illyria in the late second century see M. G. Morgan, *Athenaeum*, 1971, 271 ff. [p. 38]

7 THE METELLI. The political fortunes of this dominant family during the decade are traced by Gruen (*Rom. Pol.*, ch. iv), who believes that they won the support of the Mucii Scaevolae, Licinii Crassi, Lutatii Catuli, Rutilii Rufi, Calpurnii Pisones, and perhaps the Livii Drusi, Scribonii Curiones, and Porcii Catones, as well as taking under the wing of the *factio* promising men of no prior political influence, like Aemilius Scaurus and M. Antonius. The senatorial opposition will have been led by men raised under the tutelage of the Scipionic circle and extremists who eliminated the Gracchan movement in 121. These families soon faded from view, e.g. the Popillii Laenates, Rupillii, Opimii, Manlii, and Fabii Maximi, while others, as the Papirii Carbones, Junii Bruti and Octavii emerged again only in the hectic days of civil war in the 80s. [p. 38]

8 SCAURUS. See G. Bloch, *Mélanges d'histoire anc.* 1909; P. Fraccaro, *Opuscula*, II (1957), 125 ff. His marriage to Metella may have been much later in his life (after 102 according to F. Münzer, *Römische Adelsparteien*, 280 f.). On his lack of political principle see A. R. Hands, *JRS*, 1959, 56 ff. [p. 38]

8a M. OCTAVIUS. On his date see J. G. Schovanek, *Historia*, 1972, 235 ff., 1977, 378 ff., who argues for a date in the 90s, as does G. Rickman, *The Corn Supply in Ancient Rome* (1980), 161 ff. [p. 39]

9 MARIUS' POLITICAL CAREER. On this see especially A. Passerini, *Athenaeum*, 1934, who amongst other things tries to distinguish the pro-Marian and anti-Marian threads in Plutarch's *Life of Marius*. Marius will have used whatever means lay to his hand to gain political power: winning the patronage of the Metelli (until he offended them), gaining wealth as a *publicanus*, forming links with the Equites. A *novus homo* had to create a *factio*; only after success could be hope to lead. On Marius, beside the work of Passerini already mentioned, see T. F. Carney, *A Biography of C. Marius* (Suppl. n. 1 of *Proc. Afr. Cl. Ass.*, 1962); J. Van Ooteghem, *Gaius Marius* (Brussels, 1964); E. Badian, 'Marius and the Nobles', *Durham Univ. Journal*, 1964, 141 ff.; Gruen, *Rom. Pol.*, passim, Badian (*JRS*, 1965, 93) and Carney (*op. cit.*, 20) find greater consistency in Marius' tribunician activities than Plutarch does. On Marius' trial for *ambitus* in 116 see Carney, *Acta Juridica*, 1959, 232 ff., and for coins bearing on Marius' career, Carney, *Num. Chron.*, 1959, 79 ff. Passerini's work on Marius has now been reprinted under the title *Studi su Caio Mario* (1971). On Marius' career from 99 to 88 B.C. see T. J. Luce, *Historia*, 1970, 161 ff. The significance of Marius' importance in general is assessed by E. Gabba, *Aufstieg*, I, i, 769 ff. [p. 39]

10 FREEDMEN. Scaurus probably confined freedmen to the four urban tribes in order to keep them out of the thirty-one rustic tribes. If, however, the law of Gracchus the censor of 169, which had restricted freedmen to one urban tribe, was still in force, Scaurus' measure to place them in the four urban tribes will have been more generous in purpose. S. Treggiari, *Roman Freedmen during the Late Republic* (1969), 47 ff., argues that Scaurus' measure was repressive. [p. 39]

11 THE VESTAL VIRGINS. On the political implications of their trial see Gruen, *Rom. Pol.*, 127 ff. [p. 39]

12 THE SITE OF CIRTA. The proposal of R. Charlier (*L'Antiquité classique*, 1950, 298 ff.) that Cirta should be identified with El Kef rather than with Constantine, though it might make the geography of the campaigns more intelligible, does not seem to be firmly based. [p. 39]

13 SALLUST'S BELLUM IUGURTHINUM. This is our chief authority for the war. But Sallust, who as governor of Africa after Caesar's reorganization of the province in 47 knew the country, did not set out to write a detailed military history. Rather, he wrote a political pamphlet, related to the politics of his own day: as a staunch supporter of Caesar and the Populares, he wanted to expose the corruption of the Optimates. Hence his main theme is to show how Marius, a *novus homo* and a Popularis, successfully challenged the nobility and saved the situation which the corruption of the nobles had created. He is less concerned with strategy or chronological or topographical accuracy than with the moral and political issues. Thus his charges of corruption against the senatorial leaders may well be exaggerated and highly coloured, even if they are not groundless as suggested by G. DeSanctis (*Problemi di storia antica*, 187 ff.); see also K. von Fritz, *TAPA*, 1943, 134 ff. and W. Allen, *Cl. Ph.*, 1938, 90 ff. The curious prominence that Sallust gives to Sulla, the rival of his hero Marius, is probably due to the fact that he made use of Sulla's *Memoirs* in writing the last part of his monograph. See also W. Steidle, *Sallusts Historische Monographien* (*Historia*, Einzelschr. Heft 3, 1958); A. La Penna, 'L'interpretazione sallustiana della guerra contro Giugurta' (*Ann. della Scuola Normale Sup. di Pisa*, 1959, 45–86); D. C. Earl, *The Political Thought of Sallust* (1961), esp. ch. V. R. Syme, *Sallust* (1964), chs. X and XI; Gruen, *Rom Pol.*, ch. V. On the actual declaration of war see J. W. Rich, *Declaring War in the Roman Republic in the Period of Transmarine Expansion* (1976), 48ff. [p. 40]

14 THE MAMILIAN COMMISSION. On this, its chairman and victims, see Gruen, *Rom. Pol.*, 142 ff. On Scaurus and the prosecution see G. V. Sumner, *Phoenix*, 1976, 73 ff. [p. 40]

15 ROMAN POLICY. On equestrian influence see De Sanctis, *op. cit.* [p. 41]

16 METELLUS AND JUGURTHA. On Metellus see De Sanctis, *op. cit.*, 215 ff. On the chronology and strategy see M. Holroyd, *JRS*, 1928, pp. 1 ff. [p. 41]

17 THE TURPILIUS AFFAIR. T. Turpilius Silanus, left by Metellus in command of the Roman garrison at Vaga, had shown kindness to the inhabitants, who then treacherously massacred the Roman troops. The unfortunate Turpilius was the sole survivor. Metellus was embarrassed but had to courtmartial and execute his officer and client. If the anecdote is true that Marius, as a member of the *consilium* that tried the case, argued powerfully for condemnation, the incident will have increased ill-feeling between Marius and Metellus. Sallust's remark (*Iug.*, 69, 4) that Turpilius was scourged and executed 'nam is civis ex Latio erat' has given rise to much discussion. It is thought by some to have retrospective bearing on Drusus' legislation (see above ch. II, n. 33), but this will not be so if E. Badian's contention is right (*For. Cl.*, 196) that Turpilius was a *praefectus fabrum* and as such a Roman citizen. Does 'civis ex Latio' mean 'a man with Latin rights' or 'a Latin who has become a Roman' or 'a Roman citizen who came from Latium'?

Sallust fails to record when Cirta fell to the Romans, a clear example of his lack of interest in military details. The other sources (the Livian tradition, Plutarch, Appian and Dio) add only a little. [p. 41]

18 CAEPIO'S JUDICIARY LAW. Although Tacitus (*Ann.* 12. 60. 4) records that this measure restored the *quaestio* to the Senate, the Livian tradition that it shared the court between the Senate and Equites is probably to be preferred. For a full discussion of this bill and that of Glaucia see J. P. V. D. Balsdon, *Papers of Brit. Sch. Rome*, 1938 = Seager, *Crisis*, 132 ff. A fragment of a *lex repetundarum* has recently been found at

Tarentum: for the suggestion that it is part of Caepio's law see G. Tibiletti, *Athenaeum*, 1953, 38 ff. E. Badian has argued (*Cl. Rev.*, 1954, 101) that Cicero *Pro Balbo*, 54 applies to Caepio, not to Glaucia, but contrast B. M. Levick, *Cl. Rev.*, 1967, 256 ff. E. Badian (*Historia*, 1962, 207 ff. = Seager, *Crisis*, 13 ff.) had advocated the view that if, as is possible, other *iudicia publica* besides the extortion court had been established by this time, then Caepio's measure probably applied to them all, both permanent and special. Caepio's purpose in diluting these equestrian special tribunals with senatorial jurors would be to try to prevent further excess such as the recent Mamilian commission had provoked, cf. Gruen, *Rom. Pol.*, 159. Glaucia's subsequent law (see next note), restoring equestrian juries, will then have applied only to the *quaestio de repetundis.* Cf. also B. P. Selecky, *Klio*, 1980, 389 ff. [p. 44]

19 GLAUCIA'S JUDICIARY LAW. This law (*a*) established a legal system known as *comperendinatio* by which a trial was divided into two separate parts, (*b*) extended prosecution to accessories to a crime, and, in view of Cicero's strong statement that Glaucia 'equestrem ordinem beneficio legis devinxerat' (*Brut.* 62. 224), it (*c*) re-established equestrian juries. The date of the law is not now usually thought to be 111 (Mommsen's date), but rather some time after Caepio's bill either in 104 or 101, with a slight balance in favour of 104. On the whole question see Balsdon, *op. cit.*, n. 18. See also below, n. 23. [p. 44]

20 TOLOSA INQUIRY. Details are obscure: see J. Lengle, *Hermes*, 1931, 302 ff.; Gruen, *Rom. Pol.*, 162 ff. For other trials of 104, see Gruen, 171 ff. and *TAPA*, 1964, 99 ff. [p. 46]

21 QUAESTORS AND COMMANDERS. On the legal and conventional ties that bound quaestors and their commanding officers see L. A. Thompson, *Historia*, 1962, 339 ff. [p. 46]

22 CAEPIO'S TRIAL. This is sometimes dated as late as 95, but Licinianus (p. 21 Bonn) implies that it preceded that of Mallius which was in 103 (or 101). For arguments which place Norbanus' tribunate in 103 see Broughton, *MRR*, i, 565–6. Norbanus himself was prosecuted in 95 for his share in these disturbances on a charge of *minuta maiestas* under Saturninus' law, but was acquitted (see ch. IV, n. 2). In 103 or soon afterwards Scaurus tried to secure the conviction for extortion of C. Memmius, the popular leader of 111, and of Flavius Fimbria, consul with Marius in 104, but both were acquitted by (presumably) equestrian juries. [p. 46]

23 LEX APULLEIA DE MAIESTATE. A fragment of a Roman law has been found at Bantia in S. Italy (see Riccobono, *FIRA*, p. 82; Warmington, *ROL*, iv, 294). This has been identified with Saturninus' *lex de maiestate* by Stuart Jones (*JRS*, 1926, 171) and others. G. Tibiletti (*Athenaeum*, 1953) argues that there is nothing to connect it especially with Saturninus and that it is a *lex repetundarum* and probably is part of the *lex Servilia Glauciae.* E. J. Yarnold (*AJP*, 1957, 163 ff.) argues that it was part of Gaius Gracchus' law which forbade the passing of a capital sentence on a citizen *iniussu populi* (see p. 32). *Maiestas* is the subject of a book by R. A. Bauman. *The Crimen Maiestatis in the Roman Republic and Augustan Principate* (1967, but on this see P. Garnsey, *JRS*, 1969, 283 ff.). [p. 46]

24 LEX FRUMENTARIA. In *Ad Herennium* I. 12, 21, our only source for this bill, 'semis' should perhaps be read for 'semissibus' (i.e. the price would be $6\frac{1}{3}$ *asses*, not $\frac{5}{6}$ of an *as*, per *modius*, as suggested by H. Last (*CAH*, IX, 165), who also gives reasons for placing the measure in 103 rather than 100. If, however, the measure is put in 100 (cf. Broughton, *MRR*, i, 578), the cheaper price will be the more probable, since Saturninus was then in greater need of popular support. Two quaestors, Piso (L. Calpurnius Piso, praetor 90?) and Q. Caepio (praetor 91?), struck coins bearing the head of Saturn and two figures on a bench, together with a corn-ear and the inscription AD FRV EMV ('for

the purchase of corn'). See Crawford, *RRC.*, 33 ff., who dates them to 100 (rather than 99 as H. Mattingly, *Cl. Rev.*, 1969, 267 ff.; contra A. R. Hands, *Cl. Rev.*, 1972, 12 f.) and believes (p. 73) that Saturninus' bill was passed and that the Senate thought better of opposition and ordered the quaestors to strike money to finance it. [p. 46]

25 THE PSEUDO-GRACCHUS. A certain Equitius claimed to be a son of Ti. Gracchus until unmasked by Sempronia; thereafter he was used as a tool by Saturninus until he was killed on the first day of his tribunate of 99. [p. 47]

26 RECRUITMENT OF CAPITECENSI. This is suggested by two passages of Polybius (VI, 23, 15; 39, 15) which imply that many of the *assidui* (the men in the five classes) could no longer equip themselves properly when entering the army, and also by a speech of Ti. Gracchus (Plut. *Ti. Gr.* 9). This view may be held even by those who are not persuaded by the theory advanced by E. Gabba (*Athenaeum*, 1949, 173 ff.; 1952, 161 ff.: = *Republican Rome, the Army and the Allies* (1976), 1 ff.) that many *proletarii* had been introduced into the legions by means of reducing the minimum monetary qualification for service; he believes that the census figures included only *assidui* and not *proletarii*, and he explains the rise in the figures between 131 and 125 B.C. by some 75,000 men as the result of a recent reduction of this minimum figure. He also examines Marius' *dilectus* of 107 and suggests that many of his volunteers came from the country plebs, the *agrestes* who supported his consular candidature (Sallust, *Ing.* 73, 6). See R. E. Smith, *Service in the Post-Marian Army* (1958). Since many of Marius' African veterans were settled on allotments in Africa (cf. n. 31), his northern army will have comprised Rutilius' forces together with further volunteers. In this way he will have increased the number of men dependent on him: his *clientela* was growing. See P. A. Brunt, 'The Army and land in the Roman Revolution', *JRS*, 1962, 69 ff. On the army in general see R. E. Smith, *op. cit. supra*, J. Harmand, *L'armée et le soldat à Rome de 107 à 50 avant notre ère* (1967), E. H. Erdmann, *Die Rolle des Heeres in der Zeit von Marius bis Caesar* (1971) and E. Gabba, *RR Army*. On this theme compare also *Problèmes de la guerre à Rome*, edited by J. P. Brisson (1969). [p. 47]

27 THE PILUM. See T. F. Carney, *Cl. Qu.*, 1955, 203 ff. [p. 48]

28 MILITARY TRIBUNES. J. Suolahti (*The Junior Officers of the Roman Army in the Republican Period* (1955)) has shown how the social status of the military tribunes declined in the second century: the office tended to be ignored by older distinguished senatorial families and to be filled more by equestrian country families. At the same time Marius' tactical reforms enhanced the importance of the centurions. This, together with the increasing proletarianization of the army, gradually led to the development of a new military caste, bound more closely to the army commanders. The full significance of these developments became clear only after the Social War. Cf. also R. E. Smith, *op. cit.*, n. 26, especially ch. v, T. F. Carney, *Bibliography of C. Marius*. 32 f. [p. 28]

29 FOSSA MARIANA. Traces of this have been found by underwater exploration. See P. Diôle, *4000 Years under the Sea* (Eng. Trans., 1954), ch. 5. [p. 49]

30 AQUAE SEXTIAE AND VERCELLAE. Despite Plutarch's long account of Aquae Sextiae (*Marius*, 18–21) details are obscure. No reliance can be placed in the casualty figures (which Orosius put at nearly half a million); they may have numbered some 70,000–100,000 captured and killed. On the strategy of the Germans see F. Miltner, *Klio*, 1940, 289 ff., but E. Badian believes (*Historia*, 1962, 217 = Seager, *Crisis*, 23) that Miltner has exaggerated the ability and cohesion of the barbarians in postulating an organized three-pronged attack. On the invasions see E. Demougeot, *Latomus*, 1978, 910 ff. On the campaign of Catulus in 102 see R. G. Lewis, *Hermes*, 1974, 90 ff. On Aquae Sextiae see A. Donnadieu, *Rev. Étud. Anc.*, 1954, 281 ff. On the strategy in 101 see E. Sadée, *Klio*, 1940, 225 ff.; on Sulla's part, Sadée, *Rhein Mus.*, 1939, 43 ff. On the battle

of Vercellae see T. F. Carney, *Athenaeum*, 1958, 229 ff. For the view of J. Zennari
(*I Vercelli dei Celti*, 1956) that *vercellae* was a Celtic word and meant a metal-mining
area, and that the battle of Vercellae was fought near Ferrara, see E. T. Salmon, *Phoenix*,
1958, p. 85. [p. 49]

31 ALLOTMENTS AND COLONIES. The sources for these measures are inadequate and
obscure in detail. For the Gallic allotments see Appian, *BC*, I, 29; for the colonies in
Sicily and Greece see *de vir. illustr.* 73 (these may have been intended for the veterans of
Aquillius and Didius, whose campaigns against the Sicilian slaves and against the
Scordisci were just ending; see E. Badian, *For. Cl.*, 204 f.); for Corsica, which cannot be
dated with certainty to 100, Pliny, *N.H.* 3, 6, 80; for Cercina, see the *elogium* quoted
below. For Africa there is epigraphic evidence: the *cognomen* Mariana appears in the
third century A.D. in the titles of two settlements, Thibaris and Uchi Maius (*ILS*, 6790;
1334), while a more recently discovered inscription proclaims Marius as the *conditor
coloniae* of Thuburnica (*Comptes rend.*, 1950, 332; though Thuburnica may not technically have been a *colonia*, the reference is clearly to Marius as the originator of the
settlement there). The commissioners included C. Iulius Caesar Strabo (attested in an
inscription: *Inscr. Ital.* 13. 3. 6) and the elder Iulius Caesar who established colonists on
Cercina (*ibid.* 13. 3. 7). The proposal for allotments in Africa is dated by *de vir. ill.* 73 to
103 B.C., but the African colonies are usually assigned to 100; E. Gabba (*Athenaeum*,
1951, 12 ff.) would assign them also to 103 because he believes that only Saturninus'
legislation of 100 was repealed. On Roman colonization in N. Africa from the
time of Gracchus, to that of Augustus, see L. Teutsch, *Das Städtewesen in Nordafrika*
(1962). – Cicero (*pro Balbo*, 48) records that Marius was given the right to grant
Roman citizenship to three men in each colony (if the reading 'ternos' is correct): this
implies that the colonists were allies, not Romans, and that they had the Latin right. –
Eporedia (Ivrea) south of Aosta in the foothills of the Alps received a colony (probably
Roman) in 100 (Velleius, 1. 15. 5). There is nothing to prove that this was part of
Saturninus' legislation; it may rather have been a senatorial move, either political in
purpose, to compensate for the later cancellation of Saturninus' legislation, or strategic, designed to secure a second overland route to Gallia Narbonensis, or in connexion with the goldmines of Victimulae: on this see U. Ewins, *Papers Brit. Sch. Rome*,
1952, 70 ff., and for surviving traces of the land distribution (centuriation) see
P. Fraccaro, *Opuscula*, *III* (1957), 93 ff. See also E. Badian, *For. Cl.*, 204 ff. P. A. Brunt
has minimized the importance of the Italian settlements in Africa (*Italian Manpower
225 BC–A.D. 14* (1971), 577 ff.) and of Marius' support for allied enfranchisement (*JRS*,
1965, 106 f.). For a rejection of these interpretations see E. Badian 'Roman politics and
the Italians, 133–91 B.C.', *Dialoghi di Archeologia*, IV–V (1970–71), 402 ff. [p. 50]

32 THE PIRATE LAW. For the text see Riccobono, *FIRA*, i, 121 ff.; for a translation of part of
this interesting document see Lewis and Rheinhold, *Rn. Civ.* i, 325 f. For the more
sinister interpretation see J. Carcopino, *Mélanges, Glotz*, i, 119 ff. A second copy of what
is almost certainly this same law has been found at Cnidus in south-west Asia Minor:
for text and discussion see M. Hassall *et al.*, *JRS*, 1974, 195 ff.; cf. J. L. Ferrary, *Mélanges
d'arch.*, 1977, 619 ff. [p. 50]

33 METELLUS. Cf. E. S. Gruen, 'The Exile of Metellus Numidicus', *Latomus*, 1965, 576 ff.
[p. 51]

34 SATURNINUS' LEGISLATION. The legislation of 100 was later ignored, but was it
repealed, as argued by E. Gabba (*Athenaeum*, 1951, 13 f.)? E. Badian (*Historia*, 1962, 219
= Seager, *Crisis*, 25) has revived the objections of A. Passerini (*Athenaeum*, 1934, 348 f.)
and argues that Cicero *de leg.* 2. 14 and *pro Balbo* 48 show that it was not annulled by
the Senate. A. W. Lintott, *Violence in Republican Rome* (1968), 152 ff., also argues that

Saturninus' legislation, passed *per vim*, was not openly declared invalid: its execution was either abandoned or limited. – For the view that Marius was out-manoeuvred by Scaurus who was the master hand behind the suppression of Saturninus, see T. F. Carney, *Marius*, 43 f. For Marius' wealth, see Carney, p. 40. For the view that the decline in political support for Marius, after the suppression of Saturninus, was gradual, see E. Badian, *For. Cl.*, 210 ff. [p. 51]

CHAPTER IV

1 SOURCES FOR 99–79 B.C. See Greenidge and Clay *op. cit.* The surviving or partly surviving sources are roughly the same as those mentioned in notes 1 to chs. II and III, especially Appian (*BC*, 1, 33–106), Plutarch (*Lives of Marius* and *Sulla*), Livy, 'Periochae', 70–89, fragments of Diodorus, books 36–8, of Licinianus (dealing with 87–79 B.C.), references in Cicero (and his speech *Pro Sex. Roscio*) and in Strabo, etc. The lost works included the *Memoirs* of Sulla (of which Plutarch made use) and the *Histories* by Sempronius Asellio, which went down to 91 B.C., and by L. Cornelius Sisenna, who was praetor in 78, defended Verres in 70 and was a legate of Pompey in 67; his work, which continued Asellio's, began in 90 B.C. and went down to 82 or more probably to Sulla's death. On Sisenna see E. Badian, *JRS*, 1962, 50 ff. = *Studies*, 212 ff., and also *Athenaeum*, 1964, 422 ff., where he argues that Sisenna was in Rome during the *dominatio Cinnae* and later wrote his history in the spirit of an apologia for those who shared his experience. But see J. P. V. D. Balsdon, *JRS*, 1965, 231. An account of the Social War was written by Lucullus in Greek. On the Mithridatic War there is Appian's *Mithridatica*; a fragment from Posidonius which provides a portrait of Aristion, the leader in Athens in 88 (frg. in Athenaeus, V, 211); and the relevant part of a local history of Heraclea in Pontus written by a citizen named Memnon (Jacoby, *Frag. Griech. Hist.* IIIB, 434, 22–6). Some inscriptions and coins are mentioned below. On Sisenna see now also E. Rawson, *Cl. Qu.*, 1979, 327 ff. [p. 52]

2 FAMOUS TRIALS. These involved (*a*) Sex. Titius who was alleged to have kept a bust of Saturninus in his house (98): condemned; (*b*) P. Furius (tribune 100), who with Marius had deserted Saturninus, was accused twice: first acquitted and then lynched by the mob (98); (*c*) the younger Caepio, who had opposed Saturninus' corn-law: acquitted; (*d*) C. Norbanus, Saturninus' friend (probably in 95): though Scaurus, the Princeps Senatus, testified against him, he was acquitted; (*e*) Scaurus, accused of extortion in the East by young Caepio (92): he postponed the trial indefinitely by counter-attacking Caepio, who was acquitted. For the trials of Caepio and Norbanus, and also for Marius' supporters in these years, see E. Badian, *Historia*, 1957, 318 ff. = *Studies*, 34 ff. For all these political prosecutions in the 90s, see Gruen, *Historia*, 1966, 32 ff., and *Rom. Pol.*, 187 ff. He believes that Furius was tried once and that Scaurus was tried and acquitted. [p. 52]

2a THE LEX LICINIA-MUCIA. Despite Schol. Bob. 296, this was not an expulsion act: see E. Badian, *For Cl.*, 297, and cf. *JRS*, 1973, 127. The men condemned under this law may previously have been enrolled gradually (thus P. A. Brunt, *JRS*, 1965, 106 f.) or by the censors of 97–6 (so E. Badian, *Roman Imperialism in the Late Republic* (1968), 104f. and *Dialoghi*, 405 f. (cited in n. 31 above). [p. 53]

3 MUCIUS SCAEVOLA. E. Badian (*Athenaeum*, 1956, 104 ff.) dates the proconsulship of Scaevola in Asia to 94 B.C. He argues that Aemilius Scaurus, who led an embassy to the East, went there in 96 and realized the need for reform in Asia: hence he will have proposed that a consular governor should be sent out to Asia and have sponsored the

appointment of Scaevola. That Scaurus was the prosecutor of Rutilius may have been the erroneous belief of his descendant Mam. Aemilius Scaurus, consul in A.D. 21 (Tacitus, *Annals*, 3, 66: see E. Badian *Cl. Rev.*, 1958, 216 ff.). B. Marshall, *Athenaeum*, 1976, 117 ff., believes that Scaevola governed Asia as praetor or soon after (*c.* 98). On Scaevola's contribution to Roman law see O. Behrends, *Die Wissenschaftslehre im Zivilrecht des Q. Mucius Scaevola Pontifex* (1976). [p. 53]

4 DRUSUS' LEGISLATION. For Drusus as champion of the Senate see Cicero, *de orat.* 1. 7. 24, *pro Milone* 7. 16; Diodorus, 37, 10. The chronology of his measures is uncertain: cf. R. Thomsen, *Classica et Mediaevalia*, 1942, 13 ff. Velleius (2. 14) suggests that the franchise proposal was among the later measures, and indeed something of an afterthought. For the *lex Saufeia* see the *elogium* of Drusus (Greenidge, *Sources²*, 128); for the decemviral commission and an inscription from Vibo, *ibid*, 131. Drusus, or perhaps less probably his father (whose claim is supported by H. Mattingly, *Proc. Brit. Acad.*, xxxix, 242), carried a currency law: *octavam partem aeris argento miscuit* (Pliny, *NH*, 33. 46). That this means that Drusus arranged that one silver-plated *denarius* should be officially issued in every issue of eight ordinary silver ones has been rejected by M. Crawford (*Num. Chron.*, 1968, 57 f.; *RRC*, 616) who argues that plated coins were never officially minted and since there is no trace of debasement in *denarii* of the years immediately after 91 B.C., the story about Livius Drusus may refer to an annulled or abortive proposal. Regarding the courts, Velleius (2. 13. 2) records that Drusus wanted to restore them to the Senate, Appian (*Bell. Civ.* 1. 35) that he wanted to add 300 Equites to the Senate and to entrust the courts to this enlarged Senate, and the Epitome of Livy (71) says that he carried a law establishing mixed juries. For an attempt to reconcile the versions of Appian and Livy, see E. Gabba, *La Parola del Passato*, 1956, 363 ff. and *Annali d. Sc. Norm. di Pisa*, 1964, 1 ff., who accepts Appian's account and thinks that Livy is merely a muddled version of the same tradition. For the clause making the Equites liable to prosecution on charges of corruption to secure an unjust conviction, see Cicero, *Cluent.* 15.3; *Rabir. Post.* 16. Cf. U. Ewins, *JRS*, 1960, 94 ff. On Drusus' friends (the enemies of Marius), e.g. the Metelli, see E. Badian, *Historia*, 1957, 318 ff.; Gruen, *Rom. Pol.*, 206 ff. Some Etruscans and Umbrians went to Rome to agitate against Drusus' land law (not his citizenship law: on this see E. Badian, *Historia*, 1962, 225 f. = *Studies*, 36 ff.). J. Heurgon has found traces of Etruscan propaganda against Drusus in an Etruscan prophecy by a prophetess called Vegoia: see *JRS*, 1959, 41 ff. For further discussion of Drusus' judiciary law see E. J. Weinrib, *Historia*, 1970, 414 ff. and A. R. Hands, *Phoenix*, 1972, 268 ff. The second of Gabba's articles mentioned above is now translated in his *RR, Army*, 130 ff. [p. 54]

5 DRUSUS AND THE ITALIANS. Diodorus records (37. 13) that an army of 10,000 Italians started to march on Rome during Drusus' lifetime until persuaded that their claims would be considered. He also quotes (37. 11) an oath alleged to have been sworn by his Italian friends to Drusus. This might be a document, not necessarily genuine, produced at the subsequent trials. [p. 54]

6 LEX VARIA DE MAIESTATE. The lex Varia is usually interpreted as a law which set up a *quaestio extraordinaria* to try those 'by whose help or counsel allies had taken up arms against the Roman people'. E. S. Gruen, however, has argued (*JRS*, 1965, 59 ff.) that it did not establish a special court but redefined the charge of *maiestas* and thus superseded the existing standing court *de maiestate* which Saturninus had established; it will have continued in this form until Sulla's legislation. R. Seager (*Historia*, 1967, 37 ff.) has countered Gruen's arguments but has not convinced Gruen (see *Rom. Pol.*, 216, n. 2). However, E. Badian (*Historia*, 1969, 447 ff.) has reinforced the attack and may well be thought to have re-established the traditional position. The victims

included L. Calpurnia Bestia (*cos.* 111) who, anticipating trouble, went into exile; C. Aurelius Cotta, Drusus' friend and future consul of 75, denounced the court and went into exile; and another friend, L. Memmius. (On Memmius see T. P. Wiseman, *Cl. Qu.* 1967, 163 ff.) Three men got off; M. Antonius (*cos.* 99) thanks to his powers of oratory, Scaurus, and Q. Pompeius Rufus (*cos.* 88). It is usually believed that the court was suspended when the military situation got worse during the Social War, but H. Hill, *Roman Middle Class*, 136, argues that the evidence (Cicero, *Brut.* 304; Asconius, p. 73 Cl.) suggests that it alone continued, the other courts being temporarily suspended. Badian (*Historia*, 1969, 452 ff.) argues that the regular courts had already been suspended before Varius carried his law establishing the special court. He also shows that Varius' ultimate fate was exile, not execution. [p. 54]

7   THE LATIN CITIES. Their loyalty to Rome may be partly explained by the fact that their local magistrates had been granted Roman citizenship, perhaps from 124 B.C. As these changed annually, by 90 B.C. the nucleus of the governing class in each city would be Roman citizens, whose sympathies and loyalties would be directed to Rome. Cf. G. Tibiletti, *Rendiconti Ist. Lombardo*, lxxxvi, 1953, 45 ff. Venusia had become partly Oscanized. [p. 55]

8   AIMS OF THE ALLIES. In general see A. N. Sherwin-White, *Roman Citizenship²*, 134 ff., and P. A. Brunt, *JRS*, 1965, 90 ff. There is not much evidence for a division of loyalty within the cities on social and economic lines, though sufficient to permit Mommsen to hold that the local aristocracies were more loyal to Rome and that the rural middle classes were the real rebels. A recent view suggests that the commercial classes in the Italian cities were particularly discontented and when trading abroad felt keenly their inferior status to that of the Roman citizens (see E. Gabba, *Athenaeum*, 1954, 41–114, 293–345, a valuable discussion, although its main thesis is not acceptable). It is true that the Italians were helping to exploit the provinces, but these traders came mostly from Campania and the south rather than from the Oscan heart of the rebellion. Cf. E. Badian, *For. Cl.* 220 ff. and *Historia*, 1962, 223 ff. = Seager, *Crisis*, 29 ff. E. T. Salmon (*Phoenix*, 1962, 107 ff.) attributes the cause of the war to the 'principes Italicorum populorum', the Italian bourgeoisie, whose economic and commercial interests (especially in the provinces) were badly affected when the Equites gained control of the law courts at Rome: Roman citizenship would give them equality of privilege, and many would in fact become knights. Their resentment grew in the nineties, with the *lex Licinia Mucia* and the failure of Drusus' judiciary and citizenship laws. So they turned to war and to the old hatred of the Sabellian tribes for Rome; the masses could easily be stirred once their leaders wanted and agreed upon action. Salmon also (*Samnium and the Samnites* (1967), ch. 9) discusses the grievances of the allies which included the fact that their notable contribution to the victories over Jugurtha and the Germans 'had been rewarded by having it made clear that they were to remain second-class inhabitants of Italy' (p. 335), while the irritation caused by the Lex Licinia Mucia 'happened at a moment when a lull in the external wars left a lot of trained Italian soldiers temporarily, and dangerously, unemployed'. P. A. Brunt (op. cit.) upholds the traditional view that the allied 'demand for citizenship is essentially a demand for the *ius suffragii*' (p. 103) and argues that their desire to become Roman citizens 'reflects the success of Rome in unifying them in sentiment and was stimulated by the Cimbric war and by the career of Marius and other *novi homines* of his time' (90). They 'could reckon that enfranchisement would not substantially reduce such autonomy as they still possessed' (103). D. B. Nagle, *AJ Arch.*, 1973, 366 ff., examines Italy, region by region, and suggests that the allies found Rome's increasing pervasiveness difficult to accept. 'It was not so much the threat of renewed land commission activity that led to

the revolt as the reaffirmation implicit in Drusus' law (even though abrogated) of Rome's basic policy of allowing – and on occasion actively encouraging – her citizen landowners, large and small, to exploit the gigantic holdings of *ager publicus* added to her territory in the third and second centuries' (p. 367). An English translation of Gabba's article has now appeared in his *RR, Army*, 70 f. [p. 55]

9   THE ITALIAN CONFEDERACY. See Diodorus 37.2; Strabo, 5. 241. Roman model (Mommsen); representative government (T. Frank, *Roman Imperialism*, 301 ff.); binary league (Domaszewski, *Sitz. Ber. Wien*, 1925, and R. Gardner, *CAH*, IX, 186); primarily military and not representative government (H. D. Meyer, *Historia*, 1958, 74 ff.). See further discussion by E. T. Salmon, *Samnium and the Samnites* (1967), 348 ff., who *inter alia* believes that the government at Corfinium was similar to that of the Thessalian League which Flamininus had set up in 196. See also A. N. Sherwin-White, *Roman Citizenship*[2], (1973), 147, who (contra Meyer) doubts the existence of a primary assembly of citizens. [p. 55]

10   THE ITALIAN WAR. Our knowledge is very unsatisfactory since the account written by a contemporary writer Sisenna is lost and the surviving information from other writers is very scrappy. The Livian tradition has been analysed in detail by J. Haug, *Würzburger Jahrb. für die Altertumswiss*, 1947, 106 ff. On the coinage issued by the Italians see Sydenham, *CRR*, 89 ff.; according to A. Voirol (*Gazette Numism. Suisse*, 1953–4, 64 ff.) the issues move from bilingual to Oscan anti-Roman ones. See also M. H. Crawford, *Num. Chron.*, 1964, 145 ff. On the identification of the twelve *populi* who formed the anti-Roman league and on the generals whom they supplied to the rebel forces see E. T. Salmon, *TAPA*, 1958, 159 ff. On the war see further Salmon, *Samnium*, ch. 10. On Sisenna and the war see P. Frasinetti, *Athenaeum*, 1972, 78 ff. *La guerra sociale* (1976) by G. De Sanctis, a surviving section of the uncompleted part of his great *Storia dei Romani*, deals with the political history of 91–88 B.C. as well as with the war itself. [p. 55]

11   ALBA FUCENS. New excavations here are showing us more clearly what an early Latin colony looked like, and the strength of Alba's walls, although they may not have saved the city from capture (cf. *Archaeology*, 1959, 124). For illustrations of the site and walls see E. T. Salmon, *Roman Colonization* (1969), Plates 15 and 25. [p. 56]

12   ASCULUM AND STRABO. An interesting record of the siege is provided by sling-bullets, inscribed with such instructions as 'feri Pompeium' or even a more precise target as 'ventri' (Greenidge, *Sources*[2], 149). Many stirring tales of heroism were told about the war, e.g. how Vidacilius of Asculum broke through the Roman lines into his native city. An important document (*ibid.* 156; *ILS*, 8888) records how Strabo rewarded some Spanish horsemen who were serving under him with a grant of Roman citizenship 'in castreis apud Asculum a.d. xiv Dec. ex lege Iulia'. Members of Strabo's *consilium* included Lepidus (*cos.* 78), Catiline, and his young son, later Pompeius Magnus. See also N. Criniti, *L'Epigrafe di Asculum di Cn. Pompeio Strabone* (1970) and (on the *consilium*) H. B. Mattingly, *Athenaeum*, 1975, 262 ff. [p. 57]

13   LEX IULIA. Appian (*BC*, 1. 49) suggests that it applied to loyal communities, but Velleius (2. 16) may imply its application also to those 'qui arma ... deposuerant maturius'. For an individual grant of citizenship under the law, see n. 12 above. On the lex Iulia see further P. A. Brunt, *JRS*, 1965, 107 f., who argues that it was under this law that the new citizens were restricted to eight or ten tribes (see n. 18 below) and he rejects L. R. Taylor's view (*Voting Districts of the Roman Republic*, 107 ff.) that this restriction did not apply to the Latin colonies. [p. 57]

14   NEW MUNICIPIA. Cf. A. N. Sherwin-White, *Rom. Cit.*, 159 ff., who with others rejects the view of H. Rudolph that thereby the jurisdiction of local magistrates was abolished

and the Italians became subject to the city courts of Rome. The settlement of 90–89 did not crush all local independence. [p. 57]

15 LEX PLAUTIA PAPIRIA. For this second view see Sherwin-White, *op. cit.*, 151 ff., who argues that the clause of which we have any knowledge (Cic, *pro Arch.* 4. 7; Schol. Bob., p. 353) dealt merely with any *ascriptus* (a kind of 'honorary freeman', not an ordinary citizen) who happened not to be in residence in his adoptive city when it received citizenship under the *lex Iulia* (e.g. Cicero's friend the poet Archias, an *ascriptus* of Heraclea who was living in Rome). What else the law contained we do not know. See now E. Badian, *JRS*, 1973, 128 ff.

Plautius was also responsible for a *lex iudiciaria* by which jurors were chosen in a new way: each tribe elected 15 of its own members from any class (i.e. not only Equites) and from these 525 men the jurors for the year were to be drawn. It is not clear whether this remained in force until Sulla's law of 81 B.C. [p. 57]

16 LEX POMPEIA AND CISALPINE GAUL. The usual view, based on Asconius *in Pisonian.* p. 3, is that Strabo conferred Roman citizenship on the Cispadanes and Latin rights on the Transpadanes. It has, however, been suggested (cf. G. E. F. Chilver, *Cisalpine Gaul* (1941), 8) that the *lex Pompeia* dealt with the *whole* of Cisalpine Gaul together, granting citizenship to all Latin colonies and Latin rights to the native *oppida*. This view has been developed by U. Ewins, *Papers Brit. Sch. Rome*, 1955, 73 ff., who also revives and defends the view of E. G. Hardy (*JRS*, 1916, 66 f.) that Cisalpine Gaul was made a province in 89 under this law, and not by Sulla in 81. Cf. n. 34. This view has been rejected by E. Badian (*Proc. Afr. Cl. Ass.*, 1958, 18 = *Studies*, 103, n. 145) who doubts whether Cisalpine Gaul was a regular administrative unit even after 81 (*Historia*, 1962, 232). On the status of the Transpadani see L. R. Taylor, *The Voting Districts of the Roman Republic* (1960), ch. 9. See also A. N. Sherwin-White, *Roman Citizenship*² (1973), 157 ff. [p. 58]

17 CITIZENSHIP FOR THE REBELS. See Appian (*BC*, 1, 66. 5) and cf. Licinianus (27) 'dediticiis omnibus a senatu civitas data' and Livy, *Perioch.* 80 'Italicis populis a senatu civitas data'. The Lucanians and Samnites, who are excepted in the above passage of Appian, probably received their grant of citizenship from Cinna: cf. Appian 68. 2 and Licinianus (27) 'Cinna . . . in leges quas postulabant eos recepit.' [p. 58]

18 ENROLMENT OF NEW CITIZENS. They were confined to 8 (existing?) tribes according to Velleius or 10 new ones according to Appian. Whether or not these figures can be reconciled with the help of a fragment of Sisenna referring to 'duas novas tribus' (see Rice Holmes, *Roman Republic*, i., 356), the new citizens clearly did not receive fair play in the exercise of their public, as opposed to their private, rights. See also F. B. Marsh, *Hist. Roman World 146 to 30 BC* (2nd ed. 1953), appendix 4, E. T. Salmon, *TAPA*, 1958, 179 ff., L. R. Taylor, *Voting Districts of the Roman Republic*, ch. 8, and R. G. Lewis, *Athenaeum*, 1968, 273 ff. [p. 58]

19 DEBT. Many men were ruined by the war, money was short, and lenders began to call in their loans. A praetor of 89, Sempronius Asellio, who tried to apply an obsolete law against usury, was lynched by creditors. E. Badian, who examines the incident (*Historia*, 1969, 475 ff.), links it with the judicial lex Plotia (see above n. 15) as an attempt by the nobles to gain the support of the People against the Equites. The bronze coinage was reduced in weight: an *as* now weighed only half an ounce. One issue has the inscription LPDAP (*Lege Papiria de assis pondere*), i.e. it was issued under a *lex Papiria* (Crawford, *RRC*, n. 338). Crawford, however, would date the *lex Papiria* to 91 and regards the measure as a precaution in face of the threat from the Social War (pp. 77, 59 f., 611). [p. 58]

20 PUBLIUS SULPICIUS. The Optimate tradition, reflected in Appian, Plutarch and

Diodorus, is hostile to Sulpicius, though Cicero and the *Ad Herennium* are more favourable. His precise position is not clear: he started as an Optimate, but his measure for the new citizens was more than a vote-catching device, since they could hardly have been redistributed in time to allow them to vote for any of his other proposals. For an explanation of his conversion from Optimate to *Popularis* methods see E. Badian, *For. Cl.*, 230 ff., and *Historia*, 1969, 481 ff. When his stand on the issue of the fair distribution of the newly enfranchised Italians in the citizen body was opposed even by many of his former friends and supporters of Drusus, he found a political counterweight in Marius and in the Equites who, now that enfranchisement was an accomplished fact, would welcome the full voting power of the allied upper classes, whose interests they shared, as a counterbalance to the senatorial vote in the Comitia Centuriata (cf. Badian, *Historia*, 486 f.). This change in Sulpicius' policy will have been made only after his citizen bill had been threatened (Badian, *For. Cl.*, 230 ff.). For a rejection of the 'anti-senators' see *Historia*, 485, n. 110. Sulpicius is said to have changed his mind about the recall of exiles, which he at first opposed. These are generally thought to be primarily those banished under the Varian commission, but Badian (*Historia*, 487 ff.) argues that they were those who had suffered from the application of the Lex Licinia Mucia (see p. 52 above). A. W. Lintott, *Cl. Qu.*, 1971, 442 ff., gives a slightly different interpretation of Sulpicius' tribunate, which involves the view that Caesar Strabo sought the consulship in 88 for 87, hoping for the Mithridatic command in 87; his rival Marius will have had the same hope, thus at first not aiming to supplant Sulla in 88; but rioting and other events forced Marius into a direct challenge to Sulla. However that may be, the alliance between Sulpicius and Marius probably came late in Sulpicius' tribunate after his proposal about the new citizens had run into trouble: cf. Badian, *For. Cl.*, 232, and T. J. Luce, *Historia*, 1970, 192 ff. T. N. Mitchell writes on the volte-face of Sulpicius in 88 (*Cl. Ph.*, 1975, 197 ff.), B. R. Katz on some questions of 88–87 (*Ant. class.*, 1976, 497 ff.) and on Caesar Strabo (*Rhein. Mus.*, 1977, 45 ff.). For the view that P. Sulpicius did not have the *cognomen* Rufus see H. Mattingly, *Athenaeum*, 1975, 264 f. [p. 59]

21 MARIUS' FLIGHT. On this see T. F. Carney, *Gr. and R.*, 1961, 98 ff. An inscription of a slave of *a* C. Marius at Minturnae is, at best, doubtful evidence that the great Marius had a villa there. He had one at Misenum (but probably not another at Baiae): see E. Badian, *JRS*, 1973, 121 ff. On the declaration of Marius' followers as *hostes* see R. A. Bauman, *Athenaeum*, 1973, 270 ff., and on the immediate impact of Sulla's march on Rome see B. R. Katz, *Ant. class.*, 1975, 100 ff. [p. 60]

22 STRABO. M. Gelzer (*Vom römischen Staat*, II, 56 ff.) has attempted to some extent to rehabilitate Strabo's reputation, which the Optimate tradition has blackened, but he goes too far perhaps in suggesting that Strabo tried to adopt the role of mediator in order to obtain a personal supremacy. Cf. E. Badian, *For. Cl.*, 239 ff. Strabo's ability, aims and career must have had considerable influence on the thought of his son Pompey who had served on his *consilium* at Asculum. Cicero (*pro Cornelio* ap. Ascon., p. 79 Cl.) refers to a trial of Cn. Pompeius under the lex Varia in 89. There are great difficulties in applying this to Strabo: see E. Badian (*Historia*, 1969, 465 ff.) who accepts a correction of the text to 'Pomponium' and refers the trial to Cn. Pomponius, tribune in 90, who will then qualify for the role of 'hominem dis ac nobilitate perinvisum'.

On the siege of Rome in 87 B.C. see B. R. Katz, *Cl. Ph.*, 1976, 328 ff. [p. 61]

23 THE MARIAN MASSACRE. H. Bennett, *Cinna and his Times* (1923), 20 ff., argues that this has been exaggerated by the anti-Marian tradition and that after the initial atrocities the official execution of prominent citizens was limited. Fourteen such victims are known; seven of these deaths are attributable to Marius. Six of the victims

were consulars. See T. F. Carney, *Marius*, 65 ff., and Gruen, *Rom. Pol.*, 231 ff. C. M. Bulst (*Historia*, 1964, 313 ff.) rejects Badian's view (*Historia*, 1957, 339, n. 177) that some of the victims were former friends of Marius who had betrayed him. [p. 61]

24 ECONOMIC REFORMS. In general see C. M. Bulst, *Historia*, 1964, 330 ff. M. H. Crawford, *Proc. Cambr. Philological Soc.*, 1968, 1 ff., shows that the edict of Marius Gratidianus did not control plated coins, but ended unofficial exchange rates of silver and bronze coins (cf. notes 4 and 19 above). On the government's efforts to struggle with finance and the economy in the period 92–80 B.C. see C. T. Barlow, *AJP*, 1980, 202 ff. [p. 61]

25 REGISTRATION OF NEW CITIZENS. This possibly took place in 87–6: the repeal of Sulla's laws might imply the restoration of Sulpicius' law about the new citizens. But Livy, *Perioch.* lxxxiv, implies that it was not until 84. If so, it is not certain whether or not Sulla's imminent return will have affected the issue. [p. 61]

26 DOMINATIO CINNAE. Cinna's policy, which has been traduced by the ancient sources which rely on Sulla's *Memoirs*, has been variously interpreted. To H. Bennett (*Cinna and his Times*, 1923) Cinna was a would-be tyrant who planned to cloak 'absolute power behind the forms of constitutional government' (p. 59). Conventionally Cinna is lined up with the Equites and the new citizens against Sulla and the oligarchy. E. Badian (*JRS*, 1962, 47 ff. = *Studies*, 206 ff.) has depicted Cinna as the leader of legitimate government and Sulla at this stage as no friend of the oligarchy. T. F. Carney (*Marius*, 66) can describe Cinna as 'a moderate, a respecter of the constitution and a com-promiser'. Gruen (*Rom. Pol.*, 239 ff.), who analyses the men who co-operated in the Cinnan government, summarizes Cinna's policy as 'control of the springs of power and suppression of internal strife, and the cultivation of unity among all factions and classes' (p. 246), while 'Cinna's endeavour was a noble experiment . . . offering peace, stability and a coalescence of political groups. The combination would be wide enough to embrace Sulla also, or perhaps powerful enough to overawe him. But it was not to be. Sulla had his own following . . . hardened by war' (p. 247). C. M. Bulst (*Historia*, 1964, 307) also rates Cinna highly: 'Cinna was far more of a statesman than Sulla' (p. 277).

Badian's views (*op. cit. supra*) may be briefly summarized. He emphasizes Sulla's ruthless ambition: in 88 all but one of his officers (L. Lucullus?) refused to march with him on Rome and he showed contumacy when summoned to stand trial in Rome (but J. P. Balsdon, *JRS*, 1965, 230, finds this contumacy less extreme and questions other aspects of Badian's picture). The authority of the government in Rome was recognized by responsible opinion and in 86 no one thought of Sulla as a champion of the nobility: the Sullani were not representative senators but merely his new officers, chosen by himself: he and his army stood against the Republic. Until 85 Cinna followed a policy of *concordia*, with no sign of *dominatio*. Thus Flaccus was sent against Mithridates not against Sulla (cf. Bulst, *op. cit.*, 319 ff.). But by 85 Sulla, after his Greek victories and backed by the resources of the East, could turn to rebellion. Even Cinna's troop movement from Ancona to Illyria was not a direct move against Sulla (but to train new levies in war). But Cinnet was the turning point: the government began to disintegrate and the nobility began to go over to Sulla. [p. 61]

27 MITHRIDATES. For the kingdom of Pontus and the Mithridatic War see Th. Reinach, *Mithridate Eupator* (1890); M. Rostovtzeff, *CAH*, IX, ch. v.; D. Magie, *Roman Rule in Asia Minor* (1950), chs. 8 and 9. On Roman involvement in Asia Minor, 167–88 B.C., see A. N. Sherwin-White, *JRS*, 1977, 62 ff., and on Rome and Mithridates before 88 and in 85–73 see D. G. Glew, *Athanaeum*, 1977, 380 ff., and *Chiron*, 1981, 109 ff., respectively. [p. 61]

28 SULLA'S PRAETORSHIP. E. Badian (*Athenaeum*, 1959, 379 ff. = *Studies*, 157 ff.) has shown that this fell in 97 (not 93) and that he held a command (against the pirates?) in Cilicia: here he was instructed by the Senate to install Ariobarzanes in Cappadocia (96). This view involves some consequential adjustments in the generally accepted account of Asiatic affairs in the nineties. A. N. Sherwin-White, *Cl. Qu.*, 1977, 173 ff., argues that Ariobarzanes was restored by Sulla in 94 and ruled till *c.* 91. [p. 62]

29 MITHRIDATES AND THE ITALIANS. So far from helping the Romans, Mithridates is said to have promised help to the Italians in the Social War. A unique gold coin with an Oscan inscription may have been issued in anticipation (or on account?) of such help (see E. A. Sydenham, *CRR*, n. 643); a more common silver coin of the Italians (*op. cit.*, n. 632) depicts a man (Mithridates?) being greeted as he lands from a ship – another anticipatory issue? This may however depict the return of the exiled Marius: M. Crawford, *Num. Chr.*, 1964, 148. On the other hand, an interesting document, a senatorial decree of 78 B.C., records how three Greek ship-captains who helped Rome were rewarded by the title of 'Friend of Rome' and other honours because 'they had stood by in their ships at the outbreak of the Italian War and had rendered valiant and faithful service to our State' (see Warmington, *ROL*, iv, 444); Riccobono, *FIRA*, p. 35; Sherk, *Rom. Documents Greek East*, 22; trans. Lewis and Reinhold, *Rn. Civ.*, 267 f. The Italian War is either the Social or Sulla's war of 83–2. [p. 63]

29a GREECE AND ATHENS. On the history of Athens in the time of Mithridates see C. Habicht, *Chiron*, 1976, 127 ff; on the events of 92–87 see E. Badian, *Amer. Journ. Anc. Hist.*, 1976, 105 ff; and on Mithridates' anti-Roman propaganda in Asia Minor and Greece see E. S. Gaggero, *Contrib. in onore di A. Garzetti*, 89 ff. [p. 64]

30 CHAERONEA. The chief sources for the war in Greece are Plutarch, *Sulla*, 11–21, and Appian, *Mithr.* 28–45 and 49–50. Plutarch's account uses as a primary source the *Memoirs* of Sulla himself. Plutarch was a native of Chaeronea. On the battle see N.G.L. Hammond, *Klio*, 1938, 186 ff. [p. 64]

31 FLACCUS AND SULLA. So Memnon (Jacoby, *FGrH*, 434, F.24). For Sulla's claim that despatch of Flaccus was a stab in the back, see Plut. *Sulla*, 20, 1. Cf. E. Badian, *JRS*, 1962, 56 = *Studies*, 223 f. That Fimbria had been Flaccus' quaestor rather than legate see A. W. Lintott, *Historia*, 1971, 696 ff. On the date of their deaths see A. W. Lintott, *Historia*, 1976, 489 ff. [p. 64]

32 SETTLEMENT OF ASIA MINOR. The view of Mommsen and T. Frank, that Sulla deprived the *publicani* of the right to farm the taxes of Asia (based on Cicero, *ad Q. fr.* 1.1.33) and that it was restored by Pompey (Cic. Verr. 3.6.12), has been rejected by Rice Holmes, *RR.* I, 395, and P. A. Brunt, *Latomus*, 1956, 17 ff. How a loyal city's privileges were confirmed and even extended is seen in a letter that Sulla wrote to Stratonicea, in which he quotes the resolution of the Senate taken on this matter in 81 (for a translation of this document, *OGIS* 441 and R. K. Sherk, *Roman Documents of the Greek East*, 22, see Lewis and Reinhold, *Rn. Civ.*, 1, 337 f.). See also similar letters from Sulla and Cn.Cornelius Dolabella to Thasos: Sherk, 20,21. Sulla also responded favourably to an appeal from the Guild of Actors of Iona and the Hellespont, the Artists of Dionysus, and renewed their earlier privileges including exemption from public and military service. The favour was later confirmed by the Senate in 81: copies of the SC, together with Sulla's covering letter, were set up in various towns; that in Cos survives in part (see M. Segre, *Riv. Fil.*, 1938, 253 ff., R. K. Sherk, *Historia*, 1966, 211 ff. and *Documents*, 49; and for a translation Lewis and Reinhold, *Rn. Civ.*, 342). Sulla was greatly interested in the stage and stage-folk, including a friendship with the great actor Roscius: see further S. Garton, 'Sulla and the Theatre', *Phoenix*, 1964, 137 ff. [p. 65]

33 THE SAMNITES. E. T. Salmon has shown (*Athenaeum*, 1964, 160 ff.; *Samnium*, 377 ff.) that the Social War did not just merge into the Civil War, but that the Samnites had been at peace during Sulla's absence from Italy. But they were deliberately excluded from the treaty which Sulla signed with 'Italic peoples' in the winter of 83–82 and by driving them into hostility he could transform his personal war into a national crusade against Rome's old enemy. [p. 66]

34 PRAENESTE. For the topography see R. Gardner, *Journal of Philology*, 1919, pp. 1 ff. The temple of Fortuna there was reconstructed by Sulla. This famous sanctuary, built on the hillside on terraced slopes, is a most imposing monument. Some of the later buildings that covered it were destroyed by bombing during the last war, and the whole complex now displays something of its earlier magnificence. See F. Fasolo and G. Gullini, *Il santuario della Fortuna Primigenia a Palestrina* (1953). On the topography and siege see now R. G. Lewis, *Papers Brit. Sch. Rome*, 1971, 32 ff. [p. 66]

35 POMPEY'S TRIUMPH. The date of its celebration is. uncertain, whether 81, 80 or 79. E. Badian (*Hermes*, 1955, 107 ff.) and R. E. Smith (*Phoenix*, 1960, pp. 1 ff.) are agreed in rejecting 79: the former supports 81, the latter 80. Badian has also emphasized (*For. C1.*, 273 ff.) the seriousness of Pompey's potential threat to Sulla: *imperator* with six legions in Africa, control of Sicily, a reasonable fleet, possible support from Numidia and Mauretania, connexions in Cisalpine Gaul, the loyalty of Picenum in an Italy that was not yet completely settled; all this, together with Sertorius in the West, may well have led Sulla not to persist too far in opposing Pompey. Smith (*op. cit.*, p. 8) thinks this view exaggerates the threat which Pompey posed to Sulla at this point. [p. 66]

36 SULLA'S COLONIES. These included Arretium, Clusium, Faesulae, Interamnia, Nola, Pompeii, Praeneste. In most cases (except Pompeii) the colonists remained separate from the original inhabitants and the two communities existed side by side. For a list and discussion see E. Gabba, *Athenaeum*, 1951, 270 = *RR, Army*, 67 ff. Cf. also E. T. Salmon, *Roman Colonization* (1969), 129 ff. and P. A. Brunt, *Italian Manpower* (1971), 300 ff. Brunt argues that the pattern of land settlement in Italy was not so radically changed as some believe: confiscated latifundia may still have remained largely in the hands of *latifondisti*, now Sullans in place of Marians, while a large proportion of the Sullan colonists probably failed to make good. [p. 67]

37 SULLA FELIX. On this name see J. P. V. D. Balsdon, *JRS*, 1951, pp. 1 ff. It is disputable whether this name was officially voted to Sulla by the Senate, which by the end of 82 had ordered the erection of an equestrian statue of Sulla inscribed 'Cornelio Sullae Imperatori Felici' (Appian, *BC*, 1, 97). Sulla, who as early as 86 had named his twin children Faustus and Fausta, certainly believed in his luck. In Greece he may have used the name Epaphroditus to indicate that he enjoyed Aphrodite's favour, though Felix may not imply a cult of Venus in Italy: *felicitas* was an essential quality of a successful general (see Cicero, *De imp. Cn. Pomp.* 28; 47). Cf. also E. Badian, *Historia*, 1962, 229 = Seager, *Crisis*, 229. Another of the spoils of victory was an augurate. E. Badian (*Arethusa*, 1968, 26 ff.) has shown that Sulla added this honour to his earlier pontificate after victory and thus became one of the select few Romans to become both pontifex and augur. [p. 67]

37a VALERIUS FLACCUS. On Sulla's letter to the interrex Flaccus (Appian, *BC*, 1, 98) and the genesis of Sulla's dictatorship see H. Bellen, *Historia*, 1975, 554 ff. [p. 67]

38 CICERO'S DEFENCE OF ROSCIUS. The closing of the proscription lists did not mean the end of all suffering. The name of Sextus Roscius of Ameria, who had been murdered, was later added to the list in order that his property might be confiscated and acquired for a nominal sum by one of Sulla's agents named Chrysogonus. To avoid possible exposure Chrysogonus' accomplices charged Roscius' son with the murder of

his father, thinking that no one would dare defend him through fear of Sulla. Young Cicero, however, boldly and successfully undertook the case, which came before the *quaestio inter sicarios*. In his speech *Pro Sexto Roscio Amerino*, delivered in 80 or possibly 79, he exposed Chrysogonus, but carefully pointed out that Sulla was far too busy to be able to keep an eye on all his agents. It is symptomatic of the disordered times that Roscius' acquittal secured him his personal safety but not the restoration of his father's property. See also Gruen, *Rom. Pol.*, 265 ff. [p. 69]

39 SULLA'S NEW SENATORS. One tradition records that they were drawn from the Equites (Appian, *BC*, 1. 100. 5: 'three hundred of the best Knights'; Livy, *Perioch.* 89, 'ex equestri ordine'), another that they were 'gregarii milites' (Sall. *Cat.* 37. 6) or 'ordinary men' (Dionysius, 5. 77. 5). H. Hill, *C1. Qu.*, 1932, 170 ff., argued for the former tradition in the narrow sense of *equites equo publico* only. An attempt to reconcile the traditions has been made by E. Gabba, *Athenaeum*, 1956, 124 ff., who argues that both can be accepted: Sulla will first have drawn on normal sources including men who had served him well (cf. the filling of the Senate after Cannae by Fabius Buteo: Livy, 23, 22) and then revived the idea attributed to Gaius Gracchus and Drusus of adding 300 Equites; if the Equites were added partly because of the law-courts, this would help to explain the curious procedure by which (according to Appian, *BC*, 1, 100) they were chosen (Gabba compares the election of jurors in the centumviral tribunal). This attractive solution depends partly on the total number of the post-Sullan Senate, which Mommsen put at 600, but it would not be impossible if the figure should be only 500: Sulla would still have 350 vacancies to fill. (The highest attested attendance is 417 in 61 B.C., excluding magistrates: Cic. *ad Att.* 1. 14. 5.) For a list of the known Sullan senators see E. Gabba, *Athenaeum*, 1951, 267 ff. See also J. R. Hawthorn, *Gr. and R.*, 1962, 53 ff. For the view that Sulla wished to give the Equites (or their leaders) greater share in government, as opposed to the common theory of Sulla as an enemy of the equestrian order, see E. Gabba, *Athenaeum*, 1957, 139, *Parola del Passato*, 1956, 363 ff. Badian (*Historia*, 1962, 232) writes that 'a decisive argument against the traditional view of Sulla's hatred of the Equites' is stressed by Gabba (*PP*, 1956) namely that Sulla, unlike Drusus, did not make the Equites liable to charges of judicial corruption. Gabba (*Ann. Pisa*, 1964, 1 ff.) links Sulla's reform with that proposed by Drusus (see above n. 4). For Gabba's articles in *Athenaeum*, 1956, 1951 and *Ann. Pisa*, 1964, see now *RR, Army* 142 ff., 59 ff., 131 ff., and for the Sullan senators see C. Nicolet, *L'ordre équestre à l'époque republicaine*, I (1966), 581 ff. Sulla's general legislative programme is discussed by R. E. Marino, *Aspetti della politica interna di Sulla* (1974). [p. 69]

40 THE CENSORSHIP. G. Tibiletti (*Studia et Docum. Hist et Juris*, 1959, 121 ff.) believes that Sulla exercised censorial powers and celebrated a *lustrum*; he may have enrolled new citizens passed over in the registration of 86–85 (cf. L. R. Taylor, *Voting Districts*, 119). His power as dictator would have enabled him, in person or by delegation, to execute the tasks usually done by the censors. On the censorship in the late Republic see T. P. Wiseman, *JRS*, 1969, 59 ff. [p. 69]

41 THE TRIBUNATE. The sources are not always clear on matters of detail. Thus Livy (*Perioch.* 89) says that Sulla 'omne ius legum ferendarum ademit', but there are two laws known which may have been passed by tribunes before their powers were restored in 70 B.C. (*lex Antonia de Termessibus* and *lex Plautia de reditu Lepidanorum*; both probably in accord with senatorial wishes). Similarly, the evidence about the tribunes' veto given by Cicero does not square with what Caesar says, and there are one or two possible examples of tribunes using their veto in these years, e.g. a tribune may have vetoed proceedings against C. Antonius in 76. [p. 70]

42 LEX ANNALIS. On the *cursus honorum* see A. E. Astin, *The Lex Annalis before Sulla*

(1958). He concludes that the minimum ages for curule office were fixed and that both before and after Sulla they were 36 for aediles, 39 for praetors and 42 for consuls. It is uncertain whether there was a fixed minimum age for the pre-Sullan quaestorship (which was normally held before 30); Sulla will have established this, but with no fixed interval after the quaestorship (cf. E. Badian, *JRS*, 1959, 81 ff. = *Studies*, 140 ff.). [p. 67]

43 CISALPINE GAUL. The exact date of the formation of this province is uncertain: cf. above n. 16. If it was not established in 89, its date may be 81 and its author Sulla. But Badian (see n. 16 above) believes that there is 'good reason for doubting whether it had a separate existence (i.e. separate from the rest of Gallia) even after Sulla' (*Historia*, 1962, 232). Sulla added to his glory by extending the *pomerium*, the sacred boundary of Rome, which could be done only by one who had extended Roman territory, strictly in Italy. This has sometimes been linked with a presumed establishment of Gallia Cisalpina, but it may refer to Sulla's extension of Italy for administrative purposes from the Aesis to the Rubicon (see Badian, *Roman Imperialism in the late Republic*² (1968), 34). It may be noted, with Badian, (*op. cit.*, 31 ff.), that Sulla formed no expansionist foreign policy. He made no attempt to annex wealthy Cyrene (though the opportunity was at hand (see p. 77 and ch. v, n. 5)) nor the even wealthier Egypt (see p. 91), while he had restrained Murena from harassing Mithridates (see p. 64). Whatever the content of the *lex Pompeia*, Cisalpine Gaul will now have been in an anomalous position, containing many cities of citizens and many with Latin rights. It is uncertain whether Cisalpine Gaul was ever offered to Sulla as a proconsular province (in 88, as compensation for the temporary loss of Asia, or in 80?) as stated by Licinianus. On the population of Cisalpine Gaul see P. A. Brunt, *Italian Manpower* (1971), 166 ff. (and for the first century, 198 ff.). [p. 70]

44 PROVINCIAL COMMANDS. The view of Mommsen that Sulla passed a law which forbade consuls and praetors to leave Italy during their year of office is not now widely accepted. J. P. V. D. Balsdon, *JRS*, 1939, 58 ff., goes so far as to argue that there was not even any conventional, let alone legal, restraint on a consul leaving Rome before the end of his consular office. The very disturbed and abnormal conditions of the Seventies make it very difficult to envisage what Sulla may have hoped to establish as regular practice. The *lex de maiestate* may have forbidden generals to bring armies back undischarged to Italy. This is the view of R. E. Smith (*Phoenix*, 1960, pp. 1 ff.) who believes that it had been increasingly common for generals to leave their men abroad and to use token troops for their triumphs. Pompey's earlier insistence, against Sulla's orders, in bringing his legions back from Africa in 80 will have underlined the potential danger to the government in Rome that such conduct involved. Hence it was forbidden under Sulla's treason law. [p. 71]

45 THE QUAESTIONES. The pre-Sullan history of the courts is uncertain, but *quaestiones* certainly existed to deal with *repetundae* (149), *maiestas* (Saturninus) and *de veneficiis* (cf. Dessau, *ILS*, 45) and probably *ambitus* (perhaps by 116) and *peculatus* (by 86, perhaps in 104). Cf. E. Badian, *Historia*, 1962, 207; Gruen, *Rom. Pol.*, 117, 124 f., 258 ff. After Sulla the courts will have comprised at least: *de repetundis, de maiestate, de ambitu, de sicariis et veneficiis, de peculatu, de iniuria, de falsis.* Later other courts were established, e.g. *de vi* (see A. W. Lintott, *Violence in Republican Rome* (1968), ch. viii, who would date this to a lex Lutatia in 78 which was supplemented by a lex Plautia between 78 and 63). [p. 71]

46 SULLA'S 'MONARCHY'. For this theory, expounded with great ingenuity and learning, see J. Carcopino, *Sylla ou la monarchie manquée*, 2nd ed. 1947. For criticisms see e.g. M. I. Munro, *JRS*, 1932, 239 ff. Sulla's coinage was not monarchical in intent: see S. L. Cesano (*Rendiconti d. Pontif. Accad.* 1945–46, 187 ff.); M. H. Crawford, *Num.*

Chron., 1964, 148 ff. For the possibility that Sulla abandoned power by stages (dictator till the end of 81, consul 80, *privatus* 79) see E. Badian, *Historia*, 1962, 230 = Seager, *Crisis*, 36, *Athenaeum*, 1970, 8 ff. On Sulla's illness, T. F. Carney, *Acta Classica*, 1960, 64 ff. U. Laffi, 'Il mito di Silla', *Athenaeum*, 1967, 177 ff., 255 ff., examines the elements of Sulla's work which survived after 70 B.C. into the late Republic. He also traces the evaluation of Sulla in later historiography, including Caesar's role as the new Marius which forced Pompey to be regarded as the new Sulla who had aspired to *regnum* by way of proscriptions. With the final victory of Caesar, the anti-Sulla, the tradition hostile to Sulla triumphed. [p. 71]

CHAPTER V

1 SOURCES FOR 78–66 B.C. For 78–70 B.C. see Greenidge and Clay, *Sources*. The extant writers are roughly the same as those mentioned in note 1 to ch. IV, e.g. Appian (*BC*, 1, 107–121, and *Mithridatica*), Plutarch (Lives of *Pompey, Sertorius, Crassus, Lucullus*), Livy, *Periochae* 90–100, Dio Cassius, 36 (fragments for 69 B.C. but complete thereafter). A most important work was the *Historiae* of Sallust (cf. p. 168) which covered the years 78–67 B.C. Only fragments survive (edited by Maurenbrecher in 1891–3), but these include some speeches that Sallust put into the mouths of Lepidus, Philippus, Cotta and Macer, together with the despatch that Pompey sent to the Senate from Spain. In an *opusculum* Julius Exsuperantius (fourth century A.D.) described the civil war down to the death of Sertorius, based largely on Sallust. A major source, which now becomes important, comprises the Orations of Cicero (e.g. the *Verrines* and the *De lege Manilia*). On the period 78–49 B.C. see E. S. Gruen, *The Last Generation of the Roman Republic* (1974). [p. 73]

2 LEPIDUS' SPEECH. A fragment of Sallust's *History* gives his version of a speech by Lepidus, denouncing Sulla's tyranny. The date is uncertain: it was probably between Sulla's abdication and death, at the end of 79. Cf. Rice Holmes, *Roman Republic*, I, 363. For Lepidus' revolution see Rice Holmes, *op. cit.*, 365 ff.; N. Criniti, *Mem. Ist. Lomb* xxx (1969); E. Hayne, *Historia*, 1972, 661 ff; L. Labruna, *Il console sovversivo, Marco Emilio Lepido e la sua rivolta* (1976). [p. 73]

3 THE TRIBUNES. Lepidus is said by Sallust to have demanded the restoration of tribunician power, by Licinianus to have opposed this. The problem is which was Lepidus' first and which his second thought. [p. 73]

4 SERTORIUS. The sources for the Sertorian War are collected, with a commentary in Spanish, by A. Schulten, *Fontes Hispaniae Antiquae*, iv (1937), 160 ff. Sallust's *Historiae* (fragments) and Plutarch's *Sertorius* are more favourable to Sertorius than are Plutarch's *Pompey*, Appian or Livy (we have a fragment of Livy, xci, referring to 77 and 76 B.C.). A recent fragment of Sallust (*Catalogue of . . . Papyri in John Rylands Library*, iii) may refer to Sertorius' adventures in 81. The best modern account is A. Schulten's monograph, *Sertorius* (1926), written in German. See also Rice Holmes, *RR*, I, 369 ff., for the chronology. The fact that the sources are either pro- or anti-Sertorian makes it extremely difficult to assess his aims correctly (cf. P. Treves, *Athenaeum*, 1932, 127 ff.), with the result that modern historians tend to follow one or other of the traditions. A touchstone is provided by his negotiations with Mithridates: those who believe, with Appian, that he was willing to surrender Asia, denounce him as a traitor, while those who accept Plutarch can still regard him as a loyal patriot. An attempt to resolve the deadlock has been made by E. Gabba (*Athenaeum*, 1954, 77 ff.) by trying to analyse the political sympathies of his followers and bring them into closer relation with political

currents in Rome and Italy in the seventies. Sertorius himself was loyal to Rome, but some of his followers represent the anti-Roman views of the extremist Italian opponents of Rome in the Social War. W. H. Bennett (*Historia*, 1961, 459 ff.) argues that Sertorius was killed in 73 (not 72). On some chronological problems of the Sertorian period see B. Scardigli, *Athenaeum*, 1971, 229 ff. For Gabba's article see now *RR, Army*, 103 ff. [p. 74]

5 CYRENE. A main motive may have been to use the resources of Cyrene at a time of famine and financial need in 75: the corn shortage was relieved in 73 by the lex Terentia Cassia (see p. 78) when money had come in from Cyrene. See S. I. Oost, *Cl. Ph.*, 1963, n. 45. It is astonishing that Rome had not hitherto exploited Cyrene which had been bequeathed to her by its last king Ptolemy Apion when he died in 96 but had left the country for some twenty years in a state of unrest. Clearly the Senate was bent on limiting its administrative responsibilities, while it apparently had not been subjected to strong pressure from Equites or People. See in general S. I. Oost, 'Cyrene, 96–74 B.C.', *Cl. Ph.*, 1963, 11 ff.; E. Badian, *JRS*, 1965, 119 ff., and *Rom. Imperialism in the late Rep.*² (1968), 29 f., 35 ff., 99 f.

In 75–74 P. Cornelius Lentulus Marcellinus, a quaestor, was sent to Cyrene (*pro praetore*), perhaps at the suggestion of L. Lucullus. But Badian suggests that regular governors may not have been sent until the time of Pompey, i.e. Cyrene did not become a regular province until then, since in 67 we find Cn. Lentulus (probably Publius' brother) sent to Cyrene as Pompey's legate and acting in a manner scarcely consonant with the presence there of a regular governor. Thus Publius will have gone not as a regular governor (he was only a junior magistrate), but on a special mission to obtain money and restore peaceful conditions. A series of inscriptions referring to Cn. Lentulus has been discussed by J. Reynolds, *JRS*, 1962, 97 ff. [p. 77]

6 CLUENTIUS. Oppianicus, who was condemned, died in 72. In 66 his son charged Cluentius with murder. Cicero's defence probably secured his acquittal. The *Pro Cluentio* throws a lurid light on life in an Italian country town at this period. [p. 77]

7 POMPEY'S THREAT. E. Badian (*For. Cl.*, 279 ff.) takes Pompey's threat to return from Spain to Italy in 74 (p. 76 above) very seriously. The Optimates tried to build up power in the eastern provinces to prepare against intimidation: hence the two great *imperia* of Lucullus and Antonius (it could not be foreseen that their campaigns would miscarry and, ironically, pave the way for Pompey's two eastern commands). [p. 78]

8 LEX TERENTIA CASSIA. The details are controversial: see Rice Holmes, *RR*, i, 384. It is probable that Lepidus' corn-law had been repealed soon after 78. [p. 78]

9 SPARTACUS. Sallust in his *Historiae* seems to have given a full and vivid account of the revolt, which was not completely unfavourable to Spartacus. The tradition given by Livy and the writers who depend on him was less favourable. The two chief surviving sources, Appian and Plutarch's *Crassus*, derive in part from Sallust. For a discussion of the discrepancies and difficulties see Rice Holmes, *RR*, i, 386 ff. B. A. Marshall (*Athenaeum*, 1973, 109 ff.) follows Badian (*id.*, 1970, 6 ff.) in believing that Crassus held a praetorship before 72 (probably in 73) and that his command against Spartacus was a special grant of proconsular *imperium* to a *privatus*. See K. P. Korzera, *Klio*, 1979, 477 ff. for the treatment of Spartacus in recent Soviet historical writing. [p. 79]

10 POMPEY AND CRASSUS RETAIN THEIR ARMIES. The length of time that they did so is uncertain: see Appian, i, *BC*, 1, 21; Plut. *Crass.* 12 and *Pomp.* 23. For modern discussions see Rice Holmes, *RR*, i, 390 and F. B. Marsh, *Hist. Rom. World*, Appendix 5. The possibility of two reconciliations cannot be excluded. A. N. Sherwin-White (*JRS*, 1956, 5 ff.) argues that Appian is confused, that the armies were dismissed at the end of 71 and that the threat of force was remote since Pompey wanted the dignity of the

consulship rather than a new command or a revolution. In line with this he interprets Pompey's political actions in 70 as less anti-senatorial and as less damaging to the Sullan system than is usually supposed. However that may be, Rome must have been conscious of the personal link between the general and his army, and Pompey of the need of his veterans for land. This was probably provided under a *lex Plotia agraria* (70–69 B.C.: see Cicero, *ad Att.* 1. 18. 6) which included Metellus' Spanish veterans also; its execution was slow: see R. E. Smith, *Cl. Qu.* 1957, 82 ff. and E. Gabba, *Par. Pass.*, 1950, 66 ff. (= *RR, Army*, 151 ff.)

Pompey's rise to political power and in particular his relationships with the Metelli are discussed at length and set in a framework of factional politics by B. Twyman, *Aufstieg*, I, i. (1972), 816 ff., in contrast to the view espoused by C. Meier in *Re publica amissa* (1966; 2nd ed. 1980). D. Stockton re-assesses Pompey's consulship in 70 (*Historia*, 1973, 205 ff.). On Pompey's career in general see M. Gelzer, *Pompeius* (in German, 1949); J. van Ooteghem, *Pompée le Grand* (1954); R. Seager, *Pompey: a Political Biography* (1979); J. Leach, *Pompey the Great* (1978), a slightly more general book; P. Greenhalgh, *Pompey, the Roman Alexander* (1980) and (continued as) *Pompey, the Republican Prince* (1981). See also W. S. Anderson, *Pompey, his Friends and the Literature of the first Century BC* (1963).

On Crassus see A. Garzetti, *Athenaeum*, 1941, 1 ff., 1942, 12 ff., 1944–45, 1 ff.; F. E. Adcock, *Marcus Crassus, Millionaire* (1966); B. A. Marshall, *Crassus, a political Biography* (1976); A. M. Ward, *Marcus Crassus and the late Roman Republic* (1977); some problems of Crassus' career are also discussed by J. K. Davies and others, *Liverpool Class. Monthly*, 1978, 165 ff. [p. 81]

10a CICERO AND POMPEY. On Cicero's early relationship with Pompey see A. M. Ward, *Phoenix*, 1970, 119 ff. and *Latomus*, 1970, 58 ff. and R. J. Rowland, *Riv. stor. d' Antichita*, 1976–77, 329 ff. [p. 82]

11 TRIBUNI AERARII. This somewhat mysterious class once consisted of army pay-masters. By this time they probably included men whose property qualification (300,000–400,000 sesterces) fell just below that required for membership of the Equestrian Order. At any rate their interests were equestrian rather than senatorial. See further, Rice Holmes, *RR*, i, 391; Last, *CAH*, IX, 338; C. Nicolet, *L'Ordre Equestre*, 1 (1966), 593 ff.; T. P. Wiseman, *Historia*, 1970, 71 f., 79 f. The *lex Aurelia* is further discussed by J. L. Ferrary, *Mélanges d'arch.* 1975, 321 ff., B. A. Marshall, *Rhein. Mus.*, 1975, 136 ff. and H. Bruhns, *Chiron* 1980, 263 ff. [p. 82]

12 CAESAR'S EARLY CAREER. Several minor points of chronology and the reliability of some anecdotal material remain doubtful. See H. Strasburger, *Caesars Eintritt in die Geschichte* (1938); T. R. S. Broughton, *TAPA*, 1948, 63; L. R. Taylor, *Cl. Ph.*, 1941, 121; *TAPA*, 1942, 1 ff.; *Gr. and R.*, 1957, 10 ff.; R. Syme, *JRS*, 1944, 94 f.; E. Badian, *JRS*, 1959, 81 ff. = *Studies*, 140 ff.; T. R. S. Broughton, Suppl. to *MRR* (1960). 30. For biographies and other works on Caesar, see below ch. VII, n. 30. On Caesar and the flaminate see M. Leone, *Studi E. Manni*, 193 ff. and on his capture by the pirates (dated to 75–74), A. M. Ward, *Amer. Journ Anc. Hist.*, 1977, 26 ff. [p. 82]

13 LEGES CORNELIAE. Cornelius carried a measure that praetors should administer justice in accordance with the edicts that they had issued on entering office ('ex edictis suis perpetuis'). He proposed a severe law against men who distributed money at elections (apart from those who supplied it); a modified form of this was carried by the consul Piso, who had been elected only by scandalous bribery! Cornelius also managed to limit the granting of *privilegia* (dispensations for individuals from a law) by the Senate to meetings at which 200 members voted. With his colleague Gabinius, he secured that provincials in Rome should not, in their own interest, be allowed to

borrow money, and Gabinius secured the right of foreign embassies to meet the Senate. Cornelius' subsequent trial for *maiestas* was doubtless the outcome of his attack on senatorial prerogatives which angered the Optimates; he was defended by Cicero (see Asconius' commentary *In Cornelianam*). On the career of Gabinius, who avoided the possibility of trouble by going to Pompey in the East, see E. V. Sanford, *TAPA*, 1939, 64 ff., E. Badian, *Philologus*, 1959, 87 ff. and R. S. Williams, *Phoenix*, 1978, 195 ff. On Cornelius' tribunate and subsequent trial in 65 (when he was defended by Cicero) see R. Seager, *Hommages Renard* (1969), 680 ff., A. M. Ward, *TAPA*, 1970, 554 ff. and M. Griffin, *JRS*, 1973, 196 ff. [p. 82]

14   POMPEY'S IMPERIUM. The older view that he received *imperium maius* by land as well as sea (cf. Loader, *Cl. Rev.*, 1940, 134) can hardly be maintained. It must have been *aequum* by land as stated by Velleius, 2, 31: see e.g. V. Ehrenberg, *AJP*, 1953, 117 ff. S. Jameson, *Historia*, 1970, 539 ff, after a full discussion of the evidence concludes that Pompey's *imperium* was *maius*. [p. 82]

14a MANILIUS. On the subsequent prosecution of Manilius see E. J. Phillips, *Latomus*, 1970, 595 ff. and J. T. Ramsay, *Phoenix*, 1980, 323 ff. [p. 83]

15   SERVILIUS AND THE PIRATES. For these campaigns see H. A. Ormerod, *JRS*, 1922, 35 ff.; D. Magie, *RRAM*, 287 ff. On the status of Cilicia and Pamphylia *vis-à-vis* Rome from *c.* 102 to 74 see A. N. Sherwin-White, *JRS*, 1974, 1 ff. [p. 83]

16   POMPEY'S PIRATE CAMPAIGN. See H. A. Ormerod, *Liverpool Annals of Arch.*, 1923, 46 ff. On his settlement, see A. H. M. Jones, *CERP*, 202 ff. For new inscriptions from Cyrene, see J. Reynolds, *JRS*, 1962, 97 ff. and above n. 5. On several new inscriptions which touch on the activity of the pirates see J. Reynolds, *JRS*, 1976, 179. On Pompey's legates see P. D. Breglia, *Annali . . . Univ. di Napoli*, xiii, 1970–71, 47 ff. On his settlement of Cilicia, P. D. Breglia, *Rendiconti dell'Accad.d'Arch.* Naples, 1972, 327 ff. [p. 84]

17   NICOMEDES' WILL. Although Appian and the Livian tradition record that Nicomedes bequeathed his kingdom to Rome, the Scholia Gronoviana (ed. Strangl., p. 115) says that he died intestate, and this possibly represents Sallust's view. Caution is necessary, since the former tradition might represent an official Roman version, but since Cicero in 63 referred to Bithynia as a *hereditas (de leg. agr.* 2, 40) and Sallust falsely suggested that Rome had forged Attalus' will (ch. II, n. 38), the will should probably be accepted. [p. 85]

18   OUTBREAK OF THIRD MITHRIDATIC WAR. The date, whether 74 or 73, is uncertain. For a recent discussion, which favours 74, see T. R. S. Broughton, *MRR*, ii, 106. For a full account of the war and discussion of sources and difficulties see D. Magie, *RRAM*, 323 ff. [p. 85]

19   COTTA. Cotta was later 'liberated' by Lucullus, on whose *elogium*, later erected in the Forum of Augustus, is the claim: 'conlegam suum pulsum a rege Mithridate, cum se is Calchadona contulisset, opsidione liberavit' (Dessau, *ILS*, 60). Thereafter Cotta spent two years besieging Heraclea Pontica, which he sacked in 71. On his return to Rome he was accused by Carbo of appropriating booty and was expelled from the Senate. This is recorded in a fragment of a local history of Heraclea, written by Memnon (see ch. IV, n. 1): for a translation of this see Lewis and Reinhold, *Rn. Civ.*, I, 372. [p. 85]

20   LUCULLUS. See J. M. Cobban, *Senate and Provinces, 78–49 BC* (1935), ch. iv; J. van Ooteghem, *Lucius Licinius Lucullus* (1959), with bibliography. E. Badian, who identifies Lucullus as the one officer who marched with Sulla on Rome in 88, examines his intended settlement (*Rom. Imperialism in the Late Republic*[2] (1968), 37 ff.) and concludes: 'Lucullus' personal ambition is by no means a negligible phenomenon. Yet it is clear that, as far as foreign policy is concerned, he still stood firmly in the senatorial tradition of minimizing administrative responsibility. He set out to win glory and

wealth for himself and (as he might argue) for the Roman People. But he did not aim to annex territory, except that of Pontus, which *mos maiorum* required him to do.' [p. 86]

21 POMPEY AND THE CAUCASUS. The purpose of Pompey's advance here is uncertain: possibly it was to seek a new water-frontier for the empire, but more likely the desire to add the names of unknown peoples to his battle role of victories. The view that he wanted to develop the trans-Caspian trade route to the Far East must be abandoned if this trade route had never existed as Sir W. Tarn has cogently argued (*The Greek in Bactria and India*, 112). [p. 87]

22 POMPEY AND PALESTINE. One of the chief authorities is the Jew Josephus, *Antiquit. Jud.* xiv, 1–5. See also, E. Schürer, *The History of the Jewish People in the Age of Jesus Christ²*, I (1973, revised by G. Vermes and Fergus Millar), 233 ff. For possible reference to Pompey in the Dead Sea Qumran *Commentary on Habakkuk*, see Schürer, 241 f. [p. 87]

23 PETRA AND ARETAS. On Petra see M. Rostovtzeff, *Caravan Cities*, ch. ii. Scaurus later issued coins depicting Aretas kneeling as a suppliant beside a camel: see E. A. Sydenham, *CRR*, n. 912 and Crawford, *RRC*, n. 422. [p. 88]

24 POMPEY'S EASTERN SETTLEMENT. See especially Plut. *Pomp.* 38; Appian, *Mithr.* 114–15; Dio Cassius, 37, 7a. Cf. A.H.M. Jones, *CERP*, 157 ff., 220 ff., 258 ff.; D. Magie, *RRAM*, ch. xv. For a brief summary of the various motives which have been attributed to Pompey in his settlement, see A. J. Marshall, *JRS*, 103, n. 3; in this article Marshall shows (from *Digest*, L. 1. 1. 2) that in Bithynia-Pontus Pompey conceded to cities the right to claim citizens on the basis of their mother's (as well as father's) status: this would help to stabilize the cities by extending their hold over those liable to taxation and other civic duties. For Pompey's settlement of Syria see a useful monograph, F. P. Rizzo, *Le fonti per la storia della conquista pompeiana della Siria* (1963) and T. Frankfort, *La frontière orientale dans la politique exterieure de la république romaine* (1969). On Pompey as a founder of cities see A. Dreizehnter, *Chiron*, 1975, 213 ff. When Pompey refounded Soli in Cilicia as Pompeiopolis he placed his own portrait on the coinage (B. V. Head, *Historia Numorum* (1911), 729). [p. 88]

CHAPTER VI

1 SOURCES FOR 66–50 B.C. The narrative for these years is given by Appian (*BC*, 2. 1–35) Dio Cassius (books 36–40), Livy's *Periochae* (102–9), and writers in the Livian tradition, as Orosius, Valerius Maximus and Velleius Paterculus (2. 40–8). Sallust's *Bellum Catilinae* deals with one episode: see below n. 4. The major source is Cicero, both Orations and Letters: these provide a more intimate picture of Roman life during these years than survives for any other period of Roman history. The more important speeches are mentioned below. The standard editions of the Letters are by R. Y. Tyrrell and L. C. Purser, *The Correspondence of Cicero* (6 vols. and Index, 1885–1933), with many introductory essays; here the letters are arranged chronologically, and those written down to 50 B.C. (nos. 1–300) are in vols. I–III, and by D. R. Shackleton Bailey, *Cicero's Letters to Atticus*, 7 vols. (1965–70), *Cicero, Epistulae ad familiares*, 2 vols. (1977) and *Cicero: Epistulae ad Quintum fratrem et M. Brutum* (1981). Shackleton Bailey has also provided translations in the Penguin Classics, *Letters to Atticus* (1978) and *Letters to his Friends* (1980). See also W. W. How and A. C. Clark, *Cicero, Select Letters* (2 vols., 1925–6). Fragments of some of Cicero's lost speeches are preserved in a commentary (itself fragmentary) by Q. Asconius Pedianus, written between A.D. 54 and 57; some

information is also provided by the *Scholia Bobiensia* to several speeches. Cicero's philosophical works also are important for his political thought (see also pp. 135, 170, 174 f.). Plutarch's *Lives* include those of Pompey, Caesar (Italian edition by A. Garzetti, 1954), Crassus, Cicero (Italian edition by D. Magnino, 1963), and Cato Minor. Another biographer begins to contribute to the historiography of Rome, C. Suetonius Tranquillus (*c.* A.D. 69–140), with his life of *Divus Iulius*: see the edition by H. E. Butler and M. Cary, 1927 and cf. C. Brutscher, *Analysen zu Suetons Divus Julius und der Parallelüberlieferung* (1958). Suetonius, who was secretary to Hadrian, read widely and used both scandalous and more sober sources; he provides much valuable information, although his chronology is not always clear. For Caesar's own writings see the next chapter. For modern biographies and other works on Cicero see n. 5 to chapter VIII below. [p. 90]

2 THE FIRST CATILINARIAN CONSPIRACY. See E. G. Hardy, *The Catilinarian Conspiracy* (1924), ch. ii. Suetonius (*Iul.* 9) reports a rumour that by a *coup d'état* Crassus was to become dictator and Caesar his Magister Equitum; this is very improbable. Details about any supposed plot are extremely uncertain, and the existence of a conspiracy is denied by many scholars, e.g. by H. Frisch, *Cl. et Med.*, 1947, 10 ff.; P. A. Brunt, *Cl. Rev.*, 1957, 193 ff.; R. Seager, *Historia*, 1964, 338 ff. For a defence of the ancient tradition, C. E. Stevens, *Latomus*, 1963, 397 ff. The story *might* have arisen from the rioting, supported by Catiline and Cn. Piso, at the trial of Manilius for *repetundae* (cf. also B. Marshall, *Cl. Ph.*, 1977, 318 ff.). Another unlikely view of Suetonius (*Iul.* 8) is that Caesar hoped to start a rising among the Transpadanes: in fact he probably only showed sympathy with their desire for full citizenship (cf. p. 82). The fact, however, that by an alien act, *lex Papia*, some Transpadanes were expelled from Rome suggests that many had come to the city to agitate. See also n. 8 below. [p. 91]

3 EGYPT. Because of some dynastic uncertainties the numeration of the Ptolemies varies between I–XIV and I–XV. Ptolemy X Alexander I, after intermittent joint rule with his brother Ptolemy IX Lathyrus, was killed in battle soon after 88. E. Badian has argued (*Rhein. Mus.*, 1967, 178 ff.) that it was he who made the testament and not, as usually believed, Ptolemy XI Alexander II in 80. The remarkable aspect is that the Senate made no attempt to accept the legacy and to annex one of the richest lands in the world. [p. 91]

4 SALLUST AND CATILINE. Sallust (*Cat.* 16, 4 ff.) wrongly assigns Catiline's revolutionary schemes to 64. This is possibly due to carelessness, as Sallust was often weak on chronology, but more probably derives from the political bias of his *Bellum Catilinae*. This was published soon after Caesar's death as a pro-Caesarian pamphlet. Sallust wished to show that Caesar was not implicated in the main conspiracy of 63: he may therefore have ante-dated the beginning of the plot to 64 when Caesar could hardly be suspected of implication in it. (Caesar may have favoured Catiline's election in 64, but as a potential tool, not as a revolutionary.) Cf. also L. A. MacKay, *Phoenix*, 1962, 181 ff. [p. 92]

5 CICERO'S ELECTION. Some fragments of Cicero's *In Toga Candida* are preserved in Asconius' Commentary (A. C. Clark, O.C.T.). Advice on electioneering methods was given to Cicero in a pamphlet *De Petitione Consulatus* or *Commentariolum Petitionis*, ascribed to his brother Quintus (see e.g. Tyrrell and Purser, *Correspondence of Cicero*, i, Ep. 12). This ascription is doubted by some (e.g. M. I. Henderson, *JRS*, 1950, 8 ff., and R. G. M. Nisbet, *JRS*, 1961, 84 ff.), but is accepted by others (as F. Münzer, H. Last and recently R. Till, *Historia*, 1962, 415 ff.). Mrs. Henderson's arguments are countered by J. P. V. D. Balsdon, *Cl. Qu.*, 1963, 242 ff. Even if not by Quintus, it may contain contemporary material. The *Commentariolum* is discussed by J. M. David and others, *Aufstieg*, I, 3 (1973), 239 ff. [p. 92]

6 RULLUS' LAW (*lex Servilia*). On Cicero's speeches *De lege agraria* see E. G. Hardy, *Some Problems of Roman History*, 68 ff.; A. Afzelius, *Cl. et Med.*, 1940, 214 ff. G. V. Sumner, *TAPA*, 1966, 569 ff., argues that the measure was partly designed to meet Pompey's needs: Caesar probably supported it as Pompey's *amicus*, Crassus was inactive, and Cicero opposed because he disliked agrarian distribution. A. M. Ward, *Historia*, 1972, 244 ff. supports the more traditional view that in the proposal to annex Egypt in the Rullan land bill Crassus and Caesar were working together against Cicero and Pompey. [p. 92]

7 RABIRIUS. See Hardy, *op. cit.*, 99 ff., also L. Havas, *Acta Classica Debrecen*, 1976, 19 ff.; E. J. Phillips, *Klio*, 1974, 87 ff. [p. 93]

8 THE CATILINARIAN CONSPIRACY. For a discussion of the various problems see Hardy, *The Catilinarian Conspiracy* (1924 = *JRS*, 1917, 153–228); Rice Holmes, *RR*, 455 ff. See also N. Criniti, 'Studi recenti su Catilina', *Aevum*, 1967, 370 ff., *Bibliografia Catilinaria* (1971) and (on Catiline's reputation) *Contrib. Istit. stor. ant. Univ. S. Cu. Milan*, 1975, 121 ff. Z. Yavetz, *Historia*, 1963, 485 ff., attributes Catiline's failure to a dropping off of the support of the plebs, especially shopkeepers, since the proposed abolition of debts was a temporary expedient rather than a basic social reform. K. H. Waters has argued (*Historia*, 1970, 195 ff.) that the Catilinarian affair has been grossly exaggerated, not least by Cicero, and that there is no real evidence for a planned coup before Catiline left Rome to prepare for an armed rising. R. Seager (*Historia*, 1973, 240 ff.) also thinks that Cicero presented as parts of a grand revolutionary scheme elements (the activities of Catiline himself, Manlius' rising in Etruria and the doings of Lentulus and his confederates in Rome) which were in fact only loosely connected. In contrast to Waters and Seager, E. J. Phillips (*Historia*, 1976, 441 ff.) emphasizes the real danger from Catiline. C. R. Bradlem, *Cl. Ph.*, 1978, 329 ff., regards Catiline's slave followers as runaways, not recruits. [p. 93]

9 CICERO'S PRO MURENA. In the middle of these anxious days Cicero defended the consul-elect, L. Licinius Murena, who was accused of bribery; one of the prosecutors was Cato. Though Murena was guilty, Cicero argued that the state must have two consuls ready for the beginning of the next year in view of the dangers of the times, but he conducted the defence with a light touch; Murena was acquitted. Soon afterwards in 62 Cicero defended P. Sulla on a charge of complicity with Catiline, and also helped to vindicate the claim of his teacher Archias to Roman citizenship. [p. 93]

10 CICERO'S EXECUTION OF THE CONSPIRATORS. For a discussion of some of the legal issues involved see H. Last, *JRS*, 1943, 93 ff., who also draws attention to Sallust's references to threats to release the prisoners by force, which may well have affected the question of their fate and help to explain the Senate's backing for Cicero's quick action. T. N. Mitchell (*Historia*, 1971, 47 ff.) discusses Cicero's attitude to the *Senatus consultum ultimum* and concludes that this measure was designed to substitute in time of danger, the sovereignty of the Senate for that of individuals. [p. 94]

11 POMPEY AND NEPOS. Nepos, whose brother Metellus Celer was Pompey's brother-in-law, had been Pompey's legate in the East and now represented his interests in Rome. Nepos' mission and the resultant events are regarded by C. Meier, *Athenaeum*, 1962, 103 ff., as decisive for Pompey's future. Cf. also E. J. Parrish, *Phoenix*, 1973, 387 ff. [p. 95]

12 PERSONAL AMBITION. On this see C. Wirzubski, *Libertas as a Political Idea* (1950), esp. 64 f. A treatise on kingship by the Epicurean philosopher Philodemus (preserved on papyrus at Herculaneum) was dedicated to Piso, consul in 58. It advocates moderation in rule and its message was presumably directed to the *principes viri* of this period. See Oswyn Murray, *JRS*, 1965, 161 ff. (173 ff. for its political purpose). [p. 95]

13 OTIUM CUM DIGNITATE. On the meaning and history of this slogan see C. Wirszubski, *JRS*, 1954, 1 ff.; J. P. V. D. Balsdon, *Cl. Qu.*, 1960, 46 ff. [p. 95]

13a THE CLODIUS AFFAIR. See J. P. V. D. Balsdon, *Historia*, 1966, 65 ff., and on bribery at the trial T. Loposko, *Athenaeum*, 1978, 288 ff. [p. 96]

14 ASIATIC TAX CONTRACT. See J. P. V. D. Balsdon, *JRS*, 1962, 135 ff. [p. 96]

15 THE FIRST TRIUMVIRATE. On its crucial importance see R. Syme, *The Roman Revolution* (1939), ch. i, who adopts the same starting point as Pollio, in this outstanding study of the period from 60 B.C. to A.D. 14. Cf. also the remarks of C. Wirszubski, *Libertas*, 74 ff. The date of the formation of the triumvirate is uncertain. All sources (except Suetonius) place at least a limited agreement between Caesar and Pompey before the elections of 60, though the full agreement of the three men may have been later in the year. Cf. Rice Holmes, *RR*, i, 474 ff. G. Zecchini, *Rendi. Ist. Lomb*, 1975, 399 ff., attributes the agreement to Caesar and to two stages, before and after the elections of 60. G. R. Stanton and B. A. Marshall, *Historia*, 1975, 205 ff., regard Pompey and Crassus as the moving spirits. On the career of Afranius see M. Malavolta, *Miscell. Gr. e. Rom.*, 1977, 251 ff. [p. 97]

16 SILVAE CALLESQUE. Thus Suetonius (*D. J.*, 19, 2), the sole source. This statement has been challenged by, e.g., J. P. V. D. Balsdon, *JRS*, 1939, 180 ff., as a misunderstanding for Italy, but is widely accepted. Balsdon's view is supported further by P. J. Rhodes, *Historia*, 1978, 617 ff.: Italy was declared a token province to allow the Senate more time to assess the threat of danger from Gaul. [p. 97]

17 CAESAR'S LEGISLATION. The order and dating of his measures are uncertain, but probably the agrarian law came before the *lex Vatinia*; the first measure may have been carried by the end of January, the *lex Campana* near the end of May. For a discussion see L. R. Taylor, *AJP*, 1951, 254 ff., and (for a revised view) *Historia*, 1968, 173 ff.; C. Meier, *Historia*, 1961, 19 ff.; J. Linderski, *Historia*, 1965, 423 ff. The *lex Iulia de repetundis* is dated Aug. or Sept. by S. I. Oost, *AJP*, 1956, 19 ff. R. E. Smith, *Phoenix*, 1964, 303 ff., regards Caesar's first consulship as sealing the doom of the Republic. After attacking Caesar in edicts and pamphlets Bibulus adopted more obstructive tactics, designed to prevent business in the Comitia and to thwart Caesar; these consisted in shutting himself up at home and announcing that he was 'observing the sky' for omens. But, as pointed out by A. W. Lintott, *Violence in Republican Rome* (1968), 144 f., an announcement of an omen, to be valid, had to be made in person and therefore Bibulus' *servatio* from his house could technically be ignored by Caesar and did not invalidate the latter's *acta*. On attempts to make Caesar respect the auspices see C. Meier, *Museum Helveticum*, 1975, 197 ff. On the chronology of Caesar's legislation see further, R. Seager, *Pompey* (1979), 190 ff. [p. 98]

18 VATINIUS. On his career see L. G. Pocock, *A Commentary on Cicero In Vatinium*, an invective which Cicero delivered in 56 when he was defending P. Sestius (a quaestor of 63 who had helped him against Catiline); Vatinius was a witness against Sestius. In 59 Cicero unsuccessfully defended his former consular colleague Antonius when charged with extortion (the speech is not extant) and successfully defended L. Flaccus (speech extant). [p. 98]

19 THE VETTIUS AFFAIR. See esp. Cicero, *Ad Att.* ii, 24. Much remains obscure. Vettius tried to implicate various members of the aristocracy, e.g. Lucullus, Bibulus and Brutus, but it is improbable that there was any serious plan to murder Pompey; Vettius himself was imprisoned and died there. It is unlikely that Caesar employed him; possibly Vatinius did, as Cicero later alleged; more probably he was a free-lance. That Brutus was involved is unlikely, but the inclusion of his name is interesting and would have made the alleged plot more plausible since he was known, perhaps as early as

this, to have Republican sympathies: about this date he was mint-master and issued coins with the head of Libertas and the inscription LIBERTAS, which at any rate will have been a criticism of the triumvirs (see E. A. Sydenham, *CRR*, n. 906; Crawford, *RRC*, n. 433). Cf. P. A. Brunt, *Cl. Qu.*, 1953, 62 ff.; L. R. Taylor, *Cl. Qu.*, 1954, 181 ff.; C. Meier, *Historia*, 1961, 88 ff.; R. Seager, *Latomus*, 1965, 525 ff. [p. 98]

20 CLODIUS. A general assessment of his career is given by A. W. Lintott, *Gr. and R.*, 1967, 157 ff., while E. S. Gruen, *Phoenix*, 1966, 120 ff., also argues for Clodius' considerable independence of the triumvirs. On the support which Clodius received from his *clientela* in the East see E. Rawson, *Historia*, 1973, 219 ff. On Clodius and Cicero see W. K. Lacey, *Antichthon*, 1974, 85 ff., and W. M. F. Rundell, *Historia*, 1979, 301 ff. On the *collegia* see J. M. Flambard, *Mélanges d'arch.*, 1977, 115 ff. [p. 99]

21 CYPRUS AND CATO. See S. I. Oost, *Cl. Ph.*, 1955, 98 ff.; E. Badian, *JRS*, 1965, 110 ff. Needing money for his corn dole, Clodius proposed that Cyprus should be annexed. Since Cyprus was to be added to Cilicia, the task was to be given to Gabinius, but the latter was transferred to Syria and so Cato went to Cyprus with a specific financial commission. When joined to Cilicia it received its *lex provinciae* from P. Lentulus Spinther, the first governor of the united province. Badian, *Rom. Imperialism in late Rep.*, 77, denounces the annexation of Cyprus as 'this most disgraceful act of Roman imperialism apart from the Gallic War'. [p. 100]

22 CICERO'S DE DOMO SUA. See the edition by R. G. Nisbet (1936). Clodius attacked Cicero again in 56 about the rebuilding of his house, to which Cicero replied in *De haruspicum responsis*: n. 19, 40, where the *haruspices* warn that dissensions among the nobles may lead to one man rule (a reference to Pompey and Messius). [p. 100]

23 CICERO PRO SESTIO. Cf. n. 18 above. In this speech Cicero attacked Caesar's agents, Vatinius and Clodius and tried to rally all loyal citizens to defend the constitution. On Cicero and the *lex Campana* see M. Cary, *Cl. Qu.*, 1923, 103 ff. On the politics of 57–55 see J. F. Lazenby, *Latomus*, 1959, 67 ff. On an attempt by a tribune, probably Antistius Vetus, to prosecute Caesar, probably early in 56, see E. Badian, *Polis and Imperium* (ed. J. A. S. Evans, 1974), 145 ff. [p. 101]

23a LUCA. On the conference and its political background see E. S. Gruen, *Historia*, 1969, 71 ff., C. Luibheid, *Cl. Ph.*, 1970, 88 ff. and J. Jackson, *Liverpool Class. Monthly*, 1978. 173 ff. For a presentation of the view that Luca was less a planned summit meeting of the big three than a hastily arranged get-together, Crassus probably being absent and his interests represented by Caesar, see R. Seager, *Pompey* (1979), 122 ff. [p. 101]

24 CICERO IN 56–4. For his palinode see *ad Atticum*, 4, 5. For the *De provinciis consularibus* see the edition by H. E. Butler and M. Cary (1924). Earlier in 56 Cicero had successfully defended a brilliant young man M. Caelius Rufus, who had supplanted the poet Catullus as the lover of the notorious Clodia, Clodius' sister, and now discarded in turn was being accused by her of attempted poisoning: for Cicero's *Pro Caelio* see the edition by R. G. Austin (1960). In his *Pro Balbo*, delivered in defence of Balbus' claim to citizenship later in 56, Cicero praised Pompey. In 55 Cicero in the Senate bitterly attacked Caesar's father-in-law L. Calpurnius Piso (*cos.* 58) charging him with peculation and mis-government in Macedonia. Cicero's *In Pisonem* has been edited by R. G. M. Nisbet (1961). The (probably pseudo-) Sallustian *Oration in Ciceronem* is a reply. With less pleasure, and under pressure from Caesar, in 54 Cicero was forced to defend Vatinius, who was being prosecuted under a law carried by Crassus against bribery and the misuse of political clubs (*sodalicia*) for political purposes. Pompey insisted that Cicero should defend Gabinius, who had restored Ptolemy to Egypt, had been acquitted on a charge of *maiestas*, and was now accused *de repetundis*; he was condemned. On Gabinius see E. M. Sanford, *TAPA*, 1939, 64 ff.; E. Badian, *Philologus*,

1959, 87 ff. On the role of *amicitia* in the career of Gabinius see R. S. Williams, *Phoenix*, 1978, 195 ff., and on his trials in 54 B.C. see E. Fantham, *Historia*, 1975, 475 ff. Cicero also defended, with greater success, C. Rabirius Postumus, who had acted as Ptolemy's finance minister. Cicero also started writing in 54 his great study of political theory, *De Re Publica*. On Caelius Rufus see M. Volponi, *M. Celio rufo (Mem. dell'Ist. Lombardo,* 1971). On Cicero's relations with Milo see A. W. Lintott, *JRS*, 1974, 62 ff. [p. 102]

25 THE TERMINAL DATE OF CAESAR'S COMMAND. See especially Cicero, *ad. fam.* iii, 8, 4–9; 11, 3; *ad. Att.* vii, 7, 6; 9, 3. The precise date of the end of the command (the *legis dies*) is obviously of little importance in itself, but it becomes of vital importance because of the principle behind it, namely that Caesar wanted to step straight from his proconsular command to office in Rome, while his opponents hoped that for a short time he would become a private citizen and thus be exposed to prosecution. A vast literature has grown up on this question, from Mommsen's paper on *Die Rechtsfrage* onwards. For a summary discussion see How and Clark, *Cicero, Select Letters* (1926), appendix v; cf. Rice Holmes, *RR*, ii, 199 ff. More recent discussions include F. B. Marsh (*The Founding of the Roman Empire*, 1927, pp. 275 ff.) who puts it at 1 March 50; F. E. Adcock (*Cl. Qu.*, 1932, 14 ff.) and C. A. Gianelli (*Ann. Sc. Norm. Pisa*, 1966, 107 ff.) 13 Nov. 50; C. E. Stevens (*AJP*, 1938, 169 ff.) between July and Oct. 50; J. P. V. D. Balsdon (*JRS*, 1939, 57 ff and 167 ff.) argues that no such day was laid down by law; G. Elton (*JRS*, 1946, 18 ff.) discusses these views and returns to Mommsen's belief in 28 Feb. 49. See also R. Sealey, *Cl. Med.*, 1957, 75 ff., P. J. Cuff, *Historia*, 1958, 445 ff.; H. Gesche, *Chiron*, 1973, 179 ff.; D. Stockton, *Historia*, 1975, 232 ff. (1 March 50); K. Bringmann, *Chiron*, 1978, 345 ff.; R. Seager, *Pompey*, (1979), 193 ff., a summary, in line with Balsdon. [p. 103]

25a CICERO IN CILICIA. See M. Wistrand, *Cicero Imperator. Studies in Cicero's Correspondence 51–47 BC* (1979). [p. 103]

26 CURIO. See W. K. Lacey (*Historia*, 1961, 318 ff.) who believes that Curio was not bribed to support Caesar and that he proposed a special commission for roads (Cic. *ad. fam.* 8. 6. 1) to enable Caesar to withdraw from Gaul in peace without a consulship. On the tribunes that supported Caesar see K. Rauflaub, *Chiron*, 1974, 293 ff. [p. 104]

27 RESPONSIBILITY FOR THE CIVIL WAR. On Caesar's *dignitas* see Caesar, *Bellum Civile*, 1, 9, 2 (cf. 1, 7, 7. Cic. *ad Att.* 7, 11, 1). Cf. K. Rauflaub, *Dignitatis Contentio. Studien zur Motivation und politischen Taktik im Burgerkrieg zwischen Caesar und Pompeius* (1974). On Pompey see Tacitus, *Hist.* 2, 38, 1. Cicero admits that both Pompey and Caesar strove for their own aggrandizement: *ad Att.* 7, 3, 4; 8, 11, 2. For further discussion cf. C. Wirszubski, *Libertas*, 77 ff.; R. Syme, *Roman Revolution*, 47 ff. On the motives that drove Pompey to war see L. G. Pocock, *Gr. and R.*, 1959, 68 ff. For lists of *nobiles* and members of other senatorial families that supported Caesar, Pompey or remained neutral see D. R. Shackleton Bailey, *Cl. Qu.*, 1960, 253 ff.; H. Bruhns, *Caesar und die römische Obersicht in Jahren 49–44 v. Chr. Untersuchungen zur Herrschaftsestablierung im Burgerkrieg* (1978). [p. 104]

28 PARTHIA AND CRASSUS. On Parthia see W. W. Tarn, *CAH*, IX, ch. xiv; N. C. Debevoise, *A Political History of Parthia* (1938); M. A. R. Colledge, *The Parthians* (1967); on the cavalry, W. W. Tarn, *Hellenistic Military and Naval Developments* (1930), 73 ff. A Chinese historian of the first century A.D. describes some historical paintings which show troops attacking a city in Turkestan; some of the defenders are drawn up in a formation with interlocked shields resembling the Roman *testudo*. H. H. Dubs (*A Roman City in Ancient China*, 1957; cf. *Gr. and R.*, 1957, 137 ff.) believes that these men may represent some of the survivors of Carrhae who escaped from the Parthians and took service first with the Hun Jzh-Jzh, whose capital on the Talass River, east of the Jaxartes, was

captured, despite the help of the Romans, by the Chinese leader Ch'en T'ang (36 B.C.). They then passed to the service of Ch'en who settled them in a frontier city to which the Chinese gave their name for Rome, Li-jien. D. Timpe (*Museum Helveticum*, 1962, 194 ff.) has discussed the influence of Carrhae on later Roman policy towards Parthia and upon Roman internal politics. [p. 106]

CHAPTER VII

1 SOURCES FOR 49–44 B.C. The writers are in general those mentioned in note 1 to ch. VI: Appian (*BC*, ii, 32–117), Dio Cassius (41–44), Cicero (*Pro Marcello, Pro Ligario*, of 46 B.C. and *Pro Rege Deiotaro* of 45; Letters, nos. 301–698 in Tyrell and Purser), the Corpus Caesarianum (cf. n. 8), Livy's *Periochae* (109–16), Velleius Paterculus (2. 49–57). Plutarch, Suetonius. To these are added *Epistulae ad Caesarem* (see n. 20 below) and Lucan's *Pharsalia* (see p. 300). See also notes 5 and 8 below. Coins (cf. n. 16 and 28) and inscriptions (cf. n. 11, 21, 23) are important. [p. 107]

2 BUREBISTAS. See V. Parvan, *Dacia*, ch. v. [p. 107]

3 PRE-ROMAN GAUL. See Caesar, *Bell. Gall.*, esp. 6, 13–20; Diodorus, 5, 21–2; 25–32; Strabo, 4. The fundamental modern work is still C. Jullian, *Histoire de le Gaule*, II (4th ed., 1921). See also A. Grenier, *Les Gaulois* (1945) and T. G. E. Powell, *The Celts* (1958). For accounts of recent work on Gaul of all periods see R. Lantier, *JRS*, 1946, 76 ff.; P-M. Duval, *Historia*, v, 1956, 238 ff. Cf. M. Pobé, *The Art of Roman Gaul* (1961). [p. 108]

4 DRUIDS. See T. D. Kendrick, *The Druids* (1927); Stuart Piggott, *The Druids* (1968). [p. 108]

5 CAESAR'S GALLIC CAMPAIGNS. The chief source is Caesar's own Commentaries *De Bello Gallico* in seven books, each dealing with one year, to which his staff-officer Hirtius added an eighth book covering the years 51–50 and thus linking with Caesar's own *De Bello Civili*. Other sources add little. *Commentaries* were not strictly *historia* but rather formed the material for future historians, though Caesar brought great literary skill to their composition. They were based on the despatches that he sent back every year to the Senate in Rome. The date of their composition and publication offer many problems. Some believe that they were published annually, or in small groups of Commentaries in order to influence public opinion in Rome, while others suppose them to have been published as a single work about 51 with a view in part to future elections. On these questions see the recent discussion by Sir Frank E. Adcock, *Caesar as a Man of Letters* (1956), esp. 77 ff. An even more important question is that of their accuracy. This has been impeached in modern times on grounds of political mis-representation or the glossing over of military errors. It is too much to suppose that any man can ever achieve complete and absolute objectivity, and it would be naïve to suppose that Caesar has written the whole truth and nothing but the truth. Neverthe-less his work has stood up well to critical attacks and its essential trustworthiness is beyond question. An extreme, and as some would think in itself a tendentious, criti-cism of Caesar's veracity is found in a recent work by M. Rambaud, *L'Art de la déforma-tion historique dans les commentaires de César* (1953): for a criticism of this see J. P. V. D. Balsdon, *JRS*, 1955, 161 ff. and cf. *Gr. and R.*, 1957, 19 ff. A further attack on Caesar's reliability, especially in Book 1 and in his account of the Germans (4 and 6) is made by G. Walser, *Caesar und die Germanen* (1956), but on this see A. N. Sherwin-White, *JRS*, 1958, 188 ff. Modern works on Caesar's campaigns include C. Jullian, *Hist. de la. Gaule*, III (2nd ed. 1920); T. Rice Holmes, *Caesar's Conquest of Gaul²* (1911); L. A. Constans, *Guide illustré des campagnes de César en Gaule* (1929); C. Jullian (ed. P. M. Duval),

Vercingetorix (1963). D. Timpe, *Historia*, 1965, 189 ff., views Caesar's policy in the context of Roman tradition, but E. Badian, *Roman Imperialism in the late Rep.*, 89 ff., emphasizes the vast financial profits made by Caesar, for which 'in some cases, the opportunity had been deliberatley sought and created' (p. 77): Caesar is 'the greatest brigand of them all' (*per contra*, for the non-imperialist view of Caesar see A. N. Sherwin-White, *Gr. and R.*, 1957, 36 ff.). [p. 109]

6   CAESAR IN BRITAIN, See *Bell, Gall.* 4, 20–36; 5, 1–23. Cf. T. Rice Holmes, *Ancient Britain and the Invasions of Caesar* (1935); R. G. Collingwood, *Roman Britain and the English Settlements* (1937); S. S. Frere, *Britannia*² (1978); C. F. C. Hawkes, *Proc. Brit. Acad.*, 1977, 125 ff.; P. Salway, *Roman Britain* (1981). On Cassivellaunus' *oppidum* at Wheathampstead see R. E. M. Wheeler, *Antiquity*, 1933, 21 ff. [p. 111]

7   ALESIA AND CAESAR'S CAMPS. On the site of the preceding engagement, which is often placed near Dijon, see É. Thevenot, *Les Éduens n'ont pas trahi* (1960), 133 ff., who argues for Laignes near Vix. Caesar's great siege-works round Alesia were first excavated by the emperor Napoleon III. Other of his camps have been found near Berry-au-Bac (his campaign in 57 against the Bellovaci); at Orcet below Gergovia; and at Nointel near Clermont de l'Oise (dating from his campaign of 51 against the Bellovaci; this more recent excavation is particularly interesting: three main camps and outworks have been found, together with the *pontes* (*Bell. Gall.* 8, 14), log and brushwood causeways, which Caesar built over the marsh to enable his men to get to grips with the enemy). See O. Brogan, *Roman Gaul* (1953), 17 ff. For a fine air-photograph of the Gallic *oppidum* at Gergovia see J. Bradford, *Ancient Landscapes* (1957), pl. 69. See also for a detailed study, J. Harmand, *Une Campaigne césarienne: Alesia* (1967). [p. 112]

8   THE CIVIL WAR, 49–45. The chief sources are the *Corpus Caesarianum* and Cicero's Letters. The former comprises three books *De Bello Civili*; the *Bellum Alexandrinum*, which continues the narrative down to Zela, and was written perhaps by Hirtius (*cos.* 43) one of Caesar's officers; the *Bellum Africum* covering the winter of 47–46, and written perhaps by a tribune or centurion; and the *Bellum Hispaniense* on the Munda campaign, written by someone who took part, but who is less literate. Appian, *BC*, ii, and Dio Cassius, xli-xliii, provide narratives, while Lucan's poem, the *Bellum Civile* (or *Pharsalia*) ends with the Alexandrine war. Modern works: full discussions by Rice Holmes, *RR*, iii; see also F. E. Adcock, *CAH*, IX, ch. xvi. [p. 114]

9   DOMITIUS AHENOBARBUS. For the interesting correspondence that passed between him and Pompey see the letters preserved in Cicero *ad Attic* viii, 11. Cf. D. R. Shackleton Bailey, *JRS*, 1956, 57 ff. On the Corfinium campaign see A. Barns, *Historia*, 1966, 74 ff. [p. 114]

10 NEGOTIATIONS OF CAESAR AND POMPEY. Cf. F. B. Marsh, *Hist. Rom. World 146–30 BC*, 400 ff., and K. von Fritz, *TAPA*, 1941, 125 ff., who questions Caesar's sincerity. Difficulties arise because Caesar's version of Pompey's reply (*Bell. Civ.* i, 10, 3–4) does not quite coincide with that given by Cicero (*ad fam.* xvi, 12, 3). Further, in the negotiations after Corfinium, Caesar has not revealed the terms of Pompey's offer (*Bell. Civ.* i, 24, 5; 26, 2; cf. *ad Att.* ix, 13 A.). On the credentials of the envoys, L. Caesar and L. Roscius, see D. R. Shackleton Bailey (*JRS*, 1960, 80 ff.) who supports the view that they were sent to Caesar by Pompey and not by the Senate. The negotiations are studied in full by K. Rauflaub, *Chiron*, 1975, 247 ff. [p. 115]

11 LEX ROSCIA AND LEX RUBRIA. Two fragments of inscriptions from Ateste and Veleia in Cisalpine Gaul bear on its enfranchisement (Riccobono, *FIRA* I, nos. 20 and 19). The former, which refers to the *lex Roscia*, may be part of a supplementary measure dependent on it; the enfranchising law will then have been the *lex Roscia* (cf. E. G.

Hardy, *Problems of Rom. Hist.*, 207 ff.). Other scholars believe that the enfranchising act was a *lex Rubria* which is mentioned in the fragment from Veleia; this fragment is part of the *lex Rubria* or of a law dependent on it. For this law see Hardy, *Six Roman Laws*, 110 ff. See further U. Ewins, *Papers Brit. Sch. Rome*, 1955, 93 ff., who also suggests that Caesar was planning to settle some veterans in Cisalpine Gaul. The *lex Rubria* dealt with the judicial competence of the municipal magistrates of Cisalpine Gaul; chapters xxi and xxii, dealing with debt etc., are discussed by M. W. Frederiksen, *JRS*, 1964, 129 ff. Cf. also F. J. Bruna, *Lex Rubria. Caesars Regelung für die Richterlichen Kompetenzen der Munizipalmagistrate in Gallia Cisalpina* (1972): on which see A. N. Sherwin-White, *JRS*, 1974, 236 ff. [p. 115]

12 DEBT. On this problem in the Ciceronian age and on Caesar's legislation in particular see M. W. Frederiksen, *JRS*, 1966, 128 ff., who concludes that Caesar, faced with a debt crisis of unprecedented size, took the following steps: temporary measures in 49 and 48 that created valuations of property (*aestimationes*) at pre-war prices on the basis of which property should be legally transferred to creditors; reviving a law, and enacting in 46–45, that limited the hoarding of coin and required investment in land in Italy; and by a *lex Iulia* in 46–45 creating *cessio bonorum* which permanently helped to mitigate harsher aspects of the law of debt. (For the view that this last law was Augustan rather than Julian see L. Guénoun, *La cessio bonorum* (1920), 19 ff., and J. Crook, *Law and Life of Rome* (1967), 176 f.) [p. 116]

13 PHARSALUS. For general discussions on the battle see M. Rambaud, *Historia*, iii (1955), 346 ff., W. E. Gwatkin, *TAPA*, 1956, 109 ff., and Y. Bequignon, *Bull. Corresp. Hellen.*, 1960. 176 ff., also C. B. R. Pelling, *Historia*, 1973, 249 ff. F. Paschould, *Historia*, 1981, 178 ff., supports the view of Bequignon rather than of Pelling. [p. 117]

14 POMPEY. On Pompey see the works by Gelzer, van Ooteghem, Leach, Seager and Greenhalgh quoted above in ch. v, n. 10. On his portraiture see J. M. C. Toynbee, *Roman Historical Portraits* (1978), 24 ff. [p. 118]

15 CAESAR IN EGYPT. For the general political situation, see a Tubingen Dissertation by H. Heinen, *Rom. und Ägypten von 51 bis 47 V. Chr.* (1966), on which cf. E. Badian, *JRS*, 1968, 258 f. For the view that he did not dally in Egypt but left at the beginning of May, 47, see L. E. Lord, *JRS*, 1938, 18 ff. The story of his Nile trip is not confirmed by contemporary evidence. On the career of Cn. Domitius Calvinus see J. M. Sweeney, *Anc. W.*, I, 1978, 179 ff. [p. 119]

16 CAESAR'S DICTATORSHIP. It used to be thought that Caesar was appointed dictator II in his absence for an indefinite period (which lasted in the event until 46): one reason was that on some coins of 46 he was described as 'cos. tert., dict. iter', but this may only mean that when consul III (i.e. in 46) his last dictatorship was his second, not that he was still holding that office (there are analogies for this usage); also a coin describes him simply as 'cos. ter.', i.e. early 46 after he had given up his second but had not started his third dictatorship. He will therefore have been merely consul designate for the last months of 47. For this view see U. Wilken, *Abh. Preuss. Akad.* 1940; V. Ehrenberg, *AJP*, 1953, 129 ff.; A. E. Raubitschek, *JRS*, 1954, 70 f. [p. 119]

17 LABIENUS. He came from Picenum; he may therefore have been an old partisan of Pompey and after serving Caesar in Gaul he may have revived an older loyalty in deserting to Pompey: see R. Syme, *JRS*, 1938, 113 ff. (= *Roman Papers* (1979), i, 62 ff.). W. B. Tyrell (*Historia*, 1972, 424 ff.) interprets Labienus' departure from Caesar in 49 as a move to join the legitimate government against a revolutionary proconsul. [p. 120]

18 CATO. On Cato see L. R. Taylor, *Party Politics in the Age of Caesar* (1949), ch. viii; A. Afzelius, *Cl. et Med.*, 1941, 100 ff. On his portrait found at Volubilis in Africa see J. M. C. Toynbee, *Roman Historical Portraits* (1978), 37 ff. [p. 120]

19 LIGARIUS. See K. Kumaniecki, *Hermes*, 1967, 434 ff. [p. 121]

20 EPISTULAE AD CAESAREM SENEM DE REPUBLICA. These two works are attributed to Sallust, but some scholars believe that they are really *suasoriae* written under the Empire. Their Sallustian authorship has been maintained by many, e.g. Ed. Meyer, L. R. Taylor (*Party Politics in the Age of Caesar*, 154 ff., 185 ff., 232 ff.); others are rightly more sceptical, e.g. H. Last, *Cl. Qu.*, 1923, 87 ff., 151 ff.; F. E. Adcock, *JRS*, 1950, 139; E. Fraenkel, *JRS*, 1951, 192 ff.; R. Syme; *Museum Helveticum*, 1958, 46 ff., 1962, 177 ff. *Epistula* II is the earlier (50–49, or even 51); the first letter belongs to 46. [p. 121]

20a THE CORN DOLE. See G. Rickman, *The Corn Supply of Ancient Rome* (1980), 175 ff. After the existing list of recipients had been pruned, the number was kept down by an annual system of drawing lots (*subsortitio*) to fill the vacancies: the details of how such a system worked are shown by a third century A.D. archive relating to a corn dole at Oxyrhynchus in Egypt; see J. Rea, *Oxyrhynchi Papyri*, xl (1972). [p. 122]

21 THE SO-CALLED LEX IULIA MUNICIPALIS. This is partly preserved in a long inscription found at Heraclea in south Italy. It contains Caesar's proposed legislation about the corn-dole and roads in Rome, and the regulations for the Italian municipalities. Cf. *CAH*, IX, 698 ff. For the text see Riccobono, *FIRA*, n. 13. For translation and commentary see E. G. Hardy, *Six Roman Laws*, 149 ff.; Lewis and Reinhold, *Rn. Civ.* i, 408 ff. [p. 122]

22 PROVINCIAL ARRANGEMENTS. Further measures include the limitation of 'free legations' to one year: these were roving commissions which had been much abused by the nobility at the expense of provincials. The five-year interval between the consulship and proconsulship established by Pompey (p. 103) lapsed. A law stopped senators' sons leaving Italy and Roman citizens of military age living abroad for more than three years. [p. 123]

23 CAESAR'S COLONIES. See F. Vittinghoff, *Römische Kolonisation . . . unter Caesar und Augustus* (1952), esp. 49–95, with a list on p. 148. For the charter of Urso (Riccobono, *FIRA*, n. 21) see translation and commentary by E. G. Hardy, *Three Spanish Charters*, 23 ff.; Lewis and Reinhold, *Rn. Civ.* i., 420 ff. For the evidence afforded by coins for colonial foundations see M. Grant, *From Imperium to Auctoritas* (1946). Cf. also P. A. Brunt, *Italian Manpower* (1971), 255 ff., 319 ff. [p. 123]

24 CAESAR'S GRANTS OF CITIZENSHIP AND LATIN RIGHTS. See A. N. Sherwin-White, *Rom. Citizenship*, 136 ff. On Latin rights in Spain (extensive in Ulterior, limited in Citerior) see M. I. Henderson, *JRS*, 1942, pp. 1 ff. It is uncertain whether Caesar planned to survey the whole empire for census purposes, because this view depends on the sole authority of a fifth-century geographer. [p. 124]

25 CAESAR'S PARTY AND THE SENATE. On his supporters see R. Syme, *Rom. Rev.*, ch. v; for his senators, Syme, ch. vi, and in *Papers Brit. Sch. Rome*, 1938, pp. 1 ff. (= *Roman Papers* (1979), i, 88 ff.). On the attitude of Etruria to Caesar see E. Rawson, *JRS*, 1978, 132 ff. [p. 125]

25a LEX ANNALIS. The magistracies and the working of the lex annalis from 49 to 44 are discussed by G. V. Sumner, *Phoenix*, 1971, 246 ff. [p. 125]

26 CAESAR'S TRIBUNICIA POTESTAS. See F.E. Adcock, *CAH*, IX, 900. [p. 126]

27 CAESAR IMPERATOR. That Caesar used Imperator as a permanent title and (as Mommsen believed) to designate his extraordinary position, has been disproved by D. McFayden, *The History of the title Imperator under the Roman Empire* (1920). The coins with Caesar's portrait and the title Imperator, which were struck in 44, were not an ordinary civilian issue of the state but a military issue for the Parthian war and were signed by Caesar as commander-in-chief (see C. M. Kraay, *Numism. Chron.*, 1954, 18 ff.). On the nomenclature 'Imperator Caesar' see R. Syme, *Historia*, 1958, 172 ff. [p. 126]

28 PORTRAIT COINAGE OF 44. Two recent attempts have been made to date more
closely these interesting issues and to draw from them conclusions about Caesar's
constitutional and monarchic intentions: see A. Alfoldi, *Stüdien über Caesars Monarchie*
(1953) and K. Kraft, *Der goldene Kranz Caesars (Jahrb, f. Num.3/4)*. The latter argues that
Caesar's golden wreath represents part of the regalia of the early kings of Rome: but
it was also worn by triumphators. For a criticism of these views see R. A. G. Carson,
Gnomon, 1956, 181 ff., *Gr. and R.*, 1957, 46 ff. and Kraay, *op. cit.*, n. 27 and M. Crawford,
RRC, p. 488 (for the coins, Crawford n. 480). [p. 126]

29 CAESAR AND MONARCHY. The view that Caesar regarded monarchy as the cure for
Rome's troubles and early in his career deliberately determined to secure it by force if
need be, was advanced with great brilliance by Mommsen, who regarded Caesar
as a superman and a potential saviour of Roman society. More recently it has been
championed by J. Carcopino, *Histoire romaine*, ii (1936). The belief that Caesar aimed at
monarchy on Hellenistic lines has been advocated by Ed. Meyer, *Caesars Monarchie*[3]
(1922), who sought to contrast Caesar's monarchic rule with both the Principate of
Augustus and the 'Principate of Pompey' (i.e. Pompey, not Caesar, was the true
predecessor of Augustus). These views have been criticized by F. E. Adcock (*CAH*, IX,
718 ff.), who examines the difficult evidence at length and reaches the conclusion
that Caesar had not finally resolved to end the Republic. Cf. also R. Syme, *Rom. Rev.*,
ch. iv and *JRS*, 1944, 99 ff., and H. Last, *JRS*, 1944, 119 ff. W. Burket (*Historia*, 1962,
356 ff.) returns to the view that even before the First Triumvirate Caesar thought of
Roman monarchy, linked to the idea of Romulus-Quirinus. In 'Caesar's Final Aims'
(*Harvard Stud. Class. Phil.*, 1964, 149 ff.), V. Ehrenberg concludes 'that Caesar intended
to create his own form of monarchy – neither Roman nor Hellenistic but Caesarean',
p. 157. K. W. Welwei, *Historia*, 1967, 44 ff., also rejects a pattern of Roman or Hellenistic
monarchy but is less definite about the more positive form in which Caesar might have
clothed his power; in particular Welwei examines the meaning of the Lupercalia
episode, as also does G. Dobesch, *Caesars Apotheose zu Lebzeiten und sein Ringen um
den Konigstitel* (1966), who reaches the opposite conclusion that Caesar wished for
monarchy, the diadem and the title of king. E. Rawson (*JRS*, 1975, 148 ff.) examines the
Roman attitude to Hellenistic kings and kingship and concludes that in the light of this
tradition Caesar did not want the glorious but hated title *rex*. H. Gescher (*Historia*,
1973, 468 ff.) has argued for the view that Caesar did appoint Octavian Magister
Equitum. In *Divus Julius* (1971) S. Weinstock argues that Caesar was a religious
reformer who created new cults, stimulated the grant of extraordinary honours to
himself and was about to become a divine ruler when he was assassinated; after his
death his plan was taken up by his supporters and the new cult of Divus Iulius
inherited most of its features. The case is presented with great learning and ingenuity,
but may not convince all (e.g. those who think that the author is too credulous in
accepting some of the evidence of Dio Cassius). The book is discussed by J. North,
JRS, 1975, 171 ff. Cf. also Z. Yavetz, *Julius Caesar and his Public Image* (forthcoming).
   On the child Caesarion see ch. viii, n. 20 below, and on other rumoured sons of
Caesar see R. Syme, *Historia*, 1980, 422 ff. [p. 128]

30 CAESAR'S HEALTH. This was good, except that he twice suffered from epileptic
seizures during his campaigns and from fainting fits towards the end of his life (see
e.g. Suetonius, *Iulius*, 45), but there is no reason to believe that his mental vigour
was in any way impaired. For the view that during his last phase Caesar's character
underwent a major change, that he was corrupted by power and suffered from
megalomania see J.H. Collins, *Historia*, 1955, 445 ff. On the increasing disapproval felt
by his contemporaries towards Caesar, including his partisans as well as enemies, see

H. Strasburger, *Hist. Zeitschrift*, 1953, 225 ff., revised as *Caesar im Urteil seiner Zeitgenossen* (1968). On the last phase of his life see also J. P. V. D. Balsdon, *Historia*, 1958, 80 ff. [p. 128]

31 THE CONSPIRATORS. The motives of the conspirators were no doubt mixed. Some had private quarrels with Caesar, and some (e.g. Q. Ligarius) were Pompeians who had suffered in the civil war, but the conspiracy was in no way a resurrection of the Pompeian cause. Ex-Pompeians, as M. Brutus and Cassius, were actuated by loyalty to the Senate and constitution, Brutus being influenced by Greek ideas of the duty of tyrannicide. There is no contemporary evidence, or basis in fact, for the later legend that M. Brutus was Caesar's son: Caesar had an intrigue with Brutus' mother Servilia, but probably long after the birth of Brutus (which was probably in 85 or possibly 78). The conspirators included many Caesarians (as Decimus Brutus and C. Trebonius) who had much to hope for from Caesar (these two men had been allotted good provinces for 44); their motives must therefore have been disinterested. Cicero was not approached by the conspirators, but he approved the deed. On their choice of the Ides of March see N. Horsfall, *Gr. and R.*, 1974, 191 ff. [p. 129]

32 CAESAR. Of the two ancient Lives of Caesar that by Suetonius has been edited by H. E. Butler and M. Cary (1927; a very useful work) and that by Plutarch by A. Garzetti (in Italian; 1954). Modern biographies include W. Warde Fowler, *Julius Caesar* (1904); a welcome translation of M. Gelzer, *Caesar. Politician and Statesman* (1968); a briefer sketch by J. P. V. D. Balsdon, *Julius Caesar and Rome* (1967) and M. Grant, *Julius Caesar* (1969). H. Collins has provided 'A Selective Survey of Caesar Scholarship since 1935', *Classical World*, 1963, 45 ff., 81 ff. Various aspects of Caesar are discussed in a special bimillenary volume of *Greece and Rome*, March 1957 (IV, i), and in a volume of lectures entitled, *Caesare nel bimellenario della morte* (1956). Caesar's 'luck' is discussed by F. Boemer, *Gymnasium*, 1966, 63 ff., his honours by G. Cogrossi, *Contrib. Istit. Stor. ant. Univ. S. Cu. Milan*, 1975, 136 ff., his private fortune by A. Ferrill, *Indiana Soc. Studies Quar.*, 1977, 101 ff., his attitude to Epicureanism by F. C. Bourne, *Cl. W.*, 1977, 417 ff. and his writings by L. Radists, *Aufstieg*, I, iii (1973), 457 ff. H. Gesche's *Caesar* (1976) is a useful bibliographical review of works on Caesar. On his portraiture see J. M. C. Toynbee, *Roman Historical Portraits* (1978), 30 ff. [p. 129]

CHAPTER VIII

1 SOURCES FOR 44–31 B.C. The main narrative for these years is given by Appian (*BC*, iii–v; down to 35 B.C.) and Dio Cassius (xlv–liii). Appian is the more valuable; he made use of the *History* of Asinius Pollio (who fought on the side of Antony and later maintained a reserved attitude towards Augustus). Until his death in 43 B.C. Cicero's *Letters* and *Philippics* are an invaluable source. The poets, Horace and Virgil, begin to throw light on their age, although their major work falls after 31. The *Memoirs* of Augustus (not extant) were used by Livy (whose work here survives merely in the *Periochae*) and by Velleius Paterculus (who gives a brief narrative). Plutarch's *Life of Antony* is valuable; though not sympathetic to Antony, it provides a stirring account of his Parthian campaign (which derives from Dellius, one of Antony's officers who was an eye-witness of the campaign) and at the end (from ch. 77) it makes use of the *Memoirs* of Cleopatra's physician, Olympus. Suetonius' *Life of Augustus* and Augustus' own *Res Gestae* begin to be of service. One difficulty of the later part of the period, when Appian's narrative fails, is that both Antony and Octavian and their supporters indulged in a vicious propaganda campaign against each other: in particular by

representing his cause as that of Italy and the western tradition, Octavian over-emphasized the orientalizing of Antony's character and the influence of Cleopatra. The finest literary expression of this view, which became official with the victory of Octavian, may be found in Virgil's description of the battle of Actium (*Aeneid*, viii); it is also represented in less lofty forms. On this confusing political propaganda see K. Scott, *Mem. Amer. Acad. Rome*, 1933, pp. 1 ff.; M. P. Charlesworth, *Cl. Qu.*, 1933, 172 ff.

Modern authorities for 44–31 B.C. include T. Rice Holmes, *The Architect of the Roman Empire*, i (1928); M. A. Levi, *Ottaviano Capoparte* (1933); *CAH*. X, chs. i–iii (1934); R. Syme, *Rom. Rev.*, chs. vii–xxi; H. Frisch, *Cicero's Fight for the Republic* (1946); J. M. Carter, *The Battle of Actium* (1970), which covers the period 44–31 B.C. F. Millar (*JRS*, 1973, 50 ff.) has surveyed the Triumviral period in relation to the emergence of the principate, and in particular assesses the extent to which the institutions of the *res publica* remained active during this period when the Triumvirate was superimposed upon them but did not replace them. In the process he examines the triumviral documents from the Greek East, including some hitherto unpublished documents from Aphrodisias (among them two letters of Octavian). On this extremely important group of documents see J. Reynolds, *Aphrodisias and Rome* (1982). [p. 131]

2   ANTONY'S FUNERAL ORATION. According to Suetonius (*Iul.* 84, 2) Antony in place of a *laudatio* had read out a decree of the Senate honouring Caesar and the oath by which the Senate had pledged his safety; Antony then 'added a very few words of his own'. Appian (*BC*, ii, 144–5) attributes a short speech to him which is more conciliatory than his actions. Dio Cassius (xliv, 36 ff.) gives a very long speech. M. E. Deutsch (*Univ. California Publ. Cl. Arch.* 1928) has argued in support of Suetonius, but Cicero, *Phil.* 2, 91, may support the traditional view of a longer formal speech. [p. 132]

3   CAESAR'S ADOPTION OF OCTAVIAN. For the content of Caesar's will see above, pp. 150, 155, 156, 157. Suetonius (*Iul.* 83) records that Octavian was named first heir to three-quarters of the estate and his two cousins received the rest; then at the end of the will ('in ima cera') Octavian was adopted 'in familiam nomenque'. At best Octavian's adoption must have been conditional upon Calpurnia not bearing Caesar a post-humous son, a contingency for which Caesar had provided in his will: and there are doubts about the precise legal meaning of testamentary adoption. Such doubts have therefore led W. Schmitthenner (*Oktavian und das Testament Cäsars²*, 1973) to suggest that Octavian's adoption was achieved by him through the *lex curiata* as a political master-stroke. But although there are technical difficulties, it is probable that Suetonius is right and that in any case it was Caesar's intention that Octavian should be his adopted son as well as his heir. Cf. G. E. F. Chilver, *JRS*, 1954, 126 ff. On Octavian's rise see A. Alföldi, *Oktavians Aufstieg zur Macht* (1976). [p. 133]

4   THE PROSCRIPTIONS. Some exciting stories are told by Appian (*BC*, iv, 11–30). An inscription, the so-called *Laudatio Turiae*, commemorates the devotion of a wife to her husband (proscribed now or exiled earlier) and exposes the cruelty of Lepidus. There is an edition by M. Durry (*Éloge d'une matrone romaine*, 1950) and a translation in Lewis and Reinhold, *Rn. Civ.* i, 484 ff. [p. 135]

5   CICERO. Biographies include G. Boissier, *Cicero and his Friends* (1897); J. L. Strachan-Davidson, *Cicero and the Fall of the Roman Republic* (1894); E. G. Sihler, *Cicero of Arpinum* (1914); T. Petersson, *Cicero* (1920); H. J. Haskell, *This was Cicero* (1942); R. E. Smith, *Cicero the Statesman* (1966); and, in German, M. Gelzer, *Cicero* (1969). *Cicero*, edited by T. A. Dorey (1965), contains chapters by seven scholars on aspects of Cicero's life and work. R. J. Rowland in 'A Survey of selected Ciceronian Bibliography, 1953–1965' (*Cl. W.*, 1965, 51 ff., 101 ff.) provides a useful account and a wider one than the title might suggest. F. R. Cowell, *Cicero and the Roman Republic* (1948; Pelican

ed. 1956) is a general survey of the later Republic rather than a strict biography of Cicero. J. Carcopino, *Cicero; the Secrets of his Correspondence* (1951), is an unsuccessful attempt to undermine the historical value of Cicero's letters and to blacken Cicero's character. Two further biographies of Cicero appeared in 1971: *Cicero* by D. R. Shackleton Bailey (with emphasis on the later part of his life, from which so many of his letters survive) and *Cicero* by D. L. Stockton. E. Rawson's *Cicero* (1975) is a more balanced portrait of the whole man. His early career until 63 B.C. is handled by T. W. Mitchell, *Cicero, the Ascending Years* (1979) and his whole life is sketched by W. K. Lacey, *Cicero and the End of the Roman Republic* (1978). On Cicero's portraits see J. M. C. Toynbee, *Roman Historical Portraits* (1978), 28 ff. [p. 135]

6 CICERO'S POLITICAL THEORIES. Much has been written on the monarchical emphasis in Cicero's later writings: see, e.g. W. W. How, *JRS*, 1930, 24 ff.; E. Lepore, *Il princeps Ciceroniano* (1954). For an interpretation of his philosophic works see H. A. K. Hunt, *The Humanism of Cicero* (1954). See also S. E. Smethurst, 'Cicero's Rhetorical and Philosophical Works, 1957–1963', *Cl. W.*, 1964, 36 ff. [p. 135]

6a BRUTUS. See M. L. Clarke, *The Noblest Roman, Marcus Brutus and his Reputation* (1981). On his relations with Cassius see W. Huss, *Würzburger Jahrb. für die Alterturnswiss*, 1977, 115 ff. [p. 137]

6b THE PERUSINE WAR. See E. Gabba, *Harvard Stud. Class. Phil.*, 1971, 139 ff. for an analysis of the activities of Octavian and Antony until 36 B.C. On the Perusine war see P. Wallmann, *Talanta*, 1974, 58 ff. [p. 138]

7 THE CHILD OF VIRGIL'S FOURTH ECLOGUE. This subject has caused much speculation. For the view in the text (a future son of Antony and Octavia) see W. W. Tarn, *JRS*, 1932, 135 ff. Less likely 'candidates' are a son of Antony and Cleopatra; Asinius Gallus, son of Asinius Pollio, or his younger brother allegedly called Asinius Saloninus (whose existence has been questioned by R. Syme, *Cl. Qu.*, 1937, 39). [p. 138]

8 SEXTUS POMPEIUS. See M. Hadas, *Sextus Pompey* (1930). [p. 138]

9 AGRIPPA. See M. Reinhold, *Marcus Agrippa* (1933). Impressive remains survive of the tunnels constructed by Agrippa's architect and engineer, L. Cocceius Auctus (Strabo, 5. 4. 5): the 'Grotta di Cocceio' connected Lake Avernus with Cumae, running under Monte Grillo. Another long gallery, under the hill of Cumae itself, belongs to this system; until the real Grotto of the Sibyl was discovered in 1932, it was confused with this other work (see A. Maiuri, *I Campi Flegrei*, 1949, pp. 127 ff.). These tunnels were of course only supplementary to the vast main work of creating Portus Iulius, a major feat of engineering. See further R. F. Paget, *JRS*, 1968, 163 ff. (with plan). [p. 138]

10 RENEWAL OF THE TRIUMVIRATE. The sources are contradictory, e.g. Appian even contradicts himself (*BC*, v, 95 and *Illyr.* 28) as to whether it was legally sanctioned. See Rice Holmes, *Architect Rom. Emp.* i. 231 ff.; *CAH*, X, 59 and 902. [p. 138]

11 SELEUCUS OF RHOSUS. It was probably for services in this campaign that one of Octavian's admirals, a certain Seleucus of Rhosus in Syria, was rewarded with a grant of Roman citizenship and other privileges (immunity from taxation, etc.). Letters and an edict of Octavian to Rhosus, between 41 and 30 B.C., record this; see Ehrenberg and Jones, *Documents*, n. 301, Sherk, *Rom. Documents from Greek East* (1969), n. 58 and translation in Lewis and Reinhold, *Rn. Civ.* i, 389 ff. [p. 140]

12 OCTAVIAN'S SACROSANCTITAS. So Dio Cassius, 49, 15, 5, *contra* Appian *BC*, v, 132. See H. Last, *Rendiconti, Ist. Lombardo*, 1951, 95 ff. On Octavian's constitutional hopes in 36 see R. E. A. Palmer, *Athenaeum*, 1978, 315 ff. [p. 140]

13 TERRAMARIQUE. On this formula, A. Momigliano, *JRS*, 1942, 63. [p. 140]

14 OCTAVIAN'S ILLYRIAN CAMPAIGN. See R. Syme, *JRS*, 1933, 66 on E. Swoboda, *Octavian und Illyricum*. N. Vulic (*JRS*, 1934, 163 ff.) argues for wide conquests. See also

W. Schmitthenner, *Historia*, 1958, 189 ff., who considers it in relation to Octavian's struggle for power, and J. J. Wilkes, *Dalmatia* (1969), 46 ff. Syme's article is reprinted, with addendum, in *Danubian Papers* (1971), 135 ff. [p. 140]

15 Q. LABIENUS. He even issued a silver coinage, depicting his portrait and, on the reverse, a Parthian horse; the legend ran 'Q. Labienus Parthicus Imperator' (see E. A. Sydenham, *CRR*, n. 1356–7; Crawford, *RRC*, n. 524). [p. 141]

16 C. SOSIUS. He commemorated his victory with a coinage depicting Antony's portrait and a military trophy at the base of which sat two captives, Judaea and Antigonus (Sydenham, *CRR*, n. 1272). [p. 141]

17 THE MARRIAGE OF ANTONY AND CLEOPATRA. The date is much disputed. W. W. Tarn (*CAH*, X, 66 ff.) and others place it in 37: a new supplementary dating era started in Alexandria in 37, which may denote the regnal years of the joint reign of Cleopatra and Antony. Other possible (though less likely?) explanations of this double dating, which appears on some coins and papyri, refer it to the territorial expansion of Egypt in 37 or to Cleopatra and Ptolemy Caesar. Other historians place Antony's marriage later, after he had formally divorced Octavia. See Rice Holmes, *Architect Rom. Emp.* i, 227 ff. On Antony see R. F. Rossi, *Marco Antonio nelle lotta politica della tarda repubblica romana* (1959) and H. Buchheim, *Die Orientpolitik des Triumvirn M. Antonius* (1961). H. Bengston, *Marcus Antonius, Triumvir und Herrscher des Orients* (1977) adds little fresh. On Antony's portraits see J. M. C. Toynbee, *Roman Historical Portraits* (1978), 41 ff. [p. 142]

18 ALEXANDER HELIOS. In choosing this name for his son, Antony may have been thinking that the Persians, the predecessors of the Parthians, had been conquered by Alexander the Great, or possibly he hoped that the name would suggest the Sun-child who would, as men hoped, inaugurate a Golden Age. See W. W. Tarn, *JRS*, 1932, 135 ff. [p. 142]

19 CLEOPATRA'S AIMS. Such is the view brilliantly expounded by W. W. Tarn, *CAH*, X, 76 ff. (cf. *JRS*, 1932, 135 ff.). Others (cf. R. Syme, *Rom. Rev.* 274 f.) believe her aims to be more moderate and that many of her alleged intentions are the result of Octavian's propaganda. For the oracle (which may, but does not certainly, refer to Cleopatra) see J. Geffcken, *Oracula Sibyllina*, book iii, 350 ff. These Oracles, written in Greek hexameters, were put together over a long period of time (300 B.C.–A.D. 500) and are Greek, Jewish and Christian; book iii is mainly Jewish. [p. 142]

20 CAESARION. That Julius Caesar was in fact the father of Caesarion cannot be established beyond all doubt: some passages in the ancient authorities are inconclusive, although others (e.g. Plut. *Caes.* 49, 10) are definite in asserting it. J. Carcopino (*Ann. École Haut. Étud. Gand*, 1, 1937) has argued against Caesar's paternity and dates the birth of Caesarion to 44 rather than (as Plutarch) to 47. But see K. W. Meiklejohn, *JRS*, 1934, 191 ff. and H. Volkmann, *Cleopatra* (1958), 74 ff. J. P. V. D. Balsdon (*Historia*, 1958, 86 ff., *CR*, 1960, 69 ff.) argues that the child was born in 44 a month or two after Caesar's death and that thereupon Cleopatra invented the false story that Caesar was the father. H. Heinen (*Historia*, 1969, 181 ff.) argues for paternity of Caesar rather than Antony. [p. 143]

21 CLEOPATRA, QUEEN OF KINGS. Antony issued coins which showed Cleopatra's portrait and named her 'Queen of Kings and of her sons who are kings': the other side depicted Antony and the legend 'Armenia devicta' (Sydenham, *CRR*, n. 1210–11; Crawford, *RRC*, n. 543). Artistically these coins are poor and do not flatter the queen, but none of the other coins with her portrait (see J. M. C. Toynbee, *Roman Historical Portraits* (1978), 86 ff.) suggests that she was particularly beautiful. On Cleopatra see also H. Volkmann, *Cleopatra* (Engl. trans., 1958). Two more biographies of Cleopatra

have appeared: *Cleopatra* (1972) by M. Grant, and *Cleopatra* (1970), a somewhat more romantic account by Jack Lindsay. [p. 143]

22 THE END OF THE TRIUMVIRATE. For the view that it terminated at the end of 33 (cf. Augustus, *Res Gest.* 7: 'triumvirum rei publicae constituendae fui per continuos annos decem') and a discussion of other views, see Rice Holmes *Architect Rom. Emp.* I, 231 ff.; for more recent views see G. E. F. Chilver, *Historia*, 1950, 410 ff. On Octavian's status in 32 see H. W. Benario, *Chiron*, 1975, 301 ff., and on the crisis in Rome at the beginning of 32 see E. H. Gray, *Proc. Afr. Cl. Ass.*, 1975, 15 ff. [p. 143]

23 THE CONIURATIO. On its importance see R. Syme, *Rom. Rev.*, 284 ff., who also emphasizes its influence on the unification of Italy, *tota Italia*. After *tota Italia* (according to *Res Gestae*, 25, 2) 'the Gallic and Spanish provinces, Africa, Sicily and Sardinia swore the same oath of allegiance'. After Antony's defeat in the east, the eastern regions appear to have followed suit; later, on the accession of a new emperor, a similar oath was taken everywhere (e.g. by Cyprus to Tiberius: see ch. XIII, n. 16 below). The nature of the oath is exemplified in that taken by resident Romans and natives at Gangra in Paphlagonia in 3 B.C. soon after its incorporation in the province of Galatia: see Ehrenberg and Jones, *Documents*, 315, and for translation and discussion of this topic see P. A. Brunt and J. M. Moore, *Res Gestae* (1967), 67 f. The oath was personal and extra-constitutional, and did not confer any legal power on Octavian. For fragments of an inscription containing an oath of allegiance to Augustus taken in Samos, see P. Herrmann, *Athen. Mitteil.*, 75 (1960), 71 f.

On Octavian's followers see Syme, *op. cit.*, 292 f. and on Antony's pp. 266 ff. On the unattached votes in the Senate in 32 see P. Wallmann, *Historia*, 1976, 305 ff. [p. 143]

24 ACTIUM. For the view that Antony intended a decisive action and was let down by misunderstanding or treachery among his men see W. W. Tarn, *JRS*, 1931, 173 ff.; 1938, 165 ff. For the 'escape' theory see J. Kromayer, *Hermes*, 1933, 361 ff.; G. W. Richardson, *JRS*, 1937, 153 ff. After the battle Octavian founded a 'city of victory', Nicopolis, nearby, where he concentrated many Acarnanians and Epirots. The services of Seleucus of Rhosus, who served as his admiral, are recorded in a letter of Octavian to Rhosus (see above, n. 11). For an edict of Octavian (probably 31 B.C.), granting privileges to veterans, see Ehrenberg and Jones, *Documents*, n. 302 and translation in Lewis and Reinhold, *Rn. Civ.* i, p. 392. On Actium see also E. Wistrand, *Horace's Ninth Epode* (1958); M. L. Paladini, *A proposito della tradizione poetica sulla battaglia di Azio* (1958); J. M. Carter, *The Battle of Actium* (1970), [p. 145]

25 CLEOPATRA'S DEATH. On the chronology of her last days see T. C. Skeat, *JRS*, 1953, 98 ff. On W. Spiegelberg's view that she used an asp because, as the divine minister of the Sun-god, it defied its victim, see J. G. Griffiths, *Journ. Egypt. Arch.* 1961, 113 ff. B. Baldwin, *Journ. Egypt. Arch.*, 1964, 181 f., denies the view of Griffiths (*op. cit.*) that Cleopatra used two serpents (the double uraeaus). On Antony's will see J. Crook, *JRS*, 1957, 36 ff. [p. 145]

CHAPTER IX

1 ECONOMIC CONDITIONS. For a detailed survey see Tenney Frank, *An Economic Survey of Ancient Rome*, vol. I (1933), chs. iv and v. See also K. D. White, *Roman Farming* (1970); H. J. Loane, *Industry and Commerce in the City of Rome, 50 BC–200 A.D.* (1938); A. Burford, *Craftsmen in Greek and Roman Society* (1972); L. Schatzman, *Senatorial Wealth and Roman Politics* (1975), discusses the wealth of individual senators in the 2nd and 1st centuries B.C. In *The Ancient Economy* (1973), M. I. Finley discusses

various concepts and aspects of ancient economic life. He regards ancient economic thought and life as primitive and alien to many of the modern economic categories which are sometimes applied to it: the structure of ancient society was hostile to industry and commerce, while agriculture remained underdeveloped. For a criticism of this standpoint see M. Frederiksen, *JRS*, 1975, 164 ff. [p. 146]

2 POPULATION OF ITALY. The high figure of nearly 14 million, which included 4 million slaves, was the estimate of T. Frank (*op. cit.* p. 266). P. A. Brunt, who in *Italian Manpower, 225 BC–A. D. 14* (1971) has subjected the evidence to fresh and vigorous examination, reverts to figures of the more sober order reached much earlier by K. J. Beloch: he concludes that by 28 B.C. there were some 5–6 million Roman citizens (men, women, and children over the age of one) and that not many more than 4 million were domiciled in Italy; the total population of Italy, including infants, free foreigners and slaves, was perhaps in excess of 7 million. He believes that the number of the free population in Italy had not increased in the two hundred years before Augustus. [p. 147]

3 EMIGRATION. Besides the state-organized settlement in colonies, there was a widespread and increasing private emigration from Italy during the last two centuries of the Republic, both to the Western Mediterranean and to the Greek East. This movement has been carefully studied by A. J. N. Wilson, *Emigration from Italy in the Republican Age of Rome* (1966), who examines the volume, the kinds of communities formed overseas by the emigrants, their motives and origins, the areas settled, and the relations of the settlers with the people among whom they lived. On emigration see also P. A. Brunt, *Italian Manpower* (1971), 159 ff. [p. 148]

3a URBANIZATION. On the development of the cities of Italy in the first century B.C. see E. Gabba, *Studi classici e orientali*, 1972, 73 ff. [p. 148]

4 TRADE IN THE EAST. In general see J. Hatzfeld, *Les Trafiquants italiens dans l'Orient hellénique* (1919), and for the Italians at Delos see W. A. Laidlaw, *A History of Delos* (1933), ch. vi. Also A. J. N. Wilson, *op. cit.*, 85 ff. Brunt (*Italian Manpower*, 224 ff.) believes that the figure of 80,000 Italians who were said to have been massacred by Mithridates is grossly exaggerated, and consequently the number of Italians in Asia Minor was less than is usually supposed. [p. 149]

5 WRECKED ROMAN SHIPS. For the Mahdia wreck (cf. *Rev. Arch.*, 1911) and recent discoveries see Ph. Diôle, *Four Thousand Years under the Sea* (1954), and Fr. Benoit, *Rivista di Studi Liguri*, 1952, 237 ff. [p. 149]

6 SOCIAL LIFE. See Warde Fowler, *Social Life in Rome in the Days of Cicero* (1909). On the position of woman, see J. P. Balsdon, *Roman Women* (1962). Most aspects of the social scene are discussed in Balsdon's excellent *Life and Leisure in Ancient Rome* (1969). See also R. MacMullen, *Roman Social Relations, 50 BC–A. D. 284* (1974). [p. 151]

7 EQUITES AND THE EQUESTRIAN ORDER. See above p. 8 f. and n. 9. In the early days the Equites had served as cavalry and were enrolled in the centuriate Assembly in 18 *centuriae* as *Equites equo publico*. Later they became an élite corps whose exclusiveness was gradually undermined, and precise definition becomes increasingly difficult. This is particularly so in the period between Gaius Gracchus and Sulla. The class to whom the former transferred the *repetundae* court was more probably defined by a financial qualification than by equestrian status (cf. ch. II, n. 31 above); they were perhaps strictly *Gracchani iudices* rather than Equites, but the latter name is commonly (and conveniently) applied to them. After Sulla all reference to *equo publico* is irrelevant and membership of the Equestrian Order could apparently be claimed by any Roman citizen with sufficient wealth. Further, with the enfranchisement of Italy in 90 the

number of potential Knights was greatly increased. Thus in the late Republic the word Equites covered a great variety of people: an aristocratic group in Rome, leading men from colonies and municipia, the *publicani* many of whom had made great fortunes through their state contracts and tax-collecting and who mostly will have become socially respectable by their investment in land, and the *negotatores*, the private financiers and business men who had made good; nor must we forget the country squires, wealthy enough to qualify as members of the Order, who preferred a quiet life to the hurly-burly of either business or public service. Thus Equites were of many kinds, and it was primarily the *publicani* and Gracchan *iudices* (probably largely identical) who were interested in politics and who often clashed with the Senate. See M. R. Cimma, *Ricerche sulle società di publicani* (1981). [p. 151]

8 ATTICUS. The 16 books of Cicero's Letters to Atticus reveal the character of both men. See G. Bosisier, *Cicero and his Friends* (1897), pp. 123 ff. [p. 151]

9 THE PLEBS. See Z. Yavetz, 'Plebs sordida', *Athenaeum*, 1965, 295 ff., 'Levitas popularis', *Atene e Roma*, 1965, 97 ff., 'The Living Conditions of the Urban Plebs In Republican Rome', *Latomus*, 1958, 500 ff. (=Sealey, *Crisis*, 162 ff.), and for the late Republic *Plebs and Princeps* (1969). P. A. Brunt, 'The Roman Mob', *Past & Present*, 1966, 3 ff (reprinted in *Studies in Ancient Society*, ed. M. I. Finley, 1974, 74 ff.), and also one aspect, A. W. Lintott, *Violence in Republican Rome* (1968). [p. 152]

10 RACE MIXTURE. See T. Frank, *An Economic History of Rome*[2] (1927), 207 ff. for an extreme view. For a criticism of this see N. H. Baynes, *JRS*, 1943, 32 ff. See also S. Treggiari, *Roman Freedmen during the late Republic* (1969) (5 ff. and 32 ff. especially for race mixture). On the free and slave population of Italy see P. A. Brunt, *Italian Manpower* (1971), 121 ff. [p. 152]

11 FESTIVALS, GAMES AND VENATIONES. Of the old religious festivals (*feriae*) recorded in the Roman calander some had become relatively obscure but others (e.g. the Lupercalia and Saturnalia) remained great public holidays. The six older Games (Ludi Romani, Plebeii, Apollinares, Ceriales, Megalenses and Florales) continued alongside the new Circenses of Sulla and Caesar. See Warde Fowler, *The Roman Festivals* (1908); H. H. Scullard, *Festivals and Ceremonies of the Roman Republic* (1981). On the *venationes* see G. Jennison, *Animals for Show and Pleasure in Ancient Rome* (1937): for the Republic, especially ch. iii. For the episode in 55 see Cicero, *ad fam.* 7, 1, 3; Pliny, *NH*, 8, 7. Also J. P. V. D. Balsdon, *Life and Leisure in Ancient Rome* (1969), 306 ff. (wild beast fighting), 288 ff. (gladiators) and M. Grant, *Gladiators* (1967). On the attitude of the Romans to animals see J. M. C. Toynbee, *Animals in Roman Life and Art* (1973) and on elephants H. H. Scullard, *The Elephant in the Greek and Roman World* (1974). [p. 153]

12 THE CITY. In general see G. Lugli, *Roma antica: Il centro monumentale* (1946); T. Ashby and S. B. Platner, *Topographical Dictionary of Ancient Rome* (1929). See also E. Nash's fine *Pictorial Dictionary of Ancient Rome*, 2 vols. (1961–62) for individual buildings. See F. Coarelli, 'Public building in Rome between the Second Punic War and Sulla', *Papers Brit. Sch. Rome*, 1977, 1 ff. For Sulla's work, E. B. Van Deeman, *JRS*, 1922, pp. 1 ff. See also D. R. Dudley, *Urbs Roma* (1967), a source book of classical texts on the city and its monuments, and M. Grant, *The Roman Forum* (1970). [p. 153]

13 PROVINCIAL ADMINISTRATION. See G. H. Stevenson, *Roman Provincial Administration* (1939) and *CAH*, IX, ch. x. For a translation of some important passages see Lewis and Reihhold, *Rn. Civ.* I, ch. vi. On Roman policy towards the provinces see E. Badian, *Roman Imperialism in the late Republic*[2] (1968) and *Publicans and Sinners* (1972). [p. 154]

14 CITY SELF-GOVERNMENT. On Rome's attitude to this see A. H. M. Jones, *The Greek City* (1940), 170 ff. [p. 154]

15 CLERICAL GRADES IN THE CIVIL SERVICE. See A. H. M. Jones, *JRS*, 1949, 38 ff. [p. 156]

16 SIBYLLINE ORACLES. Cf. ch. VIII, n. 19. Part of an anti-Roman oracle, dating from the Mithridatic Wars, is translated in Lewis and Reinhold, *Rn. Civ.* I, 377 f., which also gives many passages illustrating Roman misrule (pp. 355 ff.). [p. 158]

CHAPTER X

1 FIRST CENTURY ART. See G. M. A. Richter, *Ancient Italy* (1955), chs. iii–vi, to which this section owes much; and E. Strong, *CAH*, IX, ch. xxii. In general see J. M. C. Toynbee, *The Art of the Romans* (1965); L. Crema, *L'Architettura romana* (1959); F. E. Brown, *Roman Architecture* (1961); M. Wheeler, *Roman Art and Architecture* (1964); A. Boethius and J. B. Ward-Perkins, *Etruscan and Roman Architecture* (1971); R. B. Bandinelli, *Rome, the Centre of Power, Roman Art to A.D. 200* (1970); D. Strong, *Roman Art* (1976). [p. 161]

2 PORTRAITURE. See G. M. A. Richter, *JRS*, 1955, 39 ff., where the possibility of Egyptian influence is discounted, and J. M. C. Toynbee, *Roman Historical Portraits* (1978). [p. 162]

3 LATIN POETS. In general see the histories of literature, e.g. H. J. Rose, *A. Handbook of Latin Literature* (3rd ed. 1966); J. Wight Duff, *Literary History of Rome* (3rd ed. 1960); T. Frank, *Life and Literature in the Roman Republic* (1930). See also Gordon Williams, *Tradition and Originality in Roman Poetry* (1968), detailed analysis of the essential nature of Roman poetry. [p. 162]

4 SATIRE AND LUCILIUS. See J. Wight Duff, *Roman Satire* (1937). See also W. S. Anderson, 'Recent Work in Roman Satire (1937–55)', *Class. World*, 1956, 33 ff., and *ibid.* '(1955–62)', *Cl. W.*, 1964, 293 ff., 343 ff. For text and translation of Lucilius' fragments see E. H. Warmington, *ROL*, iii. On the events of 133–129 B.C. referred to in the fragments of Lucilius, see W. J. Raschke, *JRS*, 1979, 78 ff. [p. 163]

5 TRAGEDY AND COMEDY. See G. E. Duckworth, *The Nature of Roman Comedy* (1952); M. Bieber, *The History of the Greek and Roman Theater²* (1961); W. Beare, *The Roman Stage³* (1964); *Roman Drama* (1965), ed. D. R. Dudley and T. A. Dorey, essays by seven scholars. [p. 163]

6 CATULUS AND CINNA. On Catulus' work and his supposed literary circle see H. Bardon, *La Littérature latine inconnue*, I (1952), 115 ff. On Cinna see T. P. Wiseman, *Cinna and Poet* (1974). [p. 165]

7 CATULLUS. See edition by C. J. Fordyce (1961); cf. E. A. Havelock, *The Lyric Genius of Catullus* (1939). For recent work, including the problem of the identification of Lesbia, see R. G. C. Levens, *Fifty Years of Classical Scholarship* (1954), 284 ff. See also G. Highet, *Poets in a Landscape* (1957), ch. i; T. P. Wiseman, *Catullan Questions* (1969), and in *JRS*, 1979, 161 ff. [p. 166]

8 LUCRETIUS. See C. Bailey, *Lucretius*, 3 vols. (1974). E. E. Sikes, *Lucretius, Poet and Philosopher* (1936). *Lucretius* (1965), ed. D. R. Dudley, essays by seven scholars. L. A. Holland, *Lucretius and the Transpadanes* (1979), discusses the poet's local, cultural and literary background [p. 166].

9 ROMAN HISTORIANS. For the surviving fragments of the lost Roman historians see H. Peter, *Historicorum Romanorum Reliquiae*, 2 vols., (1906–1914). See also *OCD*, s.v. Historiography, etc., and A. H. McDonald, *Fifty Years of Classical Scholarship*, 384 ff. *Latin Historians* (1966), edited by T. A. Dorey, contains a useful account of the annalists by E. Badian. E. Rawson, *Cl. Qu.*, 1972, 158 ff., argued that the *annales maximi* were not

actually widely used by Roman historians, while T. P. Wiseman, *Clio's Cosmetics* (1979), 9 ff. suggests that it was Piso rather than the *annales* that provided the annalistic framework of Roman history. [p. 166]

10 SALLUST. The fragments of his *Historiae* were edited by B. Maurenbrecher 2 vols. (1891–3). Cf M. L. W. Laistner, *The Greater Roman Historians* (1947), ch. iii; D. C. Earl, *The Political Thought of Sallust* (1961). R. Syme, *Sallust* (1964); G. M. Paul in *Latin Historians* (see n. 9), ch. iv; A. D. Leeman, *A Systematical Bibliography of Sallust, 1879–1964* (1965). [p. 168]

11 ORATORY. The surviving fragments of the Roman orators are edited by E. Malcovati, *Oratorum Romanorum Fragmenta* (2nd ed. 1955). Cf. M. L. Clarke *Rhetoric at Rome, a Historical Survey* (1953); S. F. Bonner, *Fifty Years Cl. Sch.*, 335 ff. On the orators of the late Republic see G. V. Sumner, *The Orators in Cicero's Brutus* (1973), and in general G. Kennedy, *The Art of Rhetoric in the Roman World, 300 B.C.–A.D. 300* (1972)=*A History of Rhetoric*, vol. ii. [p. 169]

12 ROMAN EDUCATION. See A. Gwynn, *Roman Education* (1926); H. I. Marrou, *A History of Education in Antiquity* (1956), 242 ff; S. F. Bonner, *Education in Ancient Rome from the elder Cato to the younger Pliny* (1977). [p. 171]

13 RHETORICA AD HERENNIUM. This has been edited by H. Caplan (Loeb Cl. Lib., 1954). [p. 171]

14 LAW AND LAWYERS. See H. F. Jolowicz, *Historical Introduction to the Study of Roman Law* (2nd ed. 1952), chs. xiii–xviii; F. Schulz, *History of Roman Legal Science* (1946), pt. ii; B. Nicholas, *An Introduction to Roman Law* (1962); J. M. Kelly, *Roman Litigation* (1966); W. Kunkel, *An Introduction to Roman Legal and Constitutional History* (1966); *id., Herkunft und soziale Stellung der römischen Juristen* (1952); and above all for law in its social setting of everyday life, J. Crook, *Law and Life of Rome* (1967). On the 'sources' of law in this period see A. Watson, *Law Making in the Later Roman Republic* (1974); he discusses topics such as the development of the praetor's edict, attitudes to the XII Tables, and (chs. 10–12) the content of the legal writings; he believes Greek influence to have been very limited [p. 171]

15 STOICS AND EPICUREANS. See M. L. Clarke, *The Roman Mind* (1956), chs. ii–iii. For Stoicism see above ch. I, n. 12. For Epicureans see A. J. Festugiere, *Epicurus and his Gods* (1955); on their activities at the end of the Republic see A. Momigliano, *JRS*, 1941, 149 ff.; B. Farrington, *The Faith of Epicurus* (1967). [p. 173]

16 CICERO'S THOUGHT. See H. A. K. Hunt, *The Humanism of Cicero* (1954). [p. 174]

17 ASTROLOGY. See F. H. Cramer, *Astrology in Roman Law and Politics* (1954), ch. ii. [p. 174]

18 ROMAN RELIGION. In general see W. Warde Fowler, *The Religious Experience of the Roman People* (1911); *id., The Roman Festivals* (1908); H. J. Rose, *Ancient Roman Religion* (1949); R. M. Ogilvie, *The Romans and their Gods* (1969). H. H. Scullard, *Festivals and Ceremonies of the Roman Republic* (1981). The two standard works are G. Wissowa, *Religion und Kultus der Römer²* (1912) and K. Latte, *Römische Religionsgeschichte* (1960). For Oriental cults see ch. XVI, n. 14 below. [p. 174]

CHAPTER XI

1 SOURCES FOR THE PRINCIPATE OF AUGUSTUS. The chief literary sources are the *Res Gestae Divi Augusti* (editions by J. Gagé³, 1977: P. A. Brunt and J. M. Moore, 1967); Suetonius, *Augustus* (edited by M. Adams, 1939); Dio Cassius, lii–lvi; Velleius Paterculus, ii, 89–128; Tacitus, *Ann.* 1. 2–15. The fragments of Augustus' own works are

collected in H. Malcovati, *Caesáris Augusti operum fragmenta* (3rd ed. 1948). The most important documents are collected by V. Ehrenberg and A. H. M. Jones, *Documents Illustrating the Reigns of Augustus and Tiberius* (2nd ed. 1955). Contemporary poets and monuments are of the first importance. For the coinage see H. Mattingly, *British Museum Catalogue of the Coins of The Roman Empire*, vol. i, *Augustus to Vitellius* (1923); H. Mattingly and others, *The Roman Imperial Coinage*, i (1923); M. Grant, *From Imperium to Auctoritas* (1946); C. H. V. Sutherland, *Coinage in Roman Imperial Policy* (1951), chs. 2–4. K. Chrisholm and J. Ferguson, *Rome. The Augustan Age* (1981), a source book in translation.

Modern works include T. Rice Holmes, *Architect Rom. Emp.*, II (1931); *Augustus, Studi in occasione del bimillenario Augusteo* (1938); R. Syme, *Rom. Rev.* (1939); J. Buchan, *Augustus Caesar* (1937); D. Earl, *The Age of Augustus* (1968); G. W. Bowersock, *Augustus and the Greek World* (1965); W. Schmitthenner (ed.), *Augustus* (1969), collected articles; A. H. M. Jones, *Augustus* (1970).

Tacitus. Since this great historian lived after the period covered by this volume and therefore his work is not described elsewhere, short reference may be made to him here at a point where his *Annals* begin to have relevance. Cornelius Tacitus was born c. A.D. 55, married in 77 the daughter of Agricola (later governor of Britain), lived through the oppressive tyranny of Domitian's last years, held the consulship in 97 in the same year as the emperor Nerva, and was proconsul of Asia about 112. Of his writings we are concerned here only with the *Annals*, probably written in eighteen books and covering the years from A.D. 14 to 68; there survive books 1–4, a fragment of 5 and 6, about half of 11, all of 12–15 and a few chapters of 16. He claimed to write 'since ira et studio', and in the facts that he gives he is accurate, but he confines his attention to certain aspects (mainly court-life and senatorial and military affairs to the neglect of other aspects of the history of the Empire), and his interpretation of the facts is often open to question. He could not shake himself free from the experiences of his own life and outlook. He was not at heart reconciled to the Principate and he looked back to the 'libertatem et consulatum', the free institutions of the Republic which he saw through rose-coloured glasses. His portrait of Tiberius may be coloured by his own experiences under Domitian, but Tacitus is not guilty of deliberate falsification: he thought that Tiberius was like that. But despite any preconceptions and unconscious temperamental bias, Tacitus sought the truth and recorded it, as he saw it, in a work of sombre magnificence and brilliant style. The standard English edition of the *Annals* is by H. Furneaux, vol. i (books 1–6, 2nd ed., 1896), II (books 11–16, by Furneaux, Pelham, Fisher, 1907). Of modern works the following may be mentioned: G. Boissier, *Tacitus* (Engl. trans. 1906); M. L. W. Laistner, *The Greater Roman Historians* (1947), chs. vi–vii; B. Walker, *The Annals of Tacitus, A study in the Writing of History* (1952); R. Syme, *Tacitus*, 2 vols. (1958); C. W. Mendell, *Tacitus, the Man and his Work* (1958). For a sceptical view of Tacitus' historical accuracy see G. Walser, *Rom. das Reich und die fremden Völker in der Geschichtsschreibung der frühen Kaiserzeit* (1951). See also T. A. Dorey (editor), *Tacitus* (1969), seven essays; F. R. D. Goodyear, *Tacitus* (*Greece and Rome*, New Surveys of the Classics, no. 4, 1970) and *The Annals of Tacitus*, vols. i and ii (1972 and 1981). [p. 176]

2 CONSENSUS UNIVERSORUM. This phrase from Augustus' *Res Gestae*, 34, is some-times interpreted as having a semi-constitutional force: the *coniuratio* of 32 B.C. gave Octavian an *imperium* to fight the war and this was widened by later general expressions of support. For a convincing criticism of this and similar interpretations see G.E.F. Chilver, *Historia*, 1950, 412 ff. See also P. A. Brunt and M. Moore, *Res Gestae* (1967), 76, who also discuss (75 f.) Octavian's constitutional position from 32 to Jan. 27 and consider what powers he may have surrendered in 28 as well as in 27

(as Dio Cassius, liii, 1–2): e.g. he allowed his colleague in the consulship, Agrippa, to hold the *fasces* alternately with himself; this implies that hitherto he had refused complete equality to his consular colleagues. On Octavian's position in January 27 see W.K. Lacey, *JRS*, 1974, 176 ff. [p.176]

3   TRIBUNICIA POTESTAS. Dio Cassius appears to say (51. 19. 6) that Octavian received *trib. pot.* in 30 B.C.; he also says that he received it in 23 (53. 32. 5). As Octavian is not likely to have relinquished it during the interval, some scholars have thought that he may have received some of the functions of a tribune in 30 and the rest in 23, but it is perhaps more probable (as argued by H. Last, *Rendiconti, Istituto Lombardo*, 1951, 93 ff.) that Dio is mistaken and that Octavian did not accept such an offer in 30 but only in 23. [p. 177]

4   THE AUGUSTAN SETTLEMENT. On the powers that Augustus received in 27 and 23 B.C. there is an immense modern literature. It is possible here to mention only some of the more recent works written in English: M. Hammond *The Augustan Principate* (1933); M. Grant, *From Imperium to Auctoritas* (1946; cf. *Greece and Rome*, 1949, 97 ff.); H. Last, *JRS*, 1947, 157 ff., and 1950, 119 ff; R. Syme, *JRS*, 1946, 149 ff.; G. E. F. Chilver, *Historia*, 1950, 408 ff. (a review of the work done on this subject between 1939 and 1950); A. H. M. Jones, *JRS*, 1951, 112 ff. (= *Studies in Roman Law and Government*, 1960, ch. 1); M. I. Henderson, *JRS*, 1954, 123 ff.; E. T. Salmon, *Historia*, 1956, 456 ff. These works will indicate the non-English literature of recent years. See also P. Grenade, *Essai sur les origines du Principat* (1961; on this see P. A. Brunt, *JRS*, 1961, 236 ff.) and P. Sattler, *Augustus und der Senat* (1960) which discusses how Augustus built up his power in face of those senators who opposed him until 17 B.C. Cf. also F. de Martino, *Storia della costituzione romana*, IV, i (1962). P. Cartledge (*Hermathena*, 1975, 35 ff.) discusses Augustus' approach to legitimizing his principate in 28–27. Recent work on Augustus is surveyed by B. Haller, *Aufstieg* II, ii, 55 ff. and by H. W. Benario, *id.*, 75 ff. [p. 178]

5   THE IMPERIUM OF AUGUSTUS. On this matter Augustus was somewhat reticent in his *Res Gestae* (whether because he thought a mention of his first grant in 43 B.C. was enough, or in order to soft-pedal the military aspect of his rule, or because the matter did not concern the Senate and People directly but rather the provinces). Though Augustus himself did not mention it, there is general agreement that the *imperium* which he exercised in the provinces from 23 was proconsular. But on the thorny question as to the nature of his provincial *imperium*, whether consular or proconsular, from 27 to 23, no agreement has been reached. Those who maintain that the consulship was essentially a domestic magistracy since Sulla's reforms, believe that Augustus' command was proconsular (cf. e.g. Salmon, *op. cit.*). For the view that it was consular see H. Pelham, *Essays* (1911), 60 ff. or M. Hammond, *op. cit.* The important distinction lies between *imperium militae* and *imperium domi*, since the former is the same whether held by a consul or proconsul. R. Syme suggests (*op. cit.*, 153) that Augustus governed his province 'while consul' rather than 'as consul'. A. H. M. Jones believes (*op. cit.*, p. 113) that in 27 the question did not arise: 'Augustus was consul, and the Senate assigned him a *provincia*: no grant of *imperium* was required'. It may well be that the approach to the problem has often been too legalistic and academic. The view of Mommsen that the grant of *imperium* gave Augustus *imperium maius* over the provinces controlled by the Senate, though followed by Von Premerstein, is not usually accepted. Nor is Premerstein's theory, based on Dio 53. 12. 1, that the Senate gave Augustus a general 'cura rei publicae', widely followed. It is probable that the grant of the *provincia* by the Senate in 27 was confirmed by a *lex* of the People. The view that Augustus' *imperium* as exercised in the provinces from 27 to 23 derived from his

consulship may receive support from a new inscription from Cyme: see H. W. Pleket, *Greek Inscriptions in the Rijksmuseum van Oudheden at Leyden* (1958) 49. This is the Greek version of a decree of Augustus and Agrippa as joint consuls in 27, ordering the restitution of sacred property (specifically in Asia, or in all senatorial provinces, or throughout the Empire?); it is followed by a letter of the proconsul of Asia, Vinicius, to the local authorities of Cyme about a case arising from it; the proconsul refers to the decree as *iussu Augusti Caesaris*. Pleket regards this as Augustus interfering in a senatorial province by virtue of consular *imperium maius*, whereas K. M. T. Atkinson (*Rev. intern. de droits de l'ant.* 1960, 227 ff.) thinks that the *iussum* refers merely to a judicial ruling given by Augustus in person when in Asia (20–19) by virtue of his *auctoritas* and therefore not bearing upon his *imperium* (and that the decree was part of a *senatusconsultum* transmitted by Augustus and Agrippa; this does not seem very probable). J. Reynolds (*JRS*, 1960, 207) points out that if the actual case at Cyme did not arise until after 23 (the date is not given), then 'the proconsul's attitude to Augustus would be more conventionally explicable'. Cf. *SEG*, XVIII, n. 555, XX, 15, and J. A. Crook, *Proc. Cambr. Philological Soc.* 1962, 23 ff. Augustus later claimed that he was acclaimed as imperator twenty-one times (*Res. Gestae*, 4,1); fourteen of these military salutations were made after he had acquired the title of Augustus. On their dates and occasions see T. D. Barnes, *JRS*, 1974, 21 ff. [p. 178]

6 CLUPEUS VIRTUTIS. Augustus records with pride this honour granted in 27 (*Res Gestae*, 34). A replica has been found at Arles, dated 26; copies of this new symbol must have been set up widely in the provinces. See W. Seston, *Comptes Rend. Ac. Inscr.* 1954, 286. See also M. P. Charlesworth, 'The Virtues of a Roman Emperor' (*Proc. Br. Acad.*, 1937). On two other attributes which were increasingly associated with the emperor during the first two centuries, see Charlesworth, 'Providentia et Aeternitas' (*Harvard Theol. Rev.*, 1936, 107 ff.). [p. 179]

7 AUGUSTUS' NAME AND POTESTAS. On the name Augustus see P.A. Brunt and J. M. Moore, *Res Gestae* (1967), 77 f. In *R.G.* 34, after saying that he excelled all men in *auctoritas* (see below, n. 9), Augustus added 'potestatis autem nihilo amplius habui quam ceteri qui mihi quoque in magistratu conlegae fuerunt'. That is, in each magistracy of his (reading quˉque, not quˉque, which would mean that Augustus was saying that 'he too had colleagues': see F. E. Adcock, *JRS*, 1952, 10 ff.), Augustus claims that his power was no greater than that of any of his colleagues in office. The interpretation is uncertain, but he is probably referring to the consulship and saying that he would not misuse the powers inherent in this office in the future: it should become normal again. This view can be used to support the belief that his provincial command was pro-consular: use of the consulship would be restricted to Italy. See further Brunt and Moore, *Res Gestae*, 78 f. [p. 179]

8 PRINCEPS. This use of the word should of course be sharply separated from the position of Princeps Senatus which Augustus also held (p. 179). Though it had Republican associations, there is no good reason to believe that he took it over from Cicero's political writings (cf. p. 135 and ch. VIII n. 6). The view of Ed. Meyer (*Caesars Monarchie und das Principat des Pompejus*, 3rd ed., 1922) that Cicero's *De Republica* suggested the creation of a Principate of Pompey and foreshadowed the ideal state created later by Augustus' Principate, is not now widely held. [p. 180]

9 AUCTORITAS. For recent discussions of its meaning see G. E. F. Chilver, *Historia*, 1950, 420 ff. The title of M. Grant's book, *From Imperium to Auctoritas* (1946), indicates its thesis that Augustus gradually shifted the basis of his power from military *imperium* to civilian *auctoritas*; but this is not acceptable because it gives to *auctoritas* a constitutional meaning that it can hardly have had. Attempts to endow it with a semi-mystic,

or 'charismatic' significance, are equally suspect. It was a personal attribute which could not be given or transferred from one man to another by law. [p. 180]

10 VARRO MURENA. K. M. T. Atkinson (*Historia*, 1960, 440 ff.) dates the trials of both Primus and Varro Murena to 22 (as Dio) and argues that the conspirator Varro was not A. Terentius Varro Murena the consul of 23 (who will have died during his year of office) but his cousin L. Murena who had probably been governor of Syria in 25. If this dating is accepted the plot cannot then have affected the constitutional settlement of 23. D. Stockton, *Historia*, 1965, 18 ff., defends the more conventional position against Mrs. Atkinson: he puts the trial of Primus in the first half of 23 and believes that it was Aulus Murena who defended him and who was involved in the conspiracy. M. Swan, *Harvard Stud. Class. Phil.*, 1966, 235 ff., argues for L. Murena and 22, as also does R. A. Bauman, *Historia*, 1965, 420 ff., who believes in two separate trials. S. Jameson, *Historia*, 1969, 204 ff., examines the events of 23 and 22 B.C. and places both trials in 23. According to B. Levick, *Gr. and R.*, 1975, 156 ff., Primus was prosecuted in 23 and defended by A. Varro Murena. [p. 180]

11 IMPERIUM MAIUS. This grant, attested by Dio Cassius (53. 32. 5), has in the past been doubted, but since the discovery of the five edicts from Cyrene (Ehrenberg and Jones, *Documents*, n. 311, translated in Lewis and Reinhold, *Rn. Civ.* ii, 36 ff.) which confirm it, the matter must surely be regarded as settled. On the edicts see further, J. G. C. Anderson, *JRS*, 1927, 33 ff.; F. de Visscher, *Les édits d'Auguste découverts à Cyrene* (1940); H. Last, *JRS*, 1945, 93. [p. 181]

12 TRIBUNICIA POTESTAS AND LEX DE IMPERIO. On the varying emphases that Augustus placed on his tribuncian power from 23 B.C. to A.D. 14 see A. K. Lacey, *JRS*, 1979, 28 ff. There survives part of a comprehensive enactment which conferred his various powers on the emperor Vespasian, the *lex de imperio Vespasiani* (Ehrenberg and Jones, *Documents*, n. 364). It is a law of the People and probably embodies a decree of the Senate; it quotes the precedents of grants made to Augustus and others. For a translation see Lewis and Reinhold, *Rn. Civ.* ii, 89 f. For a full discussion of the *lex de imperio* and these grants as made to Augustus' successors see P. A. Brunt, *JRS*, 1977, 95 ff. [p. 181]

13 AGRIPPA'S IMPERIUM. See R. Syme, *Rom. Rev.*, 337 n. 1, as against M. Reinhold, *Marcus Agrippa* (1933), 167 ff. Reinhold argued for *imperium aequum* in the imperial provinces in 23, *maius imperium* over the eastern senatorial provinces in 18, and *maius imperium* over the western provinces in 13. Despite the discovery of a papyrus fragment, which is apparently a Greek version of Augustus' *laudatio funebris* for Agrippa, the problem remains unsolved. See L. Koenen, *Zeitschrift für Papyrologie* V (1970), 217 ff., and E. W. Gray, *ibid.* VI (1970), 127 ff. The latter suggests an overall *imperium aequum* in 23, which was renewed for five years in 18, and made *maius* in 13. [p. 182]

14 AUGUSTUS' CONSULAR POWERS. This is suggested by A. H. M. Jones, *JRS*, 1951, 117 ff. (= *Studies*, 12 ff.). This interpretation of Dio 54. 10. 5 would explain how Augustus was able to command troops in Rome or Italy (Praetorian and Urban cohorts) and appoint a *praefectus urbi*, a consular prerogative. Cf. P. A. Brunt, *Cl. Rev.*, 1962, 70 ff. [p. 182]

15 LECTIONES SENATUS. Augustus stated (*Res Gestae* 8): 'senatum ter legi'. These *lectiones* probably refer to 29, 18 and 11 B.C.. He also mentioned three *census* at which the *lustrum* was celebrated in 28, 8 B.C. and A.D. 14, but a *lectio senatus* need not take place at the same time as a *lustrum*. The *lectiones* which Dio attributes to 13 B.C. and A.D. 4 should probably be rejected, the former as confused with a *recognitio equitum*, the latter as a partial census only. See A. H. M. Jones, *Studies in Roman Government* (1960), ch. II. Cf. also E. G. Hardy, *Monumentum Ancyranum*, 54 ff. A. E. Astin,

Latomus, 1963, 226 ff., believes that the *lectiones* of 13 and 11 are one and the same, begun in 13 and finished in 11, and that this *lectio* and that of 18 were carried out by virtue of *imperium consulare* and not by a grant of *censoria potestas* as in 29.

A serious problem is raised by the census figure of 29/28 which is 4,063,000 in contrast with that of 70/69 which is 910,000 *civium capita*. Did Augustus use an essentially different basis for his enumeration from those used by Republican censors, e.g. by including women and children (as argued by A. Toynbee, *Hannibal's Legacy*, I, 450 ff., following Beloch)? This view, rejected by Tenney Frank, *Cl. Ph.*, 1924, 329 ff., has again been questioned by T. P. Wiseman, *JRS*, 1969, 71 ff., who argues that a system of personal registration at Rome was replaced by a local registration, with the result that the Augustan figures bore a more realistic relation to the actual population than did the earlier figures. On the Augustan census figures see also P. A. Brunt, *Italian Manpower, 225 BC–A.D. 14* (1971), 113 ff. [p. 183]

16   LUDI SAECULARES. See J. Gagé, *Recherches sur les jeux séculaires* (1934); E. Fraenkel, *Horace* (1957), 364 ff. [p. 183]

17   ADOPTION OF TIBERIUS AND AGRIPPA POSTUMUS. H. U. Instinsky, *Hermes*, 1966, 324 ff., believes that although the adoption of Germanicus by Tiberius was a precondition of Augustus' adoption of Tiberius, nevertheless Tiberius had the freedom to choose, while Augustus' statement that the adoption was *rei publicae causa* was a political proclamation rather than a sign of resignation. B. Levick, *Latomus*, 1966, 227 ff., emphasizes that the adoption of Germanicus was to make him the equal of the younger Drusus, a wish of Augustus which Tiberius continued to respect as shown by the parallel careers of the younger men. But G. V. Sumner, *Latomus*, 1967, 413 ff., who discusses the ages of Germanicus and Drusus, concludes that Tiberius in the period of his developing ascendancy towards the end of Augustus' reign, did accelerate the career of his son Drusus.

Augustus in A.D. 4 also adopted the third son of Agrippa and Julia, born in 12 B.C. after his father's death and called Postumus. If an inscription from Trebula (*Ann. Epigr.*, 1964, no. 107) refers to Postumus and not to his father, this would provide evidence that Postumus at some point for a short time held an official position under Augustus: see J. Reynolds, *JRS*, 1966, 119. But Postumus' depraved character led Augustus to disinherit him: he was then banished (A.D. 7) and was killed immediately after Augustus himself had died. On the (improbable) story (Dio Cassius, lvi. 30, 1–2) that Augustus secretly visited Postumus on the island of Planasia (his place of banishment) during the closing months of his life, see M. P. Charlesworth, *AJP*, 1923, 146 ff. On the legal steps that Augustus took against Postumus see B. Levick, *Historia*, 1972, 674 ff. See also S. Jameson, *Historia*, 1975, 287 ff. On the last years of Augustus in the light of prosopographical studies see A. Ferrill, *Historia*, 1971, 718 ff. [p. 184]

18   PROVOCATIO. On this see A. H. M. Jones, 'I appeal unto Caesar', *Studies presented to D. M. Robinson*, 918 ff. (= *Studies*, ch. iv). P. Garnsey, *JRS*, 1966, 166 ff., questions the view that in the first century A.D. appeal was lodged *before* trial, i.e. the judge did not try the case but merely conducted a preliminary investigation; he argues that in both the first and second centuries appeal was made *after* sentence. If this is so, the classic case of St. Paul will not be a case of appeal proper at all. Mistrusting Festus and his chances of justice in Jerusalem Paul rejected the court (*reiectio*) at the hearing at Caesarea and exercised his right as a Roman citizen to appeal to Caesar, hoping for a trial in Rome. Festus, who was not obliged to agree but could have tried the case himself, decided to grant the request; in practice governors had considerable discretion. For a general survey of *provocatio* see A. W. Lintott, *Aufstieg*, I, ii (1972), 226 ff. [p. 186]

19 IMPERIAL AND SENATORIAL JURISDICTION. For a full discussion see A. H. M. Jones, *Historia*, 1955, pp. 464 ff. (= *Studies*, ch. v). Augustus also exercised appellate jurisdiction in civil cases, and so common were the appeals to him against civil judgements, both in Italy and the provinces, that he delegated the former to the urban praetor and the latter to special *consulares*. He also on occasion seems to have exercised a primary (non-appellate) civil jurisdiction. See further J. Bleiken, *Senatsgericht und Kaisergericht* (1962), on which cf. A. N. Sherwin-White, *JRS*, 1963, 203 ff.; A. H. M. Jones, *The Criminal Courts of the Roman Republic and Principate* (1972), ch. 3. [p. 186]

20 AERARIUM AND FISCUS. On this vexed problem see H. Last, *JRS*, 1944, 51 ff. and A. H. M. Jones, *JRS*, 1950, 22 ff. (= *Studies*, ch. vi). On the Aerarium and its officials, see F. Millar, *JRS*, 1964, 33 ff. Regarding the Fiscus whereas F. Millar, *JRS*, 1963, 29 ff., believes that the term *fiscus* was restricted to the emperor's personal wealth, P. A. Brunt, *JRS*, 1966, 75 ff., argues (with Jones) for wider uses as well (public funds handled by the emperor acting as a State agent) and that it came gradually to include the whole financial administration controlled by the emperor. [p. 186]

21 AUGUSTAN COINAGE. See C. H. V. Sutherland, *Coinage in Roman Imperial Policy, 31 BC–A.D. 68* (1951), chs. 2–4. [p. 188]

22 IMPERIAL AND SENATORIAL PROVINCES. F. Millar, *JRS*, 1966, 156 ff., challenges the accepted view and suggests that the division between senatorial and imperial provinces did not create a clear-cut division of responsibility and authority. He argues that, apart from the method of appointment, the only administrative difference (until the second century) was that, whereas the emperor gave instructions (*mandata*) to his *legati*, he did not so instruct proconsuls. In other respects the emperor and Senate were active in each other's sphere (though the Senate did not deal with imperial provinces as a whole); both (and especially the emperor) made regulations which were applicable everywhere and passed measures relating to places in either type of province. Cf. Millar, *The Roman Empire* (1967), 55. If this view may seem rather extreme the reassessment of the evidence must emphasize at very least that the system has too often been regarded as more rigid than it probably was. [p. 189]

23 THE IMPERIAL COUNCILS. See J. A. Crook, *Consilium Principis* (1955), a useful study of a controversial subject, which stresses the personal influence and importance of the *amici principis* as counsellors. A new papyrus fragment (see E. G. Turner, *Oxyrhynchus Papyri*, xxv, 2435) describes the reception of a deputation from Alexandria by the Consilium Principis in A.D. 13. [p. 189]

23a SENATORIAL ORDER. Augustus' handling of the senatorial census is discussed by C. Nicolet, *JRS*, 1976, 20 ff., whose views are based on the (unorthodox) belief that under the Republic entry to the Senate was *via* the equestrian order and that therefore senators had to have a census rating (at least that of the first class). [p. 189]

24 THE VIGINTIVIRATE. This group of offices comprised *iiiviri monetales* (mint-officials), *ivviri viarum curandarum* (in charge of the streets of Rome), *iiiviri capitales* (a kind of police) and *xviri stlitibus iudicandis* (who had jurisdiction in cases concerning the freedom of citizens). The two first colleges seem to have provided the surer path to later military commands in the emperor's service: see E. Birley, *Proc. Br. Acad.*, xxxix, 197 ff., who also believes that military service, as *tribunus laticlavius*, was not an essential qualification for entry into the Senate, though it was a necessary prerequisite for all senators who wished to be considered for appointment in the emperor's service. On possible variations in the early stages of the senatorial career see A. McAlindon, *JRS*, 1957, 191 ff. On the *leges annales* and the minimum age for office, see J. Morris, *Listy Filologicke*, 1964, 316 ff. [p. 189]

25 THE ELECTIONS. For this view, as opposed to the older belief that throughout his reign Augustus systematically 'rigged' the elections, see A. H. M. Jones, *JRS*, 1955, 9 ff. (= *Studies*, ch. iii). For the preponderance first of nobles, then of new men, see R. Syme, *Rom. Rev.*, 362, 372 ff., 434 f. P. A. Brunt (*JRS*, 1961, 71 ff.) has argued that Jones's theory is not supported by the Fasti: the humbler men became suffect consuls, while the ordinary consulship was reserved for men of consular lineage, and 'it should not be assumed that Augustus normally refrained from influenceing the consular elections'. In 'Imperial Control of the Elections under the Early Principate', *Historia*, 1967, 207 ff., B. Levick concludes 'in the Julio-Claudian era there were no legally defined, cut and dried rights called *nominatio, commendatio,* and *suffragatio,* which the Princeps exercised in a fixed and rigid way' (p. 228). See also R. Frei-Stobla, *Untersuchungen zu Wahlen in der römischen Kaiserzeit* (1967). A. E. Astin, *Latomus*, 1969, 863 ff., argues that *nominare* had no technical meaning in electoral contexts in the early Principate. See also E. S. Staveley, *Greek and Roman Voting and Elections* (1972), especially 217 ff. [p. 190]

26 DESTINATIO. The introduction of this procedure was revealed by the Tabula Hebana, the now famous inscription found in 1947 at Heba (Magliano) in Etruria. For the text see Ehrenberg and Jones, *Documents*² (1955), n. 94 a. There is already an immense modern literature on it; one of the most important contributions is G. Tibiletti, *Principi e magistri repubblicani* (1953). For the view expressed in the text see Jones, *JRS*, 1955, 13 ff. who dates the introduction of *destinatio* to A.D. 5; E. T. Salmon would date it to 5 B.C. (*Historia*, 1956, 475), and Tibiletti, less probably, to 27 B.C. The new inscription is a *rogatio* in honour of Germanicus in A.D. 19–20, when five new voting-centuries were established in his honour. It refers to ten earlier centuries named after Gaius and Lucius Caesar which 'destinated' consuls and praetors, and to a *Lex Valeria Cornelia* (A.D. 5) which regulated the voting procedure. See also J. Béranger, *Museum Helveticum*, 1957, 216 ff., and for a full bibliography (1947–57) G. Tibiletti, *Dizionario epigrafico di antichità romana* s.v. Lex, IV, pp. 743 ff. P. A. Brunt (see last note) believes that the purpose of the Lex Valeria Cornelia was to enhance the dignity of the upper classes rather than their political power. On *destinatio* and *nominatio* in the early Principate see D. Flach, *Chiron*, 1976, 193 ff. [p. 191]

27 PROCURATORS. Under Augustus and Tiberius the equestrian governors of imperial provinces were *praefecti*, but under Claudius the title was displaced by that of *procurator*. Cf. A. N. Sherwin-White, *Papers Brit. Sch. Rome*, 1939, 11 ff. and A. H. M. Jones, *Studies*, ch. vii. See H. G. Pflaum, *Les procurateurs equestres sous le haut empire* (1950) and below ch. XII, n. 20, and ch. XVI, n. 18. [p. 191]

28 LOWER CIVIL SERVANTS AND CAESAR'S HOUSEHOLD. For the former see A. H. M. Jones, *JRS*, 1949, 38 ff., for the latter P. R. C. Weaver, *Familia Caesaris* (1972) and G. Boulvart, *Esclaves et affranchis impériaux sous le haut-empire romaine* (1970) and *Domestique et fonctionnaire sous le haut empire romaine* (1974). [p. 192]

29 THE PLEBS. For the relationship between the city *plebs* and the Julio-Claudian emperors (as well as their role in the late Republic), see Z. Yavetz, *Plebs and Princeps* (1969). [p. 192]

30 BUILDINGS. See the works cited in ch. IX, n. 12. Augustus' Palatine house, which had belonged to the orator Q. Hortensius, is usually identified with the remains known as the House of Livia. Recent excavations have revealed traces of an earlier house just across a narrow road by the House of Livia, which are probably remains of a house which the Senate decreed should be given to him out of public funds (Dio Cassius, xlix, 15, 5); it was probably ready by 28 B.C.: G. Carettoni and N. Degrassi, *Rendi conti d. Pontif. Accad.* xxix (1966–7), 55 ff. and 76 ff; A. G. McKay, *Houses, Villas*

and Palaces in the Roman World (1975), 70 ff. Augustus' Mausoleum was built in 28 B.C. K. Kraft, *Historia*, 1967, 189 ff., argues that it was finished then and begun *c.* 32 when it will have been Octavian's propaganda answer to Antony's desire to be buried in Alexandria. On the actual work involved in running a household like that of Livia see S. Treggiari, *Papers Brit. Sch. Rome*, 1975, 48 ff. [p. 193]

31 THE VIGILES. See P. K. Baillie-Reynolds, *The Vigiles of Imperial Rome* (1926). [p. 194]

32 PRAEFECTUS URBI. On this office see G. Vitucci, *Ricerche sulla Praefectura Urbi in Età imperiale* (1956), and cf. T. J. Cadoux, *JRS*, 1959, 152 ff. [p. 194]

33 SOCIAL LEGISLATION. For details see H. Last, *CAH*, X, 441 ff. Cf. G. Williams, *JRS*, 1962, 28 ff. For an anlysis of the Augustan marriage laws see P. A. Brunt, *Italian Manpower, 225 BC–A.D. 14* (1971), 558 ff. He concludes that this legislation had little effect in increasing the number of citizens, though it may have done much to change the behaviour of the classes whom it touched. [p. 195]

34 FREEDMEN. A. M. Duff, *Freedmen in the Early Roman Empire* (1928); S. Treggiari, *Roman Freedmen during the Late Republic* (1969). [p. 196]

35 LARES COMPITALES. G. Niebling, *Historia*, 1956, 303 ff., dates the institution of an official state cult of the Lares and Genius Augusti to 7 B.C. [p. 198]

36 EMPEROR WORSHIP. In general see L. Cerfaux and J. Tondriau, *Le Culte des Souverains* (1956). See L. R. Taylor, *The Divinity of the Roman Emperor* (1931). On the formula devised by Augustus for tactfully declining divine honours, see M. P. Charlesworth, *Papers Brit. Sch. Rome*, 1939, i ff. See also K. Latte, *Römische Religionsgeschichte* (1960), ch. xi, and for the general background of thought, J. R. Fears, *Princeps a diis electus: the divine election of the Emperor as a political concept at Rome* (1977), together with P. A. Brunt's discussion in *JRS*, 1979, 168 ff. [p. 198]

37 AUGUSTAN LITERATURE. See the general books mentioned in ch. X, n. 3. Recent monographs include L. P. Wilkinson, *Horace and his Lyric Poetry* (2nd edn., 1951); *Ovid Recalled* (1955); R. Syme, *History in Ovid* (1978); E. Fraenkel, *Horace* (1957); cf. also the attractive sketches by G. Highet, *Poets in a Landscape* (1957), chs. ii–vi, and some reflections on Ovid by W. S. Maguinness (*Gr. and R.*, 1958, 2 ff.). Two books of collected essays are *Horace*, edited by C. D. N. Costa (1974) and *Ovid*, edited by J. W. Binns (1973). On the Augustan poets see T. E. Wright, *Fifty Years Cl. Sch.* (1954), 306 ff. On Livy see A. H. McDonald, *JRS*, 1957, 155 ff.; P. G. Walsh, *Livy: his Historical Aims and Methods* (1961) and *Livy* (*Greece and Rome*, New Surveys, no. 8, 1974); also *Livy* (edited by T. A. Dorey, 1971). See also C. G. Starr, *Civilization and the Caesars* (1954); G. Williams, 'Poetry in the moral climate of Rome', *JRS*, 1962, 28 ff. Unlike Williams, J. Griffin in 'Augustan Poetry and the Life of Luxury', *JRS*, 1976, 87 ff., argues that the poets reflect the luxury of contemporary social life rather than mere literary conventions about such life. [p. 199]

38 TIBULLUS, PROPERTIUS AND CORNELIUS GALLUS. See F. Cairns, *Tibullus, a Hellenistic Poet at Rome* (1979); M Hubbard, *Propertius* (1974); J. P. Sullivan, *Propertius a Critical Introduction* (1976). Another poet was C. Cornelius Gallus, a friend of Virgil and Augustus who appointed him as the first Prefect of Egypt (see above pp. 178, 212). Only one line of his love-elegies survived until 1978 when a Latin papyrus was found at Qasr Ibrim in Egyptian Nubia, preserving four complete and six fragmentary lines by Gallus. These contain references to his mistress Lycoris and to Caesar and a campaign (more probably Julius and his projected Parthian campaign than Octavian and the wars of 31–30). See R. D. Anderson *et al.*, *JRS*, 1979, 125 ff. [p. 203]

39 ASINIUS POLLIO. On his relationship to Augustus see A. B. Bosworth, *Historia*, 1972, 441 ff. [p. 204]

CHAPTER XII

1 THE PRAETORIAN GUARD. See M. Durry, *Les Cohortes prétoriennes* (1938); A. Passerini, *Le coorti pretorie* (1939). [p. 206]

2 THE LEGIONS. See H. M. D. Parker, *The Roman Legions*² (1958). On the organization of the army in general see G. Webster, *The Roman Imperial Army* (1969). On army service from the point of view of the ordinary soldier, see G. R. Watson, *The Roman Soldier* (1969). On the impact of the army upon the behaviour and destiny of the government see M. Grant, *The Army of the Caesars* (1974). [p. 206]

3 THE AUXILIA. See G. L. Cheesman, *The Auxilia of the Roman Imperial Army* (1914). [p. 207]

4 THE NAVY. See C. G. Starr, *The Roman Imperial Navy*² (1960); D. Kienast, *Untersuchungen zu den Kriegsflotten der romischen Kaiserzeit* (1966). [p. 208]

5 FORUM IULI. A fleet remained there until A.D. 69, but the base was gradually being replaced by Misenum. Excavation has revealed harbour-walls and many naval buildings, including the prefect's mansion. See A. Donnadieu, *Fréjus* (1935). [p. 208]

6 THE PROVINCES. See Th. Mommsen, *The Provinces of the Roman Empire* (1909); V. Chapot, *The Roman World* (1928); M. Rostovtzeff, *Social and Economic History of the Roman Empire* (2nd ed. 1957); H. D. Meyer, *Die Aussenpolitik des Augustus und die Augusteische Dichtung* (1961). In a discussion of this last named book P. A. Brunt (*JRS*, 1963, 170 ff.) advances the unconventional thesis that after a period of rest and pacification after the civil wars, Augustus embarked on a cautious but deliberate plan for world conquest, which was thwarted by the revolts in Pannonia and Germany in A.D. 6 and 9; only at the end of his life did he fall back on the policy of keeping the empire within its then existing boundaries. Whatever be thought of this view, at least it should be remembered that in fact Augustus added vast areas to the empire: the giver of peace was also a great conqueror. Cf. Brunt and Moore, *Res Gestae* (1967), 69. See also, in line with Brunt's views, C. M. Wells, *The German Policy of Augustus* (1972), ch. 1, and further, the first part of E. N. Luttwak's *The Grand Strategy of the Roman Empire from the first century A.D. to the third* (1976), together with discussion by J. C. Mann, *JRS*, 1979, 175 ff.

On the individual provinces under the Empire see the very detailed studies in *Aufstieg*, II, iii–ix (1975–8). [p. 208]

7 THE EASTERN PROVINCES. See A. H. M. Jones, *Cities of the Eastern Roman Provinces*² (1971); D. Magie, *Roman Rule in Asia Minor* (1950). On the Augustan governors of Asia see K. M. T. Atkinson, *Historia*, 1958, 300 ff. On the kings beyond, see M. Pani, *Roma e i re d'Oriente da Augusto a Tiberio* (1972), i.e. Cappadocia, Armenia, Media, Atropatene. [p. 209]

8 P. SULPICIUS QUIRINIUS. This *novus homo*, who was consul in 12 B.C., was legate of Syria in A.D. 6. He is the 'Cyrenius' mentioned by St. Luke, ii, 2. His career presents well-known difficulties. He was almost certainly not legate of Syria twice and may not have been the subject of a fragmentary inscription (*ILS*, 918) which has often been applied to him. As legate of Syria in A.D. 6 he supervised the assessment of Judaea after the deposition of Archelaus (see p. 211). See, briefly, R. Syme, *OCD*, s.v. On the census see E. Schürer, *The History of the Jewish People in the Age of Jesus Christ*, revised by C. Vermes and F. Millar (1973), 399 ff. [p. 209]

9 PARTHIA. N. C. Debevoise, *A Political History of Parthia* (1938); K. H. Ziegler, *Die Beziehungen zwischen Rom und dem Partherreich* (1964), M. A. R. Colledge, *The Parthians* (1967). On Roman policy to Parthia, 30–20 B.C., see D. Timpe, *Würzburger Jahrb. für die Altertumswiss.* 1975, 155 ff. [p. 209]

10 HEROD THE GREAT. See A. Momigliano, *CAH*, X, ch. xi; A. H. M. Jones, *The Herods of Judaea* (1938); M. Grant, *Herod the Great* (1971). The theory that Herod died in 1 B.C., not in 4 B.C. (with the consequent possibility of the birth of Jesus in 1 B.C. rather than in or before 4 B.C.: cf. J. Thorley, *Gr. and R.*, 1981, 81 ff.) has been revived by W. E. Filmer (*Journ. Theolog. Stud.*, 1966, 283 ff.) but refuted by T. D. Barnes, *id.*, 1968, 204 ff. (cf. Schürer, *op. cit. infra*, I, 328). On Herod's son Antipas see H. W. Hoehner, *Herod Antipas* (1972) which is not entirely satisfactory (cf. J. Rajak, *JRS*, 1974, 225).

On Jewish history in this period in general see especially E. Schürer, *The History of the Jewish People in the Age of Jesus Christ*, revised by G. Vermes and F. Millar, i (1973), ii (1976). Cf. also E. M. Smallwood, *The Jews under Roman Rule from Pompey to Diocletian* (1976) and M. Grant, *The Jews in the Roman World* (1973). [p. 210]

11 ARABIA FELIX. On the date (26–25) and purpose (conquest) of the Arabian expedition of Aelius see S. Jameson, *JRS*, 1968, 71 ff. On the site of Mariba see R. LeB. Bowen and F. P. Albright, *Archaeological Discoveries in South Arabia*, II (USA 1958). For an account of an American archaeological expedition there see W. Phillips, *Qataban and Sheba* (1955). N. Lewis argues that a papyrus fragment (*P. Oxy.* 2820) refers probably to Aelius Gallus' preparations in 25 B.C. for the expedition to Arabia Felix rather than to Cornelius Gallus. [p. 211]

12 EGYPT. See H. Idris Bell, *CAH*, x, ch. x. On the Prefects see P. A. Brunt, *JRS*, 1975, 124 ff. [p. 212]

13 ETHIOPIA. For Petronius' expedition see S. Jameson, *JRS*, 1968, 71 ff., who argues that Augustus' real intention was conquest; if so, he will have failed (as also in regard to an Elbe frontier). In general see P. L. Shinnie, *Meroe* (1967). [p. 213]

14 SPANISH WARS. See R. Syme, *AJP*, 1934, 293 ff.; W. Schmitthenner, *Historia*, 1962, 29 ff.; A. Brancati, *Augusto e la guerra di Spagna* (1963). For the sources A. Schulten, *Fontes Hispaniae Antiquae*, V (1940), pp. 183 ff. Also A. Schulten, *Los Cantabros y Astures* (1943). On Augustus' reorganization there see C. H. V. Sutherland, *The Romans in Spain* (1939), ch. vii. For romanization, J. M. Blazquez, *Emerita*, 1962, 71 ff. On the Roman conquest and later military occupation of N.W. Spain, where the mines as well as the population needed continued supervision, see R. F. Jones, *JRS*, 1976, 45 ff. [p. 213]

15 GAUL. cf. N. J. de Witt, *Urbanization and the Franchise in Roman Gaul* (1940); J. J. Hatt, *Histoire de la Gaule romaine* (1959); A. J. Christopherson, *Historia*, 1968, 351 ff., on the provincial assembly of the Three Gauls in the Julio–Claudian period. [p. 214]

16 TROPAEA AUGUSTI. For the text of this inscription see Ehrenberg and Jones, *Documents*, n. 40. [p. 215]

16a NORICUM. On the conquest and history of Noricum see G. Alfoldy, *Noricum* (1974). [p. 215]

17 THE BALKANS. The status of the cities in the new province varied. Sparta was ruled by Eurycles, who had fought for Octavian at Actium; he was rewarded with the emperor's friendship, but he stirred up so much factional strife and disturbance in Achaea that he was banished (probably between 7 and 2 B.C.); his son Laco, however, was allowed to become ruler of Sparta. On Eurycles see G. W. Bowersock, *JRS*, 1961, 112 ff. On the Augustan conquest of Dalmatia see J. J. Wilkes, *Dalmatia* (1969), ch. 5. On the conquest and history of Pannonia and Moesia see A. Mocsy, *Pannonia and Upper Moesia* (1974). [p. 216]

17a GERMANY. C. M. Wells, *The German Policy of Augustus* (1972), 211 ff., argues that the Romans established a base for two legions and auxiliaries at Oberaden (near the Lippe, N.E. of Dortmund) in 10 B.C. and held it for two years. [p. 218]

18 THE CLADES VARIANA. The site of the disaster, possibly between Osnabruck and Detmold, has been the subject of endless discussion: for some of the earlier views,

before 1931, see Rice Holmes, *Architect Rom. Emp.* ii, 166 ff. Further advance has been made in a pamphlet by W. John, *Die Ortlichkeit der Varusschlacht bei Tacitus* (1950), who argues that when Tacitus (*Ann.* I. 61) says that Germanicus, on reaching the site, found that the last stand had been made 'in medio campi', he means not 'in the middle of the battle-field', but on the 'parade-ground' within the camp: that is, the last survivors dug themselves in within a smaller area, when the ramparts of their camp had been stormed. This clue, combined with air-photography, might one day lead to a solution. Cf. W. John also in Pauly-Wissowa, *RE*, xxiv (1963), col. 922 ff. [p. 219]

19 GERMANY. On Drusus' campaign in 9 B.C., see D. Timpe, *Rhein. Mus.*, 1967, 289 ff., and on Germany under Augustus in general, *id.*, *Saeculum*, 1967, 278 ff. On the arch-aeological evidence for the Roman frontier in Germany see H. Schonberger, *JRS*, 1969, 144 ff., who starts a valuable survey with the period from 19 B.C. to A.D. 16, examining the early development of the legionary fortresses and of other forts which mark the early advances beyond the Rhine. The camp buildings were made of wood, and stone was not used before the reign of Claudius, but it was a powerful defence line. See now on the northern frontier C. M. Welles, *The German Policy of Augustus: an Examination of the Archaeological Evidence* (1972). On aspects of Augustus' German policy see also K. Christ, *Chiron*, 1977, 149 ff. [p. 219]

20 PROVINCIAL GOVERNORS. On the personnel see R. Syramkiewicz, *Les Gouverneurs de province à l'époque augustéenne: contribution à l'histoire administrative et sociale du principat*, 2 vols. (1976). On the equestrian procurators see H. G. Pflaum, *Les procura-teurs equestres sous le haut empire romain* (1950); *Les carrières procuratoriennes équestres*, 3 vols. (1960–61). [p. 220]

21 PORTORIA. See S. J. de Laet, *Portorium* (1949). [p. 220]

22 MINES. Much interesting light is thrown on the operation of mines under Hadrian by two inscriptions from the mining community at Vipasca in Lusitania: see Riccobono, *FIRA*, i, nos. 104–5; translation in Lewis and Reinhold, *Rn. Civ.* ii, 188 ff. [p. 220]

23 PROVINCIAL ADMINISTRATION. P. A. Brunt (*Historia*, 1961, 189 ff.) has examined conditions in the early Principate and concludes that abuses may have been more frequent and redress not so easy to secure as has often been supposed. Local com-munities in the provinces had the burden of providing transport in their districts for Roman officials passing through, as well as for their hospitality and for the imperial post (*cursus publicus*). An interesting inscription of *c.* A.D. 13–15 from central Pisidia shows that Augustus passed measures to regulate such state transport, with details of payment, e.g. for ox-drawn carts, mules and donkeys. For the inscription and general discussion see S. Mitchell, *JRS*, 1976, 106 ff. [p. 221]

24 LOCAL ADMINISTRATION. See F. F. Abbott and A. C. Johnson, *Municipal Adminis-tration in the Roman Empire* (1926), the second part of which comprises municipal documents. [p. 221]

25 AUGUSTAN COLONIZATION. See F. Vittinghoff, *Römische Kolonisation und Burger-rechtspolitik unter Caesar und Augustus* (1952). [p. 222]

26 THE EMPEROR'S WORK. In an important book, *The Emperor in the Roman World 31 BC to A.D. 337* (1977), Fergus Millar examines the emperors at work and what they actually did in relation to their subjects and institutions (excluding the army, emperor-worship and taxation). [p. 225]

CHAPTER XIII

1 SOURCES FOR TIBERIUS (A.D. 14–37). The chief literary sources are Velleius Paterculus, ii, 123–31, a contemporary who is favourable to Tiberius; (see A. J.

Woodman, *Velleius Paterculus, The Tiberian Narrative (2.94–131)* (1977); Tacitus, *Annals*, I–VI (most of book V is missing), edited by H. Furneaux (1907); F. R. D. Goodyear, *The Annals of Tacitus, I, II* (1972 and 1981); Suetonius, *Tiberius*; Dio Cassius, lvii–lviii. On the Julio–Claudian historians see J. J. Wilkes, *Cl. W.*, 1972, vol. 65, 177 ff. Suetonius, *Tiberius*; Dio Cassius, lvii–lviii. Documents: Ehrenberg and Jones, *Documents*. Coins: works cited in note to ch. XI, n. 1, and M. Grant, *Aspects of the Principate of Tiberius* (1950). Iconography: L. Polacco, *Il Volto di Tiberio* (1955); cf. *JRS*, 1956, 157 ff. Modern works include F. B. Marsh, *The Reign of Tiberius* (1931); R. S. Rogers, *Criminal Trials under Tiberius* (1935); D. M. Pipidi, *Autout de Tibère* (1944); G. Marañon's *Tiberius, A Study in Resentment* (1956) is popular and unreliable; R. Syme, *Tacitus* (1958), especially 420 ff.; *Tiberius* (1960) by E. Kornemann is a very subjective assessment; R. Seager, *Tiberius* (1972) and cf. R. Syme, *Historia*, 1974, 481 ff.; B. Levick, *Tiberius the Politician* (1976). Tacitus' attitude to Tiberius, especially in regard to the problems of his accession, is discussed by K. von Fritz, *Cl. Ph.*, 1957, 78 ff. For the problem of the transmission of power under the Julio–Claudians see D. Timpe, *Untersuchungen zur Kontinuität des frühen Prinzipats* (1962). On the whole period from Tiberius to Nero see the very useful book by A. Garzetti, *From Tiberius to the Antonines* (1974); the English translation of this work which was published in Italian in 1960 provides long critical notes and bibliographies which have been brought up to date to 1969. See also G. Downey, 'Tiberiana', *Aufstieg*, II, ii, 95 ff. and J. P. V. D. Balsdon on the principates of Tiberius and Gaius, *id.*, 86 ff. [p. 227]

2 DIES IMPERII. See G. Kampff, *Phoenix*, 1963, 25 ff, and K. Wellesley, *JRS*, 1967, 23 ff., who has argued that the *dies imperii*, the day on which Tiberius accepted the Principate at the hands of the Senate, was not 17 Sept., the day when divine honours were voted to Augustus, but rather early in Sept. before the 4th. Rejected by R. Seager, *Tiberius* (1972), 55. On the beginning of Tiberius' reign see D. Flach, *Historia*, 1973, 552 ff. [p. 228]

3 JULIANS AND CLAUDIANS. The so-called Julio–Claudian dynasty (Tiberius, Gaius, Claudius and Nero) were all related by blood to Augustus or Livia. Members of the imperial house with closer connexions with the Julian *gens* may have enjoyed greater popularity in some circles: thus some people would turn more readily to Germanicus who had more Julian connexions through his mother than to Tiberius' own son Drusus, who was a pure Claudian. But these differences should not be over-rated. B. Levick, *Gr. and R.*, 1975, 29 ff., points out that 'Julians' and 'Claudians' did not accurately describe groups, since because of adoption the Julians were divided. On the relations of Germanicus and Drusus see W. Allen, *TAPA*, 1941, 1 ff., and M. Stuart, *Cl. Ph.*, 1940, 64 ff. [p. 228]

4 THE NORTHERN CAMPAIGNS OF GERMANICUS. For an evaluation of these see E. Koestermann, *Historia*, 1957, 429 ff., and D. Timpe, *Der Triumph des Germanicus: Untersuchungen zu den Feldzugen der Jahre 14–16 n. Chr. in Germanien* (1968). Timpe argues that the decreeing of a triumph for Germanicus at the end of 15 shows that Tiberius regarded the war as completed and that the emperor disapproved of Germanicus' continued aggressive campaign in 16. [p. 229]

5 EDICT OF GERMANICUS. See Ehrenberg and Jones, *Documents*, n. 320b; translation in Lewis and Reinhold, *Rn. Civ.* ii. p. 562. Another edict (n. 320a; Lewis, p. 229) deprecates requisitioning. Interesting light is thrown on Germanicus' visit to Egypt by a recently published papyrus: see E. G. Turner, *Oxyrhynchus Papyri*, xxv (1959), n. 2435. It gives Germanicus' speech on arrival at Alexandria (punctuated by applause) and also the official designation of his command. On this Turner comments: 'Germanicus clearly treats Egypt as an ἐπαρχία = *provincia*, Tiberius did not.' On Germanicus in the

East see E. Koestermann, *Historia*, 1958, 331 ff. See also Weingaertner, *Die Aegyptenreise des Germanicus* (1969). [p. 229]

6 GERMANICUS' POPULARITY. This is further attested by the extravagant honours voted to him after his death which are recorded in the Tabula Hebana (Ehrenberg and Jones, *Documents*, n. 94a; see ch. XI, n. 26). See S. Weinstock, *JRS*, 1957, 144 ff. D. C. A. Shotter, *Historia*, 1968, 194 ff., discusses Tacitus' account of Germanicus' career under Tiberius. On Tacitus' portrait of Germanicus see now S. Borzsat, *Latomus*, 1969, 588 ff. On Piso see D. C. A. Shotter, *Historia*, 1974, 229 ff. [p. 230]

7 THE SENATE AND ELECTIONS. It is known that the system of *destinatio* which had been put in the hands of ten centuries of senators and knights, continued (see p. 190); five new centuries were created in honour of Germanicus in A.D. 19 (Tabula Hebana) and another five in honour of Drusus in A.D. 23 (Ehrenberg and Jones, *Documents*[2], n. 94b). At the same time the well-known statement of Tacitus (*Ann.* i, 15) that 'tum primum e campo comitia ad patres translata sunt' must be accepted. Perhaps (as suggested by G. Tibiletti) the result of the *destinatio* by the centuries, hitherto advisory, now bound the People, to whom the presiding magistrate would nominate no other names; in this case the equites will have been eliminated from the destinating assembly, probably before the end of Tiberius' reign. Alternatively (as suggested by A. H. M. Jones, *JRS*, 1955, 19) Tiberius may have proposed that the Senate should itself settle who should be candidates and should limit the number to equal the number of places to be filled: thus the elections both by the centuries and by the Comitia would become a formality. See also R. Syme, *Tacitus* (1958), 756 ff. and M. Pani, *Comitia e Senato: sulla trasformazione della procedura ellettorale in Roma nell'età di Tiberio* (1974); cf. E. S. Staveley, *JRS*, 1975, 201. The view that Tiberius did not exercise *commendatio* for the consulship has been questioned by M. L. Paladini, *Athenaeum*, 1959, 120 f. but see B. Levick, *Historia*, 1967, 207 ff., quoted above ch. XI, n. 25. See also W. K. Lacey, *Historia*, 1963, 167 ff., and D. C. A. Shotter, *Cl. Qu.*, 1966, 321 ff. R. Syme, *Historia*, 1981, 189 ff., shows that the consuls of A.D. 15–19 were not an outstanding group of men: Tiberius tended to favour the advancement of the consuls elected in Augustus' last decade. [p. 231]

8 TIBERIUS AND MAIESTAS. See F. B. Marsh, R. S. Rogers, R. Seager and B. Levick *op. cit.*, n. 1; R. A. Bauman, *Impietas in Principem* (1974); on the *lex Iulia maiestatis* see J. E. Allison and J. D. Cloud, *Latomus*, 1962, 711 ff. and for the penalties laid down by this law see B. M. Levick, *Historia*, 1979, 358 ff. C. W. Chilton has argued (*JRS*, 1955, 73 ff.) against Rogers that the only penalty laid down under the *lex Iulia de maiestate* was exile (interdictio aquae et ignis) with or without confiscation of property. Thus the death sentence, which was often exacted in Tiberius' later years, represented an extension of the penalty, imposed arbitrarily by the court (normally the Senate's rather than the emperor's court). In 21, while Tiberius was away from Rome, a Roman knight, Clutorius Priscus, was condemned by the Senate and was at once executed: on his return, Tiberius commended the only senator who had advocated exile in place of death, and caused the Senate to pass a decree ordering ten days interval between a death sentence and its execution. For the reply of R. S. Rogers to Chilton's criticism of his views see *JRS*, 1959, 90 ff. Charges of treason were often added to other charges, e.g. when C. Silanus, a former proconsul of Asia, was accused of extortion in 22. Some treason trials arose from factional politics within the Senate and nobility. Tiberius refused to admit the charge of *maiestas* against Aemilia Lepida in 20, but she was convicted on other charges: for the trial see G. B. Townend, *Latomus*, 1962, 484 ff., D. C. A. Shotter, *Historia*, 1966, 312 ff. for C. Silius' trial in 24 see Shotter, *Latomus*, 1967, 712. See in general B. Walker, *The Annals of*

Tacitus, 82 ff. On the trial of Libo Drusus see D. C. A. Shotter, *Historia*, 1972, 88 ff. [p. 232]

9   DRUSUS. See R. S. Rogers, *Studies in the Reign of Tiberius* (1943), 89 ff. [p. 233]

9a SPERLONGA. The grotto is almost certainly modern Sperlonga, where a dining-table (*triclinium*) and fine sculptures of mythological figures have been found. These illustrate Tiberius' taste in sculpture and his literary leanings (cf. Suetonius, *Tib.* 70): see A. F. Stewart, *JRS*, 1977, 76 ff. [p. 233]

10 LIVIA (JULIA AUGUSTA). Intelligent, beautiful and dignified, Livia had exercised a good influence on Augustus. The tradition about her in Tacitus derives from the propaganda of her enemies. Though she may have become somewhat masterful, the hints that she had any part in the deaths of Marcellus, Gaius and Lucius Caesar, Augustus or Germanicus, should be dismissed as pure scandal. [p. 233]

11 SEJANUS. On his family and friends see Z. Stewart, *AJP*, 1953, 70 ff., F. Adams, *AJP*, 1955, 70 ff., G. V. Sumner, *Phoenix*, 1965, 134 ff.; R. Sealey, *Phoenix*, 1961, 97 ff. for his political attachments; H. W. Bird, *Latomus*, 1969, 61 ff. The seriousness of his conspiracy (or even its existence) has been variously assessed (in the letter from Capreae, as recorded by Dio Cassius, Sejanus is not specifically charged with a plot to murder Tiberius). Sejanus possibly did not desire the death of Tiberius before he himself had received *tribunicia potestas* and his succession was reasonably assured. Thus F. B. Marsh (*The Reign of Tiberius*, 394 ff.) and others are more sceptical than e.g. R. S. Rogers. On Dio's silence see E. Koestermann, *Hermes*, 1955, 350 ff. and R. Syme, *Tacitus*, 725 ff. A. Boddington (*AJP*, 1963, 1 ff.) attributes Sejanus' fall to a powerful group of his opponents who forced Tiberius to abandon him. An inscription from Alba Fucens (*L'Année epigraphique*, 1957, n. 250) has revealed Macro's true name as Q. Naevius Sutorius Macro and the fact that he had been Praefectus Vigilum; this may help to explain how he was able to move against Sejanus with such success. On Macro see F. de Visscher, *Mélanges Piganiol* (1966), 761 ff., and *Synteleia Arangio-Ruiz* (1966), 54 ff. On Sejanus see further, D. Hennig, *L. Aelius Seianus. Untersuchungen zur Regierung des Tiberius* (1975), while J. Nicols, *Historia*, 1975, 48 ff., argues that Antonia Minor had no connections with Sejanus before 31 and her alleged links with his fall are Claudian and Flavian inventions. [p. 234]

12 FOREIGN POLICY. For a brief assessment of Tiberius' policy see G. Alfoldy, *Latomus*, 1965, 824 ff. [p. 234]

13 ARTABANUS. See U. Kahrstedt, *Artabanos und seine Erben* (1950). For the suggestion that the meeting with Vitellius fell in 37 after Tiberius' death see A. Garzetti, *Studi Calderini*, I (1956), 211 ff. [p. 235]

14 THE DRUIDS. See H. Last, *JRS*, 149, pp. 1 ff., for the view that what brought Rome into conflict with Druidism was not that it fostered disloyalty but that it preserved savage practices that were regarded as incompatible with the standards of civilization that Rome wished to see in her Empire. The suppression of Druidism in Gaul is assigned by Pliny (*NH*, xxx, 13) to Tiberius, by Suetonius (*Div. Claud.* 25) to Claudius. On Florus and Sacrovir see L. Bessone, *Num. Ant. Class. Ticens.*, 1978, 143 ff. [p. 235]

15 TACFARINAS AND THE MUSULAMII. See R. Syme, *Studies in Roman Economic and Social History in Honour of A. C. Johnson* (1951), 113 ff. For a dedication to Victoria Augusta by P. Cornelius Dolabella on Tacfarinas' death see R. Bartoccini, *Epigraphica*, 1958, 3 ff. [p. 236]

16 TIBERIUS AND EMPEROR-WORSHIP. On Tiberius' sensible attitude see Suetonius, *Tib.* 10. This is also illustrated by an inscription from Gytheum in Laconia of A.D. 15 or 16, which quotes a letter of Tiberius in reply to the city's intention to establish worship of Augustus, himself and Livia; he deprecates divine honours for himself.

See Ehrenberg and Jones, *Docum.* n. 102; partial translation in Lewis and Reinhold, *Rn. Civ.* ii. p. 560. A Cypriote oath of allegiance to Tiberius on his accession has been preserved (see T. B. Mitford, *JRS*, 1960, 75). This in itself is of interest, as also is the fact that the Cypriots swore by (among other deities) Roma and the deified Augustus, since in Asia the cult of Roma disappeared when that of the emperor was established. The Cypriots promised to worship Tiberius and all his house and proposed the voting of divine honours to Roma, Tiberius and the sons of his blood [p. 236]

16a FINANCIAL DIFFICULTIES, A.D. 33. See Tenney Frank, *AJP*, 1935, 336 ff. and C. Rodewald, *Money in the Age of Tiberius* (1976). [p. 237]

17 SOURCES FOR GAIUS. Suetonius, *Gaius Caligula*; Dio Cassius, book 59; Josephus, *Ant. Iud.* xviii, 205–xix, 211; Philo, *In Flaccum: Legatio ad Gaium*; books 7 and 8 of Tacitus' *Annals*, which dealt with Gaius, are lost. E. M. Smallwood, *Documents Illustrating the Principates of Gaius, Claudius and Nero* (1967). On the sources see M. P. Charlesworth, *Cambr. Hist. Journ.*, 1933, 105 ff. Modern works: J. P. V. D. Balsdon, *The Emperor Gaius* (1934); E. Koberlein, *Caligula und die ägyptischen Kulte* (1962). See also Balsdon on the principates of Gaius and Claudius, *Aufstieg*, II, ii, 86 ff. [p. 239]

18 THE ACCESSION OF GAIUS. The enthusiasm with which provincial cities took the oath of allegiance is shown by two inscriptions from Aritium in Lusitania (Dessau, *ILS*, 190) and Assos in Asia (Dittenberger, n. 797); they are translated in Lewis and Reinhold, *Rn. Civ.* ii, 86 f. P. Ceausescu, *Historia*, 1973, 269 ff., argues that Gaius, by curtailing the annual Games that celebrated the battle of Actium, was seeking to reconcile East and West. Unlike Augustus and Tiberius, Gaius was a *privatus* and had greater need of a comprehensive grant of legal powers by a *lex de imperio* (such as had been passed for Tiberius and possibly for Augustus); see above ch. xi, n. 12 and P. A. Brunt, *JRS*, 1977, 95 ff. [p. 239]

18a GAIUS' MENTAL STABILITY. Some historians would minimize the difference between the early and later parts of Gaius' rule: this should be attributed less to severe mental disturbance than to increased exasperation in a weak man suddenly wielding unlimited authority. Thus, e.g., A. Garzetti, *From Tiberius to the Antonines* (1974), 84. Cf. also V. Massaro and I. Montgomery, *Latomus*, 1978, 894 ff. [p. 240]

19 BRITAIN. R. W. Davies, *Historia*, 1966, 124 ff., questions the usual view that Gaius intended to invade Britain; his views have been rejected by P. Bicknell, *Historia*, 1968, 496 ff., who, very speculatively, transfers the sea-shell episode from the English Channel to the Insula Batavorum in Lower Germany! [p. 241]

19a BOSPORUS. On Gaius' policy in the Bosporus see A. A. Barrett, *TAPA*, 1977, 1 ff. [p. 241]

20 THE SENATE AT ALEXANDRIA. On the vexed question of the existence of a Greek Senate at this period, see A. Momigliano, *JRS*, 1944, 114, for the view that it did exist. [p. 241]

21 ACTA ALEXANDRINORUM. See H. A. Musurillo, *The Acts of the Pagan Martyrs* (1954) for text and commentary. [p. 242]

22 HEROD AGRIPPA. On this amiable scoundrel see M. P. Charlesworth, *Five Men: Character Studies from the Roman Empire* (1936), ch.i. [p. 242]

23 AVILLIUS FLACCUS. For this Prefect and the trouble in Alexandria see the commentary by H. Box on *Philonis Alexandrini, In Flaccum* (1939). [p. 242]

24 JEWISH EMBASSY TO GAIUS. On this see E. Mary Smallwood's useful commentary on Philo's *Legatio ad Gaium* (1961). On the chronology see A. Garzetti, *From Tiberius to the Antonines* (1974), 582 f.[p. 242]

CHAPTER XIV

1 SOURCES FOR CLAUDIUS (A.D. 41–54). The chief literary sources are Tacitus, *Ann.* xi–xii (= A.D. 47–54), the books covering the early part of the reign being lost; Suetonius, *Divus Claudius*; Dio Cassius, lx; Seneca, *ad Polybium, Apocolocyntosis*; Josephus, *Bell. Iud.* ii, 204, *Ant. Iud.* xix, 212, etc. E. M. Smallwood, *Documents Illustrating the Principates of Gaius, Claudius and Nero* (1967). On Claudius' speeches see R. Syme, *Tacitus* (1958), 703 ff. Coins: works cited in ch. XI, n. 1. Modern works: A. Momigliano, *Claudius²* (1961; with a new bibliography); V. M. Scramuzza, *The Emperor Claudius* (1940). [p. 243]

2 CLAUDIUS AND THE PRAETORIANS. He kept his debt to the Guard before the eyes of the public by two issues of coins, which depicted the Praetorian barracks and the mutual greeting, with legends, respectively, imper(ator) recept(us) and praetor(iani) recept(i in fidem): see H. Mattingly and E. A. Sydenham, *Rom. Imp. Coinage*, I, pl. v. [p. 243]

3 REFORM OF ALPHABET. Claudius proposed, and later introduced, three new letters: Ɔ = ps; Ⱶ = a sound between u and i; Ⅎ = consonantal v as opposed to the vowel. They did not survive very long. [p. 244]

4 CLAUDIUS AND THE SENATE. On Claudius and the aristocracy see a series of articles by D. McAlindon: *AJP*, 1956, 113 ff.; 1957, 279 ff.; *JRS*, 1957, 191 ff.; *CR*, 1957, 108; *Latomus*, 1957, 252 ff. From A.D. 47 Claudius' control over the Senate will have increased. It is often said that Claudius restored the elections to the Senate, but Dio Cassius (59. 20) implies that Gaius himself had already done so. On the personal part played by Roman emperors (not least Claudius) in the administration of the empire see F. Millar, 'Emperors at Work', *JRS*, 1967, 9 ff. For a revised list of consuls during Claudius' reign see P. Gallivan, *Cl.Qu.*, 1978, 407 ff. On Claudius' attitude to the Principate and his emulation of Julius Caesar see B. M. Levick, *AJP*, 1978, 78 ff. [p. 245]

5 JUDICIAL PAPYRUS. See Smallwood, *op. cit.*, n. 367, and cf. Scramuzza, *op. cit.*, 110 ff. [p. 245]

6 PROCURATORS. On their functions see Tac. *Ann.*, xii. 60, and F. Millar, *JRS*, 1964, 180 ff., and P. A. Brunt, *Latomus*, 1966, 461 ff. [p. 245]

7 FRUMENTATIONES. Claudius also, according to the usual view, transferred the distribution of corn from the senatorial *praefecti frumenti dandi* to the imperial *praefectus annonae*, and the cost of the *frumentationes* from the Aerarium to the Fiscus. This would lighten the Senate's burden, but would increase the emperor's popularity and make the dole appear as an imperial gift. G. E. F. Chilver, however, has argued (*Amer. Journ. Phil.* 1949, 7 ff.) that the *praefecti frumenti dandi* did not disappear and that in this sphere the princeps and Senate had in fact co-operated more closely than is generally believed from the time of Augustus onwards. (This view depends in part on the dating of the careers of two such *praefecti*: on this see also H. G. Pflaum, *Historia*, ii, 1954, 431 ff.) Claudius established an efficient organization for the distribution of the corn-dole at the Porticus Minucia in Rome. On the *frumentationes* see D. van Berchem, *Les distributions de blé et d'argent à la plèbe romaine sous l'empire* (1939) and G. Rickman, *The Corn Supply of Ancient Rome* (1980). The latter (73 ff., 213 ff.) takes the view that the burden of financing the corn supply was more gradually shared by emperor and Senate rather than abruptly transferred from the Senate to Claudius; the problem was the relationship of the state and the individual rather than that of Senate and emperor. [p. 245]

8 PALLAS. On his career and influence see S. I. Oost, *AJP*, 1958, 113 ff. On Narcissus see J. Melmoux, *Stud. Class.*, 1975, 61 ff. [p. 246]

9 THE HARBOUR AT OSTIA. Traces of Claudius' works survive and are revealed by air-photography: see J. Bradford, *Ancient Landscapes* (1957), 248 ff. and pls. 60 and 61. See further, R. Meiggs, *Roman Ostia*² (1973). [p. 248]

10 CLAUDIUS AND THE ALEXANDRINE JEWS. On Gaius' death fresh rioting broke out in Alexandria between Greeks and Jews (see p. 241f.) and further deputations waited on the new emperor. Claudius finally sent a letter to the Alexandrians, which is both firm and impartial: in effect he tells both Jews and Greeks to keep the peace and mind their own affairs: he refused the Jewish request for full citizen rights in Alexandria and he told the Greeks that he would not tolerate their attacks on the Jews: 'I tell you once and for all that if you do not put an end to this ruinous and obstinate mutual enmity, I shall be forced to show you what a benevolent emperor can be when turned by righteous indignation.' For the full text of this interesting and important document see Smallwood, *Documents*, n. 370; translation in Lewis and Reinhold, *Rn. Civ.* II, 366 ff. In A.D. 53 there was further trouble: according to the 'Acts of Isodore and Lampon' (see p. 242), Claudius heard a law-suit between these two anti-Jewish leaders and Agrippa II; the two men were put to death and were canonized as anti-Semitic nationalist martyrs. [p. 249]

11 'IMPULSORE CHRESTO.' Suetonius [*Claud.* 25] records: 'Iudaeos impulsore Chresto assidue tumultuantis Roma expulit' (cf. *Acts*, xviii, 2, on the expulsion). It is possible to believe that Chrestus was an unknown Jewish agitator (which is what Suetonius himself may have thought, but he may not have fully understood his source), but the identification with Jesus Christ is much more reasonable. Knowledge of Christianity may have reached the Jewish community in Rome and led to internal dissensions: in that sense Christ will have been the cause of the trouble.

Another problem arises with the imperial rescript found near Nazareth which threatens those who violate tombs with the unprecedently harsh penalty of death. The date of this inscription (see Smallwood, *Documents*, n. 377) might be Claudian and the suggestion has been made that because of these Jewish disturbances Claudius made some inquiries which revealed the anti-Christian version of the Resurrection, i.e. that the disciples had broken into the tomb and stolen the body of Jesus (cf. St. Matthew, xxviii, 12–15), and that Claudius then ordered copies of this rescript to be set up in Nazareth and Galilee to prevent similar troubles. For a discussion of the problems involved see A. Momigliano, *Claudius*, 35 ff. and F. de Zulueta, *JRS*, 1932, 184 ff. If the Claudian date for the document is not accepted, any connexion with the Resurrection is improbable. F. de Visscher (*Nouv. Clio*, 1953, 18 ff.) argues that the last four lines which threaten the death-penalty were added privately by the owner of the tomb, while J. H. Oliver (*Cl. Phil.*, 1954, 180 ff.) suggests that they were added by a local Roman authority who was not conversant with Roman practice. See also de Visscher, *Le droit des tombeaux romains* (1963), 161 ff. [p. 249]

11a MAURETANIA. On the annexation of Mauretania see D. Fishwick, *Historia*, 1971, 467 ff. [p. 250]

12 THE VOLUBILIS INSCRIPTION. See Smallwood, *Documents* n. 407. [p. 251]

13 THE ANNAUNIAN INSCRIPTION. See Smallwood, *Documents*, n. 368 (= *ILS*, 206); translation, Lewis and Reinhold, *Rn. Civ.* II, 130 f. [p. 252]

14 THE LYONS TABLET. Text in Smallwood n. 369; translation, Lewis and Reinhold, *op. cit.*, 133 ff. Tacitus' version is in *Annals* xi, 23–5. For a recent comparison of the two versions see K. Wellesley, *Gr. and R.*, 1954, 13 ff. For a discussion of some of the problems raised by this document and for Claudius' policy about citizenship in general see A. N. Sherwin-White, *Roman Citizenship*, 181 ff. [p. 252]

15 BRITISH TRIBES. A valuable source of evidence for the local dynasties in the period

before the Roman conquest is coinage (and their widespread use of coinage is in itself proof of their increasing civilization and trade); see D. Allen, *Archaeologia*, 1944, and *Problems of the Iron Age in Southern Britain* (ed. S. S. Frere, 1960), 97–308. On Camulodunum see C. F. C. Hawkes, *Reports of Research Com. of Soc. of Antiquaries*, xiv (1947), M. R. Hull, *ibid.* xx [1958]. Also C. E. Stevens, in *Aspects of Archaeology in Britain* (1951) and S. S. Frere, *Britannia* (1967), chs. 1–4. [p. 252]

16 THE CONQUEST OF BRITAIN. On Roman Britain in general see R. G. Collingwood, *Roman Britain and the English Settlements*² (1937); P. Salway, *Roman Britain* (1981); I. A. Richmond, *Roman Britain* (1955); S. S. Frere, *Britannia*² (1978); and, a brief sketch, H. H. Scullard, *Roman Britain: Outpost of the Empire* (1979). For the Claudian conquest, see Frere, *op. cit.*, ch. 5; G. Webster and D. R. Dudley, *The Conquest of Roman Britain, A.D. 43–57* (1966), a popular work. The earliest Roman fort found at Valkenburg near Leyden in Holland may have been a supplybase for Claudius' British expedition: see *JRS*, 1952, 129. For a photograph of the defences at Rutupiae see *JRS*, 1929, pl. xvii (cf. 1931, p. 246). On the battle of the Medway see A. R. Burn, *History*, 1953, 105 ff.; it may have been fought near Rochester. The career of Cogidumnus has been studied by A. A. Barrett, *Britannia*, 1979, 227 ff., in the light of the view of J. E. Bogaers, *id.*, 243 ff., that the broken stone of the famous inscription (Collingwood and Wright, *Rom. Inscr. Brit.*, n. 91) had been misread and that Cogidumnus was in fact described as 'great king of Britain' rather than as 'king and legate of Augustus in Britain' – 'REG.MAGN.BRIT.' rather than 'R.LEGAT.AVG. IN BRIT.'. The inscription gives 'R.I [. . . .] GN–BRIT'. For the attribution of the Fosse Way frontier to Plautius rather than to Ostorius Scapula see G. Graham, *Arch. Journ.*, 1958, 49 ff. On Queen Cartimandua see the article by I. A. Richmond, *JRS*, 1954, 43 ff. On the excavations at Maiden Castle, where the skeletons show the savage effects of Roman weapons, see R. E. M. Wheeler, *Reports of Research Com. of Soc. of Ant.* xii (1943). On Hod Hill see *JRS*, 1955, p. 141; I. A. Richmond and others, *Hod Hill*, II (1968). For the early occupation of Lincoln see *JRS*, 1949, 57 ff.; 1956, 22, D. F. Petch, *Arch. Journ.*, 1960, 40 ff.; and Kingsholm at Gloucester, *JRS*, 1942, 39 ff. and 1943, 15 ff., and I. A. Richmond and H. E. O'Neil, *Trans. Bristol Glos. Arch. Soc.*, 1962, 14 ff., 1965, 15 ff. On the length of Vespasian's service in Britain see D. E. Eichholz, *Britannia*, 1972, 149 ff. On the temple of Claudius at Camulodunum see D. Fishwick, *Britannia*, 1972, 164 ff., who advances the unorthodox suggestion that under Claudius there may have been only an altar to Roma and Augustus, the temple being constructed only after Claudius' death. [p. 255]

17 SOURCES FOR NERO (A.D. 54–68). The chief literary sources are Tacitus, *Annals* xiii–xvi (to A.D. 66 only); Suetonius, *Nero* (commentaries by B. H. Warmington (1977) and K. R. Bradley (1978)); Dio Cassius, lxi–lxiii. Documents: E. M. Smallwood, *Documents Illustrating the Principates of Gaius, Claudius and Nero* (1967). Coins: works cited in ch. XI, n. 1.

Modern works: B. W. Henderson, *The Life and Principate of the Emperor Nero* (1903); M. P. Charlesworth, *JRS*, 1950, 69 ff.; M. A. Levi, *Nerone e i suoi tempi* (1950); J. Bishop, *Nero* (1964): B. H. Warmington, *Nero* (1969); M. Grant, *Nero* (1970). [p. 256]

18 THE QUINQUENNIUM NERONIS. On the meaning of this phrase see J. G. C. Anderson, *JRS*, 1911, 173 ff., and F. A. Lepper, *JRS*, 1957, 95 ff.; the latter believes that it was *ben trovato*. O. Murray, *Historia*, 1965, 41 ff., attributes the phrase to Arulenus Rusticus, the biographer of Thrasea Paetus; the former wished to explain why Thrasea, later Nero's enemy, had at first co-operated with him. J. G. F. Hind (*Historia*, 1971, 488 ff.) attributes the phrase to A.D. 60–65, while M. K. Thornton (*ibid.*, 1973, 570 ff.) applies it to Nero's last years. [p. 256]

19 AGRIPPINA, SENECA AND BURRUS. For a defence of Agrippina against the charge of

having poisoned Claudius see G. Bagnani, *Phoenix*, 1946, 15 ff. Her decline and fall can be traced dramatically in the coinage. At first her portrait dominated it (see p. 257), then it appeared as the remoter of two jugate busts, then it was banished to the reverse, and finally disappeared. Cf. C. H. V. Sutherland, *Coinage in Rom. Imp. Policy*, 153 ff. The fact that Agrippina could at first control the mint types shows the *de facto* meaning of the restoration of coinage to the Senate. On Seneca see ch. XVI, n. 7; A. Garzetti, *From Tiberius to the Antonines* (1974), 607 ff. On Burrus see W. C. McDermott, *Latomus*, 1949, 229 ff., and D. Gillis, *Parola del Passato*, 1963, 5 ff. A recent inscription from Amisus in Pontus (A.D. 63–65) mentions Nero Poppaea and Britannicus and may suggest official acceptance of Nero's version of Britannicus' death: see *L'Année Epigr.* 1959, 224, and L. Robert, *Rev. Étud. Gr.*, 1958, 329. On the question of heirs and rivals of Nero see R. S. Rogers, *TAPA*, 1955, 190 ff. On the place of Agrippina's murder see R. Katzoff, *Historia*, 1973, 72 ff. [p. 257]

19a FINANCE AND CORN SUPPLY. On Nero's fiscal policy see M. K. Thornton, *Aufstieg*, II, ii (1975), 149 ff. On the African corn-supply see B. Gallotta, *Rendiconti dell' Ist. Lombardo*, 1975, 28 ff. [p. 259]

20 NERO ARTIFEX. See M. P. Charlesworth, *JRS*, 1950, 69 ff. On one aspect note also J. M. C. Toynbee, *Cl. Qu.*, 1942, 83 ff. See also H. Bardon, *Rev. Étud. Lat.*, 1936, 337 ff., on Nero's poetry. On Artifex see C. E. Manning, *Gr. and R.*, 1975, 164 ff., on the Augustales C. Gatti, *Cent. Rich. Doc. Ant. Class.*, 1976–77, 83 ff., on Nero's popularity L. Garazzi, *Atti Ist. Veneto*, 1975–76, 421 ff. [p. 259]

21 NERO CITHAROEDUS. On the coinage of 64–66 Nero is depicted as Nero–Apollo, the divine musician playing a cithara: see Sutherland, *op. cit.*, 1970 and pl. XIV, 6. [p. 260]

21a TIGELLINUS. T. K. Roper, *Historia*, 1979, 346 ff., regards Tigellinus as less powerful or terrible than as generally depicted, and as having connections with Seneca. [p. 260]

22 THE DOMUS AUREA. See J. Ward Perkins, *Antiquity*, 1956, 209 ff., and A. Boethius, *The Golden House of Nero* (1960), ch. 3. [p. 261]

23 POPPAEA. On her alleged Jewish tendencies (doubtfully based on Josephus, *Ant. Jud.* 20. 189–196) see E. M. Smallwood, *Journ. Theol. Studies*, 1959, 329 ff. [p. 261]

24 THE CHRISTIAN PERSECUTION. See especially Tacitus, *Ann.* xv, 44. The legal basis of the persecution has formed the subject of endless discussion. The three main views are (1) that a general law was passed which forbade the practice of the Christian religion, (2) that the Christians were punished without the usual forms of trial by ordinary magistrates who exercised their powers of *coercitio*, i.e. police action to enforce public order, and (3) the allegation of some specific charge, as treason or illegal assembly. The first view is not now much in favour. In line with Roman policy to the Bacchanalian cult and Druidism, which were checked only because of the crimes that they provoked, it may be that Christianity was proscribed by magisterial edict because of its supposed inherent *flagitia*, i.e. admission of the *nomen* would expose a man to magisterial *coercitio* and the magistrate would then through the normal process of *cognitio* seek to establish a *flagitium*, whether incendiarism, magic or cannibalism. On this view no general law was passed against Christianity under Nero that would affect provincial governors. For general discussions of the problem see A. N. Sherwin-White, *Journ. Theol. Studies*, 1952, 199 ff.; F. W. Clayton, *Cl. Qu.*, 1947, 81 ff.; J. Beaujeu, *L'incendie de Rome en 64 et les Chrétiens* (1960); G. E. M. de Ste Croix, *Past and Present*, 1963, 6 ff., 1964, 28 ff.; A. N. Sherwin-White, *ibid.*, 1964, 23 ff. (these articles by Sherwin-White and de Ste Croix are reprinted in *Studies in Ancient Society*, edited by M. I. Finley, 1974, 210 ff.); W. H. C. Frend, *Martyrdom and Persecution in the Early Church* (1965), 161 ff.; T. D. Barnes, *JRS*, 1968, 32 ff. [p. 261]

25 ST. PETER IN ROME. For a brief discussion of the evidence for the view that St. Peter

was one of Nero's victims see J. Lowe, *Saint Peter* (1956). Recent excavations under the Basilica of St. Peter's in the Vatican City have neither proved nor disproved the tradition that St. Peter was buried under this Church beside the site of the Circus of Nero where he is alleged to have perished. But they have revealed that below the modern church and below the Basilica that Constantine built (now beneath it) there was a large Roman cemetery and that here stood a martyr-shrine to St. Peter which is as old as *c.* A.D. 160 and was the one seen by a priest named Gaius soon after A.D. 200 (Eusebius, *Hist. Eccles.* ii, 25, 6, 7). Whether it was a tomb or a cenotaph is not known, but it is clear that the Christian community in Rome about a hundred years after St. Peter's death connected this site with him. See J. Toynbee and J. Ward Perkins, *The Shrine of St. Peter* (1956); E. Kirschbaum, *The Tombs of St. Peter and St. Paul* (1959); D. W. O'Connor, *Peter in Rome* (Columbia, 1969). On the disposal of the bodies see H. Chadwick, *Journ. Theol. Studies*, 1957, 31 ff. Excavations (1958) have revealed further burials in this area, including that of a slave of Nero who may have been connected with the administration of the Gardens of Nero. [p. 261]

26   NERO'S LIBERATION OF GREECE. An inscription from Acraephiae in Boeotia contains the text of Nero's edict summoning the Greeks to the Isthmus and of his speech of liberation. See Smallwood, *Documents*, n. 64; translation in Lewis and Reinhold, *Rn. Civ.* ii, 394. The date was 28 Nov., probably 66, possibly 67: see *CAH*, X, 735, n. 2. For another probably relevant inscription see A. Momigliano, *JRS*, 1944, 115. On the chronology of Nero's visit to Greece see K. R. Bradley, *Latomus*, 1978, 61 ff. [p. 263]

27   THE ANGLESEY HOARD. See Sir Cyril Fox, *A Find of the Early Iron Age from Llyn Cerrig Bach, Anglesey* (1946). [p. 264]

28   BOUDICCA'S REVOLT. See R. Syme, *Tacitus*, 762 ff. (who dates the outbreak in 60, not 61) and C. M. Bulst, *Historia*, 1961, 496 ff. On the governor Q. Veranius, Suetonius' immediate predecessor, see A. E. Gordon, *Univ. California Pub. in Cl. Arch.* 1952, 241 ff., and E. Birley, *Roman Britain and the Roman Army* (1953), 1 ff. The tombstone of Iulius Classicianus was found in London. The fact that he was of provincial or North Italian origin may bear on his more sympathetic policy; see E. Birley, *Antiquaries Journal*, 1936, 207 f. See D. R. Dudley and G. Webster, *The Rebellion of Boudicca* (1962) and G. Webster, *Boudicca, The British Revolt against Rome, A.D. 60* (1978). On the recall of Suetonius see M. T. Griffin *Scripta Class. Israelica*, 1976–77, 138 ff. [p. 265]

29   ARMENIA AND PARTHIA. See Tac. *Ann.* xiii, 7–9; 34–41; xiv, 23–26; xv, 1–17; 24–31; Dio Cass. lxii, 19–23. Cf. Furneaux, ed. of *Annals*, II (1907), 96 ff.; Henderson, *Nero*, 153 ff.; Anderson, *CAH*, X, 758 ff.; and for discussion of detailed and controversial points (e.g. chronology and fluctuations in Roman policy) see D. Magie, *Roman Rule in Asia Minor*, II, 1411 ff. On Corbulo see R. Syme, *JRS*, 1970, 37 ff. and on his eastern campaign see K. Gilmartin, *Historia*, 1973, 583 ff. On the Armenian settlement of A.D. 60 see A. A. Barrett, *Cl. Qu.*, 1979, 465 ff. [p. 265]

30   NERO AND THE CASPIAN. The objective, the Caspiae Portae, probably is the Dariel Pass over the Caucasus north of Tiflis. The view of W. Schur (*Die Orientpolitik d. Kaisers Nero*, 1923) that Nero was trying to 'encircle' Armenia and dominate a supposed trade-route from the Black Sea to India via the Caspian and the Oxus has not found general acceptance: see D. Magie, *op. cit.*, 1418. Against the existence of this trade-route see Sir W. W. Tarn, *The Greeks in Bactria and India* (1938), Appendix xiv. [p. 266]

31   NERO AND ETHIOPIA. On the expedition see Pliny, *NH*, vi, 181 ff.; xii, 19; Seneca, *Nat. Quaest.*, vi, 8, 3; Dio Cass. lxiii, 8, 1. Cf. M. Cary and E. H. Warmington, *The Ancient Explorers* (1929), 174 ff. For a criticism of the view that Nero intended serious warfare and wished to safeguard the Arabian coast and trade-routes in the Red Sea against the ambitions of the Axumite kingdom (cf. W. Schur, *op. cit.*), see J. G. C. Anderson, *CAH*, X,

880 ff. A fragment of papyrus describes a minor engagement between some Romans and Ethiopians: for the view that this may refer to Nero's expedition, see E. G. Turner, *JRS*, 1950, 57 ff. Cf. also ch. XII, n. 13. [p. 266]

32 THE QUMRAN COMMUNITY AND THE DEAD SEA SCROLLS. Amid the immense modern literature on this subject, reference may be made to M. Burrows, *The Dead Sea Scrolls* (1956) and *More Light on the Dead Sea Scrolls* (1958); T. H. Gaster, *The Scriptures of the Dead Sea Sect* (1957); J. Van der Ploeg, *The Excavations at Qumran* (1958); F. M. Cross, *The Ancient Library at Qumran* (1961); E. F. Sutcliffe, *The Monks of Qumran* (1960); R. de Vaux, *Archaeology and the Dead Sea Scrolls* (1973). *The Scroll of the War of the Sons of Light* (1962), which has been edited by Y. Yadin, throws light on military matters. Whether this sect were Essenes or not, is not yet established, but it was certainly not very dissimilar. The Kittim in the Scrolls are generally identified with the Romans. Their date is variously estimated, but is generally put before A.D. 70. One historical crux, the identification of the priestly enemy of the Teacher of Righteousness, has led to widely discrepant suggestions, e.g. Antiochus Epiphanes, Alexander Jannaeus, John Hyrcanus, or the Zealot Menahem (i.e. from *c.* 175 B.C. to A.D. 66). [p. 266]

33 TIBERIUS IULIUS ALEXANDER. On this man see E. G. Turner, *JRS*, 1954, 54 ff.; G. Chalon, *L'édit de Tiberius Julius Alexander* (1964). [p. 267]

34 THE JEWISH WAR. The main source is the works of Josephus, who took part: *Bellum Iudaicum* and his autobiography (*Vita*); the last book (xx) of his *Antiquitates Iudaicae* (from the Creation to A.D. 66) is also relevant here. See H. St. J. Thackeray, *Josephus the Man and the Historian* (1929). After the fall of Jerusalem some of the Sicarii managed to hold out in the fortress of Masada on the Dead Sea until they all perished in 73. For the Roman siege-works and camps here see A. Schulten, *Masada* (1933); excavation reports in *Israel Explor. Journ.*, 1956–; I. A. Richmond, *JRS*, 1962, 142 ff.; Y. Yadin, *Masada* (1967). On the Sicarii see M. Hengel, *Die Zeloten* (1961); S. Applebaum, *JRS*, 1971, 155 ff. [p. 268]

35 VINDEX AND VERGINIUS. See M. Raoss, *Epigrafica*, 1958, 46–120; P. A. Brunt, *Latomus*, 1959, 531 ff.; G. Townend, *ibid.*, 1961, 337 ff.; J. C. Hainsworth, *Historia*, 1962, 88 ff. On the development of events see now P. A. L. Greenhalgh, *The Year of the Four Emperors* (1975), and K. Wellesley, *The Long Year*, A.D. 69 (1975). On the chronology of Jan. to June, see D. F. A. Shotter, *Historia*, 1975, 59 ff., on the role of Verginius, L. J. Daly, *Historia*, 1975, 75 ff., and on the causes of the disorder of A.D. 68–69 see R. J. A. Talbert, *Amer. J. Anc. Hist.*, 1977, 69 ff. [p. 269]

CHAPTER XV

1 THE ECONOMIC LIFE OF THE EARLY EMPIRE. No ancient writer dealt with this subject. The evidence therefore has to be gathered from sources such as the geographer Strabo, Pliny the Elder's *Natural History*, the *Periplus maris Erythraei* (see n. 4 below), Petronius, and chance remarks in other writers, together with epigraphical, papyrological and archaeological material. Much of this has been brought together in Tenney Frank's indispensable *Economic Survey of Ancient Rome*, of which vol. V (1940) deals with Rome and Italy of the Empire, and vols. II–IV with the provinces.

See also Tenney Frank, *An Economic History of Rome* (2nd ed. 1927); M. Rostovtzeff, *The Social and Economic History of the Roman Empire* (2nd ed. 1957); F. M. Heichelheim, *An Ancient Economic History*, III (1970), ch. viii; M. P. Charlesworth, *Trade Routes and*

Commerce of the Roman Empire (2nd ed. 1926); K. D. White, *Roman Farming* (1970). See also A. Burford, *Craftsmen in Greek and Roman Society* (1972); M. I. Finley, *The Ancient Economy* (1973); R. Duncan-Jones *The Economy of the Roman Empire* (1974); L. Casson, *Travel in the Ancient World* (1974). [p. 272]

2 INDUSTRY AT POMPEII. See T. Frank, *Econ. Hist.*, ch. xiv, *Econ. Survey* V, 252 ff. On life in Pompeii in general see R. C. Carrington, *Pompeii* (1936); H. H. Tanzer, *The Common People of Pompeii* (1939); M. Della Corte, *Case ed abitanti a Pompeii* (2nd ed. 1954). Pompeian families (especially of the governing class) are studied by P. Castren, *Ordo Populusque Pompeianus: Polity and Society in Roman Pompeii* (1975), and Pompeian commercial life by Andreau, *Les affaires de Monsieur Jucundus* (1974). For life at Ostia, see R. Meiggs, *Roman Ostia*² (1973). [p. 273]

3 TRADE BEYOND THE EMPIRE. See Sir M. Wheeler, *Rome beyond the Imperial Frontiers* (1954); O. Brogan, *JRS*, 1936, 195 ff. on trade with the free Germans; E. H. Warmington, *The Commerce between the Roman Empire and India* (1928); J. I. Miller, *The Spice Trade of the Roman Empire 29 BC–A.D. 641* (1969). On Roma and India see W. Schmitthenner, *JRS*, 1979, 90 ff. [p. 277]

4 HIPPALUS. Our knowledge of Hippalus derives from *The Periplus of the Erythraean Sea* and Pliny, *NH*, vi, 26. The former is a sailor's guide written in Greek by an Egyptian merchant and dealing with all the seas through which Oriental trade passed. It was written in the first century A.D., perhaps about 50. The date of Hippalus is uncertain and has been placed between 80 B.C. (W. W. Tarn) and A.D. 40 (Warmington). But an Augustan date is suggested both by the date of the pottery found at Pondicherry (the actual site is two miles south at Arikamedu near a village named Virampatnam) and by an inscription from the Eastern Desert of Egypt (see *JRS*, 1953, p. 38) which refers to a slave of P. Annius Plocamus in A.D. 6, while we know that a freedman of Plocamus farmed the Red Sea taxes; his adventures at sea suggest that he did not yet know the use of the monsoon. [p. 278]

5 THE SILK ROUTE AND TITIANUS. An expedition was sent along this route, presumably to expedite trade, led by a merchant named 'Maes who was also called Titianus' (Ptolemy, i, 11, 7); he probably was a Syrian and his party got as far as the Stone Tower in Chinese Turkestan. He is usually dated about A.D. 100–120, but his expedition may have been between 20 and 1 B.C. and fit in with the interest of Augustus in the East: see M. Cary, *Cl. Qu.*, 1956, 130 ff. However, W. Schmitthenner, *JRS*, 1979, 105, thinks an Augustan date improbable. [p. 279]

6 PORTORIA. On the organization of these taxes see S. J. De Laet, *Portorium* (1949). [p. 280]

7 THE IMPORTANCE OF TRADE. For the view that this was less than is often assumed see A. H. M. Jones, *Recueil de la Société Jean Bodin* vii, 161 ff. For a wide survey of trade see K. Hopkins, 'Taxes and Trade in the Roman Empire, 200 B.C. to A.D. 400', *JRS*, 1980, 101 ff. [p. 282]

8 THE DECLINE OF THE NOBILITY. See R. Syme, *Rom. Rev.*, ch. xxxii, and *Tacitus* (1958), 585 ff. [p. 283]

9 SOCIAL LIFE IN THE EARLY PRINCIPATE. See T. G. Tucker, *Life in the Roman World of Nero and St. Paul* (1910); L. Friedlander, *Roman Life and Manners under the Early Empire* (1908 ff.); J. Carcopino, *Daily Life in Ancient Rome* (1941); C. G. Starr, *Civilization and the Caesars* (1954); J. P. V. D. Balsdon, *Life and Leisure in Ancient Rome* (1969), a valuable and entertaining survey. See also R. MacMullen, *Roman Social Relations, 50 BC to A.D. 284* (1974), and *Romans and Aliens* (1979) by J. P. V. D. Balsdon who surveys the mutual regard of Romans and other people. [p. 285]

10 CORN DISTRIBUTIONS. See D. Van Berchem, *Les Distributions de blé et d'argent à la*

plèbe romaine sous l'empire (1939). See also A. R. Hands, *Charities and Social Aid in Greece and Rome* (1968), 101 ff., a book which also deals with other forms of 'relief'. See also H. Pavis d'Escurac, *La Préfecture de l'annone: service administratif imperiale d'Auguste à Constantine* (1976) and G. Rickman, *The Corn Supply of Ancient Rome* (1980). Cf. also ch. vii, n. 7 above. [p. 287]

10a CHARIOT-RACING. On this and sport in general see H. A. Harris, *Sport in Greece and Rome* (1972). [p. 289]

11 GLADIATORS. See ch. ix., n. 11 above and L. Robert, *Gladiateurs dans l'Orient grec* (1940). [p. 289]

CHAPTER XVI

1 DOMUS AUREA. See ch. XIV, n. 22. [p. 293]

2 ROMAN PAINTING. See A. Maiuri, *Roman Painting* (1953). [p. 294]

3 LE GRAND CAMÉE DE FRANCE. On the interpretation see J. P. V. D. Balsdon, *JRS*, 1936, 252; A. Piganiol, *Histoire de Rome* (1946), 263. [p. 294]

4 THE ARA PACIS. See J. M. C. Toynbee, 'The Ara Pacis reconsidered', *Proc. Br. Acad.*, xxxix (1953), 67 ff. S. Weinstock (*JRS*, 1960, 44 ff.) has made a bold attempt to challenge the identification of the restored monument with the Ara Pacis. But see J. M. C. Toynbee, *JRS*, 1961, 153 ff. [p. 295]

5 POST-AUGUSTAN LITERATURE. H. E. Butler, *Post-Augustan Poetry* (1909); J. Wight Duff, *A Literary History of Rome in the Silver Age* (1927). On the literary chronology of the Neronian age see A. Momigliano (*Cl. Qu.*, 1944, 96 ff. = *Secondo Contributo*, 454 ff.). [p. 295]

6 DECLAMATION. See S. F. Bonner, *Roman Declamation in the late Republic and Early Empire* (1949), an interesting book which emphasizes the acquaintance of many of the declaimers with Roman law. Cf. A.D. Leeman, *Orationis Ratio* (Amsterdam, 1963). On the *suasoriae* of the elder Seneca (see p. 298 above) cf. L. A. Sussman, *The Elder Seneca* (1978). J. Fairweather, *Seneca the Elder* (1981). [p. 296]

7 SENECA. For a consideration of some recent work on Seneca see A. Garzetti, *From Tiberius to the Antonines* (1974), 606 ff.; for work on the *Apocolocyntosis* done 1922–58 see M. Coffey, *Lustrum*, 1961, 239 ff.; for work on Seneca's prose works done 1940–57 see L. Motto, *Cl. W.*, 1960. 13 ff., 37 ff., 111 ff. See also some observations by C. G. Starr, *Civilization and the Caesars* (1954), 222 ff. (where, however, the *Octavia* is attributed to Seneca). On Seneca and Christianity see A. Momigliano, *Contributo alla storia degli studi classici* (1955), 13 ff. See also M. T. Griffin, *Seneca: a Philosopher in Politics* (1976). [p. 299]

7a LUCAN. See A. M. Ahl, *Lucan: an Introduction* (1976). On Lucan and Nero see G. K. Gresseth, *Cl. Ph.*, 1957, 24 ff. [p. 299]

7b CALPURNIUS SICULUS. Though widely assigned to Nero's reign, Calpurnius' lifetime has sometimes been set much later, e.g. recently in the early third century under Severus Alexander by E. Champlin, *JRS*, 1978, 95 ff., but for the Neronian date see G. B. Townend, *JRS*, 1980, 166 ff. and R. Mayer, *id.*, 175 ff. [p. 300]

8 AUFIDIUS BASSUS. See R. Syme, *Tacitus* (1958), 697 ff. [p. 300]

9 MEDICINE. See in general J. Scarborough, *Roman Medicine* (1969). [p. 301]

10 PHILOSOPHIC OPPOSITION. In a wide-ranging survey entitled *Enemies of the Roman Order* (1967) R. MacMullen examines elements in Roman society, including many philosophers, who opposed the regime. Here chs. I and II are particularly relevant. On Musonius see M. P. Charlesworth's interesting essay in *Five Men* (1936), 33 ff.; C. F.

Lutz, *Yale Class. Stud.*, 1947, 3 ff. On the influence of Stoicism on the Principate in general see P. A. Brunt, *Papers Brit. Sch. Rome*, 1975, 7 ff. [p. 303]

11 ASTROLOGY. See F. H. Cramer, *Astrology in Roman Law and Politics* (1954), 92–131 for Thrasyllus and Balbillus. See also MacMullen, *op. cit.*, above, chs. III and IV. [p. 305]

12 THE PORTA MAGGIORE BASILICA. See J. Carcopino, *La Basilique pythagoricienne de la Porte Majeure* (1927); his belief in its connexion with Neopythagoreanism is probable, but has not been proved. [p. 305]

13 VILLA OF THE MYSTERIES. See J. Toynbee, *JRS*, 1929, 67 ff.; K. Lehmann, *JRS*, 1962, 62 ff. [p. 305]

14 ORIENTAL CULTS. See F. Cumont, *Les religions orientales dans le paganisme romain* (4th ed., 1929, Eng. trans. of 2nd ed. (1909), published in 1911 and reprinted 1956: *Oriental Religions in Roman Paganism*); J. Toutain, *Les cultes païens dans l'empire romain* (1907); W. R. Halliday, *The Pagan Background of Early Christianity* (1925); M. Rostovtzeff, *Mystic Italy* (1927); A. D. Nock, *Conversion* (1933); A. J. Festugière-Fabre, *Le monde greco-romain au temps de Notre Seigneur*, 2 vols. (1944 f.); J. Ferguson, *The Religions of the Roman Empire* (1970): R. E. Witt, *Isis in the Graeco-Roman World* (1971). On Cybele, M.J. Vermaseren, *Cybele and Attis* (1977). [p. 305]

15 JEWS AND JUDAISM. See W. O. E. Oesterly, *A History of Israel*, II (1932), G. F. Moore, *Judaism in the First Centuries of the Christian Era*, 2 vols. (1927), F. J. Foakes Jackson and Kirsopp Lake, *The Beginnings of Christianity*, I (1920), 1–168, E. Schürer, *The History of the Jewish People in the Age of Jesus Christ* (175 BC–A.D. 135), revised by G. Vermes and F. Millar, I (1973), ii (1979). [p. 306]

16 DEAD SEA SCROLLS AND CHRISTIANITY. On the lack of direct connexion see the brief but authoritative statement by H.H. Rowley, *The Dead Sea Scrolls and the New Testament* (1957); *The Teacher of Righteousness* (1957); also *The Scrolls and the New Testament*, edited by K. Stendahl (1958). M. Black, *The Scrolls and Christian Origins* (1961). On the scrolls, see further ch. XIV, n. 32. See now G. Vermes, *The Dead Sea Scrolls in English* (1962). [p. 307]

17 JESUS OF NAZARETH. In view of the immensity of the literature only a few books can be mentioned: A. Schweitzer, *Quest of the Historical Jesus* (1911); V. Taylor, *The Formation of the Gospel Tradition* (1933), *The Life and Ministry of Jesus* (1954); C. H. Dodd, *The Founder of Christianity* (1971); F. C. Burkitt, *Jesus Christ* (1932); T. W. Manson, *Jesus the Messiah* (1943); G. D. Kilpatrick, *The Trial of Jesus* (1953). See also 'The Present Position in the Controversy concerning the Problem of the Historical Jesus', by J. Jeremias, *The Expository Times*, 1958, 333 ff. For the general background see F. F. Bruce, *New Testament History* (1969). Cf. also M. Grant, *Jesus* (1977), and *Jesus and the Politics of his Day* edited by E. Bammel and C. F. D. Moule (forthcoming). On the authenticity and importance of the references to Jesus in Josephus see P. Winter in E. Schürer, *History of the Jewish People in the Age of Jesus Christ*, edited by G. Vermes and F. Millar (1973), 428 ff. [p. 307]

18 CHRONOLOGY OF THE LIFE OF JESUS. The sixth-century Christian monk, Dionysius Exiguus, who established the Christian era by equating the Roman year 753 A.U.C. with 1 B.C. and 754 A.U.C. with A.D. 1, thereby placed the birth of Jesus too late, since he was certainly born during the reign of Herod the Great who died in 4 B.C.; the date of the nativity may be as early as 7 B.C. (see above ch. xii, n. 10). The length of the Ministry of Jesus was often believed in the second and third centuries to have lasted only one year, but the tradition of the three Synoptic Gospels (more probably) suggests two years, while the Gospel according to St. John has (wrongly?) been thought to imply three years. The critical date of the Crucifixion is uncertain: it was during the procuratorship of Pilate (A.D. 26–36) and the High-priesthood of Caiaphas (18–36),

probably on a Friday and on the 14th day of the Jewish lunar month Nisan. Astronomical calculations as to when 14th Nisan fell on a Friday have resulted in little firm agreement, but the years A.D. 29, 30 or 33 are the most probable. For a discussion of the evidence for the chronology of the life of Jesus (and of the New Testament) see G. Ogg, *Peake's Commentary on the Bible*, edited by M. Black and H. H. Rowley (1962), 728 ff. [p. 307]

19 TIBERIUS AND THE CRUCIFIXION. The story that Pilate reported the death of Jesus to Tiberius, which is recorded by Tertullian (*Apolog*. 21, 24), and that Tiberius reported to the Senate 'veritatem ipsius divinitatis' (*ibid*. 5, 2), is generally rejected as deriving from the apocryphal *Acta Pilati* or other such works. Recent attempts to establish its truth have not been very happy: see S. Mazzarino, *Trattato di storia Romana*, II (1956), 165 f., who attributes its creation to the time of Domitian rather than to the second century A.D. For further literature and complete rejection of the story see T. D. Barnes, *JRS*, 1968, 32–3. A. Frova (*Rendiconti dell' Ist. Lombardo* (vol.) 95, 1961, 419 ff.) has published the new inscription of Pontius Pilate from Caesarea: '...]s Tiberievm [Pon]tivs Pilatvs [Praef]ectvs Ivdaeae.' This stone must come from a building in honour of Tiberius (a Tiberieum) dedicated by Pilate. It is noteworthy both as an epigraphic record of Pilate and also as apparently naming him *praefectus*, not *procurator*. See ch. XI, n. 27 above. [p. 308]

20 THE EARLY CHURCH. On the early Church see H. Lietzman, *History of the Early Church* (Engl. trans. 1937); J. Lebreton and J. Zeiller, *The History of the Primitive Church*, I (Engl. trans. 1942); Foakes Jackson and K. Lake, *op. cit.*, n. 15; P. Carrington, *The Early Christian Church*, I (1957), and interesting book but not adequately documented; H. Chadwick, *The Early Church* (1967), ch. 1; D. R. Griffiths, *The New Testament and the Roman State* (1970), an introductory sketch. [p. 308]

21 CHRISTIANI. On the name see H.B. Mattingly (*Journ. Theol. Studies*, 1958, 26 ff.), who compares it with 'Augustiani'. [p. 309]

22 ST. PAUL. See W. M. Ramsay, *St Paul the Traveller and Roman Citizen* (1897); A. Deissmann, *St. Paul* (1912). For a brief commentary on *Acts* see A. W. F. Blunt, volume in *The Clarendon Bible* (1923); also H. J. Cadbury, *The Book of Acts in History* (1955); in general, *Peake's Commentary on the Bible*, edited by M. Black and H. H. Rowley (1962). The chronology of Paul's life contains difficulties. His conversion to Christianity may have been five to ten years after the Crucifixion; his first missionary journey was made *c*. 57, he arrived in Rome *c*. 59–62, and his death occurred possibly in 64. His Epistles and the account of his exciting life recorded in the *Acts* throw much light on the Roman world, and on the whole the Roman authorities are seen in a favourable light, at any rate in their dealings with one who could claim *civis Romanus sum*. See also A. N. Sherwin-White, *Roman Society and Roman Law in the New Testament* (1963) and M. Grant, *St. Paul* (1976). [p. 309]

SELECT BIBLIOGRAPHY

The following is a selection of a few books (in English) which cover all or considerable parts of the political history of Rome from the Gracchi to Nero. Others, both detailed studies and works dealing more precisely with social, economic and cultural aspects, are mentioned in the Notes.

The Cambridge Ancient History, ed. S. A. Cook, F. E. Adcock and M. P. Charlesworth: ix, *The Roman Republic, 133–44 B.C.* (1932); x, *The Augustan Empire 44 B.C.–A.D. 70* (1934)

Methuen's History of the Greek and Roman World: F. B. Marsh, *History of the Roman World, 146–30 B.C.* (3rd ed. rev. by H. H. Scullard 1963) and E. T. Salmon, *A History of the Roman World, 30 B.C.–A.D. 138* (5th. ed. 1966)

M. Cary and H. H. Scullard, *A History of Rome* (3rd ed. 1975).

T. Mommsen, *The History of Rome* (Engl. trans. 1911); deals with the Roman Republic and, though old, is a classic.

A. H. J. Greenidge, *A History of Rome, 133–104 B.C.* (1904)

D. Stockton, *The Gracchi* (1979)

E. S. Gruen, *Roman Politics and the Criminal Courts, 149–78 B.C.* (1968)

T. Rice Holmes, *The Roman Republic*, 3 vols (1923), covering 78–44 B.C.

E. S. Gruen, *The Last Generation of the Roman Republic* (1974), covering 78–49 B.C.

R. Seager, *Pompey* (1979)

E. Rawson, *Cicero* (1975)

M. Gelzer, *Caesar, Politician and Statesman* (1968)

J. M. Carter, *The Battle of Actium* (1970); despite the title it deals with 44–31 B.C.

T. Rice Holmes, *The Architect of the Roman Empire*, 2 vols (1928 and 1931), deals with 44 B.C.–A.D. 14

A. Garzetti, *From Tiberius to the Antonines* (1974), a history of the Roman Empire
A.D. 14–192
B. Levick, *Tiberius, the Politician* (1976)
V. M. Scramuzza, *The Emperor Claudius* (1940)
B. H. Warmington, *Nero, Reality and Legend* (1969)

Index

Accius, L. 164–5
Achaea 138, 216, 235, 245, 250
Actium 143–5, 208
Adherbal 39–40
Aedui 109–10, 112–13, 236
Aemilianus, Scipio 3, 10–12, 19–21, 25–7, 38, 40, 163, 167
Aeneid (Virgil) 200–1
Afer, Domitius 276
Afranius, L. 96–7, 115–16, 164
Africa 66, 123, 138–9, 147, 179, 222, 236, 239, 261–3, 266, 269, 273, 277–8, 282 *see also* Mauretania; Numidia
agrarian reform 37, 50, 54, 92, 96, 98 *see also* land reform
agriculture 146–7, 248, 272–3
Agrippa, Herod 240–3, 250, 267
Agrippa, M. Vipsanius 134, 137–9, 144–5, 177, 180–2, 193–4, 208–9, 213–18, 276, 286
Agrippina the elder 230, 233–4, 237
Agrippina the younger 240, 244, 255–8
Albinus, Spurius 40–1, 267
Alexander Helios 142–3
Alexandria 91, 118, 127, 141–2, 212, 229–30, 241–2, 249, 280
Alexandrine influence 160, 165
allies of Rome 13–15, 88–9 *see also*

client-kings/kingdoms; Italian 14–15, 25–7, 50, 52–5, 77, 148
Allobroges 94, 107
Ambiorix 112
Amminius 241, 253
Amyntas 142, 208
Anatolia 62, 88
animal entertainments 152, 289–91
annalistic tradition 166–7, 202
Annals (Tacitus) 230, 252
Annius Milo, T. 66, 100
Antiochus IV 250–1
Antipas, Herod 211, 241
Antonius, M. 78
Antonius, M. (orator) 47, 50, 52, 60, 169
Antony, Marc 104, 115, 119, 137–9, 141, 143, 197; Battle of Actium 144–5; Battle of Philippi 134–7; in the East 137, 140–3; in Gaul 133–4; rise of 131–2
Apollodorus of Artemita 105
Appian 17, 204
Appius Claudius 22–3, 85
Aquilius, Manius 33, 46, 52, 63
Arabia 88, 211–12, 278
Archelaus 63–4, 142, 208, 211, 234, 265
architecture 153, 162–3, 192–3, 260
Ariobarzanes 62, 65

Ariovistus 98, 108–10
Aristobulus 87–8
aristocracy 149–50, 189–90, 283–6
Aristonicus 25, 33, 62
Armenia 62, 84–8, 106, 124, 142–3, 209–10, 229, 235, 241, 251, 263, 265–6
Arminius 218, 228–9
army 205–8, 245, 253, 262, 269, 271 *see also* legions; military conduct; military dictatorship; military officers; military reforms; influence in political life 43, 51, 134; recruitment 42, 47
Arretium 274–5
art 161–2, 260 *see also* architecture
Artabanus III 235
Artavasdes 106, 142, 209
Artaxes 209
artisan shop system 274–6
Arverni 112–13
Asculum 54–7
Asia 25, 33, 58, 61–5, 78, 82–8, 96–8, 103, 132–6, 151, 155, 188, 208, 236
Asia Minor 61–4, 84–5, 118–19, 140, 158, 208–10, 222, 250, 277, 280
assassination 240, 257–8
astrology 174, 249, 262
Atrebates 113, 253
Atta, T. Quinctius 164
Attalus 22, 33
Atticus, T. Pomponius 132, 151, 168
Augustan principate: consolidation 181–3; establishment of 176–8; first settlement 178–80; frontiers 205–19; last 25 years of 183–5; literature of 199–204; magistrates and officials 189–92; provinces 219–23; public works in Rome and Italy 192–5; relations with Senate 185–9; religious reforms 197–9; second settlement 180–1; social reforms 195–7; writings 193
Augustiani 259–60
St Augustine 174
Augustus 153, 175, 195, 227, 230, 244, 252, 276, 279, 284, 287–9 *see also* Augustan principate; Octavian;

appraisal 223–5; in the East 182, 209; honours and offices 177–9, 181–2, 184; writings 179, 193, 202, 204
Aurelius, Marcus 215, 276, 287
Autronius Paetus, P. 90–1
auxiliaries 207–8, 212–13, 217
Averni 34

Bactria 105, 162, 279
Balbillus, Ti. Claudius 262, 304
Balbus, Cornelius 97, 121, 213, 284
Bassus, Aufidius 300–1
Bastarnae 178, 216
Belgae 108, 110–11, 253–4
Belgica 214, 219
Bellovaci 110, 113
Bessi 77, 136
Bestia, L. Calpurnius 37, 40–1
Bibulus, M. Calpurnius 98–9, 102, 116–17
biography 167–8, 204
Bithynia 62–3, 77, 83, 85–6, 89, 155, 165, 208
Blaesus, Junius 236
Blossius of Cumae 21, 25, 33
Bocchus 41, 43, 68
Bohemia 215, 217, 278
Bona Dea scandal 96, 99
Bosporus 88, 118–19, 209
Boudicca 264–5
brick industry 275–6
Brigantes 254, 263
Britain 108, 214, 240–1, 245, 249–51, 263–5, 275, 277, 282; Caesar in 111–12; Claudian conquest 252–5
Britannicus 250, 255–7, 273
Brundisium 114, 117, 138
Brutus, M. Iunius 73–4, 129, 131–4, 136–7, 140–1, 149–50, 157, 173, 201
Burebistas 107, 124
Burrus, Afranius 256–9, 284
businessmen 8, 33, 39, 63, 65, 147–8, 151, 280–1 *see also* merchants

Caecina, A. 229, 269
Caelius Rufus 119, 150, 165
Caepio, Q. Servilius 44–6, 54, 56

Caesar 71, 78, 82–3, 89, 151, 153, 158, 168, 185–6, 244, 248, 284, 287; appraisal 129–30; autocracy 125–30; in Britain 111–12; Civil War 114–21; and Crassus 90–3; death of 128–9; first consulship 97–9; in Gaul 103, 107–14; in Germany 111–12; policy and administration 124–5; and Pompey 97–9, 102–4, 114–17; reform and reconstruction 121–3; in Spain 91, 115–16, 120–1, 123; triumvirate 96–7, 101; will and funeral 132–3; writings 167, 202

Caesarion 120, 127, 143, 145

calendar reform 122

Caligula *see* Gaius (Caligula)

Callistus 240, 247, 255

Calpurnia 128, 131

Calpurnius Siculus 257

Calvinus, Domitius 75, 118

Campania 55, 57, 61, 65, 79, 148, 164, 272, 275, 282

Cantabri 180, 213

Cappadocia 62–3, 84, 86, 88, 142, 208, 229, 234, 251, 265

Capreae 230, 233–4, 237–9

Caratacus 250, 253–4

Carbo, C. Papirius 26–7, 36

Carbo, Cn. 38, 44, 60–1, 65–6

Carnutes 108, 112

Carrhae 102, 106, 142

Carthage 30, 213

Cartimandua 254, 263–4

Cassius, Dio 126, 182

Cassius Longinus, C. 106, 129, 131–4, 136–7, 140–1, 157

Cassius Longinus, L. 39, 44–5

Cassivellaunus 111–12, 252

Catiline conspiracy 90–4, 108

Cato, M. Porcius the elder 17, 147, 166, 173

Cato, M. Porcius the younger 94–100, 102, 115, 120

Catullus 160, 165–6

Catulus, Q. Lutatius 47–9, 60, 68, 73–4, 82, 91–2, 153, 165

Catuvellauni 111, 252

Celtic tribes 44, 108, 154 *see also individual tribes*

centralization of administration 246–9

Chaerea, Cassius 240, 245

Chalcis 88, 250, 267

chariot races 288–9

Chatti 217, 228–9

Cherusci 217–18, 229

China 105, 279

Christianity 249, 261, 291

Cicero 81–3, 91– 104, 107, 110, 115–21, 125, 128–36, 150–3, 157–60, 164–5, 169–70, 173–4

Cicero, Q. 112

Cilicia 68, 83–6, 88, 100, 103, 142–3, 150, 155, 157, 208, 210, 234, 277

Cimbri 38, 44–5, 48–9, 52

Cinna, L. Cornelius 58, 60–1, 64, 74, 165

Cisalpine Gaul 58, 61, 65, 73, 79, 98, 107, 110–12, 132–4, 147, 165, 168, 214

citizenship 14–15, 52–5, 57–8, 61, 91, 123, 154–5, 206–7, 222, 241–2, 250–2

city life 154, 221–3, 251, 281–2 *see also* urbanization

Civil Service 191–2, 246–7, 255, 262

civil wars 60–1, 65–7, 89, 104, 114–21, 134–45, 149, 204

civitates foederatae/liberae 154–5

Claudius 202, 237, 239, 241, 276, 287–9; accession of 243–5; administration 246–9; appraisal 256; conquest of Britain 252–5; palace intrigues 255–6; provincial policy 249–52

Cleopatra 91, 118, 120, 140–5, 197

Cleopatra Selene 142–3, 213

client-kings/kingdoms 39, 88, 140, 142, 208–10, 234, 241, 250, 254–5

Clodia 150, 165

Clodius, P. 99–103, 107, 112, 150, 152, 165, 194

Coelius Antipater 168

Coelius Caldus, C. 162

Cogidumnus 254

coinage 55–6, 108, 122, 136, 162, 188, 209–10, 252–3, 257, 259, 261, 269

collegia 122, 148, 283

colonies 14, 28, 30–1, 34–5, 37, 50, 92, 123, 147, 213, 222 *see also* veteran colonies
Columella, L. Iunius 273, 301
comedy 164
Comitia 38, 59, 67–8, 98, 231
Comitia Centuriata 59, 100, 191
Commagene 88, 229, 234, 241, 250–1
commemorative art 162, 193
commerce 48, 148, 280–1
Commius 113, 253
communications 195, 215, 221, 280
Concilium Plebis 23, 25, 33, 71
conspiracies 90–3, 128–9, 180, 240–1, 248, 255, 262–3, 268–9
constitutionalism 118, 125–6
Corbulo, Cn. Domitius 250, 262, 265–6, 268
co-regencies 183, 185, 227, 231
corn dole 122, 124, 152, 268, 283, 287
corn laws 28, 46–7, 78, 99
corn trade 28–9, 46, 84, 133, 147, 248, 280
Cornelia, mother of Gracchi 20–1
Cornelia, wife of Pompey 102, 117
Cornelius, C. 82
Cornelius Nepos 168
corruption 30, 78, 149, 157
Corsica 3, 38, 50, 70, 138, 140, 297
Cotta, C. Aurelius 77–8, 112
Cotta, L. Aurelius 38, 81
Cotta, M. Aurelius 78, 85, 112
Cotys 235, 241
Crassus, Licinius 34, 37, 53–4, 169, 216
Crassus, M. Licinius 65–6, 78–82, 98, 110, 149, 178; and Caesar 90–3; Parthia 105–6; triumvirate 96–7, 101–2
Crassus Mucianus, P. 172
Crassus Mucianus, P. Licinius 22
Crassus, P. Licinius 26, 110
Crete 84, 88, 133, 154
Crimea 62, 84
criminal justice 70–1, 154, 172, 183, 248
Cunobelinus 241, 252–4
Curio, C. Scribonius 103–4, 115, 119
currency 61, 280
cursus honorum 70, 190

customs barriers 279–80
Cyprus 84, 100, 137, 142–3, 155
Cyrene 77, 83–4, 133, 186, 213, 220, 259

Dacia 107, 124, 217
daily routines 285–6
Dalmatia 140, 215–16, 245
Dardanus 64, 84
Dead Sea Scrolls 266
debt relief 60–1, 85, 93, 116, 122
Decimus Brutus 111, 115, 132–4, 136
declining standards 12–13
deification 193, 198–9, 212, 227, 240, 256, 263
dictatorship 67–9, 71, 116, 119–21, 124–6
Didius, A. 263
Didius, T. 52, 56, 74
Diodorus 167, 281
Diophanes 21, 25
diplomacy 209–10
Dolabella, Cornelius 78, 119
Dolabella, P. 131–2, 136
Dolabella, P. Cornelius 236
Domitian 232, 238
Domitius Ahenobarbus, Cn. 34, 45, 66
Domitius Ahenobarbus, L. 101, 114–15, 147, 217–18
Donations of Alexandria 143, 145
drama 164
Druidism 108, 235–6, 249, 253, 264
Drusilla, sister of Gaius 240
Drusus, brother of Tiberius 183–4, 215, 217, 244
Drusus, M. Livius the younger 28–31, 38, 53–4, 77
Drusus, son of Germanicus 233–4, 237
Drusus, son of Tiberius 227–8, 230, 232–3
dyarchic division 185–9

eastern frontier 88, 208–12, 234
Eclogues (Virgil) 138, 200
economic conditions 16–18, 32–3, 124, 146–58, 272–83
education 170–1
efficiency 247–8
Egypt 83–4, 124, 175, 177–8, 208, 212,

229–30, 273, 276–7, 279 *see also*
Cleopatra; Ptolemy dynasty of Egypt
Eleazar 267
elections 69, 102–3, 116, 119, 125,
190–1, 231, 239
emperor worship 126–7, 136, 196,
198–9, 212, 221, 236, 242, 249, 255,
263–4, 268
engineering 163
Ennius, Q. 163, 170–1, 179
epic poetry 163–4
Epicurianism 151, 166, 173, 201
Equites 7–8, 13, 28–35, 38–41, 77, 81–6,
92, 155–6, 191, 219, 231, 245–6, 281,
286 *see also* Senate/Equites relations
Ethiopia 212, 266
Etruria 55, 57, 67, 74, 79, 93–4, 148, 272
everyday life 285–6
expansion of empire 2–4, 33–4

Fabius Maximus, Q. 34
Fabius, Q. 172
factory systems 274–5, 281
Fadus, Cuspius 267
family life 150
Fannius, C. 31, 167
Felix, M. Antonius 262, 267
Festus, Porcius 267, 309
Figulus, P. Nigidius 174
Fimbria 61, 64–5
finance 85, 177, 187, 237, 247–8, 258–9
fire of Rome 260–1
fire-fighting 194
First Triumvirate: Caesar 97–9; and
Clodius 99–101; renewal and
breakdown 101–5
Flaccus, L. Valerius 60–1, 64, 67, 242
Flaccus, M. Fulvius 26–7, 31–2, 34
Flamininus 198, 263
Flavus 127
Florus, Gessius 267
Florus, Julius 235–6
foreign affairs 33–5, 37–8, 61–3,
77–8, 103–4
foreign cults 122, 174–5, 197, 231,
235–6, 242, 249, 253, 261 *see also*
Christianity; Druidism; Judaism
freeborn labourers 283

freedmen in civil service 246–7,
255, 262
Fregellae revolt 27
Frisii 217, 235, 250, 278
frontiers 205–19; eastern 88, 208–12,
234; maps 224; northeast 107, 124,
140, 211; northern 41, 77, 214–19,
228–9, 235, 250, 255, 269
Fulvia, wife of Antony 137–8

Gabinius, A. 82–3, 87, 99, 101, 118, 124
Gaetulicus, Cn Cornelius 240–1
Gaius (Caligula) 234, 237–40, 244,
249–50, 267, 284, 288; provincial
policy 240–2
Gaius Caesar, son of Julia and Agrippa
183–4, 210, 226
Galatia 62, 88, 119, 142, 208, 265–6
Galba 240, 269, 271
Galilee 211, 241, 267–8, 307–8
Gallaeci 213
Gallus, C. Cornelius 178, 212
Gannascus 250
Gaul 93, 101, 123, 178–9, 188, 199,
213–14, 220–1, 235–6, 241, 250–2,
268–9, 273–7, 281–2 *see also*
Cisalpine Gaul; Transalpine Gaul;
Transpadane Gaul; Antony in 133–4;
Caesar in 103, 107–14; Marius in
45–9
Gellius, Cn. 167
Gemellus, adopted son of Gaius
(Caligula) 237–9, 242
genealogy, Julio-Claudian 270
Georgics (Virgil) 84, 200
Germanic tribes 41, 44, 48, 108–9, 113,
216–17 *see also individual tribes*
Germanicus 184, 216, 218, 226–30,
232, 235, 244
Germany 111–12, 214, 217–19, 229,
240–1, 250–1, 269, 275, 277–8
Geta, Cn. Hosidius 250, 253
Glabrio, Acilius 29, 83, 86
gladiators 79, 152, 245, 259, 289
glass industry 275, 277
Glaucia, C. Servilius 45, 47, 50
Gracchi, importance of 32–3
Gracchus, Gaius 23, 26–7, 34–5, 99,

151, 169; legislation 27–30; opposition to 30–2
Gracchus, Tiberius 1, 5, 19, 33, 69, 145; appraisal 24–5; background 20–2; land reform 22–4
Graeco-Roman culture 159–61
Greece 63–5, 114, 116–17, 138, 141, 277, 280
Greek cities 77, 89, 116, 148, 154, 159
Greek cultural influence 8–10, 61–2, 89, 105, 108, 259, 262–3, 282, 288

Hadrian 193, 280, 283
Hannibalic War 3, 5, 16–17, 166
Hellenistic monarchy 127–8, 198–9
Helvetii 108–9
Herod see Agrippa, Herod; Antipas, Herod
Herod the Great 141, 204, 210–11, 265
Hesiod 200
Hippalus 278
Hirtuleius 75–6
historical writing 105, 166–9, 202–4
Homanades 208, 222
home-production 274
homines novi 39, 42, 44, 77, 92, 95, 284
Horace 137, 163–4, 179, 183, 197, 199–202, 215, 272
Hortensius Hortalus, Q. 78, 81–2, 169
humanitas 136, 150
Hyrcanus 87–8, 141

Iapudes 140, 215
Iceni 254–5, 264
Idumaea 211, 268
Illyricum 98, 107, 132, 140–1, 179, 188, 215–17, 227, 279
India 105, 211–12, 278–9
industry 148–9, 273–7
Isauria 83, 208
Isidore of Charax 105
Isodorus 242
Italian Confederacy 13–14
Italian War 54–8
Italy see also Rome: administration 188; allies 14–15, 25–7, 50, 52–5, 77, 148; map 290; public works 194–5
Ituraea 210, 241

Iulus Classicianus 265
Iuvenes/Iuventus 196–7, 206

Jerusalem 210, 267–8, 308–9
Jesus Christ 235, 307–9
Jews, policies towards 122, 211, 231, 235, 241–2, 249, 267–8
Juba I, king of Numidia 115, 119–20
Juba, king of Mauretania 213
Judaea 87–8, 141, 210–11, 220, 235, 240, 242, 250, 263, 267–8
Judaism 122, 211, 231, 235, 241–2, 249, 267–8
judicial legislation 30, 53–4, 70–1, 81, 245–6
Jugurtha 39–43
Julia, daughter of Augustus 138, 183–4, 226
Julia, daughter of Caesar 98, 102, 117, 150
Julia Livilla 240, 297
Julio-Claudian economy 272–83
Julio-Claudian genealogy 270
jurisdiction 186–7, 248
Juvenal 287

Laberius, Decimus 164–5
Labienus, Q. 141
Labienus, T. 92, 110, 112, 120–1, 141
Laelius 19–20
Lampon 242
land commissions 25–7, 50
land problem 16–18
land reform 19–22, 24–5; Gaius Gracchus 27–30; Tiberius Gracchus 22–4
latifundia 16–17, 272–3
Latin allies 14–15, 25–7, 50, 52–5, 77, 148
Latin rights 123, 250
Latium 55, 272–3
law-courts issues 29, 44, 46, 70–1, 78, 81, 122, 151, 186–7, 231
lawyers 171–2
legal science 171–2
legions 48, 206–7, 219, 253
legislation 186; leges Iuliae 195; lex Aebutia 172; lex Aelia Sentia 196; lex

agraria 22, 50; *lex Annalis* 45, 80; *lex Aurelia* 81; *lex Caecilia-Didia* 52, 54; *lex Campana* 98; *lex Claudia* 7–8; *lex curiata* 134; *lex de repetundis* 122; *lex Domitia* 92; *lex Fufia Caninia* 196; *lex Gabinia* 83; *lex Gellia-Cornelia* 76; *lex Hortensia* 7; *lex iudiciaria* 44; *lex Iulia de repetundis* 99; *lex Julia* 57, 156; *lex Licinia Pompeia* 102; *lex Manilia* 86; *lex Papia Poppaea* 196; *lex Plautia-Papiria* 57; *lex Plotia de reditu Lepidanorum* 82; *lex provinciae* 154–5; *lex rogata* 155; *lex Rubria* 37; *lex Terentia Cassia frumentaria* 78; *lex Valeria* 67; *lex Valeria Cornelia* 191; *lex Villia Annalis* 70

leisure 286–9
Lentulus, Cossus Cornelius 213
Lentulus Spinther 100–1
Lepidus, M. Aemilius 71, 73–4, 77, 115–16, 120–1, 125, 134, 138, 140, 183, 240; Second Triumvirate 131–2, 134–7, 139
Libo Drusus, Scribonius 232
Licinius Macer, C. 78, 167
Ligurian tribes 34, 108, 215
literature 9, 163–6, 199–204, 257
Livia 138, 226–7, 230, 233, 287
Livilla 232–3
Livius Andronicus 163, 170
Livy 202–4, 220, 244
lower classes 151–3, 283
Luca Conference 101, 110
Lucan 257, 262
Lucania 55–6, 79
Lucilius, C. 163, 171, 201
Lucius Caesar, son of Julia and Agrippa 183–4, 226
Lucretius 165–6, 173–5
Lucullus, L. Licinius 63–4, 78–9, 83–7, 89, 96, 157
Lucullus, M. 79–80
Lusitania 52, 74, 213, 258, 269
luxury goods 149–50, 252, 261
Lycaonia 33, 208
Lycia 83, 245, 249–50
Lyons Tablet 252

Macedonia 77–8, 80, 99–100, 107, 132–3, 136, 141, 178–80, 216, 235, 245, 250, 263, 280
Macedonian Wars 3–4
Macro, Sutorius 234, 238–9, 242
Maecenas, C. 134, 138, 200–1, 203–4
magistracy 70, 125, 189–92
Maiden Castle 254
Mallius, Cn. 44, 46
Mamilius, C. 40–1
Mancinus, Hostilius 21
Manilius, C. 83
Manlius, L. 93
manumission laws 196
Marcellus, C. 104
Marcomanni 214, 217–18, 235, 278
Marius 38, 74, 82, 98, 167, 171; and Africa 39–43, 47; appraisal 51; background 38–9; and Cinna 60–1; in Gaul 45–9; and Mithridates 62; and Saturninus 47; sixth consulship 49–51; Social War 56–7; and Sulla's capture of Rome 58–60
Maroboduus 217–18, 229
marriage laws 195–6
Marsi 55–6, 228
Marullus 127
Massilia 34, 45, 116
Massiva of Numidia 40
Mauretania 41, 43, 121, 212–13, 240–2, 249–51, 264
Media 142–3
Memmius, C. 40, 50, 66, 165–6
memoirs 167–9, 202
Menapii 110, 112
merchants 40, 42, 63, 280–1
Mesopotamia 106, 124
Messalina 244, 255
Messalla Corvinus, M. Valerius 203
Messalla, Valerius 137, 221
metal industry 275, 280
Metelli pre-eminence 38–9, 47
Metellus Caprarius, C. 38, 47
Metellus Celer 96–7, 165
Metellus Delmaticus, L. 37–8
Metellus Macedonicus, Q. 26
Metellus Nepos, Q. 95
Metellus Pius 65, 69, 74–6, 80

Metellus, Q. Caecilius 35, 41–2, 84, 150
Metellus Scipio 103–4
middle classes 286 *see also* businessmen; merchants
military conduct 12–13
military dictatorship 176, 179
military officers 48, 206
military reforms 47–8, 187–8, 205–8
Milo 102–3, 119, 194
mime 164–5
mining industry 280, 283
Mithridates, king of Armenia 235
Mithridates, king of Pontus 47, 57–8, 61–3, 76–8, 82–4, 87, 119, 148, 157
Mithridates of Pergamum 118–19
Mithridatic Wars 59, 63–5, 77–8, 83–8
Moesia 216, 219, 235
monarchy question 127–8
morality 150, 196–7, 201, 203, 273
Morini 110–11
municipal privileges 222–3, 251
Murena, L. Licinius 65, 93, 107
music 259, 288
mutinies 61, 116, 228, 255

Nabataeans 88, 211, 281
Naevius 9, 163
Narbonensis 33–4, 49, 75, 123, 134, 138, 188, 213, 222
Narcissus 247, 255–7
navy/naval engagements 84, 139, 143–5, 207–8
Neopythagoreanism 174, 293, 303, 305
Neoterici 165
Nero 255–6, 282, 284, 286, 288–9; and Agrippina 256–8; appraisal 269–71; and the arts 259–60; conspiracies 262–3, 268–9; fire/rebuilding of Rome 260–1; provinces under 263–8; Seneca/Burrus administration 258–9
Nero, son of Germanicus 233–4
Nervii 108, 110, 112
new men 39, 42, 44, 77, 92, 95, 284
Nicolaus of Damascus 204
Nicomedes II 62–3, 65
Nicomedes III 85
Norbanus, C. 46, 61, 65

Noricum 214–15, 219, 250
northeast frontier 107, 124, 140, 211
northern frontier 41, 77, 214–19, 228–9, 235, 250, 255, 269
Novius 164
Numidia 39–43, 47, 115, 119–20
Numidicus, Metellus 39, 44, 47, 50–1
Nymphidius Sabinus 269

Octavia, daughter of Claudius 255
Octavia, wife of Antony 138–41, 145, 193
Octavia, wife of Nero 257, 260
Octavian 140, 153 *see also* Augustan principate; Augustus; Battle of Actium 144–5; Battle of Philippi 134–7; consolidation of the West 137–40; establishment of principate 176–8; rise of 132–4
Octavius, Cn. 58, 60
Octavius, M. 23, 25, 28, 38
Odes (Carmina) (Horace) 201–2
Opimius, L. 31, 36–7, 40–1, 94
Opimius, Q. 77–8
Optimates/Optimate cause 6, 47, 58, 60, 68, 73, 77, 83, 90–1, 95–6, 99, 102, 104, 125, 171
oratory 169–70
Orodes II 105–6, 141
Ostia 46, 60, 122, 248, 259, 261, 280–2, 293
Ostorius Scapula, P. 254–5, 263
Otho 258, 269, 271
Ovid (P. Ovidius Naso) 203–4, 289

Pacorus 141
Paetus, L. Caesennius 265–6
Paetus, Thrasea 262
painting 161
palace intrigues 256
Palestine 87, 211, 235, 242, 266–8, 306–7
Pallas 247, 255–7, 267
Pamphylia 83, 208
Panaetius of Rhodes 10, 173
Pannonia 183, 215–17, 219, 227–8, 232, 236
Paphlagonia 62, 88

Papius Mutilus 56–7
Parisii 112, 214
Parthia 62, 86–8, 103–6, 124, 138–43, 157, 208–10, 229, 235, 241, 251, 265–6, 279
past, respect for 140, 178–80, 195, 197–8, 201–2, 244, 248–9
patronage 128, 151–2, 162, 199–200, 285
St Paul 261, 267, 280
Pennus, Iunius 27
People 7–8, 39–41, 45–6, 53, 59–60, 67, 69, 71, 83, 98, 186, 192, 231 see also Populares; Senate/People relations
Periochae (Livy) 202–3
Perperna, M. 33, 66, 75–6
Perusia, siege of 137
St Peter 261
Petreius, M. 116, 120
Petronius, C. 212, 262
Petronius, P. 242, 281
Pharisees 266, 268, 307, 309
Pharnaces 87–8, 118
Pharsalus 119, 129
Philip, king of Macedonia 198–9
Philip of Ituraea 211, 241
Philippi, Battle of 134–7
Philippus, L. Marcius 54, 73–4
Philo 242
philosophy 9–10, 173 see also Epicurianism; Neopythagoreanism; Stoicism
Phraates 86–7, 209–10
Phrygia 9, 33, 85, 174, 293, 306
Picenum 54–5
piety 197
Pilate, Pontius 235–6
piracy 47, 52, 65, 76–8, 82–4, 100, 140, 148, 250
Pisidia 208–9
Piso, C. Calpurnius 93, 262
Piso, Cn. Calpurnius 229–30
Piso, L. Calpurnius 11–13, 99, 166, 180, 216
Plautius, Aulus 250, 253–4
Plautus 163–4
Pliny 153, 273

Pliny the elder 238, 301–2
Plutarch 17, 167–8, 204
poetry 163–6, 199–204, 259
Polemo 142, 209, 266
political division of labour 185–9
political reforms 69–70, 77–8, 81, 99, 103, 124–5, 183, 231, 245–6
Pollio, Asinius 97, 134, 138, 141, 200, 202, 204
Polybius 4, 7, 10–11, 13, 167
Pompeii 57, 148, 154, 259, 272, 274–6, 289, 293–5, 305
Pompeius Rufus, Q. 58, 60
Pompeius, Sextus 132, 135, 138–9
Pompeius Trogus 204
Pompey Magnus 65–7, 71, 82, 91, 111, 149–50, 155–6, 167; and Caesar 97–9, 102–4, 114–17; and Cicero 95–6; and Clodius 100–2; commands of 82–3; and Crassus 80–1; and Lepidus 73–4; and Lucullus 84–6; Mithridatic Wars 84–8; pirates 83–4; senatorial administration 77–9; and Sertorius 74–7; settlement of the east 88–9; Spartacus 79–80; triumvirate 96–7
Pomponius, L. 164
pontifical law 172
Pontus 61–4, 78, 83, 85–6, 88–9, 118, 142, 155, 209, 263, 266 see also Mithridates, king of Pontus
Popillius, P. Laenas 25, 28, 37, 44–5
Poppaea 258, 260–2
Poppaedius Silo, Q. 54, 56–7
Populares 6, 23, 33, 77, 95–6
Porcia 129, 150
portraiture 162
Posidonius 160, 167, 173–4
Postumius, L. 15
Postumus, Agrippa 227
Praetorian Guard 206, 233–4, 243, 257, 260, 262, 269
Prasutagus 254, 264
Primus, M. 180
private law 171–2
proletariat 152
Propertius, Sextus 203

proscriptions 67–9, 73, 92–3, 136, 149, 264
provinces 154–8; Augustan principate 219–23; Caesar's reforms 122–3; under Claudius 249–52; division of 178–9; maps 224; under Nero 263–8; senatorial 213, 219, 236, 245, 247, 250
provincial administration 70, 99, 154; declining standards 13; and defence 212–14; governors 30, 156–7, 221; under Tiberius 234–6
provincial senators 125, 245, 252, 284
Ptolemy dynasty of Egypt 2–3, 91, 98, 101, 117–18, 141–3 see also Cleopatra
Ptolemy, king of Cyprus 100
Ptolemy, king of Mauretania 241, 250
public disturbances 24, 50, 59–60, 95, 132, 182, 241, 267–8
public games 102, 152–3, 183, 197, 231, 249, 259–60, 263, 287–9
public works 48, 122, 124, 177, 192–5, 248, 260–1, 263, 282
publicani 65, 89, 148, 151, 156–7, 220–1, 279
Punic Wars 3–4, 11
Pyrrhus 2

Quadrigarius, Claudius 167, 202
Quinctius, L. 78
Quintillian 163–4
Quirinius of Judaea 220
Quirinius, P. Sulpicius 208

Raetia 214–15, 219
realism in art 162
Regni 254–5
religion 9, 126, 174–5, 183, 231, 242, 248–9, 261, 267, 287 see also emperor worship; foreign cults; Sibylline Oracles
religious reforms 45, 197–9
Republican cause 129, 134, 136–9, 244, 262
Res Gestae (Augustus) 179, 193, 204
rhetoric 171
Rhodes 63, 83, 171, 184, 226, 258
Rhoemetalces II 235

road system 195, 214, 280
Roman rule, merits 157–8
romanization 123, 146, 195, 207, 213, 221–3, 249, 251–2, 282
Rome: administration 188; building/rebuilding 153–4, 192–5, 260–1 (see also architecture; public works); fire of 261; Sulla's capture of 58–60
Roscius, L. 115
Roscius Otho 82
Rufus, Egnatius 182, 194
Rufus, Faenius 259–60, 262
Rufus, M. Minucius 31, 38
Rufus, P. Rutilius 44, 48, 53, 157
Rupilius, P. 12, 25, 46

Sabaeans 211–12
Sabinus, Q. 110, 112
sacred law 171–2
Sacrovir, Julius 235–6
Sadducees 266–7, 307
Salassi 194, 215
Sallust 40–1, 74, 121, 167–9
Salvidienus Rufus, Q. 137–8
Samaria 268, 308
Samian ware 148, 274–5
Samnium 55, 57, 66–7
Sardinia 38, 66, 115, 138, 155–6, 231, 263
Sarmantian tribes 209, 266
satire 163, 273
Saturninus, C. Sentius 52, 62, 73, 92, 182
Saturninus, L. Appuleius 46–7, 49–50
Scaevola, P. Mucius 21–2, 24, 53, 172
Scaurus, M. Aemilius 38–40, 45–6, 53, 88
Scepticism 173
scholarship 171
science 173
Scipio, L. 61, 65
Scipio Nasica, P. 24–5, 33
Scordisci 37–8, 44, 52
Scribonianus, Furius Camillus 245, 255
sculpture 161–2
Scythian tribes 62, 209
Second Triumvirate: Battle of Actium 143–5; Battle of Philippi 134–7; Marc

Antony in the East 140–3; Octavian's consolidation of the West 137–40; rise of Marc Antony 131–2; rise of Octavian 132–4

Sejanus, L. Aelius 232–4, 237

Sempronia 21, 26

Sempronius Asellio 167

Senate/Equites relations 29–30, 43, 45, 52–4, 95, 151

Senate/People relations 23–4, 43, 45

Senate/Principate relations 185–9, 228, 230–1, 239, 245–6, 257–8, 262

senatorial administration 77–9

senatorial class 149–50, 189–90, 283–6 *see also* aristocracy; upper classes

senatorial committee 188–9, 232

senatorial government structure 4–6

senatorial provinces 213, 219, 236, 245, 247, 250

senators, provincial 125, 245, 252, 284

senatus consultum ultimum 31, 36, 73, 92–3, 104, 245

Seneca 238, 251, 256–9, 262, 264, 273, 284

Sequani 109–10

Sertorius, Q. 66, 74–8, 84

Servile Wars 12, 45–6, 52, 79–80, 152

Servilia, mother of Brutus 129, 150

Servilius Vatia, P. 83

Sextus Pompeius 120–1, 133, 137–8, 208

Sibylline Oracles 127, 158

Sicily 46, 52, 66, 78, 115, 122, 133, 138–9, 147, 155–6, 277

Silanus, M. Iunius 44–5, 257

Silius, C. 236, 255, 278

Silures 254, 263

Sisenna, L. Cornelius 169

slave-risings 45–6, 78, 152

slavery 11–13, 146, 248, 273–4, 276

social classes 149–53, 158, 255, 283–6

social life 285–91; Late Republic 146–58

social reform 32–3, 99, 183, 195–7, 201

social unrest 27, 95, 267

Social War 13, 54–8, 68, 74, 149

Sosius, C. 141, 143

Spain 38, 44, 66, 74–7, 101–2, 134, 147, 178–9, 188, 213, 222, 269, 273, 277–9, 282; Caesar in 91, 115–16, 120–1, 123

Spartacus 78–80

Stilo, L. Aelius 171

Stoicism 10, 173–4, 262

Strabo, Caesar 59–60, 74

Strabo, Cn. Pompeius 45, 56–8

Strabo of Amasia 204, 253, 278

succession issues 127, 184, 227, 230, 233–4, 237–8, 256, 269–71

Suebi 108–9, 235

Suetonius 204, 243, 250, 263–5

Sulla, L. Cornelius 42–3, 49, 73–5, 77–80, 82–5, 93, 105, 148–9, 153, 169, 284, 287, 289; capture of Rome 58–60; and Cinna 60–1; Civil War 65–7; and Mithridates 61–5; proscription 67–8; reforms 68–71; retirement 71–2; Social War 56–8

Sulla, P. Cornelius 90–1

Sulpicius, Publius 58–60

Sulpicius Quirinius, P. 208, 213

Sulpicius Rufus, Servius 60, 172

Syria 155, 178–9, 208–10, 218, 242, 251, 265–7, 276, 279–80; and Caesar 118, 124; and the First Triumvirate 99–105; and Pompey 83–4, 87–9; and the Second Triumvirate 132–3, 136–43; and Tiberius 229, 234–5

Syrus, Publilius 165

Tacfarinas 236

Tacitus 167, 181, 227, 229–30, 232, 234, 237–8, 255, 261, 265, 269

Tarentum Conference 139

Taurus, Statilius 139, 180, 183, 289

taxation 29, 34, 65, 89, 96–8, 122, 151, 155, 219–20, 236, 245, 259, 263–4, 272, 279–80

Tencteri 111

Terence 9–10, 163–4

Teutoberg massacre 184–5, 218, 227–9, 277

Teutones 38, 44–5, 48–9, 52, 107

textile industry 276

Thapsus, battle of 120

theatre 288
Thrace 37, 84, 136, 178, 180, 216, 235, 249–51
Tiberius 138, 183–5, 193, 215–18, 244, 276, 284, 289; accession of 226–8; and Africa 236, 239; appraisal 238; civil government 230–2; in the East 209; and Germanicus 228–30; last years 236–8; provincial administration 234–6; at Rhodes 184; and Sejanus 232–4
Tiberius Alexander 267
Tibullus 203
Tigellinus, Ofonius 260, 262, 269
Tigranes 62–3, 84–7, 209, 265–6
Tigurini 44–5, 49
Timagenes of Alexandria 204
Tiridates 209, 251, 263, 265–6
Titus, son of Vespasian 268
Togodumnus 253–4
trade 148–9, 211–12, 252–3, 273–9 see also businessmen; merchants
trade routes 105, 211–12, 277–8
tragedy 164
Trajan 256
Transalpine Gaul 33–4, 73, 98, 107, 114–15, 133, 138, 215
Transpadane Gaul 49, 91, 115
transport 280
treason 46, 178–82, 186, 230–4, 237–40, 245, 256–62
Trebellius 82–3
Trebonius, C. 101, 115, 132, 136
Treveri 112, 236
tribunate 69–70, 80, 82–3, 126
tribunicia potestas 177, 182–3, 186, 192, 226–7, 232
Trinovantes 111, 252, 264
Triumvirates see First Triumvirate; Second Triumvirate
Tullia, daughter of Cicero 173
Tunisia 4, 120

Ubii 139, 218
Umbria 55, 57–8, 203

upper classes 149–50, 189–90, 283–6
urbanization 154, 213, 221–3, 251, 281–2 see also city life
Usipetes 111

Valerius Antias 167, 202
Valerius Messala 137
Varius Hybrida, Q. 54
Varro, M. Terentius 77–8, 116, 147, 170–1, 180, 215
Varus, P. Attius 115
Varus, P. Quinctilius 184–5, 218, 227–9, 277
Varus, Quinctilius 218–19
Vatinius, P. 98–9, 101, 124
Velleius Paterculus, M. 227, 238
Veneti 110–11
Ventidius Bassus, P. 141
Ventidius Cumanus 267
Vercingetorix 103, 112–13
Verginius Rufus, L. 269
Verica 253
Verres scandal 13, 81, 158
Vespasian 240, 251, 253–4, 266–8, 271
Vestal Virgins 39, 143, 197
veteran colonies 47, 67, 96–8, 132, 146–7, 177, 194, 208–9, 213, 222, 250, 255; Italian 92–3, 123–4, 135–7, 259
Vettius 99
Vindex, C. Julius 268–9
Vinicianus, Annius 262
Vipsania Agrippina 184, 226
Virgil 84, 137–8, 145, 159–60, 163, 175, 198, 200–1
Vitellius 235–6, 271
Volcae 44
Vologeses I 251, 265

water-supplies 153–4, 193–4, 248, 276
wealth 11–13, 16–17, 149–50 see also luxury goods
weaponry 48
women, position of 150